Essays in American Colonial History

Edited by

Paul Goodman

UNIVERSITY OF CALIFORNIA,
DAVIS

HOLT, RINEHART AND WINSTON

New York   Chicago   San Francisco   Atlanta   Dallas
Montreal   Toronto

*The illustration on the cover is from the
I. N. Phelps Stokes Collection of American
Historical Prints, Prints Division, The
New York Public Library.*

PREFACE

The purpose of this volume is to make more readily available studies of America's colonial period that have appeared as essays in scholarly journals. These articles are concise reports of investigations, many of which have been elaborated in books, and thus they afford students a convenient, brief introduction to the scholarship of America's formative years. Instead of trying to include essays on all aspects of colonial development, I have generally chosen pieces that are interpretive. The selections are reprinted as they originally appeared except for the omission of footnotes. Preceding each essay is a brief bibliography of leading works on the subject of the essay to aid students who wish to explore further. I am grateful to Stanley N. Katz, University of Wisconsin, Seymour Shapiro, University of Massachusetts, Boston, and Gordon S. Wood, Harvard University, for valuable help in canvassing the field of prospective selections. The final choice, of course, was mine.

Davis, California   Paul Goodman
June 1967

CONTENTS

v

INTRODUCTION

Sometime before the birth of the republic in 1776, those who inhabited Britain's North American colonies came to be considered, and to think of themselves, as Americans. The sense of American nationality emerged before the concept of Americanness was embodied in a sovereign state. This national identity developed through a complex process by which European patterns of living and thinking were transformed by a century and a half of experience in a New World. Early circumstances shaped the way later generations organized political power, produced and distributed wealth, managed their spiritual affairs, and defined their communal identity. This volume explores how and why a new society developed, laying the foundations for a powerful nation.

Europeans were the ones who discovered and colonized the New World because the preconditions for overseas expansion existed in western Europe in the late fifteenth century and after. Part I of this volume illuminates the sources and methods of European expansion, especially the origins of England's thrust across the Atlantic. The first three selections analyze social changes in England that influenced the timing, direction, and manner of British settlement in America. The fourth describes French colonization, which differed from the English.

All except one of the thirteen colonies were founded in the seventeenth century. The early generations of settlers brought with them assumptions and expectations about how to proceed, based on experiences in the Old World. They usually ventured abroad in search of a better life, but did not anticipate the social disorganization that they were to meet. They expected to transfer intact to the New World patterns of social organization similar to the familiar ones they had left behind. Few foresaw that they would create a radically new social order. Circumstances in America forced settlers to modify initial colonization designs, at first in order to survive and later to prosper.

The selections in Part II examine varieties of experience during the foundations of settlement in the seventeenth century, focusing on the problems a trading company encountered in colonizing Virginia, the organization of political power, the emergence of an American social structure, the recruitment of labor, free and slave, the development of profitable patterns of commercial enterprise, and the encounters between man and God in the wilderness.

Though seventeenth-century American society clearly departed from European models, the extent of change became more apparent during the later colonial period. Part III explores in greater depth than is possible for the early years the nature and process of change in the eighteenth century. The first group of selections (Nos. 15–19) describes various aspects of the material basis of colonial society: How equally was land distributed? What problems did commercial agriculturalists face, notably tobacco planters? How adequate was the supply of currency and credit? How did membership in a mercantilist empire affect American enterprise? And how rapidly did the American economy grow? The next group of selections (Nos. 20–26) investigates the structure of colonial politics: Who ruled, the English or the Americans; and to the extent that colonists shared in governing, which of them exercised power? How was power used? How were conflicts settled?

The final group of selections (Nos. 27–32) focuses on other important aspects of the colonial social order. Social stratification in America departed from the English model, and the condition of American elites reveals some of the reasons why. A close bond existed between church and state in Europe, but in seventeenth-century America, this tie gradually weakened. Well before the American Revolution a pattern that would dominate the future was taking shape: religious tolerance prevailed in all colonies, and in some, church and state were separated, and religious bodies were private associations. By the end of the colonial period, an indigenous secular culture existed, which further explains why many on both sides of the Atlantic believed that the Americans were "a new race of men."

I

EUROPEAN APPROACHES
TO THE NEW WORLD

1. TUDOR EXPANSION*

The Transition from Medieval
to Modern History

by A. L. Rowse

Each European nation entering the race for overseas empire
had a unique colonization experience. The timing, direction,
and method of expansion and the kind of new settlements
spawned were influenced by a nation's own internal development
prior to expansion. England was late in the race for empire,
a century behind its great rival, Spain. Columbus sailed west
under the patronage of a strong monarchy that had brought
unity to Spain by completing the expulsion of the Arabs and
unifying heterogeneous elements in the Iberian Peninsula. But
while Ferdinand and Isabella were consolidating their power
in Spain, England was just emerging from a prolonged civil war

* *William and Mary Quarterly*, 3d series, vol. 14 (1957), 309–316. Reprinted by
permission of the author. Copyright 1957 by the Institute of Early American History and Culture. Footnotes have been omitted except where they are necessary for
an understanding of the text.

among rival claimants to the throne. The first century of Spanish colonization in America was a time of nation-building in England. In the following essay, A. L. Rowse argues that not until the English had left the Middle Ages behind and had developed a strong centralized state were they ready for the conquest of North America. According to Rowse, an essential precondition for expansion was the development of a powerful and highly integrated nation in place of a fragmented and unstable medieval polity. This transformation in England was the achievement of Tudor government in the sixteenth century.

For further reading: Geoffrey R. Elton, *England under the Tudors* (1956); A. L. Rowse, *The England of Elizabeth* (1950), *The Expansion of Elizabethan England* (1955); Howard M. Jones, *O Strange New World* (1964), chaps. 1–5; Trevor Aston, ed., *Crisis in Europe, 1560–1660* (1965); Wallace Notestein, *The English People on the Eve of Colonization* (1954); J. H. Parry, *The Establishment of the European Hegemony 1417–1715* (1961).

"How much the greatest event it is that ever happened in the world! and how much the best!" said Charles James Fox of the French Revolution. Charles Fox was a man of notoriously bad judgment—and I am not sure that we historians are not too generous in our estimate of the importance of revolutions. I am not speaking of their value or their merits, where bad is mixed with good, the destructive with the constructive, losses with gains. I am speaking of the *importance* of revolutions as a factor in history and wondering whether we do not overrate it. I suppose that their chief contribution lies in the release they give to forces in society that have been withheld or restrained—though not all is for the good when the safety valve is blown off.

We historians attach much significance to the Puritan Revolution in England, the Revolution of 1688, the French, the American, the Russian revolutions—many books, whole libraries, have been written about them. Yet I wonder whether there are not quieter, underlying movements, that attract less spectacular notice—the movements of peoples, the internal movements of population—which are more fundamental and achieve more durable results in the history of mankind. We in the twentieth century lie under the sinister shadow of the Russian Revolution: we are not likely to underestimate it. Yet it may well be that before long we shall come to think of the Russian colonization of Siberia, her expansion into the vast spaces of Northern Asia, as a matter of more solid and insurmountable importance for the world.

The fact is that people's attention is arrested by the drama of the revolutionary break in society: they are rather mesmerized by the cross section that is revealed and are apt not to grasp the long process in which revolution is a jolt, a disturbance, sometimes hurrying things up, sometimes obstructing or deflecting the current.

How many people have the historic imagination to realize that the making of the American nation must be the greatest single, homogeneous achievement of modern history?

Its appeal is epic rather than dramatic: a slower moving, in some ways a more subtle, appeal to the imagination. But one feels it no less strongly—and perhaps it is a deeper level of experience of life, of realization of the heroism and the pathos that it speaks to—as one moves across the prairies, down the Ohio and across the Mississippi, or out of the Cumberland Gap from Kentucky into southern Illinois and spreading fanwise across the Middle West, or along the trails from St. Louis to Oregon, to Santa Fé and across the passes into California. Again, to go back to an earlier phase, as one approaches the coast of America, one is touched to tears to think of all the effort and endurance, the sacrifice of men's lives that went into it, the hundreds and thousands of forgotten simple men along with the unforgotten—a Thomas Cavendish, most gifted young captain, second circumnavigator of the globe after Drake; a Stephen Parmenius, the Hungarian geographer, bedfellow of Hakluyt's in Oxford days, no less than a Humphrey Gilbert or a Henry Hudson, coming to his end in the ice floes of the bay now named after him. Or we remember how Gilbert beggared himself, spent his own fortune and his wife's, on his dream of the English colonization of North America; how Walter Raleigh spent similarly all that he won from the favor of the Queen upon the same great enterprise, and how, in circumstances of defeat, discouragement, disgrace, he wrote: "I shall yet live to see it an English nation."

We may regard the peopling of North America as an extension across the Atlantic of the process a thousand years before, in the time of the *Völkerwanderungen,* by which Britain was colonized by the original

Anglo-Saxon stocks: a comparable process on a much smaller scale, occupying a much longer tract of time, by which forest was felled, the frontier extended, the nation took shape out of a creative mixing, a fusion of stocks. (It would be a fine subject for a book, to have a comparative study of these parallel processes, the naming of places and similar matters separated by a thousand years.) I am to speak of the beginnings of that second process, of which the twentieth century has seen the consolidation, the fulfillment, rather than the end.

My story may be said to be concerned with the junction between the two processes, the transition from the medieval to the modern world. For, surely, this is where the transition comes between the Middle Ages and modern history, this is the factor that in the long run made the greatest difference: the discovery of the new world. We are all aware of the long and fruitful discussion as to what constituted the Renaissance—nowhere better summed up than in Wallace K. Ferguson's admirable and discriminating book, *The Renaissance in Historical Thought*—what were the factors out of which came the modern world and its characteristic experience. Whatever we may think, however much we may disagree, about the rediscovery of antiquity, the importance of the study of Greek, the new standards of criticism and scholarship, the significance of humanism, of Renaissance state and new monarchy, here is a *differentia* that is indisputable, the significance of which grows with the expanding world, with which the Middle Ages come to an end.

I often think how vividly it is brought home by that letter of a fourteenth-century bishop of Exeter, John Grandison, to a friend at the papal court at Avignon, describing the state of his remote diocese in the west: where in farthest Cornwall the people speak a language that is not even English or understood by the English, and beyond the Land's End is nothing but the great sundering flood. It is the end of the known world.

A couple of centuries later, how all that has changed! The West Country now, from being a remote backwater, is in the front line of all the maritime activity launching out across the oceans: to the Canaries and the Guinea Coast, into the South Atlantic to Brazil; from Guinea across to the Caribbean and out by the Florida Channel; to Labrador and Hudson's Bay up into the gap between Greenland and North America searching for a northwest passage to the Far East; to Newfoundland and down the coast of New England into the unknown; to the West Indies and up the coast to plant the Virginia colonies; at length direct to the coast to plant the New England colonies; into the South Atlantic with

Drake and Cavendish, to penetrate the Pacific and establish contact with the Far East. All these voyages took wing from Plymouth, in Bishop Grandison's diocese: in his days a very inconsiderable place, confined to the small change of cross-channel trade and tit-for-tat raiding, which has left its memento in the name of Bretonside by Sutton Pool. These voyages made the name and fortune of Plymouth, under the guidance of the remarkable Hawkins family and their brilliant poor relation, Francis Drake. (He did not remain a poor relation for long.) The transition from the medieval to the modern world stands well expressed in the change of name of the fortified island off Plymouth Hoe: known to the medieval people as St. Nicholas's island, to the moderns it is Drake's Island.

I realize that this is looking at the matter simply from an English perspective. But a wider one makes my point all the stronger, when one considers that by this time Portuguese and Spaniards had discovered half the world's coasts, were in occupation of much of Central and South America, and had established a regular route across the Pacific to the Far East. That brings home more powerfully than ever the difference between the Middle Ages, in this sense circumscribed and rather static, and the modern world, expansive and essentially dynamic.

The end of the Middle Ages in England was marked by contraction rather than expansion: withdrawal from the long dream of conquest in France, and, what is particularly significant, a marked shrinkage in the area of English control, of English language and civilization, in Ireland. Gaeldom came once more lapping like lake water up to the walls of the towns—Dublin, Waterford, Cork, Galway, last outposts of earlier Anglo-Irish. In the early fifteenth century, with Owen Glendower's rebellion, Wales achieved a temporary quasi independence; though it was defeated and crushed, Wales remained resentfully aloof, unabsorbed. Nor was any real progress made with the integration of Cornwall or the Scottish Borders, where they "knew no king but a Percy," into the fabric of the state. The fact was that the central institutions of the state were giving way under the strain of royal minorities, dynastic conflict, unsuccessful foreign war. The state's hold was contracting, government ineffectual, society itself inefficient and showing some signs of arrested development and decline.

The dynamic movement that initiates and motivates modern history reversed all that. The beginnings of this process form the subject of my book, *The Expansion of Elizabethan England*, and I have no wish to impose a summary of it here, apart from the unprofitability of such a procedure. But perhaps I may draw one or two conclusions from the detailed study made there.

By far the most important, and one that I had not realized before going into it, was the continuity of the process of expansion within the islands with that across the oceans, especially the phase of it which is crucial for modern history—Bismarck called it "the decisive fact in the modern world"—that across the Atlantic to the peopling of North America. These were two phases of the same movement, the second gathering momentum as it went forward, until it became the greatest single influence upon the home country in turn, a chief factor in transforming its society, making its fortune; today—it is not too much to say—constituting its fate. Without America the islands would have gone down to defeat and destruction twice in this century; without America I see no viable future for them.

The English state gathered its resources together under the Tudors and achieved an effective relation with society, particularly the leading middle elements in it—country gentry and town middle class—that enabled it to go forward with the work of expansion and internal integration.

We may see the process vividly brought home to us in the history of my native Cornwall. Small as it is, it was a little country on its own, with its own life, language, and culture. The Cornish were content with their Celtic ways—the remote people, who did not speak English, of Bishop Grandison's letter, wrapped up in their cult of the saints, their holy wells and wayside crosses, their feasts and pilgrimages, dreaming their dream of King Arthur and his return someday to the land. That self-regarding life was rudely shaken by the demand of Henry VII's government in 1497 for taxation for the defense of the Scottish Border. The Scottish Border was nothing to do with them, said the Cornish, and proceeded to raise a formidable rebellion which was only arrested outside of London, on Blackheath field. We see that the Cornish had an inadequate comprehension of the modern state, with its characteristic feature of central taxation for over-all state purposes. The Cornish were still living in the Middle Ages.

Nor were they any more reconciled half a century later when the central state imposed in 1549 a new religious uniformity upon the country with a prayer book in *English*. The English service was no better than a Christmas mumming, said the Cornish, and joined with the men of Devon in a rebellion that paralyzed government for several months in the summer of 1549, until it was crushed with some bloodshed. This time the repression was severe and the Cornish were taught a lesson they did not have to learn again. Indeed, the change of sentiment and of power within Cornwall was most marked, from the old inland families of Catholic sympathies to the newer coastal families, seafaring and Protestant, closely concerned in the ports and harbors engaged in the multifarious activities of oceanic expansion and sea warfare, their mouths open to the new world. It is surely very significant that all these families were to the fore in the voyages to America and the colonizing expeditions: one meets their names again and again in the records, Grenvilles, Killigrews, Tremaynes, Gilberts, Kendalls, Prideaux, Rouses.

Wales offers an example of integration with the state on a bigger scale, a much larger undertaking. Here the process was greatly helped and made much smoother by the Welsh capture of the throne in the person of. Henry Tudor. Never the breath of a rebellion was raised against the dynasty that was Welsh—even when the representative of the central government, Bishop Rowland Lee, was repressing the age-long delights of Welsh society, thieving and cattle stealing, stringing up thieves in hundreds, stamping out blood feuds and affrays, reducing the Welsh to English ideas of law and order.

We do not find the Welsh so much to the fore as the West Country in the American voyages. All the same we come across their names on them —Morgans and Vaughans, Floyds and Trevors. And we remember that the Welsh Captain Middleton, who bore the news of the approaching Spanish fleet to Grenville in the Azores, finished his translation of the Psalms into Welsh *apud Scutum, insulam occidentalium Indorum.* The chief field for Welsh expansionist activity—after England, where they virtually bore rule with the Tudors and the Cecils—was Ireland, to which they sent captains and soldiers for the wars, undertakers and colonists, administrators, lawyers, a Lord Deputy, and even bishops.

Ireland was a far tougher proposition for the Tudor state with its exiguous resources. It seems that historians have not even yet realized how deep was the chasm between Tudor England, in essence a modern society, and the Celtic civilization of Ireland, in many parts not even a medieval society, but pre-medieval, nomadic and pastoral, with its tribal chieftains and their endemic warfare—a culture arrested in development and run down, closer to the England of the Anglo-Saxon heptarchy than it was to the England of Elizabeth. No doubt the subjugation of Ireland could have been effected by the Tudor state earlier—if that had been its intention; or with far less difficulty in the end, if it had been able to concentrate on the objective, instead of having to regard it as one sector of a continental and oceanic struggle with Spain.

However, in the end Ireland was subjugated and a basis laid for a fruitful intermixture of the two peoples which—in spite of disappointments and the subsequent frustrations of Irish history—has led to a distinguished contribution to the world in the shape of Anglo-Irish culture. Whatever anyone may say, the basis of modern Irish society, on the land, in its property system, in law and language, is not Celtic but English. The foundation was not laid until the accession of a Scottish king came to complete the lifework of an Anglo-Welsh queen: with the union of the two kingdoms, the settlement of Ulster could go forward along with the transformation of the Scottish Borders into the middle shires of a joint kingdom. It fell to a Scottish king to proclaim the union of Britain:

> the Isle within itself hath almost none but imaginary bounds of separation, without but one common limit or rather guard of the Ocean sea, making the whole a little world within itself, the nations an uniformity of constitutions both of body and mind, especially in martial processes, a community of language (the principal means of civil society), an unity of religion (the deepest bond of hearty union and the surest knot of lasting peace).

The unification of the islands gave the basis for the great lunge forward across the Atlantic, the exodus of stocks to North America, the open door for which the Elizabethans had fought. We are all aware of the part played by the West Country, the Plymouth Company and its promoters—such men as Sir Ferdinando Gorges, John Trelawny, and John White of Dorchester—in the later beginnings of New England. But observe, what has been very little observed by historians, that it was the very people who were most deeply concerned with the plantation and colonization of Southern Ireland—Humphrey Gilbert, Walter Raleigh, Richard Grenville—who took the leading part in planting the first colonies in Virginia. It is as if Ireland were the blueprint for America.

The question of North America became one of national concern; that is to say, so many of the leading spirits of the age were interested, not a few of them engaged by it. The leading figures at Court were closely concerned—Leicester and Walsingham, Sir Christopher Hatton and Sir Philip Sidney, even Burghley in a watchful, conservative way; the Queen herself was less conservative, and she was interested in everything that affected America. She invested in at least two of Hawkins' voyages to the

Caribbean, and one of Frobisher's towards the Northwest Passage. Unbeknown to her sage Lord Treasurer, she planned Drake's great voyage with him: in that she was the principal investor and the principal recipient of the booty. It was she who granted Humphrey Gilbert the patent to settle and colonize North America; on his death she passed it on to Walter Raleigh, to whom she permitted the land to be called Virginia after her. She would never make peace with Spain without security for the liberties of the Netherlands or the open door for English settlement in North America.

On the side of action, names are legion, so many of the most famous Elizabethans took part or were involved: Drake, Raleigh, the Gilberts, Grenville, Thomas Cavendish, Frobisher, the Hawkinses. On the side of science and intellect: John Dee, the leading mathematician and cosmographer of the early part of the reign; Thomas Hariot, first mathematician of the age; Richard Hakluyt, whose lifework it was to focus their minds upon America—the priority that the American school of thought and action came to have was due to a lifetime of concentrated, educated propaganda from his brain and pen. It has been given to few men to fertilize the history of their country so prodigiously. To him we owe the survival of nearly everything we know of the American voyages. His long life proved the one continuing figure that linked the two waves of Virginia enterprise, the successive attempts of the 1580's and those that gained a permanent foothold after the Queen's death. In literature, before Shakespeare died, the impact of America upon the English imagination is already rich and evident, in Spenser and Drayton, in Raleigh and Chapman and Donne, never more beautifully than in *The Tempest*.

Perhaps then we may leave the last word to a poet, Samuel Daniel— one of Sidney's circle and a West Countryman—who glimpsed something of the limitless possibilities to come out of the unimaginable future, in that process of which we have indicated the beginnings:

> And who in time knows whither we may vent
> The treasure of our tongue, to what strange shores
> This gain of our best glory shall be sent,
> To enrich unknowing nations with our stores?
> What worlds in the yet unformèd Occident
> May come refined with the accents that are ours?

But what a difference from the accent of the Middle Ages, what a world we are away now from the medieval world!

2. STATE CONTROL IN SIXTEENTH-CENTURY ENGLAND*

by Lawrence Stone

European expansion and the creation of overseas empires
were intimately related to profound changes within Europe that
transformed not only the state but also the productive system.
The particular forms English expansion took, especially reliance
on private capital and enterprise through joint-stock companies,
which sold shares of stock to raise large sums of money, reflected
forces that were modernizing English society. The growing importance of foreign trade and industrial enterprise produced
greater national prosperity in the long run, but in the short run
they brought dislocations to the villages and towns. Older patterns of economic activity gave way to newer ones, and people
were uprooted because they were no longer able to make a
living as their forefathers had. As England become more highly
commercialized, and as regions specialized in particular tasks,
the productive system became more interdependent and highly
sensitive to fluctuations in the market place, especially on the

* *Economic History Review*, vol. 17 (1947), 103–120. Footnotes have been
omitted except where they are necessary for an understanding of the text.

continent of Europe. Recurrent instability led to distress among merchants, artisans, peasants, and landowners who sought help from the state to restore prosperity and to protect them from the uncertainties of a volatile economy. In the following selection, Lawrence Stone explores some of the political and economic consequences of national development in sixteenth-century England. According to Stone, an expansion in cloth exports during the first half of the sixteenth century resulted in a redistribution of resources which brought social dislocations and made the economy highly vulnerable to trade fluctuations. Stone rejects the view that the late sixteenth century was economically depressed, insisting that war and fear of war generated substantial industrial growth. The danger of war, he argues, rather than the pressures of depression or the dictates of economic theory, led the state to exercise greater control over the economy. A desire to promote the security of the realm, rather than to maximize profits, was the chief aim of Tudor mercantilism, but the Crown found it impossible to promote social stability through economic planning that cushioned the disruptive impact of social change, and at the same time to protect the nation against foreign dangers. National security needs led the state to seek additional revenues and to encourage economic growth, objectives which were furthered by incorporating trading companies. But these enterprises were agents of social change. Thus economic development gradually displaced people who then had to search for fresh opportunities. In the early seventeenth century, some found them in the New World, utilizing the organizational advantages of the chartered trading company.

For further reading: F. J. Fisher, "Commercial Trends and Policy in Sixteenth-Century England," *Economic History Review,* vol. 10 (1946), 95–117; R. H. Tawney, *The Agrarian Problem in the Sixteenth Century* (1912); Barry E. Supple, *Commercial Crisis and Change in England, 1600–1642* (1959); E. Lipson, *Economic History of England,* vol. 2 (1931).

The last quarter of a century has seen the publication of a number of works which have profoundly modified or enlarged previous ideas about the economic history of sixteenth-century England. New lights have been thrown upon the industrial development, the commercial expansion, and the social changes of that period.

It is possible, however, that in two respects the reaction from the ideas of the Victorian and Edwardian historians has been too great. It has been said that, in execution, Tudor social and economic policy was 'capricious and irregular and at most did no more than impose an occasional brake on the economic forces'. Undoubtedly, in some respects, that policy demanded feats of administrative efficiency that a rudimentary bureaucratic structure based on the voluntary work of local gentry was quite unable to provide. Thus attempts to enforce political Lent were confessedly a failure, as were the laws against usury, and price control of essential foodstuffs; to a certain extent the same applies to agrarian laws, although the great increase in enclosures that began during the brief experiment in relaxation of the laws at the end of the century might indicate that they were more effective than is sometimes assumed to-day. Nevertheless, in many fields in which administrative action was more easily applicable or in which the cooperation of powerful vested interests were obtained, the government exercised a determining influence upon the economic history of the Tudor period.

Secondly, the motives of the official policy have been interpreted in terms of purely economic forces, related very closely if not exclusively to the rise and fall of economic prosperity. These trends in historiography have been described as a process by which 'the twentieth century is busily recreating the sixteenth century in its own image'. But it may be doubted whether these are precisely the lessons of the present day. An interpretation which regards politics and law as but servile reflections of basic economic changes scarcely provides a suitable explanation for an age in which the pressure of war, nationalism and a theory of social justice has led the State to intervene effectively in the reorganization of the whole economic system.

I

Prosperity is an inexact and periphrastic term. Only recently, with the introduction of the concept of national income and the provision of adequate data to appreciate such a concept has the word begun to be subjected to scientific analysis. Any estimate of prosperity must depend upon a close study of domestic production, internal consumption and foreign trade. To give it social and historical content, there must be added an examination of the distribution of wealth throughout the class structure of society.

In a recent article, brilliant in analysis and fertile in ideas, F. J. Fisher has centred the study of Tudor economy and economic policy round a 'period of prosperity' followed by a 'great depression', both derived mainly from the export figures for the cloth trade. The economy of England during the first half of the sixteenth century was concentrated to an increasing degree upon a single produce handled through a single port and directed along a single trade route. When Edward VI ascended the throne, the prosperity and indeed the very existence of England depended to a very large extent on the export of cloth through London to the great international mart of Antwerp, where were obtained those import goods and manufactures demanded by the English consumer.

An examination of the figures for the export of cloth should therefore provide a quantitative illustration of some aspects of the economic changes that were in progress. But throughout the century there were two factors which operated to an unknown degree to diminish the value of any conclusions which may be drawn from trade statistics. In the first place, the volume of internal consumption is unknown. But there are indications that the sixteenth century saw a marked increase in material comfort in most sections of the population. The 'sturdy rogues and vagabonds' and the impotent poor may have existed at bare subsistence level, the younger sons of gentry may have had to content themselves with 'that which the catte left on the malt heap', the nobility may have mortgaged their estates, pawned their plate and jewels and run up enormous debts, but recent scholarship has tended to prove that the virtual freedom from taxation and the intermittent application of a sliding wage scale kept the real income of the English workman at a fairly high level during this period.

Secondly, there is the problem of how far the figures themselves may be trusted to give any real indication of trade conditions. As the century progresses, the evidence of smuggling multiplies. Gross underpayment of customs officials did not encourage honesty, and it was generally held that 'serchers are men knowne to be men that wyll be coroppted for moneye'. With the outbreak of the war in 1586 and the collapse of the

15

farming system, smuggling and interloping took on fresh vitality, and 'the stragler shipping his Clothe and other commoditie in couert manner hugger mugger and at obscure portes' became a very important factor in English overseas trade.

While these considerations tend to diminish the value of the foreign trade figures as a whole, there is no doubt that cloth export statistics can be used to provide some very rough indication of commercial trends, if not of national prosperity. Full printed figures are only available for the first half of the century, but for this period certain fairly firm statistical conclusions may be drawn.

In the first place, the direction of trade altered in a very marked manner, London gaining at the expense of the outports, squeezed out of business by the credit resources and political influence of the capital, the manipulation of the Merchant Adventurers Company by the great City magnates, and the concentration of traffic along the London-Antwerp route due to the rise of the latter city to a unique and dominating position in world trade. Thus London's relative share of traffic rose from about 70 to 90% of the whole, while the outports declined absolutely by 40%.

Wool exports suffered a slow decline of about 33%. Relatively they formed 26% in value of the boom of 1519–20, 8½% of that of 1544–5. The proportions of the trade handled by the three groups, the Adventurers, the Hansa and the other aliens remained fairly constant till 1545, taking about 55, 22, and 23% respectively. There is no sign of the Hansa or any other alien group gaining at the expense of the native merchants. The considerable temporary fluctuations that did occur were due to political factors, war, the fear of war, or arrest of goods, such as affected the Italians in 1535–8 and the Adventurers in 1545.

The overall expansion, of which so much has been said, was in fact a relatively modest affair. Taking the first and last five years of the reign of Henry VIII, cloth exports increased by exactly 50%, which is less than 1½% a year, while the value of all woollen goods exported barely increased by a third. At no time did the volume of woollen exports reach the peak of 37,700 sacks which was achieved in 1358.

The pattern of trade fluctuations divides naturally into three parts. First, a boom, in volume almost as great as the more publicized cycle of the 'forties, mostly in wool rather than cloth, building up to a peak in 1521. This expansion is of major significance in explaining the great

16

contemporary agitation over enclosures. Secondly, a period of marked annual fluctuations, but showing a slow average upward trend to 1539. Finally, a period of three cycles of increasingly dizzy booms and abysmal slumps, ending in final collapse in 1553. The explanation of these changes can be most easily studied in the latter stages. Their cause is to be sought, not in the producing area of England, nor in the entrepôt of Antwerp, nor even in the finishing towns of Brabant and Flanders, but in the consumer area around the great mart of Frankfurt. Prosperous trade conditions demanded normal political and economic relations with the Low Countries, and open communications across to north Germany and down the Rhine to the subsidiary market of Italy. Boom conditions required a good harvest in Germany to create surplus civilian purchasing power, and large armies massed on Germany's periphery to stimulate great additional military demand for clothing. These conditions were all fulfilled in the boom years of 1541, 1544–6, 1550–1. The intervening slumps of 1542 and 1547 were caused by the interruptions by war of communications between Antwerp and the consumer areas. In the latter case, a European crop failure in the autumn of 1545 was followed by a general paralysis of communications for two months by the icing up of the waterways, and succeeded in turn in the summer by the outbreak of the Smalkaldic war, which at once utterly ruined the Antwerp cloth market. Exchange depreciation played no part whatsoever in causing the first two boom cycles up to 1547, since the major decline in sterling in terms of the Flemish pound had not yet begun. Its effect upon the boom of 1550–1 is at least doubtful. All that is certain is that the crash of 1552 onwards and the subsequent reorganization of the whole export business was brought about largely by chaotic monetary conditions produced by reckless debasement and sudden deflation following swiftly and unpredictably one after another. Regular inflation sometimes stimulates export, but violent fluctuations in currency values produces a state of uncertainty which is always disastrous.

While the general increase in exports was the main cause of the dislocation of agrarian society, it was these violent trade fluctuations of the 'forties that played the largest part in creating the extreme insecurity and misery of the cloth-workers and the highly speculative nature of the traffic which were later on to unite opinion in open hostility to commercial conditions fraught with such social and economic dangers. Even the boom years limited most of their benefits to certain small sections of

Table of Exports Figures for Cloth, Wool and Worsted, 1510–47.[1,2]

DATE	CLOTH FROM OUTPORTS	CLOTH FROM LONDON	TOTAL CLOTH EXPORTS	WOOL SACKS EXPORTED	WORSTEDS EXPORTED	TOTAL VOLUME OF WOOLLENS EXPORTED	TOTAL VALUE OF WOOLLENS EXPORTED	% OF CLOTH EXPORTED BY NATIVES	% OF CLOTH EXPORTED BY HANSA	% OF CLOTH EXPORTED BY OTHER ALIENS
1510	26	50	76	8.5	6	119	97	58	14	28
1511	22	64	86	8.6	5	128	105	61	26	13
1512	20	57	77	6.5	5	110	93	59	29	12
1513	27	59	86	5.1	7	118	101	51	28	21
1514	27	66	93	7.8	6	133	113	59	22	19
1515	28	65	93	7.2	7	131	112	60	23	17
1516	23	59	82	7.6	6	121	101	61	24	15
1517	30	57	87	8.2	7	130	108	52	25	23
1518	25	67	92	9.1	7	138	115	58	23	19
1519	26	65	91	13.1	6	154	121	56	24	20
1520	31	67	98	11.5	8	156	125	62	18	20
1521	26	54	76	10.2	6	126	100	61	22	17
1522	14	50	64	5.0	3	89	76	69	22	9
1523	29	57	86	5.1	5	113	99	49	22	29
1524	21	69	90	5.1	6	118	104	58	23	19
1525	17	79	96	3.8	6	118	108	62	22	16
1526	21	70	91	4.9	7	119	106	63	20	17
1527	20	71	91	7.1	6	127	109	57	17	26
1528	19	81	100	5.6	6	130	115	58	27	15
1529	21	74	95	3.3	5	119	105	64	22	14
1530	21	71	91	4.6	5	116	103	63	23	14
1531	22	65	87	2.7	4	103	95	56	23	21
1532	20	62	82	3.0	4	99	101	54	25	21

18

Table (Continued)

DATE	CLOTH FROM OUTPORTS	CLOTH FROM LONDON	TOTAL CLOTH EXPORTS	WOOL SACKS EXPORTED	WORSTEDS EXPORTED	TOTAL VOLUME OF WOOLLENS EXPORTED	TOTAL VALUE OF WOOLLENS EXPORTED	% OF CLOTH EXPORTED BY NATIVES	% OF CLOTH EXPORTED BY HANSA	% OF CLOTH EXPORTED BY OTHER ALIENS
1533	17	83	100	2.1	5	114	107	58	25	17
1534	21	89	110	3.7	3	125	119	58	25	17
1535	14	78	92	3.8	3	111	102	61	28	11
1536	18	90	108	4.9	3	132	120	62	28	10
1537	17	86	103	3.6	2	121	111	59	33	8
1538	19	85	104	3.1	1	118	111	62	30	8
1539	17	97	114	4.3	2	135	124	53	22	25
1540	16	100	116	4.9	3	140	128	53	21	26
1541	21	110	131	4.7	2	153	141	52	20	28
1542	15	97	112	5.6	2	138	124	53	20	27
1543	18	81	99	4.2	1	118	108	54	25	21
1544	18	119	137	6.9	1	168	152	61	20	19
1545	11	136	147	4.9	1	169	158	40	22	38
1546	11	124	135	4.3	1	155	145	44	23	33
1547	13	98	109	4.7	1	130	119	57	27	16

[1] Calculated from the tables printed by G. Schanz, *Englische Handelspolitik*, II, 76–105.

[2] Figures are given in thousands of cloths or sacks of wool; figures are accurate to nearest thousand and nearest 1%.

the population, the sheep-farming landlords, the capitalist clothiers and the great London and alien merchants, while certain areas of the national economy were severely affected. The surplus agricultural labourer and evicted copyholder were reduced to the level of vagrant squatters, eking out a living on the rapidly diminishing wastes and common-lands. The outports decayed at an alarming rate as London monopolized more and more of the foreign trade. The old corporate towns were hard hit by the drift of the clothing industry to the countryside to escape guild restrictions. Long-distance foreign trade declined at a time when the seamen of western Europe were engaged in opening up the untapped resources of the Indies and the New World. Trade to West Africa and the Levant petered out. For what reason was there to tie up capital for long periods in high speculative enterprises, when there were quick and sure profits to be made by the short safe trip to Antwerp where could be obtained goods drawn from every quarter of the known world? When those profits, while remaining quick, ceased to be sure, the London capital groups began to turn their attention to opening up direct access to the sources of the exotic products they required. The sinking of capital from 1539–49 in the immense orgy of land sales organized by an improvident administration, probably played an even greater part in damping enthusiasm for foreign ventures at a time when credit facilities were extremely limited. From Antwerp 'on hoye will bryng as much in one yere as x merchantes shippes war wont to bryng from the other placees in ij years'. The result was a marked lag in shipping till in 1544 England's naval power depended on foreign shipyards. Thus the expansion in the export of cloth in the first half of the century resulted in a 'prosperity', the misshapen and unbalanced distribution of which entailed very serious economic consequences.

For the second half of the century full statistics are not at present available. Figures for London show the steady maintenance of cloth exports at a higher level than any achieved before 1540, with the exception of two acute periods of slump arising from political tension with the Low Countries. It is suspicious, however, that these London figures show no signs of the undoubted depression of 1586–7 on the outbreak of regular warfare, and of the prolonged decay in which foreign trade languished till the restoration of peace in 1604. Certain factors which were of importance during the first half of the century ceased to apply during the second. By 1550, the outports had reached a state of decay in which they remained throughout the rest of the Tudor period. The export of wool continued to decline, but it was no longer a serious factor in English economy.

But for this latter half of the century it is very unsafe to base a study of English economic history upon the export of cloth. The careful survey of the reign of Elizabeth made by Professor Scott requires much stronger weight of contrary evidence to necessitate any violent modification of his deductions. From 1559 till the outbreak of war, England embarked upon a deliberate policy of the exploitation of natural resources and the opening up of new markets. Commerce developed to Africa, Russia, Italy and the Levant. The carrying trade was captured from alien merchants. The volume of shipping quintupled, colonial ventures were undertaken, and for a time huge profits accrued from piracy and privateering. But the evidence of a general trade depression after 1586 is overwhelming. The closing of foreign markets, the recurrent threat of invasion, the drain on fluid capital by heavy taxation and investment in private naval ventures, the series of bad harvests, the catastrophic plagues of 1592 and 1602–3 all combined to create an atmosphere of stagnation and discontent. In 1591, many merchants went bankrupt for loss of traffic. As the century drew to a close, England began to suffer retribution for that orgy of piracy which she had been the first to inaugurate and by which she had so long profited.

The most remarkable phenomenon of the half-century, however, was the immense industrial revolution which created new sources of wealth by developing the natural resources of the country. It is very significant of the new pattern of English economy that the two great consumer markets for which this expanding production catered were the military needs of the State and the basic essentials of life for the poorer classes. Thus vast quantities of capital were sunk in the mining of coal, copper, zinc, iron, lead and tin. New metallurgical industries sprang up in copper, brass and iron. Brewing, building, cannon, gunpowder, steel, wire, soap and salt manufacture all expanded and developed under the new impetus. By the end of the century, the growing timber famine had not yet effectively checked this astonishing development. In the country-side, wastes were reclaimed, fens drained, and productivity increased by scientific farming. Combined with the widespread evidence of a higher level of consumption and the opening up of new foreign markets, these achievements make it impossible to dismiss the whole Elizabethan period as one of general depression. The true complexity of economic facts does not lend itself to such easy formulae.

II

It is in the highest degree unfortunate that discussion of the causes and effects of government intervention in economic policy is so frequently subordinated to ideological preconceptions of the present day. In dealing with sixteenth-century economic history, it is necessary to avoid the Scylla of naïve *étatisme* of W. Cunningham, with his conception of Burghley as an economic 'master mind', the Charybdis of Free Trade convictions, that led Professor Unwin to see nothing in company organization but Machiavellian plots by great London merchants to destroy the commerce of England for their own selfish ends; and the tempting but treacherous fairway of Marxist interpretation which conceives the Tudor statesman in the role of Aesop's fly, perched impotent but fretful upon the inexorably revolving wheel of economic causation.

The first half of the sixteenth century was a period of tentative but ever more numerous experiments in economic control, and there is no evidence for an increase in commercial freedom. The statute of 1497 only temporarily curtailed the power of the greater London merchants over the Merchant Adventurers Company. In view of Professor Tawney's conclusion that before 1571 there was not 'any substantial breach in the policy of meeting new problems with mediaeval weapons', the claim to a 'collapse of the usury laws' seems hardly substantiated. The 'relaxation of restriction upon the export of unfinished cloth' upon examination turns out to be no more than the readjustment of a monetary scale to keep pace with the depreciation of the coinage. It is hard to reconcile a 'virtual cessation of attacks upon the Hanseatic merchants' with the latter's long list of complaints at persecution and unfair discrimination at the hands of English officials, port authorities and merchants. During the war period of the 'forties, trade was less free than at any subsequent period. Ocean-going ships of every nation were arrested and requisitioned for the Navy. War decrees had prohibited aliens from exporting almost all commodities save tin. Piracy and regular naval seizures blocked the Channel. Mutual arrests of merchants' goods took place in attempts to obtain compensation for these losses.

Although the years after 1550 saw a consolidation and intensification of the previous tentative experiments at control and restriction of economic enterprise, it would be false to suggest that there was any real change in policy at this time. The continuity of method and intention was far more striking than the difference in scope and possibly in efficacy. 'The early Tudors had sought to set limits to the growth of industrial capitalism' to a degree which contrasted markedly with the deliberate encouragement by Burghley of enterprises on capitalistic lines altogether unaffected by the apprenticeship codification of 1562. That codification was itself only the culmination of a long series of local regulations and was directed mainly at the cloth trade which was regarded with much disfavour by the administration and by conservative opinion. Local monopolies, like the Newcastle Hostmen, received encouragement in their selfish ambitions. Long before 1550, price control of essential staples and of monopoly articles had begun. Bullion export was prohibited and exchange control intermittently imposed, usually with disastrous results. The Navigation Act of 1540 not merely legislated against foreign shipping but also fixed standard freight rates. Attempts were made to restrict the export of certain raw materials and the import of certain competitive foreign manufactures. With the exception of the compulsory assessment, every item of the Elizabethan Poor Law may be discovered in the act of 1536, while by 1549 both London and Norwich had adopted this last feature to complete the full programme. It was the depression of the early 'thirties and the dislocation of 1547–9 that gave rise to the Poor Law principles of the Tudor period. Thus at every point can be observed the experiments in control and restriction, drawing upon the ideas and experience of which Elizabethan statesmen were able to codify and co-ordinate a system of regulation more effective and more complete than any that had preceded it.

The concept of mercantilism has come to mean little more than a belief in the justice and efficacy of State intervention in economic activity. The policy as applied to all the countries of sixteenth-century Europe was something more precise. It was the development and the acceptance of a system of economic nationalism, the mainspring and inspiration of which was not the rise or fall of economic prosperity, but the relentless pressure of war and the fear of war. The problem of how best to avoid the problems that threatened 'if warres should chance' was one which never ceased to torment the minds of pamphleteers, merchants and statesmen. Security, not prosperity, was the main object of Tudor economic policy. The Elizabethan in particular lived in the perpetual shadow of conspiracy and invasion and was haunted by memories of the most costly war England had ever waged or was to wage again for over a century. The theory of nationalism began to assume the sanctification of philosophy: 'it be agreable to the rule of nature to prefer our owne people before strangers'. War itself acquired social justification, 'serving (as King Ferdinand had wont to say) as a Potion of Rhubarbe to waste away the choler from the body of the Realm', 'a Sovereign medicine for domesticall inconueniencies'.

It was the rearmament programme that lay behind the intensive efforts for the improvement of shipping, the reflection of which may be seen in the Navigation Acts, the enforcement of political Lent, the attempts to encourage the fishing industry, the prohibition of the sale of ships, the propaganda for colonial development, the subsidy of five shillings a ton on the construction of every ship over a hundred tons, and the restoration of strategic ports like Dover. The same factor played its part in determining government policy towards the Trading Companies—who were by charter compelled to use English vessels, and the scale of whose enterprises naturally led them to provide 'a great number of very large and serviceable Merchaunt shippes fit as well for defence of the Realme (If need were) as for Trafficque'. Measures were taken to provide the necessary raw materials for shipping. Draconian legislation was passed to preserve timber. Hemp growing for cordage was encouraged in areas where there was no danger of giving offence to the refined olfactory organ of the Queen. Somewhat ineffectual efforts were made to stimulate native manufacture of sail-cloth at Stamford. One of the primary reasons for the founding of the Muscovy Company was the need to secure a supply of tar, wax, cordage, masts and other naval stores, independent of any political accidents which might tempt the King of Denmark to close the Sound. Nor was the result of all this governmental activity altogether disappointing, as was shown by the impressive turn-out of merchant auxiliaries to assist the Queen's Navy in 1588.

The dependence of English military power upon the munitions industry of the Rhineland and north-western Europe was a source of perpetual anxiety to the Privy Council. In the great war of 1542–50 England had been obliged to import almost every military requirement: troops from Germany and Italy, money from Antwerp, shipping and naval stores from the Baltic, anchors, guns and gunpowder from the Low Countries, small arms and equipment from Milan and Brescia, food for the armed forces from Danzig and Holland, bowstaves from Switzerland and the Hansa. One of the major arguments used in 1573 for the creation of a staple at Ipswich was that by its establishment 'all maner of munitions and other thinges necessary for the Defence of this Realme wilbe brought hither as it hath bene to Andwerpe so that her Maiestie shall have in her own Realme sufficient to serve her Highness at all tymes without seking of it else where'. The plan for a public bank in 1576 was buttressed by the argument that it would serve for the 'prouisshon of munisshons and other things appartaining for defence in tyme of warre, thinges in theise trobbelsomme days thought very necessary'.

Similar motives of military security lay behind the active and friendly interest of the government in the new mining and metallurgical enterprises. The grants of monopoly patents, the earliest of their kind, were designed to improve the military preparedness of the realm. The Mines Royal were intended to make England independent of foreign copper for the manufacture of brass cannon. It was only the guarantee by the government to make large and continual purchases of copper that induced capitalists to undertake the heavy investment that was required. The Mineral and Battery Company, when granted its patent, promised to manufacture 'armure of such goodness and Temperature as shalbe thought most mete for the servis of the Quenes Maiestie'. A domestic provision of small arms and armour was assisted by the encouragement given to alien armourers to immigrate and settle at Woolwich. Iron production in the Wealde only began to expand rapidly with the invention of cast iron cannon in the 'forties, introduced to England, significantly enough, by a clergyman capitalist, Parson Levett of Buxted. By 1574, production had grown to such dimensions that the government was compelled to intervene to control sale and restrict manufacture. For the export of cannon had become a 'traid of merchandise' as a result of which it was claimed that 'the enemie is better fournished with them then our owne contry ships ar'. After Gresham's prescient warning of the importance of the question, a domestic saltpetre and gunpowder industry was given intermittent encouragement but with only moderate success till the near disaster of 1588 forced the government to take active steps to reorganize production on a large scale. The Act of 1563, prohibiting the import of certain foreign manufactures, was motivated in part by the balance of trade theory and the desire to provide domestic employment. It is noticeable, however, that most of the goods mentioned in the Act were articles of military equipment.

The reorientation of English economy that occurred after 1550 was in part the result of individual enterprise and investment of private capital. But the direction taken by that flow of capital and energy was in no small way guided by a system of governmental favours and inhibitions. Burghley, supported by conservative and responsible opinion, directed the economic life of England towards the creation of an autarkic state. For fear of the dangers of economic warfare lay heavy upon the commercial life of Elizabethan England. Thus the food policy of increased corn production and low prices was inspired as much by a desire for self-sufficiency as a sense of social paternalism. The reasons for the Act of 1597–8 were that 'the said husbandrie and tillage is a cause that the realme doth more stand upon itselfe without dependinge upon forraine Cuntries', the decay of which subjected 'the realm to the discretion of foreign states . . . to help us with corn in time of dearth'. Restrictions on taverns and the restraint of wine import was based on the wisdom 'not to laye down the vse of our natural foods ("ale and beare") for the entysement of a forrayn that by occasion of warrs may be kept from us'. The great expansion of native industry was made economically possible partly by the interruption of foreign trade due to political events and by the improved credit facilities of London but partly also by the protective barriers deliberately created by the government to foster economic self-sufficiency.

Richelieu observed that 'l'argent . . . est le point d'Archimède qui étant fermement établi donne moyen de mouvoir tout le monde'. *Pecunia nervus belli* was a generally accepted truism that the paradoxical suggestion of Machiavelli had done nothing to confound. The vicious and all pervasive fiscalism that was such a marked feature of Elizabethan policy was itself but one aspect of the pressure of war upon every facet of sixteenth-century life. The normal revenue of the Crown was perfectly capable of meeting the ordinary requirements of the administration. But the passionate desire to acquire a war chest in time of peace and the desperate search for ways and means to meet the cost of military enterprises in time of war exercised a persistent and ever-increasing influence upon economic policy. In every discussion of economic ideas during the reign whether in favour of the protection of the new drapery, a patent of monopoly, a new bullion policy, or against State control of exchange and the new impositions on cloth, all writers were at pains to point out, whatever the improbability of the claim, that 'the Queenes Customes shall much increase yearly'.

It is not surprising therefore if opportunist motives of war finance can be detected behind the favours showered by the Crown upon the Trading Companies. After a careful study of the fact, Professor Unwin concluded that 'whatever the results of the connexion between the government and the Merchant Adventurers, it had its origin and mainspring, not in any disinterested desire of the government to realise any particular theory of trade, but in the urgency of the Crown's own immediate needs'. The connexion between the establishment of a monopoly limited to an inner ring of great merchants and the regular loans to the Crown and the two seizures of cloth in 1553 and 1559 has been established beyond all doubt. It was war finance, not depression economics, that gave the merchant capitalists their chance. Similarly, the Muscovy Company provided extended credits to the government for the purchase of naval stores; the Levant Company offered a new imposition on currants and made the Crown a shareholder, the Spanish Company paid a lump sum down for its privileges; industrial monopolies were auctioned to the highest bidder. The flood of patents of every type at the end of the reign reflects the desperate state of the Crown finances, which led the Queen to sacrifice her popularity for the meagre returns rendered by the host of optimistic projectors and patentees. Even price control and the policy of deflation and exchange regulation was influenced to no small extent by the fact that 'the highe price of all thinges is . . . the cheyfiste cawse the Kings maiestie cannot without expence of wonderful great sommes of money menteigne his warres against his eneymies'.

A further cause of government activity was the problem of unemployment. 'That lothesome monster Idelnesse (the mother and breeder of Vacaboundes) . . . that pestilent Canker' 'which is the root of all mischief' was regarded with intense hostility by moralists on the one hand and by politicians on the other. The essential truth was rediscovered that industrial workers in general and textile workers in particular 'ar of worss condition to be quyetly governed than the husband men'. 1536 and 1548 had left an indelible impression upon the minds of contemporaries, which accounts for the particular interest shown by the government in every crisis of the cloth trade. They lived in fear that 'for lack of vent, tumult will follow in clothing counties', and it was the need to 'stay the fury of the inferior multitude' that lay behind much of the administrative activity to provide cheap food and fuel and to maintain employment.

But the paradox of Tudor administration and perhaps the ultimate cause of the collapse of the whole system is to be found in the extent to which its programme of the paternalist state, of social justice and conservatism, was sacrificed to the implementation of the more pressing needs of planned autarky and opportunist war finance. All Tudor governments were the most resolute theoretical opponents of those social changes and those new *bourgeois* classes from which they are supposed to have derived most support. That hostility may be seen—though more perhaps in words than in deeds—from Henry VII, through Wolsey, Cromwell, Somerset and Burghley right down to Robert Cecil, and beyond to Bacon and Laud. Its most idealistic expression is found in the writings of Latimer and Hales; its most concrete and far-reaching programme is Burghley's draft proposals to set before the parliament of 1559. That Burghley's ideas were never translated into legislation was due to the hostility of the classes represented in the Commons to any such fixation of the class structure. Only those who had already arrived could afford to shut the door upon new aspirants to a raised social standing. Nevertheless, till the turn of the century, public opinion was generally hostile to those new forces in society, the rack-renting landlord, the dry exchanger, the corrupt chevisauncer, the insatiable usurer, the forestaller, regrater and engrosser, the patentee and monopolist, each 'a great taker of advantages', all conveniently and collectively summed up as 'caterpillars of the Common weal'.

III

Man is not exclusively an economic animal. Prejudice or passion, ignorance or idealism, not infrequently make him act in a manner directly contrary to his material interests. Thus this social conservatism was accepted by many whose career was only made possible by the dissolution of the existing class system. How many sheep-farming landlords voted in the Commons for the Depopulation Acts, how many clothiers for the Statute of Apprentices? Their compliance, however, must not exclusively be attributed to sentimentality. The propertied classes of the Elizabethan period were faced with a turbulent and unruly proletariat, half industrial workers, half professional unemployed. The State had no police force, no standing army, to quell disorder. It was the fear of a jacquerie by these 'swarms of poor loose wandering people . . . dangerous to the State' that led the rising merchants and progressive gentry to accept restraints upon their activity; for they had the sense to realize that the methods they employed to acquire their fortunes were at the same time precisely those that accentuated the threat of social revolution. Like the statesmen and courtiers who held the reins of political power, they were perpetually afraid lest 'the people of the realm . . . fall into violence to feed and fill their lewd appetites with the open spoil of others'.

The reign of Edward VI was the critical period in sixteenth-century England. Society itself seemed in danger of imminent dissolution. Religious anarchy and extremism, administrative corruption, financial collapse, currency and exchange chaos, agrarian unrest, extravagant and fruitless military enterprises, political control by a group of most unscrupulous and irresponsible careerists, all combined with the most violent fluctuations in the main export trade to produce a situation of acute crisis. Rightly or wrongly, two conclusions were drawn in the economic sphere. Excessive dependence upon the cloth trade was thought to be a cause of military weakness, agrarian disturbance, a shortage of labour in agriculture and other essential industries, a decay in shipping and in general a deformation of the economic life of the country. Further, the key to foreign trade was held to lie in a favourable exchange rate, the maintenance of which was constantly endangered by the transfer operations of a host of small merchants, trading on short-term credit. The first conclusion resulted in a series of measures designed to control further expansion of the cloth trade. The second, coupled with the fiscal needs of the state and the existence of a powerful class of great merchants, led to a number of agreements between the government and high financial interests which found expression in the creation of industrial monopolies and of joint stock trading companies. The necessity for capital concentration to increase efficiency and productivity clearly played a part in influencing this growth. This need, however, does not explain the monopolistic and oligarchic system as it developed in the latter half of the sixteenth century. Thus the great industrial and commercial expansion of the time was financed and directed behind artificial barriers which confined investment and control to some two or three score of great London merchants, a few enterprising courtiers like Burghley and Leicester, and a handful of progressive-minded industrialists and land-owners. Extensive economic control and a measure of social conservatism were achieved at the price of a free hand for big business.

For it is altogether false to see company organization as a reaction to restriction in the face of a depression. In boom and slump alike, the motive force behind the trading companies was the desire by the great merchants to increase their profits by placing restrictions on their lesser competitors, and by making price-rigging agreements between themselves to prevent cut-throat competition. The principle that actuated them was set out in Lionel Cranfield's suggestion to his fellow-magnate Sir Arthur Ingram that 'we may join together faithfully to raise our fortunes by such casualties as this stirring age shall afford', instead of seeking 'to advance our estate by each other's loss'—which was not perhaps quite what Bacon had in mind when he declared that 'Trading in Companies is most agreeable to the English nature.'

The Companies were formed to obtain the maximum profits for a minimum number, most of them during a period of expansion. The Spanish Company was created in 1577 to skim the cream of the trade to the Peninsula which had been reopened in 1574, the Eastland Company in the middle of the prosperous decade of 1575–85. Nor is there any clear connexion between a slump in trade and the growth of restrictionism. The 'limitation of the vend' by the Newcastle Hostmen was enforced at a time of immense expansion in the coal trade. The restrictive regulations of the Merchant Adventurers continued in full force during the post-war boom of the early years of the reign of James I, as well as the depression period of 1586–1603. The expulsion of the Hansa, of which so much play has been made, was due to the end of the war and the expansion of English shipbuilding, which made dependence upon Hanseatic sea-power no longer necessary, and to the dominant influence over government finance exerted by a small group of Merchant Adventurers. Excessive interest in Hakluyt's personal preoccupations has led to the disguising of many of the ventures of exploration and colonization of the period as quests for new markets for surplus domestic cloth. The examination of other witnesses shows clearly that the primary object of these voyages and Companies was that of the simple treasure-hunter—the passionate search for new passages to the land of gold and silver, jewels and spices.

If it is inaccurate to describe company organization as 'the restrictions of a great depression', it is no more justifiable to attribute the attacks on these restrictions at the end of the century to the fact that 'conditions for trade expansion had once more come into being'. The most cursory examination of the chronology of the attack shows that precisely the reverse is true. The search for the causes of the depression of the 'fifties had led to a successful campaign against the cloth industry and the small merchants and retailers. The same search for the causes of the depression of the 'nineties led to the attack, less successful on this occasion, upon the industrial monopolies and trading companies. It was at the height of the slump, in 1597, that Parliament first set on foot the inquiry into its origins that led to the attacks upon industrial monopolies and patents during the next few years. Nor was the great outcry against the trading companies in 1604 a spontaneous reaction to peace and the reopening of European trade routes, but had its origin at least four years back. For it was to confound the critics that Wheeler wrote his celebrated defence of the Merchant Adventurers in 1601. The whole process looks suspiciously like an attempt by those outside the ring, not to destroy the system, but to force an opening just sufficiently wide for themselves to enter into a share of the profits. By 1602, London was paying 80% of the customs of all the ports in the country, and a little later James I could observe that 'with time England will only be London'. Prevailing dissatisfaction at the depression seemed a convenient opportunity to renew the war against the Capital, which the provincial merchants had waged intermittently albeit unsuccessfully during the whole of the past century. Thus the driving force behind the attack on the Companies was provincial jealousy of London by West Country merchants, using Sir Edwin Sandys as a convenient political mouthpiece.

IV

A hundred years of active historical research have done much to deepen the understanding and fill in the pattern of Tudor economic history. As in all other fields, however, increase of knowledge has done little to facilitate generalization. The article by F. J. Fisher upon commercial trends and policy in sixteenth-century England marked a great step forward in the study of the complex evolution of the period. But this complexity does not lend itself easily to any simple explanation of the relationship between the rise and fall of economic prosperity and the development of State control and restrictionism.

The continuity of purpose and effort of State control was more striking than any change in scale of operations. Its motives were less a passive reaction to depression or the interpretation of economic theory than a system of economic nationalism inspired primarily by a fear of war and on a secondary plane by an ideal of social conservatism. The success of the Elizabethan administration in particular in imposing its will upon the community was due to the loyalty which the middle-classes felt towards a regime which provided security against internal unrest and external attack. More positive support was derived from the great capitalist groups of merchants and financiers, whose interests were actively favoured by the methods of control through the 'chosen instrument' of a monopolistic company.

Fundamentally the growing hostility to the system of control at the end of the century was a symptom of the rise of a new class of gentry, lawyers, small merchants and entrepreneurs, retailers and middle-men, hitherto excluded from the major benefits of the economic system and hampered in their activity by the official policy—both of which they were finally to sweep away by force in 1640. For if the Elizabethan and early Stuart system reserved its richest rewards for a limited number of courtiers and great merchant financiers, the economic developments of the century nevertheless brought in their trail the rise of a broad-based lesser *bourgeoisie* who progressively strengthened their hold upon the national wealth and their influence in the Lower House of Parliament. Half a century had elapsed without any serious rioting or rebellion by the poor and the fear of social unrest had consequently faded. Foreign invasion had so often threatened without result that even that menace had now grown stale. Gratitude for the benefits of the regime now therefore gave way to a spirit of criticism of its more unpopular features. The ring was cleared of interference by the poor or by the Spaniard, and the battle between the conservative aristocracy and the new middle-classes was engaged in earnest.

Thus the economic history of the sixteenth century possesses a unity of its own that justifies its examination in relative isolation to preceding and subsequent events. Its character, moreover, is peculiarly sympathetic to the present-day, when State control of economic enterprise and the distortion of society by the threat and actuality of war are the two dominant features of a restless and uncertain age.

3. PURITANISM AS A REVOLUTIONARY IDEOLOGY*

by Michael Walzer

English colonization began. during a period of profound social instability and rapid national development. The transition from a medieval to a modern social order involved creating powerful national states by centralizing political power and increasing rationalization and commercialization of the productive system. It was also necessary to formulate a value system and code of behavior appropriate to a new order. Those experiencing social change no longer found the faith of medieval Catholicism a meaningful interpretation of experience or an adequate guide for responding to the forces unsettling their lives. Protestantism attempted to supply an ideology attuned to the needs of people living through the breakup of an old social order and the painful emergence of a new one.

Students of social change have long sought to discover the roots of the ideology of the middle class, an ill-defined group

* *History and Theory*, vol. 3 (1961), 59–90. Copyright © 1961 by *History and Theory*. Reprinted from vol. 3, no. 1, of *History and Theory* by .permission of Wesleyan University Press. Footnotes have been omitted except where they are necessary for an understanding of the text.

credited with inventing both modern capitalism and liberal democracy. In the following essay, Michael Walzer reexamines critically the three most influential accounts of the process by which men become middle class in their thinking and behavior. Finding none of them satisfactory, Walzer formulates another hypothesis based on his understanding of the experiences of English Calvinists, the Puritans. "Puritanism," he argues, "appears to be a response to disorder and fear, a way of organizing men to overcome the acute sense of chaos" stemming from the breakdown of habitual routines and values. Experiencing profound anxiety generated by "exile, alienation, and social mobility," people struggled "to regain control of a changing world" and in the process found themselves compelled to attack the ungodliness of the old order, including hierarchy and patriarchy. Puritanism provided a new faith and discipline with which troubled souls hoped to achieve mastery over themselves and their society. Though at first men tried to purify the world in which they lived, the hostility of established forces discouraged and endangered Puritans so that many abandoned England to establish their Holy Commonwealth in a New World.

For further reading: Michael Walzer, *The Revolution of the Saints* (1965); Max Weber, *The Protestant Ethic and the Spirit of Capitalism* (1948); Richard H. Tawney, *Religion and the Rise of Capitalism* (1926); Robert W. Green, ed., *Protestantism and Capitalism* (1959).

I

Ideas, like men, play many parts. They are used casuistically to justify behavior; they rationalize interests; they shape character; they inspire fanaticism and presumption. No unified theory is likely to explain all the possible connections of thought and action. The connections are different at different moments in history and at any single moment they are different for different men. Recent studies of revolutionary movements and totalitarian governments clearly suggest the shifting role of ideas during periods of crisis and relative stability. To reduce all this to a single formula would be to impoverish our historical and sociological speculation. This was probably the initial effect of Marxism upon the history of ideas, even though the theory of ideology was surely the most subtle and valuable contribution yet made to that history. The Marxist epigone, ignoring the master's metaphysics, explained the creation, spread and decay of ideological systems in terms of a unilinear economic history and a theory of "reflection" never satisfactorily developed in either psychological or epistemological terms. His was a view obviously inadequate to the understanding of religious thought (where the original Marxist idea of alienation might be fruitfully applied) and artistic creativity. But it was also inadequate precisely where he claimed it to be most useful—in the interpretation of revolutionary ideology.

The Marxist insisted, correctly enough, upon the catastrophic character of social change; but he never studied the effects of catastrophe upon the mind and spirit of men. He tended, instead, to view revolutionary thought as the rational expression of the interests of a rising class, and he imagined interests to be objective, narrowly based in economic life, and more or less automatically expressed. This sort of analysis seems best suited to post-revolutionary periods; it hardly reaches beyond the conventional forms of selfishness, self-deception and hypocrisy. Thus the Marxist historian "understands" the Puritans after 1660 far better than he understands Oliver Cromwell; and similarly, the enthusiasm of a Robespierre is far less comprehensible to him than the everyday vulgarity of a Balzac bourgeois.

Of the Dissenting businessman and the nineteenth-century bourgeois, it has often enough been said that their ideas determine only the character of the lies they tell. Selfishness moves these men, but they call it enterprise; success rewards them, but they call it salvation, or happiness. An acute insight into these forms of self-justification—at times very witty and at times a little misanthropic—underlies the Marxist theory of ideology. But the theory moves beyond this insight; even the epigone is not content merely to expose lies, but seeks to understand the strange and complex process by which men become prisoners of the lies they tell. There comes a time when the mind is no longer open to the free play of interests, when opportunity is missed, or even pridefully disdained. At such a time, the casuistry of morality or honor cannot simply be equated with hypocrisy; it also sets limits, finds some lies acceptable, others not. Thus ideologies "harden" and fasten the men who believe them to a conventional mode of thinking and behaving, a mode which is increasingly irrational the more it lags behind the ongoing forces of history. Were it not for this irrationality, old ruling groups might readily adapt themselves to the opportunities offered by social change and there would be no revolutions.

There is a corollary to this view of the imperviousness of established ideological systems which Marxists have rarely drawn. Revolutionary ideologies must, in their turn, be intensely negative and destructive. They must foster what Max Weber has called "an unusually strong character", a kind of fanaticism, if they are to help men break through the hardened structure of convention and routine. Now, human beings are open to fanaticism only at certain moments in history; more often they are closed to it, safe from whatever it is that inspires devotion, dogmatism and presumption, and then disdainful of all "enthusiasm"— as for example, in eighteenth-century England. This openness is not made comprehensible by the casual invocation of a "rising" class, although it may well coincide with certain moments in a class history. Nor can the character of the fanaticism be explained solely in terms of the economic interests of a class.

The purpose of this paper is to suggest another explanation and to explore in some detail the part played by ideas during a period of rapid social change and revolution. The startling spread of Puritanism in England during the late sixteenth and early seventeenth centuries will provide a case history and suggest in dramatic form the (often ugly) kinds of discipline and self-control which revolutionary ideology can develop in men and the strength of character it can inspire. And since Puritanism has already been the subject of so many explanations, the English example will provide the opportunity for a critique of several earlier views of the significance of the Calvinist faith, and of various methods of studying revolutionary ideology.

II

Puritanism has twice been assigned a unique and creative role in Western history. Neither of these assignments was made by a Marxist historian; it was rather the Whigs and the Weberians who found modernity in the mind of the saints. But in a curious fashion, Marxists have been driven to adopt the insights of both these groups of writers, since both have defended and elaborated the historical connection which the Marxists themselves have so persistently sought to establish—that is, the connection of Puritanism with capitalism and liberalism.

Whig historians of the nineteenth and twentieth centuries saw in Protestantism in general, but more particularly in English Calvinism, the seed-bed of liberal politics. The purely individualistic relationship of the saint to his God, the emphasis upon voluntary association and mutual consent to church government among the saints themselves, the extraordinary reliance upon the printed word, with each man his own interpreter—all this, we have been told, trained and prepared the liberal mind. And then the natural alliance of Puritans and parliamentarians created the liberal society. It is a clear implication of this view, though one not often expressed by Whig writers, that Puritanism *is* liberalism in theological garb, that is, in a primitive and somewhat confused form.

Max Weber credited Puritanism with a rather different character and a different but related contribution to Western development. Writing in a more modern vein and free, up to a point, from Whig prejudices, he suggested that Calvin's ideas—again, especially in England—played a decisive part in the creation of the "spirit of capitalism". His views are so familiar that they need not be described in any detail here. But it should be said that they involve two rather distinct arguments, which will be considered separately below. Weber thought that Puritanism had sponsored a significant rationalization in behavior, especially in work: it had trained men to work in a sustained, systematic fashion, to pay attention to detail, to watch the clock. In this sense, the Calvinist ethic is related to that long-term process which culminates, but does not end, in a rational-legal (bureaucratic) society. Weber argued in addition to this that Puritanism had produced an extraordinary and apparently *irrational* impulse toward acquisition, which is more directly connected with the rise of a capitalist economy. The source of both impulses, toward rationalization and endless gain, lay in the anxiety induced by the theory of predestination—but the two are not the same and it is at least plausible to imagine the first without the second.

A Marxist historian would obviously deny the views of historical causation expressed or implied by both Whigs and Weberians, but he would defend ardently the close connection of Puritanism with the liberal and capitalist worlds. So ardently, indeed, would he do so, that he would probably concede, for the sake of the connection, a kind of "interaction" between economics, politics and religion, and thus open the way for an eclectic amalgamation of the three different points of view. Thus, contemporary Marxist writers tend still to describe Puritanism as the reflection of a rising bourgeoisie, though not necessarily its direct reflection (and this point—suggested, for example, by Tawney's notion of a "magic mirror"—is none too clear). But they then go on to argue that the reflection reacts somehow upon the original subject, reinforcing latent, perhaps underdeveloped class characteristics, meeting psychic needs, and generally accelerating the progressive evolution. This second argument is made in terms with which Whigs and Weberians would hardly disagree—especially since it constitutes a Marxist appropriation of their own insights. Such an eclecticism may incidentally make more sophisticated the history of all who adopt it; but it does not necessarily do so, for it provides no new insights and often involves the suspension of criticism for the sake of coherence. Giving up the hapless debate over whether Puritanism or capitalism came first would be, perhaps, no such loss. However, it would be a great loss indeed if no one called the union itself into question and sought to work out in a new way the historical experience of the saints.

The resemblance between the Calvinist covenant and the capitalist contract—often invoked and elaborated by Marxist writers—will serve to suggest the kind of questions which need to be raised. The voluntarism of both covenant and contract clearly distinguished them from earlier traditionalistic relationships; but they are also distinguished from one another by two facts which the Marxists have surely underrated. First, they are based upon very different, indeed, precisely opposite, views of human nature. The contract assumes trust, a mutual recognition of economic rationality and even of good will. The covenant, as will be argued below, institutionalizes suspicion and mutual surveillance. If it is true that sober-minded capitalists preferred to do business with members of the Puritan brotherhood, this may well have been because they knew that the brethren were being watched. Secondly, the two forms of association serve very different human purposes. Puritan godliness and capitalist gain have, perhaps, something to do with one another, though they have little enough in common. The suggestion that they are *really the same thing*, or one the mere reflex, in thought or in action, of the other, has long distorted our understanding of the saints and their English enterprise. In order to grasp the precise nature of this distortion it is necessary not only to point out the basic incompatibility of Puritanism with both liberalism and capitalism, but also to discuss the various methods by which their similarity has been discovered and to attack the attitude toward historical experience which these methods imply.

A number of recent writers have gone so far as to describe the Puritan saints as traditionalists in both politics and economics, a description which has the virtue of standing the older theorists neatly on their heads, but which also makes the revolution incomprehensible. This is not the view which will be argued here; it describes at best only the cautious conformity of Puritan preachers in dealing with such conventional topics as monarchy, rebellion, usury and charity. On the other hand, it is not difficult to detect the sharply anti-traditionalist ideology of these same men working itself out in their attacks upon hierarchy, their new views of ecclesiastical organization, their treatises on family government, their almost Manichean warfare against Satan and his worldly allies, their nervous lust for systematic repression and control. The last two of these are obviously not compatible with liberal thinking (or with entrepreneurial activity). They point directly to the revolution, when the struggle against Anti-Christ would be acted out and, for a brief moment, the repressive Holy Commonwealth established. In the years before the actual revolution, the nature of Puritanism was best revealed in the endless discussions of church government and in the practices of such Puritan congregations as already existed. These practices can by no means be called liberal, even though they were founded upon consent. Precisely because of this foundation, however, they cannot be called traditionalist either. The experience of the saints suggests something very different.

III

It was, perhaps, not without a certain malice that the early Puritans were called "disciplinarians". But malice has its insights and this one is worth pursuing. The association of the brethren was voluntary indeed, but it gave rise to a collectivist discipline marked above all by a tense mutual "watchfulness". Puritan individualism never led to a respect for privacy. Tender conscience had its rights, but it was protected only against the interference of worldlings and not against "brotherly admonition". And the admonitions of the brethren were anxious, insistent, continuous. They felt themselves to be living in an age of chaos and crime and sought to train conscience to be permanently on guard against sin. The extent to which they would have carried the moral discipline can be seen in the following list of offenses which merited excommunication in one seventeenth-century congregation:

> for unfaithfulness in his master's service.
> for admitting cardplaying in his house . . .
> for sloth in business.
> for being overtaken in beer.
> for borrowing a pillion and not returning it.
> for jumping for wagers . . .
> for dancing and other vanities.

Had the saints been successful in establishing their Holy Commonwealth, the enforcement of this discipline would have constituted the Puritan terror. In the congregation there was already a kind of local terrorism, maintained by the godly elders as the national discipline would have been by an élite of the saints. Thus, Richard Baxter reported that in his Kidderminster parish the enforcement of the new moral order was made possible "by the zeal and diligence of the godly people of the place who thirsted after the salvation of their neighbours and were in private my assistants".

It was for this moral discipline that the saints fought most persistently, and it was over this issue that Baxter and his colleagues left the Established Church in 1662. Their failure to win from Charles II's bishops the congregational rights of admonition and excommunication finally forced them—as the political Restoration had not done—to acknowledge the failure of their revolutionary effort to turn "all England into a land of the saints". By that time, however, the effort had had a certain prosaic success—not at all of the sort which Puritan preachers once imagined.

The crucial feature of the Puritan discipline was its tendency to transform repression into self-control: worldlings might be forced to be godly, but saints voluntarily gave themselves to godliness. Liberalism also required such voluntary subjection and self-control but, in sharp contrast to Puritanism, its political and social theory were marked by an extraordinary confidence in the possibility of both a firm sense of human reasonableness and of the ease with which order might be attained. Liberal confidence made repression and the endless struggle against sin unnecessary; it also tended to make self-control invisible,

to forget its painful history and naively assume its existence. The result was that liberalism did not create the self-control it required. The
Lockeian state was not a disciplinary institution, as was the Calvinist
Holy Commonwealth, but rather rested on the assumed political virtue
—the "natural political virtue"—of its citizens. It is one of the central
arguments of this essay that Puritan repression has its place in the
practical history, so to speak, of that strange assumption.

It is not possible, of course, to judge the effectiveness of this repression or the extent of the social need for it. For the moment it can
only be said that Puritans knew about human sinfulness and that Locke
did not need to know. This probably reflects not only different tempera-
ments, but also different experiences. The very existence and spread
of Puritanism in the years before the Revolution surely argue the
presence in English society of an acute fear of disorder and "wickedness". The anxious tone of Tudor legislation—which Puritan leaders
like William Perkins often vigorously seconded—is itself a parallel
argument. On the other hand, the triumph of Lockeian ideas suggests
the overcoming of that anxiety and fear, the appearance of men for
whom sin is no longer a problem. In a sense, it might be said that
liberalism is dependent upon the existence of "saints"—that is, of men
whose good behavior can be relied upon. At the same time, the secular
and genteel character of liberalism is determined by the fact that these
are men whose goodness (sociability, self-discipline, moral decency, or
mere respectability) is self-assured and relaxed, entirely free from the
nervousness and fanaticism of Calvinist godliness.

This, then, is the relationship of Puritanism to the liberal world: it
is perhaps one of historical preparation, but not at all of theoretical
contribution. Indeed, there was much to be forgotten and much to be
surrendered before the saint could become a liberal bourgeois. During
the great creative period of English Puritanism, the faith of the saints
and the tolerant reasonableness of the liberals had very little in common.

Roughly the same things can be said about the putative connection
of Calvinism and capitalism. The moral discipline of the saints can be
interpreted as the historical conditioning of the capitalist man; but the
discipline was not itself capitalist. It can be argued that the faith of
the brethren, with its emphasis upon methodical endeavor and self-
control, was an admirable preparation for systematic work in shops,
offices and factories. It trained men for the minute-to-minute attentive-
ness required in a modern economic system; it taught them to forego

their afternoon naps—as they had but recently foregone their saints' day holidays—and to devote spare hours to bookkeeping and moral introspection. It somehow made the deprivation and repression inevitable in sustained labor bearable and even desirable for the saints. And by teaching self-control, it provided the basis for impersonal, contractual relationships among men, allowing workmanlike cooperation but not involving any exchange of affection or any of the risks of intimacy. All this, Calvinism did or helped to do. Whether it did so in a creative fashion or as the ideological reflection of new economic processes is not immediately relevant. The saints learned, as Weber has suggested, a kind of rational and worldly asceticism, and this was probably something more than the economic routine required. They sought in work itself what mere work can never give: a sense of vocation and discipline which would free them from sinfulness and the fear of disorder.

But Weber has said more than this; he has argued that systematic acquisition as well as asceticism has a Calvinist origin. The psychological tension induced by the theory of predestination, working itself out in worldly activity, presumably drove men to seek success as a sign of salvation. The sheer willfulness of an inscrutable God produced in its turn, if Weber is correct, the willfulness of an anxious man, and set off the entrepreneurial pursuit of better business techniques and more and more profit. At this point his argument breaks down. If there is in fact a peculiar and irrational quality to the capitalists' lust for gain, its sources must be sought elsewhere than among the saints. For Puritanism was hardly an ideology which encouraged continuous or unrestrained accumulation. Instead, the saints tended to be narrow and conservative in their economic views, urging men to seek no more wealth than they needed for a modest life, or, alternatively, to use up their surplus in charitable giving. The anxiety of the Puritans led to a fearful demand for economic restriction (and political control) rather than to enterpreneurial activity as Weber has described it. Unremitting and relatively unremunerative work was the greatest help toward saintliness and virtue.

The ideas of Puritan writers are here very close to those of such proto-Jacobins as Mably and Morelli in eighteenth-century France, who also watched the development of capitalist enterprise with unfriendly eyes, dreaming of a Spartan republic where bankers and great merchants would be unwelcome. The collective discipline of the Puritans

—their Christian Sparta—was equally incompatible with purely acquisitive activity. Virtue would almost certainly require economic regulation. This would be very different from the regulation of medieval corporatism, and perhaps it was the first sense of that difference which received the name *freedom*. It was accompanied by a keen economic realism: thus the Calvinist acknowledgement of the lawfulness of usury. But Calvinist realism was in the service of effective control and not of free activity or self-expression. Who can doubt that, had the Holy Commonwealth ever been firmly established, godly self-discipline and mutual surveillance would have been far more repressive than the corporate system? Once again, in the absence of a Puritan state the discipline was enforced through the congregation. The minutes of a seventeenth-century consistory provide a routine example: "The church was satisfied with Mrs. Carlton," they read, "as to the weight of her butter." Did Mrs. Carlton tremble, awaiting that verdict? Surely if the brethren were unwilling to grant liberty to the local butter-seller, they would hardly have granted it to the new capitalist. The ministerial literature, at least, is full of denunciations of enclosers, usurers, monopolists, and projectors—and occasionally even of wily merchants. Puritan casuistry, perhaps, left such men sufficient room in which to range, but it hardly offered them what Weber considers so essential—a good conscience. Only a sustained endeavor in hypocrisy, so crude as to astonish even the Marxist epigone, could have earned them that. The final judgment of the saints with regard to the pursuit of money is that of Bunyans' pilgrim, angry and ill-at-ease in the town of Vanity, disdainful of such companions as Mr. Money-love and Mr. Save-all.

The converse is equally true: to the triumphant bourgeois sainthood, with all its attendant enthusiasm and asceticism, would appear atavistic. And this is perhaps the clearest argument of all against the casual acceptance of the Whig or Weberian views of Puritanism. It suggests forcefully that the two views (and the Marxist also, for surprisingly similar reasons) are founded upon anachronism. Even if it is correct to argue that Calvinist faith and discipline played a part in that transformation of character which created the bourgeois—and too little is known about the historical development of character to say this without qualification—the anachronism remains. The historical present is hopelessly distorted unless the tension and repression so essential to the life of the saint are described and accounted for. Even more important, the effort to establish a holy commonwealth (to universalize the tension and repression) is rendered inexplicable once liberalism and capitalism are, so to speak, read into the Puritan experience. For then Puritanism is turned into a grand paradox: its radical voluntarism culminates in a rigid discipline; its saints watch their neighbors with brotherly love and suspicion; its ethic teaches sustained and systematic work but warns men against the lust for acquisition and gain. In fact, of course, these seeming contrasts are not paradoxical. The saints experienced a unity, common enough among men, of willfulness and repression, of fanatical *self-control.* Latter-day historians do the Puritans little honor when they search among the elements of the Puritan faith for something more liberal in its political implications or more economically rational. Indeed, the methods of that search invite in their turn the most searching criticism.

IV

Whigs, Weberians and Marxists have reconstructed Puritanism in terms of two other constructs which they know far better and love far more: liberalism and capitalism. The Whig reconstruction is the most crude and the least historical. Whig historians describe liberalism as if it were a kind of Community Chest to which nations, groups of men, and particular thinkers have made contributions. History is a catalogue of the contributors, whose actual intentions and circumstances count for little. The contributions mount up; the world perfects itself. This is a view obviously close to that of the French progressists of the eighteenth century who saw history as a (more or less) steady accumulation of facts, of moral and scientific truths. But the French thinkers at least regarded religious fanaticism as an enemy, a sign that they had some acquaintance with it. Revolutionaries that they were, the very fervor of their attack upon priestly and monkish zeal suggested the coming cult of progress—the new fanaticism. The Whigs, on the other hand, were altogether free from zeal and could neither understand nor even hate the zealot; they did not recognize in him a fellow creature. Thus, at the same time as they described the saints as their own (somewhat lusty) progenitors, they expelled Oliver Cromwell from the moral universe and called the millenarians "insane". But Cromwell was surely a representative figure and the millenarians achieved little more than a logical extension of ideas basic to all Puritan thinking. If they cannot be included in the world the liberals recognize and understand, then that world is false.

Whig writers continually fail to achieve historicity—the quality of truly engaging the past. Perhaps this is because they are so unwilling to criticize, even retrospectively, potential contributors to the liberal consensus. Such moral trepidation makes virtually impossible honest, that is, comprehensive and virile, characterizations of men whose historical labor is deemed valuable. Thus, liberal historians, under the impact of Marxism, have tentatively suggested the connection of Puritanism with the rising middle class, but have been entirely unable to describe realistically the human experience of "rising"—again, perhaps, because it is not always an ennobling experience. They fail to make the complex connections of the new religion with the new men in any way specific. They merely suggest vaguely that an enlightened class embraced an enlightened faith . . . and left us all an inheritance of enlightenment. So we know the past only by its contribution, as if nothing had been lost in the giving. As for the men who, like the millenarians, had nothing to give—had it not been for our own experience with totalitarian movements they might have vanished from history.

Nor did Max Weber reconstruct the historical reality of the Puritan saint. His real interests, like those of the Whigs, lay elsewhere. Studying the psychological effects of Puritan faith, he created a new *deus absconditus* for the capitalist world—Calvin's God. But like all mortals, he learned the attributes of that God (and of his human instruments) by studying his creation. Weber constructed Puritanism as a composite of capitalist (specifically, economically rational) elements, very much as the Marxists do, for all his criticism of their monistic historiography. This obviously required a selection, in which the restrictionist attitudes described above—as well as all that is irrational in Puritan thought— were necessarily ignored. Thus it matters very little whether the saint is the creator of the capitalist or merely his reflection; in the work of the historian the known determines the unknown—and the saint is an unknown man.

Indeed, it seems at times that Weber turns Puritanism into a virtual equivalent of the capitalist spirit. He argues, for example, that among the saints rational labor (conceived by Weber exclusively in economic terms) is a form of worship and worship itself a strenuous and systematic labor. The spirit of capitalism is *first embodied in a religious ideology,* and from this ideology it derives the moral force necessary to break through convention and routine. Without Puritanism, Weber believes, the capitalist spirit might never have taken a historically viable form. Calvinist theology was somehow the crystallizing agent, but at the same time, Puritanism was the crystallization. For nothing is added, according to Weber's account, by the subsequent secularization of capitalist endeavor; hence it must be said that the original form was complete. What existed at first exists still, more ugly, perhaps, as its theological meaning gradually is forgotten. But this virtual confusion of the Puritan and capitalist spirits, which inevitably follows from Weber's work, points to a radical defect in his argument. Briefly put, the defect is this: Weber's explanation of acquisitive behavior—in terms of anxiety over salvation and the desperate need to win some conviction of grace—will serve as well to explain Puritan saintliness. Granted the connection, at best incomplete, the psychological mechanisms which shape the two seem identical. In history, the salvation panic, the concern and self-doubt which Weber describes, is quite common. It is the psychological crisis which culminates in conversion; out of it emerges the self-confident, austere and zealous saint. The saint's anxiety does not begin *after* his conversion, though it may in some manner be maintained by his new religious ideology—"a man at ease is a man lost", wrote the Puritan minister Thomas Taylor. And thus the saint does not become a capitalist through any subsequent psychological process; his acquisitiveness—given Weber's point—is only an aspect and in no historical sense a result of his saintliness. But it is not possible to explain capitalism in terms of Puritanism (that is, Puritanism can be neither a cause nor even a "decisive factor" in the development of capitalism) if both are generated by the same experience. Looked at in this light, Weber hardly raises the problem of causation, for he never asks what are obviously the crucial questions: Why did men become Puritans? Why did they make the experience of anxiety so central to their lives? Why were they open to the extraordinary character change which their new faith presumably effected?

The argument can be put differently. Weber assumes that the cause of anxiety is an anxiety-inducing ideology. He never concerns himself with the origins of Calvinist faith or with that "elective affinity" which its converts presumably experienced. Now ideologies are modes of perceiving the world, and one perceives, up to a point, what one needs to see. That is, ideologies organize and sharpen feelings and sensitivities which are already present. The future saint who "elects" Calvinism is not in utter ignorance of the salvation panic it may induce. He chooses Calvinism, and not some other religious ideology, precisely because it explains a world in which he is already anxious—worried, confused, neurotic or whatever—and it is this original anxiety which must be explained if his eventual conversion and salvation are, so to speak, to be anticipated. The terms and character of the conversion are conditioned by Calvinist thought, but not explained by it. Indeed, a later generation of Puritans, without losing their beliefs, would find conversion enormously difficult.

All this is really a Marxist critique of Weber, but no Marxist has yet undertaken a description of the state of mind of the men who became Calvinist saints, or even of their historical experience. The reason undoubtedly is that the Marxist knows the beginning of Puritanism as well as Weber knew the end: at the beginning and the end is capitalism.

There is another defect in Weber's argument, and it also stems from a failure to ask historical questions about the saints. Neither Weber nor any of his followers have ever demonstrated that the men who actually became Puritans, for whatever reasons—who really believed in predestination and lived through the salvation panic—went on, presumably for the same reasons, to become capitalists. They have not immersed themselves in the history of the period. This by no means precludes all insight: Weber's discussion of the activity of the saint and the energizing effects of predestination—despite a logic which seems to lead to passivity and quiescence—is a triumph of psychological speculation. But his particular judgments are guesswork at best. There is, for example, considerable evidence to show that many of the most sensitive of the saints went on, after the crisis of their conversion, to become ministers, and very little evidence that many went on to become capitalist businessmen. Among lay Puritans, the weight of the diaries, letters and memoirs clearly suggests that the most significant expression of their new faith was cultural and political rather than economic. The saints were indeed activists and activists in a far more intense and "driven" fashion than the men who came after: Scottish peasants learned to read; English weavers worked with a book propped up over the loom; gentlemen attended to parliamentary affairs with a new assiduousness; godly mothers trained their sons to a constant concern with political life. In their sermons, Puritan ministers urged many forms of activity, from methodical introspection to organized philanthropy to godly warfare. Addressing the gentry and their urban associates, the ministers spoke most often of *magistracy* and described a kind of political commitment and zeal which would have its effects in the revolution. Of business, apart from general injunctions to avoid idleness and work hard, they said very little.

But of business they are made to say a great deal through the anachronistic historiography not only of Weber but of the Marxists as well. Both, for example, place an emphasis on the Calvinist acceptance of usury which is totally unwarranted by the texts themselves. Marxists understand this acceptance as a reflection of changing economic conditions. If so, it is a weak reflection indeed of such a common practice, and one which could hardly have brought much comfort to the new man staring hard and moodily into his ideological mirror. The difficulty with the theory of reflection is that one can see in the mirror only what one already sees in front of it. And here is an opening for the endless anachronistic errors into which Marxists fall. In front of the mirror-image of Puritanism they firmly set the capitalist man, a figure who has, for anyone familiar with the nineteenth century, the odd quality of being *déjà vu*. Inevitably, what results is a distortion—the mirror is "magic" indeed! Thus the extraordinary, intense, and pervasive seventeenth-century concern with personal salvation is hardly noticed by Marxist students of the mirror-image, and the scanty texts on usury are brought into the forefront of historical vision. The Puritan covenant is glimpsed in the mirror and all too quickly understood; the intentions and aspirations of the signers themselves are not studied, for real historical motives exist, so to speak, only on this side of the glass. The Puritan hatred of the economic vices, like laziness and profligacy, is sharply reflected, but the vast depths of sin and demonism are obscured. In the Marxist world of economic reason, beggars are duly whipped, witches untouched by the flame. It would be possible, of course, to put a different man in front of the mirror. But in order to know what man to choose, one would first have to look at the image—that is, to reverse the procedures of the usual Marxist methodology. This reversal will be taken up below.

Engels himself, aware up to a point of these difficulties, suggested a somewhat different epistemology in an effort to explain the Calvinist theory of predestination. This invocation of God's arbitrary willfulness, he wrote, was the "religious expression" of the functioning of a market economy, where a man's fate depends on impersonal forces over which he has no control. The method of the "expression" is analogical reasoning and not mere reflection. The particular analogical leap from market forces to divine decree is comprehensible, says Engels, given the general religious atmosphere. This presumably explains the upward direction of the leap, but it is somewhat more of an explanation than is logically necessary. In fact the idea of analogy opens the way for a virtually indeterminate individual creativity. What are the limits of the analogical imagination? Men see shapes in clouds and inkblots and while the shapes they see undoubtedly tell us something about the men, the historian or the psychologist has extraordinary license in interpreting what that something is. And this is a license which works both ways: one may well wend one's way back from the theory of predestination and discover some material counterpart other than the market economy. The truth of the discovery cannot be judged formally; it will depend on how well the men who did the original thinking or imagining are known by the historian. At the very least the unraveling of such complex modes of thought as analogy or, in the seventeenth century, allegory, should not be prejudged. It is easy to see in Bunyan's *Pilgrim's Progress*, for example, a working out of such bourgeois themes as mobility, calculation and individualism, but not of accumulation, thrift or even sustained work in a calling. And it is never easy to say who are the Christians of this world.

V

To make Christian a petty-bourgeois is to ignore the fact that he was . . . Christian, a pilgrim bound for the heavenly city, and that many of the readers of *Pilgrim's Progress* were in some sense his colleagues. Indeed, the Marxists are no more committed than are Whigs or Weberians to the world of experience which this pilgrimage represents. They are as disinclined to encounter the saints in history; but in their case the disinclination has a methodological reason. They tend to treat such an experience as Christian's journey as an epiphenomenon of objective existence, of what Marx called "real life". This is not to say that the pilgrimage was not actually made. Rather, it involves the assertion that it can only be understood by putting aside Christian's ideology— his perceptions, feelings, thoughts, aspirations—and confronting directly those economic and social processes which somehow underlie and cause the actual journey. But the distinctions presupposed by this kind of explanation are hopelessly precise. Many critics have pointed out that ideas play a vital role in what Marxists call the objective world: no economic relationship is conceivable, for example, which does not involve some shared notions of profit and loss, of security, trust, love or interest. Ideas are intrinsic to any relationship among men, as they are to any perceived sequence of events. It is simply not possible to treat them as reflections or epiphenomena because one can't imagine or satisfactorily construct "reality" without them.

Thus there is, so to speak, no journey but *only* a pilgrimage. One cannot separate the physical motion from the sense of destination and describe the one as an example of increased social mobility and the other as an illusion, a piece of religious confusion, the result of Bunyan's failure to understand social change.

In sharp contrasts to the pilgrim Christian, Defoe's Moll Flanders is something of a Marxist heroine, an economic woman; despite her ideology she is never confused. Defoe at least suggests that ideas and "real life" can easily be distinguished. But this is only true when ideas have become conventional—like Moll's moralizing—and even then it is not entirely true. For ideology is a way of perceiving and responding to the experienced world, so it is always itself an aspect of experience. In relatively peaceful or stable times (when no-one is a pilgrim), perceptions may be widely shared, even inherited, and responses predictable. For ordinary men, ideology may indeed become a reflex, automatic and inescapable, and then the way be opened for all sorts of evasion, hypocrisy, and platitudinizing. Writing about such periods, Marxists have had their greatest success: thus have they struck off the bourgeois ideology. They have done much less well in confronting sharp discontinuities of perception and response. For all his concern with revolution, Marx was himself the product of the same world which produced the great social novels, those elaborate, many-volumed studies of manners, status and class relationships in which the fundamental stability of the society as a whole and of character (what would today be called "identity") within the society was always assumed. And Marx never questions the second of these assumptions: bourgeois and proletarian appear in his work as *formed characters*, free at least from psychological instability even while their struggle with one another tears apart the social order. But in a time like that of the Puritans, Christian's colleagues, there is an enormous range in perception and response, and—more important—an enormous range in the clarity of perception (even if it be the clarity of madness) and in the intensity of response. Ideology cannot be consistently linked with class experiences because those experiences no longer take place in a regular and predictable order. Hence character is not stable; its very formation, so to speak, is problematic.

It is obvious that Bunyan's pilgrim would hardly set out on his strange journey in such a stable bourgeois society as that of nineteenth-century England. Nor, since Christian is everyman and no medieval saint, would he set out from a stable feudal society. He "corresponds" to what can roughly be called a time of transition. But the time of transition, a time of instability and chronic danger, is only the *condition* of his journey—its cause is ideological. And it is the journey in its ideological setting, complete with purpose and meaning, which constitutes the experience and needs to be explained.

In order to get at the world of experience, it may well be necessary to construct some highly abstract model of economic processes and social change. But this construct is not "real life". It is only an intellectual approach to reality and only one among several possible approaches. The Marxist historian seeks to reconstitute the world which is perceived, while at the same time detaching himself from the particular perceptions of historical men. But it ought to be those very perceptions which direct his work. Reality is too complex, too detailed, too formless: he can never reproduce it. He must seek, instead, to reproduce only those aspects of historical existence which were, so to speak, absorbed into the experience of particular men. And if he is to avoid anachronistic reconstructions, his guide must be the men themselves. It would be absurd to assume *a priori* that what is of central importance in late sixteenth- and early seventeenth-century history is, for example, the growth of the coal industry. One must look first to see what impact such a phenomenon had upon the lives of men. It is not, of course, only a question of whether they talked about it, but of whether they *felt* it, directly or indirectly, consciously or unconsciously. If they did not, then its significance must be sought in the future.

Marxists become the victims of the very alienation they claim to understand so well when they reverse this procedure and make experience dependent upon what is originally only a creation of the mind. When Tawney writes that Puritanism is the "magic mirror" in which the middle-class man saw himself ennobled and enhanced, he is in no sense enlightening us as to the historical process by which Puritanism

51

developed and spread. For the Puritan is a real man, who can be encountered in history. But the middle-class man is made up, and it is sheer anachronism to describe him as a historical figure, articulate, already in search of an enhanced image. It has been suggested above that Puritanism is a part of the process (the long succession of perceptions and responses) by which men *become* middle-class. But to know the particular perceptions upon which it is based or the responses it prescribes, it is necessary to know the Puritan. There is, in fact, no magic mirror; sainthood is no mere enhancement of an already established (even if worrisome) identity. It is a far more active thing than that; it is indeed what Weber suggests—a way of forming an identity.

What must be studied, then, is a mind, or a group of minds, coping with problems and not passively reflecting them. For the mind mediates between the "objective" situation and the human act and if the act is to be understood, the mind must first be known. The problems it faces are posed by an environment which can of course be analyzed in some objective fashion—for example, statistically. But different aspects of this environment are experienced by different men with different results in consciousness and behavior. Hence the "objective" construct is of no independent value and has no prior significance in explanation. The first task of the historian is to establish his familiarity with the experience of particular men, with their difficulties, aspirations and achievements, and with the styles in which all these are expressed. This is not to suggest that the historical record should be taken at face value, or the assumption casually made that men always mean what they say. There is, for example, false piety and evasion among the saints which the historian must expose. There is caution and conformity which he must respect, but not too much. For hindsight is also insight into the concealments of respectability and of "Aesopian" prose; and it is often insight as well into purposes half-understood and patterns of thought not yet fully worked out. Hence the methods of the historian must be sceptical, devious and experimental, even while his general approach is open and sympathetic. But ultimately his sympathy is the key to all else: the best judgment of face value will be made by men with some intuitive understanding of other levels of thinking and feeling.

The problem of the Puritan belief in witchcraft and demonology has already been suggested and may profitably be developed at greater length as an illustration of the above argument. One sees in the mirror (that is, in experience and thought) images which have no easy or readily explained connection with the supposed subject, middle-class man. Witchcraft indeed suggests a world altogether apart from the Marxist universe of interest. In his book *Navaho Witchcraft*, Clyde Kluckhohn has analyzed the psychological basis of the belief in terms of the concepts of hostility and anxiety and has sought to give these concepts some precision. He has discussed the possible ways in which historical events or particular social structures may generate those anxious or hostile feelings which presumably lead to the perception of witches (or of oneself as a witch) and to the responses of persecution and cruelty. Now the history of the persecution of witches in England (also the history of the practice of witchcraft) directly parallels the career of the Puritans. The first enactments were produced by the returning Marian exiles; the persecution reached its height during the revolutionary period and in the centers of Puritan sentiment; interest in and fear of witches declined after the Restoration. Perhaps Marxists have paid so little attention to witchcraft precisely because it had no future; it was neglected in that final process of selection which constituted the bourgeois world. The point here is that this piece of knowledge about Puritan feeling and behavior suggests certain possibilities in the "objective" environment to which Marxists have been singularly blind.

Anxiety seems to appear in acute form only among men who have experienced some great disorder or who are caught up in a process of rapid, incomprehensible change: the breakdown of some habitual system of conventions and routines, a departure to an unaccustomed world, the aftermath of epidemic or war. Events of this sort leave men without customary restraints upon their behavior and no longer responsible to revered authorities. The result often is that extraordinary panic which Erich Fromm has somewhat misleadingly called a "fear of freedom." In human experience, this is more likely a dread of chaos, and one of its aspects is a sharp, if often delusory perception of danger and of dangerous men.

If Puritanism is studied with these ideas in mind, a new light is thrown on sixteenth- and seventeenth-century history. One searches more deeply in the life experience of the saints for those feelings of fearfulness which parallel the belief in witches—and for the sources of such fear. One searches for sudden changes in environment, habits, authorities. The result is a hypothesis which is in striking contradiction to that of the Marxists: Puritanism appears to be a response to disorder and fear, a way of organizing men to overcome the acute sense of chaos. With this hypothesis it becomes possible to understand, for example, the as yet fragmentary evidence which suggests that the Calvinist faith, especially in its more radical forms, appealed most of all to men newly come to London and not, as Marxists have always assumed, to experienced city dwellers. For coming to the city was an event in a man's life which might well sharpen his sense of danger and even lead him to seek that discipline which has been described above as central to Puritan association. Thus, the sudden increase in London's population between roughly 1580 and 1625 takes on new significance: it may well be that London did not so much prepare men to become "saints" as that sainthood helped them, through the hard transition period, to become Londoners. Once they had become *urbane*, they were in fact unlikely to remain faithful to the original Calvinist creed; they became revisionists. Similarly, it is somewhat less of a paradox than Marxists might suppose that witchcraft should range more widely in the southeast of England, where economic development was most advanced. For it may be—and this, perhaps, can be investigated—that witchcraft helped solve, in the minds of the people, some of the problems raised by that very development and by its impact upon traditional ways of doing things. (This is, of course, only speculation, but it is speculation which begins at the right place: with a concern for the concerns of the Puritans themselves.)

It seems likely that certain modes of perception and response parallel certain basic historical experiences; if so, comparison is possible and one might arrive at general propositions. But the relationship between, for example, urbanization and some ideological response to urbanization (once again, it must be said that these are not distinct "spheres") must be understood in dynamic terms. Perhaps it would be best to figure to oneself an energetic man continually struggling to understand and cope with the surrounding world. Undoubtedly, energy and struggle are not universal in history: ways of thinking quickly become habitual, as does experience itself. But it is the creative moments which require explanation and at such moments ideology is never a mere habit or reflex, but a willful activity. For perhaps a hundred years after the original creative achievement of Calvin, the spread of Puritanism can still be described in the active tense: men, with their own problems and aspirations, continually rediscovered for themselves, with all the enthusiasm which must have attended the first discovery, the truths of the new faith. The historian who begins with these ideology-producing men may then work outward, so to speak, re-experiencing their world and only after this subjecting that world to such further analysis as will improve his own understanding of it.

The Puritan saints are such men, making their ideology, and making themselves. The sources and nature of this creativity must next be considered.

VI

The study of the Puritans is best begun with the idea of discipline, and all the tension and strain that underlies it, both in their writing and in what can be known of their experience. It is strange that theorists have had so little to say on this topic, especially since the rebellion against Puritan repression, or rather against its ugly remnants—devoid, as Weber's capitalism is, of theological reason—is still a part of our own experience. The persecution of witches, of course, was not a vital aspect of Puritan endeavor, but the active, fearful struggle against wickedness was. And the saints imagined wickedness as a creative and omnipresent demonic force, that is, as a continuous threat. Like Hobbes, they saw disorder and war as the natural state of fallen men, out of which they had been drawn by God's command and by the painful efforts of their own regenerate wills. But they lived always on the very brink of chaos, maintaining their position only through a constant vigilance and, indeed, a constant warfare against their own natural inclinations and against the devil and his worldlings.

The goal of this warfare was repression and its apparent cause was an extraordinary anxiety. It is by no means necessary to argue that these two constitute the "essence" of Puritanism, only that their full significance has not been realized. In Calvin's own work anxiety is presented as central to the experience of fallen man: this is anxiety of a special sort; it is not the fear of death and damnation, but rather the fear of sudden and violent death. Hobbes would recognize it as the dominant passion of man in his natural state. Thus Calvin:

> Now, whithersoever you turn, all the objects around you are not only
> unworthy of your confidence, but almost openly menace you, and seem
> to threaten immediate death. Embark in a ship; there is but a single
> step between you and death. Mount a horse; the slipping of one foot

55

endangers your life. Walk through the streets of a city; you are liable to as many dangers as there are tiles on the roofs. If there be a sharp weapon in your hand, or that of your friend, the mischief is manifest. All the ferocious animals you see are armed for your destruction. If you endeavor to shut yourself in a garden surrounded with a good fence, and exhibiting nothing but what is delightful, even there sometimes lurks a serpent. Your house, perpetually liable to fire, menaces you by day with poverty, and by night with falling on your head. Your land, exposed to hail, frost, drought and various tempests, threatens you with sterility, and with its attendant, famine. I omit poison, treachery, robbery and open violence, which partly beset us at home and partly pursue us abroad . . . You will say that these things happen seldom, or certainly not always, nor to every man, [and] never all at once. I grant it; but we are admonished by the examples of others, that it is possible for them to happen to us. . . .

Among the saints such terrible fearfulness was overcome, and that was the great benefit of sainthood: it did not so much promise future ecstasy as present "tranquillity". "When the light of Divine Providence," wrote Calvin, "has once shined on a pious man, he is relieved and delivered not only from the extreme anxiety and dread with which he was previously oppressed, but also from all care." But relief was not rest in the Calvinist world; it was rather that security of mind which might well manifest itself as self-righteousness—or as fanaticism.

In Puritan literature this same fearfulness is made specific in social terms. Once again, it is a fear which Hobbes would understand: the fear of disorder in society. It is apparent in the nervous hostility with which Puritan writers regarded carousal, vagabondage, idleness, all forms of individualistic extravagance (especially in clothing), country dances and urban crowds, the theater with its gay (undisciplined) audiences, gossip, witty talk, love-play, dawdling in taverns—the list could be extended. The shrewdest among their contemporaries sensed that this pervasive hostility was a key to Puritanism—though they could hardly help but regard it as hypocritical. Ben Jonson's Zeal-of-the-land Busy is a caricature based, like all good caricatures, on a kernel of truth. Zeal-of-the-land is, for all his comical hypocrisy, insistently and anxiously concerned about the world he lives in—and the aim of his concern is supervision and repression.

At times, Puritan preachers sounded very much like Hobbes: ". . . take sovereignty from the face of the earth," proclaimed Robert Bolton, "and you turn it into a cockpit. Men would become cut-throats and cannibals . . . Murder, adulteries, incests, rapes, robberies, perjuries, witchcrafts, blasphemies, all kinds of villainies, outrages and savage cruelty would overflow all countries." But secular sovereignty was not their usual appeal. They looked rather to congregational discipline, as has been argued above. Thus Thomas Cartwright promised that the new discipline would restrain stealing, adultery and murder. Even more, it would "correct" sins "which the magistrate doth not commonly punish"—he listed lying, jesting, choleric speeches. It need hardly be said that John Locke, a century later, was not terribly worried about such sins. Walsingham's spies reported in the 1580's and '90's that Puritan agitators were promising "that if discipline were planted, there should be no more vagabonds nor beggars". John Penry foresaw the "amendment" of idleness and hence, he thought, of poverty. Now none of these concerns was unusual in Tudor or early Stuart England, but the intensity and extent of Puritan worry and the novelty of the proposed solution have no parallel among statesmen or traditional moralists. These latter groups also watched with apprehension the growth of London, the increasing geographic and social mobility, and the new forms of individualistic experimentation. It must be said, however, that the tone of their writings rarely reached a pitch of anxiety and fearfulness comparable to, for example, the diary of the Puritan minister Richard Rogers, endlessly worried about his own "unsettledness". Nostalgia was a more common theme, satire and mockery a more frequent defense among moralists like Thomas Dekker. And the world they would have substituted for Renaissance England was an already romanticized version of medieval England. Not so the Puritans. Their discipline would have established dramatically new forms of association: the anxiety of the minister Rogers led him to join with his brethren in a solemn covenant—and these brethren were neither his immediate neighbors nor his kinfolk.

What Rogers sought from his covenant was a bolstering of his faith, a steeling of his character. "The sixth of this month [December, 1587] we fasted betwixt ourselves," he reported in his diary, ". . . to the stirring up of ourselves to greater godliness." The need for this "stirring up" is so pervasive among the Puritans that one might well imagine that what they feared so greatly was rather in themselves than in the society about them. In fact, what they feared was the image in themselves of the "unsettledness" of their world. Puritan fearfulness is best explained in terms of the actual experiences of exile, alienation, and social mobility about which the saints so often and insistently wrote. Discipline and repression are responses to these experiences, responses which do not aim at a return to some former security, but rather at a vigorous control and a narrowing of energies—a bold effort to shape a personality amidst "chaos". Thus might be explained the extraordinarily regimented life recorded in Margaret Hoby's diary. Mrs. Hoby was a merchant's daughter, married to a gentleman (the son of the Elizabethan ambassador Sir Thomas Hoby, translator of Castiglione) and carried off to a country estate in Yorkshire where all her neighbors were Catholic and, in her eyes, rowdy and sinful men. There she spent her time in earnest conversations with her minister, reading and listening to sermons and laboriously copying them out in her notebook, adhering to a strict routine of public and private prayer, assiduous in her daily self-recrimination:

> I talked of some things not so as I ought when I had considered of them, but I find what is in a man if the Lord's spirit do never so little hide itself . . . but this is my comfort, that my heart is settled to be more watchful hereafter. . . .

How many men have settled since for the same "comfort"!

Undoubtedly, Margaret Hoby's behavior might be differently explained, but not so as to account so well for the similar behavior of her brethren. These people felt themselves exceptionally open to the dangers about them and this must have been, in part, because they were cut off, as were the men who succumbed to chaos—beggars and vagabonds—from the old forms of order and routine. It is this sense of being cut off, alien, that is expressed in the endless descriptions of the saint as a stranger and pilgrim which are so important in Puritan writing. Pilgrimage is, perhaps, one of the major themes in all Christian literature, but it achieves among the Puritans a unique power, a forcefulness and intensity in its popular expression which culminates finally in Bunyan's classic. Over and over again, with the detail which only experience or, perhaps, a continually engaged imagination can give, Puritans describe life as a journey (or, in the image which Hobbes later made famous, as a race) through alien country. And yet, at the same time, they write of the vagabond with venomous hatred: he is a dangerous man because he has not disciplined and prepared himself for his journey. "Wandering beggars and rogues," wrote William Perkins, "that pass from place to place, being under no certain magistracy or ministry, nor joining themselves to any set society in church or commonwealth, are plagues and banes of both, and are to be taken as main enemies of [the] ordinance of God . . ." The bitterness of this passage suggests the self-hatred of the Puritan pilgrim, pitying and worrying about his own "unsettledness". When the famous preacher Richard Greenham told a Puritan audience "Paradise is our native country", some of his listeners surely must have winced to think: *not England.* "We dwell here as in Meshech and as in the tents of Kedar, and therefore we be glad to be at home." It was painful, but inevitable, that the saints should live in tents. Perkins himself wrote in the same vein, for all his hatred of the wanderer: "Alas, poor souls, we are no better than passengers in this world, our way it is in the middle of the sea." For many Puritans, if not for Perkins himself, who grew old in Cambridge, these words must have had a meaning both literal and poignant. Since the days of Mary, exile had been a common experience for the saints. And a generation after Perkins wrote, the "middle of the sea" would become a path for tens of thousands.

The fanatical self-righteousness of that first Puritan John Knox, a Scottish peasant's son, set loose in Europe by war and revolution, is surely in some sense a function of his exile: righteousness was a consolation and a way of organizing the self for survival. The "unsettledness" of Richard Rogers was due in part to his devious struggles with the corporate church and its bishops; but Rogers, who remembered his Essex birthplace as a "dunghill", was ever an outsider, and Puritanism his way of stirring up his heart. When William Whitgift, the future archbishop, cruelly taunted the Puritan leader Thomas Cartwright for "eating at other men's tables", he was perhaps suggesting an important source of Cartwright's vision of congregational unity and holiness. Margaret Hoby's life would have been different indeed had she been raised in a traditional country family: there would, for example, have been dancing at her wedding, and her life thereafter would hardly have allowed for time-consuming religious exercises. Deprived of such a life, because of her social background (and the ideas which were part of it) or, perhaps, because of basic changes in rural life, she willfully sought new comforts. Country gentlemen like John Winthrop and Oliver Cromwell, educated at Cambridge, knowledgeable in London, suddenly turned upon the traditional routine of English life as if it were actually vicious.

Half in, half out of that routine, they anxiously sought a new certainty. "Oh, I lived in and loved darkness and hated light; I was a chief, the chief of sinners", wrote Cromwell of his seemingly ordinary and conventional life before conversion. But now, he went on, "my soul is with the congregation of the first born, my body rests in hope; and if here I may honor my God either by doing or by suffering, I shall be most glad."

All this suggests once again the view of Puritanism as a response of particular men to particular experiences of confusion, change, alienation and exile. Now Calvinism obviously made men extremely sensitive to disorder in all its forms. It is more important, however, that it gave meaning to the experience of disorder and provided a way out, a return to certainty. It was an active response, and not a mere reflection of social confusion, for indeed other men responded differently. There is no rigid pattern in these responses. It seems probable that members of a rising middle class most sharply experienced that alienation from old England which drove men to the exercises of sainthood. On the other hand, there were both gentlemen and citizens who certainly enjoyed the new freedoms of mobility, extravagance, individuality and wit, and eagerly sought entrance to the Renaissance court, where freedom was cultivated. And from among these men undoubtedly came many future capitalists. It would not be easy to explain in particular cases why the court held such attractions for some men, while it was vicious and iniquitous in the eyes of others. No more is it readily comprehensible why some of the newcomers to the burgeoning city of London merged into the mob or explored the exciting underworld, while others hated the wickedness of the city and sought out virtuous brethren in the radical conventicles. What is important for the present is that Puritanism was a response to an experience which many men had; it provided one way of understanding the experience and of coping with it.

Coping with it meant being reborn as a new man, self-confident and free of worry, capable of vigorous, willful activity. The saints sometimes took new names to signify their rebirth. If alienation had made them anxious, depressed, unable to work, given to fantasies of demons, morbid introspection or fearful daydreams such as Calvin had suggested were common among fallen men, then sainthood was indeed a transformation. Cromwell's pledge to honor his God "by doing" was no idle boast: he was obviously capable of just that. Perhaps this transformation gave businessmen the confidence necessary for innovation or freed them from the necessity of feeling guilty about routine connivance, usury, extortion. Thus argue Marxists and Weberians alike. But innovation was more likely due to the recklessness of the speculator than to the self-confidence of the saint; indeed, the saints hated the "projectors" who lived in and about the court, currying favor and waiting for opportunity. The congregational discipline, as has been seen, would have established controls hardly compatible with businesslike hard dealing. Cromwell's "doing" was obviously of a different order, and Cromwell was a representative man. His life suggests that the Puritan experience produced first of all a political activist.

The Puritan new man was active not so that success might reinforce his self-esteem, but in order to transform a world in which he saw his own ever-present wickedness writ large. In a sense, his was a struggle to free himself from temptation by removing all alternatives to godliness, by organizing his own life as a continuous discipline and society as a regiment. His activity was political in that it was always concerned with government—though not only or, perhaps, not most importantly, at the level of the state. Puritans often imagined the congregation as a "little commonwealth", replacing the organic imagery of Anglicans and Catholics with expressions deliberately drawn from the world of coercion and sovereignty. Thus they made manifest their own pervasive concern with *control* rather than with harmony or love. Their treatment of the family was similar: they saw it as a field for the exercise of discipline by a godly father usually described as a "governor". Puritan interest in the family parallels that of Jean Bodin (though, in contrast to Robert Filmer, also a Bodinian, the saints had little to say about paternal affection and benevolence) and probably has the same source. The insistence upon the absolute sovereignty of the father and upon the family as an institution for repressing and disciplining naturally wicked, licentious and rebellious children derives in both cases from an extraordinary fear of disorder and anarchy. Thus two Puritan preachers in a famous treatise on "family government":

> The young child which lieth in the cradle [is] both wayward and full of affections: and though his body be but small, yet he hath a great heart, and is altogether inclined to evil. . . . If this sparkle be suffered to increase, it will rage over and burn down the whole house. For we are changed and become good, not by birth, but by education. . . . Therefore parents must be wary and circumspect, that they never

smile or laugh at any words or deeds of their children done lewdly . . .
naughtily, wantonly . . . they must correct and sharply reprove their
children for saying or doing ill. . . .

The father was continually active, warily watching his children; the
elders of the congregation were ever alert and vigilant, seeking out the
devious paths of sin; so also the godly magistrate. "In you it is now to
cleanse, to free your country of villainy," a Puritan minister told the
judges of Norwich, ". . . consider your power to reform . . . if you be
faithful, and God's power to revenge if you be faithless." In Puritan
writings, political activity was described as a form of work: it required
systematic application, attention to detail, sustained interest and labor.
Much that the godly magistrates undertook might be called, in Marxist
terms, progressive; some of their activity, however, would clearly im-
pede free economic activity. But description in these terms is valuable
only if one seeks to understand those aspects of Puritan activity which,
through a subsequent process of selection, became permanent features of
the modern world. In the seventeenth century, Puritan politics obviously
had an interest rather different from that suggested by the term "progress". Its immediate purpose was to regain control of a changing world;
hence the great concern with method, discipline, and order, and the
frequent uneasiness with novelty. When the saints spoke of reform, they
meant first of all an overcoming of social instability and all its moral
and intellectual concommitants. Godly magistracy was a bold effort to
seize control of society, much as sainthood had been an effort to control
and organize the self. And the first of these followed from the second: in
this way did Puritanism produce revolutionaries. In much the same way,
it may be suggested, did the Jacobin man of virtue become an *active
citizen*, and the hardened and "steeled" Bolshevik first a *professional*
revolutionary and then, in Lenin's words, a "leader", "manager", and
"controller".

These revolutionary men do not simply attack and transform the old
order—as in the Marxist story. The old order is only a part, and often
not the most important part, of their experience. They live much of their
lives amidst the breakdown of that order, or in hiding or exile from it.
And much of their rebellion is directed against the very "unsettledness"
that they know best. The analogy with the Bolsheviks is worth pursuing.
Lenin's diatribes against "slovenliness . . . carelessness, untidiness, un-

punctuality, nervous haste, the inclination to substitute discussion for action, talk for work, the inclination to undertake everything under the sun without finishing anything" were intended first of all as attacks upon his fellow exiles—whatever their value as descriptions of the "primitive" Russia he hated so much. The first triumph of Bolshevism, as of Puritanism, was over the impulse toward "disorganization" in its own midst: here, so to speak, was Satan at work where he is ever most active—in the ranks of the godly. And it must be said that this triumph was also over the first impulses toward freedom. Thus the Puritans vigorously attacked Renaissance experimentation in dress and in all the arts of self-decoration and hated the free-wheeling vagabonds who "crowd into cities [and] boroughs . . . roll up and down from one lodging to another", never organizing themselves into families and congregations. Similarly, the Jacobin leader Robespierre attacked the economic egotism of the new bourgeoisie and spitefully connected the radical free thought of the Enlightenment with anti-revolutionary conspiracy. Atheism, he declared, is aristocratic. And again Lenin, preaching with all the energy of a secular Calvinist against free love: "Dissoluteness in sexual life is bourgeois, [it] is a phenomenon of decay. The proletariat is a rising class . . . It needs clarity, clarity and again clarity. And so, I repeat, no weakening, no waste, no destruction of forces."

In fact, Lenin's morality had little to do with the proletariat, and the "dissoluteness" he attacked had little to do with the bourgeoisie. He might as well have talked of saints and worldlings as the Puritans did. The contrast he was getting at was between those men who had succumbed to (or taken advantage of!) the disorder of their time—speculators in philosophy, vagabonds in their sexual life, economic Don Juans —and those men who had somehow pulled themselves out of "unsettledness", organized their lives and regained control. The first group were the damned and the second the saved. The difference between them was not social but ideological.

Puritans, Jacobins and Bolsheviks did tend to come from the same social strata—that is, from the educated middle classes, preachers, lawyers, journalists, teachers, professional men of all sorts. But this is not because such men are representatives of larger social groups whose interests they defend. It has already been shown that the connection between Puritan theory and bourgeois interests is at best a difficult one, which is in no sense implicit in the theory, but is rather worked out later in a long process of corruption, selection and forgetting. Men like the godly ministers speak first of all for themselves: they record most sensitively the experience of "unsettledness" and respond to it most vigorously. For reasons which require further investigation, such men seem less integrated into their society—even in the most stable periods —and more available, as it were, for alienation than are farmers or businessmen. This is not, of course, to reduce their moral discipline (or their radical politics) to the psychological therapy of alienated intellectuals. The alienation which John Knox or Richard Rogers experienced, with all its attendant fearfulness and enthusiasm, sometimes disfiguring and sometimes ennobling, was only a heightened form of the feelings of other men—in a sense, of all men, for ultimately the sociological range of the Puritan response was very wide.

But the historian must also record that "unsettledness" was not a permanent condition and that sainthood was only a temporary role. For men always seek and find not some tense and demanding discipline, but some new routine. The saints failed in their effort to establish a holy commonwealth and, in one way or another, their more recent counterparts have also failed. What this suggests is not that the holy commonwealth was an impractical dream, the program of muddled, unrealistic men. In fact, Puritan ministers and elders (and fathers!) had considerable political experience and the holy commonwealth was in a sense achieved, at least among those men who most needed holiness. Nor is it correct to argue from the failure of the saints that Puritanism in its revolutionary form represents only a temporary triumph of "ideas" over "interest", a momentary burst of enthusiasm. For such moments have their histories, and what needs to be explained is why groups of men, over a fairly long span of time, acquired such an intense interest in ideas like predestination and holiness. Puritan ideology was a response to real experience, therefore a practical effort to cope with personal and social problems. The inability of the saints to establish and maintain their holy commonwealth suggests only that these problems were limited in time to the period of breakdown and psychic and political reconstruction. When men stopped being afraid, or became less afraid, then Puritanism was suddenly irrelevant. Particular elements in the Puritan system were transformed to fit the new routine—and other elements were forgotten. And only then did the saint become a man of "good behavior", cautious, respectable, calm, ready to participate in a Lockeian society.

VII

The argument of the preceding section may now be concluded: Puritanism was not a revolutionary ideology in the Marxist sense, reflecting the interests of a rising class. Such interests are in the seventeenth century better represented by parliamentarians and common lawyers who had their own ideology. The faith of the saints was rather a peculiarly intense response to the experience of social change itself, an experience which, in one way or another, set groups of men outside the established order. It should be obvious that this may be the result of either "rising" or "falling" in economic terms; mobility itself is the key, especially if the old social order is traditionalist, dependent for its stability upon popular passivity. The Puritan response produced revolutionaries, that is, saints, godly magistrates, men already disciplined (before the revolution begins) for the strenuous work of transforming all society and all men in the image of their own salvation. Such men, narrow, fanatical, enthusiastic, committed to their "work", have little to contribute to the development of either liberalism or capitalism. To expect freedom from their hands is to invite disappointment. Their great achievement is what is known in the sociology of revolution as the *terror*, the effort to create a holy commonwealth and to force men to be godly.

The contribution of these men to the future is the destruction of the old order. Alienated from its conventions and routines—from its comforts—they feel no nostalgia as they watch its slow decay. They are capable not only of establishing, underground, an alternative system, but also of making a frontal assault upon the old order itself, in the case of the Puritans, upon hierarchy and patriarchy, the central principles of traditional government. Their extraordinary self-confidence, won at some cost, as has been seen, makes them capable finally of killing the king. Here Weber's analysis is undoubtedly closer to the truth than that of the Marxists: the saints are entrepreneurs indeed, but in politics rather than in economics. They ruthlessly (and anxiously) pursue not wealth or even individual power—never rely on great men, warned a Puritan preacher—but *collective control* of themselves, of each other, of all England.

The Puritan struggle for collective control is not unique in history. The illustrations already drawn from Jacobin and Bolshevik experience suggest at least the possibility of a comparative study of revolutionary ideology. To "set up" such a comparison has been one of the purposes of the foregoing argument. It remains only to defend its usefulness: it is useful primarily, of course, because the encounter with sainthood is a part of our own experience.

On the level of ideology, of perception and response, comparisons of the Calvinist elect with the Jacobin men of virtue and the Bolshevik vanguard would not provide any test of the hypothetical description of Puritanism as a response to breakdown, disorder, and social change. They would demonstrate only that the hypothesis can be extended to cover other cases: other men have also lived through the experience of exile and alienation and have shaped their characters in opposition to their environment. Other men have won a self-assurance akin to that of the saints, and it has permitted them similar forms of activity—radical, ruthless, experimental. This extension of the range of analysis is useful even if it does not permit scientific testing of the hypothesis. Comparison always brings new insight: the additional examples often require elaboration and correction of the original hypothesis, and at the same time the discovery of significant differences in similar cases defines its limits. Working back and forth between, say, Puritans and Bolsheviks may also avoid some of the dangers of anachronistic judgment which are probably inherent in a commitment to a single progress—to English history, for example, with its solemn advance from precedent to precedent. For if the foregoing argument is at all correct, then the saints are likely to be similar not to the men who came before or after them in English history, but to other men in other countries who lived through a similar time and shared some of the same experiences.

The conditions of these experiences obviously may be compared in a more systematic fashion. Measurements of social mobility of various sorts and careful studies of economic change both might be useful here, though it must be said again that recording such measurements or carrying out such studies does not bring one face to face with "real life". Mobility, for example, is a different experience for different men. Nevertheless, it can surely be argued that urbanization under more or less similar conditions—which can be investigated and the details quarrelled over—makes a limited number of ideological responses likely, the appearance of a limited variety of new men probable. All these men may not be present in every case, but on a broad enough national scale and over a sufficient span of time, they are all likely to appear: the lost worldling whom the Puritans called damned, the exciting (and often creative) speculator in freedom, the fearful man who desperately seeks authority, and the saint himself.

But it is probably not possible in any particular place, at any moment in time, to predict the appearance of the last of these men—though it can be suggested, on the basis of the argument outlined above, that he will not be absent in a time of full-scale revolution. The ideas which shape his character are not automatic products of some objective development—indeed, very little is yet known about their production—and it is not easy to guess when they will take hold or what their precise nature will be. And here comparative work can only serve to increase the sensitivity of the student. If a science is not possible, then one must resort to an older form of knowledge, to that intuition which comes, above all, from the practice of history.

4. AN EXPERIMENT IN "FEUDALISM"

French Canada in the Seventeenth Century*

by Sigmund Diamond

Spain, France, and England each approached the New World differently. Precisely how each went about creating an overseas empire depended on the social order prevailing in the mother country; a nation's methods of operation abroad were shaped by the way it managed affairs at home. In the following selection, Sigmund Diamond examines the French colonization design for New France (Canada) and shows how it was modeled on the French idea of a well-ordered society. The French discovered that assumptions rooted in European experience were inappropriate to the Canadian wilderness. Yet, rather than alter them, they tried to impose their system under circumstances that doomed them to failure. When the struggle with Britain for the control of North America reached a climax in the middle of the eighteenth century, French Canada could not match

---

* *William and Mary Quarterly*, 3d series, vol. 18 (1961), 1–34. Footnotes have been omitted except where they are necessary for an understanding of the text.

English America in population, wealth, or extent of development. The loss of its North American colonies was the price France paid for its "Experiment in 'Feudalism.' " By studying the French experience, it is possible to achieve a clearer understanding of the distinctive way Britain settled North America and the reasons for its greater success. How did the British approach to the New World differ from the French and why? In what ways was it more appropriate to American conditions?

For further reading: Clarence H. Haring, *Spanish Empire in America* (1952); Edward G. Bourne, *Spain in America* (1905); Silvio Zavala, *New Viewpoints on the Spanish Colonization of America* (1943); J. H. Parry, *The Spanish Seaborne Empire* (1966).

I

The history of sixteenth- and seventeenth-century colonization provides an almost unique opportunity for the study of certain problems in social organization. The very requirement, as in the case of the British and French in North America, to establish settlements "where none before hath stood," or, as in the case of the Spanish in Central and South America, to devise a mode of accommodation with pre-existing societies, imposed the necessity of considering problems of social organization with a clarity and directness rarely before achieved. Nor was this entirely a matter of necessity. The creation of new societies raised thought about appropriate forms of organization to a new level of consciousness, not only because the situation created the need, but also because it created the opportunity. Man had now the possibility, so at least it seemed, of making a fresh beginning. Was it really necessary that he be forever burdened with the residue of the iniquity and folly of past history? Was it not possible to devise a new form of social organization in which at least some of the less desirable characteristics of the old would be eliminated? From consciousness of both necessity and opportunity came the impetus to create forms of social organization appropriate to achieve the ends held by the leaders of colonization ventures—whether corporations, private individuals invested with almost regal authority, or the crown.

How were the members of the new societies to be recruited? How were they to be motivated to accept the obligations attached to their positions in these new societies? How was order to be maintained between persons of different statuses? What should be the proper balance among ethic, reward, and sanction in getting persons to behave in the proper fashion? Would the family detach persons from their loyalty to the colonizing organization, or would it increase their satisfaction with their lot in the New World? What special features of social organization would have to be created to accommodate the new societies to sponsorship by joint-stock companies, and how might these be different in colonies undertaken by individuals or by government?

Simply to state these questions is to suggest that implicit in the history of early modern colonization is the problem of planned social action, and that this history may be re-examined with the view in mind of analyzing the discrepancy between the plan for the new society and the actual outcome of the effort to apply the plan. If, as appears to be the case, the effort to plan certain aspects of a social system may have unanticipated effects elsewhere in the system—effects that may negate the very purposes of the planners—an examination of the sources of these unanticipated effects may reveal to us more than we now know of the ways in which the different parts of a society are related, and how that society worked.

II

In New France, as in Virginia, the first persistent instrument used to achieve the purposes of colonization was the chartered commercial company. Society was brought to both Jamestown and Quebec in the ships of a commercial company, in both cases for the same reasons and with much the same consequences. The form of organization devised by the company proved incapable not only of balancing the somewhat contradictory objectives of the merchants—and others—who invested and the government which patronized, but even of solving the strictly business problem of recruiting the supplies of capital and labor necessary for the survival of the company. To take but one example, the great Company of One Hundred Associates, the most prominent of several that failed in New France before 1663, undertook by the terms of its charter to transport four thousand settlers between 1627 and 1642. It was, however, unable to devise a form of social organization that could reconcile its own interests in deploying its labor force into the most profitable economic pursuits with the interests of the government in fixing immigrants to the land and in establishing a polity, and with the interests of the population in receiving as many as possible of the rewards for undertaking the hazardous task of bringing society to a wilderness. Colonization under commercial auspices was considered a failure, and with the demise of the company in 1663, it devolved upon the government in France, as it had upon the government in England in the case of the Virginia Company in 1624, to create a more adequate form of social organization. The cost of recruiting a population, of supplying it, of motivating it to work, of defending it against its enemies became a charge upon government and not upon private business.

What followed was a remarkable experiment in creating a society according to plan, an attempt to utilize existing institutions—religion, family, land tenure, law—and to adapt them, under government auspices, to the objectives of the planners and the needs of an immigrant population under frontier conditions. The administrative demands entailed in such an effort were staggering. Hundreds of manuscript volumes of home and colonial decrees and an even larger mass of correspondence, court decisions, and other official documents stand today as mute testimony to the scope of the attempt. What, above all, characterizes the plan is that it bore so clearly the stamp of that passion for rationality —the desire to achieve order, symmetry, and harmony—which is the hallmark of bureaucratic endeavor. It would be anachronistic and yet truthful to describe the objective of the French authorities in Canada after 1663, not as the creation of a society to be governed by political means, but as the creation of an administrative system in which persons would have fixed positions in a table of organization, would behave in the way deemed appropriate for those positions, and would be manipulated, deployed, and disciplined by measures more compatible with the requirements of a formal organization than of a society.

To a degree, of course, this desire to rationalize the operations of the system of governance was already highly developed in France. The attempt of the seigniors of the *ancien régime* to bring order into their own economic activities and into their relations with tenants is by now well known; even better known is the celebrated effort of the monarchy under Louis XIV and his successors to reform the system of administration. What permitted the same effort to be carried even further in Canada was the possibility of beginning at the beginning. Where a society did not already exist, there was no necessity to make the best of a bad situation, to compromise the goal of rationality by having to reckon with the need to adjust to established institutions and traditions.

Instructing the Dauphin in the desirability of recruiting only persons of moderate social position into the civil service, Louis XIV wrote: "It was not to my interest to select subjects of higher degree. It was important that they should not conceive hopes any higher than it pleased me to grant them, something which is difficult among persons of high birth." The tendency betrayed by the King's instructions to regard his civil servants as instruments to aid him in achieving his own purposes had an even wider extension in Canada, for there everyone was looked upon as the King viewed his civil servant, as an agent of the state. The letter of Jean Baptiste Colbert to Marquis Prouville de Tracy upon the latter's assumption of the governorship is exceptional only because Tracy's position in the administration imposed the necessity of greater explicitness. "The first thing that I must insist upon," wrote Colbert, "is that, since the king takes note of all of his affairs, you must address yourself directly to him in making reports and receiving his orders. It would be well for you to observe this in the future, for although I inform him of everything written to me, those, like you, who hold positions of trust ought to have it as a maxim to have their main relationship with His Majesty."

Relying upon the loyalty of their direct subordinates and the self-discipline of the population, the metropolitan authorities aimed at the creation of a society in Canada in which the vast majority of persons would be firmly fixed to the land, would live peaceably in their villages, and would respond obediently to the commands of their superiors. The reins of legitimate power were held firmly in the hands of the administrative authorities and their designated surrogates, and any tendency toward the development of competing authority, even when it conformed to practices already established in France, was rigorously suppressed.

Every aspect of life in Canada was subject to rational calculation and was alterable by purposeful action. Political institutions, the family, Indian affairs, the range of permissible trades and occupations, the amount of prestige and honor to be associated with each status in the society were all carefully regulated. The behavior of each major segment of the population was prescribed in the minutest detail, even to the point of regulating the order of precedence in religious and secular ceremonies, the appropriate forms of address, and the types of weapons that each might bear. The total corpus of these regulations betrays the assumption, central to the conception of the administrator, that each person is essentially the occupant of a position in an organization and that his behavior can be made to conform to the needs of the system for order and stability.

Precautions were taken that nothing should interfere with the flow of authority in the established chain of command. Though occasional meetings of the population were held to discuss problems and to hear proposed programs, never did these assume the character of representative assemblies; they were *ad hoc* bodies, summoned to listen and not to argue. When, elated by his own cleverness, Governor Louis de Buade, Comte de Frontenac, informed Colbert in 1672 that he had administered an oath of loyalty to the seigniors and, for convenience, to a group of habitants acting on behalf of all, he received a blistering reply. "Since our Kings have long regarded it as good for their service not to convoke the Estates-General of the Kingdom in order perhaps to abolish insensibly this ancient usage, you, on your part, should very rarely, or, to speak correctly, never, give a corporate form to the inhabitants of Canada. You should even, as the colony strengthens, suppress gradually the office of Syndic, who presents petitions in the name of the inhabitants, for it is well that each should speak for himself and no one for all."

Nothing was permitted to escape the hawklike eyes of those responsible for seeing that the colonists behaved according to plan, and no problem was too small to be taken to the highest official. Jérôme de Pontchartrain himself, the minister of colonies in Paris, was called upon to decide disputes involving a cow strayed into someone's garden, a brawl at a church door, the virtue of a certain lady. Colbert had to be informed, as evidence of the degree to which prescriptions for proper behavior were observed, that two captains had been married, one lieutenant engaged, and "four ensigns are in treaty with their mistresses, and are already half engaged." Jean Talon, struck with the thought that population increase might be achieved by the intermarriage of Indians and French, studied the reproductive capacity of Indian women and reported that it was impaired by their nursing children longer than necessary; but, he added, "this obstacle to the speedy building up of the colony can be overcome by a police regulation."

In short, what was planned was a society in which all persons would be under a jurisdiction and patronage that were at once French, royal, and orthodox. Stability would be guaranteed by each person's having a precise place and acting in accordance with the behavior defined as appropriate to that place. The elements of this society were, of course, diverse—government regulation of economic activity, a special system of land tenure, an elaborate code of law, an established church, royal patronage of the institution of the family—and every effort was made to weld them together into an organization in which discipline would be achieved because each man would remain loyal to the institutions to which he was attached.

The fur trade, which had been at once a blessing and a curse to the colony, was the subject of endless consideration by government officials. Although the form of regulation varied, the trade was controlled at virtually all times so as to restrict the number and influence of persons engaged in it. The privileged few were thus to be attached to the government with the ties of gratitude that flow from profit, while the mass of the population would not be diverted from the performance of necessary agricultural tasks. The *coureurs de bois* were to be quarantined so that their lawlessness could not contaminate what was hoped would be an obedient agricultural society. Men who desert the land to enter the forests, said Talon, are men, "without Christianity, without sacraments, without religion, without priests, without laws, without magistrates, sole masters of their own actions and of the application of their wills . . . ."

Population growth, recognized by government officials as indispensable to increasing agricultural production and, at least indirectly, to reducing the overhead costs of administering the colony, was promoted through immigration, encouragement of marriage, family subsidies, and attempts to mobilize the Indians into the labor force. The policy of "Francisation," which included conversion, domiciliation, intermarriage, and education of the Indians in the ways of the white man, was undertaken in the hope that, made tractable by their re-education, they would swell the labor force. It quickly became evident that the policy had failed, and that population growth would have to come about through immigration and natural increase.

In 1668 Colbert suggested to Talon that those "who may seem to have absolutely renounced marriage should be made to have additional burdens, and be excluded from all honors; it would be well even to add some marks of infamy." The Intendant was quick to take the hint; bachelors were barred from the right to hunt, fish, trade with the Indians, and even to enter the woods. By act of the Sovereign Council of Canada, "any inhabitant having in legitimate marriage ten living children, not priests, *religieux* or *religieuses* shall be paid three hundred livres a year, and those who have twelve shall be paid four hundred livres a year." Young men who married before the age of twenty were given a bonus. Fathers whose sons were not married by the age of twenty or whose daughters were still vestals at the age of sixteen were to be fined and summoned to the court every six months.

But to encourage marriage the government would have to take the initiative in providing women, unless it were willing—which it was not —to tolerate "a thousand disorders in the settlements . . . where the women are very glad to have several husbands and where the men cannot get even one wife." Marriage, it was anticipated, would not only increase the birth rate but would lead to a more settled and orderly life. As in Virginia, therefore, the government assumed the responsibility of shipping from France "demoiselles" for the military officers and what pious Mother Marie de l'Incarnation called "une marchandise mêlée"— mixed goods—for the ordinary settlers, something more than a thousand altogether.

Still French Canada's population growth, dependent overwhelmingly upon natural increase and very little upon immigration, lagged far behind Canadian requirements. As late as 1710 Governor Philippe de Rigaud, Marquis de Vaudreuil, complained that there was not enough labor for the seigniors to cultivate even half their estates; six years later he was recommending that condemned salt smugglers in France be shipped as indentured servants at the expense of the farmers-general. In 1733 Governor Charles de la Boische, Marquis de Beauharnois, and Intendant Gilles Hocquart echoed the complaint: "The scarcity of men, and the high wages of both agricultural and urban labor, considerably diminishes the revenues of landlords and merchants." Despite every effort of a government that exhorted and a people that produced, the population of French Canada amounted to only about 5 per cent of the population south of the St. Lawrence River by the middle of the eighteenth century.

But neither government regulation nor family attachments were, in the view of the French authorities, sufficient to maintain social discipline; religion, too, was counted on to disseminate an ethic calculated to remind each man to keep to his allotted place. From the beginning of New France, the Roman Catholic Church was given major responsibility for enforcing the ban on Protestants in Canada, and the zealousness with which it responded to the task of rooting out unorthodoxy in both its Jansenist and Protestant forms revealed that secular as well as religious discipline was its proper concern. The importance of orthodoxy from the religious viewpoint was self-evident. "On the side of the state," wrote Bishop François Xavier de Laval, "it appears to be no less important. Everyone knows that Protestants in general are not so attached to His Majesty as Catholics . . . . To multiply the number of Protestants in Canada would be to give occasion for the outbreak of revolutions."

Doctrinal conflict was minimized, therefore, by screening prospective immigrants, but the church played a no less significant role in disciplining colonists once they had arrived. The keynote was sounded in a letter from Louis XIV to Bishop Laval: "As I have been informed of your continued care to hold the people in their duty towards God and towards me by the good education you give or cause to be given to the young, I write this letter to express my satisfaction with conduct so salutary, and to exhort you to persevere in it." The nature of this education may be inferred from the list of virtues commended to boys, drawn from the rulebook of the Petit Séminaire in Quebec: "humility, obedience, purity, meekness, modesty, simplicity, chastity, charity, and an ardent love of Jesus and his Holy Mother." All schools but one were under control of the church, and that single exception—the School of Mathematics and Hydrography—passed under its influence early in the eighteenth century.

In its role as custodian of morals and, though its pretensions in this area were disputed, of law, the church went even further. It regulated the style of clothing; it censored books; it established with meticulous accuracy the order of priority of both religious and secular officials on ceremonial occasions; it attacked usury and supported its attack by refusing confession to usurers; it shipped back to France immoral men, including those who were so unmindful of their situation in life as to fall in love with more highly placed girls; and it attempted to cultivate an ethic of obligation and obedience, of simplicity and austerity.

Most important of all, however, it threw the weight of ecclesiastical discipline behind the effort to fix the population into assigned positions; the sanction of excommunication itself was invoked against those who left the land without permission and traded illegally for furs with the Indians. Although there were disputes between secular and religious officials when either tried to exercise authority that pinched the other, they were as one in recognizing the importance of the church in disciplining the inferiors of both, in urging upon them acceptance of a code of beliefs that would confine their behavior within the limits desired by higher authority. We must "multiply the number of parishes and . . . render them fixed . . . ," wrote Governor Jacques-René de Brissay, Marquis de Denonville, to Colbert in 1685. "This undertaking . . . would be a sure means of establishing schools, with which the *curés* would occupy themselves and thus accustom the children at an early hour to control themselves and become useful." Finally, in its capacity as landowner, the church assumed the role of model seignior, and attempted by the force of its own example to influence the behavior of other landlords. By 1750 the church held over two million arpents of land, more than one-third of all the grants that had been made.

But the most characteristic institution of the old regime in Canada— the one that gave tone to the entire society—was the seigniorial system. There was much in it that was reminiscent of medieval feudalism, but only reminiscent. Feudalism in France was an organic growth; in Canada it was a transplanted institution, and the French administration saw to it that in the transplanting it was pruned of less desirable characteristics. The French monarchy had established itself in the teeth of feudal opposition and was in no mood now to offer the seigniors sufficient independence and power so as to require repetition of the experience. When Governor Tracy and Intendant Talon drew up their "Projet de Règlement" in 1667, they warned that since "obedience and fidelity [two words obscured] are more likely to suffer attenuation in distant provinces of the state than in the neighbors of the Sovereign Authority, which resides mainly in the person of the prince and has more force and virtue there than in any other person, it is the part of prudence to prevent in the establishment of the growing state of Canada all those vexatious revolutions which might render it monarchical, aristocratic, or democratic, or even—by a balanced power and authority between subjects—divide it into parts and give rise to such a dismemberment as France suffered by the creation of such sovereignties within the kingdom as Soissons, Orleans, Champagne, and others." In their concern lies the clue to the essential difference between French and Canadian feudalism. The landed seignior in Canada was entitled to many of the rights possessed by his counterpart in France—potential membership in the nobility; ceremonial rights like fealty and homage; judicial rights like holding private courts; and more lucrative rights such as the collection of rents and mutation fines, the imposition of labor services, and the monopoly of all milling—and the enforcement of these rights was presumably guaranteed by the extension to Canada of the law code known as the Custom of Paris and the beneficent protection of the royal authority. Nevertheless, the position of the Canadian seignior was far different from that of the French.

The right to have a private court was his, but the use of the term *haute, moyenne, et basse justice* in Canada must not delude us into thinking that it held the same meaning as in France. The existence of the competing royal court eventually limited private jurisdiction to relatively simple cases about seigniorial dues and obligations, and even in these the habitant had free right of appeal to the royal court. Nor were the profits of justice as lucrative in Canada as in France; where population was sparse, the opportunity to squeeze income from it in the courts was limited by the small number of cases and by the fear that too much repression would cause the seignior's labor force to move to the lands of a less exacting landlord. "I will not say that the Goddess of Justice is more chaste and impartial here than in France," wrote Baron Louis Armand de la Hontan, "but at any rate, if she is sold, she is sold more cheaply." In Canada the problem was not so much to check the encroachments of the seigniorial courts as to force the reluctant seigniors to accept the profitless and limited jurisdiction the Crown imposed on them.

So, too, the seigniors of Canada had the rights of *banalité* and *corvée*. Under conditions of severely limited population, however, these were drained of most of their significance. The intendants of Canada, conscious of the fact that onerous obligations on the peasantry would hamper immigration, restricted the size of the payments to the seigniors and forced them to improve their mills. So profitless were these rights that, as with private courts, the problem was not so much to control their abuse as to get the seigniors to exercise them at all. In 1686 a royal decree was issued requiring the seigniors to build mills on their land grants on penalty of losing their monopoly, but for twenty years the seigniors sabotaged enforcement of the decree by not promulgating it.

What under other circumstances would have been a profitable privilege was for the Canadian seignior a burdensome cost.

Even the conditions under which he held land and could legitimately demand payments from his sub-infeudees were different from those in France. Squirm though he might, never could the seignior wholly evade the scrutiny of the intendants, who were determined to prevent the payments owed by the *censitaires*, the peasants, from becoming too burdensome. Even more, his power to dispose of his own domain was limited in such a way as to reduce his maneuverability and to make him essentially an agent of the Crown in the achievement of its purposes. After several preliminary gestures, the King, through the Arrêts of Marly in 1711, decreed that all seigniorial grants not settled and developed through sub-infeudation would revert to the Crown, and that the payments to seigniors from sub-infeudated lands must be uniform and limited. In the minds of the administrators, the seigniors were less proprietors than trustees, entitled to occupy the land only if they performed the essential tasks required of them.

Though the Canadian seignior was sometimes able to evade some of the restrictions imposed upon him, there can be little doubt that his rights were more limited than were those of the French. Still, they were believed sufficient to get him to assume the tasks for which the Crown held him responsible—to clear the land, to settle it with farmers, to support the church and the state, and to keep his subordinates in their places. For those who did their tasks well, there was the added incentive of possible ennoblement: We must grant titles, Talon told Colbert in 1670, to "fill the officers and richer seigniors with a new zeal for the settlement of their lands in hope of being recompensed with titles as well." Having deprived the seignior of many of the attributes that permitted him to be a seignior, the King's administrators yet hoped he would act like one.

As with the seigniors, so with the *censitaires*. They, too, had rights and obligations differing somewhat from their brothers' in France. They had to clear the land lest it revert to the seignior; they owed him rent and mutation fines; they worked for him and gave him part of their catch of fish; they paid him deference; they were not allowed to engage in the fur trade. Yet, their duties were less onerous than in France, and they were protected from excessive exploitation by a solicitous officialdom. Besides, the prospect of improvement was such, so it was anticipated, as to induce them willingly to accept their position. "There are so many strong and robust peasants in France," wrote Father Paul Le Jeune, "who have no bread to put in their mouths; is it possible they are so afraid of losing sight of the village steeple, as they say, that they would rather languish in their misery and poverty, than to place themselves some day at their ease among the inhabitants of New France, where with the blessings of earth they will more easily find those of heaven and of the soul?" In short, the seigniorial system in Canada was transformed by the authorities into an agency of land settlement, an instrument for peopling the country, and a mechanism for insuring social stability.

III

How did the system actually work? If long-term stability and social discipline were the objectives desired by the authorities, they were not the objectives attained.

The *sine qua non* of successful colonization was the mobilization of an adequate labor force. In Canada, as in British North America, experiments in the use of forced labor and of the local Indians failed, and it soon became necessary to recruit labor by voluntary means. To do so, however, such substantial concessions had to be made that the real position occupied by the labor force in the new society was utterly different not only from its position in Old World society but even from what the planners of the system had intended.

The companies before 1663 recognized the necessity of offering incentives, but sought to minimize them in an effort to keep costs low. Louis Hébert, the Paris apothecary who became the first settler at Quebec, had been offered full support for himself and his family for a period of two years plus two hundred crowns per year for three years as inducement to emigrate. After he arrived, however, the company imposed harsher terms: he was given only one hundred crowns per year; his entire family and his servant were required to work for the company for three years, after which time he was required to sell all his produce to the company at prices current in France; he could work on clearing his land and building his house only when the chief factor did not need his services; he was not to engage in the fur trade; and he was to offer his professional services free of charge to the company.

Samuel de Champlain had been quick to see that the terms were not sufficiently attractive to encourage immigrants. "The Companies having refused to give them the means of cultivating the land," he wrote, "had thus taken away all reason for them to become settlers. At the same time, these Companies gave out that there were numerous families in the country; the truth is that, being entirely useless, they served only to count, and burdened the settlement more than they helped it . . . . That was not the way to create a great desire on the part of anyone to go and people a country, when a man cannot have any free enjoyment of its returns . . . ."

Men who knew the country best, like Father Le Jeune, could only agree with him. Those who emigrate for regular wages, he argued, do not provide the most efficient labor force; they "try to be like some of our neighbors, who, having scarcely passed the line of the Equator, all begin to call themselves Gentlemen, and no longer care to work; if they felt constrained to do it for themselves, they would not sleep over it." The right of ownership, even if limited, was his solution. He explained that immigrants ought to "engage themselves to some family for five or six years on the following conditions:"

That they should be boarded during all this time without receiving any wages, but also that they should possess entirely and in their own right one-half of all the land they clear. And, as they will need something for their own support, the contract should provide that all they get every year, from the lands they have already cleared, should be shared by half; this half, with the little profits they can make in the Country, would be enough to keep them, and to pay after the first or second year for half the tools which they will use in clearing and tilling the land. Now if four men could clear eight arpents of land a year, doing nothing else, winter or summer, in six years forty-eight arpents would be cleared, of which twenty-four would belong to them. With these twenty-four arpents they could support thirty-six persons, or even forty-eight, if the land is good. Is this not a way of becoming rich in a little while?

Throughout the long history of New France, the concessions offered to immigrants assumed many different forms, but in the final analysis they amounted to the same thing—the promise, even the guarantee, of social mobility.

Those who came at their own expense had the promise of land and even, if they performed "notable service" in the interests of the authorities, of titles and patents of nobility. If, as now appears to be the case, most of the *engagés* did not have the promise of land at the time they agreed to their contracts of engagement, many did receive land after completion of their term of service; and, in any case, the wages they could expect in Canada allowed them a substantial increase in living standards.

To induce soldiers to remain in Canada after the period of their enlistment, land and financial subsidies were promised according to rank. Nearly 1500 remained, "finding there land that they would not perhaps have had in their own country." For skilled artisans there was not only the guarantee of high wages but, significantly, the promise that they would not forever be tied to the same position. Throughout the entire French occupation of Canada, ordinary craft restrictions on the achievement of mastership were loosened, and the opportunity to return to France in the higher status was freely granted. To be sure, the lure of the carrot was not the only means used; there was also the stick. Servants were forbidden to leave their masters and others to hide them on pain of severe punishment; marriage without consent of the master was banned; artisans were forced to do whatever their masters required, even when that meant working outside their trades; wages of unskilled workers were regulated.

The net effect of the administration's policy was to introduce slackness rather than rigidity into the society, even to the point of seriously compromising its own ability to obtain revenue. The state *corvée* had to be curtailed, eventually suppressed, for fear that word of its existence would restrict emigration from France and would antagonize the labor force, which, in another capacity, was counted on to provide militia service. The billeting of soldiers, always a source of complaint, was progressively limited until in 1683 it was entirely abolished and became a regular fixed charge upon the state. Direct payments in the form of seigniorial rents and ecclesiastical tithes were reduced considerably below the level prevailing in France. Indeed, *liberté* and *tranquilité*— eventually the major objectives of colonial policy—were seen as attainable only by offering concessions to induce a labor force to migrate and increase its productivity. "Such are the means of attracting colonists and keeping them," wrote M. Petit in his treatise on colonization. "But the most important of all is gentleness and moderation in the government, in extending its hand so that the colonists find, at least in the legitimate use of authority, compensations for the harshness of their labor and the sacrifice of their health in establishments recognized as so useful to the state."

Despite all inducements, the population of Canada never reached the desired quantity and quality. From beginning to end, the reports to the authorities bemoaned the scarcity of labor and its lack of discipline. "Sixty indentured servants have been sent to this country again this year with the notion that they would be immediately useful," Intendant Jacques de Meulles wrote to the Marquis de Seignelay, Colbert's son, in 1684. "The oldest is not seventeen, and . . . I believe that those who sent them are making a mockery of us, there being no one of an age to render service." Send us no more gentlemen, Governor Denonville pleaded in 1686, only "sturdy peasants . . . used to hatchet and pickaxe." "We entreat, you, Monseigneur," wrote Beauharnois and Hocquart to Minister Jean-Frédéric Phélypeaux, Marquis de Maurepas, in 1730, "to stop sending libertines to the colony. There is already a very great number, and it is more difficult to restrain them in this country than anywhere else because of the facility they have for escaping and the difficulty in convicting them." By 1712 the seigniory of Isle Perrot, granted in 1672, had only one inhabitant; those of Chicouanne and Boisseau, granted that same year, had none; Pointe du Lac, granted early in the seventeenth century, had one settler; Lussaudière, granted in 1672, had none; the seigniory of Jacques Cartier, granted in 1649, had only one inhabitant—he fished for eels—and dozens more were so sparsely inhabited as to be profitless to their owners and to the state. The problem of maintaining an adequate labor force was made even more difficult by the flight into the wilderness of those who were expected to remain fixed to the land. Throughout the eighteenth century, when the population of able-bodied adult males was always pathetically small, an average of three hundred men were absent each year, won over to the freedom of forest life, deserters to the English, or seekers after their fortune in Louisiana. Above all, however, the problem of disciplining labor and raising its productivity was exacerbated by the refusal of the population to behave in the expected manner.

The continued loyalty of the seignior to the system depended on his ability to profit from his privileges, and his privileges were such as to require a large and expanding population. But in Canada, unlike France, land was plentiful and people scarce; and the competition was among seigniors for tenants and not among tenants for land. And even the land system itself conspired against the desire of the authorities to fix people to the land and against the ability of the seigniors to make their living from it. The estates, laid out in parallelograms with the short side fronting on the St. Lawrence River, became split up into ever-narrowing ribbons of farms as, with the passage of time, they were divided among heirs; and agricultural productivity suffered accordingly. Instead of wealth and the grandeur of privileged status, poverty was the lot of most seigniors. "It is necessary to help them," wrote Denonville to Seignelay, "by giving them the means of . . . livelihood for, in truth, without that there is great fear that the children of our nobility . . . will become bandits because of having nothing by which to live."

What was a bad situation to begin with was worsened by the propensity of many seigniors to adopt a style of life better in accord with their expectations than with realities. "The Gentlemen that have a Charge of Children, especially Daughters," wrote Baron La Hontan, "are oblig'd to be good Husbands, in order to bear the Expence of the magnificent Cloaths with which they are set off; for Pride, Vanity, and Luxury, reign as much in *New France* as in *Old France*." "One finds here no rich persons whatever," Father Pierre F. X. de Charlevoix wrote. "In New England and the other British colonies there reigns an opulence by which the people seem not to know how to profit; while in New France poverty is hidden under an air of ease which appears entirely natural. The English colonist keeps as much and spends as little as possible; the French colonist enjoys what he has got, and often makes a display of what he has not got."

To persist in behaving in New France in ways that were appropriate to Old France was to fly in the face of reality. When the Sieur de Frédéric, captain in the Carignan-Salières regiment and nephew of its colonel, punished a habitant for complaining to the intendant about injury done to his crops when Fréréric rode over his land, he doubtless felt that the propriety of his behavior could not be impeached. He was, however, returned to France by Intendant Talon. In France, conscience required that sympathy be extended to peasants whose fields were trampled by seigniors. In Canada, the reverse was true: "divers persons so [abuse] the goodness of the seigneurs of this island [Montreal], who allow them such freedom, that they hunt and fish everywhere on the superior's private domain . . . where they kill the pigeons on pretence of their being other game, and break down all the fences, even threatening the overseer, a most worthy man placed there by the seigneur." So widespread was the abuse that the seigniors had to beg the protection of the authorities.

The protection to the ego offered by keeping up appearances at all costs rather quickly reached its limits. Louis Hamelin, the seignior of Grondines, was himself reduced to working his own mill when his miller was called to military service. Even such notable families as Saint-Ours, Vercheres, Repentigny, and Aubert de la Chesnaye were impoverished and forced to besiege the King with petitions for military commands, judicial posts, licenses to trade in furs, pensions—anything that might provide income. Others gave up entirely and returned to France. When the owners of the seigniory of Monts-Pelées donated it to the Dames Religieuses de la Miséricorde de Jesus, they wrote wistfully and pathetically: "the present donation is made because the donors find themselves at a very advanced age which does not permit them to work to gain their livelihood and because the little property they have is not sufficient to produce enough income to support them in sickness or in health for the rest of their days; they are, moreover, abandoned by all their relatives and friends." In the circumstances, the seigniors began to behave not as their role prescribed, but as conditions seemed to require.

They violated their obligations to their tenants, attempting to exact from them rights to which they were not entitled. They "grant to their habitants leave to cut timber on the ungranted lands, on condition that they pay 10 per cent of the value of the boards obtained therefrom," Intendant Michel Bégon wrote Victor Marie d'Estrées, president of the Conseil de Marine, in 1716. "When they concede woodlands they reserve for themselves all the oak and pine timber thereon without compensation to the habitants, and they are able to exact any price they please for this wood . . . ." They attempted to squeeze more labor through the *corvée* than they were entitled to, made attractive verbal promises to the habitants and then stiffened the terms in writing, induced tenants to clear land for pasture which they later sold, and extorted illegal payments.

Instead of using land for agriculture and settlement, they used it for speculation. Without themselves making any improvements or insisting that their tenants do so, the seigniors, so the local authorities reported to Paris, encouraged the habitants to buy and sell land so that they might collect the mutation fine that went with every change in ownership. "There will always be some people," Intendant Jean Bochart de Champigny informed Minister Louis de Phélypeaux, Comte de Pontchartrain, in 1691, "who will seek land concessions in distant places . . . for the sole purpose of going there to trade . . . without thought of settling."

Instead of doing their duty in the preservation of law and order, the seigniors connived with lawbreakers. Fearful in Canada as in the Antilles that the establishment of too many taverns would distract workmen and increase delinquency, the authorities sought to use the seigniors as direct agents of social control. "The trade of tavern-keeper has attracted all the rogues and lazy people who never think of cultivating the land," Denonville wrote Seignelay in 1685: "far from that, they deter and ruin the other inhabitants. I believe, Monseigneur, that in the villages, the Seigneur should hire and dismiss the tavern-keeper according to his good and bad conduct, and the Seigneur would be responsible for him. I know of seigneuries where there are only 20 houses and more than half are taverns. . . ." But instead of upholding the law against tavern-keepers, they helped them to break it; as, indeed, they helped others also to break the law. "I must not conceal from you," Intendant Jacques Duchesneau wrote Colbert, "that the disobedience of the *coureurs de bois* has reached such a point that everybody boldly contravenes the King's interdictions . . . . I have enacted ordinances against the *coureurs de bois;* . . . against the gentlemen . . . who harbor them; and even against those who have any knowledge of them, and will not inform the local judges. All has been in vain; inasmuch as some of the most considerable families are interested with them . . . ."

The seigniors broke the law themselves, especially when the authorities put them in such a position that to act in accordance with their status as loyal servant of the state seemed to conflict with the pressures on behavior that followed from their position as seignior. On October 21, 1686, a royal edict ordered all seigniors to establish mills on their property, but for twenty years the law remained a dead letter because, contrary to orders, it was not promulgated by the Superior Council in Quebec.

Above all, the seigniors failed in their obligation to support the social system that they, more than anyone else, were counted on to uphold. In making use of the major opportunity that existed to escape the discipline of the system—participation in the fur trade—they provided an example that others were quick to follow. "These disorders," wrote Denonville, "are much greater in the families of those who are gentlemen or who want to be so, either because of indolence or vanity. Having no other means of subsistence but the forest, because they are not accustomed to hold the plow, the pick, or the ax, their only resource being the musket, they must spend their lives in the woods, where there are no priests to restrain them, nor fathers, nor governors to control them. . . . I do not know, Monseigneur, how to describe to you the attraction that all the young men feel for the life of the savage, which is to do nothing, to be utterly free of constraint, to follow all the customs of the savages, and to place oneself beyond the possibility of correction."

At times even the authorities recognized that a vast discrepancy had developed between the real position of the Canadian seignior and the one he had been given, and that the pressure of new necessities was a more powerful influence on behavior than the designs of the administrators. Contrasting the behavior of the Canadians with that of the young men in the Antilles, Beauharnois and Hocquart reported to the King that most Canadians "prefer voyages and trade, which give them the means of livelihood. It is not surprising that the young men of the Islands seek to fill vacancies for the position of councilor, because not only are their customs different from those of the Canadians, but, having been born with money, they are ambitious only for honors. Poverty reigns in Canada; men seek to escape from it and obtain a little comfort."

Conditions that were poison for the seigniors were meat for the *censitaires*, though they, too, disrupted the social organization by refusing to behave in accordance with expectations or even frequently as custom and law dictated. In the design of the administrators, the *censitaires* were intended as a docile and obedient labor force. The very concessions, however, that were offered to entice them into the labor force—concessions that took the form both of direct incentives and limitations on the authority of their seigniorial masters—made it impossible to keep them in their assigned position or to fix their behavior in the desired mold. Their situation in the New World was a very decided improvement over their situation in the Old World, and they acted less in response to old prescriptions than to new imperatives.

In classic feudalism, institutions and rules existed which empowered the seigniors to compel obedience. Marc Bloch has observed:

> Now, in the hands of the seigniors the almost unrestricted exercise of the rights of justice placed an infinitely powerful weapon of economic exploitation. It reinforced their power of command, which in the language of the time . . . was called their "ban." "You can compel us to observe these rules" (those relating to the oven), the inhabitants

of a village in Roussillon tell the Templars, masters of the place, in 1246, "even as a seignoir can and ought to compel his subjects." . . . Among the multiple applications of this discipline, one of the most significant and, in practice, the most important, was the formation of seigniorial monopolies . . . . With very sure instinct, the jurists, when they began in the thirteenth century to create a theory of society, found themselves in agreement in linking the *banalités* with the organization of justice. The right to judge had been the strongest prop of the right to command.

These were the rules and institutions that permitted the seigniors to maintain distance between themselves and the *censitaires* and that compelled the latter to accept the discipline imposed on them. In Canada, these institutions did not exist—or, at least, they existed in a most attenuated form—and it proved impossible to subject the *censitaires* to a discipline that implied a far wider distance between themselves and their superiors than in fact was the case. Not only were the seigniors' traditional monopolies emptied of meaning and their authority curbed by the administration, but the *censitaires* now competed directly with them in areas that had once been their private preserve. It was the *censitaires*, not the seigniors, who were appointed to the position of *capitaine des milices*, a post that involved the exercise of civil as well as military authority; and the complaints of the seigniors, faced with declining prestige, were to no avail. "You should," wrote Minister Jérôme de Pontchartrain to Governor François de Galiffet of Three Rivers, "make the seigniors of the parishes in your jurisdiction understand that the *capitaines des milices* must not communicate to them the orders that they receive from the governors and intendants before executing them; that is not due to them and they have no right to demand it of the *capitaines*, who might do so as a matter of courtesy, however, when it is of no interest to the service."

The *censitaires* hunted and fished almost at will, they were occasionally called in to offer advice on government policy, and they were urged to report all "torts, exces, violances" committed by the seigniors. Small wonder, then, they responded to their new situation by surrounding themselves with some of the trappings of the status that had so long been denied them. Though the government appealed to their own self-interest in urging them to concentrate on the production of cattle, pigs, and sheep, and though it imposed ban after ban on the raising of horses, they continued to breed horses and to ride through the countryside, as if in unconscious remembrance of the age-old connection between *cheval* and *chevallerie*.

Even in the area of landownership, they reduced the distance between themselves and the seigniors. In 1712 Gédéon de Catalogne, a military engineer, made a survey of the more than ninety seigniories that then existed in Canada. Excluding those granted to religious orders, it is possible—by comparing the secular owners in 1712 with the original owners —to arrive at some estimate of the degree to which the barriers of privilege and aristocracy were melting away. Of the seventy-six secular grants for which it is possible to find the names both of the persons to whom they were originally granted and who held them in 1712, only forty-five, or 59 per cent, were in the hands of the same families. Of the seigniories issued from 1670 to 1710, 62 per cent remained in the original families. Clearly, time was on the side of mobility. And equally significant, Catalogne's report shows that of the seventy-six secular seigniories in 1712, at least twenty-two were owned by families of bourgeois or lower origin.

Though the intention of the administration and the wish of the seigniors was that the *censitaire* should behave with the oxlike placidity of the peasant, he refused to do so because he was not, in truth, a peasant. As Baron La Hontan wrote: "The peasants there are at their ease. What, did I say peasant? Honorable apologies to these gentlemen! That term, taken in its usual meaning, would put our Canadians into the fields. A Spaniard, if he should be called a rustic, would not wince, nor twirl his mustache more proudly. These people are not wrong after all; they do not pay the salt tax nor the poll tax; they hunt and fish freely; in a word they are rich. Then how can you compare them with our wretched peasants? How many nobles and gentlemen would throw their old parchments into the fire at that price."

That the Canadian *censitaire* had ceased to be a French peasant received stunning confirmation in the eighteenth century, but by then time had run out on the French government. Taking pity on those displaced Acadians who had managed to return to France, the government devised a variety of plans to attach them "à la glebe de France," all of which involved tenurial terms far superior to those of the generality of peasants and at least one of which was drawn up on the basis of the most advanced physiocratic theory. Each attempt to place the Acadians on the land proved a fiasco, for the way in which they had assimilated their own history made them unfit to assume the status of peasant. "I think, really, that the Acadians are mad," wrote the Commissaire Général in 1772. "Do they imagine that we wish to make seigniors of them? The intention of the government is to put them on the level of the cultivators in the provinces where they might be established, giving them the means to subsist by their labor. They seem offended by the fact that we wish to treat them like our peasants."

Not all *censitaires*, of course, did well in Canada. But, whether the peasant profited under the system or suffered under it, how was it possible to retain him in the same subordinate position he had held in France? Indeed, he rejected the very title of *censitaire* because of its connotation of servility and succeeded in having himself referred to even in official documents simply as "habitant." Corresponding to this change in title was a change in his behavior.

Instead of obedience to the seignior, there were "mutinerie et l'indépendence." The state, too, on occasion felt the wrath of its citizens, and even the church, though protected by the loyalty of the people to Catholicism, became the target of popular hostility. When Bishop Laval introduced the French tithe into Canada in 1663, the resistance was so widespread that he was quickly forced to offer concession after concession—reduction from one-thirteenth to one-twentieth and finally to one-twenty-sixth; exemption of fish, eggs, timber, and livestock; and a five-year exemption on newly cultivated land. For more than fifty years the conflict raged between church and inhabitants, and not even the refusal to grant absolution to those who withheld the tithe or who paid in spoiled wheat could quell the "great murmuring at the door of the church." "Many individuals," wrote Duchesneau in 1677, "through plain disobedience . . . and scorn of the church not only refuse to pay the tithes, but are even carried away to the point of violence." As late as 1727 the inhabitants of the parish of St. Antoine-de-Tilly had to be *ordered* by the intendant to pay their tithes to the curé.

Worst of all, their disobedience took the form of wholesale desertion of agricultural tasks. Despite the severe sanctions imposed by church and state, increasing numbers of people, "excited by the bad example of the *coureurs de bois* and by the profits that they had made," left the field for the forest in search of furs. In the year 1680 approximately one-third of the adult male population had escaped the discipline of society by entering the fur trade. At no time does the proportion of the adult male labor force engaged in trapping and hunting seem to have been less than one-quarter or one-fifth. Not only did they deplete an already inadequate labor force, but they infected those who remained with the example of their rebelliousness. "We weare Cesars, being nobody to contradict us," said Pierre Radisson, greatest of all the *coureurs de bois*. If his was a self-image too elevated for the many to aspire to, they felt themselves at least to be captains of their own fate. "The genius of the people of New England," Minister Maurepas wrote to Beauharnois in 1728, "is to work hard at cultivating the land and to establish new settlements one after the other. . . . The inhabitants of New France think differently. They would like always to move forward without getting tangled up in interior settlements, because they gain more and are more independent when they are more remote." "One part of our youth is continually rambling and roving about," wrote Father Charlevoix, "and . . . it infects them with a habit of libertinism, of which they never entirely get rid; at least, it gives them a distaste for labour, it exhausts their strength, they become incapable of the least constraint, and when they are no longer able to undergo the fatigues of travelling . . . they remain without the least resource, and are no longer good for anything. Hence it comes to pass, that arts have been a long time neglected, and great quantity of good land remains still uncultivated, and the country is but very indifferently peopled."

Litigious, independent, insubordinate, the habitants joined the seigniors in making a mockery of the behavior defined for them. No longer were they willing to act as instruments of those who planned the system; they acted now out of concern for their own survival or improvement. At times, as we have seen, they deliberately violated the norms of their society; at times, they violated them unwittingly because, under conditions of rapid change, it became problematic as to how the norms were to be applied. But the society was turned upside down when its sworn defenders themselves subverted it. "Profit, my dear Vergor, by your place," wrote Intendant François Bigot to Louis Du Pont du Chambon, Sieur de Vergor, commandant of Fort Beauséjour; "trim, lop off; all power is in your hands; do it quickly so that you may be able to come and join me in France and buy an estate near mine." Instead of enforcing the laws against illegal fur traders, the intendants permitted them to carry on and they cut themselves in on the profits. They traded in flat violation of the orders they received from Paris. "Trading is prohibited to persons in office," wrote the President of the Navy Board. "They are placed there only to protect it, not to carry on even the most legitimate, and for the strongest reasons should abstain from dealing in concessions and monopolies that they ought to prevent with all their power . . . . What is certain is, that . . . it can only be regarded as criminal on the part of all those who have taken part in it or those who have favored it or even fostered it, and above all for persons employed in the service . . . ."

The circle was complete when what had once been regarded as deviance came later to be recognized as the norm. "I believe," wrote Denonville to Seignelay, "that Monseigneur should not determine to cease to give letters of nobility but that it would be well to give them only to those who will . . . enter into whatever commerce makes a noble in this country." In 1685 the Canadian noblesse—which had been created as the apex of the seigniorial system—was allowed without derogation of rank "to engage in commerce by land as well as by sea, to buy and sell goods wholesale as well as retail." Never did the French nobility obtain such blanket permission to trade, and such permission as they did obtain came later than in Canada.

The medicine, however, only worsened the disease. Trade "serves but to . . . reduce the number of people in the houses; to deprive wives of their husbands, fathers and mothers of the aid of their children . . . ; to Expose those who undertake such journeys to a thousand dangers for both their Bodies and their souls. It also causes them to incur very many expenses, partly necessary, partly Useless, and partly Criminal; it accustoms them not to work . . . . It Takes them away from all the holy places . . . . So long as all the young men devote themselves to no other occupation . . . There can be no hope that the Colony will Ever become flourishing . . . for it will always lose thereby What would most enrich it,—I mean the labor of all the young men." Church might mourn and anathematize and King complain and legislate, but the trend could not be reversed. Instead of docility, disobedience was the rule; instead of agriculture, trade; instead of remaining on the land, the people flocked to the cities; instead of simplicity and austerity, the extremes of grinding poverty and the glitter and tinsel "d'un fort bon ton." Canada had become "a tableau of abuses, and not a body of rules."

So disrupted had the society become, then, and so profitless to its sponsors, that only the merchants of the seaport towns of France objected when Canada was lost to the British. On February 10, 1763, the very day the Treaty of Paris was signed, Voltaire wrote Étienne François, Duc de Choiseul: "Permit me to compliment you. I am like the public; I like peace better than Canada and I think that France can be happy without Quebec."

IV

The French government was faced with the twofold problem of maintaining order and stability in Canada and of motivating its subjects to perform the tasks given them. It sought to assign each man a status, the behavior of which was defined and regulated; when men behave according to prescription, each can act toward the other with the certainty that his own behavior will be understood and with the expectation that the other's responses will be the appropriate ones. At the same time, however, the government was faced with the necessity of recruiting a labor force, and the means it used involved offering such a variety of concessions and incentives that the position of the labor force in the society that was actually created was utterly different from its position in the society that had been contemplated. The government of France, like the General Court of the Virginia Company of London, was fully conscious of its problems, but—again like the Virginia Company—the solution it adopted for the problem of motivation made it impossible to solve the problem of order. Rigor and severe discipline, the distinguishing characteristics of the first social order in Canada as in Virginia, broke down in the face of the need to recruit a *voluntary* labor force. By her own actions, France created in Canada a social basis for disobedience, a society in which deviance became the only means of survival and of taking advantage of such opportunities as existed.

In a sense, a drama was taking place on the North American continent that had been played out before in Europe. At various times in late medieval and early modern Europe, especially in periods of considerable stress, the seigniors had to offer concessions to their tenants, even to the point of enfranchisement, to prevent, by their emigration to "free" lands, the loss of their labor force. In 1439 the Hospitaliers de la Commanderie de Bure enfranchised their serfs of Thoisy: "all the 'houses and barns which are at the said Thoisy have been burned and destroyed . . . and no one wants to live . . . in the town. . . . in this way everyone withdraws and goes to live in free places.' " In 1628, when the Sire de Montureux-les-Gray, in Comté, freed his serfs, he did not conceal his hope that the "enfranchised village will be 'better inhabited and populated,' and, 'consequently,' that the seigniorial rights 'would produce greater revenue.' "

"Misery was sometimes the creator of liberty," says Marc Bloch. So it undoubtedly was in Europe; in North America, the need to recruit a voluntary labor force was the mother of liberty.

II

FOUNDATIONS OF SETTLEMENT: THE SEVENTEENTH CENTURY

5. THE SIGNIFICANCE OF THE SEVENTEENTH CENTURY*

by Oscar Handlin

According to Oscar Handlin, the seventeenth century was a formative period in the development of uniquely American ideas and institutions that have shaped the nation ever since. Those who migrated to the New World brought with them expectations rooted in the social patterns of Europe. Their assumptions about organized power in the state, spiritual life in the church, and material resources in the productive system proved impractical as they learned that they could not transfer Old World institutions to a wilderness. Whereas in Europe the modernization of medieval societies involved centralization of authority, in the new American settlements power became fragmented and decentralized despite vigorous efforts to construct the social order on European models. The conflict between European assumptions and American realities generated tensions within the colonists; the origins and dimensions of these tensions are explored in the following essay. The validity of Handlin's hypothesis can be tested by determining how well it accounts for the social changes analyzed in succeeding essays.

* James M. Smith (ed.), *Seventeenth-Century America* (Chapel Hill: University of North Carolina Press, 1959), pp. 3–12. Footnotes have been omitted except where they are necessary for an understanding of the text.

The historian is trained to see the past in its own terms. He studies the seventeenth century as the product of that which had gone before it, and he attempts to reconstruct the culture and society of the American colonies as those might have seemed to the men who lived in them.

This is the necessary perspective for an understanding of the period. An impressive body of recent studies has shown that the settlements along the coast of North America were elements of imperial systems that had their counterparts in many other regions of the world. We have learned that the institutional life of the colonies can only be understood against a background that reaches back to the medieval past. The labor system, the forms of government, even the modes of thought of the seventeenth century extended patterns that had long before been developing in Europe. To see in them the forerunners or prototypes of what would emerge in the eighteenth or nineteenth century is grievously to misinterpret them.

But our purpose in celebrating the 350th anniversary of the settlement of the Jamestown colony must be somewhat different. The seventeenth century should have general meaning, for we—and the historians along with the rest of us—live, after all, in the twentieth century; and we expect somehow that the experiences of the men who began to come off the ships at Jamestown have also a meaning for us in the twentieth century. A commemorative occasion is a time for retrospection—for looking backward from the present to take account of the way we have come. It has its picturesque and interesting aspects, of course. But its true value arises from the opportunity it offers us to acquire perspective on the present and the future. From that point of view, it is our obligation to look back to the seventeenth century for what it can reveal of the antecedents of our own culture.

In that respect the seventeenth century was immensely significant. In the decades after the settlement at Jamestown, three generations of Americans—the first Americans—began to shape the social order, the way of life, and an interpretation of their own experience that would influence much of subsequent American history. Pick up the story where you will—in the eighteenth or nineteenth century or in our own times—and invariably in these matters the threads lead back to the seventeenth century. It will be worth while to discuss each of these developments briefly.

The colonists who settled at Jamestown and elsewhere along the coast after 1607 brought with them fixed conceptions of what a social order should be like. Their whole effort thereafter was devoted to re-creating the forms they had known at home. Yet in practice their experience persistently led them away from the patterns they judged desirable. The American social order that finally emerged was abnormal. That is, it not only diverged from the experience of the European society from which the newcomers emigrated, but it was also contrary to their own expectations of what a social order should be.

The settlers were loyal to the governments from which they emi-grated, and they were conservative in their attitudes toward existing institutions. Repeatedly they explained that their emigration was not intended to disrupt but rather to preserve and improve the society they left. Nevertheless they were constantly moving off on tangents through the force of circumstance and the pressure of the environment. A number of examples will clarify this point.

The forms of colonial government developed slowly and erratically. The first settlers transplanted two forms commonplace in the practice of Europeans in this period. The chartered commercial companies, as in Virginia and Plymouth, carried across to their plantations institutions that went back to the medieval boroughs. The proprietary colonies rested on old feudal precedents. Both efforts at imitation quickly proved unstable, however, and the colonies of either sort passed through a period of rapid change.

The problem of changing political forms was, of course, also troubling Europe in the seventeenth century. But in the Old World this era witnessed the emergence of the centralized bureaucratic state. Theory and practice moved in the same direction, toward the derivation of all authority from a single source, such as the Crown, however defined.

The colonies accepted the theory. Their most prominent men were surprisingly legalistic and had no inclination to dispute the authority under which their government functioned. But practice took another direction. Power tended to devolve to its local sources. Whether that involved the town, as in New England, or the local powers sitting in the vestry, as in Virginia, the characteristic political organization was decentralized. Whatever acknowledgment might be given to the authority of the Crown, political institutions were decisively shaped by the neces-sity of defining connections to local power. Significantly, the most stable colonies of this period were Connecticut and Rhode Island, where the organization of local government in the towns preceded and re-mained basic to the organization of central political institutions.

The dispersal of power to local sources was, however, characteristic of other, nonpolitical institutions also. The churches developed a *de facto* congregational form, despite the fact that their communicants theoretically held to a belief in centralized authority. Apart from the Plymouth Separatists, there was no disposition to challenge the traditional hierarchical and centralized structure of the church. Yet, the New England Puritans, once here, found themselves closer to the Separatists than to the Church of England of which they had expected to remain adherents. Most strikingly, the members of the Church of England throughout the colonies continued to acknowledge that a bishop was essential to the full practice of their religious duties. Yet in practice, delays, obstructions, and evasions prevented the emergence of an episcopate before the Revolution. Religious functions too seemed to devolve to their local sources.

These developments were related to the structure of the population, which was also anomalous in the sense that it ran contrary to the expectations of those who planted the colonies. The founders expected that their societies would consist of functionaries and peasants. The companies anticipated plantations populated by servants, that is, by soldiers and clerks, who would carry forth the business of trade and defense. The proprietors looked forward to a population of native or imported peasants who would reconstruct some sort of manorial system in the New World. This was evident, even toward the end of the seventeenth century, in the plans of the Carolina proprietors.

Instead, surprisingly, all the colonies developed a society of yeomen and artisans—not by plan, and often, it seemed, simply through the want of an alternative. Yet the consequences were radical. There developed in the mainland colonies of the seventeenth century a wide variety of social types, a microcosm of the Old World as it were, ranging from slaves and servants at the bottom through yeoman farmers and artisans, to a gentry at the top. Within this variety of types there were both the recognition of actual stratification and a high degree of mobility. The fact that a servant was different from a yeoman and yet that a servant could become a yeoman led to the definition of a new concept of freedom and to the development of distinctive social institutions.

In the structure of the population, therefore, as in the evolution of governmental and other institutions, the seventeenth-century colonies followed an abnormal path, one which was different from the experience of Europeans at home or in other parts of the world and one which was contrary to their own expectations. The causes of this abnormality were complex. In part it was due to the extensive quality of the land to which these settlers came. They had pitched upon the edge of an almost empty continent; and the existence of open space to which men could withdraw remained a constant condition of their life. That in itself was an element tending toward looseness of social structure.

Furthermore, they encountered no going society with fixed institutions of its own. The Indians who inhabited the region had a culture, of course. But they were so few in number and so little prepared to resist as to have relatively little effect upon the whites. The Europeans of the same period in India or even in Africa were significantly influenced by the institutions they encountered there; those in America, hardly at all. Indeed the American colonists were often disappointed in their natives. The continued inclination to refer to the Indian kings, queens, and nobility reflected an eagerness to discover in the red men a fixity of forms that did not exist. Its absence was a further source of instability.

But most important, the institutional looseness of the seventeenth century was related to the way of life that developed in the colonies. The American seventeenth-century social order was disorderly by the expectations of normal men. But the settlers were not normal men. The terms of American existence compelled frequent and serious deviations from the norms of behavior accepted by the men who peopled the colonies. Every aspect of their existence combined to produce disorder.

The century was occupied by a succession of waves of immigration, so that the experience of transplantation was not limited to one group or to one moment, but was repeated again and again. And that experience caused enormous shocks in the personal and social relationships of those involved in it. The circumstances of the crossing at once threw these men and women into disorder. It takes an effort of the imagination to conceive of the conditions of life on the three ships which came to Jamestown in 1607. These vessels of 100, 40, and 20 tons, respectively, were laden with the gear and the supplies and provisions for the voyage and also with all that the plantations would at first require. Yet, there was also room on these tiny craft for 140 people. The settlers were almost five months in transit, at the mercy of the winds and weather and of the unknown sea. Later voyages involved larger ships—but not much larger; and the time spent in crossing shrank, although not dependably. But accommodations were never commodious and the experience was never pleasant. Few immigrants recovered quickly from the difficulties of crowded and uncomfortable weeks at sea in tiny ships that carried them to their strange destinations.

Many of those who made the crossing were people whose life was already in disorder. Often, they had already been displaced and compelled to move once; their stamina had already been tried. The residents of London who came to the colonies had, as likely as not, been born in the country and had drifted to the city. Others among the newcomers, like the Pilgrims, like the Finns who settled on the Delaware, like the German sectarians, were already uprooted and had already deviated from the settled life of stable societies.

Hard conditions of life compounded the disorder for a greater or lesser time in each of the colonies. Everywhere the settlers who survived could look back upon a starving time, a period when the margin between life and death narrowed perilously and when the very existence of the feeble societies hung by a thread. So, in retrospect, the Virginia burgesses looked back to the administration of Sir Thomas Smith and recalled:

> The allowance in those tymes for a man was only eight ounces of meale and half a pinte of pease for a daye the one & the other mouldy, rotten, full of Cobwebs and Maggots loathsome to man and not fytt for beasts; which forced many to flee for reliefe to the Savage Enemy, who being taken againe were putt to sundry deaths as by hanginge, shootinge and breakinge upon the wheele; & others were forced by famine to filch for their bellies, of whom one for steelinge 2 or 3 pints of oatmeale had a bodkinge thrust through his tongue and was tyed with a chaine to a tree untill he starved. Yf a man through his sickness had not been able tow worke, he had no allowance at all, and so consequently perished. Many through these extremities, being weery of life digged holes in the earth and hidd themselues till they famished. . . . So lamentable was our scarsitie that we were constrained to eat Doggs, Catts, ratts, Snakes, Toad-Stooles, horsehides and wt nott; one man out of the mysery he endured, killinge his wiefe powdered her upp to eate here, for wch he was burned. Many besides fedd on the Corps of dead men, and one who had gotten unsatiable, out of custome to that foode could not be restrayned, until such tyme as he was executed for it, and indeed soe miserable was our estate that the happyest day that eyer some of them hoped to see, was when the Indyands had killed a mare they wishing whilst she was boyling that St *Tho*: *Smith* [the Governor] was uppon her backe in the kettle.

Later prosperity never dimmed the memory of the early difficulties; and there remained always areas where the trying experience of survival was being repeated. As settlement spread, there was always at its edge a brutal and disorderly struggle for existence.

Some of the harsh features of pioneer life disappeared with the development of settled communities. But others endured for a long time. A high death rate remained constant and throughout the century embittered the personal relationships of the colonists. In the first winter at Plymouth, one-half the Pilgrims died. Between 1606 and 1623 about five thousand immigrants came to Virginia. They had children and raised families. Yet at the end of that period there were only one thousand left.

Nor was this cruel mortality simply a condition of initial settlement. It remained characteristic of seventeenth-century life. Infant mortality was murderous; and although many children were born, the number of survivors was distressingly low. It was rare in this century that a husband and wife should live into old age together. The frequency of remarriages by widowers and widows showed how familiar a factor in life was death.

More generally, constant nagging difficulties intruded in the management of the details of home or farm or shop. Old habits did not apply to new circumstances; and it was hard for individuals to fulfill the personal, family, religious, or communal roles they were expected to play. This, perhaps, explains the harsh judgments that the colonists were always making of one another. The lack of stability or orderliness even in the home was particularly troublesome. In the tight quarters of the seventeenth-century houses, large families had to learn to live with one another, and also with the Negroes and other strange servants. Emotional strains were inevitable and weak community discipline sometimes led to violence, desertion, or criminality. The lack of permanence, the constant mobility that shifted individuals and families about through the continent exacerbated all these tensions. By contrast, the old homes of the Old World in retrospect came to embody orderliness. Often, in thinking of what they had left in Europe, the colonists expressed a poignant sense of separation from the source of stability and culture.

Finally, their life was rendered harsh by the apparent hostility of the elements. The wilderness itself created problems for men accustomed to open spaces. In the folk literature of Europe the forests were peopled by wild, inhuman creatures often hostile to man. In America even the climate and the changes of the seasons were unfamiliar. Most important, the denizens of the wilderness were a constant threat to the flimsy structure of civilization. The Indians grew more and more fearsome as the century advanced; and on the borders French and Spanish Papists were a continuing threat. In the face of all these dangers, there was no security in the settlements. The precariousness of existence was at the root of the disorder that overwhelmed them. Everywhere from the moment they boarded ship the first Americans found risks of the greatest order inseparable from the conduct of their lives.

The native-born, that is, the second and third, generations were more at home in the wilderness and, never having known Europe, were less pressed by the necessity of making comparisons with that which had been left across the ocean. They had sources of instability of their own, in their heightened rootlessness and mobility. But they were likely to accept the disorder and precariousness that troubled their immigrant parents or grandparents as a way of life and to adjust to its conditions.

The men subject to so many elements of abnormality and disorder necessarily interpreted their own experiences in a distinctive way. They were constantly driven to ask questions that other men had no need to raise. People whose families had lived generations without end in the same village had no cause to wonder why they were where they were or to speculate on the significance of having been placed where they were. But the immigrants whose conditions of life and whose institutions had been driven so far from every ordinary course necessarily had to seek answers to such questions.

The necessity was particularly urgent in the seventeenth century when men ascribed to every event a deep meaning. Nothing that occurred was taken as simply random. Everything was the product of the intent of some mover. A tree did not fall; it was felled. If a monstrous child was born or a school of porpoises seen, that was a sign of something. In the same way, there was necessarily a significance to the painful shift of population that created colonial society. In an era in which men believed literally in signs, portents, curses, spells, and imprecations, to say nothing of witches, they had to seek a meaning to their own unusual experiences.

The first Americans continued the habit of explaining every occurrence in terms of a familiar dichotomy. On the one hand, they could see in some events good impulses, derived from God and reflecting a divine intent. But they also found abundant evidence of evil impulses or dark desires emanating from satanic intentions. The fearful men who lived with risk and disorder were constantly on the lookout for the means of identifying and interpreting what happened to them. As a simple matter of a guide to personal life, it was essential to know whether an incident was the product of divine or devilish interference.

The same confrontation of good and evil could be seen in the social world that surrounded the individual. There in the external wilderness, in the savagery of life without reliable guides, were the sources of corruption. Were not the Indians imps of Satan, and the Papists, creatures of the Devil, and was not therefore the whole American experience one which endangered man's salvation? On the other hand, was it not possible to identify that which lay across the ocean with that which was good and conducive to man's salvation? Europe, from the American perspective, was the source of morality, of law, of order, and of Christianity. But in that event, how was the colonist to explain his migration, away from order to disorder, away from law to savagery, away from Christianity to the spiritual perils of the New World?

The questions thus raised could be answered on both the personal and the social level; and the answer on the one offers an analogy to the answer on the other. The character of this response may be discerned in the poem that a grieving grandmother wrote in the 1660's to explain to herself the death of three grandchildren within four years. All were under the age of four. Surely these tender innocents had been stricken down through no fault, no evil deed, of their own. There was, however, a reason. Anne Bradstreet explained:

> By nature Trees do rot when they are grown.
> And Plumbs and Apples thoroughly ripe do fall,
> And corn and grass are in their season mown,
> And time brings down what is both strong and tall.
> But plants new set to be eradicate,
> And buds new blown, to have so short a date,
> Is by his hand alone that guides nature and fate.

An unnatural misfortune of this sort was thus in itself evidence of a particular divine concern. While the nature of God's intentions might be inscrutable to men and closed to fallible human understanding, the event itself nevertheless was a sure indication of some particular purpose. It could even supply a kind of assurance of divine interest and oversight.

It was also true that a way of life out of the usual course was evidence of some particular design. The whole character of the plantation of these settlements, by its very abnormality, indicated that there had been some special purpose to the coming to America. The fact that this whole area had been withheld from previous human habitation indicated that there was some special intention for its use. The fact that their institutions and their course of life did not follow any usual pattern was itself a sign that these settlements had an unusual destiny.

As the immigrants examined their own coming, they could see evidence of a larger will in their own careers. Their migration was largely the product of their own helplessness, of social forces over which they had no control—persecution by the Established Church, changes in agriculture and the unavailability of land, the disruption of the wool trade and the growth in the number of men without employment. But on the other hand, the migration was also the product of their own choice. Not all those who were persecuted or displaced or unemployed had come. Migration stemmed from a compulsion that forced the emigrant to leave and also the positive act of will by which he decided to go. The emigrant might thus be compared to a legate dispatched on a mission by a potentate, a legate who accepted the errand voluntarily. The fact, too, that not all those who went arrived reflected a process of survival and seemed to imply a kind of selection of some from among the rest.

In no other way could these people account for the experience but by the conclusion that somehow they had been chosen to depart from the ways of ordinary men and to become in their own lives extraordinary for some special purpose.

Among some of the colonists this intention was spelled out with considerable sophistication. New England Puritans thought of themselves as led by Divine Providence to a new Canaan where they were to create a new kind of society that would be a model for the whole world. Their city upon a hill would ultimately be emulated by all other men. It was a part of the scheme of divine redemption, occupying the stage at a critical turn in the cosmic drama that had begun with the Creation, that had been continued in the Reformation, and that would end in the Second Coming.

Elsewhere the explanation was less sophisticated, less explicit, and less literate. But there nonetheless emerged again and again expressions of conviction in a sense of mission—to convert the Indians or to civilize the wilderness. The newness of a New World reserved for some ultimate purpose and waiting for those who would bring it under cultivation or use it as the setting for their own experiments in salvation confirmed the successive groups of immigrants, in the seventeenth century and later, in the belief that there was a profound importance to their coming.

The second and third generations were different in this respect also. They were natives, not subject to the strains of the decisions that had burdened their parents or grandparents. Indeed, in the eyes of the immigrants, the second generation seemed a ruder, less cultivated, and wilder people. That accounts for the complaints about declension and about the loss of the sense of mission that began to be sounded in the last quarter of the century.

But the second generation had actually not lost the sense of mission so much as transformed it beyond the recognition of their predecessors. The very fact that they were a wilderness people, at home in the New World, gave them a sense of power. They could deal with the forest and the savage as their parents could not. Out of contact with the standards of the Old World, they developed their own, and their ability to do so generated confidence in their own capacity for achievement.

Therefore they too, although in a different form, were moved by a conviction of the grandeur of their destiny; and they could link that conviction to the potentialities of the land, which was not alien to them as it had been to their parents. Pride in their own power and in the future greatness of their homes created for them a picture of themselves as a people destined to conquer, an idea to be eloquently expressed just after the turn of the century by Robert Beverley.

In a variety of forms, the sense of mission has remained a continuing theme in American life. In the eighteenth century Jefferson's generation gave it secularized liberal expression. The nineteenth century imbued it with the spirit of liberal reform. And at the opening of the twentieth century, it was woven into the ideology of imperialism. So, too, social disorder, the acceptance of risk, and the precariousness of life that developed in the seventeenth century long remained characteristic of America. It was the significance of the seventeenth century to bring into being peculiarities of character and institutions, the influence of which was long thereafter felt in the history of the United States.

6. FROM ORGANIZATION TO SOCIETY

Virginia in the Seventeenth Century*

by Sigmund Diamond

The first permanent British settlements in North America were made under private rather than public auspices. The colonization of Virginia was the work of a trading company whose objective was to make money rather than to found a new society. The Virginia Company modeled its enterprise on the experiences of earlier English trading companies that had done business in distant places such as Russia, the Mediterranean, and India, and on the example of Spanish traders who had quickly found wealth in America. But the Virginia Company discovered that its assumptions and expectations did not fit the circumstances it encountered. The company could survive only by modifying its objectives and methods and by becoming a colonizing enterprise. As it did so, it found that the tasks of

* *American Journal of Sociology*, vol. 63 (1958), 457–475, by permission of The University of Chicago Press. Copyright 1958 by The University of Chicago Press. Footnotes have been omitted except where they are necessary for an understanding of the text.

recruiting a labor force of appropriate size and quality, obtaining sufficient capital to finance the necessary investments a new society required, and administering these resources efficiently and productively exceeded its ability and transformed its original design. Adjustments to American conditions came too late to save the company from dissolution but, nevertheless, it had laid the foundations for the development of one of the largest and most influential settlements in colonial America.

For further reading: Wesley F. Craven, *Dissolution of the Virginia Company* (1932) ; *Southern Colonies in the Seventeenth Century* (1949). .

Fad and fashion play their roles in the world of scholarship as elsewhere, and often products of the intellect may assume the quaint air of artifacts for no better reason than that, with the passage of time, they are made obsolete by the appearance of new, if not necessarily better, models. But in scholarship, if not in manufacturing, novelty is a virtue that has limits; and even old ideas and interests may be resurrected if they demonstrate the existence of problems or give promise of solving problems for which more recent ideas have proved inadequate. So it is that historical sociology, though conceded to be one of the roots from which the discipline itself emerged, has, in this country at least, suffered from the competition of more stylish fashions. And so it is, too, that there is increasing evidence today that historical sociology, so long an outmoded form of inquiry, is once again commending itself as an important subject of research. What follows is, frankly, an attempt to aid in the rehabilitation of historical sociology, not by exhortation, but, it is hoped, by a persuasive demonstration that questions of considerable importance for sociological theory may be raised when problems are examined in historical perspective. Our interest in this essay is in the utilization of certain aspects of the history of Virginia in the early seventeenth century to suggest significant questions concerning the creation of new statuses and the circumstances under which the character of an organization may be so altered as to be transmuted into something which is not, properly speaking, an organization at all but a society.

109

I

It must be conceded at the outset that the group we have selected for study was pathetically small. In 1607, when the Virginia Company established a settlement at Jamestown, its population numbered 105; and in 1624, when the crown revoked the charter of the Company, the population of Virginia amounted to just over 1,200, despite the fact that the Company had sent more than 5,000 emigrants during that seventeen-year period. But, just as a limited duration of time is no necessary detriment to a study of this kind, because there are periods of history when the rate of change is accelerated, so, too, the limited size of the group affords no accurate measure of the importance of the enterprise. Judged in terms of its outcome, its importance is self-evident. But, judged even in terms of the criteria of importance imposed by contemporaries, the verdict must be the same. The articles on the Virginia settlement in the *Kölnische Zeitung* and the *Mercure françoise;* the running series of reports from the Venetian ambassadors in London to the Doge and Senate; the letters from Jesuit priests in England to the Propaganda Fide in Rome and the newsletters from Venice and Antwerp in the Vatican archives; the continuing stream of dispatches from the Spanish ambassadors to King Philip III, pressing him to attack Jamestown, advising him of the latest decisions of the Virginia Company, and relating their efforts to recruit English spies; and the existence in the royal archives at Simancas of a description of the layout of Jamestown and the earliest known map of the town, the work of an Irish spy in the service of Spain—all this is eloquent testimony of the position of Virginia in the international relations of the seventeenth century and of the concern felt in the capitals of Europe in the Virginia Company's undertaking. Nor was the expression of this concern merely verbal. In August, 1613, when the population of Virginia barely exceeded 200, the settlement at Jamestown had a decidedly cosmopolitan cast, for it contained eighteen prisoners—fifteen Frenchmen, including two Jesuits and several members of the nobility; a Spanish spy, Don Diego de Molina; a renegade Englishman in the pay of Spain; and an Indian princess, Pocahontas.

At the May Day, 1699, exercises at the College of William and Mary, one of the student orators—who must have been a sophomore—exclaimed:

Methinks we see already that happy time when we shall surpass the Asiaticians in civility, the Jews in religion, the Greeks in philosophy, the Egyptians in geometry, the Phoenicians in arithmetic, and the Chaldeans in astrology. O happy Virginia.

We may be intrigued by the ingenuousness of the student, but we are interested in the statement as evidence of the fact that in 1699— and for some time earlier—Virginia was a society and Virginians were nothing if not ebullient about its prospects. For it had not always been so.

At its inception—and for a number of years thereafter—it had been a formal organization, and, if the joyous outburst of the student reflects its character at a later date, its earlier character is better revealed by the instructions given by the Virginia Company to Sir Thomas Gates on the eve of his departure for Jamestown in May, 1609:

You must devide yor people into tennes twenties & so upwards, to every necessary worke a competent nomber, over every one of wch you must appointe some man of Care & still in that worke to oversee them and to take dayly accounte of their laboures, and you must ordayne y^t every overseer of such a nomber of workemen Deliver once a weeke an accounte of the wholle comitted to his Charge . . . you shall doe best to lett them eate together at reasonable howers in some publique place beinge messed by six or five to a messe, in wch you must see there bee equality and sufficient so that they may come and retourne to their worke without any delay and have no cause to complain of measure or to excuse their idleness upon ye dressinge or want of diet. You may well allowe them three howers in a somers day and two in the winter, and shall call them together by Ringinge of a Bell and by the same warne them againe to worke.

And, if in later years "O happy Virginia" could be a spontaneous outcry of its citizens, it could not have been earlier. Testifying in 1625 about conditions under the administration of Sir Thomas Dale in 1614–16, Mrs. Perry, one of the fortunates who survived more than a few years in the first quarter-century of Virginia's history, revealed that

in the time of Sr: Thomas Dales Government An leyden and June Wright and other women were appoynted to make shirts for the Colony servants and had six nelds full of silke threed allowed for

111

making of a shirte, wch yf they did not p'forme, They had noe allowance of Dyott, and because theire threed naught and would not sewe, they tooke owt a ravell of ye lower p^{te} of ye shirte to make an end of ye worke, and others y^t had threed of thiere owne made it up wth that, Soe the shirts of those wch had raveled owt proved shorter then the next, for wch fact the said An leyden and June Wright were whipt, And An leyden beinge then wth childe (the same night thereof miscarried).

Our first inquiry, then, must be into the characteristics of the original settlement at Jamestown—characteristics which changed so markedly during the course of the next quarter-century.

Virginia was not established as a colony to take its place among the territories governed by the British crown; it was not a state, and, properly speaking, it was not a political unit at all. It was property, the property of the Virginia Company of London, and it was established to return a profit to the stockholders of that company. Under the political and economic conditions of seventeenth-century England, speculators in overseas expansion could count on no support from the government except verbal encouragement and some legal protection—and sometimes precious little of these. Under the circumstances, therefore, colonization had to be undertaken as a private business venture, and the first charge imposed on the property was the return on the shareholder's investment. Traditionally, this episode has been dealt with primarily in terms of the motivation of participants—did they come to establish religious freedom, to seek a haven for the politically persecuted, or to found a "First Republic"?—and it is true that those who joined the Virginia enterprise did so for many reasons. Some, like Richard Norwood, were foot-loose and fancy-free after having completed their apprenticeships. Robert Evelin wrote his mother that he was "going to the sea, a long and dangerous voyage with other men, to make me to be able to pay my debts, and to restore my decayed estate again . . . and I beseech you, if I do die, that you would be good unto my poor wife and children, which God knows, I shall leave very poor and very mean, if my friends be not good unto them." In its promotional literature the Virginia Company took advantage of this broad spectrum of motives and cast its net wide to snare the purses and bodies of all sorts and conditions of persons in support of a venture in which

> . . . profite doth with pleasure joyne,
> and bids each chearefull heart,
> To this high praysed enterprise,
> performe a Christian part.

But, from the point of view of the managers of the enterprise, recruitment was perceived less as a problem of motivation than of achieving an organizational form through which the resources and energies of the participants could be mobilized. The basic objectives of the promoters in establishing a plantation in Virginia are quite clear: to exploit the mineral resources which they were certain were there; to search for that elusive will-o'-the-wisp—a water route to the Pacific through North America—and to monopolize whatever local trade existed and whatever oriental trade would be developed with the opening-up of the northwest passage.

The organizational form adopted for the venture was not created by the promoters; the roots of the joint-stock company, though it was still subject to considerable experimentation, lay deeply imbedded in English history. Nor were the proprietors themselves totally without experience in the establishment of plantations or unaware of the experience of others. Sir Thomas Smythe, a leader of the Virginia enterprise, was one of the merchant princes of London, a governor of the East India Company, the Muscovy Company, and many others. And they had before them the experience—which was, as we shall see, not entirely an unmixed blessing—of the colonizing efforts of Sir Walter Raleigh and Sir Humphrey Gilbert, of the trading posts established by the great commercial companies, of Spain and Portugal, and of the founding of plantations in Ireland.

What they established was a business organization; and, though the form of that organization was changed at various times during the Company's history, those changes were at all times dictated by the need to make the business pay, which, in the words of Sir Edwin Sandys, one of the two great leaders of the Company, was "that whereon all men's eyes were fixed." Its problems were those of any business organization. It sold shares, begged contributions, and organized lotteries to raise the necessary funds; it was concerned to recruit a proper labor force; it had to cope with the problem of adequate supervision and administration so as to maintain its authority; and it engaged in a

113

full-scale advertising campaign to sell to potential adventurers and planters the glories of a land where the "horses are also more beautiful, and fuller of courage. And such is the extraordinarie fertility of that Soyle, that the Does of their Deere yeelde Two Fawnes at a birth, and sometimes three." And it was confronted with the petty harassments of cajoling those whose good will was needed for the success of the organization. "Talking with the King," wrote the Earl of Southampton to Sir Robert Cecil, "by chance I told him of the Virginia Squirrills which they say will fly, whereof there are now divers brought into England, and hee presently and very earnestly asked me if none of them was provided for him. . . . I would not have troubled you with this but that you know so well how he is affected by these toyes."

But though the Company's plans were eminently rational, its grand design suffered from a fatal flaw: reality was far different from what the Company expected. Its model had been the East India Company, and its dream had been to reproduce the Spanish looting of a continent; but conditions in Virginia were not those of India or Mexico and Peru. "It was the Spaniards good hap," wrote Captain John Smith later in the history of the Virginia Company,

> to happen in those parts where were infinite numbers of people, whoe had manured the ground with that providence that it afforded victuall at all times; and time had brought them to that perfection they had the use of gold and silver, and the most of such commodities as their countries affoorded; so that what the Spaniard got was only the spoile and pillage of those countries people, and not the labours of their owne hands. But had those fruitfull Countries been as Salvage, as barbarous, as ill-peopled, as little planted laboured and manured, as Virginia; their proper labours, it is likely would have produced as small profits as ours. . . .
>
> But we chanced in a land, even as God made it. . . . Which ere wee could bring to recompence our paines, defray our charges, and satisfie our adventurers; wee were to discover the country, subdue the people, bring them to be tractable civil and industrious, and teach them trades that the fruits of their labours might make us recompence, or plant such colonies of our owne that must first make provision how to live of themselves ere they can bring to perfection the commodities of the countrie.

But though the error in conception made by the leaders of the Virginia Company was, from their viewpoint, a grievous one, it is also thoroughly understandable. It is true that the late sixteenth and early seventeenth century was a period of rapid expansion in the organization of trading companies; no less than thirty-four were chartered during that time. But the significant point is that the Virginia Company was the eighteenth to be founded, and, of the previous seventeen, whose experience could be taken as models, all dealt with countries within the European seas, with settled communities along the African coast, or with the advanced societies of Asia. For them, the problem was to exploit the already existing labor force of a settled society. For the Virginia Company, the problem—and it is in this that the crucial difference lies—was to recruit a labor force.

It must be understood, therefore, that in conformity with its objectives and organizational form, the establishment planted by the Virginia Company at Jamestown was a private estate, which, in the absence of an amenable local labor force, was worked on the basis of imported labor. Basic policies were laid down in London by the General Court of the Company, the body of those who had purchased the £12 10s. shares or who had been admitted for favors in the Company's behalf; the management and direction of affairs were intrusted to agents of the shareholders; and the supervision of those whose labor in Virginia was necessary for the attainment of the Company's objectives was placed in the hands of officials appointed in London.

Under the circumstances there were many potent inducements to English investors to purchase the Company's £12 10s. shares, a price, incidentally, which was the Company's estimate of the cost of transporting a settler to Virginia. Under the charter of 1606 they were guaranteed that after a five-year period, during which the settlers in Virginia would be supported by a stream of supplies sent at Company expense, the profits gained through trade and the discovery of minerals would be divided among the investors in proportion to the number of shares they held, and grants of land would be made to them on the same basis. But what were to be the inducements to become the labor force of a company trading post?

It should be noted at once that the English imitated the Spaniards in attempting to mobilize native labor. For the Company the key to the integration of the Indians into the labor force was in the ease with which, it was anticipated, they could be converted to Christianity and thereby won over as well to the secular values of Europeans. To them would accrue spiritual benefits; the Company, already blessed with

115

those, would receive something more substantial. As a certain "Maister Captaine Chester" put it:

> The land full rich, the people easilie wonne,
> Whose gaines shalbe the knowledge of our faith
> And ours such ritches as the country hath.

But though the Company succeeded for a time in exacting some tribute from the local tribal chiefs in the form of goods and weekly labor services, the Indians proved unwilling to accept the Company's spiritual and secular offerings. Long before the Indian uprising of 1622 gave an excuse to the settlers to engage in a campaign of extermination, it was clear that the Virginia Company would be forced to import its own labor force.

Between 1607 and 1609, when its charter was changed, the Virginia Company sent over 300 persons to Jamestown. They were a disparate crew of adventurers and roughnecks, imbued with the hope that after a short period in Virginia they would return home with their fortunes in their purses. The social composition of the original labor force, the tasks they were expected to perform, and the nature of the settlement they were expected to establish can all be inferred from the passenger lists of the first expedition and the three subsequent supplies that were sent out by the Company before its charter was modified in 1609. The original expedition numbered 105 persons, of whom we have the names of 67. Of these 67, 29 were listed as gentlemen and 6 were named to the local council; the rest were listed by occupation—1 preacher, 4 carpenters, 12 laborers, 1 surgeon, 1 blacksmith, 1 sailor, 1 barber, 2 bricklayers, 1 mason, 1 tailor, 1 drummer, and 4 boys—and 2 were unidentified. In the three succeeding supplies, the rather high proportion of gentlemen was not substantially reduced, nor did the range of occupations alter significantly. Seventy-three of the 120 persons in the first supply of 1608 can be identified. In this group, gentlemen exceeded laborers 28 to 21. The remainder was made up of an odd assortment of craftsmen, including jewelers, refiners, and goldsmiths—bespeaking the expectations of the Company—apothecaries, tailors, blacksmiths, and—mute testimony to the fact that gentlemen must be gentlemen whether in the wilds of Virginia or a London drawing room—a perfumer. In brief, the two most striking characteristics of this original labor force are the presence of so high a proportion of gentlemen and the absence of any occupations indicative of an intention to establish a settled agricultural community.

From the point of view of the promoters of the Virginia enterprise, these men were not citizens of a colony; they were the occupants of a status in—to use an anachronistic term—the Company's table of organization, and the status was that of workman. Such other qualities or attributes that they possessed might have been of importance when they were in London, Norwich, or Bristol, but what counted in Virginia was that they should accept the directions of their superiors and that they should be willing to work.

Even under the best of circumstances, the problem of maintaining discipline and authority would have been crucial to the success of the Company. But these were hardly the best of circumstances, for the very social composition of the original labor force intensified what in any case would have been a grievously difficult problem. In the long intervals between the arrival of supplies under the direction of the Company's admiral, Christopher Newport, conditions in Jamestown bordered on anarchy; men were beaten by their officers, plots were hatched to escape the country, and insubordination was rampant. The Company's administrative methods, characterized by the utmost laxness, could not cope with the situation. "I likewise as occation moved me," wrote President Wingfield, discussing the supplies in Virginia, "spent them in trade or by guift amongst the Indians. So likewise did Captain Newport take of them . . . what he thought good, without any noate of his hand mentioning the certainty; and disposed of them as was fitt for him. Of these likewise I could make no accompt." Nor did the high percentage of aristocrats help matters. Unused to the heavy work of axing timber, they cursed so much at their blisters that the president of the council ordered that at the end of the day's work a can of cold water be poured down the sleeve of each offender for every curse he had uttered. To Captain John Smith, the problem was the presence of too many gentlemen: "For some small number of adventrous Gentlemen . . . nothing were more requisite; but to have more to wait and play than worke, or more commanders and officers than industrious labourers was not so necessarie. For in Virginia, a plaine Souldier that can use a Pickaxe and spade, is better than five Knights."

Clearly, even if the mortality figures had been less gruesome than they were—in July, 1609, between 80 and 100 were alive of the 320 who had been sent since 1607—qualitative considerations alone would

117

have dictated a change in the composition of the labor force. For the Company the situation was brought to a head with the realization that there were to be no quick returns from metals and trade and that profits would have to be made through the exploitation of agricultural resources.

Never did the Company rely fundamentally on the recruitment of involuntary labor, but so desperate were its labor requirements and so necessary was it to keep the good will of those authorities who favored the transportation of undesirables that it felt compelled to resort to forced labor.

As early as 1609, a letter from Lisbon revealed that the Portuguese were transporting fifteen hundred children over the age of ten to the East Indies and suggested that the same be done in the case of Virginia. Shortly thereafter the Privy Council notified the mayor of London that the plagues of the city were due mainly to the presence of so many poor persons and recommended that a fund be raised, with the help of the commercial companies, to send as many of these as possible to Virginia. The Virginia Company promptly gave an estimate of the expenses involved and of the terms that would be offered to the emigrants; but, though a large sum of money was raised, no persons were actually transported at that time. In 1617, however, the City of London raised £500 to pay the cost of shipping one hundred children to Virginia, where they were to be apprenticed until the age of twenty-one, thereafter to be the fee-simple owners of fifty acres of land each. So delighted were the Company and the Virginia planters that they continued the practice, but it is evident that not all the children were equally pleased by the future arranged for them. In January, 1620, Sandys wrote to Sir Robert Naunton, the king's principal secretary, that "it falleth out that among those children, sundry being ill-disposed, and fitter for any remote place than for this Citie, declare their unwillingness to goe to Virginia: of whom the Citie is especially desirous to be disburdened; and in Virginia under severe Masters they may be brought to goodness." Since the City could not deliver and the Company could not transport "theis persons against their wills," Sandys appealed to the Privy Council for the necessary authority. It was quickly given. Exact figures cannot be determined, but, before the demise of the Company in 1624, additional shipments of children had been delivered to Virginia, and it is evident that several hundred must have been involved.

Concerning the shipment of convicts and rogues and vagabonds the information is scanty. Some convicts were certainly in Virginia before 1624, though we do not know how many; but the Virginia Company was antagonistic to the importation of such persons, and, in any case, convict-dumping on a large scale did not become a characteristic of the colonial scene until the second half of the seventeenth century. So, too, was the Company antagonistic to the importation of rogues, possibly because, unlike the case of the London children, it was forced to assume the cost of transportation. It engaged in the practice under pressure from King James I. For one group of fifty boys sent out in 1619, the Company expected to receive £500 in tobacco from the planters to whom they were indentured; but as late as October, 1622, it had received only £275.15.6, and Governor Yeardley was told that the planters "should be caused to make satisfaccon for the 224^{li}4:6:wch is remayninge due unto the Companie this yeare in good leafe Tobacco." That still others were sent is certain; the Court Book of Bridewell Hospital records that in 1620 Ellen Boulter was "brought in by the Marshall for a Vagrant, that will not be ruled by her father or her friends," to be kept at her father's charges to go to Virginia.

But throughout its history the Company was dependent upon the recruitment of voluntary labor, and especially was this true when it realized that profits would have to be made from agricultural staples and not minerals. The change in objective not only emphasized the necessity of recruiting a larger labor supply but required that it be qualitatively different from the earlier one, for now that the glitter of gold was vanishing the Company needed not soldiers of fortune but sober workmen who would be able to extract from the land the food supplies necessary for their own support and the staples whose export would produce profit for the shareholders. But what could the Company offer as sufficient inducement to motivate large numbers of persons to come to Virginia, especially when—as the evidence indicates—enthusiasm for emigration from England was confined to the wealthy, who themselves were hardly likely to exchange the comforts of life in England for the dangers of life in Virginia? The difficulties the Company faced in this respect were exacerbated by the whispering campaign started by settlers who had already returned from Virginia. "Some few of those unruly youths sent thither," said a Virginia Company broadside in 1609,

> (being of most leaued and bad condition) and such as no ground can
> hold for want of good direction there, were suffered by stealth to get

aboard the ships returning thence, and are come for England againe, giving out in all places where they come (to colour their owne misbehaviours, and the cause of their returne with some pretence) most vile and scandalous reports, both of the Country itselfe, and of the Cariage of the business there.

The Company now determined to be discriminating in the selection of settlers:

> And for that former experience hath too clearly taught, how muche and manie waies it hurtheth to suffer Parents to disburden themselves of lascivious sonnes, masters of bad servants and wives of ill husbands, and so to dogge the business with such an idle crue, as did thrust themselves in the last voiage, that will rather starve for hunger, than lay their hands to labor.

It was conceded that some "base and disordered men" might inveigle themselves into the body of settlers, but they could not do too much harm, for, as the Reverend William Crashaw said on the departure of Governor de la Warr to Virginia, "the basest and worst men trained up in a severe discipline, sharp lawes, a hard life, and much labour, do prove good members of a Commonwealth. . . . The very excrements, of a full and swelling state . . . wanting pleasures, and subject to some pinching miseries," will become "good and worthie instruments."

Clearly, if prospective settlers in Virginia faced "severe discipline, sharp lawes, a hard life, and much labour," substantial concessions would have to be offered to induce them to emigrate. The status the Company was asking them to accept was that of servant, employee of the Company, but it was one thing to create a position and quite another to get men to fill it. Since perpetual servitude was obviously no inducement, the Company was required to limit the period of service and to make other concessions. Every settler over the age of ten, whether he paid his own way or was shipped at Company expense, was promised one share of stock in the Company, with potential dividends from the profits of trade and a land grant to be made at the time of the first division after seven years. Every "extraordinarie" man—such as "Divines, Governors, Ministers of State and Justice, Knights, Gentlemen, Physitions" or such as were "of worth for special services"—was given additional shares according to the value of his person. The Company expected, in return for assuming all the costs of maintaining the plantation and providing supplies to the emigrants, that each settler would work at tasks assigned him under the direction of Company-appointed officers. For a period of seven years, all supplies were to be distributed through the Company store, all exports were to be shipped through the Company magazine, and all land was to be held by the Company. In effect, the Company created the status of landowner in order to induce persons to accept the status of non-landowner; it was asking emigrants to accept the present burdens of membership in a lower status in anticipation of the future benefits they would receive upon promotion to a higher status. From the point of view of the structure of an organization, this was simply automatic progression—promotion to a higher position in the table of organization after a limited tenure in a lower position. From the point of view of a society, however, this was a guaranty of social mobility, and, as we shall see, it seriously compromised the Company's ability to secure its organizational objectives.

That the Company expected the combination of limited servitude and potential landownership to solve its labor problem is quite clear; sufficient numbers of workmen would be induced to emigrate to Virginia and, having arrived, would be motivated to do the work that was essential to the Company's success. Virginia planter and London adventurer were to be united in a single relationship. Do not discourage the planters, the London stockholders were admonished, "in growing religious, nor in gathering riches, two especiall bonds (whether severed or cojoined) to keepe them in obedience, the one for conscience sake, the other for fear of losing what they have gotten." How the planter's concern for his own interests was to benefit the Company was quite clear. "The Planters," wrote Alderman Johnson, "will be in such hope to have their owne shares and habitations in those lands, which they have so husbanded, that it will cause contending and emulation among them, which shall bring foorth the most profitable and beneficiall fruites for their ioynt stock."

But land for the settlers and profits for the stockholders were affairs of the future, and both were dependent upon the skill and speed with which the planters could be molded into an efficient labor force. It was of the utmost importance, therefore, that the Company establish its authority in Virginia and maintain discipline, and for the achievement of these purposes the Company was not content to rely simply on the self-discipline it hoped would be the by-product of the effort to obtain profits. The first step was taken with the issuance of the new charter of 1609. During its first three years in Virginia, the Company felt, "experience of error in the equality of Governors, and some outrages, and follies committed by them, had a little shaken so tender a body." To avoid the evils of divided authority, "we did resolve and obtain, to renew our Letters Pattents, and to procure to ourselves, such ample and large priviledges and powers by which we were at liberty to reforme and correct those already discovered, and to prevent such as in the future might threaten us . . . under the conduct of one able and absolute Governor." But changes in the formal structure of authority were not sufficient.

Religion, too, was counted upon to do its part in maintaining order. Doctrinal conflict was minimized from the start by the ban on Catholics, but what really distinguishes the role of religion under the Virginia Company was it conscious utilization for disciplinary purposes. No less an authority on colonization than Richard Hakluyt had pointed to the advisability of taking along "one or two preachers that God may be honoured, the people instructed, mutinies better avoided, and obedience the better used." The Company was quick to take the hint. Religion was used to screen prospective planters before their arrival in Virginia, and it was used to discipline them after their arrival. "We have thought it convenient to pronounce," stated the Company in a broadside of 1609, "that . . . we will receive no man that cannot bring or render some good testimony of his religion to God." And during the time that Sir Thomas Dale's code of laws was sovereign in Virginia—from May, 1610, to April, 1619—the settlers were marched to church twice each day to pray for relief from dissension and for the showering of blessings upon the shareholders:

> O Lord . . . defend us from the delusion of the devil, the malice of the heathen, the invasions of our enemies, & mutinies & dissentions of our own people. . . . Thou has moved . . . the hearts of so many of our nation to assist . . . with meanes and provision, and with their holy praiers . . . and for that portion of their substance which they willingly offer for thy honour & service in this action, recompence it to them and theirs, and reward it seven fold into their bosomes, with better blessinges.

In a society of ranks and orders, deference is owed to certain persons by virtue of their social position, and the Company attempted to maximize the potentiality for discipline in such an arrangement by appointing to leading posts in Virginia those persons to whom obedience was due because of their high status. Insofar as it was possible, the Company selected only persons of high birth to be governor; when it was not possible, as in the case of Governor Yeardley, it quickly, and it seems surreptitiously, secured for him a knighthood. And at all times the governors were urged to surround themselves with the pomp and circumstance of high office, the better to impress the governed. "You shall for the more regard and respect of yor place," read the Company's instructions to Sir Thomas Gates,

> to beget reverence to yor authority, and to refresh their mindes that obey the gravity of those lawes under wch they were borne at yor discrecon use such formes and Ensignes of government as by our letters Pattents wee are enabled to grant unto you, as also the attendance of a guarde uppon your pson.

Ultimately, however, the Company relied upon a military regimen and upon the imposition of force to obtain labor discipline. Governor de la Warr had been instructed that his men were to be divided into groups and placed under the charge of officers "to be exercised and tryned up in Martiall manner and warlike Discipline." Settlers were forbidden to return to England without permission, and their letters were sealed and sent first to the Company in London before being forwarded. But the full code of military discipline was not worked out until the arrival in Jamestown of Captain Thomas Dale, marshal of the colony, who had been granted a leave of absence from his post in the Netherlands army at the behest of the Company. Dale supplemented the usual list of religious offenses and crimes against the state and the person with a series of enactments designed to protect the Company's interests. Slander against the Company, its officers, or any of its publications; unauthorized trading with the Indians; escaping to the Indians; theft; the killing of any domestic animal without consent; false accounting by any keeper of supplies—all were punishable by service in the galleys or death. Failure to keep regular hours of work subjected the offender to the pain of being forced to lie neck and heels together all night for the first offense, whipping for the second, and one year's service in the galleys for the third.

Moreover, Dale created a military rank for every person in Virginia and specified the duties of each in such a way as to provide us with important clues into the nature of labor discipline and what was expected to provide the motivation to work.

> Because we are not onely to exercise the duty of a Souldier, but that of the husbandman, and that in time of the vacancie of our watch and ward wee are not to live idly, therefore the Captaine . . . shall . . . demand . . . what service, worke, and businesse he hath in charge, from the Governor . . . in which worke the Captaine himselfe shall do exceeding worthily to take paines and labour, that his Souldiers seeing his industry and carefulnesse, may with more cheerfulnesse love him, and bee incouraged to the performance of the like.

Of the corporal:

> His duty is to provide that none of his Squadron, be absent, when the drumme shall call to any labour, or worke, or at what time soever they shall be commanded thereunto for the service of the Collonie, in the performance of which said workes he is to be an example of the rest of his Squadron by his owne labouring therein . . . that thereby giving incoraging to his superior officers he may be held by them worthy of a higher place.

Of the private soldier:

> He shall continue at his worke until the drumme beat, and . . . be conducted into the church to heare divine service, after which he may repayre to his house or lodging to prepare for his dinner, and to repose him until the drumme beate shall call him forth againe in the afternoone . . . the Generall having understanding of his promptitude and dilligence may conferre upon him, and call him into place of preferment and commaund.

What is so striking about Dale's Code is the way in which it stripped from people all attributes save the one that really counted in the relationship which the Company sought to impose on them—their status in the organization. Behavior was expected to conform to a set of prescriptions the major characteristic of which was that the rights and obligations of persons depended on their position within the organization. In this respect, the contrast between Dale's Code and the first set of laws the settlers were able to enact for themselves at the General Assembly of 1619 is startling. For then, considerations other than status within an organization were fundamental:

All persons whatsoever upon the Sabaoth days shall frequente divine service and sermons both forenoon and afternoone. . . . And everyone that shall transgresse this lawe shall forfeicte three shillinges a time to the use of the churche. . . . But if a servant in this case shall wilfully neglecte his Mr's commande he shall suffer bodily punishment.

Or consider the following petition drafted by the Assembly:

. . . that the antient Planters . . . suche as before Sir T. Dales' depart were come hither . . . maye have their second, third and more divisions successively in as lardge and free manner as any other Planter. Also that they wilbe pleased to allowe to the male children, of them and of all others begotten in Virginia, being the onely hope of a posterity, a single share a piece.

For the planters in Virginia, considerations of length of residence and of varying degrees of freedom now affected the rights and obligations of persons. No longer could relations be determined exclusively by the positions persons held within a single system—the organization of the Company. By 1619 Virginia was becoming a society, in which behavior was in some way determined by the totality of positions each person held in a network of sometimes complementary, sometimes contradictory, relationships. The key to this transformation from organization to society lies in the concessions the Company was forced to offer to induce persons to accept positions in the organizational relationship; for those concessions so multiplied the number of statuses and so altered the status of persons that a system of relationships was created where only one had existed before.

The fact is that the reforms the Company instituted in 1609 were not sufficient either to swell the supply of labor migrating to Virginia or to motivate the planters who were there to work with the will the Company expected. The Company had hoped that by its reforms it would be able to obtain not "idle and wicked persons; such as shame, or fear compels into this action [but] fit and industrious [persons], honest sufficient Artificers." Yet so unproductive were they that as late as 1616 John Rolfe could indicate to Sir Robert Rich that what had been was still the Company's most serious problem. Our greatest want, he wrote, is "good and sufficient men as well of birth and quality to command, soldiers to marche, discover and defend the country from invasion, artificers, labourers, and husbandmen." And so dissatisfied had the settlers become with their situation that, in a letter smuggled to the Spanish ambassador in London with the connivance of English sailors, Don Diego de Molina, the prisoner in Jamestown, reported that "a good many have gone to the Indians . . . and others have gone out to sea . . . and those who remain do so by force and are anxious to see a fleet come from Spain to release them from this misery." The hope that Don Diego attributed to the colonists was, no doubt, the wish of the patriotic Spaniard; but it is nevertheless true that some settlers did flee to the Indians, that the Company did succeed in obtaining authority to deport to Virginia those settlers who had escaped back to England, and that Coles and Kitchins, who had been Don Diego's guards, were executed in 1614 for organizing a plot to escape to Florida.

Nor did the concessions granted to superior colonists in 1614, including a kind of modified right to private property and some relief from the obligation to work on the Company lands, suffice to solve the labor problem. For the simple fact was, as Captain John Smith wrote, that "no man will go from hence to have less liberty there then here." The Company, determined in 1619 to make a final effort to create of Virginia the profitable investment it had always hoped it would be, took his advice to heart. Though it was faced with declining financial resources, with internal bickering, and with increasing evidence that the king was losing patience with its meager achievement, the Company decided to pin its hopes on a quick return. The key to profits, it felt, lay in raising the value of the Company lands through increasing population and in diversifying products through the importation of labor skilled in many trades. The success of the effort, obviously, rested upon the strength of the additional inducements that could be offered to both investors and potential emigrants.

As always, one of the principal devices used by the Company to attract labor and to increase productivity was that of easing the terms on which land could be acquired. The effect of the reform was to create within the Company a new group of statuses differentiated from one another in terms of the amount of property attached to each or the length of time required to obtain land on the part of those who were not yet entitled to it:

1. "Ancient planters" who had come to Virginia at their own cost before 1616 received 100 acres per share in perpetuity rent-free.

2. "Ancient planters" who had come to Virginia at Company expense received 100 acres at an annual rent of 2s. after the completion of their seven-year period of servitude on the Company's land.

3. All persons who came to Virginia after 1616 at their own expense received 50 acres at an annual rent of 1s.

4. All persons who came to Virginia after 1616 at Company expense were to receive 50 acres after having worked on the Company's land for seven years, during which time half their produce belonged to the Company and half to themselves.

5. All tradesmen received a house and 4 acres of land so long as they plied their trades.

6. All persons who paid for the transportation of emigrants received 50 acres per person.

7. Company officers not only were entitled to their regular land grants but were supported by the labor of tenants-at-halves on large tracts of land reserved by the Company for that purpose.

8. Indentured servants, whose transportation was paid by the Company or by private associations of investors and who were then sold to planters on their arrival in Virginia, were entitled to "freedom dues"—including a land grant—on the expiration of their servitude.

Nor was this all. Determined to improve the morale of the colonists and, eventually, to relieve the Company of the burdensome cost of transporting labor from England, Sandys also began in 1620 to ship women to Virginia to become wives of the planters. There had been marriages in Virginia before, of course, but the supply of single women, restricted to the few female servants of married couples, was far smaller than the demand. Now, however, the Company organized the shipment of women on a business basis, forming a separate joint-stock company for the purpose. Though the women were, in any case, to be paid for by the planters at the rate of 120 pounds of the best leaf tobacco per person and though the Company conceded that it was dubious as to its authority to control marriages—"for the libertie of Mariadge we dare not infrindg"—it nevertheless discriminated between classes of planters in the bestowal of the women. "And though we are desireous that mariadge be free according to the law of nature," the Company wrote to the Governor and Council of Virginia, "yett would we not have these maids deceived and married to servants, but only to such freemen or tenants as have meanes to maintaine them."

Finally, in a radical departure from previous policy, the Company limited the scope of martial law and ordered Governor Yeardley to convene an assembly of elected representatives from each district in Virginia. The Company did not intend to diminish its own authority, for the Governor was given the right to veto all enactments of the Assembly, and the General Court of the Company in London retained the right to disallow its decisions. Rather was it the Company's hope that the degree of acceptance of its program would be increased if it had the added sanction of approval by representatives of the planters themselves.

In a sense, the Company's reforms succeeded too well. Lured by the new prospects in Virginia, about 4,800 emigrants departed from England between November, 1619, and February, 1625, nearly twice as many as had gone during the entire period from 1607 to 1619. But, while the Company's propaganda could refer blandly to "each man having the shares of Land due to him" and to "the laudable forme of Justice and government," actual conditions in Virginia were quite different. Goodman Jackson "much marviled that you would send me a servant to the Companie," young Richard Freethorne wrote to his parents:

> He saith I had beene better knocked on the head, and Indeede so I fynde it now to my great greefe and miserie, and saith, that if you love me you will redeeme me suddenlie, for wch I doe Intreate and begg. . . . I thought no head had beene able to hold so much water as hath and doth daylie flow from mine eyes. . . . But this is Certaine I never felt the want of ffather and mother till now, but now deare friends full well I knowe and rue it although it were too late before I knew it.

"To write of all crosses and miseries wᶜh have befallen us at this tyme we are not able," said Samuel Sharp. "So the truth is," Edward Hill wrote to his brother, "we lyve in the fearefullest age that ever Christians lived in."

Though Company policy was not responsible for all the suffering endured by the settlers, it was responsible for intensifying their sense of deprivation by having promised too much. "My Master Atkins hath sould me," Henry Brigg wrote to his brother, Thomas:

> If you remember he tould me that for my Diett the worst day in the weeke should be better then the Sonday, & also he swore unto you that I should never serve any man but himselfe: And he also tould us that there they paled out their groundes from Deare & Hoggs. But in stead of them we pale out oʳ Enemyes.

"If the Company would allow to each man a pound of butter and a pounde of Chese weekely," wrote a planter to Sir John Worsenholme,

> they would find more comfort therin then by all the Deere, Fish & Fowle is so talked of in England of wch I can assure yo^u yor poore servants have nott had since their cominge into the Contrey so much as the sent.

"I am pswaded," George Thorp wrote to John Smyth of Nibley,

> that more doe die of the disease of theire minde then of theire body by having this country victualls over-praised unto them in England & by not knowing, they shall drinke water here.

No doubt the chasm between expectation and reality contributed to the planters' alienation from the organizational relationship into which they had been lured by the Company's promises. But that relationship was affected even more by the development of a network of relations that followed inevitably from the inducements to get men into the Company.

At one time in Virginia, the single relationship that existed between persons rested upon the positions they occupied in the Company's table of organization. As a result of the efforts made by the Company to get persons to accept that relationship, however, each person in Virginia had become the occupant of several statuses, for now there were rich and poor in Virginia, landowners and renters, masters and servants, old residents and newcomers, married and single, men and women; and the simultaneous possession of these statuses involved the holder in a network of relationships, some congruent and some incompatible, with his organizational relationship.

Once the men in Virginia had been bachelors who lived in Company-provided barracks. Now they lived in private houses with their families, and, though the Company attempted to make use of the new relationship by penalizing each "Master of a family" for certain crimes committed by those under his authority—hoping thereby that the master would use his authority to suppress crime—it can hardly be doubted that its action involved the head of the family in a conflict of loyalties.

Once all persons had been equal before Company law, and penalties had been inflicted solely in accordance with the nature of the offense.

Now, the General Assembly found that "persones of qualitie" were "not fitt to undergoe corporall punishment."

Once length of residence was irrelevant in determining the obligations of persons to the Company. Now, however, it was enacted that all "Y^e olde planters, y^t were heere before, or cam in at ye laste cominge of Sr. Tho: Gates they and theire posteritie shalbe exempted from theire psonall service to ye warres, and any publique charge (Churche dewties excepted)."

Once Virginians had been governed administratively through a chain of command originating in the Company's General Court. Now an authentic political system existed, and the members of the Assembly demanded the same right to disallow orders of the General Court that the Court had with respect to the Assembly.

Once all land had been owned by the Company. Now much of it was owned by private persons, and even more had been promised to them, and the opportunities for the creation of private fortunes involved the planters in a new relationship with the Company. No longer was the planter willing to have his tobacco exported through the Company at a fixed price, when, as a free landowner, he might strike his own bargain with the purchaser. No longer was the planter willing, at a time when labor meant profit, for the Company to commandeer his servants. Even officers of the Company, expected to administer its program in Virginia, saw the chance to subvert it to their own purposes; "The servants you allow them, or such as they hire," Captain John Smith told the Company, "they plant on their private Lands, not upon that belongeth to their office, which crop alwaies exceeds yours." Indeed, it became increasingly difficult to get planters to accept Company positions:

> Sr George is taken up with his private. . . . Capt. Hamor is miserablie poore and necessities will inforce him to shift. . . . Capt: Mathews intends wholie his Cropp, and will rather hazard the payment of forfeictures, then performe our Injunctions. . . . Mr Blanie is now married in Virginia, and when he hath discharged your trust in the Magazine wilbee a Planter amongst us. . . . And I would you could persuade some of qualities and worth to come out.

The increase in private wealth tended to subordinate status in the Company to status in a different relationship among the planters. The muster roll of early 1625 shows 48 families bearing various titles of distinction, most of which had been earned in Virginia. They alone held 266 of the approximately 487 white servants in Virginia, 20 of the 23 Negro servants, and 1 of the 2 Indian servants. These were the families at the apex of Virginia society, determined to uphold their rights as over against other persons and sometimes going beyond their rights. Acting through the General Assembly, they insisted upon scrupulous enforcement of contracts of servitude, forbade servants to trade with the Indians, and, so as not to lose their labor, regulated the right of their servants to marry. Nor, as the chronic complaints bear witness, were they loath to keep their servants beyond the required time. That aspect of the relationship between master and servant was eloquently revealed in a petition to the Governor by Jane Dickenson in 1624:

> [She] most humblie sheweth that whereas her late husband Ralph Dickenson Came ov^r into this Country fower Yeares since, obliged to Nicholas Hide deceased for ye tearme of seaven yeares, hee only to have for himselfe & yor petitioner ye one halfe of his labors, her said husband being slaine in the bloudy Masacre, & her selfe Caried away wth the Cruell salvages, amongst them Enduring much misery for teen monthes. At the Expiration it pleased God so to dispose the hartes of the Indians, y^t for a small ransome yor petitioner wth divers others should be realeased, In Consideration that Doctor Potts laid out two pounds of beades for her releasement, hee alleageth yor petitioner is linked to his servitude wth a towefold Chaine the one for her late husbandes obligation & thother for her ransome, of both wch shee hopeth that in Conscience shee ought to be discharged, of ye first by her widdowhood, of the second by the law of nations, Considering shee hath already served teen monthes, two much for two pound of beades.
>
> The pmises notwthstanding Dr Pott refuseth to sett yor peticioner at liberty, threatning to make her serve him the uttermost day, unless she pcure him 150^{li} weight of Tobacco, she therefore most humbly desireth, that you^u wilbe pleased to take w^t Course shalbe thought iust for her releasement fro' his servitude, Considering that it much differeth not from her slavery wth the Indians.

But that was only one aspect of the relationship. Conditions in Virginia were now more fluid than they had been, and persons of low estate might also rise. Secretary of State John Pory wrote Sir Dudley Carleton that "our cowekeeper here of James citty on Sundays goes accowtered all in freshe flaminge silke; and a wife of one that in England had

131

professed the black arte, not of a scholler, but of a collier of Croydon, wears her rought bever hatt with a faire perle hat band." The Company was opposed to such unseemly displays of wealth on the part of persons of low estate, but it could not prevent them.

The ultimate stage in the transition of Virginia from organization to society was reached when the settlers came to feel that the new relationships in which they were now involved were of greater importance than the Company relationship, when their statuses outside the organization came largely to dictate their behavior. For at that point they were no longer willing to accept the legitimacy of their organizational superiors. William Weldon warned Sir Edwin Sandys that the planters who now had land were grumbling at Company policy:

> I acquainted them wth my restraint of plantinge Tobacco wch is a thinge so distastefull to them that they will wth no patience indure to heare of it bitterly Complayninge that they have noe other meanes to furnish themselves with aparell for the insuinge yere but are likely as they say (and for aught I Can see) to be starved if they be debarred of it.

From general discontent it was but a short step to ridicule of Company officials and outright refusal to accept a Company assignment. Wrote planter William Capps to John Ferrar:

> The old smoker our (I know not how to terme him but) Governor, so good so careful mild, Religious, iust, honest that I protest I thinke God hath sent him in mercie for good to us, he undergoeth all your cares & ours and I feare not but god will bless him in all his pceedinges but who must be th'Instrument to make all this whole againe? Why Capps: all voyces can sett him forth about the business: But who must pay him his hyre? The Contrey is poore and the Companie is poore and Cappes is poore already, & poorer he will be if he follow this course.

Like other men, planter Capps believed that "Charity first beginnes at home," and he divorced his own interest from that of the Company:

> I will forsweare ever bending my mind for publique good, and betake me to my own profit with some halfe a score men of my owne and lie rootinge in the earthe like a hog, and reckon Tobacco ad unguem by hundrethes, and quarters.

That the Company could no longer expect to command obedience was clear, for even its officers in Virginia perceived themselves as having a set of interests distinct from those of their London superiors and turned their backs to their authority. "Such is the disposition of those who glorie in their wisdomes," wrote George Sandys, the treasurer in Virginia, to his brother, Sir Miles,

> that they will rather Justifye and proceed in their Errors than to suffer a supposed disgrace by reforming them. . . . Who clere themselves by the wrongings of others; objecting unto us their Instructions, whereof manie are infeasible and the most inconvenient, for to say the truth they know nothing of Virginia.

"Such an Antipathy is there between theyr vast Comands and o^r grumbling Obedience," Sir Francis Wyatt wrote to his father:

> Mingling matters of honor and profitt often overthrow both. They expect great retournes to pay the Companies debt. . . . For me I have not a third part of my men to inable me to either. . . . I often wish little Mr Farrar here, that to his zeale he would add knowledge of this Contrey.

In 1607 there had been no "Contrey," only the Virginia Company. It was the Company's fate to have created a country and to have destroyed itself in the process. More than a century later, James Otis wrote bitterly: "Those who judge of the reciprocal rights that subsist between a supreme and subordinate state of dominion, by no higher rules than are applied to a corporation of button-makers, will never have a very comprehensive view of them." His comment was intended as an observation on contemporary political affairs, but we can detect in it a verdict on the past as well.

The Company had been faced with the problems of motivating its members to work for the ends which it was created to achieve and, at the same time, of maintaining the discipline that was essential for its organizational integrity. The solution it adopted for the first problem made it impossible to solve the second; and the burden of achieving order and discipline now became the responsibility not of an organization but of a society.

Among the papers in the Sackville collection is a document entitled "A Form of Policy for Virginia," written when it was already apparent that the Company had failed. The proposal was never adopted, but it is significant nonetheless, for, as Professor Fernand Braudel reminds us,

> victorious events come about as a result of many possibilities, often contradictory, among which life finally has made its choice. For one possibility which actually is realized innumerable others have been drowned. These are the ones which have left little trace for the historians. And yet it is necessary to give them their place because the losing movements are forces which have at every moment affected the final outcome.

The significance of the document, drafted as a royal proclamation, lies in its awareness of the problems of motivation and order, in its realization that they could no longer be solved by instructions handed down through a chain of command, and in its conscious application of particular social inventions to solve them:

> Wee . . . knowinge that the perfection and happinesse of a commonwealth, lyeth . . . first and principally in the government, consisting in the mutuall duties of commandeing and obeyeing, next in the possessing thinges plentifully, necessarie for the life of man, doe professe that . . . we intend wholely the good of our subjects . . . endeavouringe to cause both England and Virginea, to endowe each other with their benefittes and profitts that thereby layeing aside force and our coactive power, we may by our justice and bountie marrye and combinde those our provinces to us and our soveraigntye in naturall love and obedience.

The problem of order was solved by the meticulous enumeration of every social status that was to exist in Virginia, with a specification of the rights and obligations that inhered in each. The problem of motivation was solved by the granting of both economic rewards and social privileges to each status and by the opportunity given to move from one to another:

> The meanest servant that goeth (God soe blessing him and his endeavours, that hee can purchase and [an] estate in England or compasse to carrie over or drawe over with him of his friends and adherences the number of 300 men) he may become a lord patriot which is the greatest place the commonwealth canne beare.

The problem of consensus was solved through devices to enhance the mutual affection of persons in these statuses:

> To the end that love may be mayntayned, and that theise degrees may not estrange the upper orders from the lower, we wish that the heirs and eldest sonnes of the upper orders may marrie with the daughters of the lower orders. . . . And that the daughters of the upper orders being heires may marrye with the sonnes of the lower orders, makeing choice of the most vertuous . . . that all degrees may bee thereby bound togeather in the bonds of love that none may be scorned but the scorner. To this end alsoe, although we would not have you imitate the Irish in their wilde and barbarous maners, yet we will commend one custome of theires unto you, which is that the poorer sort sueing to gett the nurseing of the children of the lordes and gentrie, and breedeinge upp in their minorities as their owne, this breedinge . . . doth begett anoether nature in them to love their foster children and brethren, as if they were naturally bread of the same parentes.

Written in the margin of the document, by whom we do not know, is a lengthy commentary. Concerning the importance of status and order, the following is written: "This maintenance of theire degrees will immoveably fixe the frame of the collonie." Concerning the importance of mobility and motivation, the following is written: "Soe framinge the government that it shall give all men both liberty and meanes of riseinge to the greatest places and honours therein, whereby they will receave such content that they will all strive to maintaine it in the same forme we shall now settle it."

Shakespeare had written:

> Take but degree away, untune that string
> And hark, what discord follows.

The author of the document agreed. He rested his hopes for stability on the attachment of each person to a position in which recognized rights and responsibilities inhered. What he did not realize is what may be learned from the history of the Virginia Company—that each man is attached to many positions, that each position involves him in a separate relationship that imposes its own necessities, and that his behavior is the product of all the positions he holds and, because he has a memory, of all the positions he once held.

II

The generalizations that emerge from our study are of two kinds: those directly tied to the events of the time and place that we have analyzed and those of a more abstract kind that derive from the analysis of these historical particulars but can be stated in such a way as to be of more general applicability.

There seems little room for doubt about some of the conclusions we have drawn: that the character of seventeenth-century North American society was shaped decisively by the fact that, in contrast to the situation in Latin America, the creation of the society was accomplished through the recruitment of a voluntary labor force; that higher statuses in that society were created as a result of the need to induce persons to accept positions in lower statuses; and that the behavior of persons in that society was determined not only by opportunities for advancement, as Whiggish interpreters of our history would have us believe, but, as well, by the fact that these opportunities were less than people had been led to expect.

With respect to more general hypotheses, it may be suggested that the mechanism by which the change from organization to society was accomplished lay in the very effort to apply the blueprint that was intended to govern the relations between persons, for this so multiplied the number of statuses persons held, and therefore the relationships in which they were involved, as to alter their behavior in a decisive fashion.

The testing of these hypotheses, of course, would involve the examination of still other consciously selected historical situations for the purpose of comparison—the experience of the British in establishing other colonies in North America and in coping with a totally different problem in India, of the French in Canada and the Spanish in South America, of the reasons for the difference between the blueprint in accordance with which utopian communities were planned and the outcome of their establishment, and the like. Herein lies the design for a research in historical sociology.

7. THE THEORY OF THE STATE AND OF SOCIETY*

by Perry Miller and Thomas H. Johnson

Those who came to the New World desired to establish an ordered society in a wilderness where no social organizations -existed. The settlers brought with them from Europe commonly held notions about the functions of the state and the way power should be distributed. In the following selection, Perry Miller and Thomas H. Johnson explore the social thought of New England Puritans to determine how it shaped the polities created in Massachusetts and Connecticut and especially the connection between the state and church. Despite religious beliefs and aspirations which distinguished Puritans from others, most Englishmen shared similar assumptions about the nature and purpose of government and the relationship between the individual and the community. Though colonists diligently strove to model their societies on traditional principles, they were eventually forced by necessity to modify their social theory and forms of government.

---

* Perry Miller and Thomas H. Johnson (eds.), *The Puritans* (New York: Harper & Row, 1938), vol. 1, 181–194. Footnotes have been omitted except where they are necessary for an understanding of the text.

137

For further reading: Perry Miller, *Errand into the Wilderness* (1956); Edmund S. Morgan, *The Puritan Dilemma* (1958); Clinton Rossiter, *Seedtime of the Republic* (1953), chs. 6–8; Sumner C. Powell, *Puritan Village: The Formation of a New England Town* (1963).

It has often been said that the end of the seventeenth and the beginning of the eighteenth century mark the first real break with the Middle Ages in the history of European thought. Even though the Renaissance and Reformation transformed many aspects of the Western intellect, still it was not until the time of Newton that the modern scientific era began; only then could men commence to regard life in this world as something more than preparation for life beyond the grave. Certainly if the eighteenth century inaugurated the modern epoch in natural sciences, so also did it in the political and social sciences. For the first time since the fall of the Roman Empire religion could be separated from politics, doctrinal orthodoxy divorced from loyalty to the state, and the citizens of a nation permitted to worship in diverse churches and to believe different creeds without endangering the public peace. Various factors contributed to effecting this revolution; the triumph of scientific method and of rationalism made impossible the older belief that government was of divine origin; the rise of capitalism, of the middle class, and eventually of democracy, necessitated new conceptions of the rôle of the state. Social leadership in England and America was assumed by a group of gentlemen who were, by and large, deists or skeptics, and to them all religious issues had become supremely boring. At the same time the churches themselves, particularly the newer evangelical denominations, were swinging round to a theology that made religious belief the subjective experience of individual men, entirely unrelated to any particular political philosophy or social theory.

In order to understand Puritanism we must go behind these eighteenth-century developments to an age when the unity of religion and politics was so axiomatic that very few men would even have grasped the idea that church and state could be distinct. For the Puritan mind it was not possible to segregate a man's spiritual life from his communal life. Massachusetts was settled for religious reasons, but as John Winthrop announced, religious reasons included "a due forme of Government both ciuill and ecclesiasticall," and the civil was quite as important in his eyes as the ecclesiastical. Only in recent years has it become possible for us to view the political aspects of Puritanism with something like comprehension and justice. For two centuries our social thinking has been dominated by ideas which were generated in the course of a sweeping revolt against everything for which the Puritans stood; the political beliefs of the Puritans were forgotten, or, if remembered at all, either deplored or condemned as unfortunate remnants of medievalism. Puritanism has been viewed mainly as a religious and ethical movement. But of late years the standards of the eighteenth century have for the first time come under serious criticism and in many quarters are showing the strain. In these circumstances the social philosophy of Puritanism takes on a new interest, and quite possibly becomes for us the most instructive and valuable portion of the Puritan heritage.

The Puritan theory of the state began with the hypothesis of original sin. Had Adam transmitted undiminished to his descendants the image of God in which he had been created, no government would ever have been necessary among men; they would all then have done justice to each other without the supervision of a judge, they would have respected each other's rights without the intervention of a policeman. But the Bible said—and experience proved—that since the fall, without the policeman, the judge, the jail, the law, and the magistrate, men will rob, murder, and fight among themselves; without a coercive state to restrain evil impulses and administer punishments, no life will be safe, no property secure, no honor observed. Therefore, upon Adam's apostasy, God Himself instituted governments among men. He left the particular form to be determined by circumstance—this was one important human act on which the Puritans said the Bible was *not* an absolute and imperious lawgiver—but He enacted that all men should be under some sort of corporate rule, that they should all submit to the sway of their superiors, that no man should live apart from his fellows, that the government should have full power to enforce obedience and to inflict every punishment that the crimes of men deserved.

There was a strong element of individualism in the Puritan creed; every man had to work out his own salvation, each soul had to face

his maker alone. But at the same time, the Puritan philosophy demanded that in society all men, at least all regenerate men, be marshaled into one united array. The lone horseman, the single trapper,
the solitary hunter was not a figure of the Puritan frontier; Puritans
moved in groups and towns, settled in whole communities, and maintained firm government over all units. Neither was the individualistic
business man, the shopkeeper who seized every opportunity to enlarge
his profits, the speculator who contrived to gain wealth at the expense
of his fellows, neither were these typical figures of the original Puritan
society. The most obvious lesson of the selections printed herein is
that Puritan opinion was at the opposite pole from Jefferson's feeling
that the best government governs as little as possible. The theorists
of New England thought of society as a unit, bound together by inviolable ties; they thought of it not as an aggregation of individuals
but as an organism, functioning for a definite purpose, with all parts
subordinate to the whole, all members contributing a definite share,
every person occupying a particular status. "Society in all sorts of
humane affairs is better then Solitariness," said John Cotton. The
society of early New England was decidedly "regimented." Puritans
did not think the state was merely an umpire, standing on the side
lines of a contest, limited to checking egregious fouls, but otherwise
allowing men free play according to their abilities and the breaks of
the game. They would have expected the rule of "laissez-faire" to
result in a reign of rapine and horror. The state to them was an active
instrument of leadership, discipline, and, wherever necessary, of coercion; it legislated over any or all aspects of human behavior, it not
merely regulated misconduct but undertook to inspire and direct all
conduct. The commanders were not to trim their policies by the desires of the people, but to drive ahead upon the predetermined course;
the people were all to turn out as they were ordered, and together
they were to crowd sail to the full capacity of the vessel. The officers
were above the common men, as the quarter-deck is above the fore-
castle. There was no idea of the equality of all men. There was no
questioning that men who would not serve the purposes of the society
should be whipped into line. The objectives were clear and unmistakable; any one's disinclination to dedicate himself to them was obviously so much recalcitrancy and depravity. The government of
Massachusetts, and of Connecticut as well, was a dictatorship, and
never pretended to be anything else; it was a dictatorship, not of a

single tyrant, or of an economic class, or of a political faction, but of the holy and regenerate. Those who did not hold with the ideals entertained by the righteous, or who believed God had preached other principles, or who desired that in religious belief, morality, and ecclesiastical preferences all men should be left at liberty to do as they wished —such persons had every liberty, as Nathaniel Ward said, to stay away from New England. If they did come, they were expected to keep their opinions to themselves; if they discussed them in public or attempted to act upon them, they were exiled; if they persisted in returning, they were cast out again; if they still came back, as did four Quakers, they were hanged on Boston Common. And from the Puritan point of view, it was good riddance.

These views of the nature and function of the state were not peculiar to the Puritans of New England; they were the heritage of the past, the ideals, if not always the actuality, of the previous centuries. That government was established by God in order to save depraved men from their own depravity had been orthodox Christian teaching for centuries; that men should be arranged in serried ranks, inferiors obeying superiors, was the essence of feudalism; that men should live a social life, that profit-making should be restrained within the limits of the "just price," that the welfare of the whole took precedence over any individual advantage, was the doctrine of the medieval church, and of the Church of England in the early seventeenth century. Furthermore, in addition to these general principles, there were two or three more doctrines in the New England philosophy which also were common to the age and the background. All the world at that moment believed with them that the church was to be maintained and protected by the civil authority, and a certain part of the world was contending that government was limited by fundamental law and that it took its origin from the consent of the people.

Every respectable state in the Western world assumed that it could allow only one church to exist within its borders, that every citizen should be compelled to attend it and conform to its requirements, and that all inhabitants should pay taxes for its support. When the Puritans came to New England the idea had not yet dawned that a government could safely permit several creeds to exist side by side within the confines of a single nation. They had not been fighting in England for any milk-and-water toleration, and had they been offered such religious freedom as dissenters now enjoy in Great Britain they would have scorned to accept such terms. Only a hypocrite, a person who did not really believe what he professed, would be content to practice his religion under such conditions. The Puritans were assured that they alone knew the exact truth, as it was contained in the written word of God, and they were fighting to enthrone it in England and to extirpate utterly and mercilessly all other pretended versions of Christianity. When they could not succeed at home, they came to America, where they could establish a society in which the one and only truth should reign forever. There is nothing so idle as to praise the Puritans for being in any sense conscious or deliberate pioneers of religious liberty—unless, indeed, it is still more idle to berate them because in America they persecuted dissenters from their beliefs after they themselves had undergone persecution for differing with the bishops. To allow no dissent from the truth was exactly the reason they had come to America. They maintained here precisely what they had maintained in England, and if they exiled, fined, jailed, whipped, or hanged those who disagreed with them in New England, they would have done the same thing in England could they have secured the power. It is almost pathetic to trace the puzzlement of New England leaders at the end of the seventeenth century, when the idea of toleration was becoming more and more respectable in European thought. They could hardly understand what was happening in the world, and they could not for a long time be persuaded that they had any reason to be ashamed of their record of so many Quakers whipped, blasphemers punished by the amputation of ears, Antinomians exiled, Anabaptists fined, or witches executed. By all the lights which had prevailed in Europe at the time the Puritans had left, these were achievements to which any government could point with pride. In 1681 a congregation of Anabaptists, who led a stormy and precarious existence for several years in Charlestown, published an attack upon the government of Massachusetts Bay; they justified themselves by appealing to the example of the first settlers, claiming that like themselves the founders had been nonconformists and had fled to New England to establish a refuge for persecuted consciences. When Samuel Willard, minister of the Third Church in Boston, read this, he could hardly believe his eyes; he hastened to assure the authors that they did not know what they were talking about:

> I perceive they are mistaken in the design of our first Planters,
> whose business was not Toleration; but were professed Enemies of it,
> and could leave the World professing they *died no Libertines*. Their
> business was to settle, and (as much as in them lay) secure Religion
> to Posterity, according to that way which they believed was of God.

For the pamphlet in which Willard penned these lines Increase Mather
wrote an approving preface. Forty years later, he and his son Cotton
participated in the ordination of a Baptist minister in Boston, and he
then preached on the need for harmony between differing sects. But
by that time much water had gone under the bridge, the old charter
had been revoked, there was danger that the Church of England
might be made the established church of the colonies, theology had
come to be of less importance in men's minds than morality, the tone
of the eighteenth century was beginning to influence opinion—even
in Boston. Increase was old and weary. Puritanism, in the true sense
of the word, was dead.

Of course, the whole Puritan philosophy of church and state rested
upon the assumption that the word of God was clear and explicit,
that the divines had interpreted it correctly, and that no one who was
not either a knave or a fool could deny their demonstrations. Ergo,
it seemed plain, those who did deny them should be punished for
being obstinate. John Cotton said that offenders should not be disciplined for their wrong opinions, but for persisting in them; he said
that Roger Williams was not turned out of Massachusetts for his conscience, but for sinning against his own conscience. Roger Williams
and John Cotton debated the question of "persecution" through several
hundred pages; after they had finished, I think it is very doubtful
whether Cotton had even begun to see his adversary's point. And still
today it is hard to make clear the exact grounds upon which Roger
Williams became the great apostle of religious liberty. Williams was
not, like Thomas Jefferson, a man to whom theology and divine grace
had become stuff and nonsense; on the contrary he was pious with a
fervor and passion that went beyond most of his contemporaries. So
exalted was his conception of the spiritual life that he could not bear
to have it polluted with earthly considerations. He did not believe
that any man could determine the precise intention of scripture with
such dreadful certainty as the New England clergy claimed to possess. Furthermore, it seemed to him that even if their version were

true, submission to truth itself was worth nothing at all when forced upon men by the sword. Williams evolved from an orthodox Puritan into the champion of religious liberty because he came to see spiritual truth as so rare, so elevated, so supernal a loveliness that it could not be chained to a worldly establishment and a vested interest. He was a libertarian because he contemned the world, and he wanted to separate church and state so that the church would not be contaminated by the state; Thomas Jefferson loved the world and was dubious about the spirit, and he sought to separate church and state so that the state would not be contaminated by the church. But John Cotton believed the state and church were partners in furthering the cause of truth; he knew that the truth was clear, definite, reasonable, and undeniable; he expected all good men to live by it voluntarily, and he was sure that all men who did not do so were obviously bad men. Bad men were criminals, whether their offense was theft or a belief in the "inner light," and they should be punished. Moses and Aaron, the priest and the statesman, were equally the viceregents of God, and the notion that one could contaminate the other was utter insanity.

The two other ideas which we have noted as being derived from the background of the age, rule by fundamental law and social compact, were the special tenets of English Puritanism. For three decades before the settlement of Massachusetts the Puritan party in England had been working hand in glove with the Parliament against the King. The absolutist Stuarts were allied with the bishops, and the Puritan agitator and the Parliamentary leader made common cause against them both. As a result of this combination, the Puritan theorists had taken over the essentials of the Parliamentary conception of society, the contention that the power of the ruler should be exercised in accordance with established fundamental law, and that the government should owe its existence to a compact of the governed. Because these ideas were strategically invaluable in England, they became ingrained in the Puritan consciousness; they were carried to New England and were preached from every pulpit in the land.

The Puritans did not see any conflict between them and their religious intentions. In New England the fundamental law was the Bible. The magistrates were to have full power to rule men for the specific purposes to which the society was dedicated; but they as well as their subordinates were tied to the specific purposes, and could not go beyond the prescribed limits. The Bible was clear and definite on the form of the church, on the code of punishments for crimes, on the general purposes of social existence; its specifications were binding on all, magistrates, ministers, and citizens. Consequently, the Puritans did not find it difficult to conclude that in those matters upon which the Bible left men free to follow their own discretion, the society itself should establish basic rules. The New England leaders and the people frequently disagreed as to what these rules were, or as to how detailed they should be made, but neither side ever doubted that the community must abide by whatever laws had been enacted, either by God or by the state. The government of New England was, as we have said, a dictatorship, but the dictators were not absolute and irresponsible. John Cotton was the clerical spokesman for the Massachusetts rulers, but he stoutly demanded "that all power that is on earth be limited."

The belief that government originated in the consent of the governed was equally congenial to the Puritan creed. The theology is often enough described as deterministic, because it held that men were predestined to heaven or hell; but we are always in danger of forgetting that the life of the Puritan was completely voluntaristic. The natural man was indeed bound in slavery to sin and unable to make exertions toward his own salvation; but the man into whose soul grace had been infused was liberated from that bondage and made free to undertake the responsibilities and obligations of virtue and decency. The holy society was erected upon the belief that the right sort of men could of their own free will and choice carry through the creation and administration of the right sort of community. The churches of New England were made up of "saints," who came into the church because they wanted membership, not because they were born in it, or were forced into it, or joined because of policy and convention. Though every resident was obliged to attend and to pay taxes for the support of the churches, no one became an actual member who did not signify his strong desire to be one. The saints were expected to act positively because they had in them a spirit of God that made them capable of every exertion. No doubt the Puritans maintained that government originated in the consent of the people because that theory was an implement for chastening the absolutism of the Stuarts; but they maintained it also because they did not believe that any society, civil or ecclesiastical, into which men did not enter of themselves was worthy of the name.

Consequently, the social theory of Puritanism, based upon the law of God, was posited also upon the voluntary submission of the citizens.

As men exist in nature, said Thomas Hooker, no one person has any power over another; "there must of necessity be a mutuall ingagement, each of the other, by their free consent, before by any rule of God they have any right or power, or can exercise either, each towards the other." This truth appears, he argues, from all relations among men, that of husband and wife, master and servant; there must be a compact drawn up and sealed between them.

> From *mutuall acts* of consenting and ingaging each of other, there is an impression of *ingagement* results, as a *relative bond*, betwixt the contractours and confederatours, wherein the *formalis ratio*, or *specificall nature* of the covenant lieth, in all the former instances especially *that of* corporations. So that however it is true, the rule bindes such to the duties of their places and relations, yet it is certain, it requires that they should *first freely ingage* themselves in such covenants, and *then* be carefull to fullfill such duties. A man is allowed freely to make choice of his wife, and she of her husband, before they need or should perform the duties of husband and wife one towards another.

The rules and regulations of society, the objectives and the duties, are erected by God; but in a healthy state the citizens must first agree to abide by those regulations, must first create the society by willing consent and active participation.

These ideas, of a uniform church supported by the civil authority, of rule by explicit law, of the derivation of the state from the consent of the people, were transported to New England because they were the stock ideas of the time and place. What the New England Puritans added of their own was the unique fashion in which they combined them into one coherent and rounded theory. The classic expression of this theory is the speech on liberty delivered by John Winthrop to the General Court in 1645. In that year Winthrop was serving as lieutenant governor, and as such was a justice of the peace; a squabble broke out in the town of Hingham over the election of a militia officer; Winthrop intervened, committing one faction for contempt of court when they would not give bond to appear peaceably before the legislature and let the affair be adjudicated. Some of the citizens were enraged, and the lower house of the General Court impeached Winthrop for exceeding his commission and going beyond the basic law of the land. He was tried and acquitted; thereupon he pronounced this magnificent oration, setting before the people the unified theory of the Puritan commonwealth.

As he expounds it, the political doctrine becomes part and parcel of the theological, and the cord that binds all ideas together is the covenant. The New England divines had already refashioned the original theology of Calvinism to bring it more into accord with the disposition of Englishmen, their most important addition being their statement of the relationship between the elect and God in the form of a covenant. As they saw it, when a man received the spirit of God, he availed himself of his liberty to enter a compact with the Deity, promising to abide by God's laws and to fulfill God's will to the best of his ability. In turn God guaranteed him redemption. A regenerate man was thus by definition committed by his own plighted word to God's cause, not only in his personal life and behaviour, but in church affairs and in society. Winthrop argues that individuals, in a natural state, before grace has been given them, are at absolute liberty to do anything they can, to lie, steal, murder; obviously he is certain that natural men, being what they are, will do exactly these things unless prevented. But when men become regenerate they are then at "liberty" to do only what God commands. And God commands certain things for the group as a whole as well as for each individual. Regenerate men, therefore, by the very fact of being regenerate, come together, form churches and a state upon explicit agreements, in which they all promise to live with one another according to the laws and for the purposes of God. Thus the government is brought into being by the act of the people; but the people do not create just any sort of government, but the one kind of government which God has outlined. The governors are elected by the people, but elected into an office which has been established by God. God engenders the society by acting through the people, as in nature He secures His effects by guiding secondary causes; the collective will of regenerate men, bound together by the social compact, projects and continues the will of God into the state. As John Davenport expressed it, "In regular actings of the creature, God is the first Agent; there are not two several and distinct actings, one of God, another of the People: but in one and the same action, God, by the Peoples suffrages, makes such an one Governour, or Magistrate, and not another." So, when men have made a covenant with God they have thereby promised Him, in the very terms of that agreement, to compact among themselves in order to form a holy state in which His discipline will be practiced. As one of the ministers phrased it:

> Where the Lord sets himselfe over a people, he frames them unto a willing and voluntary subjection unto him, that they desire nothing more then to be under his government . . . When the Lord is in Covenant with a people, they follow him not forcedly, but as farre as they are sanctified by grace, they submit willingly to his regiment.

When men have entered these covenants, first with God, then with each other in the church and again in the state, they have thrice committed themselves to the rule of law and the control of authority. Winthrop can thus insist that though the government of Massachusetts is bound by fundamental law, and though it takes its rise from the people, and though the people elect the officials, still the people's liberty in Massachusetts consists in a "liberty to that only which is good, just and honest." By entering the covenant with God, and the covenant with each other, the citizens renounce all natural liberty, surrender the right to seek for anything that they themselves might lust after, and retain only the freedom that "is maintained and exercised in a way of subjection to authority."

The theory furnishes an excellent illustration of the intellectual ideal toward which all Puritan thought aspired; in the realm of government as of nature, the Puritan thinker strove to harmonize the determination of God with the exertion of men, the edicts of revelation with the counsels of reason and experience. On one side, this account exhibits the creation of society as flowing from the promptings and coaction of God; on the other side it attributes the origination to the teachings of nature and necessity. The social compact may be engineered by God, but it is also an eminently reasonable method of bringing a state into being. Delimitation of the ruler's power by basic law may be a divine ordinance to restrain the innate sinfulness of men, but it is also a very natural device to avoid oppression and despotism; the constitution may be promulgated to men from on high, but it is in fact very much the sort which, had they been left to their own devices, they might have contrived in the interests of efficiency and practicality. Men might conceivably have come upon the erection of governments through explicit compacts, in which they incorporated certain inviolable regulations and a guarantee of rights, quite as much by their own intelligence as by divine instruction. As always in Puritan thought, there was no intention to discredit either source, but rather to integrate the divine and the natural, revelation and reason, into a single inspiration. "Power of Civil Rule, by men orderly chosen, is Gods Ordinance," said John Davenport, even if "It is from the Light and Law of Nature," because "the Law of Nature is God's Law." The Puritan state was thus from one point of view purely and simply a "theocracy"; God was the sovereign; His fiats were law and His wishes took precedence over all other considerations; the magistrates and ministers were His viceroys. But from another point of view, the Puritan state was built upon reason and the law of nature; it was set up by the covenant of the people, the scope of its power was determined by the compact, and the magistrates and ministers were the commissioned servants of the people.

As this theory stands on paper it is, like so many edifices erected by the Puritan mind, almost perfect. When it was realized in practice, however, there were at least two difficulties that soon became apparent. For one, not all the people, even in New England, were regenerate; in fact, the provable elect were a minority, probably no more than one fifth of the total population. But this did not dismay the original theorists, for they had never thought that mere numerical majorities proved anything. Consequently, though the social compact furnished the theoretical basis of society in New England, nevertheless it was confined to the special few; the election of officers and the passing of laws was given to those only who could demonstrate their justification and sanctification. The Congregational system, with its membership limited to those who had proved before the church that they possessed the signs of grace, offered a ready machinery for winnowing the wheat from the chaff. Therefore, under the first charter the suffrage in Massachusetts was limited to the church members. In Connecticut the franchise was not officially restrained in this fashion, but other means served as well to keep the electorate pure and orthodox. The "citizens," as they were called, elected delegates to the General Court, chose judges, and passed laws. The others, the "inhabitants," had equality before the law, property rights, police protection; they were taxed no more than the citizens or submitted to no indignities, but they were allowed no voice in the government or in the choice of ministers, and only by the mere force of numbers gained any influence in town meetings.

The restriction of the franchise to church membership seemed to solve the first difficulty confronted by the Puritan theorists. But in time it only brought them face to face with the second and more serious problem: the whole structure of theory which Winthrop outlined in his speech, and which the sermons of Mitchell, Stoughton, and Hubbard reiterated, fell apart the moment the "citizens" were no longer really and ardently holy. Just as soon as the early zeal began to die down, and the distinction between the citizens and the inhabitants became difficult to discern, then the purely naturalistic, rational, practical aspect of the political theory became detached from the theological, began to stand alone and by itself. As the religious inspiration waned, there remained no reason why all the people should not be held partners to the social compact; the idea that God worked His ends through the covenant of the people grew vague and obscure, while the notion that all the people made the covenant for their own reasons and created the state for their own purposes took on more and more definite outlines. As toleration was forced upon the colonies by royal command, or became more estimable as religious passions abated, the necessity for the social bond being considered a commitment of the nation to the will of God disappeared. Instead, men perceived the charms and usefulness of claiming that the compact had been an agreement of the people, not to God's terms, but to their own terms. The divine ordinance and the spirit of God, which were supposed to have presided over the political process, vanished, leaving a government founded on the self-evident truths of the law of nature, brought into being by social compact, instituted not for the glory of God, but to secure men's "inalienable rights" of life, liberty, and the pursuit of happiness. Until Jefferson rewrote the phrase, the three interests which were to be furthered and guaranteed by the government were more candidly summarized as life, liberty—and property.

The sermon of Samuel Willard, delivered in the 1690's, betrays the merest beginnings of the change from the theological version of political principle to the purely rational and naturalistic variant, but the real revolution in the thought was first decisively proclaimed by the Reverend John Wise. He wrote his pamphlet in defence of church government only; he was aroused by a proposal that had been tentatively suggested several years previously among a group of Boston ministers, that the local autonomy of individual congregations had perhaps been carried too far and that possibly a more centralized administration would help check the degeneration of the religious spirit. Wise wrote his vindication of the Congregational system in order to demolish this ecclesiastical proposal, but in working out the philosophy of church government he had to overhaul the fundamentals of all government. The revolution he inaugurated in the thinking of New England consisted in the very organization of his book; where the early defenders of the church system discussed the Biblical and rational arguments together, or forced them to coalesce into one argument, Wise deliberately separated them into two distinct and independent chapters. He compressed into the first section of his book a recital of all the passages of scripture that had been held to substantiate the Congregational system, and then hurried on to the argument from unaided natural wisdom. The radicalism of his pamphlet is compressed into one sentence, into his suggestion that the scheme of government might be said to have originated with nature and reason, and only subsequently to have "obtained the Royal Approbation." Where the early writers had maintained that government springs from the action of God upon the reason, Wise separates divine commands and the dictates of reason into independent sources, and establishes a direct line of communication with God through the natural reason, without any real necessity for consulting scripture. Instead of the unity of early Puritan theory, this account is actually out-and-out rationalism, and the function of the Bible is reduced to supplying a secondary confirmation of the reasonable. From Wise to the philosophy of the Declaration of Independence is a clear and inevitable progress. Barnard and Mayhew mark further steps in that development, and with Mayhew the right of revolution, the right to resist the government when it oversteps the limits established by the social compact and the fundamental law, becomes the most important doctrine in the theory. With Jonathan Mayhew the separation of God's will from man's is complete; or rather, with him, the divine will has been made over into the image of the human. The purposes of society are no longer the deity's, but the subject's; the advantages to be derived from corporate existence are no longer salvation, but the well-being of the citizen. The power of the Puritan God, and of the English King, is bound by the terms of this compact and by the basic law; we are by now certain that God will respect the law we have agreed upon, but as for the King—if he impose a tax on tea to which we do not ourselves consent, and if we thereupon resist him, "even to the dethroning him," we are not criminals, but have only taken "a reasonable way" of vindicating our natural rights.

8. "PREPARATION FOR SALVATION" IN SEVENTEENTH-CENTURY NEW ENGLAND*

by Perry Miller

English Puritans migrating to America brought with them an elaborate theology and social theory, the result of efforts by several generations of English Protestants to understand anew God's design and to remodel beliefs and institutions in accordance with His commands. Massachusetts and Connecticut offered Puritans their best hope to found a new world, unencumbered by inherited error which seemed entrenched in Europe. Yet once Calvinists were free of English authority and were busy erecting and sustaining their Bible Commonwealth, they quickly discovered that the conquest of power, even in a region as isolated as New England, forced them subtly to remold their doctrines in order to make them more appropriate for the experiences of the wilderness. In the following essay, Perry Miller explores how Calvinists, committed to a belief in divine determinism, nonetheless strove ingeniously to find some arena for man's will, not only to buttress the faith but also to strengthen the community's ability to command moral behavior from the populace.

---

* *Journal of the History of Ideas*, vol. 3 (1943), 253–286. Footnotes have been omitted except where they are necessary for an understanding of the text.

For all their theological ingenuity, New England Calvinists could not modify predestinarian Calvinism without undermining the foundations of the faith. In doing so they were Americanizing religious belief. Whatever circumstances in England had made the first settlers Calvinists, their children, born in America, did not experience them. The terms of their lives and the direction of their aspirations were defined, not by the covenant with God, but by the prospects of settling a new land. For both generations the Puritan faith sanctioned hard work and perseverance, and it enjoined them to pursue their callings energetically; but where the first generation had subordinated worldly functions to spiritual ambitions, not without a struggle, their descendants found this increasingly difficult. Their experiences in the New World taught them that while on earth men were not prisoners of some prearranged social fate but possessed free will, the ability to advance their worldly fortunes. Departures from the original mission of the first settlers generated tension and guilt because, even though later generations no longer entirely believed in the ancient faith, they could not simply abandon it or accept themselves as renegades. Instead, men sought ways of relieving their anxiety and purging their guilt to gain the peace and strength needed to complete tomorrow's tasks on the wharves, oceans, and fields, tasks which increasingly occupied their minds and absorbed their energies.

For further reading: Perry Miller, *Errand into the Wilderness* (1956); *The New England Mind: The Seventeenth Century* (1939); "Declension in a Bible Commonwealth," *Proceedings, American Antiquarian Society*, vol. 51 (1941), 37–94; *From Colony to Province* (1953); Michael Walzer, *The Revolution of the Saints* (1965); Edmund Morgan, *The Puritan Dilemma* (1958); *Visible Saints* (1963); Samuel Eliot Morison, *The Intellectual Life of Colonial New England* (1956); H. W. Schneider, *The Puritan Mind* (1930).

In the second half of the seventeenth century the clerical and political leaders of the Puritan colonies in New England became convinced that their societies were steadily degenerating. From about 1650 on, as the founders were laid to rest and the second generation attempted to take up the work, it seemed to every pious observer that the spirit of the fathers was dying with them. In sermon after sermon, especially those delivered on formal and public occasions, to the General Courts on annual election days or to particular congregations on the days appointed for public fasts, the ministers traced the accelerating "declension," and repeatedly called upon the people to repent their sins and reform their ways lest the God who had blessed their fathers should now wreak a terrible vengeance upon them. Afflictions and disasters, such as plagues, crop-failures or Indian wars, were exhibited as the preliminary manifestations of His wrath, to be followed by still more terrible judgments if the reform were not forthcoming. In 1679 the ministers met at Boston in a formal Synod, drew up a systematic survey of the evils, and launched an even more vigorous campaign to incite the people to recovery.

Whether the colonies had in fact so woefully fallen off need not concern us. The point is that the ministers, and in all probability most of the people, believed that the case was desperate, and the staggering tabulation of sins, crimes, and offenses published by the Synod in 1679 furnished sufficient documentation. What does concern us is that the leaders of these Calvinist communities, believing that they were faced with destruction, called upon their people to reform, although not a man among them yet entertained any serious doubts about the doctrine of divine determinism. They maintained the absolute sovereignty of God and the utter depravity of man; they held that whatever came to pass in this world was ordained by providence, and they attributed the success of the founders not to human abilities or to physical opportunities, but solely to God, who had furnished the abilities and brought about the opportunities by His providential care. Therefore the question was bound to present itself to divines and statesmen of the second generation, could any merely human effort arrest the moral decline? Was not it a fact in the irresistible plan of God, just as the triumph of the first generation had been decreed in Heaven? If God was withholding His grace, could the people be expected to become saints, and if He was depriving them even of "restraining grace" could they possibly avoid yielding to every temptation? And if God, even while rendering them powerless to resist, was at the same time augmenting the temptations, what point could there be in summoning the society to repent?

Any other nation, having such absolute control over all the agencies for molding public opinion, might have gone directly to work. But a Puritan state, anxious though it was to excite the populace, could not merely preach repentance and expect the mass of men to obey. Before it could call upon them to reform, it had first to prove that there were legitimate provisions in the accepted theory of the community for assuming that they could if they would. Was there any authorization in the Word of God—as it had been definitively expounded by the founders—for summoning the populace to this work? For the Puritan, this was the all-important question. If he could not prove that the founders had bequeathed him a principle to serve in the emergency, he could not invent one of himself, for that would be to commit the horrid crime of "innovation."

Unfortunately the leaders in the second half of the century were aware that in one fundamental respect their situation differed from anything the founders had foreseen. John Winthrop had declared that the societies of New England were in a direct covenant relationship with Jehovah, exactly as the chosen people of the Old Testament had been; they had agreed with Him to abide by the rules of righteousness, to practice the true polity, to dedicate themselves to doing His will on earth. If they lived up to their promise, He would reward them with material prosperity; if they faltered, He would chastise them with physical affliction until they reformed. When he proclaimed this national covenant, Winthrop had not been troubled by the fact that a majority of the settlers were presumably not regenerated. Only one-fifth of the adult population could give such evidence of their sanctification as would admit them to the covenant of a particular church, but Calvinist theory did not prevent the remaining four-fifths, even though unnumbered among the visible saints, from sharing in the covenant of the nation or from acting their part in its fulfillment. According to the doctrine of all Reformed communities, there existed a realm of conduct which was within the competence of a merely "natural" ability, wherein unregenerate men could be expected to behave one way rather than another because of ordinary pressures, the law, the police, moral persuasion or the promptings of their conscience. Whether they were saints or not, all men could be required to furnish the state a purely "external" obedience, to abstain from murder or theft, to take no usury and to pay their debts. A holy state, received into a covenant with God, differed from an uncovenanted one not because all its citizens were saints but because therein saints could determine and administer the laws and the natural inhabitants be either incited or compelled to obey. In Massachusetts and Connecticut these conditions were fulfilled. The mass of the planters were earnest beings who, by voluntarily migrating, demonstrated that they were eager to do whatever was within the command of their "natural ability." Furthermore, the leadership was a monopoly of certified saints, who were enabled through grace not only to practice good laws but to enforce obedience upon the body politic. Thus the terms of the national covenant could be complied with, though but a small minority were capable of entering the personal Covenant of Grace. The national covenant bound men only to "external" righteousness, without presuming the essential sanctity of every individual. In his great oration of 1645 Winthrop explained that all those who enter a civil society—he obviously meant both the godly and the ungodly—no longer have the right to exercise their impulses to evil, but are now committed, by their own assent, to obeying the authority which is set over them for their own good, and to doing only that which is inherently good, just, and honest. Hence he could summon all inhabitants, church members or not, to a public repentance. The national covenant obliged the community only to an outward rectitude, and required that God punish all violations with a physical affliction, but it also promised that an outward reformation would procure an immediate deliverance. No doubt God would never consent to take a society into such a national covenant which did not contain some men sanctified by the Spirit, inwardly as well as externally, but a core of them was adequate as long as they were in control.

For the founders there did exist a real distinction between the realms of nature and of the Spirit, and such actions as required no supernatural assistance were altogether sufficient to ensure the public welfare. The original saints could earn their liberation from all social distresses by carrying their unconverted neighbors to at least a constrained compliance with the good, just, and honest—which would fully satisfy the public justice of God. But thirty or forty years later the ministers had built up the picture of a universal depravity, and it seemed clear that the society was no longer responding to providential corrections, let alone to the laws against usury and excessive apparel. They put the blame upon all alike, and called for action from all. One of their principal complaints was the infrequency of sound conversions, and the purely numerical consideration, which had been of no consequence to John Winthrop, thus became tremendously important. It was now absolutely imperative that the vast number of non-members, who had supposedly committed themselves to the extent of their natural ability (or been committed by their fathers), who were regularly convened on the days of humiliation and urged to repent, be assured that they could do something. The children of the saints were troubled about their own calling and election, which to many was not so "sure" as that of their fathers had been; a large number were members by only a "Half-Way" covenant which left their inward condition in some perplexity, and they also had to be convinced, whether they were truly regenerate or not, that they could achieve at least the external obedience. Certainly the mass could no longer be carried or driven by the saints, for the saints were not equal to the task. Had it been merely a matter of recalling approved Christians from temporary lapses, the clergy would have had clear sailing, but in 1679 they had to face the fact, by their own admissions, that the whole body politic was in a bad way, and that a reform which touched only a segment would not be enough. In order to effect a national recovery, the whole nation had to be recovered; the declension was a social phenomenon, and it seemed to bring social consequences, plagues, wars, and famines. Hence these determinists were the more obliged to find some method for appealing to natural men, for persuading the unregenerate that they could achieve enough sanctity to preserve the society, though they might never be able to save their souls. The whole people, citizens and inhabitants, church members and non-members, recorded their vow to repent and reform on the many days of humiliation, but their promise would remain an empty gesture unless they could be convinced that they did have the power to keep it without first having to be numbered among the spiritually elect.

It might seem, when the leaders returned to first principles and studied the works of their fathers, that they were caught in the inexorable logic of Calvin. All things in their world were ordained by God, and if He decreed that a people were to decline, no human hand could fend off the appointed outcome. So the founders had conceived the world. They had, it is true, carved out a small island of liberty in the sea of determinism, which was the Covenant of Grace, but even that Covenant was a very slight curtailment of God's awful despotism. The great English theologians from whom New England learned the "federal" doctrine had delivered themselves without equivocation. William Perkins, for instance, condemned all "Pelagians" who would seek the cause of predestination in men, as if God ordained them only after He foresaw which would receive or reject the offer of salvation. The decrees have no cause beyond God's arbitrary pleasure, and Perkins dismissed as "subtile deuices" all attempts to mitigate this "hard sentence." William Ames worked out more carefully the rationality of the Covenant, but he always insisted upon the irrationality of a transcendent might behind it, and agreed that no foreknowledge of God should ever be presupposed to His determinations. John Preston would argue that according to the logic of the Covenant men were justly condemned for not doing what they could do, but he would also declare, "God hath kept it in his power to draw whom he will, to sanctifie whome he will," and would expound the natural freedom of men with this qualification, "yet it is not in any mans power to beleeve, to repent effectually." Hence John Ball's *A Treatise of the Covenant of Grace*, published in 1645, in some respects the most daring excursion in the whole literature, could not avoid the embarrassing question: "To what end doe the promises and threatenings [of the Covenant] tend . . . if God doe worke all things by his effectual power in them that believe?" Ball could not answer his own question, and took refuge in the conventional distinction between God's revealed and hidden will. Openly He demands obedience of all men, but secretly He gives the ability only to the few already elected: "That is, he invites many in the Ministry of his Word, and externall administration of the Covenant, whom he doth not inwardly instruct and draw." If you concluded, therefore, that the offer of the Covenant was a "giftelesse gift," Ball could reply only that you were an unthankful servant and perverse being. But the ministers of New England by 1679 had to deal with a race of the unthankful and perverse.

The founders faithfully echoed such teachers. Cotton pointed out that God could pour His grace upon the most abominable sinners, so that "If he take pleasure to breathe in a man, there is nothing can hinder him, it will blow upon the most noysome dunghill in any place, and be never a whit the more defiled." Logic compelled him to suggest that the best way to become a saint might be "to have run a lewd course of life," since a Calvinist God would then be the more challenged to show His power, but such reflections were sadly out of order in 1679. Thomas Hooker seemed to be no more helpful: man is darkness and God is light, he said, and darkness is unalterably opposed to light; "Thou canst resist a Saviour, but not entertaine him, doe what thou canst."

In fact, the ministers, who in the *Report* of the Synod bade all men reform, also renewed their allegiance to the *Westminster Confession,* which explicitly stated that "God from all eternity did by the most wise and holy Counsel of his own Will, freely and unchangeably ordaine whatsoever comes to pass," and further declared that until grace comes the natural spirit must be "passive" and utterly incapable of moral action. "A natural man being altogether averse from that good, and dead in sin, is not able by his own strength to convert himself, or to prepare himself thereunto." With what right, therefore, could the divines rally depraved generations to repent in the name of the fathers, who had taught that a people to whom God chooses not to give His grace are impotent? If men may sit all their lives under the most clear dispensations of the Gospel and yet remain impenitent—Samuel Willard testified at the end of the century, "woful experience tell[s] us that there are a great many that do so"—with what face could the ministers preach reformation? What inducement could they offer the average man or what hope of success could they hold out?

It was at this point that the second and third generations began to perceive the advantages in an idea which the founders themselves had devised, which they had heroically vindicated against all opposition and bequeathed to their children as an indispensable part of New England orthodoxy. Though Calvinism pictured man as lifeless clay in the potter's hand, and the *Westminster Confession* asserted that the natural man could not convert himself or even "prepare himself thereunto," the New Englanders had been able to maintain that there did exist a state of "preparation for salvation." We should note at once that the seeds of this difficult and dangerous idea are to be found in the writers whom the New Englanders studied even before the migration. Perkins, Preston, and Ames were Calvinists, and undoubtedly had no intention of propounding any belief at variance with the accepted creed, but they were also the formulators of the Covenant or "federal" version of Calvinism, in which they managed to present Jehovah as consenting to deal with sinners according to the terms of a covenant. As soon as the relationship of God to man was conceived in this fashion, the corollary became obvious that the terms of a covenant may be known in advance. Men must still receive grace, which is dispensed arbitrarily according to sovereign decrees, but the very fact that God does propose terms means that there may be a moment in time between absolute depravity and the beginning of conversion in which the transaction is proposed. Men may not be able to do anything until they are regenerated, but until then they can listen and meditate. Grace is a covenant, and the essence of a covenant, these theologians never wearied of explaining, is an agreement between two agents, both of whom must know the conditions. If election be a flash of lightning that may strike at any moment, men cannot place themselves in its path, nor cultivate any anticipatory attitudes, but when it comes as a chance to enter a contract, they must first of all learn what is to be contracted. Though God gives His son freely, Preston said, "yet except we take him, that gift is no gift; therefore there must be a taking on our part." A man must have his quill sharpened for the signature and the wax warmed for his seal. God has graciously put aside His overwhelming might in order to treat with men in a rational negotiation, "that we might know what to expect from God, and upon what termes." If we may know the terms, we may be encouraged, in advance of our conversions, even while we possess nothing more than our "natural gifts," to commence a course of obedience. Once regeneration was conceived not as a sudden prostration but as a gradual process commencing with an initial stage of negotiation, it became possible, even probable, that men should undergo a preliminary state of "preparation" before they actually were called.

The English formulators were concerned chiefly to establish the fact that regeneration is a process in time, capable of being analyzed into temporal units. They concentrated attention not so much on the crisis of conversion but on the moment just preceding it, when the Covenant of Grace was being tendered to a sinner but was not yet taken up. In Perkins the idea of preparation first appeared as little more than a conventional instruction to preachers that they should spare no pains with their people: "This preparation is to bee made partly by disputing or reasoning with them, that thou mayest thorowly discerne their manners and disposition, and partly by reproving in them some notorious sinne, that being pricked in heart and terrified, they may become teachable." Among his successors the idea took on increased dimensions. We can trace through their works an expanding realization that previous to the signing of a covenant there must be a period in which man is instructed and solicited, that before a simple regeneration he may be careless but before a covenant he must learn to stipulate. The federalists denounced Arminianism because they said that no amount of good works merited any consideration from God, but at the same time they taught sinners provisions for their possible conversion. Preston, for example, said that the worst of sinners may be called without any antecedent humbling of the heart, just as a sick man does not need a sense of sickness in order to be cured, but nevertheless "if he be not sicke, and have a sense of it, he will not come to the Physitian." Coming to the physician will not in itself work a cure, but it may be "a preparative sorrow." Though a reprobate may have the sense and yet never be saved, the elect are seldom taken into the Covenant of Grace until after they too have had it. In general the evidence indicates that these theologians had succeeded, even before 1630, in investing the word "preparation" with a distinct connotation, making it mean a period in time during which men could acquire a "sense" which was not yet an actual conversion but which might be a forerunner of it, an experience that all men might have, since it was not limited merely to the elect, which could be construed as a hopeful augury of ultimate success and could be demanded of all men, whereas an authentic work of the Spirit would have to wait upon the disposition of God.

To establish this thesis the covenant theologians undertook a labor which won them fame throughout Protestant Europe and which was assiduously carried on by their New England disciples, a subtle analysis of the temporal process of regeneration, so that they were able to give elaborate descriptions of every step, beginning with the most minute diagnosis of the dawning of a premonition. Yet all this while, their loyalty to the basic Protestant doctrine of salvation by faith required them to insist that, no matter how slight this first movement might be, it should be attributed to no effort of man but solely to the grace of God. Hence their conception of a state of preparation, as something that came before even the most infinitesimal rumble of faith, was exceedingly welcome. Preparation did not need to be called a saving act of the human will; it could be set forth as no meritorious work in any Arminian sense, not even as part of faith at all, but as a mere inclination to accept faith, should faith ever come. This much a corrupt man might do, for it was really no motion of his soul; it was no lifting of himself by his own bootstraps, but simply an attitude of expectancy. Had the mechanism of regeneration still been phrased exclusively in the language of Calvin, as a forcible seizure, a holy rape of the surprised will, there would have been no place for any period of preparation, which would have been conceivable only as the first moment of an effectual calling. But when regeneration was understood to be the offer and acceptance of a covenant, even though the power to accept it must come from God, men could make themselves ready to entertain it, since they could know in advance what form it would assume and what response it would entail. Though God might do as He pleased, it was noted that normally those who most strove to prepare themselves turned out to be those whom He shortly took into the Covenant of Grace.

So far as the somewhat obscure passages from the early writers can now be made out, they do not exhibit any interest in the social implications of the idea. These writers still assumed the distinction between the realms of nature and of grace; at this point they were concerned with salvation, not with politics. The conduct of society, the observance of the moral law in domestic and business affairs, was to them a matter of regulation and compulsion. Good laws were to be enforced, and even the most drastic forms of Calvinism always assumed that men had the physical power to obey whatever laws the state imposed. Such actions had nothing to do with salvation, and were not a part of preparation. Of course a saint would endeavor to be a good citizen, but the performance of his civic duties did not earn his redemption. The idea of preparation, as formulated by Perkins, Preston, and Ames, met a spiritual need; it encouraged men to seek holiness in the midst of a determined universe. But almost as soon as the idea was propounded, it began to reveal that it did in fact have social as well as spiritual consequences, for while a man was undergoing a work of preparation in the hope that it might be followed by a conversion, he would be making every effort, out of his own volition, to perfect his external behavior. He would have a positive incentive to righteous conduct, although he could not yet be said to be a true saint or even to have a hope of salvation. But though he might finally go to Hell, if while he lived in this world he prepared himself, he would *ipso facto* fulfill the terms of the national covenant. Thus the rapid development of the idea, first among the theologians of English Puritanism and then among the leaders of New England, is a symptom of the change that came over the Puritan movement as it became concerned more with the conquest of power than with the pursuit of holiness. Sixteenth-century Puritans were driven by one consideration above all others, the salvation of their souls, and they set out to cleanse the Church as a proof of their sainthood, but in the seventeenth century Puritans became organized into a political party and thereupon had to take more thought for the strategy of winning a political victory. The problem of determinism never bothered men who were already convinced of their election, for they were free to do God's will; but when saints banded together to capture the English state, or after they had captured the new states in New England, they had to find more effective means of getting all the people, the mass of the unregenerate whom they were now to govern, started on the road they had travelled in the sheer exuberance of zeal. In the practical terms of social regulation, their problem now was to excite the people to moral action. Almost from the beginning the leaders perceived that to depend merely upon the sanctions of the law, upon the coercion of natural abilities, was not enough. Yet according to Calvinist doctrine, if men were ever to perform anything beyond the limits of nature, they had to be supplied with grace. Hence for the sake of the social welfare, as much as for the welfare of particular souls, it became necessary that men be made gracious. Yet grace was dispensed only by God, according to the secret pleasure of His will, and men could not be converted by any amount of external compulsion. But preparation was not a supernatural work. All men could achieve it, and all men therefore could be called upon to prepare for grace, and thereby to exert themselves in precisely such a course of moral conduct as was required of all the society by the national covenant.

We should not be surprised that Thomas Hooker, the virtual dictator of Connecticut and one of the most socially minded among the early ministers, should be also the greatest analyst of souls, the most exquisite diagnostician of the phases of regeneration, and above all the most explicit exponent of the doctrine of preparation. Thomas Shepard and Peter Bulkeley followed his lead. All three agreed that preparation was not a meritorious work; they took infinite precautions lest their doctrine be construed in any Catholic or Arminian sense. Hooker would explain that no natural action can prepare for supernatural grace, and that the effectual operation of the Word must never be thought to depend upon anything that a man may do by himself, "not upon any preparation which was done, nor any performances . . . but meerly upon the power and good pleasure of the Lord." After justification the will has acquired a new power, "whereby it is able to set forth it selfe into any holy action," but in the first stage it is merely wrought upon, "and I am a patient and doe onely endure it: but I have not any spirituall power to doe any thing of myself." Bulkeley put it in the language of the federal theology: after God has taken us into a covenant with Him, He requires a positive performance of its terms, but "first the Lord doth dispose us and fit us to a walking in Covenant with him," and in these hours we must remain passive. In fact Hooker and his friends were so eager to prove their orthodoxy that they would indulge in statements as extreme as any to be found in the history of New England, and consequently their real position had been generally misrepresented. Since the sinner must be at first "meerly patient," said Hooker, God is at liberty to give or to deny grace to whom He pleases, and may justly refuse it to the most prayerful and conscientious, *"for it is not in him that wils and runs, but in God that shews mercy."* By the same token God may bestow it "upon such who neither prize nor profit at al they have." The Puritan God was a capricious Jehovah whose favor did not follow upon any good work of man—it "hangs not upon that hinge."

We may very well ask what Hooker and his group could conceivably accomplish when they prefaced the doctrine of preparation by such qualifications. To appreciate the significance of their work we must remember that had they definitely broken with the Calvinist system, had they openly advocated the natural freedom of men to perform deeds that would secure salvation, they would have been branded as Arminians. So Hooker was extremely careful to insist upon the natural impotence of the unregenerate. He was not endeavoring to preach even the possibility that holy actions might be performed by natural men, but he was endeavoring to mark off a number of chronological phases in the sequence of regeneration and then to argue that the first might be undergone by some who ultimately did not continue through the others, who finally proved to be reprobates. The important point was to establish the factual existence of this probationary period, to demonstrate that regeneration was not a precipitate or instantaneous transformation and that the first degree did not always or necessarily lead to the second. There is an "order" in God's proceedings, Hooker said: first He takes away the resistance of the soul by an irresistible operation, whereupon the soul "comes to be in the next passive power" and is disposed to a spiritual work—*"vult moveri."* In his preface to Rogers' *Doctrine of Faith,* a handbook much prized among the people, Hooker called attention to a passage wherein Rogers wrote that we cannot tell exactly when faith is born, whether after a man has fully apprehended Christ or when he first hungers for Him; this, Hooker remarked, ought to settle all disputes about preparation, for all should agree that in the first stage "there is as it were the spawne of Faith, not yet brought to full perfection." But this first conviction need not be regarded as a "fruit" of faith, only as a preliminary negotiation. Of course such beginnings must be initiated by the Lord—"I have no power of my selfe, but onely receive it from the Lord"; when the will is first turned toward God, it is "not onely the bare power and faculty of the naturall will" at work, but that will turned by God's efficiency, yet at this point God is still acting from the outside, as when He moves any object in nature, not from within as He does after He has filled the heart with His Spirit. Hence there is a space between depravity and sanctity, a hiatus during which the human will is being influenced but is not yet transformed, a state which Hooker characteristically illustrated in a metaphor, comparing it to the moment when a clock that was running out of order is stopped but not yet repaired. At that moment, "the clocke is a patient, and the workman doth all," yet whenever the workman is the Holy Ghost and "where ever it is soundly wrought," the operation "will in the end be faith and grace." Hooker's reputation among Puritans was great because he was the expert chronometer of regeneration, offering the most acute discriminations of preparation, vocation, justification, adoption, and sanctification, but his most impressive thought was devoted to the first action in the series. Through this doctrine he did more than any other to mold the New England mind.

However, his teachings were not universally accepted by all Puritans. They were opposed even by some of the federalists, who saw in them, despite Hooker's elaborate safeguards, a sophistical form of Arminianism. Pemble, for example, without mentioning Hooker by name, attacked his doctrines in the *Vindiciae Gratiae,* declaring that such actions as Hooker identified with preparation could not be encompassed by the unconverted. "They are not antecedents, but consequents and parts of true conversion," whereas any preparative actions produced merely by human efforts could be "no efficient causes to produce grace of conversion." Giles Firmin attacked both Hooker and Shepard specifically, on the ground that their doctrine caused seekers after God much unnecessary discouragement since it made them distrust the first acting of the Spirit for fear it might prove no more than an abortive preparation. They demanded more of men than God required and called upon them not merely to repent but to go beyond repentance, whereas according to Firmin the battle was won just as soon as men were able to lament their sins.

The majority of New England divines followed Hooker, but there was one ominous exception. John Cotton generally figures as the chief "theocrat" of Massachusetts and is popularly remembered as the dictator of its intellect, yet in fact he differed widely from his colleagues, and his dissent came near to causing his ruin. On this fundamental point Hooker's influence eclipsed Cotton's, and his share in the formation of American Puritanism is correspondingly the larger. The full story of the opposition is difficult to reconstruct, because the authorities made every effort to play it down; nevertheless, the noise of their disagreement resounded through the Calvinist world. Enemies of the New England Way were quick to make the most of it, the Presbyterian Baillie, for instance, scoring a blow when he sneered that Winthrop and Welde, in their narrative of the Antinomian episode, did all they could "to save Mr. *Cottons* credit," yet they could not so falsify the story but what "they let the truth of Mr. *Cottons* Seduction fall from their Pens." The halting sentences in which Cotton endeavored to reply do more to confirm our suspicions of a difference than to persuade us of the asserted agreement, nor do we need to search very far into his writings to find the theological basis for his divergence.

Cotton's position was simplicity itself. Though he was a "federalist," he was first of all the man who sweetened his mouth every night with a morsel of *The Institutes*. He was persuaded that between the natural and the regenerate man lay a gulf so immense that only divine grace could bridge it. If a man performs a single action appropriate to the elect, he has then and there become one of them. There can be no halfway conversion; a man is either one or the other, and those who once receive grace will infallibly persevere through all short-comings to an ultimate glorification. Therefore what Hooker and Shepard called preparation was for Cotton simply the impact of grace, and the prepared were already saints. "A man is as passive in his Regeneration, as in his first generation." If we are "fitted" for good deeds, the first motion must be a work solely of God, who alone can fit us, and once He gives the smallest competence, He has thereby signified His irrevocable favor. Hence, as Cotton saw it, the first motion no less than the last is "true spirituall Union between the Lord & our souls"; define it as closely as possible, it is still from God. The natural heart is totally "drowsie," and "for our first union, there are no steps unto the Altar." Can a blind man prepare himself to see? Hooker's doctrine creates a false sense of security, for it tells men that preparation consists in a disposition to wait upon Christ, and those who have brought themselves by their own efforts to such a seeming surrender thereupon give over striving. The supreme refinement of deceptive faith has always been a self-induced determination to wait upon Christ: "there is no promise of life made to those that wait & seek in their own strength, who being driven to it, have taken it up by their own *resolutions.*" Should we try to reassure ourselves by reflecting that if we cannot work we can believe, or that if we cannot believe we can wait until we come to believe, "here is still the old roote of *Adam* left alive in us, whereby men seeke to establish their owne righteousnesse." There can be no safe building upon such resolves, for they are produced by mechanical causes, even when induced by the persuasive eloquence of the pastor at Hartford.

Cotton was the better Calvinist, and he knew it: not only would he plead the authority of federalists like Pemble in rejecting preparation, he would also cry out, "Let *Calvin* answer for me." Nevertheless Hooker triumphed in New England, for the good and sufficient reason that Cotton's doctrine fathered the awful heresy of Antinomianism. Modern historians often find the technicalities of this dispute so abstruse as to lead them comfortably to conclude that it was meaningless, but its social consequences became immediately apparent when Mrs. Hutchinson declared that she had come to New England "but for Mr. Cotton's sake" and added, "As for Mr. Hooker . . . she said she liked not his spirit." Mr. Hooker, it will be remembered, aided by Shepard and Bulkeley, was the principal prosecutor in her trial before the Synod, and did not check the expression of his satisfaction upon her expulsion.

Anne Hutchinson took her stand upon Cotton's doctrine of a radical distinction between regeneration and unregenerateness, asserting that in no sense whatsoever could works have anything to do with justification, that they could not even be offered as "evidence," and that a true saint might consistently live in any amount of sin. She wiped out all Hooker's fine-spun discriminations between a state of preparation and a state of adoption; she presented the clear-cut alternatives of an absolute union with Christ or an utter disseverance. Her followers regarded preparation as the most offensive among the tenets of the New England clergy, and cited Hooker and Shepard as proof positive that the ministers were preaching a "covenant of works." If Hooker would allow that a man could do something, anything, before he was redeemed, which could also be done by those who eventually went to perdition, what was this but Popery? The Antinomians emphatically declared that the sinner "for his part, must see nothing in himselfe, have nothing, doe nothing, only he is to stand still and waite for Christ to doe all for him." They disapproved any preaching of the "law," any pressing of duties upon the unconverted, any calling them to faith and prayer; to exhort even the elect to fulfill their obligations was superfluous, not because saints would be perfect but because those who are concerned about their conduct are still under the obsolete covenant of the law. To them it seemed that Hooker, though he professed the impotence of nature, set men to work of themselves and promised the unconverted that somehow they might take the first step toward grace if only they would try; therefore, as Anne Hutchinson saw it, the people were misled into thinking themselves justified no further than they could perceive themselves enabled to perform good works, although the essence of Protestantism was the assurance of justification through the free promise of forgiveness. Election did not admit of degrees proportioned to the extent of the endeavor, nor could any amount of sin reverse the divine decree; justification was absolute and final, in and by itself.

Anne Hutchinson announced that she had learned her doctrine from Cotton, and throughout her ordeal wrapped herself in the mantle of his authority, to the consternation of the authorities. Even after the Antinomians were exiled, and Cotton had utterly renounced them, they would not give him up. In the heat of the conflict the elders brought Cotton to a conference, "drew out sixteen points, and gave them to him, entreating him to deliver his judgment directly in them." Winthrop remarks that many copies of his reply "were dispersed about"; seven years later, one Francis Cornwell published in England what purported to be an authentic version, with a dedication to Sir Harry Vane—for that erstwhile friend of Mrs. Hutchinson was now a power in the land. The book was so popular that two more editions appeared in 1646 and a fourth in 1647, and when copies were brought to Boston there must have been anguish in the parsonage of the First Church. Winthrop says that at the conference Cotton cleared some doubts, "but in some things he gave not satisfaction"; in Cornwell's version he appears to have given none at all. The issue in 1637, says the editor, came down to this: the renegade clergy "would not believe themselves justified, no further than they could see themselves work; making their Markes, Signes, and Quallifications, the causes of their Justification," whereas the Antinomians upheld the true Protestant position that the evidence of justification is to be discerned "onely by Faith in the Free Promise." Cornwell exhibited Cotton adhering to the Antinomian sense. Being

168

asked whether there are any conditions in the soul before faith "of dependance unto which, such promises are made," he replied roundly, no: "To works of creation there needeth no preparation; the almighty power of God calleth them to be his people, that were not his people." In other answers, still according to Cornwell, Cotton asserted that to evidence one's justification by his sanctification is Popery, that "Such a Faith as a practicall Sillogisme can make, is not a Faith wrought by the Lords Almighty power," that no conviction wrought by natural means, even by evangelical preaching, should be confounded with a true work of faith, for "the Word without the Almighty power of the Spirit is but a dead Letter," that God does not give His grace upon condition of our becoming prepared, because "it is not his good pleasure to give us our first comfort . . . from our owne righteousnesse." In these words the Antinomians were content that their cause be stated; they then appealed to the judgment of Protestantism whether the divines in New England, following the way of Hooker and of preparation, had not betrayed the Bible Commonwealth.

Anne Hutchinson said that but one minister besides Cotton remained faithful, her brother-in-law, John Wheelwright, who came to grief when, on the fast-day appointed for a public lamentation over the controversy, he delivered a sermon which the authorities found "incendiary." The text of that discourse does not immediately suggest, to an age insensitive to the fine shading of theological dispute, exactly wherein it was subversive, but if it be read in the light of the times, in view of the then agitated state of the question of preparation, its inflammable substance becomes all too evident. Wheelwright later repudiated Mrs. Hutchinson, or at least the errors charged upon her; yet like Cotton he opposed the doctrine of preparation and therefore by implication accused his colleagues of apostasy. "To preach the Gospell," he declared, "is to preach Christ . . . & nothing but Christ . . . so that neither before our conversion nor after, we are able to put forth one act of true saving spirituall wisdome, but we must haue it put forth from the Lord Jesus Christ, wth whom we are made one." Hooker, Shepard, and Bulkeley were bending all their ingenuity to tabulating the successive periods of conversion, but Wheelwright flatly announced that when the Lord converts a soul, He "revealeth not to him worke, & from that worke, carieth him to Christ, but there is nothing revealed but Christ, when Christ is lifted vp, he draweth all to him, that belongeth to the election of grace." If men think they are on the highway to salvation after they have traversed the first mile but are not yet united to Christ, "they are saued wthout the Gospell." "No, no," he exclaimed, "this is a covenant of works." If so, then the ministers of New England were not Protestants, and the friends of Wheelwright might warrantably conclude that Christians should refuse them a hearing, that they might take even more violent measures against them.

Therefore Wheelwright was banished, but John Cotton was not. There were many reasons why the authorities were unwilling to send away their most renowned scholar, but one is forced to suspect that he owed his preservation to the fact that he was still more reluctant to go. Wheelwright would disown the extravagances of the Antinomians, but he would not compromise on preparation; Cotton bent before the storm and saved his standing in the holy commonwealth at the expense of his consistency. Perhaps this statement is too severe, for in works presumably written after 1638 Cotton still stressed the strictly Protestant version of the Covenant of Grace, which, he said in a book published five years after his death, "is not of our will, but of the Lords, that takes away our strong heart, and gives us a soft heart before any preparation." Nevertheless, it is clear that Cotton learned at least a degree of caution from his unhappy experience, and his subsequent references inevitably suggest that he so moderated his opinions as to make himself no longer able to speak frankly. The account which he gave in his reply to Roger Williams is so patently evasive, so utterly fails to correspond to the narrative of Winthrop, and is so denuded of feeling that every line rings with a hollow sound. He had never, according to his own account, given any countenance to the "sundry corrupt, and dangerous errors" of the "Familists," but instead had publicly preached against them. The orthodox brethren had then said to the erring party, "See, your Teacher declares himselfe clearly to differ from you," and they had replied, "No matter . . . what he saith in publick, we understand him otherwise, and we know what he saith to us in private." On no other grounds than these was bred a "jealousie" in the country "that I was in secret a Fomenter of the Spirit of Familisme, if not leavened my selfe that way." In this account and in others he confessed that he had meditated fleeing from Massachusetts, since in the opinion of many, "such a Doctrin of Union, and evidencing of Union, as was held forth by mee, was the *Trojan* Horse, out of which all the erroneous Opinions and differences of the Country did issue forth," yet, he protested, he did not have to go, not because he changed his mind, but because "private conference with some chiefe Magistrates, and Elders" revealed the welcome fact that he was in essential agreement with them after all! At the Synod he at last discovered the "corruption of the Judgement of the erring Brethren" and saw the fraudulence of their pretense of holding forth nothing but what they had received from him, "when as indeed they pleaded for grosse errors, contrary to my judgement," and therefore he "bare witnesse against them." This happy resolution was not a matter of his being recovered, but "the fruit of our clearer apprehension, both of the cause and of the state of our differences, and of our joynt consent and concurrence in bearing witnesse against the common heresies, and errors of Antinomianisme, and Familisme, which disturbed us all." Therefore he could reply to Baillie that there had never been any question of his "Seduction"—"all of us hold Union with Christ, and evidencing of Union by the same Spirit, and same Faith and same holinesse."

But what of Cornwell's embarrassing pamphlet? Cotton could do nothing but denounce it as a forgery and publish what he swore were the replies he had given in the cross-examination of 1637. The student finds himself wondering how, if Cornwell's version is accurate, Winthrop could have said at the time that Cotton cleared some doubts, or how, if Cotton's own version is true, Winthrop should have added that in other things he gave no satisfaction. At any rate, what Cotton now presented sounds strangely different from his previous statements. He described himself replying to the question of whether our union with Christ be complete before and without faith, that though from one point of view we are united to Christ as soon as He elects us, "yet in order of nature, before our faith doth put forth it self to lay hold on him," we may be among the elect without a final union—an admission that gave Hooker every right to introduce a period of preparation. When asked if justification could be evidenced by a "conditionall" promise—a word he formerly had denounced—he hedged: "The Spirit doth Evidence our Justification both wayes, sometimes in an absolute Promise, sometimes in a conditionall," and though he would still hestitate to take "saving qualifications" as a "first evidence" of justification, he would generously grant that "A man may haue an argument from thence (yea, I doubt not a firm and strong argument)." Since Hooker had carefully defended his thesis against Arminian constructions, Cotton could seek refuge in the same disavowals; the promises of the Covenant, he could say, have no efficacy in themselves to bring

171

men to faith unless the Spirit accompanies them, "yet this is the end to which God giveth them, to stir up the Sons of men." Consequently, men are not to rest but are to be exhorted "to provoke themselves and one another, to look after the Lord." He would still insist that in the first work of conversion a man must be passive; nevertheless, urged on by his colleagues, he would say, "There are many sins which a man lives in, which he might avoid by very common gifts, which would he renounce, God would not be wanting to lead him on to further grace." This was exactly what Hooker meant by "preparation."

Cotton was much too valuable to be sacrificed unnecessarily, and in the 1640's he vindicated the wisdom of the authorities by rendering the New England Way yeoman service in its dispute with the Presbyterians, but on this point he never dared again to speak with authority. If he touched upon it, he would preface his remarks, "Reserving due honour to such gracious and precious Saints, as may be otherwise minded." Eager as he was to prove the basic unanimity of New England, he could not altogether conceal his well-known opinions, and he had to admit a degree of difference: "though some may conceive the Union wrought in giving the habit, and others rather refer it to the act: and some may give the second place to that, whereto others give the first." Yet his strategy was always to minimize the importance of these differences; he went conspicuously out of his way to approve the treatises of Shepard and Hooker, particularly Hooker's *The Sovles Preparation*, and smoothed over his former objections with the mild qualification, "wherein . . . they sometime declare such works of Grace to be preparations to conversion, which others do take to be fruits of conversion." In every case, he protested that he and they were entirely at one upon all essentials, holding alike that whosoever did come under a saving work of the Spirit had to experience a preparation of some sort. His effort to drape the conflict in the robes of harmony was assiduously seconded by the other spokesmen for New England, their deliberate obscurantism indicating not only how wide but how dangerous the breach had been. The issue made a deep impression upon the seventeenth century, and as late as 1690 George Keith, then speaking as a Quaker and hailing in Anne Hutchinson a forerunner of George Fox, embarrassed his New England opponents by reminding them that Cotton had been closer to his doctrine and to hers than to theirs. Even at the end of the century the leaders were maintaining the defensive tactics of the founders; in a preface to Cotton Mather's *The Everlasting*

Gospel in 1700, Higginson granted that Cotton had "differed from some of his Brethren in *The Souls Preparation for Christ"* and had contended that "some" took certain works to be *"preparations to Conversion, which others take to be fruits of Conversion"*; however, Higginson insisted, the disagreement never became a serious issue, because all agreed that such works must be achieved by every person who undergoes the effectual influence of the Spirit. *"And so the Difference is but Logical, and not Theological."*

The fact of the matter is, however, that in 1637 the difference had been not only theological but social and political, and had Cotton stood his ground either he would have had to flee or the society been torn asunder. He did not stand his ground, and his uneasy references to the affair in subsequent years are oblique admissions that he and not Hooker made the concession. Hooker seemed to be tightening his victory when, in sermons delivered at Hartford in the 1640's, he began an exposition of preparation with the remark, "I shall not only speak mine own Judgment, but the Judgment of all my fellow Brethren, as I have just cause, and good ground to beleeve," and then proceeded to expound preparation in direct contradiction to the views of Cotton. After guaranteeing their orthodoxy by a blanket assertion that they were not Arminians, Hooker and his brethren serenely defined preparation as a work that should be demanded of all men as a "condition" of their salvation. The Antinomians had succeeded only in convincing them of the supreme need for a more vigorous pressing of moral responsibility upon all the people; the horror of Anne Hutchinson's heresy was simply that "most of her new tenets tended to slothfulnesse, and to quench all indevour in the creature." She had declared before the Synod, "The Spirit acts most in the Saints, when they indevour least," and the Synod had answered, "Reserving the special seasons of Gods preventing grace to his owne pleasure, In the ordinary constant course of his dispensation, the more wee indevour, the more assistance and helpe wee find from him." The last embers of Antinomianism had to be beaten out, and Hooker showed the clergy how to wield the one flail that would serve, the doctrine of preparation. With Cotton subdued, Hooker preached repeatedly upon it. "The soule of a poore sinner must bee prepared for the Lord Jesus Christ, before it can receive him." The people must do something to receive God or else never expect Him: "only he watcheth the time till your hearts be ready to receive and entertaine him." When the soul perceives—if it listened to Hooker it could not help but perceive— that it cannot save itself, it "falls downe at the foot of the Lord, and is content to be at Gods dispose," and though at that moment it has no dominion over its sin, "yet it is willingly content that Jesus Christ should come into it." Hooker never preached long without a metaphor: a sharp sauce, he explained, will not "breed a stomacke, yet it stirres up the stomacke," and so a godly preparation, though it may not breed faith, may yet stir up the stomach of faith—and conduct.

The connection of the Antinomian outburst with the further development of the idea of preparation can be traced explicitly in the works of Thomas Shepard. When he described a sort of heretics who hold that there is no sorrow for sin but what is common to both the reprobate and the elect and who insist that genuine grief can come only after the soul is in Christ by faith, his listeners had no trouble knowing whom he meant, or in following his assertion that such heretics are in error because a man who gives no previous thought to his sins is in no position to receive grace, even the irresistible grace of God. No doubt it would be Pelagian to say that a man can dispose himself of his own power, but some antecedent disposition is necessary; a form cannot be joined to matter until the matter is prepared, until it is made "such a vessel which is immediately capable" of the union. Shepard acknowledged that this is a difficult doctrine; even angels may be "posed" by the problem of explaining how men may yield themselves to Christ so that all their fruit comes from Him and not from themselves, but Shepard was certain that before any soul experiences a supernatural change it must learn to "lie like wax" beneath the seal. This learning was what he and Hooker understood by preparation.

The real import of a Puritan doctrine is seldom found in the formal statement. To protect their orthodoxy, theologians would hedge every proposition with innumerable qualifications; but once they had proved and vindicated a doctrine, they were free to reveal its true meaning in their "applications." In their exhortations Hooker and Shepard disclosed the great utility of the doctrine of preparation, namely that they could demand of every man, no matter how sinful, that he make the requisite and feasible preparations, and they could blame him for his own damnation if he refused. Of course, Hooker would explain, if a man's relief depended upon his own endeavors, he would certainly fail: the soul cannot choose Christ "out of the power of nature"; nevertheless, an inn must be prepared to receive the guest, else He will pass by to another lodging. In another characteristic simile, he declared that it is with the soul as with a woman in child-birth: "when her throwes come often and strong, there is some hope of deliverance; but when her throwes goe away, commonly the child dies, and her life too." If a man should argue, "I can do nothing for my self, therefore I will take a course that no man shall do any thing for me," humanity would call him mad; instead, he can and must conclude, since he is able to do nothing of himself, "therefore I must attend upon God in those means which he useth to do for all those he useth to do good unto." Assuredly, unregenerate though he be, a man can avoid the grosser temptations; it is not in your power to make the Gospel "effectual," but it is in your power to "doe more than you doe, your legs may as well carry you to the word, as to an Ale-house." You can read pious books as well as "Play-books"; "you may sing as well Psalmes as idle songs." By the doctrine of preparation, in short, the people of New England, nominally professing a rigid Calvinism, could still be told, "doe what you are able to doe, put all your strength, and diligence unto it." At the very least, if they could not resist the ale-house and the play-book, they could "wait" upon God:

> It is true indeed, we cannot doe it, but by Christ, it is the grace of Christ, the power of Christ, the spirit of Christ that doth help us to get our selves from under iniquitie; yet notwithstanding we must labour to get our selves from under it, and Christ will help us. . . . It is the Lords Almighty power that hath possesst us with this libertie and freedome from iniquitie, but yet notwithstanding before we can come to inioy a full libertie from all iniquitie, we must fight for it, and wage the battels of the Lord.

The people could not excuse themselves by pleading that they were disabled, for with the very argument they showed that they were "*not yet* WILLING *to be made* ABLE." Hooker never hesitated to exhort the unregenerate: "It is possible for any Soule present (for ought I know or that he knows) to get an humble heart." The customary ending of a Hooker sermon was an encouragement to all men "that you would indeavour, and be perswaded to get an interest in Christ." Likewise, Thomas Shepard held it a "slothful opinion" to believe that since no activity of grace can be received except from God, men should attempt nothing. Peter Bulkeley indicated the connection of the doctrine with the federal theology by reasoning that, since grace is an offer of a contract, a man can humble himself before God, confess his depravity and intreat God for a chance to enter the covenant. Generally, Bulkeley promised, God will receive those who come to Him, and "Thus you see the way to enter into Covenant with God."

Here at last was a fulcrum for the lever of human responsibility, even in a determined world. Here was something a man could do, here was an obligation that could be urged upon him, no matter how impotent his will. He could at least prepare, he could wait upon the Lord. Of course, his preparation would be worthless if it did not lead to faith, but it was not, like faith itself, so far above the reach of a mortal being that he could do nothing toward attaining it. Whatever was lost or gained in this restatement, one thing was sure: it ruled out all forms of Antinomianism. In 1657 Hooker's fellow Congregationalists in England, Goodwin and Nye, published his *Application of Redemption* with their hearty endorsement, admitting that Hooker had been accused of "urging too far, and insisting too much upon that as *Preparatory*, which includes indeed the beginnings of true Faith," but they were now ready to agree with him, because they in England were suffering what New England had endured in 1637, a wave of Antinomian fanaticism, and they hoped that Hooker's volume would set to rights "those that have slipt into *Profession*, and Leapt over all both *true* and *deep Humiliation* for sin, and *sence of their natural Condition*." With this to recommend the doctrine, that it provided both an antidote to Antinomianism and a working basis for stirring up the sinful will without running to the opposite extreme of Arminianism, no wonder it became a prized possession of the New England mind! And no wonder that as the decades passed and the leaders became more and more worried over the declension, as they were obliged to find means for stimulating the zeal of the flagging generations, they enlarged and magnified the scope of preparation.

The next stage in the development of the doctrine is marked by John Norton's *The Orthodox Evangelist*, published in 1657, which was a treatise upon the particular "evangelical truths" that were then being widely opposed "in this perilous hour of the Passion of the Gospel." There were many Antinomians, mystics, seekers, and Quakers abroad, and therefore Norton devoted three long chapters to preparation; he did not so much extend Hooker's idea as give it systematic formulation, but by that very act, by stripping off Hooker's rhetoric, he caused further implications to emerge. He was compelled, for instance, to

distinguish between works which are preparatory in the sight of God
—which are achieved only by the elect—and those judged by man, which
are to be measured by the rule of charity and to be considered in
many cases merely as grounds for hope, not as the signs of a completed
redemption. Leaving secret things to God, Norton was able to insist
that preparatory works in the second sense might legitimately be required of everybody. His definitions emphasized the temporal element,
making preparation a period in which a man is neither a sinner nor
a saint, but in some tentative half-way condition: "By preparatory
Work, we understand certain inherent qualifications, coming between
the carnal test of the soul in the state of sin, and conversion wrought
in the Ministry." It is a "common work of the Spirit," whereby "the
soul is put into a Ministerial capacity of believing immediately," whereas
"the unprepared soul is incapable of directly receiving faith." He stressed
constantly that God works conversion not by a violent invasion of
the psyche but by degrees: " 'Tis in the works of Grace, as we ordinarily
see in the works of Nature; God proceeds not immediately from one ex-
tream unto another, but by degrees." Norton again recited all the safeguards against Arminianism; he denied that preparatory works have
any causal influence upon vocation, and repeated that even the preparing soul is passive. Yet he carried the analysis so far beyond Hooker
that not only was he able to describe preparation as a part of the process
of conversion, but to dissect preparation itself into a process, with
an array of component stages: believing in the holiness of the law,
realizing the nature of sin, learning the message of Christ, comprehending the need for repentance, and finally waiting upon Christ in the
use of means under the Gospel Covenant. All this, let us remember,
was presented as pertaining only to preparation, during which the
soul remains passive! Preparation, as Norton said, "worketh not any
change of the heart, yet there are in it, and accompanying of it, certain
inward workings, that do dispose to a change." He did not demand that
every individual run through all the stages he marked out; in fact,
he declared, the least measure is enough to put a soul into a "preparatory capacity," and since certainty of election is not always possible
in this life, a work of preparation among the as yet unconverted, even
if it be not followed by a visible operation of the Spirit, must still be
taken as a hopeful sign. In any event, it was clear that preparation
could be accomplished by the unregenerate. Arminians and Pelagians
allowed too much to preparation—one wonders what more they could

allow!—but Norton's chief concern was to counter those "Enthusiasts" who were denying the usefulness or indeed the very existence of any preparation. Hence the conclusion for him, even more explicitly than for Hooker, was the moral duty of all men to seek for preparation, even though it would not guarantee their salvation: "That it is the duty of every one that hears the Gospel to believe, and that whosoever believeth shall be saved; but also it ministers equal hope unto all (answerable to their preparatory proceeding) of believing, and being saved." That the soul should first be prepared and then called to faith, instead of being called without warning, "is the method of the Gospel, ought to be the direction of the Ministry, and course of the Soul; Christs own way, and therefore the most hopefull and most speedy way for attaining of faith and salvation thereby."

Increase Mather came back to Boston in 1661, believing it the last stronghold of Protestantism and resolved to maintain all doctrines in their most rigorous form; just as he at first opposed the Half-Way Covenant, even though his father was a principal advocate, so also he held to Cotton's views on preparation. In 1669 he declared conversion a miracle, far beyond the power of nature to produce or even approach, and in 1674 was preaching "men are altogether *passive* in their *Conversion*." But meanwhile New England sank into the mire of apostasy, and he above all others thundered the need for reform. Very shortly he found himself obliged to remodel his thinking, starting not from abstract doctrines but from the facts with which he was contending. He changed sides on the Half-Way Covenant, and before long he also altered his views of preparation, declaring that while the gate is indeed strait, yet God requires men to strive for entrance, and consequently "they should do such things as have a tendency to cause them to Believe." Others in his generation, under the same circumstances, likewise found charms in the same thought. Samuel Willard was too skilled in the traditional theology ever to lose sight of natural inability; he would explain that when a man repents, "it is God by his Spirit that enforms him with this power and grace," and he held it an error to "put a Divine honour upon Moral swasion, as if it could of it self attract and draw the heart after it," yet whenever he exhorted the congregations, he pointed out that in preparation, as apart from regeneration, they have a power of working upon themselves. "It is one of Satans cheats, to tell us we must wait before we resolve." In his *Compleat Body of Divinity* he defined preparation as that time in which the soul is not yet redeemed but is merely in *"a posture and readiness for the exerting of the act of Faith, which follows thereupon."* Even at this date there were debates among the orthodox, and many whom Willard respected still denied the existence of any preparatory works; but he repeated the arguments of Hooker and Norton, and added a few of his own, to prove once more that men may be called upon to prepare themselves if not to convert themselves. In 1690 a committee of ministers attempted to moderate the confusion that followed the revolution against Andros by issuing a manifesto of the ancient creed of New England; admitting that men are saved or rejected entirely by the will of God, they hastened to insist, nevertheless, that there are "some previous and preparatory common works" which may be accomplished by all, though in those who afterwards fall away "we deny them to be the beginnings of true justifying or saving faith." Most sermons in the last decades of the century exhibit the same alternation between an assertion of human impotence and an incitation to preparation, and in one breath denounce the "insignificant and unsavoury" belief that men's efforts have any value while in the next they exhort men to greater efforts. The inconsistency no longer bothered the preachers, and once having stated the conventional inability, they were at liberty to press upon their congregations an obligation to act, as though John Calvin had never lived. If accused of Pelagianism they answered that preparation was not salvation and therefore not a matter of grace. How may I know that I have Christ? the people would ask, and Samuel Mather could reply, "As Your *Conviction* is, such your faith is: as is the preparation work, such is the closing with Christ. It is a *sure rule;* and this is the reason why we so much, and so often press for *preparation* work. . . . And there is more *preparation* needful, than many think for."

The culmination of this development, the enlargement of preparation to a point beyond which it could not be extended without bursting the bonds of orthodoxy, is to be seen in the writings of Cotton Mather. Even at the beginning of his career he was so far heedless of first principles as to represent his brother Nathaniel entering into a covenant with God *before* being converted, which then became "an influence into his *Conversion* afterwards." Cotton Mather never had any other conception of grace than as a process that could be "cherished and promoted"; though he paid the usual lip service to total depravity, he always heartily exhorted depraved men to set their house in order, and their provisions, according to his instructions, would have included almost every action of the religious life. "You may make a *Tryal*"; there can be no harm in trying, for "Never, I am perswaded, never any Soul miscarried, that made such Applications." True, God has not promised to give grace to those who seek it, nevertheless—there is always a "nevertheless" in Cotton Mather's discourse—" 'Tis many ways Advantageous, for an *Vnregenerate* Man, to Do as much as he *can*," for "there is a probability that God intends to help him, so that he shall *do* more than he *can*." Certainly, if a man makes his "*Impotency* a Cloak for his *Obstinacy*, it will Aggravate his Condemnation at the Last." The way to be recovered—"the way of the *New-Covenant*"—is very simple: "*Try* whether you can't give that Consent; if you *can*, 'tis done!" By the beginning of the eighteenth century, preparation had come to mean for all practical purposes, that every man was able to predispose himself for grace, that his fate was in his own hands, even though grace was given of God. The memory of John Cotton's dissent remained a monitor of caution, but the preachers were no longer capable of comprehending why he had dissented.

The premise of clerical thinking in the new century remained ostensibly what it had been in the old, the inherent nature of a covenant, whether among men or between man and God. But in the later treatment, the fact that a covenant not only permits but requires a preliminary negotiation and that the terms of salvation must therefore be known to every sinner, became not a condescending mercy of God but a utilitarian convenience. The federal theology began by permitting what strict Calvinism would not, some sort of anticipatory behavior among those who desired redemption, but successive theologians steadily enlarged the field of such behavior by shifting the focus of attention from the awful majesty of God to the concrete and manageable propositions of a business transaction. "For this reason," Willard put it in 1700, "the *Gospel Promises* are exhibited on terms; and these terms therein proposed, do not only tell us what it is that God requires of Sinners in the treaty of Peace which he opens and manageth with them . . . but they do also give us to understand after what manner God will by his Grace convey a pardon to Sinners." Puritans of the seventeenth century always assumed that God alone could fully enable men or nations to take up a covenant, but from the beginning the federalists had insisted that there is "an order in which he brings them to a participation"; hence the rationalizing, secularizing tendencies of the age did not need to appear in New England as a frontal attack upon the terrible decrees of election and reprobation, but could be satisfied by a cautious translation of the initial action in the order of grace into the language of a commercial parley. The infusion of grace itself, said Cotton Mather, is immediately done by God's almighty arm, "But then, the Spirit of God, because He will deal with us as *Rational Creatures*, He also puts forth a *Moral Efficiency* for our *Conversion;* We are capable of *Treaties*, of *Proposals*, of *Overtures;* and He therefore *Exhorts* us, and Uses a variety of *Arguments* to perswade us."

Once more, we must remark that the first federal theologians set forth the idea that conversion is a logical process following a discernible "order," beginning with a period of preparation, not for social but for evangelical reasons. They wished to incite men to preparedness, not in order that laws might be obeyed, but that souls might be saved. Yet they did dignify certain motions, admittedly within the attainment of the unregenerate, as the prologues to conversion. Thereupon they made the national covenant a logical possibility, for not only God but all the people could bear their part: "As in a Covenant there are Articles of agreement betweene party and party; so betweene God and his people." To become a holy society, a people must know the terms of holiness and be able to observe them; the doctrine of preparation secured both conditions, and so Massachusetts and Connecticut could conceive of themselves as societies in which all men, saints or not, were pledged to observe the externals of religion. But once these societies began to decline, the inhabitants to grow remiss and be duly punished by plagues and financial losses, they could all be informed "they shall seek to him for a pardon, and upon their so doing, they shall find it." Within a few decades the preparation that was first urged upon all men for the salvation of their souls was being pressed upon them for the preservation of the state. They could do what was required, and though they might miss their redemption they could reform their manners. There were still limits to what men could do merely in a way of preparation, but by staying away from the ale-houses and putting off their luxurious clothes they could make the difference between social prosperity and ruin.

But at this point a new question intruded itself upon the leaders: would men bestir themselves in order to save the society when they had no hope of escaping Hell? Might not the unregenerate understandably object that there was no reason why they should strive for a goal they could not attain merely in order that the saints might grow rich? That this question, in some form, could not be avoided is abundantly testified by the sophistries of Cotton Mather, and in him the worst forebodings of Anne Hutchinson were finally vindicated, for he began, though in the most tentative fashion, to suggest that whoever would prepare himself would almost certainly go to Heaven! First of all, he was concerned that men keep up the outward observances. "Men have a *Natural Power*, as to the *External part of Religion*"—there was no longer any qualification in his mind. Therefore it followed, "If men do not in Religion, what they have a *Natural Power* to do, they cannot with any modesty complain of the Righteous God, that He does not grant them the *Higher Power*, to Exert those Acts of Religion, which are Internal." By the same token it followed that those who did exercise the lower power were practically assured of receiving the higher: "If men did in Religion, more than they do, & *All* that they could by a *Natural Power* do, there would be a greater Likelihood, (I say not, a *Certainty*, but a *Likelihood*,) that God would grant them that *Higher Power*." The founders had taken for granted that a holy society could force the proper manners upon the unregenerate; Cotton Mather could not persuade the unregenerate to mend their manners without luring them with the promise of an almost sure chance of salvation, even though they still were deficient in grace and faith.

It was but a short step from such thinking to an open reliance upon human exertions and to a belief that conversion is worked entirely by rational argument and moral persuasion. The seeds of what Jonathan Edwards was to denounce as "Arminianism" in the mid-eighteenth century were sown in New England by Hooker and Shepard, who, ironically enough, were the two most evangelical among the founders and the most opposed to seventeenth-century forms of Arminianism. The subsequent development of their doctrine is not a mere episode in the history of a technical jargon. It is nothing less than a revelation of the direction in which Puritanism was travelling, of the fashion in which the religious world of the seventeenth century was gradually transformed into the world of the eighteenth. A teleological universe, wherein men were expected to labor for the glory of God, wherein they were to seek not their own ends but solely those appointed by Him, was imperceptibly made over into a universe in which men could trust themselves even to the extent of commencing their own conversions, for the sake of their own well-being, and God could be expected to reward them with eternal life. Even while professing the most abject fealty to the Puritan Jehovah, the Puritan divines in effect dethroned Him. The fate of New England, in the original philosophy, depended upon God's providence; the federal theology circumscribed providence by tying it to the behavior of the saints; then with the extension of the field of behavior through the elaboration of the work of preparation, the destiny of New England was taken out of the hands of God and put squarely into the keeping of the citizens. Even while invoking the concept in an effort to stem the tide of worldliness, the ministers contributed to augmenting the worldly psychology: if the natural man was now admittedly able to practice the external rules of religion without divine assistance, and if such observance would infallibly insure the prosperity of society and most probably the redemption of souls, if honesty would prove the best policy and if morality would pay dividends, then the natural man was well on his way to a freedom that would no longer need to be controlled by the strenuous ideals of supernatural sanctification and gracious enlightenment, but would find adequate regulation in the ethics of reason and the code of civic virtues.

9. HOW DEMOCRATIC WAS ROGER WILLIAMS?*

by Alan Simpson

Like thousands of others who left England for Massachusetts in the 1630s, Roger Williams came to find a new life in a land where God's word and spirit might prevail. Though he shared the hopes and beliefs of other Puritans, he quickly became estranged from political and religious authority in the Bay Colony. He challenged the power of the magistrates and the ministers, charging that they betrayed Calvinist ideals. They promptly declared him a heretic whose errors could not be permitted to infect the community. Forced to flee from Massachusetts, Williams became a seeker, but precisely what he sought and what propelled him throughout his long life have not always been clear. In the following essay, Alan Simpson argues that those who think of Williams as an early American democrat have read their own values back into the seventeenth century. To achieve an accurate understanding of Williams, Simpson insists, one must appreciate that the preoccupying concern of Williams' generation did not include either political democracy or social equality. A Calvinist, Williams was pre-eminently a

* *William and Mary Quarterly*, 3d series, vol. 13 (1956), 53–67. Footnotes have been omitted except where they are necessary for an understanding of the text.

religious man whose spiritual search explains why he left England, rejected the authority of the Bay Colony, and established another settlement on different principles, which, like those he rejected, represented man's search to comprehend God's design.

For further reading: Perry Miller, *Roger Williams, His Contribution to the American Tradition* (1962); Theodore P. Greene, ed., *Roger Williams and the Massachusetts Magistrates* (1964); Alan Simpson, *Puritanism in Old and New England* (1955); Ola Elizabeth Winslow, *Master Roger Williams* (1957).

The special character of American history—its deceptive resemblance to a short story with a simple plot—offers peculiar temptations to the practice of the cult which delights in revealing our ancestors as the pioneers of modern times. Most of us have learned to smile at the complacency of Macaulay in studying English history as an experiment in Whiggery, but nothing seems more natural than to go on studying American history as an experiment in democracy. Our best textbooks can find no more suitable title, and a good portion of our scholarship has always consisted in grooming the remoter personalities in our history into the torchbearers of the grand idea. Admittedly, the further back the investigator went, the harder it grew, until astonishing powers of audacity or ignorance were required to make the early Puritan conform to type; but even here—if not among the orthodox Puritans, at least among the rebels—glittering prizes awaited the brave. Who could fail to be thrilled by the nonconformist who hurled defiance at the oligarchy, founded his own colony on a radical separation of church and state, did his best to thrust the Englishmen in England up the same enlightened path, and lived to boast, among the wrecked hopes of the revolutionary generation, that nowhere on earth was such liberty enjoyed as in Rhode Island? Such a figure, discovered precisely where the darkness of European history should have been first dissipated on these shores, seemed like a luminous beacon lighting the way to the century of the common man.

Of course these heady excitements have always been resisted in some quarters. And even students have been known to open one of Roger Williams's pamphlets, under the impression that they were going to meet a familiar figure, only to shut it hastily again with the feeling that there must have been some mistake. More recently there has been a thorough reinspection of the Puritan mind by a group of scholars who have nothing in common with the myth-makers. But as long as there existed no passable biography of Williams and no short cut through the wilderness of his writings, the endearing image of the "Irrepressible Democrat" was likely to endure. It had enough plausibility to make demolition awkward, and it warmed the hearts of all but the learned who wrote for the learned.

One of these deficiencies has at last been supplied. Perry Miller, a sensitive, sure-fingered guide, has led us through as much of Williams's prose as the modern reader is ever likely to examine. However, this admirable commentator has been content to shrug off the myth with a few contemptuous asides and to confine himself to exhibiting the evolution of a prophet in the sphere of religious ideas. This leaves the implications of these ideas for politics and the political activity of their author only partially explored, while the general reader is left to make his own guess as to how and where the inventors of the great democrat went astray.

Any attempt to understand Roger Williams must begin with the fact that from first to last he was a religious enthusiast. We cannot, of course, say the same of all the people of his generation who used the language of religion as their normal mode of expression. Many were simply following a convention. Many began with a zeal for purer worship only to become progressively absorbed in the defense of careers, the protection of class interests, or the reconstruction of social institutions for their independent values. It has been suggested that Williams is really one of these, in spite of all appearances to the contrary. However sincere his personal religion, however formidable his attachment to Puritan methods of thought, we were encouraged to look elsewhere for the real significance of his career. One authority called him a "freethinker more concerned with social commonwealths than with theological dogmas"; another insisted that he was essentially a political thinker, whose principle of religious liberty grew out of his theory of the state and whose best efforts after 1640 were not given to theology but to the construction of a democratic commonwealth; a third left the impression that the most admirable feature about him was his lonely struggle for social democracy.

All of these views were unfortunate. There is no trace whatever in Roger Williams of that gradual secularization of interest which is such a marked feature in the history of the Levellers. There is not the slightest point in confusing his "seekerism"—an assertion that the divinely authenticated form of church government was yet to be revealed—with any skepticism about the fundamentals of Christian belief. There is every evidence that his principle of religious liberty was derived both formally and emotionally from his sense of what was due to God. And there are clear indications that his standards of political conduct, even though often recommended by himself on humane rather than Christian grounds, were in fact emanations from a Christian experience.

When a Puritan viewed the world, he saw it as a twofold system of nature and grace. There was the unregenerate mass of mankind, living their perishable lives outside the circle of mercy, and there were those whom grace had saved from the doom that awaited the natural man. Views about the government of each order and their mutual relationships varied indefinitely, but there was no disagreement about the transcendent importance of election or about the duty of the elect to wean themselves from the affections of this life. For a man whose physical vitality carried him through some eighty years of strenuous activity, Williams sustained a remarkable sense of his own corruptibility and a steady disrespect for all those seductions of "profit, honour, and pleasure" which beguile the unregenerate. He did not profess to know who was saved and who was damned in this world, but he knew that salvation was all that mattered and that in the nature of things most men would not escape the fate that all had deserved. This in no way deterred him from the most ardent efforts to assist in the conversion of the few, or to defend the many in such rights as God intended them to have; but it gave him a perspective on the problems of this fallen world that was decidedly remote from our own.

So far as the political order was concerned, Williams had really only one revolutionary statement to make. He denied that the state had any responsibility for the only form of life which has absolute importance— the life of the soul—and he set himself the infinitely difficult task of convincing his contemporaries that this was consistent with Scripture, reason, and experience.

Others had preceded him in this quest for an escape from the contradictions of an age which strove to reconcile the tradition of religious uniformity with the new variety of opinions; but perhaps no Englishman demanded such freedom so early or with such sweeping rigor. The immediate impulse to the development of the views expressed in the *Bloudy Tenent* and its sequels came from a collision between the conscience of a religious separatist and the orthodoxy which Massachusetts was erecting through a partnership of church and state. The principle which gives coherence to the quarrels between Williams and the authorities is the determination of the separatist, in the interest of religious truth, to purify the church from all pollution. Thwarted at every point and ultimately banished by the combined action of ecclesiastical and civil authority, he was led to deny any coercive power by either authority over the religious conscience. And unlike any European, he was in a position to found a community on his principle and to begin the experiment of making it work. It is not surprising, then, that when the revolutionary debate opened in England and it seemed to him that another movement for religious reformation was threatened with a fatal confusion of the church and the world, he plunged in with a breath-taking boldness.

Williams's arguments were addressed to the faithful, without the slightest concession to any reader who had not been drilled in the discipline of Puritan disputation. The formal argument involved three principal features: an exposition of New Testament texts to demonstrate that the most erroneous conscience imaginable is not to be disturbed in its errors by force; a ruthless disposal of all the Old Testament precedents by the device of "typology"; and a series of scattered but perfectly clear-cut expositions of the nature of church and state as utterly different societies. But he had also absorbed within his formidable framework many of the arguments generated by the discussions of his predecessors during the previous century; and all this makes it notoriously difficult to summarize the decisive considerations. Yet on at least one occasion, he expressed himself with refreshing simplicity when he offered to defend, in public debate, three positions:

1. That forced worship stinks in God's nostrils;
2. That forced worship denies the coming of Christ by insisting on the national church of the Jews;
3. That religious liberty is the only prudent, Christian way of preserving peace in the world.

When Williams reflected on the history of the effort to enforce a religious orthodoxy, two forcible impressions seemed to occur to him: such efforts ignore the church—that is to say, they are incompatible with the true nature of those who profess to be, or who hope to discover themselves to be, the elect; and they destroy that peace which God has ordained for both the elect and the natural man during their earthly pilgrimage. Since the welfare of the church transcends the welfare of natural man, the first consideration has the priority. The real sufferers from the doctrine of forced worship have always been the saints. It places them at the mercy of any error which clerical authority may commit, as Williams himself found in his clash with the Massachusetts hierarchy. It invites the natural man, through his representative, the civil power, to impose standards in a realm where he is absolutely unfit to have an opinion. It fosters the delusion that the "garden of the church" was ever intended to embrace "the wilderness of the world." It obscures the true nature of the fallen conscience as a faculty which inevitably judges differently throughout the world and will continue to do so until enlightened by divine grace. The only escape from those monstrosities is to realize that regeneration is a spiritual process, to be promoted through spiritual means, and that the purity of the regenerate depends upon their freedom to separate themselves from the contamination of the world. "Forced worship stinks in God's nostrils."

But if forced worship stinks in God's nostrils, how about the national church of the Old Testament? Here Williams delivered a frontal assault on the main difficulty which the Puritan experienced in conceding full religious liberty—a difficulty well illustrated by the Whitehall Debates of 1648 among professed advocates of liberty of conscience in England. Henry Ireton, speaking for those with reservations, checked the appeal to Christ's ministry with the obvious retort: It is not enough to show us what Christ preached; it is necessary to show us how the power given to the magistrate under the Old Testament has been superceded under the New. Williams disposed of this problem by a sweeping use of that principle of typology which enabled the Reformers to perform almost as many feats with Scripture as allegory had permitted in earlier days. The church of the Jews simply typified the spiritual church of Christ, and for John Cotton or anybody else to invoke it as a literal model for a national church was in effect to deny Christ's coming.

But forced worship stinks for the further reason that, besides perverting God's plan for the regeneration of souls, it has also frustrated his command that the regenerate man and the natural man should live together in peace. The saint is not "of the world," but he must live in it;

and God willed that the spiritual community of the chosen, scattered throughout the infinitely larger community of the damned, should live under a temporal regime of law. But what security can men enjoy in their bodies and goods so long as the world is trapped, as it has been so agonizingly during the last century, in the fallacies of forced worship? The agency for providing this security is the state, and the natural reason given by God to all men serves to guide its activities. Civil peace has been enjoyed by communities who have never heard the name of Christ, and man's hope of enjoying this good is made less, not more, certain by intruding the claims of saints. God gave His saints no commission to rule the world—as we might guess, if no other reason existed, from the fact that He chooses them from ranks which are rich in faith but poor in worldly skill. It is upon the gifts of the damned, Williams is almost driven to say, that we mainly rely, under the providence of God, for the peace of our earthly pilgrimage.

When we turn from his definition of the province of the state to his views about its constitution, we find that though Williams wrote reams to vindicate the true character of the church from the misunderstandings of Presbyterians, Congregationalists, Baptists, Quakers, and their lay auxiliaries, he never wrote a pamphlet in his life to explain the principles of civil government. His views about these have to be derived from passages in his attacks on persecution, from fragments in his letters, and from conjectures based on the imperfect records of his practical activity as a founder of colonial institutions. The temptation to erect bold structures on slender evidence has not always been resisted. One favorite source for the admirers of his "democracy" has been the passages in the *Bloudy Tenents* affirming the sovereignty of the people in civil government; but it hardly seems to have been noticed that in their context those passages have one purpose only—to reduce to absurdity the religious claims of the magistrate by showing that as the representative of natural men he cannot know what he is talking about. Williams uses his maxims to show how the world should not be allowed to judge the church and scarcely begins to consider what they imply for the structure of political institutions. But perhaps the most notable example is the way in which the modern mind has allowed itself to be excited by two lines in a single letter: "I have been charged with folly for that freedom and liberty which I have always stood for; I say liberty and equality, both in land and government." We shall see later how the magic word "equality" has cast its usual spell over modern readers.

Judged from his general observations about civil government, Williams held the following views. Government was ordained by God for the safety of our bodies and goods. He has enjoined obedience for these purposes in Scripture, but the duty is equally evident where Scripture does not run, as it rests on natural reason. God has not enjoined any specific form of government, and it is therefore to be inferred that forms of government will vary with the "several natures, dispositions, and constitutions of mankind." A political community, whether monarchical, aristocratic, democratic, or any mixture of these conventional types, is to be conceived as an agreement of the people, for their mutual security, under the forms deemed appropriate to them. The rulers are trustees, and the terms of the trust (though not, of course, its purposes, or the principles of natural justice) are alterable at the will of the people. But just who the people are, who is entitled to speak for them, and how their rights are to be vindicated under an abuse of justice are questions which are left decidedly vague. It will be noticed that he adopted the proposition that many other Puritans in his generation found convenient: "Civil government is derived mediately from God, immediately from the people." But he never, like his friend Milton or like the English Levellers, developed a doctrine of natural rights beyond the point implicit in the generalizations just mentioned. The reason for this may lie simply in the fact that the problem of justifying rebellion or regicide never presented itself directly to the man whose task was to build a colony in the wilderness; but it seems more probable that if he had stayed in England to fight the English struggle, his sense of the role of circumstances in civil government would have deterred him, as it deterred Oliver Cromwell and Ireton, from doctrinaire philosophy.

When we turn from Williams's writings to his practical activity as a founder of a colony and an intermittent participant in the English Revolution, what are we entitled to say of his aims? We can say that he was primarily concerned with an experiment in religious liberty; that civil liberty was an important but secondary aim; that no belief in social equality ever entered his head; and that some of his most characteristic pleas in the world of politics sprang from a Christian sentiment of love.

Perhaps enough has been said to suggest the primacy of religious liberty in all his activity; but as the emphasis once put on it has undergone some curious shifts, it may be worth while to recapitulate the evidence. There is the sustained plea for freedom of worship in his major works and the absence in these writings of any comparable

191

concern with the ordering of the civil state after it has been stripped of its religious duties. There is his striking lack of interest in England's effort to solve its civil, as distinct from its religious, problems. There is the absence of any evidence that he found the civil constitution of Massachusetts obnoxious, except where it interfered with religion; indeed, he praised it and sought advice from John Winthrop about how to establish his own colony. There is the patent fact that he intended his plantation to be first and foremost a haven for persecuted consciences, as we can see from the priority given to "soul liberty" in all his boasts and entreaties. And there is the misunderstood fact that it is essentially the effort to separate church and state that constitutes the real challenge for this community. Few observers, on either side of the Atlantic, thought that separation could be accomplished without desperate injury to both institutions. The great problem for the founders of Rhode Island was a dual one: preservation against the threat of extermination from without, and the protection of internal unity against the extravagances of the emancipated conscience. The crucial domestic problem was not one of organizing civil liberty, still less of organizing social democracy, but simply of reconciling religious liberty with social order in the face of individuals who invoked the rights of conscience to destroy the elementary obligations of civil life—office-bearing, taxpaying, submission to legal process, acceptance of social distinctions, and respect for political authority. The hopes of the founders are accurately stated by John Clarke in an appeal to Charles II for a renewal of the charter: "[they] have it much on their hearts (if they may be permitted) to hold forth a lively experiment, that a flourishing civil state may stand, yea, and best be maintained, and that among English spirits, with a full liberty in religious concernments."

Perhaps it may be urged that Williams desired both religious and civil liberty and sought them equally. That he desired both, and contrived to secure both in his colonial situation, is true, but that he sought them equally is far from clear. There is little in his writings to suggest that he could not have lived contentedly under any system of government that guaranteed religious freedom and protected its subjects in their persons and property. The system he chose for Rhode Island guaranteed a high degree of civil liberty; but it was simply an adaption of English representative principles to a frontier situation, for which he claimed no universal validity and which he was perfectly content to derive as a unique privilege from English authority, whether Parliament, dictator, or restored monarch, as the case might be. And if some features of this system, such as the rights of self-government in legislation and taxation, were valued for the security they offered for "bodies and goods," they must have seemed even more valuable for the security they offered for the grand design of spiritual freedom. He naturally felt, as Puritans did everywhere, that the best security for his ideals was to have power entrusted to those who believed in them, which in this case was the whole body of free men.

Perhaps the sharpest light is thrown on the subordination of the interest in civil liberty when we look at his activity and associates in the English scene. There were "irrepressible democrats" in England—the Levellers—but he never paid the slightest attention to them. There were problems about the constitution of the Rump calculated to worry any democrat or republican, but it was not these that worried Williams: all that concerned him, so far as the record goes, was the necessity for completing the only program that really mattered—the final emancipation of the religious conscience. There were infinitely worse problems about Cromwell's position. But in spite of certain differences of opinion there is little to suggest that Williams's predominant feeling for Cromwell was not one of respect. This apparent indifference to the failure of the English Revolution to fulfill its promise of civil liberty can only mean that its promise of religious liberty seemed vastly more important.

This raises the interesting question whether Williams would ever have been able to maintain in England, had he lived there continuously, the positions which have made him famous in Rhode Island. In his plantation he could deny to the godly any claim to rule the state, just as he could deny to the state any duty to uphold the godly, because the community was founded on the assumption that liberty of conscience was fundamental. But in England he appears as the friend and supporter of men who upheld the right of the godly to rule, against all the traditional claims of Englishmen to be ruled through their elected representatives. Milton, Cromwell, Sir Harry Vane invariably placed their ideal of Christian liberty above their concern for civil liberty where the two conflicted. Is there any probability that Williams would have done otherwise? Certainly there is nothing in the evidence to suggest that the oligarchies which governed England after 1649 could not have sustained themselves in his favor by eliminating "forced worship" and by striving in their capacity as self-appointed trustees "to do justly, and to love mercy, and to walk humbly with God."

This dilemma did not arise in the frontier situation, and Williams's pride in being able to combine civil liberty with religious liberty is well known. What is less clearly understood is that it was *civil liberty*, and not some kind of experiment in social equality. What he obtained from English authority were powers of local self-government similar to those held in Massachusetts, the only crucial differences being those caused by the withdrawal of the church from the state. These differences were admittedly profound. They meant that one kind of privilege—clerical—was swept away from voting and office-holding and that all the problems of political justice could be studied in isolation from Mosaic precedents. But a belief in social equality was no necessary consequence of this, and the notion that Williams entertained any seems ill-founded.

The case for treating Williams as a pioneer of social democracy (*equalitarianism* is the inelegant term usually employed) seems, at bottom, to rest on two familiar but treacherous notions: the belief that the religious radical of the Protestant Reformation became almost inevitably a social radical as well, and the belief that the frontier is capable of generating only one political philosophy. Williams is introduced to us in general terms as the product of these two influences. More specifically, we are asked to believe that he smarted under class distinctions in England, resented them in Massachusetts, and labored heroically in Rhode Island to level all barriers to either political or economic opportunity. We are told that he failed, just as his alleged allies in the same struggle, the Levellers, failed in England, but that we ought to salute him as a lonely champion of true democracy against the encroaching forces of colonial privilege.

The English Levellers are a clear case of a seventeenth-century faction whose thought did actually revolve around the idea of equality. They bore all the marks of a class movement; protested vehemently against every kind of special privilege; demanded manhood suffrage; and asserted, in language that would warm the heart of any Jacksonian democrat, their complete confidence in the capacity of the common man to deal adequately with any problem of government. But if we test Williams (who, as we have said, ignored the Levellers) by either his writings or his practical work, we find nothing of this in his character. The suggestion that he smarted under the snobbery of student life at Cambridge or under a social system which denied him the pleasure of a marriage above his station, may be dismissed as mere Americana. His conception of government as an art demanding special skills is purely traditional, as may be gathered from his frequent comparisons between the ruler and the pilot or the physician. His ideal of "civility" has all the overtones of gentility—respect for education, good manners, and social distinctions. He was always on his guard against the tendency to draw improper conclusions from the idea of Christian equality, and he made only the most limited use of the other line of thought which the Levellers used to justify their views—the doctrine of natural rights. The scraps from his writings which are offered as evidence of doctrinal democracy usually turn out to be one of two things: either a separatist attack on clerical privilege, or simply a Christian protest against acquisitiveness.

Of course, the final answer to this question depends on the impression left by his prolonged struggles with the proprietors of Providence—the early settlers who eventually entrenched themselves as a privileged oligarchy. This is not the place to attempt a detailed reconstruction of this history, each phase of which has been used to fortify the conception of Williams as the "Irrepressible Democrat." One can only say that the skeptical doubts are unquenched.

When Williams conveyed his initial land purchases to a group of associates, among whom he himself was one, he intended to set up a trust which would manage this domain on behalf of the future town. It would be a fellowship, open to qualified newcomers, that would combine the duties of government and land-management in a public-spirited way. The domain would supply settlers with holdings appropriate to their means and needs; the purchase fees obtained would be first applied to liquidating the original costs and would then form a source of public revenue; and the undistributed land would be held for the future needs of the community—especially for the future refugees from religious persecution, for whom this haven was really being created. Such a community would be "democratic" in the sense that Providence would never reproduce the social variety of Boston, let alone of Old England, and also in the sense that the members of the town fellowship would enjoy equal privileges. But equality, either in land or political privilege, was never envisaged for the community as a whole.

Williams began by assuming that firstcomers would naturally enjoy advantages and that the normal subject of political rights would not be the individual but the master of a family, with his traditional authority over children, wife, and servants. He found nothing objectionable in the crystallization of three classes within the slowly growing town—the proprietor, the twenty-five-acre man, and the freeman with a smaller holding. And if he became associated in the politics of Providence with the championship of a popular faction against a proprietary faction, this was essentially because the proprietors, in his opinion, were bent on converting a public trust into a private estate. If they had fulfilled his conception of a trustee, in their relation with the Indians, with Massachusetts, with their own poorer neighbors, and with the religious refugees, there is little reason to suppose that he would have quarreled with their privileges. And the most he ever contends for is the principle that the management of the town lands should be in the town meeting and not in a closed corporation of greedy monopolists.

When he protests, in the letter previously mentioned, that he has always been for "liberty and equality in land and government," it is a matter of conjecture what precisely he had in mind. The probable answer would be his willingness to share his original purchase with a group of associates; his persistent efforts to get these associates to deal justly with claims of others; his stand against clerical privilege; and his efforts to secure a free constitution. Williams spent his life repeating the things that really mattered to him. If the principle of equality had ever meant for him what it meant for an English Leveller, we would not have been left to divine his doctrine from a couple of sentences.

If we are looking for a guiding principle in Williams's political conceptions, other than his attachment to the common-law tradition and to certain standards of public spirit which he shared with the best gentry of his day, we should really seek it in the idea of Christian love. It is the old commandment, enlarged and enriched by his reflection on persecution, that rouses his impetuous devotion. His God appears to him as a God of Mercy and Love, hating greed and cruelty in all its forms, revealing a community beneath the rivalries of race, nation, and sect, and blessing the peacemakers. Williams was prepared to secularize the state in the faith that the natural conscience of mankind provided an adequate basis for civil order; but the virtues he demanded of society, in both its internal and external relations, remained heroically Christian.

Sometimes, in conformity with his thesis, he tries to argue a particular duty from natural reason; but more often he simply appeals to the common Christian legacy. "How far from Nature is the Spirit of Christ Jesus that loves and pities, prays for and does good to enemies. . . . Our God is a God of Mercy. . . . We have great cause to sigh at the unChristian ways of punishment. . . . I humbly ask how it can suit with

Christian ingenuity to take hold of some seeming occasions for their [the Indians'] destructions. . . . Concerning liberty of conscience . . . I hope . . . that not only the necessity, but the equity, piety and Christianity of that freedom will more and more shine forth, not to licentiousness, as all mercies are apt to be abused, but to the beauty of Christianity and the lustre of true faith in God and love to poor mankind."

Like John Winthrop, though in different terms, he had dreamt of establishing in the wilderness "a city set on a hill"; but he had even longer than Winthrop to discover that the American experiment was turning sour. "Sir," he wrote to Winthrop's son in 1664, "when we that have been the eldest, and are rotting, (to-morrow or next day) a generation will act, I fear, far unlike the first Winthrops and their Models of Love: I fear that the common Trinity of the world, (Profit, Preferment, Pleasure) will here be the *Tria omnia,* as in all the world beside: that Prelacy and Papacy too will in this wilderness predominate [and] that God Land will be (as now it is) as great a God with us English as God Gold was with the Spaniards. . . ."

Need one repeat that the fading dream of this passionate pilgrim had been no vision of modern times?

10. SOCIAL ORIGINS OF SOME EARLY AMERICANS*

by Mildred Campbell

The first Americans had to create a productive system from scratch. In Europe, economic development was a slow, evolutionary process that occurred over many centuries. The modernization of European economies was built on the accumulated human and material resources of past generations. But in the American colonies, though natural resources were abundant, a labor force was nonexistent, since the Indians proved intractable. To survive the initial years of settlement and to satisfy greater material wants later required recruiting a labor force. By 1660, about 75,000 people inhabited the colonies, and population grew rapidly, reaching about two million a century later.

What kind of people migrated to a wilderness, from what strata of society did they come, and why did they uproot themselves and leave behind loved ones and familiar places? How was this vast migration organized and financed? In the seventeenth century, involuntary labor, notably Negro slaves,

* James M. Smith (ed.), *Seventeenth-Century America* (Chapel Hill: University of North Carolina Press, 1959), pp. 63–89. Footnotes have been omitted except where they are necessary for an understanding of the text.

was not nearly as important a source of labor as the English indentured servants studied by Mildred Campbell in the following essay. Those who left home were neither very rich nor very poor but were people from the middling strata who had some expectations. The poorest often accepted their lot as decreed by fate; the well-to-do had too much to risk and too little to gain by migrating. But young farmers and artisans could not be sure that if they remained at home they would enjoy a position equal to their fathers'. Economic change was squeezing the smaller agriculturalists off the land, and in the towns and cities old trades were decaying, unable to compete with more efficient methods of industrial organization. Changes in the English economy displaced people from their traditional occupations and sent them searching for new ways of making a living. At the same time, religious tensions related to social change intensified the instability of life in England during much of the seventeenth century. The forces that disrupted English society eventually spread over the face of Europe and sent millions across the ocean during the three centuries when America welcomed all who wanted to come.

For further reading: Mildred Campbell, *The English Yeoman under Elizabeth and Early Stuarts* (1942); Abbot E. Smith, *Colonists in Bondage* (1947); Richard B. Morris, *Government and Labor in Early America* (1946); Marcus Lee Hansen, *The Atlantic Migration* (1940); Oscar Handlin, *The Uprooted* (1951).

A study of American origins must eventually lead to the structure and functioning of many Old World societies, for the national fabric is woven of many threads. But the people who came first in their sturdy ships of fifty to a hundred tons, who kept coming throughout the seventeenth century until the small seaboard settlements had moved out of their first precarious existence to a more certain future—these have a special claim upon us. Indeed, one wonders whether individuals ever meant as much to any enterprise as did those who filled the emigrant ships in that first century of colonization. Emigration across the Atlantic has never ceased from their day to ours, but only then did actual survival depend on the arrival of a relatively few people.

It was also only in the first century that those who came were a fairly homogeneous group in terms of national origins. For despite the Dutch on the Hudson, and small groups of Swiss, Swedes, Finns, and French Huguenots pocketed along the coast, the small vessels which set out on the American voyage were chiefly English built and English manned. Their cargoes, moreover, consisted largely of Englishmen and, later and in smaller numbers, Englishwomen. Even the Scots and Irish, who in the next century would crowd the harbors of the New World, were a minority in the first century.

We have long been accumulating a vast amount of information about these early settlers, and able historians have exploited the material with skill and insight. Only in more recent years, however, have serious attempts been made to push the story further back. We now try to discover their social origins. We want to know more about what they brought with them; not their material possessions—the *Susan Constant* and her sister ships provided space for only the barest minimum of necessities—but that other luggage which every individual perforce carries about with him, his heritage. That heritage was the sum total of his own experiences and the environment in which he grew up; it had made him what he was and determined, to an extent, what he would become. The impact of the New World might, and we know often did, produce marked changes in a settler which, for good or ill, would affect his whole future. It could never entirely obliterate his past.

Let us admit at the outset that we shall never know the past of these first Americans, still English in their own eyes and in the eyes of others, as well as we should like to know it; nor shall we be able to answer half the questions about them that can be asked. An appallingly large number of them never lived to play their part in the enterprise to which they were so important. Thousands either died on the voyage or during the first year after their arrival. Most of those who came never kept personal records and no records were kept about them. Except for the concern of a ship captain or his agent that there be a profitable cargo for the outgoing voyage, their homeland in most cases took little note of their leaving. And the New World soon made it clear that their past mattered less than what they could do in the "needful" present. But the search is worth while if one can know even a little more about the lives of these people in their native England: the social strata from which they sprang, the fabric of life in their home communities, the reasons why the New World made its appeal—all matters about which we have thus far little concrete information.

The scene of the search is England under the Stuarts and in the Cromwellian interlude. Recent decades have taught us much about the entire social background of this period. Professors Trevelyan and Rowse paint the larger canvas in the bold strokes they use so effectively. Wallace Notestein perhaps comes nearer than anyone else to taking up residence among seventeenth-century Englishmen and learns from his close acquaintance both big and little things about them that are revealing. Others have dealt more narrowly with special segments of society, or have done what the English scholars do so well—shown what life was like in specific localities. The Tawney–Trevor Roper controversy over the gentry has also added light as well as heat. Such studies have enabled us to read a broadside addressed to "earls, lords, knights, gentlemen, and yeomen," with a better knowledge of what those terms mean. There remains, however, a multitude of shadings to vex us, especially in the lower groups and in the more mobile and intricate relationships of urban society.

In searching for the origins of American settlers we shall not be concerned equally with all of the social strata. Yet two basic aspects of seventeenth-century social philosophy which affected everyone must be kept in mind: first, the universal acceptance of the concept of social gradation and a complete belief in its rightness; and second, the belief, held simultaneously, that differences in rank, although normally to be observed, were not unalterable. One will not, of course, forget that the period of the Civil Wars produced a handful of Diggers on St. George's Hill who espoused a doctrine of communistic living, or that John Lilburne and his fellow-soldiers turned a part of the Cromwellian army into a debating society on political democracy. The issues of these debates would one day assume great importance; but they are probably remembered more for their later significance than because of any immediate effect they had on social structure. Degree, priority, and place, as Shakespeare described it, as the clergy taught and preached it, and as the people of all ranks lived it, was the accepted social philosophy of the day. "For that infinite wisdom of God which hath distinguished his angels by degrees . . . hath also ordained kings, dukes . . . and other degrees among men."

The normal expectation of the members of every class was to see their children settled and married within their own social group. On the other hand, if a man came to a position of substance and outlook more in keeping with another class above or below him, he eventually moved into its ranks. This practice had long lent a freshness and toughness to the fiber of English society. Now in the fast changing and more competitive conditions of the Tudor and Stuart era, social fluidity was greater than it had ever been. Some deplored the current development in which "Joan is as good as My Lady," where "Citizen's wives have of late growne Gallants," and "the yeoman doth gentilize it." But most people considered it a source of national strength that "in England the temple of honour is bolted against none."

It worked both ways though. A man could go down as well as up. Inflationary prices, a fluctuating land market, defective land titles, precarious investments, and bad debts created a milieu which gave some men their opportunity and brought dismal failure to others. Every social category had its crop of new men. Increased competition placed a higher premium on personal initiative than had been known in an earlier England. In emphasizing the manner in which pioneer colonial life developed individual initiative, it may be that we have not sufficiently recognized that much initiative was already present in the society from which the early settlers came, that indeed this may partially explain their coming.

In England tales of discovery and exploration had enlisted the interest and stretched the imagination of people of every class. But those at the top of the social hierarchy rarely were concerned with actual settlement. In terms of patronage and investment, however, many of them were active. Lord Baltimore had able friends among his own associates to aid in the Maryland enterprise; and no fewer than eight earls, one viscount, and a bishop helped to launch the Virginia Company under its second charter in 1609. Interest in colonial schemes became a favorite hobby, more than a hobby in some cases, with noblemen at the court of Charles II. But in answer to the query, "Who would venture their persons and who their purses?" the noblemen usually answered in favor of the latter, and few members of the nobility actually emigrated with the intention of remaining in the colonies.

Below the nobility came the knights and country gentry: "gentlemen of the blood," of ancient lineage. But with them also were newly landed men, office holders, members of the professions, university men, and many with business and mercantile interests—these too were known as "gentlemen." Dozens of such men became involved in colonial activities.

Indeed, one wonders if seventeenth-century America would have advanced much beyond the trading-post stage had it not been for their money, vision, and perseverance. They were the men who instituted, to a great extent financed, and almost wholly ran the great companies under which the first colonies were started. The wealthier and more important, men like Sir Ferdinand Gorges, Sir John Popham, Matthew Cradock, Sir Thomas Smith, carried on their work from England. But others came in person to lead the new plantations: younger sons of the financial backers, gentry of lesser pretensions, clergymen, and merchants. This was especially true in the earlier years, partly because leadership from below had not yet had time to develop, and partly because it seems to have been the original intent that the colonies should be led by individuals of the upper classes, a policy in keeping with the philosophy of the time. It is also apparent that in the beginning such men had little idea that the demands made upon them by the New World would be so different from those to which they had been accustomed at home.

More is known about these leaders than about any of the other settlers and for obvious reasons. They were the articulate ones. They themselves wrote and kept records, though not perhaps as many records as we should like, and others wrote about them. They were the clergymen about whom Perry Miller, Alan Simpson, and a host of writers tell us, those who preached *Puritanism in Old and New England* and made frequent journeys back and forth. Among them are some of Louis Wright's *First Gentlemen of Virginia* and some of John Pomfret's proprietors of *The Province of West New Jersey*. They wander through the pages of Bernard Bailyn's *New England Merchants in the Seventeenth Century*. In terms of social origins, less illustrious people also belong in this group: bankrupt businessmen; ill-starred younger sons and brothers of the gentry; proverbial ne'er-do-wells whose families hoped that a change of scene would set them on a better path, youths like Lady Finch's unruly son, "whom she sent to Virginia to be tamed." Sometimes family hopes for reformation were realized. Often enough, however, parents had to face the fact that the voyage across the Atlantic was not sufficient to bring about the moral transformation desired. Despite this unpromising contingent, men of the rank of knight or gentleman (whether that rank came by birth or acquisition) played a role in colonial society out of proportion to their numbers. And the more we know about them, the better off we shall be. They are recognized by the title "Sir" if they were knights, or merely by "Mr.," a term not applied below the gentry. In many colonial narratives they are spoken of as "the better sort" and in lists of ships' passengers are usually identified as the "men of quality." Thus one ship carried "eighteen men of quality and eighty-seven others." Another speaks of "seven gentlemen and sixty-four others." And again, we read of "about a score of men of quality and a hundred and four others." One becomes familiar with the pattern.

But who were "the others"? Practically nothing is known about them, although the passenger lists make it perfectly clear that they account for the overwhelming numbers in the emigrant ships. "How to people His Majesty's dominions with people?" becomes a kind of recurrent refrain in the plantation literature of the seventeenth century. It was "the others" who chiefly furnished the answer to that query. Because there were so many of them and because our information about them is so woefully scant they have perhaps a special claim to attention. Who actually were they? Did they belong chiefly to the "middling people"— yeomen and artisans? Were they largely the poor agricultural laborers whose sorry plight in this period is well known? Or were they mostly riffraff from the streets of London and Bristol, the poor who had so increased under the Tudors as to demand state action; or beggars, and condemned persons who filled the prisons? We know that all of these were represented among the early colonists. But beyond that we have had little concrete information about them, and slight knowledge of the relative degree with which the various groups responded to the appeals from the New World for settlers.

Two sets of seventeenth-century manuscripts merit attention for what they have to offer about the identity of "the others." They record the departure of slightly more than 11,000 emigrants from Bristol and London in the second half of the seventeenth century. The Bristol record, the more important of the two, contains the names of some 10,000 people who shipped from that port between 1654 and 1685. It provides a small amount of data for the entire group over the whole period; but the fuller part of the record, and that part which contains information pertinent to the subject of social origins, covers approximately the first 7 years and deals with upwards of 3,000 people. The London record includes approximately 750 men and women who left for the New World in the year 1683-84. Although a smaller sample, it contains the same type of information (including several additional items) as found in the Bristol record, thus providing comparative material from another area. The London and Bristol records list only a few of the many thousands of men and women who made their beginning in the New World as indentured servants before the American Revolution. But they originated in a period for which data are scarce; hence, though neither record is statistically perfect, both deserve careful consideration.

The first significant fact about both records is that they deal entirely with people who were coming to America as indentured servants. This is perhaps fortunate; for studies made in the last two decades have demonstrated that a far larger percentage of our colonial population entered the country under indenture than was formerly thought. One-half of the total is held to be a conservative estimate. On the question of their social origins, moreover, almost no concrete information is available.

The plan of indenture has been so fully treated by scholars that only a brief definition is required here. Under the indenture terms, a prospective settler agreed to serve a master in one of the colonies for a period of years (usually four or five), in return for free passage across the Atlantic and certain "Freedom dues" when his term of service was over. One aspect of indenture, however, has not been sufficiently considered: the fact that within the framework of English society, as it actually functioned in the seventeenth century, such a practice would be considered not only natural but salutary. This is of great importance if we look at the New World from the point of view of the prospective emigrant still in England, or of the family of a young person contemplating settlement. The whole idea of service and services in return for land, training, protection—in short, for social and economic security—was an idea basic to medieval thinking and practice and one that had by no means disappeared. The practice of apprenticeship, for example, was not legalized and specifically defined until 1563, but it had been the general practice for generations.

The same mental and social outlook that found positive values in the seven-year apprenticeship for young children would see social values in a four- or five-year indenture for a young man—and even more for a young woman—who was preparing to set out on a journey of three thousand miles in the hope of eventually establishing himself. Promotion literature advised young single men—particularly those with small means —to go into service for a few years and especially recommended indenture for young women. Some tales that came back across the water about the life of an indentured servant in the American colonies made it clear that it was often very different from the version presented in the promotion literature. But stories of those settlers who had been fortunate circulated in England as well; and the practice of indenture, which was based on the long-accepted principle of service, could weather reports of abuse and failure.

Historians have long been interested in the social status of the colonists who came under indenture; but throughout the first third of the twentieth century it remained a subject of the widest conjecture, despite the tremendous amount of excellent work done in the colonial field. Professor Andrews, who often deplored our lack of sufficient knowledge on the subject, said of the indentured servants in Virginia: "Some of them, perhaps many, seem to have been in origin above the level of menials, to have good family connections in England, and in a few instances to have been even of gentle birth." Marcus Jernegan believed they came chiefly from the undesirables and the agricultural class who under conditions in England had no chance to better themselves. In his *First Americans*, Professor Wertenbaker shared this view. The bulk of the indentured servants were, he said, "poor laborers who were no longer content to work in misery and rags in England while opportunity beckoned them across the Atlantic." Fifteen years later he had accepted what Abbot Smith, Richard Morris, and others were saying, namely, that "all kinds came." An analysis of the Bristol and London records helps to define that phrase and to show in what proportions different social groups were represented.

It is a matter of considerable interest that approximately twenty-five percent of the Bristol group are women. We shall have something more to say of them later. Among the men, yeomen and husbandmen are in the majority; they account for about thirty-six percent, with the yeomen outnumbering the husbandmen. Artisans and tradesmen number approximately twenty-two percent; laborers account for about ten percent; gentlemen and professional men make up a little less than one percent. Thus the farmers outnumber the skilled workers almost two to one, and the combined farmers and skilled workers outnumber the laborers more than five to one.

In the smaller London sampling, the women are somewhat under the twenty-five percent of the Bristol records. The skilled workers outnumber the yeomen and husbandmen in almost the reverse proportion to the Bristol record: approximately two to one. This difference is, of course, to be expected in the records of an urban center. The husbandmen are also more numerous than the yeomen. But as in the case of the Bristol servants, the number of farmers and skilled workers in comparison with the laborers is in a ratio of about five to one.

A question may be raised concerning the authenticity of the status terms. Would not an ordinary laborer, knowing that masons, bricklayers, and carpenters were in great demand in the colonies at high wages, possibly try to assume a skill for which he had no training? Some may have tried this deception, and it is possible that the number of artisans should be slightly lowered to take care of self-styled craftsmen. But two factors weigh in favor of the general validity of the terms. First, the number and variety of the skills listed in the records suggest accuracy: there are ninety-eight trades, many of which, such as the tuckers, fullers, and button makers, were not those most sought after by the colonial agents. Secondly, men in the seventeenth century were still accustomed to being recorded in terms of their status or occupation. They were so listed in court records, wills, deeds, leases, and business transactions of all kinds. It would have seemed natural and prudent to give the same information for this record as for all others. Hence, allowing for a certain margin of error and even some false reporting, the evidence still points to a large majority of farmers and tradesmen over laborers.

The relatively low number of laborers was at first puzzling. According to writers of the period, the laborers' status was the lowest in the social hierarchy. They were the most numerous and poorest members of England's working population. Although their wages rose slightly during the first half of the century, they tended to remain constant, even in some places to drop a little, from then until the end of the century. Those who worked by the year for an annual wage ranging from three to five pounds were perhaps the most fortunate. They had a roof over their heads and something to eat. We think it a hardship that the medieval serf could not escape the land, but neither, it may be well to remember, could the land get away from him. His life was meager, often harsh, but economically it was more secure than that of his successor, the landless laborer.

In the comments of some of their contemporaries may lie a partial explanation of the laborers' lack of enthusiasm for emigration. Thomas Ludwell, a Somerset man, received a request for servants from his brother in Virginia. He answered that there were workmen in his neighborhood to spare, but "they will live meanly and send their families to the parish to be relieved rather than hear of such a long journey to mend their condition." Robert Southwell, who had had poor luck in his attempt to recruit laborers in 1669, said of them: "They are loth to leave the smoke of their own cabin if they can but beg neere it." There are other comments in the same vein. The laborers were accustomed to little; they could do with little. In times of dearth they would be hungry; but they had rarely had full stomachs, and while they might come close to starvation, the parish would not let them die. In addition, they were a superstitious lot and quite possibly would have been frightened by the tales about the dangers of the long voyage over strange waters.

If the London and Bristol records can be taken as a fair sample (and they are in accord with other recent studies), it is clearly a mistaken assumption to think that the laborers formed the large part of those who came to America as indentured servants. The majority were farmers and skilled workers.

Most of the women in the list were not classified according to status except as "singlewoman" or "spinster," the latter term being used at this period to describe either a married or an unmarried woman. A number of "widows" were listed, and a few women were classified according to the skill or occupation which they hoped to have in the homes of their new masters—"dairy maid," "lady's maid," and the like. Young women often went in twos and threes from the same village, and now and then the lists show members of the same family. It is quite possible that a larger percentage of women than men came from among the laborers. Country folk had their own measuring rods in terms of social codes and behavior patterns; a yeoman or tradesman of some standing would feel more reluctant to see his daughter set off on such a journey than would a laborer. Yeomen and husbandmen worked alongside farm laborers getting in the crops and mingled with them in the village alehouse. Yet it was not considered the proper thing for the daughters of yeomen to work in the fields, although the wives and daughters of laborers did so as a matter of course. Daughters of yeomen and tradesmen, however, often went into the service of families in their neighborhoods, and in certain industries such as lacemaking, girls were apprenticed in the usual way.

There are women listed in both these records who were going in answer to personal requests from planters in Maryland and Virginia for servants of various skills. Charles Peck of London was sending one to his brother Tom in Virginia at the latter's request. She was to serve in his own home, and "not be soulde unless to some planter for a wife." It was commonly accepted that a husband was the chief inducement the New World had to offer a young girl. Nor would she have much trouble getting one, although the match was not always with the wealthy planter that the promotion literature promised. It is interesting that promoters were becoming a bit more discriminating in their advice respecting the women who were wanted. They were somewhat on the defensive about the women who had been sent over from the houses of correction: "But if they come of honest stock, and have good repute they may pick their husbands out of the better sort of people." Three months, one of them thought, was as long as one could hope to keep a good maid before "some proper young fellow" would come after her.

Servants sought as wives were purchased either in pounds sterling or tobacco. This businesslike way of approaching marriage strikes a wrong note in our generation. But it would have seemed quite normal to the seventeenth century, where every girl (except those of the very lowest groups, who were not too particular about such things) was accustomed to a marriage that was largely a business arrangement. Women who went to the colonies, however, may not always have accepted husbands immediately, even if they were not under indenture; there was plenty of work at good pay for them until such time as they did marry. Later in the century when many servants were going to Pennsylvania, Gabriel Thomas lamented about the exorbitant wages women could command: "They are not as yet very numerous which makes them stand on high terms for their several services." He added, however, "They are usually marry'd before they are twenty years of age."

Practically all of the servants were young. Indeed, it is clear that the whole plan for indentured service was designed for the young unmarried man and woman. It is easier for the young to be uprooted, and a new-found land across the sea would beckon to twenty-one as it would not to fifty. The Bristol record does not give ages, but they are given in the London group. The majority were between the ages of eighteen and twenty-four, with twenty-one and twenty-two predominating—just the age when the young tradesmen were finishing their apprenticeship. The large number of farmers and skilled workers going under indenture demonstrates the appeal which this method of emigration made to single young men of small means and even to those whose parents could perhaps have managed the passage money.

A young man just out of his apprenticeship would not, if he remained in England, set up for himself at once. Likewise, a yeoman's son, unless he were the eldest or his father were able to buy land for him, would work at home or for a neighboring yeoman or gentleman through his earlier years while he accumulated piecemeal holdings of his own. English yeomen were a canny lot. Perhaps farmers everywhere are. To be able to get to America without any expense to himself or his family would appeal to a lad brought up as these had been. Besides if a young man went to America alone without enough money to buy labor, reputed to be both high and scarce, what could he do with the fifty or a hundred acres of land that he hoped to get? Nobody knew better than a farmer's son that it took more than one pair of hands to get crops in the ground and to harvest them. These were some of the facts that would have been in the minds of the yeomen and husbandmen, carpenters, tilemakers, and weavers whose names are enrolled in the Bristol and London lists.

A few married men went without their wives, leaving them sometimes provided for, sometimes not. And there were a few married couples going together, but not many, for this practice was discouraged because of complications likely to arise on the other side. Finally in 1682 an order prohibiting a married man from going as an indentured servant went into effect. But it is doubtful if recruiting agents looked into the matter too closely. There are examples in other records of groups of married people who paid their own passage, but were apparently somewhat older and better established. They took along with them single young men and women under indenture—their neighbors, friends, and kinspeople. They would thereby get the "headright" lands for having brought them over, and the young people coming as servants were with friends and kinsfolk during their early years in a strange country. Hundreds who were not so fortunate left it to chance to place them in the hands of a good master or a poor one when the ship docked.

It is significant that the married people referred to above who took their families and paid their own passage were for the most part farmers and tradesmen of the same social rank as the servants they took with them. This was, I believe, generally the case. For one of the gratifying byproducts of the information concerning status that comes from these records is that through them we are also able indirectly to determine the status of the remainder of "the others" who filled the emigrant ships. If the laborers at the bottom of the economic scale account for a relatively small number of those coming under indenture, it is certain that they were not widely represented among those who paid their own passage. The reluctance of the laborers to go as servants has already been shown.

If one adds to that the crucial fact that they simply would not have had the five or six pounds required to pay their own passage, it is clear that there would be few of them in that group. Individuals or small groups sometimes came over in the personal service of men of better substance, but this would not account for many. If, therefore, the laborers at the bottom of the social and economic hierarchy were a minority, as were also the "men of quality" at the other extreme, we can but conclude that "the others," both those who came under indenture and those who paid their own fare, were drawn from the middling classes: farmers and skilled workers, the productive groups in England's working population. The difference between those who came as servants and those who paid their own fare was partly economic, with the poorer farmers and "decayed" tradesmen coming under indenture; and partly, as we have seen, it was a matter of age, experience, and marital position.

Status is basic to the quest for social origins. But before attempting further to spell out its meaning in terms of actual living conditions, we must pay our respects to one other relatively small group among the Bristol servants, the children. The term of service set down in the indenture provides the key for determining their numbers. The vast majority of adult terms are for four or five years, the four-year term slightly predominating, although now and then a servant went for two or three years, or more rarely, even for one. Children, however, were sent for longer terms in order that they should reach adulthood by the time their service was over. Their average term was seven years, as was that of the ordinary apprentice in England; but in both cases it might be as high as ten or twelve years, depending on the child's age.

About eight percent of the Bristol group went for a term of six years or more, chiefly seven. But seven years or longer is also the term assigned to those recalcitrants whom the justices of the peace sent to the colonies for the punishment of minor crimes. How can we know that the emigrants with terms of seven years or more were not these delinquents rather than minors? It is likely that some of them were, for delinquents of this type were sent along with other servants and we know of some who were in this group. Fortunately, the London indentures containing the actual ages for everyone are of assistance in this problem. For they show that almost all of the indentures for long terms (about six percent in this record) apply to children under fifteen. Only occasionally is an older person given a longer term. An examination of Quarter Sessions court records, where instances of forced emigration for minor crimes were documented, offers supporting evidence during the years in question that this type of punishment was apparently used sparingly by the county officials. Hence, unless there was a larger percentage of delinquents in the Bristol group than among those going from London, which hardly seems likely, we may assume that the majority of Bristol's eight percent assigned to long terms were also minors.

Not infrequently, of course, some of the individuals deported for misdemeanors were likewise minors; often the children who went as servants were orphans or problem children whom someone wished to dispose of. We glimpse them now and again in the records. John Morgan, a Bristol upholsterer, appeared in July, 1659, with an uncancelled indenture that had been made out for David Thomas, a Glamorgan boy who was bound to him. He should have been registered earlier: "But in regard he was on shipboard, and could not be brought up for fear of his running away, he was not enrolled in the middle of the book." A fourteen-year-old girl in London was taken out of White Chapel jail to which she had been committed for "pilfering lace" and with the consent of her father and mother was indentured for service in America. A stray letter among the London indentures tells the story of Robert Redman. An uncle in Cambridge had sent him up to London to be put aboard *The Hopewell*. He writes that in the boy's trunk "is his best and worst cloathes, an extra shirt, 2 pr. stockins, 6 neck cloathes, 6 handkerchers, 2 caps, 1 hatt, 1 pr. shoes." Instructions are given that anything else needful is to be provided. "If 9 years or tenn yeares service be required," the uncle writes, "I am contented provided he have his bellefull of food, with cloathes to keep him warm and warm lodgin at night." He asks to be told when the boy is "disposed of" and to whom and "how to rit a letter to his master and to him." It is apparent that things have not gone well. Young Redman is not to be given the keys to his trunk for fear he will either sell or give away his belongings. "I could keep him no longer," the uncle says; yet he hopes he will have a good voyage, and has sent along "Balsome and salve" for the ship's surgeon to use in treating an injury on the boy's leg. After a somewhat formal ending according to the fashion of the day, a postscript adds that "Thers a Rage to dress his wounded leg with."

Aside from the delinquents, both minor and adult, sent by the justices, two groups of indentured servants entered into their contracts under compulsion: convicts and, during both the Commonwealth and Restoration period, political prisoners. Neither group will be considered here; for with the few possible exceptions which have been considered among those holding long terms, it seems clear that these records deal with the ordinary men and women who went to America under indenture of their own volition. Therefore, we turn again to the two basic records for additional clues which will make possible at least a fragmentary reconstruction of the environment they were leaving behind them.

Next in importance to the status term is that part of the record which gives the emigrant's place of origin; for without this information, it would be impossible to enlarge our understanding of the American settler's background. Both records show how widely the New World ventures were known in England. The Bristol names include representatives from every English county except Rutland, and many from Wales. An overwhelming majority are from the West, with Somerset, Gloucestershire, and Wiltshire taking the lead among the English counties and Monmouthshire first among the Welsh. Proximity to Bristol undoubtedly accounts partly for this concentration; but it is significant that some western counties are much more sparsely represented. Outside the heavy concentration in London and Middlesex, Yorkshire furnished the largest number to the London group.

The place of origin carries significance beyond the servant group; for if large numbers of servants were coming from certain centers, it is almost certain that there were also large numbers from these same centers who paid their own passage. The largest number of servants recorded in the Bristol group, slightly more than half, booked for Virginia. One is therefore not surprised to come upon the following passage from James Southall's sketch of a Virginia family, in which he discusses the section in England that was the source of so many of Virginia's early settlers. He describes an area

> about thirty miles north of Bristol in the west of England, running due north and south for a distance of about ten miles and with an average breadth of three miles, where a . . . ridge of the Malvern Hills divides the county of Hereford from the county of Worcester and on the southeast of these, on the south bank of the upper Severn, with yet ampler dimensions stretches the county of Gloucester, all three counties touching each other at a common point near the city of Gloucester.

It was in this district, the author says,

> and from Somersetshire, and the neighboring counties of Wales . . . from Warwick on the north, Devon in the southwest, Herts and the

213

Isle of Wight in the south, and across the Bristol Channel from the coast of Ireland, that in Virginia, the counties of Henrico, James City, Charles City, Isle of Wight, Gloucester, Surrey, and Prince George were largely settled.

Except for including Ireland and the Isle of Wight, he has described almost exactly the area chiefly represented by the Bristol record. Along with East Anglia, and Lincolnshire and Yorkshire in the north, the West Country was the homeland of thousands of the early settlers. From the beginning there was in the West a strong tradition for the American adventure. The New World would not seem so far away to West Country boys, many of whose fathers and brothers earned their living as mariners and seamen on ships that plied between Plymouth, Bristol, and lesser ports to the New World. They were not, said a contemporary, of "the In-land sort," who were "wedded to their native soils like a Snaile to his shell, or . . . a mouse to his chest." Their grandfathers would have sailed or known people who sailed with Drake and Raleigh—and grandfathers are all alike. It was natural that Hugh Peter, telling the House of Lords in 1665 about his departure to New England, should say that he "by birth in Cornwall was not altogether ignorant of that place." It is then to the West Country that we must turn. For here lay the farm lands and villages from which almost eighty-five percent of the Bristol emigrants came.

Three centuries have inevitably changed the West Country. The most conspicuous difference is the growth of modern urban centers; yet there has been less change than in some parts of England, and one can drive through miles of rural Gloucestershire, Wiltshire, and Somerset, where the country must look much the same as it did three centuries and a half ago when many of its humbler people were preparing to leave. There are evidences now of more intensive agriculture, but the contours of hills and green sloping meadows remain the same. It is a good land to look upon. So also they must have thought who were departing from it. For it is a great mistake to assume that emigration, for whatever purpose, meant that people left home and familiar surroundings with no regrets. Even the most rabid of the New England Puritan clergy, full of spleen and invective, frequently expressed devotion to old England and the "mistaken ones" who stayed behind. These folk who left the West Country were not very articulate; they could not have said what they felt as did a later West Country man:

'Tis time, I think, by Wenlock town
The golden broom should blow.

But chance words and phrases that appear in prosaic colonial records betray the same nostalgia. It was probably sheer homesickness that overcame the boy from a Gloucestershire village who went to Bristol with a friend intent on shipping to Virginia—he let the other boy go on without him, the record says, and "came back home."

The houses they lived in, especially the homes of the lesser folk, were made of whatever natural building materials the locality afforded. Some of the small stone houses that can be seen today in Cotswold villages were there then, some newly built, some already old—all evidence of the prosperity that Cotswold wool had brought to the locality. Beyond the Cotswolds to the west in the Severn Valley, a redder sandstone furnished excellent building material, but it was hard to quarry and in general was reserved for churches and the houses of great men. Farmers and tradesmen built their houses mostly of a combination of wood and some kind of plaster spread often over a wattle framework. "Cob," as it was called, used largely in Devon farmhouses, was a mixture of mud, straw, gravel, and chalk. These houses were small, varying from the two to three rooms of the less well-to-do to as many as eight or nine in the houses of wealthy yeomen, small clothiers, and tradespeople of some substance. The homes of the laborers have not survived; they were probably little more than hovels and, except for some very newly built, were almost certainly without much light. John Aubrey, himself a West Country man, wrote of Wiltshire in 1671 and remarked that within his remembrance the use of glass had been restricted: "Copyholders and ordinary poor people had none." The inventories attached to wills supply details of the interiors of these crude homes. Trestled furniture was still being used, although sometimes "joined" tables are mentioned. Pewter dishes were by now a commonplace in the cupboards of the middling people, but wooden trenchers were still in everyday use. Occasionally there were a few prized silver teaspoons. Their standards of both comfort and cleanliness would, of course, be scorned by people of like position in modern society.

It is understandable that promoters found these middling people of the West Country satisfactory settlers and made special efforts to induce them to go to the colonies. It was not merely their skills that were wanted. They had other qualities born of the kind of lives they had lived that would stand them in good stead. They were not, it is true, accustomed to the peculiar type of pioneer hardship that prevailed in America, but their lives in England had known little comfort or ease. The craftsmen were accustomed to working from five in the morning until seven or eight at night. Farmers labored outside from daylight until dark and carried on indoor tasks by fire and candlelight. A man could not be idle and hold his own in the demanding world in which they lived. Idlers there were, of course, but lower and middle class families did not have the means to care for loafers.

Men of the West Country like those elsewhere were forced to adapt themselves to the competitive and acquisitive society common to their age. Those with a greater margin of wealth could weather the crises better. Because of their fairly simple standard of living and the fact that they were practically self-supporting, the farmers were less affected by the high prices of outside products than almost any other group. Despite market fluctuations, they could usually sell their sheep and grain at a very good profit.

Wealthy yeomen of the West Country not only had glass and chimneys in their houses, but were now installing wainscoting in their "halls" and "parlours." The members of this class were aggressive, and if they held their land in a good tenure—that is, if it were freehold or of that particular kind of copyhold which carried similar security—they were most probably affluent. But circumstances which brought success to many meant failure for others. Land hunger was rife among all classes. Wealthy clothiers, drapers, and merchants who had done well and wished to set themselves up in land were avidly watching the market, ready to pay almost any price for what was offered. Even prosperous yeomen often could not get the land they desired for their younger sons; and indeed those who did not hold their own land in a good tenure ran the risk of losing it.

The West Country was good farming country, especially for sheep raising. Somerset in particular also had excellent land for tillage, and its farmers were noted for their skill. Yet even if the title to his land were clear, a West Country farmer could fare badly compared with farmers in some sections of England. For the West was a conservative part of the country. Change came slowly there, and only a beginning had been made with inclosures. More than a century later George Turner, writing of farming conditions in the vale of Gloucestershire, could still say: "I know one acre which is divided into eight lands, and spread over a large common field, so that a man must travel two or three miles to visit it all. . . . But this is not the worst. . . ." And he continued to recite the woes that West Country farmers were still enduring.

A great deal of the land was still copyhold, and large landholders kept the village economy almost on a feudal basis. The farmers from Tetbury, Chipping Sodbury, and other Gloucestershire villages were still performing services that had long since been discarded in many parts of England. The tendency, moreover, to retain long leases (ninety-nine years was the most common), once an advantage to the leaseholders, was now catching up with western farmers. Many leases which had been made out in Elizabeth's reign were now "falling in," leaving the tenant to face increased fines and rents or the likelihood of seeing his land go to someone else. It is not surprising if farmers facing these and similar conditions lent a sympathetic ear to the tales of ship captains and their agents, colonial promoters, and returned travellers—tales of a country where land was to be had for the asking, or nearly so, where leases did not "fall in," nor rents come due, where, in short, a man was his own landlord. That these promises were often highly exaggerated, that there was not land in many places, at any rate, suitable land, to be had for the asking did not alter the landlord dream. It is a commonplace to say that land was the greatest inducement the New World had to offer; but it is difficult to overestimate its psychological and social importance to people in whose minds land had always been identified with security, success, and the good things of life. "Now we can get few English servants," said a member of the Barbados Assembly in 1665, "having no lands to give them at the end of their time which formerly was their main allurement." Tradesmen as well as yeomen and husbandmen looked forward to becoming landholders. Richard Norton was a Bristol millwright and John Hatten a watchmaker, but they, no less than John Rose, a Wiltshire husbandman, and Morgan Jones, son of a Monmouthshire yeoman, carried with them indentures that called for fifty acres of land in Virginia or Maryland. This was in 1655. In later years the Carolinas and Pennsylvania would make even more attractive land offers.

With the bulk of the family land going to the eldest son, it had been the traditional pattern for farmers in every section of England to apprentice one or more of their other sons to trade. This was especially true in the West Country, where the cloth trade had for generations been a source of employment. Hard times among the East Anglian clothworkers made it easier for Winthrop and the other Puritan leaders to gain recruits for New England. The exodus of West Country clothworkers to America in the second half of the century is less well known but merits equal attention. The plight of the West Country was made considerably worse by economic disruption during and after the Civil Wars. No part of the nation was unaffected by this conflict, but the West was especially hard hit. As a key city Bristol early became a major objective and was successively under the control of both armies. The neighboring countryside suffered accordingly. "This England," said one, "is merely the ghost of that England which it was lately." Ships rotted in Bristol harbor; Gloucestershire woolen mills were plundered; clothworkers in Somerset were left without employment for months.

Nor did matters improve when the wars were over. Returned soldiers found themselves without work. Slack periods in the cloth business came in close succession. Prices fluctuated. Problems growing out of the plight of war widows, disabled soldiers, and an increasing number of poor rose to plague local officials and cast a pall of gloom over village communities. "I wish I could hear what condition you live in," an Essex tradesman had written a few years earlier to his Virginia kinsman, "for I fear if these times hold long amongst us we must be all faine come to Virginia." If the emigrant records can be taken as a key, many West Country men and women were now thinking the same thing. The annual exodus of servants shipping from Bristol rose from slightly less than 300 in 1655 to almost 800 in 1659, and hundreds more emigrants were going with their families and paying their own fare.

Discontent in the West Country cloth towns was not new. The trade had suffered somewhat earlier in the century, but it was not until after the Civil Wars that the complaints so increased in volume and bitterness. Modern scholars are inclined to think that the depression in the cloth trade traditionally assigned to the late Commonwealth and early Restoration years was not as damaging to the industry as was earlier thought. They tend to see the complaints from clothiers as disgruntlement over a shift to new men and new methods rather than a decline in the industry itself. But they all agree on the bad effects of the situation for the workers. The local records at Taunton and Trowbridge and Gloucester are filled with the hardships of the clothworkers: those who "toiled in their cottages from Castle Colne and Malmsbury on the edge of the Cotswold country" and in the industrial towns on the Avon, "to Westbury, Edington and the other villages under the plain." And it was from

Castle Colne, Malmsbury, Westbury, and other villages under the plain that John Niblett, the clothmaker, Thomas Allen, the worsted comber, Edward Webb, the feltmaker, and John Davis, the tailor, with dozens of their friends and neighbors, made their way to Bristol during the late fifties and early sixties, to sign the indentures which assured their free passage to America. Other tradesmen and farmers in the nearby countryside were likewise affected, for hard times cannot come to a basic industry in a rural area without affecting auxiliary trades and the whole working population.

Tradesmen, like farmers, were worried not merely by present uncertainties but by the lack of future opportunity. It had once been the expectation of journeymen that they would advance their status three or four years after apprenticeship. Many were beginning now to find that they would have to be wage earners all their lives. Skilled workers of certain kinds much needed in the colonies could sometimes get special favors written into their agreements. John Walker and Samuel Minor, both carpenters, had made such arrangements. Walker's term was only three years, with a wage of forty pounds per annum while he was still in service. Minor, probably younger, was bound for five years, to receive twenty pounds the first three years and twenty-five the last two. Most of the servants, however, were either not that forehanded or their skills were not such as would be so much needed in America. Land and high wages were counted on to make up for that.

Despite the fact that industry and the land had each its peculiar character and concerns, their interaction in the general economy was very marked. What each could offer or failed to offer to the individual was of paramount importance. Together they provided the economic framework within which West Country farmers and tradesmen shaped the course of their lives. The laborers, whether agricultural or urban, were perhaps most immediately affected by the current fluctuations common to both Cromwellian and Restoration years. They eked out a meager living on their daily wage if there was work for them. If the cloth works were "still" or harvests were thin, they became a public charge; the local records bear eloquent testimony to the efforts of harassed parish officials to look after their poor. For such among them as were ambitious there was little or no opportunity. Emigration offered it and, as we know, there were some who took advantage of the offer. But most of them were not ambitious. Their niche in the social and economic scale was not threatened as was often that of small landed men or craftsmen.

It would, however, be a great error to assume that these West Country people thought only of economic matters. It should also be remembered that numerous though the emigrants were from any region, far more people stayed at home than left. To think otherwise would be to distort the view of the background of American immigration. There had long been a good deal of mobility among England's working population, particularly among young single men who moved around in search of work when times were bad in their own communities. In some cases families whose sons emigrated to America were already accustomed to having them away from home. The life of country communities would not be markedly changed because here and there a young person or a few families left. Those at home would carry on with the normal pursuits of daily life as dictated by their rank and position in the community and by individual and group interests.

Aside from the demands of daily occupations, perhaps the central focus of their activities was religion. Their scale of values was in large part determined by it, and it profoundly affected the shape and substance of their mental and social outlook. To the middling people of the West Country, as to many of their kind elsewhere, religion meant non-conformity. It was not, of course, all of one brand—that is the essence of non-conformity. "How many ways do you make it to heaven in this place?" a royalist chaplain had asked in 1647 as he deplored the "rabble of heresies" around Bristol. The years under Cromwell had not eased their troubles as much as many had hoped for. There was probably not much actual religious persecution, although it was not wholly absent; Quakers were cruelly treated at Bristol in 1654–56 and hunderds of them went to America in the following years. A comparison of the Bristol list with Besse's "Sufferers" shows an identity of almost five hundred names. Granting the error which may originate in the prolific repetition among West Country names, these figures cannot be entirely without significance. And not only Quakers were troubled. The West was indeed as the royalist chaplain had found, a hotbed of activity of the various sects. The rise in the Bristol emigration for 1659 has already been indicated. It is significant that the largest annual exodus came in 1662, when the first Restoration statutes against dissenters went into effect. Between eight and nine hundred servants went to America in that year from this one port. If the non-conformists of the West Country had not fared too well in the Commonwealth, they certainly did not expect the return of the Stuarts to help matters. Nor did it.

George Herbert, earlier tracing the cycle through which he thought
religion ran her course, startled some of his friends by saying:

> Religion stands on tiptoe in our land
> Readie to pass to the American strand.

Nor had he been unaware of the social and economic implications:

> Then shall Religion to America flee;
> . . . .
> My God, Thou dost prepare for them a way,
> By carrying first their gold from them away,
> For gold and grace did never yet agree
> Religion alwaies sides with povertie.

Josiah Child was only the best known of various writers in the second
half of the century who pointed out the "great swarms of new inhabitants" whom the New World received because of the restrictions placed
on dissenters in England.

Nowhere were non-conformity and the ferment which it bred more
deeply rooted than in the clothmaking centers. Richard Baxter, a Puritan
clergyman of yeoman origins, pointed out this relationship as he looked
back upon the part played by the various classes in the Civil Wars. Writing in 1683, he said,

> On the side of Parliament were the smaller part (as some thought) of
> the gentry in most of the countries and the greatest part of the
> Tradesmen and Freeholders, and the Middle sort of men; especially
> in those corporations and countries [counties] which depend on
> Cloathing and such Manufactures.

The preoccupation of the middling classes with non-conformity has often
been noted. It was, says Alan Simpson, "weavers at their looms, tradesmen in their shops, and yeoman farmers in their homes" among whom
Puritanism chiefly took root. Certainly non-conformity, clothmaking,
and emigration were active influences in East Anglia in the first half of
the century. It was also a combination that was active in the West Country in the second half. Restrictions on non-conformity and the impover-
ishment of the clothmaking industry gave the New World a double

appeal. By no means, of course, were all of these Somerset farmers and Wiltshire and Gloucestershire clothworkers deeply religious people. Far from it. But most of them had been brought up in non-conformist groups which had, to a great extent, shaped the pattern of their lives. As Oscar Handlin has said about the effect of the church on later comers to America, it was not so much that they "rationally accepted doctrines" as that their beliefs were "closely wrapped in the day-to-day events of their existence." And as was true of most people in seventeenth-century England, whatever their religious persuasion they accorded it intense loyalty and were ready to defend it with all of the energy—to say nothing of the invective—at their disposal. Religious controversy was in the very air they breathed; and it inevitably colored personal and neighborhood activities which often had nothing to do with religion.

With certain Puritan clergymen, religious conviction may well have been the primary motive for emigration. It may have motivated some other people, but this would not, I think, have been true of most. Among the farmers and tradesmen who left their native villages, religion was a kind of cement which gave unity and security to those who were thinking of moving to a new life in strange surroundings. Families would be readier to permit their young people to make the voyage if they went with neighbors of the same religious persuasion as their own. Threats and discrimination, moreover, were no balm to people already disgruntled; hence one more factor was added to the existing restiveness, one that provided the emotional and psychological stimulus sometimes needed to translate economic wants and needs into action.

The New World was the beneficiary of this state of mind. For many it seemed to provide the best answer to their needs and hopes. "They say there's bread and work for all, and the sun shines always there." The gospel of this line from an emigrant song of a later period was at the heart of the movement from its beginning. For West Country men and women Bristol was the nearest port from which ships went almost weekly during the summer months. For others it was London or one of the lesser ports. Laborers went if they could be persuaded. Convicts and, on several occasions, political prisoners were forced to go. But over the course of the years, the majority of "the others" who found shipping in the trading vessels that regularly plied the western waters were England's middling people—the most valuable cargo that any captain carried on his westbound voyage.

11. SLAVERY AND THE GENESIS
OF AMERICAN RACE PREJUDICE*

by Carl Degler

Though Negroes came to America along with the first generation of permanent white settlers, there were relatively few
until the end of the seventeenth century. On the eve of the
American Revolution, however, Negroes comprised about 20
percent of the population and were a vital part of the labor force,
and slavery was firmly fixed in the Southern colonies. Despite
the importance of slavery in early America, historians have not
been able to agree on its origins. Some contend that slavery
evolved well after the first Africans arrived, arguing that initially Negroes were treated very much like indentured white
servants and were not considered an inherently inferior or degraded race. Others insist that from the beginning Negroes were
regarded as inferior, treated differently from white servants,
and condemned to slavery even before that status was clearly
defined in law. In the following selection, Carl Degler takes
issue with the provocative account of slavery's genesis by

* *Comparative Studies in Society and History,* vol. 2 (1959), 49–66, 488–495.
Footnotes have been omitted except where they are necessary for an understanding
of the text.

Oscar and Mary F. Handlin, who rebut Degler in an exchange of correspondence.

For further reading: Oscar Handlin, *Race and Nationality in American Life* (1957), chap. 1; David B. Davis, *The Problem of Slavery in Western Culture* (1966); Stanley Elkins, *Slavery: A Problem in American Institutional and Intellectual Life* (1959); James Baldwin, *The Fire Next Time* (1962).

Over a century ago, Tocqueville named slavery as the source of the American prejudice against the Negro. Contrary to the situation in antiquity, he remarked: "Among the moderns the abstract and transient fact of slavery is fatally united with the physical and permanent fact of color." Furthermore, he wrote, though "slavery recedes" in some portions of the United States, "the prejudice to which it has given birth is immovable". More modern observers of the American past have also stressed this causal connection between the institution of slavery and the color prejudice of Americans. Moreover, it is patent to anyone conversant with the nature of American slavery, particularly as it functioned in the nineteenth century, that the impress of bondage upon the character and future of the Negro in the United States has been both deep and enduring.

But if one examines other societies which the Negro entered as a slave, it is apparent that the consequences of slavery have not always been those attributed to the American form. Ten years ago, for example, Frank Tannenbaum demonstrated that in the Spanish and Portuguese colonies in South America, slavery did not leave upon the freed Negro anything like the prejudicial mark which it did in the United States. He and others have shown that once the status of slavery was left behind, the Negro in the lands south of the Rio Grande was accorded a remarkable degree of social equality with the whites. In the light of such differing consequences, the role of slavery in the development of the American prejudice against the Negro needs to be reexamined, with particular attention paid to the historical details of origins.

224

I

Tannenbaum showed that in the Portuguese and Spanish colonies there were at least three historical forces or traditions which tended to prevent the attribution of inferiority to the Negro aside from the legal one of slavery. One was the continuance of the Roman law of slavery in the Iberian countries, another was the influence of the Roman Catholic Church, and the third was the long history—by Anglo-American standards—of contacts with darker-skinned peoples in the course of the Reconquest and the African explorations of the fifteenth and sixteenth centuries. Roman law, at least in its later forms, viewed slavery as a mere accident, of which anyone could be the victim. As such it tended to forestall the identification of the black man with slavery, thus permitting the Negro to escape from the stigma of his degraded status once he ceased to be a slave. The same end, Tannenbaum showed, was served by the Roman Church's insistence upon the equality of all Christians and by the long familiarity of the Iberians with Negroes and Moors.

In North America, of course, none of these forces was operative—a fact which partly explains the differing type of slavery and status for Negroes in the two places. But this cannot be the whole explanation since it is only negative. We know, in effect, what were the forces which permitted the slave and the Negro in South America to be treated as a human being, but other than the negative fact that these forces did not obtain in the North American colonies, we know little as to why the Negro as slave or freedman, occupied a degraded position compared with that of any white man. A more positive explanation is to be found in an examiniation of the early history of the Negro in North America.

It has long been recognized that the appearance of legal slavery in the laws of the English colonies was remarkably slow. The first mention does not occur until after 1660—some forty years after the arrival of the first Negroes. Lest we think that slavery existed in fact before it did in law, two historians have assured us recently that such was not the case. "The status of Negroes was that of servants," Oscar and Mary Handlin have written, "and so they were identified and treated down to the 1660's". This late, or at least, slow development of slavery complicates our problem. For if there was no slavery in the beginning, then we must account for its coming into being some forty years after the introduction of the Negro. There was no such problem in the history of slavery in the Iberian colonies, where the legal institution of slavery came in the ships with the first settlers.

The Handlins' attempt to answer the question as to why slavery was slow in appearing in the statutes is, to me, not convincing. Essentially their explanation is that by the 1660's, for a number of reasons which do not have to be discussed here, the position of the white servant was improving, while that of the Negroes was sinking to slavery. In this manner, the Handlins contend, Negro and white servants, heretofore treated alike, attained different status. There are at least two major objections to this argument. First of all, their explanation, by depending upon the improving position of white servants as it does, cannot apply to New England, where servants were of minor importance. Yet the New England colonies, like the Southern, developed a system of slavery for the Negro that fixed him in a position of permanent inferiority. The greatest weakness of the Handlins' case is the difficulty in showing that the white servant's position was improving during and immediately after the 1660's.

Without attempting to go into any great detail on the matter, several acts of the Maryland and Virginia legislatures during the 1660's and 1670's can be cited to indicate that an improving status for white servants was at best doubtful. In 1662, Maryland restricted a servant's travel without a pass to two miles beyond his master's house; in 1671 the same colony lengthened the time of servants who arrived without indenture from four to five years. Virginia in 1668 provided that a runaway could be corporally punished and also have additional time exacted from him. If, as these instances suggest, the white servant's status was not improving, then we are left without an explanation for the differing status accorded white and Negro servants after 1660.

Actually, by asking why slavery developed late in the English colonies we are setting ourselves a problem which obscures rather than clarifies the primary question of why slavery in North America seemed to leave a different mark on the Negro than it did in South America. To ask why slavery in the English colonies produced discrimination against Negroes after 1660 is to make the tacit assumption that prior to the establishment of slavery there was none. If, instead, the question is put, "Which appeared first, slavery or discrimination?" then no prejudgment is made. Indeed, it now opens a possibility for answering the question as to why the slavery in the English colonies, unlike that in the Spanish and Portuguese, led to a caste position for Negroes, whether free or slave. In short, the recent work of the Handlins and the fact that slavery first appeared in the statutes of the English colonies forty years after the Negro's arrival, have tended to obscure the real possibility that the Negro was actually *never* treated as an equal of the white man, servant or free.

It is true that when Negroes were first imported into the English colonies there was no law of slavery and therefore whatever status they were to have would be the work of the future. This absence of a status for black men, which, it will be remembered was not true for the Spanish and Portuguese colonies, made it possible for almost any kind of status to be worked out. It was conceivable that they would be accorded the same status as white servants, as the Handlins have argued; it was also possible that they would not. It all depended upon the reactions of the people who received the Negroes.

It is the argument of this paper that the status of the Negro in the English colonies was worked out within a framework of discrimination; that from the outset, as far as the available evidence tells us, the Negro was treated as an inferior to the white man, servant or free. If this be true, then it would follow that as slavery evolved as a legal status, it reflected and included as a part of its essence, this same discrimination which white men had practised against the Negro all along and before any statutes decreed it. It was in its evolution, then, that American colonial slavery differed from Iberian, since in the colonies of Spain and Portugal, the legal status of the slave was fixed before the Negro came to the Americas. Moreover, in South America there were at least three major traditional safeguards which tended to protect the free Negro against being treated as an inferior. In summary, the peculiar character of slavery in the English colonies as compared with that in the Iberian, was the result of two circumstances. One, that there was no law of slavery at all in the beginning, and two, that discrimination against the Negro antedated the legal status of slavery. As a result, slavery, when it developed in the English colonies, could not help but be infused with the social attitude which had prevailed from the beginning, namely, that Negroes were inferior.

II

It is indeed true as the Handlins in their article have emphasized that before the seventeenth century the Negro was really called a slave. But this fact should not overshadow the historical evidence which points to the institution without employing the name. Because no discriminatory title is placed upon the Negro we must not think that he was being treated like a white servant; for there is too much evidence to the contrary. Although the growth of a fully developed slave law was slow, unsteady and often unarticulated in surviving records, this is what one would expect when an institution is first being worked out. It is not the same, however, as saying that no slavery or discrimination against the Negro existed in the first decades of the Negro's history in America.

As will appear from the evidence which follows, the kinds of discrimination visited upon Negroes varied immensely. In the early 1640's it sometimes stopped short of lifetime servitude or inheritable status—the two attributes of true slavery—in other instances it included both. But regardless of the form of discrimination, the important point is that from the 1630's up until slavery clearly appeared in the statutes in the 1660's, the Negroes were being set apart and discriminated against as compared with the treatment accorded Englishmen, whether servants or free.

The colonists of the early seventeenth century were well aware of a distinction between indentured servitude and slavery. This is quite clear from the evidence in the very early years of the century. The most obvious means the English colonists had for learning of a different treatment for Negroes from that for white servants was the slave trade and the slave systems of the Spanish and Portuguese colonies. As early as 1623, a voyager's book published in London indicated that Englishmen knew of the Negro as a slave in the South American colonies of Spain. The book told of the trade in "blacke people" who were "sold unto the Spaniard for him to carry into the West Indies, to remaine as slaves, either in their Mines or in any other servile uses, they in those countries put them to". In the phrase "remaine as slaves" is the element of unlimited service.

The Englishmen's treatment of another dark-skinned, non-Christian people—the Indians—further supports the argument that a special and inferior status was accorded the Negro virtually from the first arrival.

Indian slavery was practised in all of the English settlements almost from the beginning and, though it received its impetus from the perennial wars between the races, the fact that an inferior and onerous service was established for the Indian makes it plausible to suppose that a similar status would be reserved for the equally different and pagan Negro.

The continental English could also draw upon other models of a differentiated status for Negroes. The earliest English colony to experiment with large numbers of Negroes in its midst was the shortlived settlement of Providence island, situated in the western Caribbean, just off the Mosquito Coast. By 1637, long before Barbados and the other British sugar islands utilized great numbers of Negroes, almost half of the population of this Puritan venture was black. Such a disproportion of races caused great alarm among the directors of the Company in London and repeated efforts were made to restrict the influx of blacks. Partly because of its large numbers of Negroes, Old Providence became well known to the mainland colonies of Virginia and New England. A. P. Newton has said that Old Providence

> forms the connecting link between almost every English colonising enterprise in the first half of the seventeenth century from Virginia and Bermuda to New England and Jamaica, and thus it is of much greater importance than it actual accomplishments would justify.

Under such circumstances, it was to be expected that knowledge of the status accorded Negroes by these Englishmen would be transmitted to those on the mainland with whom they had such close and frequent contact.

Though the word "slave" is never applied to the Negroes on Providence, and only rarely the word "Servant", "Negroes", which was the term used, were obviously *sui generis*; they were people apart from the English. The Company, for example, distrusted them. "Association [Tortuga island] was deserted thro' their mutinous conduct", the Company told the Governor of Old Providence in 1637. "Further trade for them prohibited, with exceptions, until Providence be furnished with English." In another communication the Company again alluded to the dangers of "too great a number" of Negroes on the island and promised to send 200 English servants over to be exchanged for as many Negroes. A clearer suggestion of the difference in status between an English servant and a Negro is contained in the Company's letter announcing the forwarding of the 200 servants. As a further precaution against being overwhelmed by Negroes, it was ordered that a "family of fourteen"—which would include servants—was not to have more than six Negroes. "The surplusage may be sold to the poor men who have served their apprenticeship". But the Negroes, apparently, were serving for life.

Other British island colonies in the seventeenth century also provide evidence which is suggestive of this same development of a differing status for Negroes, even though the word "slave" was not always employed. Though apparently the first Negroes were only brought to Bermuda in 1617, as early as 1623 the Assembly passed an "Act to restrayne the insolencies of Negroes". The blacks were accused of stealing and of carrying "secretly cudgels, and other weapons and working tools". Such weapons, it was said, were "very dangerous and not meete to be suffered to be carried by such Vassals . . .". Already, in other words, Negroes were treated as a class apart. To reinforce this, Negroes were forbidden to "weare any weapon in the daytyme" and they were not to be outside or off their master's land during "any undue hours in the night tyme . . .".

During the 1630's there were other indications that Negroes were treated as inferiors. As early as 1630 some Negroes' servitude was already slavery in that it was for life and inheritable. One Lew Forde possessed a Negro man, while the Company owned his wife; the couple had two children. Forde desired "to know which of the said children properly belong to himself and which to the Company". The Council gave him the older child and the Company received the other. A letter of Roger Wood in 1634 suggests that Negroes were already serving for life, for he asked to have a Negro, named Sambo, given to him, so that through the Negro "I or myne may *ever* be able" to carry on an old feud with an enemy who owned Sambo's wife.

There is further evidence of discrimination against Negroes in later years. A grand jury in 1652 cited one Henry Gaunt as being "suspected of being unnecessarily conversant with negro women"—he had been giving them presents. The presentment added that "if he hath not left his familiarity with such creatures, it is desired that such abominations be inquired into, least the land mourne for them". The discrimination reached a high point in 1656 when the Governor proclaimed that "any Englishman" who discovered a Negro walking about at night without a pass, was empowered to "kill him then and theire without mercye". The proclamation further ordered that all free Negroes "shall be banished from these Islands, never to return eyther by purchase of any man, or otherwise . . .". When some Negroes asked the Governor for their freedom in 1669, he denied they had any such claim, saying that they had been "purchased by" their masters "without condition or limitation. It being likewise soe practised in these American plantations and other parts of the world."

In Barbados Negroes were already slaves when Richard Ligon lived there in 1647–50. "The Iland", he later wrote, "is divided into three sorts of men, viz: Masters, servants, and slaves. The slaves and their posterity, being subject to their masters for ever," in contrast to the servants who are owned "but for five years . . .". On that island as at Bermuda it was reported that Negroes were not permitted "to touch or handle any weapons".

On Jamaica, as on the other two islands, a clear distinction was made between the status of the Negro and that of the English servant. In 1656 one resident of the island wrote the Protector in England urging the importation of African Negroes because then, he said, "the planters would have to pay for them" and therefore "they would have an interest in preserving their lives, *which was* wanting in the case of bond servants . . .".

It is apparent, then, that the colonists on the mainland had ample opportunity before 1660 to learn of a different status for black men from that for Englishmen, whether servants or free.

III

From the evidence available it would seem that the Englishmen in Virginia and Maryland learned their lesson well. This is true even though the sources available on the Negro's position in these colonies in the early years are not as abundant as we would like. It seems quite evident that the black man was set apart from the white on the continent just as he was being set apart in the island colonies. For example, in Virginia in 1630, one Hugh Davis was "soundly whipped before an Assembly of Negroes and others for abusing himself to the dishonor of God and the shame of Christians, by defiling his body in lying with a negro". The unChristian-like character of such behavior was emphasized ten years later when Robert Sweet was ordered to do penance in Church for "getting a negro woman with child". An act passed in the Maryland legislature in 1639 indicated that at that early date the word "slave" was being applied to non-Englishmen. The act was an enumeration of the rights of "all Christian inhabitants (slaves excepted)". The slaves referred to could have been only Indians or Negroes, since all white servants were Christians. It is also significant of the differing treatment of the two races that though Maryland and Virginia very early in their history enacted laws fixing limits to the terms for servants who entered without written contracts, Negroes were never included in such protective provisions. The first of such laws were placed upon the books in 1639 in Maryland and 1643 in Virginia; in the Maryland statute, it was explicitly stated: "Slaves excepted".

In yet another way, Negroes and slaves were singled out for special status in the years before 1650. A Virginia law of 1640 provided that "all masters" should try to furnish arms to themselves and "all those of their families which shall be capable of arms"—which would include servants—"(excepting negros)". Not until 1648 did Maryland get around to such a prohibition, when it was provided that no guns should be given to "any Pagan for killing meate or to any other use", upon pain of a heavy fine. At no time were white servants denied the right to bear arms; indeed, as these statutes inform us, they were enjoined to possess weapons.

One other class of discriminatory acts against Negroes in Virginia and Maryland before 1660 also deserves to be noticed. Three different times before 1660—in 1643, 1644 and 1658—the Virginia assembly (and in 1654, the Maryland legislature) included Negro and Indian women among the "tithables". But white servant women were never placed in such a category, inasmuch as they were not expected to work in the fields. From the beginning, it would seem, Negro women, whether free or bond, were treated by the law differently from white women servants.

It is not until the 1640's that evidence of a status for Negroes akin to slavery, and, therefore, something more than mere discrimination begins to appear in the sources. Two cases of punishment for runaway servants in 1640 throw some light on the working out of a differentiated status for Negroes. The first case concerned three runaways, of whom two were white men and the third a Negro. All three were given thirty lashes, with the white man having the terms owed their masters extended a year, at the completion of which they were to work for the colony for three more years. The other, "being a Negro named John Punch shall serve his said master or his assigns for the time of his natural Life here or elsewhere". Not only was the Negro's punishment the most severe, and for no apparent reason, but he was, in effect, reduced to slavery. It is also clear, however, that up until the issuing of the sentence, he must have had the status of a servant.

The second case, also of 1640, suggests that by that date some Negroes were already slaves. Six white men and a Negro were implicated in a plot to run away. The punishments meted out varied, but Christopher Miller "a dutchman" (a prime agent in the business) "was given the harshest treatment of all: thirty stripes, burning with an "R" on the cheek, a shackle placed on his leg for a year "and longer if said master shall see cause" and seven years of service for the colony upon completion of his time due his master. The only other one of the seven plotters to receive the stripes, the shackle and the "R" was the Negro Emanuel, but, significantly, he did not receive any sentence of work for the colony. Presumably he was already serving his master for a life-time—*i.e.*, he was a slave. About this time in Maryland it does not seem to have been unusual to speak of Negroes as slaves, for in 1642 one "John Skinner mariner" agreed "to deliver unto . . . Leonard Calvert, fourteen negro-men-slaves and three women-slaves".

From a proceeding before the House of Burgesses in 1666 it appears that as early as 1644 that body was being called upon to determine who was a slave. The Journal of the House for 1666 reports that in 1644 a certain "mulata" bought "as a slave for Ever" was adjudged by the Assembly "no slave and but to serve as other Christian servants do and was freed in September 1665". Though no reason was given for the verdict, from the words "other Christian servants" it is possible that he was a Christian, for it was believed in the early years of the English colonies that baptism rendered a slave free. In any case, the Assembly uttered no prohibition of slavery as such and the owner was sufficiently surprised and aggrieved by the decision to appeal for recompense from the Assembly, even though the Negro's service was twenty-one years, an unheard of term for a "Christian servant".

In early seventeenth century inventories of estates, there are two distinctions which appear in the reckoning of the value of servants and Negroes. Uniformly, the Negroes were more valuable, even as children, than any white servant. Secondly, the naming of a servant is usually followed by the number of years yet remaining to his service; for the Negroes no such notation appears. Thus in an inventory in Virginia in 1643, a 22-year old white servant, with eight years still to serve, was valued at 1,000 pounds of tobacco, while a "negro boy" was rated at 3,000 pounds and a white boy with seven years to serve was listed as worth 700 pounds. An eight-year old Negro girl was calculated to be worth 2,000 pounds. On another inventory in 1655, two good men servants with four years to serve were rated at 1,300 pounds of tobacco, and a woman servant with only two years to go was valued at 800 pounds. Two Negro boys, however, who had no limit set to their terms, were evaluated at 4,100 pounds apiece, and a Negro girl was said to be worth 5,500 pounds.

These great differences in valuation of Negro and white "servants" strongly suggest, as does the failure to indicate term of service for the Negroes, that the latter were slaves at least in regard to life-time service. Beyond a question, there was some service which these blacks were rendering which enhanced their value—a service, moreover, which was not or could not be exacted from the whites. Furthermore, a Maryland deed of 1649 adumbrated slave status not only of life-time term, but of inheritance of status. Three Negroes "and all their issue both male and female" were deeded.

Russell and Ames culled from the Virginia court records of the 1640's and 1650's several instances of Negroes held in a status that can be called true slavery. For example, in 1646 a Negro woman and a Negro boy were sold to Stephen Charlton to be of use to him and his "heyers etc. for ever". A Negro girl was sold in 1652 "with her Issue and produce . . . and their services forever". Two years later a Negro girl was sold to one Armsteadinger "and his heyers . . . forever with all her increase both male and female". For March 12, 1655 the minutes of the Council and General Court of Virginia contain the entry, "Mulatto held to be a slave and appeal taken". Yet this is five years before Negro slavery is even implied in the statutes and fifteen before it is declared. An early case of what appears to be true slavery was found by Miss Ames on the Virginia eastern shore. In 1635 two Negroes were brought to the area; over twenty years later, in 1656, the widow of the master was bequeathing the child of one of the original Negroes and the other Negro and her children. This was much more than mere servitude—the term was longer than twenty years and apparently the status was inheritable.

Slavery and the Genesis of American Race Prejudice

Wesley Frank Craven, in his study of the seventeenth-century Southern colonies, has concluded that in the treatment of the Negro "the trend from the first was toward a sharp distinction between him and the white servant". In view of the evidence presented here, this seems a reasonable conclusion.

Concurrently with these examples of onerous service or actual slavery of Negroes, there were of course other members of the race who did gain their freedom. But the presence of Negroes rising out of servitude to freedom does not destroy the evidence that others were sinking into slavery; it merely underscores the unsteady evolution of a slave status. The supposition that the practice of slavery long antedated the law is strengthened by the tangential manner in which recognition of Negro slavery first appeared in the Virginia statutes. It occurred in 1660 in a law dealing with punishments for runaway servants, where casual reference was made to those "negroes who are incapable of making satisfaction by addition of time", since they were already serving for life.

Soon thereafter, as various legal questions regarding the status of Negroes came to the fore, the institution was further defined by statute law. In 1662 Virginia provided that the status of the offspring of a white man and a Negro would follow that of the mother—an interesting and unexplained departure from the common law and a reversion to Roman law. The same law stated that "any christian" fornicating "with a negro man or woman . . . shall pay double the fines imposed by the former act". Two years later Maryland prescribed service for Negroes "durante vita" and provided for hereditary status to descend through the father. Any free white woman who married a slave was to serve her husband's master for the duration of the slave's life, and her children would serve the master until they were thirty years of age. Presumably, no penalty was to be exacted of a free white man who married a Negro slave.

As early as 1669 the Virginia law virtually washed its hands of protecting the Negro held as a slave. It allowed punishment of refractory slaves up to and including accidental death, relieving the master, explicitly, of any fear of prosecution, on the assumption that no man would "destroy his owne estate".

In fact by 1680 the law of Virginia had erected a high wall around the Negro. One discerns in the phrase "any negro or other slave" how the word "negro" had taken on the meaning of slave. Moreover, in the act of 1680 one begins to see the lineaments of the later slave codes. No Negro may carry any weapon of any kind, nor leave his master's grounds without a pass, nor shall "any negroe or other slave . . . presume to lift his hand in opposition against any christian", and if a Negro runs away and resists recapture it "shalbe lawful for such person or persons to kill said negroe or slave . . .".

Yet it would be a quarter of a century before Negroes would comprise even a fifth of the population of Virginia. Thus long before slavery or black labor became an important part of the Southern economy, a special and inferior status had been worked out for the Negroes who came to the English colonies. Unquestionably it was a demand for labor which dragged the Negro to American shores, but the status which he acquired here cannot be explained by reference to that economic motive. Long before black labor was as economically important as unfree white labor, the Negro had been consigned to a special discriminatory status which mirrored the social discrimination Englishmen practised against him.

IV

In the course of the seventeenth century New Englanders, like Southerners, developed a system of slavery which seemed permanently to fasten its stigma upon the Negro race. But because of the small number of Negroes in the northern provinces, the development of a form of slavery, which left a caste in its wake, cannot be attributed to pressure from increasing numbers of blacks, or even from an insistent demand for cheap labor. Rather it seems clearly to be the consequence of the general social discrimination against the Negro. For in the northern region, as in the southern, discrimination against the Negro preceded the evolution of a slave status and by that fact helped to shape the form that institution would assume.

References to the status of the Negroes in New England in this period are scattered, but, as was true of the Southern provinces, those references which are available suggest that from the earliest years a lowly, differential status, if not slavery itself, was reserved and recognized for the Negro—and the Indian, it might be added. The earliest date asserted in the sources for the existence of Negro slavery in Massachusetts is that of 1639. John Josselyn tells of a Negro woman held on Noddles Island in Boston harbor. Her master sought to mate her with another Negro, Josselyn says, but she kicked her prospective lover out of the bed, saying that such behavior was "beyond her slavery . . .". Though the first legal code of Massachusetts, the Body of Liberties of 1641, prohibited "bond-slavery" for the inhabitants, it clearly permitted enslavement of those who are "sold to us", which would include Negroes brought in by the international slave trade.

Such use of Negroes was neither unknown nor undesirable to the Puritans. Emanuel Downing wrote to John Winthrop in 1645 about the desirability of a war against the Indians so that captives might be taken who, in turn, could be exchanged

> for Moores, which wilbe more gayneful pilladge for us then [*sic*] wee conceive, for I doe not see how wee can thrive untill wee gett into a stock of slaves sufficient to doe all our busines, for our children's children will hardly see this great Continent filled with people, soe that our servants will still desire freedome for themselves, and not stay but for verie great wages. And I suppose you know verie well how we shall maynteyne 20 Moores cheaper than one English servant.

The following year the Commissioners of the United Colonies recommended that in order to spare the colonies the cost of imprisoning contumacious Indians they should be given over to the Englishmen whom they had damaged or "be shipped out and exchanged for Negroes as the cause will justly serve". Negroes were here being equated with Indians who were being bound out as prisoners: this was treatment decidedly a cut lower than that visited upon white servants. That enslavement of Negroes was well known in New England by the middle of the century at the latest is revealed by the preamble to an act of Warwick and Providence colonies in 1652. It was said that it "is a common course practised amongst Englishmen to buy negers, to that end they may have them for service or slaves forever . . . ".

By mid-century, Negroes were appearing in the inventories of estates and, significantly, the valuation placed upon them was very close to that found in Virginia inventories of the same period. Their worth is always much more than that of a white servant. Thus in 1650 "a neager Maide" was valued at £ 25; in 1657 the well-known merchant, Robert Keayne left "2 negros and a negro child" estimated to be worth £ 30. "A negro boy servant" was set at £ 20 in an estate of 1661. A further indication of the property character of Negroes was the attachment by the constable of Salem in 1670 of a Negro boy "Seasar" as the "proper goods of the said Powell".

Despite the small numbers of Negroes in New England in this early period, the colonies of that region followed the example of the Southern and insular provinces in denying arms to the blacks in their midst—a discrimination which was never visited upon the English servant. In 1652 Massachusetts provided that Indians and Negroes could train in the militia the same as whites, but this apparently caused friction. The law was countermanded in 1656 by the statement "henceforth no negroes or Indians, altho servants of the English, shalbe armed or permitted to trayne". Although as late as 1680 it was officially reported to London that there were no more than thirty "slaves" in Connecticut, that colony in 1660 excluded Indians and "negar servants" from the militia and "Watch and Ward".

Edward Randolph in 1676 reported that there were a few indentured servants in Massachusetts "and not above two hundred slaves", by which he meant Negroes, for he said "they were brought from Guinea and Madagascar". But it was not until 1698 that the phrase "Negro slave" actually appeared in the Massachusetts statutes. The practice of slavery was preceding the law in Massachusetts precisely as it had in the South. Though an official report to London in 1680 distinguished between Negro slaves and servants in Connecticut, the law of that colony did not bother to define the institution of slavery. Indeed, as late as 1704, the Governor gave it as his opinion that all children born of "negro bond-women are themselves in like condition, i.e., born in servitude", though he admitted that there was no statute which said so. His contention was, however, that such legislation was "needless, because of the constant practice by which they are held as such . . .".

During the last years of the seventeenth century, laws of Connecticut and Massachusetts continued to speak of Negroes as "servants", but it was very clear that the Negro's status was not being equated with that of the white servant. The General Court of Connecticut observed in 1690 that "many persons of this Colony doe . . . purchase negroe servants" and, since these servants run away, precautions have to be taken against such eventualities. It was therefore laid down that all "negroe or negroes shall" be required to have a pass in order to be outside the town bounds. Any inhabitant could stop a Negroe, free or slave, and have him brought before a magistrate if the black man were found to be without such a pass. Moreover, all ferrymen, upon pain of fine, were to deny access to their ferries to all Negroes who could not produce a pass. Massachusetts in 1698 forbade trade with "any Indian, or negro servant or slave, or other known dissolute, lewd, and disorderly person, of whom there is just cause of suspicion".

By the early years of the eighteenth century, the laws of Connecticut and Massachusetts had pretty well defined the Negro's subordinate position in society. Massachusetts acted to restrict the manumission of slaves by providing in 1703 that "molatto or negro slaves" could be free only if security was given that they would not be chargeable upon the community. Another law set a curfew upon Indians, mulattoes and Negroes for nine o'clock each night. In 1705 Massachusetts became the only New England province to prohibit sexual relations between Negroes and mulattoes and Englishmen or those of "any other Christian nation". Moreover, "any negro or mulatto" presuming to "smite or strike" an English person or any of another Christian nation would be "severely whipped". In 1717 Negroes were barred from holding land in Connecticut.

Thus, like the colonists to the South, the New Englanders enacted into law, in the absence of any prior English law of slavery, their recognition of the Negroes as different and inferior. This was the way of the seventeenth century; only with a later conception of the brotherhood of all men would such legal discrimination begin to recede; but by then, generations of close association between the degraded status of slavery and black color would leave the same prejudice against the Negro in the North that it did in the South.

It would seem, then, that instead of slavery being the root of the discrimination visited upon the Negro in America, slavery was itself molded by the early colonists' discrimination against the outlander. In the absence of any law of slavery or commandments of the Church to the contrary—as was true of Brazil and Spanish-America—the institution of slavery into which the African was placed in the English colonies inevitably mirrored that discrimination and, in so doing, perpetuated it.

Once the English embodied their discrimination against the Negro in slave law, the logic of the law took over. Through the early eighteenth century, judges and legislatures in all the colonies elaborated the law along the discriminatory lines laid down in the amorphous beginnings. In doing so, of course, especially in the South, they had the added incentive of perpetuating and securing a labor system which by then had become indispensable to the economy. The cleavage between the races was in that manner deepened and hardened into the shape which became quite familiar by the nineteenth century. In due time, particularly in the South, the correspondence between the black man and slavery would appear so perfect that it would be difficult to believe that the Negro was fitted for anything other than the degraded status in which he was almost always found. It would also be forgotten that the discrimination had begun long before slavery had come upon the scene.

Letters to the Editor

To the Editor:

We are constrained to reveal serious errors of fact and interpretation in Professor Degler's recent article, "Slavery and the Genesis of American Race Prejudice" in your October, 1959 issue. We find it necessary to do so because of the intrinsic importance of the subject and because Professor Degler's analysis takes issue with our studies, "The Origins of the Southern Labor System," *William and Mary Quarterly*, VII (1950), 199 ff.; and *Race and Nationality in American Life* (Boston, 1957). We shall not here repeat the arguments advanced in these works; nor shall we attempt to correct all the mistakes Professor Degler has made. We shall rather limit ourselves to a consideration of his major misunderstandings of the historical evidence.

Professor Degler does not use the significant terms of his discussion, "slavery" and "prejudice," with any precision. At the very outset he confuses the issue by an inept comparison of slavery in English and Latin America. Slavery in the Spanish and Portuguese colonies, he asserts, "did not leave upon the freed Negro any thing like the prejudicial mark which it did in the United States." Hence that prejudicial mark must have antedated slavery. But the very authorities he cites in his footnotes 3 and 4 explain slavery did not have the same consequences in Brazil as in Virginia because slavery in Brazil was not the same institution as in Virginia, in such important respects as family or communal organization or the impact upon individual personality. The effects were different because the institutions Degler loosely comprehends within the term "slavery" were different. Nowhere does he show an understanding of the need for distinguishing the various meanings of the term in the continental colonies, in the West Indies or in Latin America.

By the same token, the loose reference to race prejudice in Professor Degler's usage conflates at least two different phenomena and obscures them both. The attitude which de Tocqueville and others perceived to be a product of slavery was one which rested upon the belief that the Negroes were a species of being inherently different from and inferior to the whites. Professor Degler offers no evidence of the existence of that assumption among sixteenth- or seventeenth-century Englishmen or Americans. In those centuries, as Englishmen established contacts with every part of the world, they had numerous occasions to encounter men of other colors. In the voluminous accounts of their travels, we know of no such expressions of racial prejudice.

Professor Degler does present evidence of discrimination against the Negroes in the treatment of seventeenth-century American servants, but he does not understand that this is not the same phenomenon as that involved in his first usage of the term, "race prejudice." He not only errs in the implication that our treatment failed to recognize these discriminations; more important, he fails to perceive that such differential treatment was directed not against Negroes alone but against all sorts of strangers—white, red, and black. There were laws against "the insolencies of the Irish" just as there were laws against "the insolencies of the Negroes."

Englishmen, in the Old World and the New could, of course, perceive the differences between themselves and Negroes, or, for that matter, between themselves and Frenchmen, Dutchmen, Irishmen, Germans, Welsh and even Scots. The English had an ethnocentric preference for their own kind and looked down upon the queerness of any strangers; Elizabethan literature is full of slurs expressive of that attitude. But a "prejudice" against foreigners, which includes Irishmen or Hollanders, is far different from the race prejudice directed against the Negro in the nineteenth century. One can find the former in the seventeenth century, but not the latter.

Handicapped as he is by the inability to use his terms properly, Professor Degler cannot comprehend the subtle process by which changes in attitudes occur. One example will suffice. He questions the connection we established between the deterioration of the position of Negroes and the improvement in the condition of white servants after the 1660's. He does so by asserting that the position of the Negroes could not have declined for this reason in New England "where servants were of minor importance." There is no footnote to this astounding statement which runs counter to all the evidence. We cannot, of course, expect that Professor Degler should have known William Towner's unpublished dissertation on the subject. But we do have a right to expect some familiarity with the evidence in his own footnote 68. Weeden's *History*, there cited, points out that trade in indentured servants "went on more or less from the beginning. Besides the influx of freemen and freewomen, gentle or yeoman, there was a number of banished convicts and a steady stream of laborers, forced to sell their service to pay the expense of this transfer to the better opportunities of the New World" (II, 520).

Professor Degler further compounds his own confusion by reference to three Virginia and Maryland laws—of 1662, of 1668, and of 1671. Professor Degler may not himself know what he intends to show by them. He summarizes these laws in a paragraph which begins by asserting that they "indicate that an improving status for white servants was at best doubtful" and which ends by suggesting that "the white servant's status was not improving."

But whatever his interpretation, even if the laws cited said what Professor Degler claims they do, they would not contradict our proposition that major changes occurred after the 1660's. Surely it is a naive view that would expect social attitudes transformed in the 1660's to be immediately reflected in every legislative action of the decade.

Anyway, the laws do not say what Professor Degler thinks they do. The text of the acts in question supports our view. The Virginia statute is brief enough to be quoted in full:

WHEREAS it hath been questioned whether servants running away may be punished with corporall punishment by their master or magistrate since the act already made gives the master satisfaction by prolonging their time by service. *It is declared and enacted by this assembly* that moderate corporall punishment inflicted by master or magistrate upon a runaway servant, shall not deprive the master of the satisfaction allowed by the law, the one being as necessary to reclayme them from persisting in that idle course, as the other is just to repair the damages sustayned by the master. (Hening, *Statutes at Large*, II, 266.)

This text makes evident: first, that this is an enactment declaratory of intent, not new legislation; and second, that it is evoked by questioning based upon an enlarging view of the rights of servants. The re-affirmation of such a law is evidence of the significance of the questioning of it.

Similarly, the Maryland laws of 1662 and 1671 are reenactments of earlier laws. The antecedent of the statute on length of service survives and proves to be identical with its reenactment. Had Professor Degler compared the two he might have been led to speculate as to why the Assembly found it necessary twice to extend the duration of service from four to five years. It might even have occurred to him that the second measure was an indication of the difficulty of securing conformity with the first (*Maryland Archives*, I, 451; II, 147, 335).

An inappropriately framed problem, loosely-used terms and obtuseness to the dynamics of social change have served Professor Degler badly. The history of American slavery must be approached from an altogether different point of departure. Analysis of the interplay of social, cultural, economic and intellectual forces reveals a gradual transformation of both attitudes and law in which differences in treatment, based upon the helplessness and the strangeness of the Negro, slowly defined his status; and in which the necessity for explaining and justifying that status ultimately evoked the prejudices and the ideology of racism.

OSCAR AND MARY F. HANDLIN
Harvard University

To the Editor:

Knowing Professor Handlin's skill in verbal assault, I was not surprised at the studiously pejorative nature of the rebuttal signed by him and his wife. But I must confess to being surprised that they would naively characterize differences in interpretation as "errors" and "mistakes". To be sure, they speak of "serious errors of fact" in my article, but since none is cited in their rebuttal, their criticisms concern matters of interpretation only. One thing their criticism has done is to give me an opportunity to point up the central issue between us in a way I could not do in my article.

Let us turn, then, to my so-called errors of interpretation. I am taxed with "confusing the issue" and making "an inept" comparison between slavery in the English and South American colonies. Actually I made no comparison of slavery in the two areas at all; I merely noted that the Negro entered society in North and South America through the agency of slavery and since the consequences for the Negro and society were different in the two regions I thought the usual conclusion of seeing "slavery" as the cause of American attitudes toward the Negro needed reexamination. I drew no conclusions other than the fact that in view of the experience of the Iberian colonies, slavery was not a sufficient explanation. As for my not understanding that slavery in North and South America were different institutions, I thought anyone who read my article would not fail to see that I assumed all through my article that slavery was quite different in the two areas. Moreover, nowhere did I say, as the Handlins assert, that because race prejudice did not follow slavery in South America as it did in North America, "hence that prejudicial mark must have antedated slavery." If I had said that, there would have been little need for the rest of the article.

Then I am criticized for a "loose reference to race prejudice" and for "conflating" a number of phenomena. Actually, as any careful reading will show, I took some pains *not* to use the term "race prejudice" when discussing the seventeenth century data. The phrase apparently caught the Handlins' eyes in the title (where it is justified by its being tied to the word "genesis") and they never forgot it. It is true, as they say, that I did not show that there were racist beliefs expressed in the seventeenth century, but that was not the task I set myself. The primary purpose of my article—as I wrote on p. 52—was to show that a pattern of discrimination against the Negro antedated legal slavery.

Since the Handlins have raised the question of the causes for the discrimination, I might say, in passing, that unlike them, I am not at all sure of the bases for the discrimination. In my article (p. 53) I did no more than suggest that racial, cultural, and religious differences were involved. It is worth pointing out, though, since the Handlins say, "We know of no . . . expression of racial prejudice in the literature of the seventeenth century," that there were certainly some. Morgan Godwyn's *The Negro's and Indian's Advocate*, published in 1680, which the Handlins cite in their original article on another point, contains many references suggesting that Negroes were viewed as "inherently different from and inferior to the whites," to use the Handlins' definition. For example, Godwyn says that one commonly held argument against Negroes was that *"Negro's* are conceived to be but Brutes."

Godwyn also tells of a West Indian who asserted "That *Negro's* were beasts, and had no more Souls than Beasts, and that Religion did not concern them." Still another person told him that baptism did no more good to a Negro "than to her black Bitch" (pp. 38–40). Godwyn also devotes many pages (43–61) to defending the Negroes against the curse of "Cham"—a variation of a familiar nineteenth-century pro-slavery argument that Negroes were inferior by virtue of their descent from Ham, the cast-out son of Noah. Reference to the curse of Cham is also to be found in an English pamphlet of 1675, *Two Voyages to New England.* There are even references in Shakespeare's plays which suggest that, in the popular mind, the Negro's inferior position was tied to his physical appearance. In *Titus Andronicus*, Tamora, who is in love with the Moor Aaron, is reviled with these words: "Believe me, queen, your swarth Cimerian doth make your honour of his body's hue, spotted, detested and abominable." Similar references connecting the allegedly low character of the black man with his appearance are to be found in *Othello.*

Indeed, in the light of Lewis Hanke's studies on Spanish attitudes toward the Indians, many literate sixteenth and seventeenth-century Europeans must have been familiar with a racist conception of colored peoples. Professor Hanke, in his recent *Aristotle and the American Indians, A Study in Race Prejudice in the Modern World* (London, 1959), observes that the first person to apply the Aristotelian doctrine of natural slavery to the Indians was a Scottish professor living in Paris in 1510, one John Major (Hanke, p. 14). Furthermore, in the great debate held at Valladolid in 1550–1 between Las Casas and Sepúlveda, the latter argued at length that the Indians were inherently inferior. The substance of Sepúlveda's position was quickly known throughout Europe through the summaries and commentaries which appeared in several languages, including English (Hanke, pp. 76, 78, 90).

As I say, I make no claim for the widespread acceptance of a racist view of colored peoples in the seventeenth century, for the evidence is too skimpy, but in the face of books like Godwyn's, it seems rather cavalier to write, as the Handlins do, that "we know of no such expressions of racial prejudice."

I do assert, though, that the Negro was generally accorded a lower position in society than any white man, bound or free. It will be remembered that the Handlins in their original article asserted that until the

1660's the treatment of Negro and white "servants" was substantially the same. And their statement was more than a casual one—paragraphs were devoted to showing that the word "slave" had no special meaning and that "until the 1660's the statutes on the Negroes were not at all unique. Nor did they add up to a decided trend." (P. 209 of their original article. The several factual errors in their article I pointed out in this connection, they have not denied in their rebuttal.) The same kind of discrimination, they said, was visited upon other strangers and, therefore, evidence of discrimination against Negroes was not significant.

The nub of our disagreement, then, is whether the treatment of the Negro was the same as that accorded other non-Englishmen. In my article I showed that a number of examples of discrimination against the Negro appear in the records before the 1660's, so many in fact, that they seemed to me to justify the conclusion that the Negro occupied an especially low place in colonial society. This is not the place to repeat the evidence in my article or that in the Handlins'. But I will say that I am convinced that an examination of their article will show no examples of discrimination against white men comparable in degree of discrimination with those I cited involving Negroes—examples having to do with bearing arms, being taxable, being punished, the length of service, and the like. Indeed, the Handlins offer very few examples of any kind to buttress their assertion, repeated in their rebuttal, that many kinds of strangers other than Negroes and Indians were discriminated against. Since the point at issue between us is a matter of the evidence, the final determination must be left to those who carefully read both articles and compare the evidence therein given.

When the ammunition for attack is running low it is an old device to drag in matters peripheral to the main argument. The Handlins have resorted to this tactic in a number of their criticisms; these can be easily dealt with. They ask for a footnote for my "astounding statement" that servants were of minor importance in New England. They provide me with a contrary one from Weeden's *History* which is remarkable for its irrelevance to the question at hand. The quotation is obviously non-quantitative when the question it is cited to answer is essentially quantitative—that is, how numerous were indentured servants. Besides, in context it is clear that Weeden is merely showing that there were indentured servants in New England. It is curious, moreover, that the Handlins should have cited in their own behalf Weeden's old, general history when R. B. Morris, *Government and Labor in Early America,* and Abbot Smith, *Colonists in Bondage,* two much more recent and authoritative books on the subject, are available. From these books I cite the footnotes I never dreamed anyone would need for such a point: Morris, pp. 35–36, 313, 326 for the paucity of servants in New England, and Smith, pp. 316, 324 and 329 for a comparison of servants in the South and New England which show how minor indentured servitude was in the latter section.

Then we come to the matter of the position of the indentured servants. The Handlins say the Maryland statute of 1671, which extended the terms of servants without indenture from four to five years, was really a reenactment of a previous law; this repetition shows, they continue, that the statute was not having the desired effect of lengthening servants' terms. Therefore, they argue, the position of the servant was actually improving rather than worsening as the terms of the act seem to say. The principle that reenactment implies lack of compliance is valid when properly applied, but in this instance, it provokes more questions than it settles. For the question must be asked: who was refusing to obey the law and therefore necessitating its reenactment? Certainly it couldn't be the servants, for without a contract they had no choice in the matter. Are we to believe that the justices were refusing to apply the law for the longer term? What could be their purpose since, as we know from Abbot Smith and others, they were often masters themselves? Or do the Handlins expect us to believe that the masters themselves were refusing to get five years out of their servants when the law gave them every right to; are we to believe that the legislature which passed the law had a greater interest in advocating a longer term than the masters themselves? To ask the questions is to answer them.

Furthermore, this practice of taking statutes which restate previous acts as proof of evasion can cut both ways. On p. 214 of their original article, the Handlins cite a Virginia law of 1661–2 as evidence for the improving position of the servants because it tells how a servant can appeal to a magistrate in the event of mistreatment by a master. Portions of this act, in identical language, appear in *two* previous laws, one in 1642–3 and one in 1657–8 (Hening, *Statutes,* I, 254–5, 440). Should I argue, à la Handlins, that we can infer from this that the position of the servants by 1660–1 was really worsening because this was the third time the legislature had to point out that servants could appeal to commissioners for protection against their masters?

The Handlins might take me seriously and answer that, unlike their own instances, the reenactments I cite are not identical in wording and therefore not comparable with theirs. Actually, the two Maryland laws (those of 1662 and 1671) which they assert in their rebuttal are mere reenactments, turn out, upon examination, not to be identical either. The text of the law of 1662 contains a reference to a statute of 1650, but, since the 1650 law does not survive, we cannot know whether the 1662 law was the same or not; all we know is that both statutes dealt with the problem of runaways. As for the law of 1671, it is true, as the Handlins say, that it was preceded by the law of 1666. But these two acts, contrary to the Handlins' contention, are not identical; the second law differs in one important matter from the first, a fact which may well explain, after all, why there were two laws. In the 1666 act a "penalty of 1,000 pounds of tobacco" was to be levied against any master who did not register the age of his servant with the courts so that the servant's time of service might be adjudged. The justification given in the law for the fine was "for depriving the Courts of such opportunity of view [sic] of the parties." The act of 1671 omitted the fine and, since it also repealed all previous laws on the subject, we must conclude that the fine was no longer imposed by law. Such a removal of a penalty upon masters certainly constitutes no gain for servants. In place of a fine for failure to bring a servant before the court, the law of 1671 set the servant's term at five years, regardless of the servant's age. Such a statute, rather than weakening the resolve to lengthen the term from four to five years, as the Handlins argue, actually strengthens it by making the law more workable.

Finally, something deserves to be said about the Virginia statute they quote in full in their rebuttal. Contrary to their assertion it is not at all clear that this act is merely a restatement of an old one. No previous act that I know of—and the Handlins cite none—made it clear that whipping was permissible along with added time. The previous statute providing for the punishment of runaways, passed in 1661–2 (Hening, *Statutes*, II, 116–7) contains no references to corporal punishment. It is hard to see how the Handlins can argue that an act which makes it clear that whipping is permissible constitutes a lightening of the servant's lot when heretofore the statutes were silent on the subject.

So much for our points of disagreement. Actually, our two positions are not as far apart as the Handlins' remarks would lead one to believe. I can, for example, subscribe to the final sentence of their rebuttal without abandoning anything that I wrote in my article. I can also agree with them on the slow and ambiguous evolution of the Negro's status and of slavery, on the fact that discrimination against the Negro was at first based on other than just racial grounds, on the fact that freedom in the seventeenth century was a matter of degree and not absolute, and on the quite different history of slavery in the North American colonies as compared with the South American. But I cannot agree that whites and Negroes were treated alike before 1660. The question of *why* they were not—a matter of prime importance—is still wide open for further investigation.

CARL N. DEGLER
Vassar College

12. MODERN TENSIONS AND THE ORIGINS OF AMERICAN SLAVERY*

by Winthrop D. Jordan

Winthrop D. Jordan, in the following essay, argues that the evidence does not support either Degler's or the Handlins' account of slavery's origins. Jordan reviews the historiography, suggesting that changing interpretations reflect shifting attitudes toward the Negro and slavery. Renewed interest in slavery's genesis in the 1950s, he argues, was stimulated by the contemporary revolution in race relations, which gave an old historical controversy new life and relevance. Historians must rely on fragmentary and inconclusive data concerning the period before the end of the seventeenth century, and Jordan's evidence indicates that some, though not all, Negroes were treated differently from white indentured servants. Rather than choosing between the Degler hypothesis that racial prejudice led to the Negro's enslavement and the Handlins' contention that slavery generated racism, Jordan suggests that "both may have been equally cause and effect." This question has proved so vexing because institutions often evolve subtly, slowly, and informally, and the evidence is susceptible to different interpretations.

Modern Tensions and the Origins of American Slavery

Thanks to John Smith we know that Negroes first came to the British continental colonies in 1619. What we do not know is exactly when Negroes were first enslaved there. This question has been debated by historians for the past seventy years, the critical point being whether Negroes were enslaved almost from their first importation or whether they were at first simply servants and only later reduced to the status of slaves. The long duration and vigor of the controversy suggest that more than a simple question of dating has been involved. In fact certain current tensions in American society have complicated the historical problem and greatly heightened its significance. Dating the origins of slavery has taken on a striking modern relevance.

During the nineteenth century historians assumed almost universally that the first Negroes came to Virginia as slaves. So close was their acquaintance with the problem of racial slavery that it did not occur to them that Negroes could ever have been anything but slaves. Philip A. Bruce, the first man to probe with some thoroughness into the early years of American slavery, adopted this view in 1896, although he emphasized that the original difference in treatment between white servants and Negroes was merely that Negroes served for life. Just six years later, however, came a challenge from a younger, professionally trained historian, James C. Ballagh. His *A History of Slavery in Virginia* appeared in the *Johns Hopkins University Studies in Historical and Political Science*, an aptly named series which was to usher in the new era of scholarly detachment in the writing of institutional history. Ballagh offered a new and different interpretation; he took the position that the first Negroes served merely as servants and that enslavement did not begin until around 1660, when statutes bearing on slavery were passed for the first time.

There has since been agreement on dating the statutory establishment of slavery, and differences of opinion have centered on when enslavement began in actual practice. Fortunately there has also been general agreement on slavery's distinguishing characteristics: service for life and inheritance of like obligation by any offspring. Writing on the free Negro in Virginia for the Johns Hopkins series, John H. Russell in 1913 tackled the central question and showed that some Negroes were indeed

* *Journal of Southern History*, vol. 28 (1962), 18–30. Copyright 1962 by the Southern Historical Association. Reprinted without footnotes by permission of the Managing Editor.

servants but concluded that "between 1640 and 1660 slavery was fast becoming an established fact. In this twenty years the colored population was divided, part being servants and part being slaves, and some who were servants defended themselves with increasing difficulty from the encroachments of slavery." Ulrich B. Phillips, though little interested in the matter, in 1918 accepted Russell's conclusion of early servitude and transition toward slavery after 1640. Helen T. Catterall took much the same position in 1926. On the other hand, in 1921 James M. Wright, discussing the free Negro in Maryland, implied that Negroes were slaves almost from the beginning, and in 1940 Susie M. Ames reviewed several cases in Virginia which seemed to indicate that genuine slavery had existed well before Ballagh's date of 1660.

All this was a very small academic gale, well insulated from the outside world. Yet despite disagreement on dating enslavement, the earlier writers—Bruce, Ballagh, and Russell—shared a common assumption which, though at the time seemingly irrelevant to the main question, has since proved of considerable importance. They assumed that prejudice against the Negro was natural and almost innate in the white man. It would be surprising if they had felt otherwise in this period of segregation statutes, overseas imperialism, immigration restriction, and full-throated Anglo-Saxonism. By the 1920's, however, with the easing of these tensions, the assumption of natural prejudice was dropped unnoticed. Yet only one historian explicitly contradicted that assumption: Ulrich Phillips of Georgia, impressed with the geniality of both slavery and twentieth-century race relations, found no natural prejudice in the white man and expressed his "conviction that Southern racial asperities are mainly superficial, and that the two great elements are fundamentally in accord."

Only when tensions over race relations intensified once more did the older assumption of natural prejudice crop up again. After World War II American Negroes found themselves beneficiaries of New Deal politics and reforms, wartime need for manpower, world-wide repulsion at racist excesses in Nazi Germany, and growingly successful colored anticolonialism. With new militancy Negroes mounted an attack on the citadel of separate but equal, and soon it became clear that America was in for a period of self-conscious reappraisal of its racial arrangements. Writing in this period of heightened tension (1949) a practiced and careful scholar, Wesley F. Craven, raised the old question of the Negro's original status, suggesting that Negroes had been enslaved at an early date. Craven also cautiously resuscitated the idea that white men may have had natural distaste for the Negro, an idea which fitted neatly with the suggestion of early enslavement. Original antipathy would mean rapid debasement.

In the next year (1950) came a sophisticated counterstatement, which contradicted both Craven's dating and implicitly any suggestion of early prejudice. Oscar and Mary F. Handlin in "Origins of the Southern Labor System" offered a case for late enslavement, with servitude as the status of Negroes before about 1660. Originally the status of both Negroes and white servants was far short of freedom, the Handlins maintained, but Negroes failed to benefit from increased freedom for servants in mid-century and became less free rather than more. Embedded in this description of diverging status were broader implications: Late and gradual enslavement undercut the possibility of natural, deep-seated antipathy toward Negroes. On the contrary, if whites and Negroes could share the same status of half freedom for forty years in the seventeenth century, why could they not share full freedom in the twentieth?

The same implications were rendered more explicit by Kenneth M. Stampp in a major reassessment of Southern slavery published two years after the Supreme Court's 1954 school decision. Reading physiology with the eye of faith, Stampp frankly stated his assumption "that innately Negroes *are*, after all, only white men with black skins, nothing more, nothing less." Closely following the Handlins' article on the origins of slavery itself, he almost directly denied any pattern of early and inherent racial antipathy: ". . . Negro and white servants of the seventeenth century seemed to be remarkably unconcerned about their visible physical differences." As for "the trend toward special treatment" of the Negro, "physical and cultural differences provided handy excuses to justify it." Distaste for the Negro, then, was in the beginning scarcely more than an appurtenance of slavery.

These views squared nicely with the hopes of those even more directly concerned with the problem of contemporary race relations, sociologists and social psychologists. Liberal on the race question almost to a man, they tended to see slavery as the initial cause of the Negro's current degradation. The modern Negro was the unhappy victim of long association with base status. Sociologists, though uninterested in tired questions of historical evidence, could not easily assume a natural prejudice in the white man as the cause of slavery. Natural or innate prejudice would not only violate their basic assumptions concerning the dominance of culture but would undermine the power of their new Baconian science. For if prejudice was natural there would be little one could do to wipe it out. Prejudice must have followed enslavement, not vice versa, else any liberal program of action would be badly compromised. One prominent social scientist suggested in a UNESCO pamphlet that racial prejudice in the United States commenced with the cotton gin!

Just how closely the question of dating had become tied to the practical matter of action against racial prejudice was made apparent by the suggestions of still another historian. Carl N. Degler grappled with the dating problem in an article frankly entitled "Slavery and the Genesis of American Race Prejudice." The article appeared in 1959, a time when Southern resistance to school desegregation seemed more adamant than ever and the North's hands none too clean, a period of discouragement for those hoping to end racial discrimination. Prejudice against the Negro now appeared firm and deep-seated, less easily eradicated than had been supposed in, say, 1954. It was Degler's view that enslavement began early, as a result of white settlers' prejudice or antipathy toward the first Negroes. Thus not only were the sociologists contradicted but the dating problem was now overtly and consciously tied to the broader question of whether slavery caused prejudice or prejudice caused slavery. A new self-consciousness over the American racial dilemma had snatched an arid historical controversy from the hands of an unsuspecting earlier generation and had tossed it into the arena of current debate.

Ironically there might have been no historical controversy at all if every historian dealing with the subject had exercised greater care with facts and greater restraint in interpretation. Too often the debate entered the realm of inference and assumption. For the crucial early years after 1619 there is simply not enough evidence to indicate with any certainty whether Negroes were treated like white servants or not. No historian has found anything resembling proof one way or the other. The first Negroes were sold to the English settlers, yet so were other Englishmen. It can be said, however, that Negroes were set apart from white men by the word *Negroes*, and a distinct name is not attached to a group unless it is seen as different. The earliest Virginia census reports plainly distinguished Negroes from white men, sometimes giving Negroes no personal name; and in 1629 every commander of the several plantations was ordered to "take a generall muster of all

the inhabitants men woemen and Children as well *Englishe* as Negroes."
Difference, however, might or might not involve inferiority.

The first evidence as to the actual status of Negroes does not appear
until about 1640. Then it becomes clear that *some* Negroes were serving
for life and some children inheriting the same obligation. Here it is
necessary to suggest with some candor that the Handlins' statement to
the contrary rests on unsatisfactory documentation. That some Negroes
were held as slaves after about 1640 is no indication, however, that
American slavery popped into the world fully developed at that time.
Many historians, most cogently the Handlins, have shown slavery to
have been a gradual development, a process not completed until the
eighteenth century. The complete deprivation of civil and personal
rights, the legal conversion of the Negro into a chattel, in short slavery
as Americans came to know it, was not accomplished overnight. Yet
these developments practically and logically depended on the practice
of hereditary lifetime service, and it is certainly possible to find in the
1640's and 1650's traces of slavery's most essential feature.

The first definite trace appears in 1640 when the Virginia General
Court pronounced sentence on three servants who had been retaken
after running away to Maryland. Two of them, a Dutchman and a Scot,
were ordered to serve their masters for one additional year and then
the colony for three more, but "the third being a negro named John
Punch shall serve his said master or his assigns for the time of his
natural life here or else where." No white servant in America, so far
as is known, ever received a like sentence. Later the same month a
Negro was again singled out from a group of recaptured runaways; six
of the seven were assigned additional time while the Negro was given
none, presumably because he was already serving for life. After 1640,
too, county court records began to mention Negroes, in part because
there were more of them than previously—about two per cent of
the Virginia population in 1649. Sales for life, often including any
future progeny, were recorded in unmistakable language. In 1646
Francis Pott sold a Negro woman and boy to Stephen Charlton "to the
use of him . . . forever." Similarly, six years later William Whittington
sold to John Pott "one Negro girle named Jowan; aged about Ten
yeares and with her Issue and produce duringe her (or either of them)
for their Life tyme. And their Successors forever"; and a Maryland
man in 1649 deeded two Negro men and a woman "and all their issue
both male and Female." The executors of a York County estate in 1647

disposed of eight Negroes—four men, two women, and two children—
to Captain John Chisman "to have hold occupy posesse and inioy and
every one of the afforementioned Negroes forever[.]" The will of Rowland Burnham of "Rapahanocke," made in 1657, dispensed his considerable number of Negroes and white servants in language which
clearly differentiated between the two by specifying that the whites
were to serve for their "full terme of tyme" and the Negroes "for ever."
Nor did anything in the will indicate that this distinction was exceptional or novel.

In addition to these clear indications that some Negroes were
owned for life, there were cases of Negroes held for terms far longer
than the normal five or seven years. On the other hand, some Negroes
served only the term usual for white servants, and others were completely
free. One Negro freeman, Anthony Johnson, himself owned a Negro.
Obviously the enslavement of some Negroes did not mean the immediate
enslavement of all.

Further evidence of Negroes serving for life lies in the prices paid
for them. In many instances the valuations placed on Negroes (in
estate inventories and bills of sale) were far higher than for white
servants, even those servants with full terms yet to serve. Since there
was ordinarily no preference for Negroes as such, higher prices must
have meant that Negroes were more highly valued because of their
greater length of service. Negro women may have been especially
prized, moreover, because their progeny could also be held perpetually.
In 1645, for example, two Negro women and a boy were sold for 5,500
pounds of tobacco. Two years earlier William Burdett's inventory listed
eight servants (with the time each had still to serve) at valuations
ranging from 400 to 1,100 pounds, while a "very anntient" Negro was
valued at 3,000 and an eight-year-old Negro girl at 2,000 pounds, with
no time-remaining indicated for either. In the late 1650's an inventory
of Thomas Ludlow's large estate evaluated a white servant with six
years to serve at less than an elderly Negro man and only one half of a
Negro woman. The labor owned by James Stone in 1648 was evaluated
as follows:

	lb tobo
Thomas Groves, 4 yeares to serve	1300
Francis Bomley for 6 yeares	1500
John Thackstone for 3 yeares	1300
Susan Davis for 3 yeares	1000

Emaniell a Negro man	2000
Roger Stone 3 yeares	1300
Mingo a Negro man	2000

Besides setting a higher value on the two Negroes, Stone's inventory, like Burdett's, failed to indicate the number of years they had still to serve. It would seem safe to assume that the time remaining was omitted in this and similar documents simply because the Negroes were regarded as serving for an unlimited time.

The situation in Maryland was apparently the same. In 1643 Governor Leonard Calvert agreed with John Skinner, "mariner," to exchange certain estates for seventeen sound Negro "slaves," fourteen men and three women between sixteen and twenty-six years old. The total value of these was placed at 24,000 pounds of tobacco, which would work out to 1,000 pounds for the women and 1,500 for the men, prices considerably higher than those paid for white servants at the time.

Wherever Negro women were involved, however, higher valuations may have reflected the fact that they could be used for field work while white women generally were not. This discrimination between Negro and white women, of course, fell short of actual enslavement. It meant merely that Negroes were set apart in a way clearly not to their advantage. Yet this is not the only evidence that Negroes were subjected to degrading distinctions not directly related to slavery. In several ways Negroes were singled out for special treatment which suggested a generalized debasing of Negroes as a group. Significantly, the first indications of debasement appeared at about the same time as the first indications of actual enslavement.

The distinction concerning field work is a case in point. It first appeared on the written record in 1643, when Virginia pointedly recognized it in her taxation policy. Previously tithable persons had been defined (1629) as "all those that worke in the ground of what qualitie or condition soever." Now the law stated that all adult men and *Negro* women were to be tithable, and this distinction was made twice again before 1660. Maryland followed a similar course, beginning in 1654. John Hammond, in a 1656 tract defending the tobacco colonies, wrote that servant women were not put to work in the fields but in domestic employments, "yet som wenches that are nasty, and beastly and not fit to be so imployed are put into the ground." Since all Negro women were taxed as working in the fields, it would seem logical to conclude that Virginians found them "nasty" and "beastly." The essentially racial nature of this discrimination was bared by a 1668 law at the time slavery was crystallizing on the statute books:

> Whereas some doubts, have arisen whether negro women set free were still to be accompted tithable according to a former act, *It is declared by this grand assembly* that negro women, though permitted to enjoy their ffreedome yet ought not in all respects to be admitted to a full fruition of the exemptions and impunities of the English, and are still lyable to payment of taxes.

Virginia law set Negroes apart in a second way by denying them the important right and obligation to bear arms. Few restraints could indicate more clearly the denial to Negroes of membership in the white community. This action, in a sense the first foreshadowing of the slave codes, came in 1640, at just the time when other indications first appear that Negroes were subject to special treatment.

Finally, an even more compelling sense of the separateness of Negroes was revealed in early distress concerning sexual union between the races. In 1630 a Virginia court pronounced a now famous sentence: "Hugh Davis to be soundly whipped, before an assembly of Negroes and others for abusing himself to the dishonor of God and shame of Christians, by defiling his body in lying with a negro." While there were other instances of punishment for interracial union in the ensuing years, fornication rather than miscegenation may well have been the primary offense, though in 1651 a Maryland man sued someone who he claimed had said "that he had a black bastard in Virginia." There may have been nothing racial about the 1640 case by which Robert Sweet was compelled "to do penance in church according to laws of England, for getting a negroe woman with child and the woman whipt." About 1650 a white man and a Negro woman were required to stand clad in white sheets before a congregation in Lower Norfolk County for having had relations, but this punishment was sometimes used in ordinary cases of fornication between two whites.

It is certain, however, that in the early 1660's when slavery was gaining statutory recognition, the colonial assemblies legislated with feeling against miscegenation. Nor was this merely a matter of avoiding confusion of status, as was suggested by the Handlins. In 1662 Virginia declared that "if any christian shall committ ffornication with a negro man or woman, hee or shee soe offending" should pay double the usual fine. Two years later Maryland prohibited interracial marriages:

> forasmuch as divers freeborne English women forgettful of their free Condicōn and to the disgrace of our Nation doe intermarry with Negro Slaves by which alsoe divers suites may arise touching the Issue of such woemen and a great damage doth befall the Masters of such Negros for prevention whereof for deterring such freeborne women from such shamefull Matches . . . ,

strong language indeed if the problem had only been confusion of status. A Maryland act of 1681 described marriages of white women with Negroes as, among other things, "always to the Satisfaccōn of theire Lascivious & Lustfull desires, & to the disgrace not only of the English butt allso of many other Christian Nations." When Virginia finally prohibited all interracial liaisons in 1691, the assembly vigorously denounced miscegenation and its fruits as "that abominable mixture and spurious issue."

One is confronted, then, with the fact that the first evidences of enslavement and of other forms of debasement appeared at about the same time. Such coincidence comports poorly with both views on the causation of prejudice and slavery. If slavery caused prejudice, then invidious distinctions concerning working in the fields, bearing arms, and sexual union should have appeared only after slavery's firm establishment. If prejudice caused slavery, then one would expect to find such lesser discriminations preceding the greater discrimination of outright enslavement.

Perhaps a third explanation of the relationship between slavery and prejudice may be offered, one that might fit the pattern of events as revealed by existing evidence. Both current views share a common starting point: They predicate two factors, prejudice and slavery, and demand a distinct order of causality. No matter how qualified by recognition that the effect may in turn react upon the cause, each approach inevitably tends to deny the validity of its opposite. But what if one were to regard both slavery and prejudice as species of a general debasement of the Negro? Both may have been equally cause and effect, constantly reacting upon each other, dynamically joining hands to hustle the Negro down the road to complete degradation. Mutual causation is, of course, a highly useful concept for describing social situations in the modern world. Indeed it has been widely applied in only slightly altered fashion to the current racial situation: Racial prejudice and the Negro's lowly position are widely accepted as constantly reinforcing each other.

This way of looking at the facts might well fit better with what we know of slavery itself. Slavery was an organized pattern of human relationships. No matter what the law might say, it was of different character than cattle ownership. No matter how degrading, slavery involved human beings. No one seriously pretended otherwise. Slavery was not an isolated economic or institutional phenomenon; it was the practical facet of a general debasement without which slavery could have no rationality. (Prejudice, too, was a form of debasement, a kind of slavery in the mind.) Certainly the urgent need for labor in a virgin country guided the direction which debasement took, molded it, in fact, into an institutional framework. That economic practicalities shaped the external form of debasement should not tempt one to forget, however, that slavery was at bottom a social arrangement, a way of society's ordering its members in its own mind.

13. COMMUNICATIONS AND TRADE*

The Atlantic in the Seventeenth Century

by Bernard Bailyn

The survival of the first generation of settlers depended on their finding a staple such as tobacco or fish that they could export to finance the importation of essential goods and the development of their societies. Though the great majority of colonists were agriculturalists, a native merchant group quickly emerged to accumulate surpluses for export and to purchase and distribute imports. In the following essay, Bernard Bailyn describes the formative years of the American merchant community, emphasizing the role kinship played in business relationships. Commercial development differentiated the leading ports which had regular contact with England and the Atlantic basin from the smaller towns and rural communities which were cut off from the outside world. American merchants enjoyed extensive autonomy from English control until the latter decades of the seventeenth century when laws regulating trade and an inflow of English officials forced them to adjust to new pressures. Those who gained access to English authority enjoyed advantages and privileges denied others and achieved a degree of eminence, based on political connections, that created divisions within the mercantile community that persisted down to the American Revolution.

For further reading: Bernard Bailyn, *The New England Merchants in the Seventeenth Century* (1955); James B. Hedges, *Browns of Providence Plantations* (1952); William T. Baxter, *The House of Hancock* (1945); Frederick B. Tolles, *Meeting House and Counting House* (1948).

In the first half of the seventeenth century the northern mercantile nations of Europe followed Spain and Portugal in flinging their commercial frontiers westward to the New World. By the end of the century they had surpassed the Iberian nations in western trade and made of the Atlantic basin a single great trading area. Their economic enterprises created not only a crisscrossing web of transoceanic traffic but also a cultural community that came to form the western periphery of European civilization. The members of this community were widely separated, scattered across three thousand miles of ocean and up and down the coasts of two continents. But the structure of commerce furnished a communication system that brought these far-flung settlements together. The same structure proved to be a framework upon which certain important elements in colonial society took form. My purpose is to sketch certain characteristics of the Atlantic colonies in the seventeenth century which relate to these social consequences of commercial growth.

The formative period of northern Atlantic trade was the second third of the seventeenth century. In those years there were important commercial developments on the American continent by the English, the Dutch, and the French; but the swiftest advance took place in the Caribbean. "After 1625," A. P. Newton writes, "swarms of English

---

* *Journal of Economic History*, vol. 13 (1953), 378–387, copyright New York University for the Economic History Association. Footnotes have been omitted except where they are necessary for an understanding of the text.

and French colonists poured like flies upon the rotting carcase of Spain's empire in the Caribbean, and within ten years the West Indian scene was changed forever." The Lesser Antilles became a battleground of the expanding European empires. The island of St. Christopher in the Leewards was jointly possessed by the French and English; Barbados, Nevis, Antigua, and Montserrat were indisputably English; Guadeloupe and Martinique were French; and Curaçao, St. Eustatius, and Tobago were in the hands of the Dutch.

The feverish activity that lay behind these developments resulted from the belief of numerous Europeans that wealth could be readily extracted from the places in the New World with which they were acquainted. But for every success there were a dozen failures. Hopes were held for commercial designs that strike us now as ill-conceived, even stupid. Yet to contemporary merchants, cautious men who built fortunes on their ability to judge investments shrewdly, they were at least as promising as the schemes that succeeded.

Remarkable only for its subsequent fame but typical in its results was the Plymouth Company's colony at the mouth of the Sagadahoc River in New Hampshire. Behind the failure of this venture lay the belief that exploiters of North America, like those of Asia, had only to build coastal trading factories, to which throngs of natives would haul precious piles of goods to exchange for tinkling bells and snippets of bright cloth. English merchants invested approximately £15,000 in the Lynn Ironworks, which collapsed within two decades of its promising start in the early 1640's. At least three major fur companies foundered on the belief that the heartland of American pelts lay in the swampy margins of a mythical "Great Lake of the Iroquois," from which were supposed to flow all the main rivers emptying into the Atlantic. The Virginia settlements after the mid-twenties gradually gained a solid economic base, but only after a decade and a half of continuous failure. In the Caribbean islands, experimentation in all sorts of commodities preceded and accompanied the development of sugar as a staple crop.

Patterns of trade were established, of course, around the poles of successful economic ventures, and it was, therefore, only after the broad wave of failures had receded, leaving behind clear indications of natural possibilities, that the commercial system in its familiar form became evident.

The result was a network of trading routes woven by the enterprises of merchants, shipmasters, and colonists representing all the leading mercantile nations of western Europe. The character of each nation's involvement in the web of traffic was determined largely by the resources it controlled and its place in European affairs. Holland's concentration on the carriage of other nations' goods shaped its position; the commerce of France came to rest upon Canadian furs and West Indian sugar; England's position was determined by the very variety of her colonial products and of the interests of her merchants.

The form of England's commercial system was an interlocked group of irregular circles linking the fixed points of port towns in the British Isles, Newfoundland, the American mainland, the West Indies, the Wine Islands, and the continent of Europe. Outward from the larger ports in the British Isles flowed shipping, manufactures, and investments in colonial property, the enhanced value of which returned as colonial products to be sold at home or abroad. No important part of this flow was self-sufficient. Merchants in the colonies, who profited by injecting into the flow goods of their ownership which would be carried one or more stages closer to the ultimate resolution, became important agents in maintaining the efficiency of this mechanism. Their commerce was not independent, and if it appeared to be so to some of them that was because the efficiency of the system permitted them to operate successfully within a limited area. A breakdown in any major part of the mechanism affected all other parts. When, at the outbreak of the American Revolution, the link between England and her colonies was broken, the whole system, in so far as it affected the colonial merchants, was destroyed.

To contemporaries, the commercial system, which we may describe in abstract, geometrical terms, was not something impersonal existing above men's heads, outside their lives, to which they attached themselves for purpose of trade. Unconcerned with abstract economic forces, they knew that their trade was the creation of men and that the bonds that kept its parts together were the personal relationships existing among them.

Overseas commerce in the seventeenth century was capricious. Arrangements were interminably delayed by the accidents of sailing. Demand fluctuated almost incalculably, as one unforeseen crop failure could create a market which the arrival of a few ships could eliminate overnight. Reliable factors and correspondents were, therefore, of paramount importance, for the success of large enterprises rested on their judgment. In such a situation the initiation and continuance of commerce demanded deep personal commitments between people separated by hundreds of miles of ocean. How could such commitments be made? Not, in these early years, by impersonal correspondences between men brought into temporary contact by complementary business needs. The logic of the situation demanded that they follow preexistent ties of blood or long acquaintance.

To a striking degree first commercial contacts were secured by the cement of kinship. Very frequently brothers, sons, and "in-laws" became the colonial agents of their European relatives. In the middle years of the seventeenth century a number of European—especially English and French—trading families spread out over the Atlantic world. Sons of Londoners seeking their fortunes entered trade in the West Indies and drew on their London connections who were themselves anxious to profit from the importation of colonial goods. Thus Richard Povey, brother of the famous London merchant-politician Thomas Povey, looked after the family interests in Jamaica, while another brother, William, attended to affairs in Barbados. Not infrequently the same family had other relatives on the American mainland who joined in the growing enterprise. The Winthrop family, starting with representatives in England and Massachusetts, ended with ties to Rhode Island, New London and Hartford, Connecticut, Teneriffe in the Canaries, and Antigua in the West Indies. Typical of the reports by young Samuel Winthrop of his progress in securing the last-named contacts are these sentences from a letter of 1648 to his father:

> Captain Clement everet a Justice of peace [in St. Christopher], who being our country man and hearing our name vsed me verry Courtiously, and assisted me much in my law suites which were there verry many. Justice Froth, who was of your acquantance in England (as he informes me), was his Granfather. I haue left in his handes my busines in St. Christpors.

Jean Bailly of La Rochelle conducted his West Indian trade through two relatives in the Caribbean islands, especially Clerbaut Bergier in Martinique. But the most complete family commercial system of which we have any knowledge is that of the Hutchinsons; it is an almost ideal type of this sort of arrangement.

The Hutchinson family trading unit was based upon the continuous flow of manufactures exported from London by the affluent Richard Hutchinson to his brothers Samuel and Edward and his nephews Elisha and Eliakim in Boston, Massachusetts. They, together with Thomas Savage, who had married Richard's sister, retailed the goods in the Bay area and, through middlemen, sold also to the inland settlers. They conducted a large trade with the West Indies, sending provisions and cattle in exchange for cotton and sugar which they sold for credit on London. This West Indian trade of the Hutchinsons was largely handled for them by Peleg Sanford of Portsmouth, Rhode Island, whose mother was another sister of Richard and who was, hence, cousin and nephew of the Boston merchants of the family. Peleg, who had started his career as a commercial agent in the West Indies, exported their horses and provisions to Barbados where they were sold by his brothers, the Barbadian merchants William and Elisha Sanford.

The Hutchinsons with their Rhode Island and West Indian relations formed a self-conscious family group which considered it unfortunate but not unnatural that Edward Hutchinson should go to jail, as he did in 1667, as a consequence of his support of his nephew Peleg in a law suit.

Since commerce was so dependent upon personal relationships, the weaving of a network of correspondences was greatly facilitated by the migrations within the colonial area. Many mainland settlers transplanted themselves to the Caribbean islands and became factors in the West Indies for the merchant friends they had left behind. On the other hand, several merchants were involved in the movement of people among and out of the West Indies, and some of them became residents of the continental colonies. Thus, John Parris, a relative of the New Englander John Hull, moved from the West Indies to Boston where he engaged in large operations in an attempt to stock his Barbados plantation with slaves. Men who moved south to the Indies or north to the continent carried with them friendships and a knowledge of affairs in their old home towns which were used in broadening the foreign contacts of the colonial merchants.

A further consequence of the personal nature of commercial ties in this early period was the consistency, long before mercantilist legislation became effective, with which Frenchmen and Britishers dealt with their fellow nationals in trade. Correspondences with foreigners were difficult to establish and maintain. To British colonials in this period, it seemed that little reliance could be placed on the bonds of Frenchmen who desired nothing more than the collapse of the British settlements in the New World. In long-distance transactions Englishmen preferred to deal with their relatives and friends who, if necessary, could be brought to law in the British courts far more easily than could Frenchmen. Richard Wharton, one of the most enterprising colonial merchants of the seventeenth century, failed to extend his contacts into the French West Indies because of his inability to secure reliable French correspondents. The later enforcement of mercantilist legislation was greatly facilitated by this early tendency of overseas merchants to favor connections with, if not relatives or old friends, at least fellow countrymen.

Through channels of trade created by personal ties among Europeans scattered about the Atlantic world flowed not only physical commodities but the human communications that related the settlers to European life. The orbits of commerce formed by lines drawn between the fixed points of correspondents helped shape the character of urban development and the structure of society in the colonial settlements.

On the American continent, as certain trading centers became poles in the primary cycles of trade, others slipped back toward ruralism. In the passage of generations the communities involved in the major orbits came into closer cultural relations with Europe than they did with some of the neighboring backwoods villages. The Boston merchants' meeting place in their Townhouse Exchange was in every way, except geographically, closer to the "New-England walke" on the London Exchange than to the market places of most inland towns. Study of any of the continental trading regions reveals the varying degrees of provincialism that followed the solidification of the routes of commerce.

In New England, the most important commercial center in North America during the seventeenth century, Boston, with its excellent harbor and access to the provincial government and to flourishing agricultural markets, became the major terminus of traffic originating in Europe. With the exception of Salem and Charlestown, the other promising mercantile centers of the 1630's and 1640's fell back into secondary economic roles and relative seclusion from the cultural life of the Atlantic community. Plymouth, which had been the first trading center east of Manhattan, was described in 1660 as "a poor small Towne now, The People being removed into Farmes in the Country," and New Haven, whose optimistic merchant leaders had laid out "stately and costly houses," was "not so glorious as once it was," with its "Merchants either dead or come away, the rest gotten to their Farmes." This is not to say that these essentially rural districts had no trade. On the contrary, there were men in the Connecticut River towns and along Long Island Sound who managed a considerable exchange of goods; but their dealings were different from those of the Bostonians. Engaged in secondary orbits of trade, they sent small but steady flows of local produce only to other American colonies or occasionally to the West Indies. The Connecticut River grandees were, like the younger Pynchon, primarily landed squires and only secondarily merchants. The few men in the small coastal villages who did devote themselves primarily to trade operated within a commercial sphere subordinate to that of the Bostonians and the Dutchmen.

Life in the inland areas and in the minor ports came to differ significantly from that in the commercial centers in direct contact with Europe. While Boston and New York assumed characteristics of British provincial outports and while their leading residents groped for an understanding of their place as colonials in British society, towns like Scarborough, Maine, and Wethersfield, Connecticut, became models of new types of communities; and their inhabitants, restricted in experience to the colonial world, came to lack the standards by which to measure or even to perceive their provincialism. Fashion, patterns for styles of living, and the emulative spirit of provincialism followed the routes of trade, which, throughout the colonial world, became important social boundaries.

This fact became particularly evident in the last third of the century when national rivalries, both military and economic, required the presence of official representatives in the colonies from the home countries. These officers, civil and military, settled for the most part in the large trading centers, close to the main objects of their supervision. Their presence in what might be called the focuses of the primary trading orbits had a most important social consequence. These home country representatives were quickly surrounded by a number of Europeans new to the colonies: men seeking careers in the quickly expanding colonial administrations. Customs functionaries, lesser bureaucrats, fortune hunters in official positions—these newcomers, grouped around the chief European representatives, came to constitute colonial officialdom, which in all the main colonial ports became a major social magnet for the residents. For not only did it represent cosmopolitan fashion and political influence, but, in its access to those who controlled government contracts and who wielded the weapon of customs regulations, it offered great economic opportunities.

Toward these groups, therefore, moved every colonial with ambition and the slightest hope of success. The threshold of officialdom became a great divide in the society of the commercial towns. Next to this principle of association, "class," in the traditional European sense, was meaningless. In Europe the word "merchant" meant not only an occupation but a status and a way of life. In America, where, as Madam Knight discovered in her famous journey of 1704, they gave the title of merchant to every backwoods huckster, trade was not so much a way of life as a way of making money, not a social condition but an economic activity. Similarly, how could the well-known American mariner, Captain Cyprian Southack, be prevented from describing himself, as he did on occasion, as "gent."?

The limits of officialdom, however, were palpable. No merchant would confuse failure with success in obtaining favors from customs officials or in gaining contracts for provisions and naval stores. It was well worth a merchant's noting, as Samuel Sewall did in his *Diary*, that he was not invited to the governor's dinner parties or to the extravagant funerals staged by the members of his group.

It was as true in the seventeenth century as it is now that the introduction of an important new social barrier necessarily intrudes upon a variety of interests. The advent of officialdom was attended by upheavals throughout the Atlantic world. Wherever we turn in this period we find evidence of social dislocation as successful resident entrepreneurs came to terms with this important new force in the colonial world.

One of the first successful agricultural districts in Carolina was Albemarle County. Behind the barrier of shifting sand bars that blocked Albemarle Sound to all but the most shallow-draft ocean-going vessels lived, in the 1670's, approximately 3,000 settlers—farmers, coastal backwoodsmen, many of them tough, stubborn refugees from better-organized communities. Their one cash crop was tobacco, of which they prepared nearly one million pounds a year. This they disposed of to northerners on peddling voyages in exchange for the commodities they needed. The Navigation Law of 1673 levied duties on tobacco at the port of lading, and Albemarle, like all other commercial centers, was soon visited by a customs collector. The settlers resisted, fearing an increase in the price of goods if their tobacco was taxed, and they forced the governor to remit to the traders three farthings in every penny taken. In 1677 the appointment of an imperious collector of customs determined to enforce the law led to a rebellion of the settlers headed by one John Culpeper. Until the legal authorities could regain control, Culpeper acted as collector, formed a temporary government, and barred the royal comptroller and surveyor of the customs at Albemarle from the exercise of his office.

Culpeper's rebellion, though it was soon quelled and finds little mention in American history, was a significant event. It is a simplified example of what was taking place throughout the colonies. We do not yet have a full account of Leisler's rebellion which kept New York in turmoil for two years. But when we do, it will be found that it was in great part the culmination of resentments that accompanied the introduction of English officialdom into that province. Leisler's career, in fact, can only be understood against the background of family rivalries that grew up around this pre-eminent principle of association. Edmund Andros, famous for his difficulties as the governor of the Dominion of New England, had a less notorious but equally important reign as the Duke of York's governor in New York. In this position he precipitated social differences among the merchants who resisted when they could not take advantage of his influence. He was finally recalled on charges of excessive fee-taking and profiteering.

The rebellion of 1689, which overthrew his administration of the Dominion of New England, divided the northern merchants on lines not of ideology but of interests defined by the degree of proximity to officialdom. No ideology, no religious belief, no abstract political principle or party loyalty separated the Boston merchants Richard Wharton and Charles Lidget, but in 1689 they were on opposite sides of the political fence. Lidget ended up in the Boston jail with Andros because his connections, inherited from his father who had built the family fortune on the timber he sold to the Navy mast contractors, linked him to the leaders of the official group. Wharton died in the midst of his fight for the removal of Andros whose favor he had been denied. The fact that Lidget was one of the founders of the first Anglican Church in New England does not indicate a religious or ideological orientation different from Wharton's. The latter, if he was not an active Anglican, certainly was not a dissenter. Both men married heiress daughters of nonconformist New Englanders.

In the West Indies the same principle was at work during most of the seventeenth century. But toward the end of the century controversies touched off by the intrusion of officialdom diminished in the islands as a consequence of the consolidation of large plantations and the growth of absenteeism. The resident nonofficial population became less active politically as the large planters returned to the home country, leaving their estates in the hands of managers and agents. But battles over the economic benefits of political and social advantage were not ended; they were merely transferred to London where they punctuated the history of the West India interest.

By the end of the century this principle of association in the commercial centers was deeply woven into the fabric of American society. Its importance did not diminish thereafter. Recently, Oliver Dickerson in his book *The Navigation Acts and the American Revolution* destroyed a number of myths by pointing out the importance of what he called "customs racketeering." From his researches it appears that the merchant group was as deeply divided on the eve of the Revolution as it was in 1689. Both John Hancock and Thomas Hutchinson were leading Boston merchants, but the former was clearly victimized by the strategy of the Hutchinson-Bernard clique which controlled the channels of prerogative. And in South Carolina, Henry Laurens, probably the richest merchant in the southern colonies, whose mercantile connections were with the opponents of the King's Friends, suffered equally from the rapacity of the official group.

Further study of the merchants as a social group may reveal that this principle of association, which emerged as an important social force when the nations of Europe undertook to draw together the threads of trade spun by seventeenth-century entrepreneurs, was a major determinant of the movement that led to Revolution.

14. POLITICS AND SOCIAL STRUCTURE IN VIRGINIA*

by Bernard Bailyn

Efforts to reproduce the English social order in the American colonies proved impractical. In the following essay, Bernard Bailyn describes how social stratification evolved in Virginia and how it differed from the order of society in England. Since Virginia lacked an established and experienced aristocracy to provide leadership and manage public affairs, an American elite literally had to be recruited in a hurry. Bailyn explores the social sources of the Virginia elite and the methods by which men achieved eminence and political power. As the contours of colonial society took shape during the seventeenth century, the process by which some became rulers over others generated tensions which sometimes broke out in violence. Yet the rebellions of the latter half of the seventeenth century were not evidence of a chronic revolutionary situation but rather of a new society experiencing growing pains. Though conflicts erupted in violence, they were quickly and easily subdued, and rivals learned to accommodate one another peacefully. Nevertheless political instability was persistent and perhaps inherent in the peculiar kind of social structure that evolved in early America.

Politics and Social Structure in Virginia

For further reading: Louis B. Wright, *First Gentlemen of Virginia* (1964); Wilcomb E. Washburn, *The Governor and the Rebel* (1957); Jerome R. Reich, *Leisler's Rebellion* (1953); Michael G. Hall *et al.*, eds., *The Glorious Revolution in America* (1964).

By the end of the seventeenth century the American colonists faced an array of disturbing problems in the conduct of public affairs. Settlers from England and Holland, reconstructing familiar institutions on American shores, had become participants in what would appear to have been a wave of civil disobedience. Constituted authority was confronted with repeated challenges. Indeed, a veritable anarchy seems to have prevailed at the center of colonial society, erupting in a series of insurrections that began as early as 1635 with the "thrusting out" of Governor Harvey in Virginia. Culpeper's Rebellion in Carolina, the Protestant Association in Maryland, Bacon's Rebellion in Virginia, Leisler's seizure of power in New York, the resistance to and finally the overthrow of Andros in New England—every colony was affected.

These outbursts were not merely isolated local affairs. Although their immediate causes were rooted in the particular circumstances of the separate colonies, they nevertheless had common characteristics. They were, in fact, symptomatic of a profound disorganization of European society in its American setting. Seen in a broad view, they reveal a new configuration of forces which shaped the origins of American politics.

In a letter written from Virginia in 1623, George Sandys, the resident treasurer, reported despondently on the character and condition of the leading settlers. Some of the councilors were "no more then Ciphers," he wrote; others were "miserablie poore"; and the few substantial planters lived apart, taking no responsibility for public concerns. There was, in fact, among all those "worthie the mencioninge" only one person deserving of full approval. Lieutenant William Peirce "refuses

---

* James M. Smith (ed.), *Seventeenth-Century America* (Chapel Hill: University of North Carolina Press, 1959), pp. 90–115. Footnotes have been omitted except where they are necessary for an understanding of the text.

273

no labour, nor sticks at anie expences that may aduantage the publique." Indeed, Sandys added, Peirce was "of a Capacitie that is not to bee expected in a man of his breedinge."

The afterthought was penetrating. It cut below the usual complaints of the time that many of the settlers were lazy malcontents hardly to be preferred to the Italian glassworkers, than whom, Sandys wrote, "a more damned crew hell never vomited." What lay behind Sandys' remark was not so much that wretched specimens were arriving in the shipments of servants nor even that the quality of public leadership was declining but that the social foundations of political power were being strangely altered.

All of the settlers in whatever colony presumed a fundamental relationship between social structure and political authority. Drawing on a common medieval heritage, continuing to conceive of society as a hierarchical unit, its parts justly and naturally separated into inferior and superior levels, they assumed that superiority was indivisible; there was not one hierarchy for political matters, another for social purposes. John Winthrop's famous explanation of God's intent that "in all times some must be rich some poore, some highe and eminent in power and dignitie; others meane and in subieccion" could not have been more carefully worded. Riches, dignity, and power were properly placed in apposition; they pertained to the same individuals.

So closely related were social leadership and political leadership that experience if not theory justified an identification between state and society. To the average English colonist the state was not an abstraction existing above men's lives, justifying itself in its own terms, taking occasional human embodiment. However glorified in monarchy, the state in ordinary form was indistinguishable from a more general social authority; it was woven into the texture of everyday life. It was the same squire or manorial lord who in his various capacities collated to the benefice, set the rents, and enforced the statutes of Parliament and the royal decrees. Nothing could have been more alien to the settlers than the idea that competition for political leadership should be open to all levels of society or that obscure social origins or technical skills should be considered valuable qualifications for office. The proper response to new technical demands on public servants was not to give power to the skilled but to give skills to the powerful. The English gentry and landed aristocracy remained politically adaptable and hence politically competent, assuming when necessary new public functions, eliminating the need for a professional state bureaucracy. By their amateur competence they made possible a continuing identification between political and social authority.

In the first years of settlement no one had reason to expect that this characteristic of public life would fail to transfer itself to the colonies. For at least a decade and a half after its founding there had been in the Jamestown settlement a small group of leaders drawn from the higher echelons of English society. Besides well-born soldiers of fortune like George Percy, son of the Earl of Northumberland, there were among them four sons of the West family—children of Lord de la Warr and his wife, a second cousin of Queen Elizabeth. In Virginia the West brothers held appropriately high positions; three of them served as governors. Christopher Davison, the colony's secretary, was the son of Queen Elizabeth's secretary, William Davison, M.P. and Privy Councilor. The troublesome John Martin, of Martin's Brandon, was the son of Sir Richard Martin, twice Lord Mayor of London, and also the brother-in-law of Sir Julius Caesar, Master of the Rolls and Privy Councilor. Sir Francis and Haute Wyatt were sons of substantial Kent gentry and grandsons of the Sir Thomas Wyatt who led the rebellion of 1554 against Queen Mary. George Sandys' father was the Archbishop of York; of his three older brothers, all knights and M.P.'s, two were eminent country gentlemen, and the third, Edwin, of Virginia Company fame, was a man of great influence in the city. George Thorpe was a former M.P. and Gentleman of the Privy Chamber.

More impressive than such positions and relationships was the cultural level represented. For until the very end of the Company period, Virginia remained to the literary and scientific an exotic attraction, its settlement an important moment in Christian history. Its original magnetism for those in touch with intellectual currents affected the early immigration. Of the twenty councilors of 1621, eight had been educated at Oxford, Cambridge, or the Inns of Court. Davison, like Martin trained in the law, was a poet in a family of poets. Thorpe was a "student of Indian views on religion and astronomy." Francis Wyatt wrote verses and was something of a student of political theory. Alexander Whitaker, M.A., author of *Good Newes from Virginia*, was the worthy heir "of a good part of the learning of his renowned father," the master of St. John's College and Regius Professor of Divinity at Cambridge. John Pory, known to history mainly as the speaker of the first representative assembly in America, was a Master of Arts, "protege and disciple of Hakluyt," diplomat, scholar, and traveler, whose writings from and about America have a rightful place in literary history. Above all there was George Sandys, "poet, traveller, and scholar," a member of Lord Falkland's literary circle; while in Jamestown he continued as a matter of course to work on his notable translation of Ovid's *Metamorphoses.*

There was, in other words, during the first years of settlement a direct transference to Virginia of the upper levels of the English social hierarchy as well as of the lower. If the great majority of the settlers were recruited from the yeoman class and below, there was nevertheless a reasonable representation from those upper groups acknowledged to be the rightful rulers of society.

It is a fact of some importance, however, that this governing elite did not survive a single generation, at least in its original form. By the thirties their number had declined to insignificance. Percy, for example, left in 1612. Whitaker drowned in 1617. Sandys and Francis Wyatt arrived only in 1621, but their enthusiasm cooled quickly; they were both gone by 1626. Of the Wests, only John was alive and resident in the colony a decade after the collapse of the Company. Davison, who returned to England in 1622 after only a year's stay, was sent back in 1623 but died within a year of his return. Thorpe was one of the six councilors slain in the massacre of 1622. Pory left for England in 1622; his return as investigating commissioner in 1624 was temporary, lasting only a few months. And the cantankerous Martin graced the Virginia scene by his absence after 1625; he is last heard from in the early 1630's petitioning for release from a London debtor's prison.

To be sure, a few representatives of important English families, like John West and Edmund Scarborough, remained. There were also one or two additions from the same social level. But there were few indeed of such individuals, and the basis of their authority had changed. The group of gentlemen and illuminati that had dominated the scene during the Company era had been dispersed. Their disappearance created a political void which was filled soon enough, but from a different area of recruitment, from below, from the toughest and most fortunate of the surviving planters whose eminence by the end of the thirties had very little to do with the transplantation of social status.

The position of the new leaders rested on their ability to wring material gain from the wilderness. Some, like Samuel Mathews, started with large initial advantages, but more typical were George Menefie and John Utie, who began as independent landowners by right of transporting themselves and only one or two servants. Abraham Wood, famous for his explorations and like Menefie and Utie the future possessor of large estates and important offices, appears first as a servant boy on Mathews' plantation. Adam Thoroughgood, the son of a country vicar, also started in Virginia as a servant, aged fourteen. William Spencer is first recorded as a yeoman farmer without servants.

Such men as these—Spencer, Wood, Menefie, Utie, Mathews—were the most important figures in Virginia politics up to the Restoration, engrossing large tracts of land, dominating the Council, unseating Sir John Harvey from the governorship. But in no traditional sense were they a ruling class. They lacked the attributes of social authority, and their political dominance was a continuous achievement. Only with the greatest difficulty, if at all, could distinction be expressed in a genteel style of life, for existence in this generation was necessarily crude. Mathews may have created a flourishing estate and Menefie had splendid fruit gardens, but the great tracts of land such men claimed were almost entirely raw wilderness. They had risen to their positions, with few exceptions, by brute labor and shrewd manipulation; they had personally shared the burdens of settlement. They succeeded not because of, but despite, whatever gentility they may have had. William Claiborne may have been educated at the Middle Temple; Peirce could not sign his name; but what counted was their common capacity to survive and flourish in frontier settlements. They were tough, unsentimental, quick-tempered, crudely ambitious men concerned with profits and increased land holdings, not the grace of life. They roared curses, drank exuberantly, and gambled (at least according to deVries) for their servants when other commodities were lacking. If the worst of Governor Harvey's offenses had been to knock out the teeth of an offending councilor with a cudgel, as he did on one occasion, no one would have questioned his right to the governorship. Rank had its privileges, and these men were the first to claim them, but rank itself was unstable and the lines of class or status were fluid. There was no insulation for even the most elevated from the rude impact of frontier life.

As in style of life so in politics, these leaders of the first permanently settled generation did not re-create the characteristics of a stable gentry. They had had little opportunity to acquire the sense of public responsibility that rests on deep identification with the land and its people. They performed in some manner the duties expected of leaders, but often public office was found simply burdensome. Reports such as Sandys' that Yeardley, the councilor and former governor, was wholly absorbed in his private affairs and scarcely glanced at public matters and that Mathews "will rather hazard the payment of fforfeitures then performe our Injunctions" were echoed by Harvey throughout his tenure of office. Charles Harmar, justice of the peace on the Eastern Shore, attended the court once in eight years, and Claiborne's record was only slightly better. Attendance to public duties had to be specifically enjoined, and privileges were of necessity accorded provincial officeholders. The members of the Council were particularly favored by the gift of tax exemption.

The private interests of this group, which had assumed control of public office by virtue not of inherited status but of newly achieved and strenuously maintained economic eminence, were pursued with little interference from the traditional restraints imposed on a responsible ruling class. Engaged in an effort to establish themselves in the land, they sought as specific ends: autonomous local jurisdiction, an aggressive expansion of settlement and trading enterprises, unrestricted access to land, and, at every stage, the legal endorsement of acquisitions. Most of the major public events for thirty years after the dissolution of the Company—and especially the overthrow of Harvey—were incidents in the pursuit of these goals.

From his first appearance in Virginia, Sir John Harvey threatened the interests of this emerging planter group. While still in England he had identified himself with the faction that had successfully sought the collapse of the Company, and thus his mere presence in Virginia was a threat to the legal basis of land grants made under the Company's charter. His demands for the return as public property of goods that had once belonged to the Company specifically jeopardized the planters' holdings. His insistence that the governorship was more than a mere chairmanship of the Council tended to undermine local autonomy. His conservative Indian policy not only weakened the settlers' hand in what already seemed an irreconcilable enmity with the natives but also restricted the expansion of settlement. His opposition to Claiborne's claim to Kent Island threatened to kill off the lucrative Chesapeake Bay trade, and his attempt to ban the Dutch ships from the colony endangered commerce more generally. His support of the official policy of economic diversification, together with his endorsement of the

English schemes of tobacco monopoly, alienated him finally and completely from the Council group.

Within a few months of his assuming the governorship, Harvey wrote home with indignation of the "waywardness and oppositions" of the councilors and condemned them for factiously seeking "rather for their owne endes then either seekinge the generall good or doinge right to particuler men." Before a year was out the antagonisms had become so intense that a formal peace treaty had to be drawn up between Harvey and the Council. But both sides were adamant, and conflict was inescapable. It exploded in 1635 amid comic opera scenes of "extreame coller and passion" complete with dark references to Richard the Third and musketeers "running with their peices presented." The conclusion was Harvey's enraged arrest of George Menefie "of suspicion of Treason to his Majestie"; Utie's response, "And wee the like to you sir"; and the governor's forced return to England.

Behind these richly heroic "passings and repassings to and fro" lies not a victory of democracy or representative institutions or anything of the sort. Democracy, in fact, was identified in the Virginians' minds with the "popular and tumultuary government" that had prevailed in the old Company's quarter courts, and they wanted none of it; the Assembly as a representative institution was neither greatly sought after nor hotly resisted. The victory of 1635 was that of resolute leaders of settlement stubbornly fighting for individual establishment. With the reappointment of Sir Francis Wyatt as governor, their victory was assured and in the Commonwealth period it was completely realized. By 1658, when Mathews was elected governor, effective interference from outside had disappeared and the supreme authority had been assumed by an Assembly which was in effect a league of local magnates secure in their control of county institutions.

One might at that point have projected the situation forward into a picture of dominant county families dating from the 1620's and 1630's, growing in identification with the land and people, ruling with increasing responsibility from increasingly eminent positions. But such a projection would be false. The fact is that with a few notable exceptions like the Scarboroughs and the Wormeleys, these struggling planters of the first generation failed to perpetuate their leadership into the second generation. Such families as the Woods, the Uties, the Mathews, and the Peirces faded from dominant positions of authority after the deaths of their founders. To some extent this was the result of the general insecurity of life that created odds against the physical survival in the male line of any given family. But even if male heirs had remained in these families after the death of the first generation, undisputed eminence would not. For a new emigration had begun in the forties, continuing for close to thirty years, from which was drawn a new ruling group that had greater possibilities for permanent dominance than Harvey's opponents had had. These newcomers absorbed and subordinated the older group, forming the basis of the most celebrated oligarchy in American history.

Most of Virginia's great eighteenth-century names, such as Bland, Burwell, Byrd, Carter, Digges, Ludwell, and Mason, appear in the colony for the first time within ten years either side of 1655. These progenitors of the eighteenth-century aristocracy arrived in remarkably similar circumstances. The most important of these immigrants were younger sons of substantial families well connected in London business and governmental circles and long associated with Virginia; family claims to land in the colony or inherited shares of the original Company stock were now brought forward as a basis for establishment in the New World.

Thus the Bland family interests in Virginia date from a 1618 investment in the Virginia Company by the London merchant John Bland, supplemented in 1622 by another in Martin's Hundred. The merchant never touched foot in America, but three of his sons did come to Virginia in the forties and fifties to exploit these investments. The Burwell fortunes derive from the early subscription to the Company of Edward Burwell, which was inherited in the late forties by his son, Lewis I. The first William Byrd arrived about 1670 to assume the Virginia properties of his mother's family, the Steggs, which dated back to the early days of the Company. The Digges's interests in Virginia stem from the original investments of Sir Dudley Digges and two of his sons in the Company, but it was a third son, Edward, who emigrated in 1650 and established the American branch of the family. Similarly, the Masons had been financially interested in Virginia thirty-two years before 1652, when the first immigrant of that family appeared in the colony. The Culpeper clan, whose private affairs enclose much of the history of the South in the second half of the seventeenth century, was first represented in Virginia by Thomas Culpeper, who arrived in 1649; but the family interests in Virginia had been established a full generation earlier: Thomas' father, uncle, and cousin had all been members of the original Virginia Company and their shares had descended in the family. Even Governor Berkeley fits the pattern. There is no mystery about his sudden exchange in 1642 of the life of a dilettante courtier for that of a colonial administrator and estate manager. He was a younger son without prospects, and his family's interests in Virginia, dating from investments in the Company made twenty years earlier, as well as his appointment held out the promise of an independent establishment in America.

Claims on the colony such as these were only one, though the most important, of a variety of forms of capital that might provide the basis for secure family fortunes. One might simply bring over enough of a merchant family's resources to begin immediately building up an imposing estate, as, presumably, did that ambitious draper's son, William Fitzhugh. The benefits that accrued from such advantages were quickly translated into landholdings in the development of which these settlers were favored by the chronology of their arrival. For though they extended the area of cultivation in developing their landholdings, they were not obliged to initiate settlement. They fell heirs to large areas of the tidewater region that had already been brought under cultivation. "Westover" was not the creation of William Byrd; it had originally been part of the De la Warr estate, passing, with improvements, to Captain Thomas Pawlett, thence to Theodorick Bland, and finally to Byrd. Lewis Burwell inherited not only his father's land, but also the developed estate of his stepfather, Wingate. Some of the Carters' lands may be traced back through John Utie to a John Jefferson, who left Virginia as early as 1628. Abraham Wood's entire Fort Henry property ended in the hands of the Jones family. The Blands' estate in Charles City County, which later became the Harrisons' "Berkeley" plantation, was cleared for settlement in 1619 by servants of the "particular" plantation of Berkeley's Hundred.

Favored thus by circumstance, a small group within the second generation migration moved toward setting itself off in a permanent way as a ruling landed gentry. That they succeeded was due not only to their material advantages but also to the force of their motivation. For these individuals were in social origins just close enough to establishment in gentility to feel the pangs of deprivation most acutely. It is not the totally but the partially dispossessed who build up the most propulsive aspirations, and behind the zestful lunging at propriety and status of a William Fitzhugh lay not the narcotic yearnings of the disinherited but the pent-up ambitions of the gentleman *manqué*. These were neither hardhanded pioneers nor dilettante romantics, but ambitious younger sons of middle-class families who knew well enough what gentility was and sought it as a specific objective.

The establishment of this group was rapid. Within a decade of their arrival they could claim, together with a fortunate few of the first generation, a marked social eminence and full political authority at the county level. But their rise was not uniform. Indeed, by the seventies a new circumstance had introduced an effective principle of social differentiation among the colony's leaders. A hierarchy of position within the newly risen gentry was created by the Restoration government's efforts to extend its control more effectively over its mercantile empire. Demanding of its colonial executives and their advisors closer supervision over the external aspects of the economy, it offered a measure of patronage necessary for enforcement. Public offices dealing with matters that profoundly affected the basis of economic life—tax collection, customs regulation, and the bestowal of land grants—fell within the gift of the governor and tended to form an inner circle of privilege. One can note in Berkeley's administration the growing importance of this barrier of officialdom. Around its privileges there formed the "Green Spring" faction, named after Berkeley's plantation near Jamestown, a group bound to the governor not by royalist sympathies so much as by ties of kinship and patronage.

Thus Colonel Henry Norwood, related to Berkeley by a "near affinity in blood," was given the treasurership of the colony in 1650, which he held for more than two decades. During this time Thomas Ludwell, a cousin and Somerset neighbor of the governor, was secretary of state, in which post he was succeeded in 1678 by his brother Philip, who shortly thereafter married Berkeley's widow. This Lady Berkeley, it should be noted, was the daughter of Thomas Culpeper, the immigrant of 1649 and a cousin of Thomas Lord Culpeper who became governor in 1680. Immediately after her marriage to Berkeley, her brother Alexander requested and received from the governor the nomination to the surveyor-generalship of Virginia, a post he filled for twenty-three years while resident in England, appointing as successive deputies the brothers Ludwell, to whom by 1680 he was twice related by marriage. Lady Berkeley was also related through her mother to William Byrd's wife, a fact that explains much about Byrd's prolific office-holding.

The growing distinctiveness of provincial officialdom within the landed gentry may also be traced in the transformation of the Council. Originally, this body had been expected to comprise the entire effective government, central and local; councilors were to serve, individually or in committees, as local magistrates. But the spread of settlement upset this expectation, and at the same time as the local offices were falling into the hands of autonomous local powers representing leading county families, the Council, appointed by the governor and hence associated with official patronage, increasingly realized the separate, lucrative privileges available to it.

As the distinction between local and central authority became clear, the county magistrates sought their own distinct voice in the management of the colony, and they found it in developing the possibilities of burgess representation. In the beginning there was no House of Burgesses; representation from the burghs and hundreds was conceived of not as a branch of government separate from the Council but as a periodic supplement to it. Until the fifties the burgesses, meeting in the Assemblies with the councilors, felt little need to form themselves into a separate house, for until that decade there was little evidence of a conflict of interests between the two groups. But when, after the Restoration, the privileged status of the Council became unmistakable and the county magnates found control of the increasingly important provincial administration pre-empted by this body, the burgess part of the Assembly took on a new meaning in contrast to that of the Council. Burgess representation now became vital to the county leaders if they were to share in any consistent way in affairs larger than those of the counties. They looked to the franchise, hitherto broad not by design but by neglect, introducing qualifications that would ensure their control of the Assembly. Their interest in provincial government could no longer be expressed in the conglomerate Assembly, and at least by 1663 the House of Burgesses began to meet separately as a distinct body voicing interests potentially in conflict with those of the Council.

Thus by the eighth decade the ruling class in Virginia was broadly based on leading county families and dominated at the provincial level by a privileged officialdom. But this social and political structure was too new, too lacking in the sanctions of time and custom, its leaders too close to humbler origins and as yet too undistinguished in style of life, to be accepted without a struggle. A period of adjustment was necessary, of which Bacon's Rebellion was the climactic episode.

Bacon's Rebellion began as an unauthorized frontier war against the Indians and ended as an upheaval that threatened the entire basis of social and political authority. Its immediate causes have to do with race relations and settlement policy, but behind these issues lay deeper elements related to resistance against the maturing shape of a new social order. These elements explain the dimensions the conflict reached.

There was, first, resistance by substantial planters to the privileges and policies of the inner provincial clique led by Berkeley and composed of those directly dependent on his patronage. These dissidents, among whom were the leaders of the Rebellion, represented neither the downtrodden masses nor a principle of opposition to privilege as such. Their discontent stemmed to a large extent from their own exclusion from privileges they sought. Most often their grievances were based on personal rebuffs they had received as they reached for entry into provincial officialdom. Thus—to speak of the leaders of the Rebellion—Giles Bland arrived in Virginia in 1671 to take over the agency of his late uncle in the management of his father's extensive landholdings, assuming at the same time the lucrative position of customs collector which he had obtained in London. But, amid angry cries of *"pittyfull fellow, puppy* and *Sonn of a Whore,"* he fell out first with Berkeley's cousin and favorite, Thomas Ludwell, and finally with the governor himself; for his "Barbarous and Insolent Behaviors" Bland was fined, arrested, and finally removed from the collectorship. Of the two "chiefe Incendiarys," William Drummond and Richard Lawrence, the former had been quarreling with Berkeley since 1664, first over land claims in Carolina, then over a contract for building a fort near James City, and repeatedly over lesser issues in the General Court; Lawrence "some Years before . . . had been partially treated at Law, for a considerable Estate on behalfe of a Corrupt favorite." Giles Brent, for his depredations against the Indians in violation of official policy, had not only been severely fined but barred from public office. Bacon himself could not have appeared under more favorable circumstances. A cousin both of Lady Berkeley and of the councilor Nathaniel Bacon, Sr., and by general agreement "a Gent:man of a Liberall education" if of a somewhat tarnished reputation, he had quickly staked out land for himself and had been elevated, for reasons "best known to the Governour," to the Council. But being "of a most imperious and dangerous hidden Pride of heart . . . very ambitious and arrogant," he wanted more, and quickly. His alienation from and violent opposition to Berkeley were wound in among the animosities created by the Indian problem and were further complicated by his own unstable personality; they were related also to the fact that Berkeley finally turned down the secret offer Bacon and Byrd made in 1675 for the purchase from the governor of a monopoly of the Indian trade.

These specific disputes have a more general aspect. It was three decades since Berkeley had assumed the governorship and begun rallying a favored group, and it was over a decade since the Restoration had given this group unconfined sway over the provincial government. In those years much of the choice tidewater land as well as the choice offices had been spoken for, and the tendency of the highly placed was to hold firm. Berkeley's Indian policy—one of stabilizing the borders between Indians and whites and protecting the natives from depredation by land-hungry settlers—although a sincere attempt to deal with an extremely difficult problem, was also conservative, favoring the established. Newcomers like Bacon and Bland and particularly landholders on the frontiers felt victimized by a stabilization of the situation or by a controlled expansion that maintained on an extended basis the existing power structure. They were logically drawn to aggressive positions. In an atmosphere charged with violence, their interests constituted a challenge to provincial authority. Bacon's primary appeal in his "Manifesto" played up the threat of this challenge:

> Let us trace these men in Authority and Favour to whose hands the dispensation of the Countries wealth has been commited; let us observe the sudden Rise of their Estates [compared] with the Quality in wch they first entered this Country. . . And lett us see wither their extractions and Education have not bin vile, And by what pretence of learning and vertue they could [enter] soe soon into Imployments of so great Trust and consequence, let us . . . see what spounges have suckt up the Publique Treasure and wither it hath not bin privately contrived away by unworthy Favourites and juggling Parasites whose tottering Fortunes have bin repaired and supported at the Publique chardg.

Such a threat to the basis of authority was not lost on Berkeley or his followers. Bacon's merits, a contemporary wrote, "thretned an eclips to there riseing gloryes. . . . . (if he should continue in the Governours favour) of Seniours they might becom juniours, while there younger Brother . . . might steale away that blessing, which they accounted there owne by birthright."

285

But these challengers were themselves challenged, for another main element in the upheaval was the discontent among the ordinary settlers at the local privileges of the same newly risen county magnates who assailed the privileges of the Green Spring faction. The specific Charles City County grievances were directed as much at the locally dominant family, the Hills, as they were at Berkeley and his clique. Similarly, Surry County complained of its county court's highhanded and secretive manner of levying taxes on "the poore people" and of setting the sheriffs' and clerks' fees; they petitioned for the removal of these abuses and for the right to elect the vestry and to limit the tenure of the sheriffs. At all levels the Rebellion challenged the stability of newly secured authority.

It is this double aspect of discontent behind the violence of the Rebellion that explains the legislation passed in June, 1676, by the so-called "Bacon's Assembly." At first glance these laws seem difficult to interpret because they express disparate if not contradictory interests. But they yield readily to analysis if they are seen not as the reforms of a single group but as efforts to express the desires of two levels of discontent with the way the political and social hierarchy was becoming stabilized. On the one hand, the laws include measures designed by the numerically predominant ordinary settlers throughout the colony as protests against the recently acquired superiority of the leading county families. These were popular protests and they relate not to provincial affairs but to the situation within the local areas of jurisdiction. Thus the statute restricting the franchise to freeholders was repealed; freemen were given the right to elect the parish vestrymen; and the county courts were supplemented by elected freemen to serve with the regularly appointed county magistrates.

On the other hand, there was a large number of measures expressing the dissatisfactions not so much of the ordinary planter but of the local leaders against the prerogatives recently acquired by the provincial elite, prerogatives linked to officialdom and centered in the Council. Thus the law barring office-holding to newcomers of less than three years' residence struck at the arbitrary elevation of the governor's favorites, including Bacon; and the acts forbidding councilors to join the county courts, outlawing the governor's appointment of sheriffs and tax collectors, and nullifying tax exemption for councilors all voiced objections of the local chieftains to privileges enjoyed by others. From both levels there was objection to profiteering in public office.

Thus the wave of rebellion broke and spread. But why did it subside? One might have expected that the momentary flood would have become a steady tide, its rhythms governed by a fixed political constellation. But in fact it did not; stable political alignments did not result. The conclusion to this controversy was characteristic of all the insurrections. The attempted purges and counterpurges by the leaders of the two sides were followed by a rapid submerging of factional identity. Occasional references were later made to the episode, and there were individuals who found an interest in keeping its memory alive. Also, the specific grievances behind certain of the attempted legal reforms of 1676 were later revived. But of stable parties or factions around these issues there were none.

It was not merely that in the late years of the century no more than in the early was there to be found a justification for permanently organized political opposition or party machinery, that persistent, organized dissent was still indistinguishable from sedition; more important was the fact that at the end of the century as in 1630 there was agreement that some must be "highe and eminent in power and dignitie; others meane and in subieccion." Protests and upheaval had resulted from the discomforts of discovering who was, in fact, which, and what the particular consequences of "power and dignitie" were.

But by the end of the century the most difficult period of adjustment had passed and there was an acceptance of the fact that certain families were distinguished from others in riches, in dignity, and in access to political authority. The establishment of these families marks the emergence of Virginia's colonial aristocracy.

It was a remarkable governing group. Its members were soberly responsible, alive to the implications of power; they performed their public obligations with notable skill. Indeed, the glare of their accomplishments is so bright as occasionally to blind us to the conditions that limited them. As a ruling class the Virginian aristocracy of the eighteenth century was unlike other contemporary nobilities or aristocracies, including the English. The differences, bound up with the special characteristics of the society it ruled, had become clear at the turn of the seventeenth century.

Certain of these characteristics are elusive, difficult to grasp and analyze. The leaders of early eighteenth-century Virginia were, for example, in a particular sense, cultural provincials. They were provincial not in the way of Polish *szlachta* isolated on their estates by poverty and impassable roads, nor in the way of sunken *seigneurs* grown rustic and old-fashioned in lonely Norman chateaux. The Virginians were far from uninformed or unaware of the greater world; they were in fact deeply and continuously involved in the cultural life of the Atlantic community. But they knew themselves to be provincials in the sense that their culture was not self-contained; its sources and superior expressions were to be found elsewhere than in their own land. They must seek it from afar; it must be acquired, and once acquired be maintained according to standards externally imposed, in the creation of which they had not participated. The most cultivated of them read much, purposefully, with a diligence the opposite of that essential requisite of aristocracy, uncontending ease. William Byrd's diary with its daily records of stints of study is a stolid testimonial to the virtues of regularity and effort in maintaining standards of civilization set abroad.

In more evident ways also the Virginia planters were denied an uncontending ease of life. They were not *rentiers*. Tenancy, when it appeared late in the colonial period, was useful to the landowners mainly as a cheap way of improving lands held in reserve for future development. The Virginia aristocrat was an active manager of his estate, drawn continuously into the most intimate contacts with the soil and its cultivation. This circumstance limited his ease, one might even say bound him to the soil, but it also strengthened his identity with the land and its problems and saved him from the temptation to create of his privileges an artificial world of self-indulgence.

But more important in distinguishing the emerging aristocracy of Virginia from other contemporary social and political elites were two very specific circumstances. The first concerns the relationship between the integrity of the family unit and the descent of real property. "The English political family," Sir Lewis Namier writes with particular reference to the eighteenth-century aristoracry,

> is a compound of blood, name, and estate, this last . . . being the most important of the three. . . . The name is a weighty symbol, but liable to variations . . . the estate . . . is, in the long run, the most potent factor in securing continuity through identification. . . . Primogeniture and entails psychically preserve the family in that they tend to fix its position through the successive generations, and thereby favour conscious identification.

The descent of landed estates in eighteenth-century England was controlled by the complicated device known as the strict settlement which provided that the heir at his marriage received the estate as a life tenant, entailing its descent to his unborn eldest son and specifying the limitations of the encumbrances upon the land that might be made in behalf of his daughters and younger sons.

It was the strict settlement, in which in the eighteenth century perhaps half the land of England was bound, that provided continuity over generations for the landed aristocracy. This permanent identification of the family with a specific estate and with the status and offices that pertained to it was achieved at the cost of sacrificing the younger sons. It was a single stem of the family only that retained its superiority; it alone controlled the material basis for political dominance.

This basic condition of aristocratic governance in England was never present in the American colonies, and not for lack of familiarity with legal forms. The economic necessity that had prompted the widespread adoption of the strict settlement in England was absent in the colonies. Land was cheap and easily available, the more so as one rose on the social and political ladder. There was no need to deprive the younger sons or even daughters of landed inheritances in order to keep the original family estate intact. Provision could be made for endowing each of them with plantations, and they in turn could provide similarly for their children. Moreover, to confine the stem family's fortune to a single plot of land, however extensive, was in the Virginia economy to condemn it to swift decline. Since the land was quickly worn out and since it was cheaper to acquire new land than to rejuvenate the worked soil by careful husbandry, geographical mobility, not stability, was the key to prosperity. Finally, since land was only as valuable as the labor available to work it, a great estate was worth passing intact from generation to generation only if it had annexed to it a sufficient population of slaves. Yet this condition imposed severe rigidities in a plantation's economy—for a labor force bound to a particular plot was immobilized —besides creating bewildering confusions in law.

The result, evident before the end of the seventeenth century, was a particular relationship between the family and the descent of property. There was in the beginning no intent on the part of the Virginians to alter the traditional forms; the continued vitality of the ancient statutes specifying primogeniture in certain cases was assumed. The first clear indication of a new trend came in the third quarter of the century, when the leading gentry, rapidly accumulating large estates, faced for the first time the problem of the transfer of property. The result was the sub-division of the great holdings and the multiplication of smaller plots while the net amount of land held by the leading families continued to rise.

This trend continued. Primogeniture neither at the end of the seventeenth century nor after prevailed in Virginia. It was never popular even among the most heavily endowed of the tidewater families. The most common form of bequest was a grant to the eldest son of the undivided home plantation and gifts of other tracts outside the home county to the younger sons and daughters. Thus by his will of 1686 Robert Beverley, Sr., bequeathed to his eldest son, Peter, all his land in Gloucester County lying between "Chiescake" and "Hoccadey's" creeks (an unspecified acreage); to Robert, the second son, another portion of the Gloucester lands amounting to 920 acres; to Harry, 1,600 acres in Rappahannock County; to John, 3,000 acres in the same county; to William, two plantations in Middlesex County; to Thomas, 3,000 acres in Rappahannock and New Kent counties; to his wife, three plantations including those "whereon I now live" for use during her lifetime, after which they were to descend to his daughter Catherine, who was also to receive £ 200 sterling; to his daughter Mary, £ 150 sterling; to "the childe that my wife goeth with, be it male or female," all the rest of his real property; and the residue of his personal property was "to be divided and disposed in equall part & portion betwix my wife and children." Among the bequests of Ralph Wormeley, Jr., in 1700 was an estate of 1,500 acres to his daughter Judith as well as separate plantations to his two sons.

Entail proved no more popular than primogeniture. Only a small minority of estates, even in the tidewater region, were ever entailed. In fact, despite the extension of developed land in the course of the eighteenth century, more tidewater estates were docked of entails than were newly entailed.

Every indication points to continuous and increasing difficulty in reproducing even pale replicas of the strict settlement. In 1705 a law was passed requiring a special act of the Assembly to break an entail; the law stood, but between 1711 and 1776 no fewer than 125 such private acts were passed, and in 1734 estates of under £ 200 were exempted from the law altogether. The labor problem alone was an insuperable barrier to perpetuating the traditional forms. A statute of 1727, clarifying the confused legislation of earlier years, had attempted to ensure a labor force on entailed land by classifying slaves as real property and permitting them to be bound together with land into bequests. But by 1748 this stipulation had resulted in such bewildering "doubts, variety of opinions, and confusions" that it was repealed. The repeal was disallowed in London, and in the course of a defense of its action the Assembly made vividly clear the utter impracticality of entailment in Virginia's economy. Slaves, the Assembly explained, were essential to the success of a plantation, but "slaves could not be kept on the lands to which they were annexed without manifest prejudice to the tenant in tail. . . . often the tenant was the proprietor of fee simple land much fitter for cultivation than his intailed lands, where he could work his slaves to a much greater advantage." On the other hand, if a plantation owner did send entailed slaves where they might be employed most economically the result was equally disastrous:

the frequent removing and settling them on other lands in other counties and parts of the colony far distant from the county court where the deeds or wills which annexed them were recorded and the intail lands lay; the confusion occasioned by their mixture with fee simple slaves of the same name and sex and belonging to the same owner; the uncertainty of distinguishing one from another after several generations, no register of their genealogy being kept and none of them having surnames, were great mischiefs to purchasers, strangers, and creditors, who were often unavoidably deceived in their purchases and hindered in the recovery of their just debts. It also lessened the credit of the country; it being dangerous for the merchants of Great Britain to trust possessors of many slaves for fear the slaves might be intailed.

A mobile labor force free from legal entanglements and a rapid turnover of lands, not a permanent hereditary estate, were prerequisites of family prosperity. This condition greatly influenced social and political life. Since younger sons and even daughters inherited extensive landed properties, equal often to those of the eldest son, concentration of authority in the stem family was precluded. Third generation collateral descendants of the original immigrant were as important in their own right as the eldest son's eldest son. Great clans like the Carters and the Lees, though they may have acknowledged a central family seat, were scattered throughout the province on estates of equal influence. The four male Carters of the third generation were identified by contemporaries by the names of their separate estates, and, indistinguishable in style of life, they had an equal access to political power.

Since material wealth was the basis of the status which made one eligible for public office, there was a notable diffusion of political influence throughout a broadening group of leading families. No one son was predestined to represent the family interest in politics, but as many as birth and temperament might provide. In the 1750's there were no fewer than seven Lees of the same generation sitting together in the Virginia Assembly; in the Burgesses they spoke for five separate counties. To the eldest, Philip Ludwell Lee, they conceded a certain social superiority that made it natural for him to sit in the Council. But he did not speak alone for the family; by virtue of inheritance he had no unique authority over his brothers and cousins.

The leveling at the top of the social and political hierarchy, creating an evenness of status and influence, was intensified by continuous inter-marriage within the group. The unpruned branches of these flourishing family trees, growing freely, met and intertwined until by the Revolution the aristocracy appeared to be one great tangled cousinry.

As political power became increasingly diffused throughout the upper stratum of society, the Council, still at the end of the seventeenth century a repository of unique privileges, lost its effective superiority. Increasingly through the successive decades its authority had to be exerted through alignments with the Burgesses—alignments made easier as well as more necessary by the criss-crossing network of kinship that united the two houses. Increasingly the Council's distinctions became social and ceremonial.

The contours of Virginia's political hierarchy were also affected by a second main conditioning element, besides the manner of descent of family property. Not only was the structure unusually level and broad at the top, but it was incomplete in itself. Its apex, the ultimate source of legal decision and control, lay in the quite different society of England, amid the distant embroilments of London, the court, and Parliament. The levers of control in that realm were for the most part hidden from the planters; yet the powers that ruled this remote region could impose an arbitrary authority directly into the midst of Virginia's affairs.

One consequence was the introduction of instabilities in the tenure and transfer of the highest offices. Tenure could be arbitrarily inter-rupted, and the transfer to kin of such positions at death or resignation —uncertain in any case because of the diffusion of family authority—

could be quite difficult or even impossible. Thus William Byrd II returned from England at the death of his father in 1704 to take over the family properties, but though he was the sole heir he did not automatically or completely succeed to the elder Byrd's provincial offices. He did, indeed, become auditor of Virginia after his father, but only because he had carefully arranged for the succession while in London; his father's Council seat went to someone else, and it took three years of patient maneuvering through his main London contact, Micajah Perry, to secure another; he never did take over the receivership. Even such a power as "King" Carter, the reputed owner at his death of 300,000 acres and 1,000 slaves, was rebuffed by the resident deputy governor and had to deploy forces in England in order to transfer a Virginia naval office post from one of his sons to another. There was family continuity in public office, but at the highest level it was uncertain, the result of place-hunting rather than of the absolute prerogative of birth.

Instability resulted not only from the difficulty of securing and transferring high appointive positions but also and more immediately from the presence in Virginia of total strangers to the scene, particularly governors and their deputies, armed with extensive jurisdiction and powers of enforcement. The dangers of this element in public life became clear only after Berkeley's return to England in 1677, for after thirty-five years of residence in the colony Sir William had become a leader in the land independent of his royal authority. But Howard, Andros, and Nicholson were governors with full legal powers but with at best only slight connections with local society. In them, social leadership and political leadership had ceased to be identical.

In the generation that followed Berkeley's departure, this separation between the two spheres created the bitterest of political controversies. Firmly entrenched behind their control of the colony's government, the leading families battled with every weapon available to reduce the power of the executives and thus to eliminate what appeared to be an external and arbitrary authority. Repeated complaints by the governors of the intractable opposition of a league of local oligarchs marked the Virginians' success. Efforts by the executives to discipline the indigenous leaders could only be mildly successful. Patronage was a useful weapon, but its effectiveness diminished steadily, ground down between a resistant Assembly and an office-hungry bureaucracy in England. The possibility of exploiting divisions among the resident powers also declined as kinship lines bound the leading families closer together and as group interests became clearer with the passage of time. No faction built around the gubernatorial power could survive independently; ultimately its adherents would fall away and it would weaken. It was a clear logic of the situation that led the same individuals who had promoted Nicholson as a replacement for Andros to work against him once he assumed office.

Stability could be reached only by the complete identification of external and internal authority through permanent commitment by the appointees to local interests. Commissary Blair's extraordinary success in Virginia politics was based not only on his excellent connections in England but also on his marriage into the Harrison family, which gave him the support of an influential kinship faction. There was more than hurt pride and thwarted affection behind Nicholson's reported insane rage at being spurned by the highly marriageable Lucy Burwell; and later the astute Spotswood, for all his success in imposing official policy, fully quieted the controversies of his administration only by succumbing completely and joining as a resident Virginia landowner the powers aligned against him.

But there was more involved than instability and conflict in the discontinuity between social and political organization at the topmost level. The state itself had changed its meaning. To a Virginia planter of the early eighteenth century the highest public authority was no longer merely one expression of a general social authority. It had become something abstract, external to his life and society, an ultimate power whose purposes were obscure, whose direction could neither be consistently influenced nor accurately plotted, and whose human embodiments were alien and antagonistic.

The native gentry of the early eighteenth century had neither the need nor the ability to fashion a new political theory to comprehend their experience, but their successors would find in the writings of John Locke on state and society not merely a reasonable theoretical position but a statement of self-evident fact.

I have spoken exclusively of Virginia, but though the histories of each of the colonies in the seventeenth century are different, they exhibit common characteristics. These features one might least have expected to find present in Virginia, and their presence there is, consequently, most worth indicating.

In all of the colonies the original transference of an ordered European society was succeeded by the rise to authority of resident settlers whose influence was rooted in their ability to deal with the problems of life in wilderness settlements. These individuals attempted to stabilize their positions, but in each case they were challenged by others arriving after the initial settlements, seeking to exploit certain advantages of position, wealth, or influence. These newcomers, securing after the Restoration governmental appointments in the colonies and drawn together by personal ties, especially those of kinship and patronage, came to constitute colonial officialdom. This group introduced a new principle of social organization; it also gave rise to new instabilities in a society in which the traditional forms of authority were already being subjected to severe pressures. By the eighth decade of the seventeenth century the social basis of public life had become uncertain and insecure, its stability delicate and sensitive to disturbance. Indian warfare, personal quarrels, and particularly the temporary confusion in external control caused by the Glorious Revolution became the occasions for violent challenges to constituted authority.

By the end of the century a degree of harmony had been achieved, but the divergence between political and social leadership at the topmost level created an area of permanent conflict. The political and social structures that emerged were by European standards strangely shaped. Everywhere as the bonds of empire drew tighter the meaning of the state was changing. Herein lay the origins of a new political system.

III

THE STRUCTURE OF COLONIAL SOCIETY: THE EIGHTEENTH CENTURY

The Productive System

15. LAND SPECULATION AND THE SETTLEMENT OF KENT, 1738–1760*

by Charles S. Grant

The colonial land system influenced the development of the economy and the social structure. The abundance of rich, virgin lands that could be bought cheaply, free from the manorial obligations that pressed on the European peasantry, located on streams and rivers that gave husbandmen access to markets, encouraged the spread of family farms and the emergence of plantations. Instead of satisfying people's land hunger, the availability of land intensified the desire to accumulate larger holdings. According to Charles S. Grant, land speculation was not confined to any particular occupational or social group but appealed to urban and rural folk as well as to small-scale yeomen investors and relatively large-scale absentee speculators. Rapid growth and shifts of population led people to expect land values to rise; if one located investments in the right place, the profits were thought to be considerable. Frontier land was appealing to farmers who wanted to abandon soils worn out by wasteful methods of farming and move to fresh lands farther west. Except for trade and farming, there were practically no other outlets for their savings—no banks or insurance companies, few government securities, and no corporate stocks and bonds. Moreover, in a society where wealth defined social position and land was the primary form of wealth, the ambitious understandably sought broad acres. Yet despite the colonists' preoccupation with speculation, Grant's study of Kent, Connecticut, suggests that speculation did not result in a markedly unequal distribution of land, with a few absentee proprietors engrossing most of the best acreage. Perhaps there was too much land for that to happen; nevertheless there were exceptions. New York's Hudson River Valley was carved into large manorial estates whose owners rented but did not sell the land. As a result, immigrants preferred to settle in other colonies where opportunities for acquiring their own farms were greater; therefore New York's development lagged. Though it is apparent that the social consequences of land speculation did not generally lead to monopolization, where the economic consequences led is less clear. Was land speculation the best use of savings or did it limit the investment capital available for more productive kinds of economic activity that could have promoted more rapid economic growth?

For further reading: Roy H. Akagi, *Town Proprietors of New England* (1924); Shaw Livermore, *Early American Land Companies* (1939); Charles S. Grant, *Democracy in the Connecticut Frontier Town of Kent* (1961).

Kent, on the extreme western border of Connecticut, was one of that colony's "notorious" auction townships, sold in fifty-three shares to bidders gathered at Windham, Connecticut, for the "vendue" on March 8, 1738. The settling of Kent and its sister towns by 1740 was a final step in the filling up of Connecticut's frontier.

---

* *New England Quarterly*, vol. 28 (1955), 51–71. Footnotes have been omitted except where they are necessary for an understanding of the text.

Land Speculation and the Settlement of Kent, 1738-1760

Recent historians have been interested in the unwholesome aspects of the eighteenth-century New England frontier: the orgy of speculation in the new towns, the evils of absenteeism, the conflicts of proprietors versus non-proprietors, and the exploitation of debtor-pioneer farmers by wealthy easterners. Kent was a frontier town inflicting severe hardships on a group of Congregational pioneers, who cleared land, erected rough cabins, and lived the subsistence-farming kind of life typical of the New England frontier of the period. But Kent was an exception to the standard picture. The purpose of this essay is twofold: first, to develop the story of speculation in local lands so that Kent, as a representative of prosperous, harmonious towns, can be placed on the scales as a counter balance for communities steeped in controversy and rancor; second, to suggest that the investigation of more towns along the lines followed here may establish that there was generally less clashing between absentee speculators and local residents than standard accounts would imply.

One of the darkest pictures of the eighteenth-century frontier is that of Curtis Nettels in his *Roots of American Civilization*.

> The frontier farmers viewed the speculators as their natural enemies who withheld land from cultivation, waged war against squatters, forced the price of land upwards, controlled town governments as absentee voters, and failed to contribute toward the defense and welfare of the new communities. . . . The most important legacy of speculation was this sharpened antagonism between seaboard wealth and frontier poverty.

Almost as gloomy are James Truslow Adams, Louis M. Hacker, Oliver P. Chitwood, and other writers of general surveys. They have distinguished predecessors in Lois K. Mathews and Frederick Jackson Turner, who studied "restless democracy, resentfulness over taxation and control, recriminations between the western pioneer and the eastern capitalist." Probably the outstanding monograph on problems of New England's eighteenth-century frontier is Roy H. Akagi, *The Town Proprietors of the New England Colonies*. Part II of his study is entirely devoted to land speculation and the attendant evils. His work is a documentation of the earlier Turner assumptions and is often cited.

These historians responsible for the standard "gloomy" line have possibly tended to seek out bitterness and controversy. Certainly Turner was looking for patterns of antagonism found later in Shays' Rebellion and the Populist Revolt. Seeking controversy or not, most writers have used sources that emphasize sore spots on the New England scene. In particular, they have relied on the more striking town histories such as that of Westminster. Adams wrote, ". . . we have let down our lines here and there to take soundings." Hovering over 1,000 New England towns, the historians dropped their lines and nearly all hit Westminster. Kent, and perhaps scores of towns like it, presented a scene poles apart from Westminster. But lacking spectacular events, lacking adequate local histories, Kent-type towns have been ignored. Their stories, too, deserve attention before a final verdict is recorded.

*   *   *

Kent emphatically bears out the standard contention on the prevalence of speculation. The most conspicuous economic fact which emerges from an analysis of Kent Land Records is that nearly all Kent land figured in speculative transactions. The figures are surprisingly large considering the small size of Kent (about 200 families in 1760). During the period 1738–1760 a total of 872 different men bought and sold Kent land. James Lassell of Windham engaged in thirty-nine separate transactions during this period. The famous William Samuel Johnson of Stratford did not start until 1755 but between that year and 1792 he figured in one hundred separately recorded Kent land deals. Altogether, there were over 6,000 land transactions in this frontier settlement between 1738 and 1760 for an average of better than seven deals per man.

However, Turner, Akagi, Nettels, and others have failed to note the speculative activity of the lower-class, on-the-spot settler. Historians have pictured the frontiersman as too poor to speculate, as belonging to a class antagonistic to that of the rich eastern speculator. At Kent, however, the humblest pioneers were apparently speculating their heads off.

The way these farmers made land deals among themselves is astonishing. The first division naturally contained the best land for farming and home-building. The fifty-three lots of this division lay on both sides of the "twelve-rod highway to Cornwall" now U.S. Route Seven. This choice land came into the hands of the settlers almost immediately but, instead of remaining stable and inactive, the first-division lots were bought and sold more often than any other plots in Kent. For example, lot 46 was drawn by proprietor-settler Thomas Beeman at the first division in Windham in 1738. By 1748 this farm lot had reached Jethro Hatch, but a glance at its gyrations in between Beeman and Hatch is instructive.

Lot 46, First Division
1738–to Thomas Beeman by draw

West part of Lot	*East part of Lot*
1739–Thomas Beeman to Ebenezer Barnum, Sr. No price.	1739–Thomas Beeman to Nathaniel Robards for 114 pounds.
1743–Ebenezer Barnum Sr. to Jonathan and Samuel Skeels for 100 pounds.	1741–Nathaniel Robards to Ebenezer Barnum, Jr. for 162 pounds.
1743–Jonathan and Samuel Skeels to Ebenezer Barnum, Jr. for 120 pounds.	

1745–Ebenezer Barnum, Jr. to Amos Barnum for 413 pounds.

1745–Amos Barnum to Ephraim Fisher for 512 pounds.

1746–Ephraim Fisher to John Beeman (brother of original owner, Thomas). No price.

1748–John Beeman to Jethro Hatch. No price.

Every man listed above was a local settler. These same settlers, and almost all other settlers in Kent, were dealing in similar fashion with other first-division lots. Lot 6 changed hands seven times, lots 22 and 29 changed ten times each, and lots 36 and 46 changed eight times each. The average turnover for all fifty-three lots during the period 1738–1760 was four, this being reduced by seven lots for which there is no record of any sales. It seems hardly an exaggeration to say that each pioneer wanted a piece of five or six other home lots. Abel Wright owned at various times parts of eleven first-division lots; Nathaniel Berry held in ten, John Mills in seven, Joseph Pratt in six, and Reuben Swift in five. The Barnums collectively were in sixteen of the lots and the Comstocks, Hatches, Hubbells, and Fullers were almost as widespread.

Since all these men were settlers, it might be reasoned that the trading represented an effort to consolidate holdings. However, evidence indicates that only a small percentage of the purchases were for this purpose. One need only establish the home lot of an individual and then look to see where he did his buying. Usually he bought on the other side of town or in some inexplicable, crazy-quilt pattern. The writer has studied many of these lots which were traded most frequently among the local pioneers to see if some special feature might account for their popularity. In no case was there anything unusual, such as iron-ore land, water-power land, or a good cross-roads site for a tavern. The deed descriptions and present-day inspection show merely good farming lots. One may then conclude that most of these purchases were purely speculative. Here was a steadily growing town with a considerable population turnover. Land was easy to buy, easy to sell, and best of all, prices were steadily rising.

Although the Kent records support standard-version writers on the prevalence of land speculation, they produce a far different version as to who the speculators were. Eastern land jobbers, class conflicts, and evils of absenteeism were barely evident. In Kent there was a central group of pioneers who endured hardships, raised tremendous families, and reaped the largest share of speculative profits. There were, of course, a few wealthy absentees and some poverty-stricken locals. The full Kent story deserves to be written around the dominant majority of sturdy farmer-speculators rather than in terms of a struggle between insignificant ne'er-do-wells and seaboard aristocrats.

By using land records, church records, tax lists, vital statistics, and lists of town officers, it is possible to determine the name of every person who speculated in Kent land as an absentee and of almost every man who took up residence in the town. The minutes of the town meetings and proprietors' meetings are especially helpful in affording insight as to character and economic status of different citizens. More important, all sources tend to interweave and produce some sort of sketch for each individual.

The investigator would like to know three things: first, the numerical breakdown between absentees and residents (what percentage of all property owners were absentee?); second, profits gained (who were the active traders and profiteers?); and third, actual acreage owned by the two groups (what percentage of total acreage did absentees hold at any given time?).

Of the 772 persons who owned land in Kent between 1738 and 1760, 474, or sixty-one per cent, took up residence in Kent. Thus sixty-one per cent were prepared to endure frontier hardships, which were extremely severe in 1740 and still moderately rugged by 1760. True, many settlers did not stay more than four or five years but moved on to New York, Pennsylvania, or Vermont. Such movement was characteristic of the time affecting all towns and classes. As to the 298 absentees (thirty-nine per cent), were they the notorious land jobbers, the class apart, which Turner, Akagi, and Nettels found settlers viewing with bitter distrust? When one examines this group of 298 absentees, one finds little basis for class distinction. They will be grouped forthwith into relatives, neighbors, combination neighbor-relatives, small investors, and finally large absentee land jobbers.

A well-known phenomenon of the time, illustrated effectively at Kent, was the large family, often with ten or twelve children. This situation quite possibly exerted a strong influence against class antagonism. After all, a colonial tended to compete in a world populated by his own brothers and cousins, some of whom had risen to the gentry class while the black sheep had dropped to the bottom of the social heap. Yet family loyalty and unity served as a wire network interlacing top, middle, and bottom classes. The frontiersman could hardly be called a class antagonist of the absentee speculator when the latter was his own father, son, or brother! At Kent it would seem that the heart of a family, or clan, would arrive en masse leaving behind a mere scattering of less energetic brothers. Of the Swifts, who came from Sandwich, Massachusetts, it was the vigorous, resourceful, and soon-wealthy Jabez, Nathaniel, and Reuben who left behind their apparently less energetic brothers, Zephania and Jira. With the Hatches of Tolland, the Hubbells of Newtown, and the Barnums of Danbury, it was not the ne'er-do-wells who traipsed off to Kent; rather, it was the heads of the families that led the way. The Barnums, in time to become a leading iron family of New England, helped fill Kent with Amos, David, Ebenezer, Ebenezer Junior, Gidion, Gidion Junior, Jehiel, Joshua, and Richard. Left behind in Danbury were Abel, Epharm, and Nathaniel. Similarly, during the 1738–1760 period there were eight adult Beemans at Kent, ten Fullers, fourteen Rowlees, and over twenty families with four or more adult members in Kent.

Of the 298 absentees, 109 were stay-at-home members of Kent families. They represented all levels of the social and financial scale and were connected to Kent through a variety of relationships. But they had one thing in common. They avoided the stigma of "callous, absentee, land jobber." At the top of the scale Jared Eliot, the famous Killingsworth pastor-scientist, owned valuable Kent lands. He gave these in 1757 to sons Jared Nathan, Wathernon, and Aaron. All but the last moved immediately to Kent and became prominent in the community. Eliot descendants remained until the 1840's. Philip Cavarly of Colchester might appear to conform to the standard caricature. However, he gave his lands to daughter Abigail, who was the wife of Josiah Strong of Colchester. By 1756 the Cavarly lands were owned and farmed by grandsons Philip and Julian Strong. One of the most active absentee traders was James Lassell of Windham. He was a proprietor who engaged in thirty-nine Kent land deals. But his brother, Joshua Lassell, was one of the original and most prominent Kent settlers. Joshua was selectman (town's highest office), highway surveyor, tythingman, and grand juryman between 1740 and 1755.

The above group of 119 relative absentees takes a substantial bite from the total of 298 absentees. A second group of forty-two absentees takes a second bite from the "callous-land-jobber" category on the grounds that its members were immediate neighbors of Kent. These Kent land owners had their homes mostly in New Milford (bordering Kent to the south), and Sharon (to the northwest), with a scattering in Cornwall. There were also New Yorkers from the Oblong, Dover, and Amenia. Inasmuch as these neighbors farmed the same rocky soil and endured the same hardships as the Kent pioneers, they obviously were not a class apart. In some cases, notably the Bostwicks of New Milford and Benoi Pack of Cornwall, their Kent lands lay on the border and were cultivated as part of the home farm. Absentees Pack and Bostwick lived closer to the Kent meetinghouse than did many actual occupants of the eastern part of the town.

Most neighbors, however, owned Kent land for speculative rather than farming purposes. In 1754 the Barnums decided to sell off the iron-ore mine they had selected in the seventh division (pitch 43). This small piece of land up above present-day Kent Falls Park was sold in 128 shares which brought about five pounds apiece. There were twenty-six purchasers of these shares who came from the neighboring towns (mostly Sharon) thus accounting for over half of the neighbor group. Without exception these neighbors were obscure persons making small purchases. It would seem that the speculative mania reached to the bottom of the economic scale and that where the wealthy might purchase large tracts in distant towns, the humble would take a few pounds and buy part of a lot in a neighboring town.

A third group of nineteen absentees is furthest of all from the standard concept of the eastern capitalist. This is a combination relative-neighbor group whose members would be eligible for, but have not been counted in either of the groups discussed above. It seemed that as large families moved into Kent, they would drop off a few brothers or sons in the neighboring towns. The Swifts, swarming into Kent from Sandwich, left Jabez' son Heman (a Revolutionary general) in Cornwall. All the while, Heman owned a parcel of Kent land. Enough Sanfords came to Kent to leave their name to "Sanford Brook" but brother Elihu never got beyond New Milford. And so it went with Hambelton, Strong, Sealey, Brownson, and many other families. They had relatives close by, living the same sort of life, but were absentee through the technicality of owning Kent land while residing just over the border.

With the fourth group of "small-investor absentees" we come closer to the usual picture of the eighteenth-century land speculator. This group contains names of ninety-one Kent land owners who had no known close ties with Kent either through relatives using their land or their own proximity to the town. The men comprising this group fail, however, to support the thesis of class conflict and absentee control of land and political institutions because of the utter insignificance of their holdings. None held more than 150 pounds' worth of Kent land at any one time. The average for the group was thirty pounds and the average length of ownership was less than three years. One suspects that these "little fellows" from distant Hartford, Lebanon, Windham, and New London were valued customers rather than antagonists of the Kent settlers. What harm if Nat Baker, John Alford, or Peleg Brewster bought a Kent mountain wood lot for seventy pounds and sold it three years later for 110?

For the most part these ninety-one small purchasers were customers of the big absentees in their respective towns. Wherever an absentee proprietor was located, there appeared a cluster of small-fry purchasers to take the assorted lots and pitches off the proprietor's hands. Twenty-seven absentees, mostly small, lived in Windham alone; and this surprising concentration can be attributed to the dealings of such Windham proprietors as James Lassell and David Ripley. Proprietors John Davis and Ebenezer Marsh had their circle of customers in Litchfield as did the Silsbeys in Lebanon. This tendency for absentees to trade with absentees did keep some blocks of land out of cultivation and off the Kent tax lists. (This situation lends some support to the standard view on evils of absenteeism.) At Kent, however, there is no evidence of resentment. Enough Kent settlers did buy from absentees to suggest

307

there was a wide-open market and a rapid turnover. That a Windhamite sold Kent land most often to another Windhamite suggests merely that the latter was the handiest customer. The picture is certainly not one of good land being held off the market with frustrated settlers struggling to wrest ownership from a group of wealthy absentees.

Of the 298 absentees, 261 have been discussed above and have been more or less eliminated from the wealthy, land-jobber category. Some of the remaining thirty-seven men are at last the type of speculator that Turner, Akagi, and Nettels have written about. In this group are some of Connecticut's prominent "aristocrats" to whom Kent was just a wilderness corner where land profits might be made. William Williams the prominent patriot and signer of the Declaration of Independence, was a partner with Nathan Cerary in a quick 3000-pound transaction. Williams' Tory opponent, Dr. Benjamin Gale, is among the thirty-seven as are Richard Jackson, Connecticut's Colonial Agent in London, and Oziel Hopkins. Most famous, and also most active, was William Samuel Johnson, a founding father at the Philadelphia Constitutional Convention in 1787. On the other hand, over half the thirty-seven "large investors" were relatively obscure men and made the "large" list only because their holdings exceeded a 150-pound arbitrary dividing line between large and small.

It seems significant, therefore, that of a grand total of 772 persons owning Kent land between 1738 and 1760, only thirty-seven, or five per cent, were the type around which so much of the history of land policy has been written.

The second point under consideration, comparison between number of transactions and profits of residents on the one hand and absentees on the other, helps confirm the relative insignificance of the absentee land speculators. For judging speculative activity, the writer has examined the 126 proprietors of Kent of whom eighty, or sixty-four per cent, were residents. An arbitrary scoring system has been set up wherein each man is rated according to the number of lots he received in divisions (reflecting how many proprietary shares he held and how long he held them) and his total number of ordinary transactions (reflecting to some extent his interest, activity, and profit taking).

On the basis of this system, local settler Joshua Lassell was the clear leader with 137 points. He was followed by three more solid Kent citizens, John Mills, Ebenezer Barnum, and Nathaniel Berry. The first absentee, William Samuel Johnson, was number five in the ranking with 102 points. In the top ten, Johnson was the only absentee. In the top twenty-five there were but three and in the top fifty, but nine. Men ranking fifty-one through one hundred, on the other hand, included twenty-nine absentees. And of the twenty-six tail-enders, nineteen were absentees including all the last six.

As for profits, the same pattern appears to hold as with trading activity. The locals were the big profiteers while the absentees sold out too early. This statement applies most strongly to the forty-one original proprietors who first journeyed to Windham in 1738 and bought their fifty shares at the auction. Of these forty-one original proprietors, twenty-five were absentees who never came to Kent while the remaining sixteen moved to their newly bought land, erected cabins, and led in the founding of the town. All forty-one proprietors, local and absentee alike, stood to make a "killing." The average price paid for a proprietary share, or right, was 185 pounds (lowest acceptable bid, 165 pounds; highest, 201). This share entitled the proprietor to a lot in each of ten successive divisions. After 1740 as the settlement survived and flourished, land prices rose to a point where the value of a single division lot was higher than the original cost of the entire proprietary share. By 1755 good land was bringing two to three pounds per acre and most of the early divisions each bestowed fine hundred-acre lots on the holders of proprietary shares.

A proprietor who held his share through all divisions and then sold all his accumulated lots and pitches could realize about a tenfold increase over his original investment. No proprietor followed this precise course, however. The Kent resident proprietors not only held on pretty well to the end but in addition engaged in much trading among themselves, with newcomers, and with absentees. As land prices continued to rise (they are said to have increased fourfold between 1750 and 1812), these local proprietors apparently reaped a harvest greater even than the tenfold bonanza from the proprietary shares. On the other hand, the absentee proprietors sold out in two or three years. They did not even wait for the secure settlement of the town. Thus their gain was a mere ten to fifty per cent instead of the 1000 to 4000 per cent profits of the locals.

It is the twenty-five absentee proprietors who bought shares at Windham who have attracted the attention of the historians. Akagi has checked the turnover of such proprietary shares in other towns and noted that few men lasted long as proprietors, thus offering evidence of absenteeism and speculation. What the situation in Kent shows, however, is that the absentee proprietors, at first a majority, sold their shares at insignificant profits to Kent residents. These absentees sold out and constituted thereafter an insignificant minority. Two of the original absentee proprietors sold to Kent pioneers within a month of their purchases at Windham auction. The first, Samuel Benedict, sold to Josiah Starr for the exact purchase price, 189 pounds, five shillings. The second, Ebenezer Bishop, made a nice profit of forty-six pounds selling to settler Nathaniel Slosson. For two years there was relative inactivity while all proprietors collected lots in divisions one through four. Then the absentees unloaded in a rush. Between May 5, 1739 and April 4, 1740, nineteen of the remaining twenty-three absentees sold their shares in quick succession. In selling, they conveyed not only the right, or proprietary share, but also all land accumulated in divisions. Because the town was not yet firmly established and land prices were low, their average profit was only about thirty pounds, or fifteen per cent. Of these nineteen original absentees, Elisha Williams profited most by buying his share at Windham for 193 pounds and selling out for 250. Jacob Wanzer gained the least; indeed he sold out for the same price he had paid two years earlier.

This mass sell-out in 1739 left only four absentee proprietors from the original group of twenty-five. These four, Philip Cavarly, John and Knel Mitchell, and John Smith, all had family members using their lands. They were the only original absentee proprietors to hang on and make large profits but their family ties with Kent disqualify them from being rated absentees in the "callous, class-apart" sense.

There was a good reason for this sudden sell-out of absentees to locals. In order to avoid the evils of absenteeism, the Connecticut legislature provided that titles to this auction land would be confirmed only if the proprietor moved to Kent and ". . . by himself or his agent within the space of two full years enter upon the said granted premises, build and finish one house thereon not less than 18 feet square and seven feet stud; clear and fence seven acres of said land and continue thereon for the space of three successive years . . . ." Local historians have pointed with pride to such requirements but more sophisticated writers have minimized them and suggested poor enforcement. The conditions in Kent surely emphasize that the requirements were highly respected. As the two-year deadline came due, every proprietor either moved to Kent, established a son or brother on the property, or else sold out to a Kent resident.

While the absentee proprietors were selling out, what of the resident proprietors? The sixteen original resident proprietors were augmented by sixty-four more, who had bought from absentees, and these eighty locals constituted the backbone of the town. As the years passed, they reaped a bountiful harvest of lots and pitches. Almost all unloaded the land to newcomers and members of their own families and thus the records invariably show them making more sales than purchases. Sometimes the ratio of sales over purchases was five to one.

A significant aspect was the generous habit of making gifts of land to sons. Daniel Comstock, the shoemaker, gave his first-division lot to son Abel, his second-division lot to son Garshom, third to Eliphalet and so on down through a large family. Old Daniel ended up not much richer than when he started but the town was dotted with prosperous Comstock farms. This policy was followed by nearly every family. Today an entire area is named Skiff Mountain for the many Skiffs who reaped eventual benefits from Joseph Skiff's original share and speculative dickerings. The names Fuller Mountain, Spooner Hill and Geer Mountain all testify to the fecundity and generosity of proprietors Joseph Fuller, William Spooner, and Ezra Geer. The greater part of the sons sold the division lots their fathers had given them and moved on to Vermont, New York, the Wyoming Valley, and the Western Reserve. The point is that they each went forth with a 200-pound stake, as much as their own fathers had used to buy the original share in Kent. We thus have a financial basis for the expansion, if not of all New England, at least of Kent.

One of the most important tasks in making a definitive examination of the relationship between absentee and local is the determination of comparative amounts of land held at any one time. What percentage of the total Kent acreage was owned by the absentees in, say, 1750? Important, but also a task of almost insurmountable complexity. By 1750 Kent was a patchwork of perhaps 1500 separate slices of land each of which had been bought and sold an average of three times. These slices were sold to absentees one year, bought back by locals the next, sold in complex, multiple transactions, and sold under descriptive conditions (piles of stones, old chestnut trees) that are meaningless today. It would take a lifetime's work to assemble the crazy quilt of lots and produce precise figures.

A number of clues suggest, however, that the percentage of absentee-owned acreage at any given time was small. First of all, there were no really big absentee land owners. Nowhere does one find individual holdings larger than 600 acres and these plots were located on the extreme borders of the town. When, in 1751, land west of the Housatonic River was added to Kent and sold by the General Assembly, one might have expected big absentee land jobbers to do the buying. Absentees did buy (being on the spot at Hartford); but the twenty lots into which the region was divided were small (about 100 acres each) and no one bought more than three lots. The average price for this poor land was less than one pound per acre and none of the buyers in selling to Kent residents made a profit of more than forty pounds.

In 1751 a complicated negotiation resulted in the granting by the General Assembly of 280 acres west of the Housatonic to William Williams. This was an eye-catching transaction, the sort that has figured prominently in creating the standard version on land jobbing by wealthy easterners. However, "land-jobber" Williams sold this land within a year to John Mills and Joseph Fuller of Kent. This transaction thus illustrates a second point. Even where absentees obtained fairly valuable plots, they seldom held on to them for long. Thus the proportion of locally owned land would tend to remain high despite the quick in-and-out thrusts of prominent absentees.

Probably the best systematic method for comparing resident and absentee holdings is to take the early divisions containing the best land and trace the ownership of each lot. The writer has followed this procedure with the first and fourth divisions. As already mentioned, there was a spectacular turnover of lots, some changing hands ten times in twenty years. But when the dust had settled, local pioneers were in possession. When the first division was completed in 1738, twenty-eight of the fifty lots went to residents and twenty-two to absentees. By 1739 seven of the absentees had sold out to residents leaving fifteen absentee lots. By the next year eight more had sold out (this was the year the settlement really got underway) and by 1745 three more had sold to locals. Of the last four absentees holding first division lots, one sold to a resident in 1755, a second, Richard Hubbell, was a member of the prominent Kent Hubbell family, and the last two absentee holders left no evidence of any kind. Their lots, 39 and 43, simply disappear from the records.

The fourth division tells a similar story. It started in 1739 with thirty-eight local owners and twelve absentees. By 1745 three of the absentees had sold to locals, by 1750, four more, and by 1760, one more. Four lots remained in the hands of absentees until late in the century.

Summarizing, it seems safe to make these generalizations: the absentees made small purchases and held them for short periods of time; they dealt in the less desirable lands; and their total ownership of Kent lands probably did not amount to more than ten per cent of all Kent acreage at any given time after settlement in 1740. Adding these determinations to the earlier conclusions, that only five per cent of the land owners were the sort of absentee jobbers described by Turner, Akagi, Nettels, et al. and that their profits were insignificant compared to those of the locals, one may conclude that Kent offers a notable exception to the standard picture.

Kent's history suggests that many writers may have been too eager to sort out and then wrap up colonials in neat class packages. Following Turner, they drop the "poor restless" package on the frontier and place the "prosperous gentry" package in the comfortable eastern towns. Antagonism follows. Kent, however, featured a hybrid package, a mass of settlers in neither extreme camp. Local speculator John Mills gained wealth to match his poise, dignity, and qualities of leadership. Eastern gentry type? He would hardly seem so when one notes his rough cabin, his back-breaking labors, and his dangerous life (he was drowned while working at Bull's Bridge). Even Mills's sons preserved the "which-class?" confusion. Two were educated at Yale and Samuel Mills went on to fame as a clergyman-author. Grandson Samuel is covered in the *Dictionary of American Biography*. But Philo Mills became Kent's tavern keeper, Lewis Mills ran the village trading post, and Peter Mills carried on the family farm. These hybrid Kent settler-speculators—Millses, Comstocks, Fullers, Barnums, Swifts, and Hatches—poured into and through Kent, scheming, land jobbing, taking profits, clearing the wilderness.

There can be no denying the existence of absenteeism, indebtedness, and violent controversies in many towns, particularly in Vermont, New Hampshire, and western Massachusetts. That bitter story, that side of the balance sheet, has been emphasized, as might have been expected during the years when class-struggle literature was most popular. Kent seems important, however, not only because it shows the bright side of the balance sheet, but also because its records suggest undercurrents of harmony and prosperity that may have existed in all towns more than hitherto suspected. The dealings of the big absentee speculators that have been studied are relatively prominent in central archives; the stories of their local rivals and of relative percentages, profits and acreages have gathered dust in local town clerks' offices.

16. THE MARKET SURPLUS PROBLEM
OF COLONIAL TOBACCO*

by L. C. Gray

The economic development of the colonies hinged on the production and export of agricultural surpluses. In Virginia, Maryland, and parts of North Carolina tobacco became the chief staple. In the following essay, L. C. Gray explores the development of commercial agriculture in the tobacco colonies where plantations developed which required considerable investments of capital, employed slave labor supervised by overseers, and grew tobacco on a scale greater than was possible on a family farm. Though the fortunes of the leading families in these colonies rested on tobacco, planters were plagued by chronic price fluctuations and imbalances between supply and demand as well as by persistent indebtedness to British merchants. Gray attempts to account for overproduction and describes the efforts made to stabilize production and prices. Though the bulk of the tobacco crop was sold on the European continent, its marketing was monopolized by British merchants and channeled through British ports where it was heavily taxed by the Crown. The marketing system profoundly influenced the development of the tobacco industry, especially the emergence of large units of production such as plantations. It is not readily apparent that it was more efficient to grow tobacco on large plantations than on family farms to reap the benefits from economies of scale. Tobacco producers, unlike other farmers who grew commodities such as wheat, which was not marketed through Britain, sent their crops to Britain and thereby gained access to English and Scottish capital. London or Glasgow merchants found it advantageous to extend credit to planters to expand the scale of operations. Once in debt, the planter was more firmly tied to the merchant-creditor since he had to mortgage next year's crop to secure necessary funds. Furthermore, by increasing the volume of tobacco passing through their hands, middlemen multiplied the charges for services connected with distribution and marketing. By serving as bankers, investing their capital in American agriculture, British merchants thus enabled husbandmen to acquire additional land, slaves, and equipment needed to transform a farm into a plantation.

For further reading: L. C. Gray, *History of Agriculture in the Southern United States to 1860* (1933); Jacob Price, "The Economic Growth of the Chesapeake and the European Market, 1695–1775," *Journal of Economic History,* vol. 25 (1964), 496–511.

I have been moved to select the subject of this paper because of the paramount interest of the present problem of market surpluses, and because in the history of colonial tobacco may be found many analogies and parallelisms with the present-day aspects of the problem.

Early Artificial Level of Prices and Its Collapse

At the time it first began to be planted by the Virginia colonists in 1610–11 tobacco in the English market was essentially a luxury product. In the seven years preceding 1622 there had been imported from Spain an annual average of about 60,000 pounds of high-grade tobacco pro-

---

* *Agricultural History,* vol. 2 (1928), 1–34. Footnotes have been omitted except where they are necessary for an understanding of the text.

duced in the West Indies, with probably about as much more introduced by smugglers. In 1619 it was stated that the Spanish product customarily sold for eighteen shillings sterling per pound, an enormous price considering the high value of sterling in that period. Virginia tobacco as made in these earlier years was of much poorer quality than the Spanish product, and though it was assessed in the English "Book of Rates" at ten shillings the pound, actually sold at less than half this amount in the latter part of 1619. However, in 1620 it sold as high as eight shillings in the London market. Under these conditions it is not surprising that tobacco was mainly used by the wealthy and was retailed on the London streets by the pipeful.

On the basis of these high prices the Virginia Company in 1618 authorized its representatives in the Colony to allow three shillings for the best grades and eighteen pence for that of second quality in trade at the company's warehouse. Naturally such prices stimulated a frenzy of activity in colonial tobacco planting comparable with the feverish spirit of a mining camp. The volume of production and of exports was rapidly expanded. From 1615 when the first colonial shipment reached England until 1622 the exports had increased to 60,000 pounds, and six years later to 500,000 pounds, or more than eight times the amount of official imports of England a little more than a decade earlier. The next decade witnessed a three-fold increase, the annual exports averaging 1,395,063 pounds for the four years, 1637–1640, inclusive.

Prices fell precipitately from their unnatural levels, in spite of frantic efforts by the Crown and the Company to maintain them. By 1630 Governor Harvey was complaining that the merchants were buying tobacco in Virginia for less than a penny per pound.

The Behavior of Prices, 1630–1774

From this time forward prices never returned to their original high levels, but until the outbreak of the Revolutionary War ranged between about three pence per pound as a maximum down to a half penny or less. Indeed at times even this minimum price was purely nominal, for tobacco was practically unsalable. It was rarely higher than two pence.

I shall not attempt in this paper to trace the course of prices year by year, but it is desirable to devote some attention to the behavior of prices for longer periods.

The data indicate not only fluctuations from year to year, reflecting the seasonal variations in yield and consequently in volume of production, but also the periodical emergence of long periods of acute depression. It is desirable to trace briefly the record of these depressions. As already noted, the precipitate fall of prices from the original high levels had brought tobacco by 1630 to what then appeared to be an absurdly low price. For several years thereafter prices were ruinously low, and various legislative attempts were made to deal with the problem.

The crop of 1638 was two and a half times as large as the average for the other years from 1637 to 1640, inclusive, and being thrown into an already sagging market, caused prices again to collapse. In 1638-9 prices were so low that planters could not subsist by them, and there resulted a series of attempts at legislative price-fixing which will be described later. The probability is that in spite of the rather generous official rates placed on tobacco during the next two or three years, prices did not recover until the situation was relieved by the short crop of 1644.

While the outbreak of the civil war in England appears for a short time to have depressed prices, the activity of the illicit trade with the Dutch tended to sustain prices fairly well, with only occasional years of low prices until after the Restoration. In the latter part of the sixth decade there began a period of depression which, excepting a slight improvement in 1663, continued until 1667. It is probable that the acreage planted to tobacco had become excessive by reason of the rapid migration to the colonies induced by the disturbances of the period of the Civil War and the Protectorate. Probably another factor was the extension and more rigid application of the navigation policy in 1660 and the following years and the restrictions on Dutch competition. The situation was further complicated by the unusually large yield of the crop of 1666, and by the demoralization of the market due to the plague in London, which was so severe that in 1665 the tobacco fleet did not go to the colonies at all. The depression was relieved by the great storm of 1667 which destroyed from two-thirds to four-fifths of the crops in Virginia and by the destruction of twenty tobacco ships by the Dutch.

For about a decade conditions appear to have been somewhat improved, but with a tendency for prices to sag to very unprofitable levels in particular years, as in 1671, 1673, 1678. Apparently throughout this period the tobacco acreage was so large as to permit reasonably good prices only following years of small yield with a constant tendency toward entirely unprofitable prices in years of good crops.

The Market Surplus Problem of Colonial Tobacco

The enormous crop of 1677, said to be in Virginia as large as the total production of three normal years and in Maryland the largest "ever heard of" precipitated another crisis. In 1680 Governor Culpeper, of Virginia, wrote the British authorities that the low price of tobacco "staggered" him and that its continuance would prove "the fatal and speedy ruin of this once noble Colony." The crop of that year, however, proved again unusually large, and added to an already abnormal carry-over so glutted the market that tobacco became practically worthless. For several years the depression continued, leading in 1682 to plant-cutting riots in New Kent, Gloucester, and Middlesex counties, Virginia. As a result of the destruction of about 10,000 hogsheads of tobacco by the rioters the price of tobacco was improved in 1683.

From this time forward until after the outbreak of the war of the Spanish Succession in 1702 was a period of generally favorable tobacco prices. It was a period of expanding demand, and years of poor yields occurred with sufficient frequency to prevent the accumulation of an abnormal carry-over.

One of the most desperate periods of depression in the history of the industry began to make its influence felt in 1703 and continued for a decade. The good prices just preceding the war had stimulated production and a gradually increasing carry-over. The war cut off the tobacco trade to Spain, France, Flanders, and part of the Baltic States, leaving only Holland as the principal foreign market. Since the Dutch preferred the brighter variety of Oronoke, the Dutch market had been glutted with the brown type. The depression grew worse as the war continued. In 1704 several thousand hogsheads of consignment tobacco brought the planters no return whatever, and the returns from some of it were not sufficient to pay the freight. In 1705 complaints were made of "the extraordinary low price of tobacco of this year beyond what hath been known for several years past." Conditions continued to get worse. In 1710 it was said the merchants in Maryland would make no advance on tobacco. In Virginia tobacco was nominally rated at a penny per pound, but large quantities were actually unsalable. Toward the close of the war William Byrd wrote that poor people could not make enough to clothe themselves, while the larger planters were getting deeper and deeper in debt. Many had been forced to sell part of their lands and negroes to meet debts, while still others had emigrated to the Carolinas and elsewhere.

Good prices continued for four years after the close of the war. This relief, however, was but temporary, and merely served to stimulate expansion of production, which again brought low prices in 1720, continuing until 1724, when a crop failure brought temporarily good prices. Then followed a decade of severe depression. Thus the industry appears to have suffered from extreme depression for a period of fourteen years with the exception of one year, and during a period of thirty-two years depression had prevailed except for one interval of four years and another of one year of good prices.

After 1734 there ensued a period of a quarter of a century free from a serious and protracted price depression, although there were occasional years of low prices. Even the War of the Austrian Succession and the Seven Years War did not bring serious price depression, such as had prevailed during the War of the Spanish Succession, for the tobacco trade had become so important both to England and to France that during the two later wars an indirect and informal arrangement was made between England and France whereby tobacco ships, whether British or neutral, engaged in carrying tobacco from England to France were given special passes exempting them from capture, very curious instances of the deliberate continuance of trade relations by belligerent nations. An examination of trade statistics indicates that neither of the later wars seriously affected the volume of the tobacco trade; and prices do not appear to have been abnormally affected, with the exception of the last two years preceding the peace of Paris. The inflation of the Virginia currency which accompanied the course of the war began to manifest itself in a general rise of prices in 1760, which continued until 1764. However, tobacco appears to have lagged behind in the general advance. It appears probable that in spite of the higher nominal prices paid for tobacco there was a period of almost continuous depression from about 1760 or 1761 until about the beginning of the eighth decade, followed in turn by several years of good prices.

I shall not undertake to say how much the behavior of tobacco prices, as revealed by this summary of the experience of a century and a half, is characteristic of the price history of other agricultural products and of other periods, nor to what extent the conditions responsible for it have prevailed elsewhere. To some extent, probably, these conditions are generic in a sense, but to some extent they were peculiar to the production and marketing of colonial tobacco. I shall turn my attention therefore to a brief consideration of these conditions.

The Foreign Market for Colonial Tobacco

As we have seen, when Virginia tobacco first began to appear in the English market it encountered the Spanish-American product, and for a few years this competition caused the Virginia Company and its satellite, the Somers Isles Company, much concern. For several years the question of exclusion or restriction was an important issue in the struggle between the Crown and the Parliamentary party. In 1624 the king accepted the policy of restriction as a part of the scheme to monopolize the tobacco trade, but for several years after 1625 the policy with regard to Spanish leaf was vacillating, the issue being employed as a club to force the acceptance of the royal monopoly schemes. However, the rapid expansion of the Virginia and Maryland production in a few years made the Spanish competition comparatively insignificant. By 1685 to 1688 the annual average quantity of Spanish tobacco brought to London was only 16,000 pounds, as compared with an annual average of 14,500,000 pounds of English colonial tobacco.

For some years after 1630 tobacco from the new settlements in the British West Indies was a more important competitive factor than was the Spanish-American product. However, the rise of the sugar industry and the absorption of the small tobacco plantations gradually reduced the importance of this phase of competition.

In the early years of the tobacco industry another source of threatening competition was the development of tobacco growing in England. The royal interest in the growing revenues from imported tobacco, combined with some solicitude for the newly developing colonial establishments and some concern as to the sumptuary consequences of the rapidly developing use of tobacco in England, resulted in the latter part of 1619 and the early part of 1620 in royal proclamations prohibiting this industry, and with a few minor interruptions this policy was continued until 1779, when the American Revolution made it desirable to permit tobacco production in Ireland and England. However, the problem of enforcement proved about as difficult a task as modern prohibition. It was stoutly opposed as an unwarrantable restriction of personal liberty. Until the outbreak of the Civil Wars the administrative machinery was wholly inadequate to suppress the British industry, and during the Civil Wars and the Commonwealth there was but little official repression. During this period the industry grew to such proportions that

the determined efforts of the Crown, after the Restoration, to exterminate it resulted in a bitter struggle which continued for at least three
decades. As late as 1703 a little was still growing near Bristol, but the
British industry was no longer an important competitive factor.

The character of the foreign market for tobacco was largely influenced by British commercial policy in combination with its fiscal
policy. It is not necessary before this group to describe in detail the
evolution of the Navigation Acts. While the tobacco colonies were
interested in the broadest possible market for their product, the British
Crown was anxious to prevent the resulting loss in import duties. Consequently, in October, 1621, a peremptory order required all tobacco to
be brought to England, and this became the established policy of the
Crown with respect to tobacco long before it was generalized and
applied to other commodities by the Parliamentary enactment of 1651,
1660, 1672, and 1673. Gradually also during the Stuart period it became
apparent that the practical administration of the policy could only be
accomplished if foreign ships were excluded from the carrying trade, a
policy that had long been recognized as justified by the principles of
mercantilism and the exigencies of naval rivalry. This policy was also
extended and consolidated later by Parliamentary enactments.

There was but little effective enforcement during the English Civil
Wars and the Commonwealth period, and considerable evasion for
several decades after the Restoration, but gradually the administrative
machinery was improved, and during the remainder of the eighteenth
century evasion was intermittent rather than continuous.

The significance of the requirement that tobacco must first be
brought to English ports before it could be shipped to other markets
can be fully appreciated only if considered in relation to customs and
drawback policies and the development of the foreign market.

In 1615, the year before Virginia tobacco was first brought to the
British market, the customs and impost duties on imported tobacco
were revised so as to make the total duties payable equivalent to two
shillings per pound. During the last few years of the Virginia Company
the question of the duties on Virginia tobacco in relation to various
exemptions granted in the several charters was a matter of continued
controversy, resulting in a number of temporary adjustments. The duty
on Virginia tobacco was fixed at one shilling in 1620, and in 1623 was
lowered to nine pence (three pence for customs and six pence for impost). In 1632 the combined customs and impost duty was lowered to

four pence, and in 1640 to two pence, which was continued for two years. The exigencies of civil war compelled an increase in customs duties and the addition of heavy excise taxes; but these so discouraged consumption that it was necessary to lower them a number of times, until by March, 1644, the taxes on tobacco consisted only of a penny for customs and two pence for excise, the latter being lowered to a penny by 1657.

The first Parliament after the Restoration removed the excise on British colonial tobacco, but while retaining the old ad valorem poundage rate of five per cent, which at the established valuation of the "Book of Rates" was equivalent to a specific duty of a penny, the act provided for an additional penny nine months after importation, to be repaid on re-exportation within a certain period, together with one-half the poundage duty. Thus, tobacco consumed in England was taxed two pence per pound for customs but on re-exportation enjoyed a drawback of a penny and a half. This provision was continued until 1685 when three pence was added, making the total duty five pence. Further additions in 1697 and 1703 raised the duty to $6\frac{1}{3}$ pence, which was continued until 1748, when the duty was increased to $7\frac{1}{3}$ pence. In 1758 it was again increased to $8\frac{1}{3}$ pence. As a consequence of the large increases after 1685 the duties on tobacco until the close of the colonial period were from three to seven times as high as the usual range of prices in the colonies.

The significance of these rates, however, was greatly modified by the drawback policy. With the succession of large increases in duties on tobacco beginning in 1685 the policy of allowing a drawback for all but the one-half penny provided for at the Restoration was continued until 1723, in which year it was arranged that the entire duty on re-exported tobacco should be remitted. Thus, the net effect of the fiscal policy after 1685 was to impose a high duty on tobacco consumed in Great Britain, but to remove as far as possible all burdens on the trade to the Continent.

The significance of this policy lies in the fact that with the progress of time the trade to the Continent became much the more important. In 1693 and again in 1698 it was estimated that two-thirds of the total imports were re-exported. After the Peace of Utrecht the proportion of re-exports continued to increase until by the last five years preceding the outbreak of the American Revolution approximately eighty-three per cent of the tobacco imported into England was re-exported, and nearly ninety-eight per cent of the Scotch imports were re-exported, so that for Great Britain as a whole ninety per cent of British imports were sent abroad, leaving only about ten per cent to pay the heavy duties on tobacco consumed in Great Britain. Toward the close of the seventeenth century Spain, the former competitor of Virginia in the English market, was annually buying about 2,000 hogsheads a year in the British market. France was taking 18,000 to 20,000 hogsheads. These Latin countries had obtained much of their tobacco by way of Holland, but in the interval between the Peace of Ryswick and the beginning of the War of the Spanish Succession the British developed a large direct trade with France. British merchants had also achieved a profitable trade with the Baltic States in the poorer grades of brown Oronoke tobacco. In the last two decades of the seventeenth century an important trade in manufactured Virginia and Maryland tobacco was developed with Russia by means of monopolistic concessions granted by the Czar, who endeavored to get the concessionnaires to teach the mystery of tobacco manufacture to his own people. The regular tobacco merchants of Great Britain strongly protested, and in the early years of the eighteenth century the British foreign office adopted the policy of trying to induce the Czar to abandon the monopolistic policy and accept free trade, and similar negotiations were opened with Spain, Portugal and Sweden.

The War of the Spanish Succession destroyed most of the British direct trade with France and the Baltic countries, which went to Holland. The Dutch purchased the bright leaf grades of Oronoke, which they mixed with large quantities of low grade tobacco produced in Holland and German states, thus leaving the lower grades of Oronoke tobacco practically a drug on the market. The Dutch learned the trick of steaming and rolling tobacco stems so as to slice them up for smoking mixtures with various proportions of English and Dutch leaf. They also made roll tobacco composed of one-half English and one-half Dutch mixtures to meet the requirements of the French tobacco monopoly. As a result, Dutch production had increased to 20,000,000 pounds by 1706, an industry producing 20,000,000 pounds had developed in Pomerania and Brandenburg, and another 20,000,000 pounds had come to be produced around Strassburg, Frankfort, and in Hungary.

It appears, then, that colonial tobacco producers were almost entirely dependent on the foreign market as affected by wars, trade restrictions of various kinds, and heavy taxation on imports into the mother country; and although enjoying substantial exemption in case of re-export, tobacco was subject to various impositions and trade restrictions in the continental countries of Europe and to various types of exploitation by merchants in British and continental markets. In order to understand these conditions it is desirable to devote some attention to the mechanism of marketing.

Mechanism of Marketing

In the first decade of the colony of Virginia the Virginia Company practically monopolized the trade of the colony, although under the charters of 1606 and 1609 private traders were allowed to come in provided they paid certain fees to the company. Later a subsidiary corporation for exclusive trade was organized by certain members of the Virginia Company. However, this subsidiary trading monopoly proved unprofitable, and early in 1620 it was resolved to wind up its affairs and throw the trade open to the public.

In the last three years of the company period ships of the subsidiary colonizing corporations and private adventurers carried on the bulk of the trade, and for a number of years afterward the colony was compelled to rely on peripatetic merchant ships which came irregularly. As they went about from plantation to plantation collecting the cargo the planter found himself largely at their mercy, for if he failed to sell on the terms offered, another ship might not come his way. The lack of any knowledge of market conditions, except neighborhood hearsay, increased the planters' disadvantage in bargaining. These conditions were responsible for a number of acts against engrossing and forestalling, and also for the earlier attempts to establish port towns or concentration markets at Jamestown and St. Mary's, attempts which failed through the influence of the merchants.

Increasing competition, especially that of the Dutch, gradually reduced the extreme dependence of the planter on the casual appearance of a single ship. Development during the Dutch wars of the practice of sending the majority of the English merchant ships in a fleet under convoy also tended to improve the market situation in some respects through the simultaneous arrival of the fleet.

However, though the policy of operating in a fleet was promoted by frequent wars and by danger from pirates, there was no continuity in the practice. Furthermore, the practice itself at times promoted collu-

325

sion and resulting restriction of competition. Thus, in 1695 Governor Nicholson, of Maryland, complained that the merchants from the outports tended to arrive earlier than the majority of the London ships, and together with some of the forerunners of the latter made a practice of spreading the news that not much tobacco would be wanted and that it would be cheap. He declared, "The merchants make their own market by such bad news, which is very often false." In the years 1704–7, while the War of the Spanish Succession was raging, Colonel Quary, colonial representative in London, attributed the demoralization in prices in part to the fact that four separate fleets had proceeded to the tobacco colonies within fourteen months. He argued that the so-called "smokers' fleet" (probably the outport ships), which arrived first in the colonies, placed a high price on British goods with the result that the planters held off until the arrival of the London fleet. The latter, however, being made up mainly of ships of merchants trading on consignment, carried but a small quantity of goods because it was believed that the planters' wants would have been supplied by the earlier fleet. On returning to England the "smokers' fleet" found no market, for buyers held off until the arrival of the later fleet, resulting in a glut. He urged as a remedy a single fleet.

If the system of casual trading which prevailed in the early years whereby the ship captain brought a cargo of miscellaneous goods to be traded for tobacco wherever he could make a bargain often placed the planter at a serious disadvantage, it also subjected the merchant to very great risks, especially after competition for cargoes became keen. He was forced to make the long voyage without assurance that he would obtain a cargo, and frequently his stay was greatly protracted and he was put to great expense in going about from place to place looking for a cargo. In making credit advances to unknown planters the risk of bad debts was enhanced. Furthermore, on returning to England with no established market he was compelled to seek a purchaser, involving additional delay and risk.

One important step in the evolution of a more effective mechanism of marketing was the development of a class of merchants specializing in the trade of a particular province. Thus, in time mention is made of the "Virginia merchants" and the "Carolina merchants" as being two separate groups. We also hear of "Exchange in the Virginia Walk" in London, suggesting a definite place where Virginia merchants met for trade. Since tobacco was practically the only important product brought from Virginia and Maryland the merchants dealing with these colonies were necessarily tobacco merchants who were specialists in sorting, processing, and selling that product and who had developed a definite relationship to the British and continental markets. From a very early time and throughout the colonial period the tobacco merchants exerted a large influence on legislation affecting tobacco and were frequently consulted by administrative officials and Parliamentary committees. Furthermore, they achieved a considerable degree of unity of action.

Another step was the development of a definite relationship between the tobacco merchant and the producer of tobacco. This took the form first of the consignment system, which was more or less connected with and dependent upon the practice of the ships going about collecting the cargo from the various plantations instead of obtaining it from a central market. The system of importation was equally simple, for the same ship which took the planters' tobacco usually brought goods from England or other places, in many cases on the special order of the planter. In the pure form of the consignment system the merchant acted only as the agent of the planter, who was his regular client. The merchant advanced transport cost, market charges, and various fees and taxes, sold the crop on his client's account, and placed the net proceeds to his credit. It was but a step from this to advancing him goods, slaves, and funds beyond the amount of his balance, and consequently for a large proportion of the planters indebtedness to the merchant was a chronic condition, which greatly increased their dependence. The merchant executed various special orders for his client, such as purchasing on specification plate, drapery, shoes, and tailored clothing, and frequently performed more intimate services such as looking after visiting relatives in England. For some decades it is probable that the practice of direct marketing connected with direct importation was more economical than would have been centralized collection. It is probable that the consignment system grew up largely through the preference of the British merchants who were thus relieved of the great risks involved in buying outright months before the product could reach the market under the slow methods of transport in the early colonial period.

Gradually, however, planters began to buy from other sources than from the merchant who handled their tobacco. Moreover, serious abuses and disadvantages from the standpoint of the planter grew up in connection with the system of consignment. The indebtedness of the planter placed him largely at the mercy of his merchant and compelled him to accept the results obtained by the latter, however unsatisfactory. Even if the merchant was honest and reliable, the results were necessarily frequently disappointing, but the system involved an undue reliance on the honesty and fairness of the merchant and naturally contributed to the suspicion of falsified accounts and "rigged" sales, a suspicion no doubt frequently justified. In 1785 James Madison wrote R. H. Lee, complaining that both private planters and native merchants had "received accounts of sales this season which carry the most visible and shameful frauds in every article."

In part, of course, this suspicion was a manifestation of the age-long distrust of the merchant, which was frequently expressed throughout the colonial period. In 1730 the popular feeling was reflected in a stanza of the poem, *Sotweed Redivivus,* which reads:

> "Nor should Crop Merchants correspond,
> "On t'other side the Herring-Pond,
> "Their pick'd and cull'd Tobacco send,
> "In weighty Cask, to some sly Friend," etc.

There were numerous complaints against the British monopoly and the "Engrossers of the Commodity at Home." About the middle of the nineteenth century N. F. Cabell recorded the recollection of mercantile domination of Virginia agriculture in the following words which show how closely the colonial attitude of farmers toward the middleman resembled that of the present day: "We remember to have heard one of our elder and wiser brethren, one well versed in our history, and who habitually weighed his words,—declare it his belief 'that no civilized people on earth had *been so badly paid for their labor* (sic) as the planters of Virginia during the Colonial era, and for long years afterwards' * * * Merchants, he said, 'had done more to produce the mischief than all the ignorant empiricism, ill-judgment, and alleged indolence of the planters'. A delegation of the former would meet annually and settle the price of tobacco for the year."

In shipping on consignment the planter was forced to assume the risks not only of price changes, but also of the large charges involved for transport, taxes, and marketing, which in the aggregate were several times the domestic price in the colonies. Furthermore, the tobacco was sold by the wholesale merchants to retailers on long credits at the planter's risk. If the purchaser went bankrupt or otherwise failed to meet his indebtedness, the planter not only lost his tobacco, but was out the heavy charges, amounting in 1733 to eighteen or nineteen pounds sterling per hogshead. Among these costs were a number of petty marketing charges which, though originally arbitrarily imposed, had become fixed by custom. These are illustrated by a typical account of sales published in 1737 for a hogshead of tobacco weighing 732 pounds net at sale in London.

	£		sh.		d.
British duties	16	—	18	—	2
Maryland export duty	0	—	2	—	9
Freight	1	—	15	—	0
Primage and petty charges	0	—	2	—	1
To entry inwards, etc.	0	—	1	—	6
To entry outwards, etc.	0	—	2	—	0
To cooperage	0	—	2	—	0
To porterage, etc.	0	—	1	—	0
To warehouse rent	0	—	3	—	6
To brokerage	0	—	2	—	0
To postage of letters	0	—	1	—	0
To drafts (4 lbs. of tobacco)	0	—	0	—	9
To loss of weight (allowing 14 lbs. for natural loss on shipboard, 44 lbs. of tobacco)	0	—	8	—	3
To commission of 2½ per cent on duties and on selling price	0	—	12	—	0
	£20	—	12	—	0

Some of these petty charges were a source of great irritation to the planters, who keenly resented them. They believed that a number of them redounded to the merchant's own profit. They also resented the fact that the merchant's commission of 2½ per cent was applied to all these charges, and the arbitrary character of the charges offended the same sense of independence which objected to taxation without representation. They also disliked the custom which permitted the gouging of hogsheads in order to obtain samples which was the occasion for a good deal of petty pilfering by stevedores, sailors, and others. At the close of the eighteenth century the custom was so prevalent that negro stevedores were accustomed to supply choice tobacco obtained by pilfering on the special order of discriminating patrons in England.

In the early years of the eighteenth century, the tidewater lands having been largely occupied, the tobacco industry began to expand westward into the interior. The planters on these new lands found it less easy to maintain direct relationship with the English merchants, and this condition, together with the various causes of dissatisfaction with the consignment system, led to the extensive development of outright purchase in the colonies. This development was largely promoted by the aggressive methods of the outport merchants, particularly the Scotch, who developed a considerable illicit trade before the Union, in 1707, but after that time increased their share of the business so rapidly that by 1775 they handled about one-half of all the tobacco brought to Great Britain. While the relative importance of shipment on consignment and of outright purchase varied somewhat, according to price conditions, the latter method had gained in importance so rapidly that by the close of the colonial period three-fourths of the tobacco was purchased outright in the colonies. In 1769 the merchant, Roger Atkinson, wrote, "The spirit of consigning is broke * * * ye Scotch are become ye engrossers."

In addition to the tendency to differentiate and partially specialize the various marketing functions originally performed by peripatetic merchant-traders, there was also a tendency to specialize the function of transport through the practice of hiring cargo space. Thus the use of transport facilities was rendered more elastic, and thereby more economical.

Corresponding to the commercial mechanism in Great Britain for the marketing of tobacco there also developed a commercial mechanism in the colonies. In the first place, many of the larger planters who maintained wharves of their own early began shipping tobacco for smaller neighboring planters not located on navigable water or not possessing wharves. Thus there developed a class of merchant planters who found the joint function advantageous. As a planter the expenses of marketing were reduced and some of the elements of exploitation removed. It was also possible to control somewhat the time of marketing his crop and to be in closer touch with marketing conditions. Servants to stock his plantations could be transported cheaply on return voyages, and the headrights provided a means of acquiring large land holdings. As a merchant there was greater certainty of obtaining a cargo, and if such could not be obtained plantation slaves could be employed in preparing a cargo of pipe staves, clapboards, and other timber for shipment to the West Indies. By reason of his British connections the colonial merchant-planter enjoyed unusual facilities for obtaining capital which he invested not only in planting but in various other enterprises, and thus there were many colonial merchants who, like William Byrd (the first), at one and the same time were planters, colonizers, wholesale exporters and importers, retail storekeepers, lumbermen, Indian traders, millers, and prospectors for ores.

The merchant-planter operated in various ways. These are well illustrated by the activities of William Fitzhugh. To a large extent he served merely as a resident factor representing one or more British firms for whom he developed a permanent clientele of planters whose business he solicited, and collected indebtedness due his British correspondents. However, when he saw a chance of profit Fitzhugh bought on his own account tobacco from neighboring planters, and at times he wrote apologetically to his correspondents in England because of the smallness of his consignment business, and continued to ship small quantities merely as a means of maintaining their good will.

In the latter part of the colonial period there developed a specialized class of merchants in the tobacco colonies, some of whom were acting as junior partners of British firms or as salaried representatives, and in some cases as independent merchants with foreign correspondents. As the tobacco industry expanded westward, some of these mercantile agencies developed chains of stores in the back country for selling goods and slaves on long credits of nine months or more in exchange for tobacco and other products.

Conditions Responsible for Inelasticity of Production

The long periods of price depression which were traced in an earlier part of this paper were due in large part to the great inelasticity of production, that is, the failure to adjust volume of production quickly to the quantitative demands of the market. In part these elements of inelasticity are inherent in the very nature of business enterprise, whether agricultural or industrial. In part, the inelasticity arose from conditions peculiar to agriculture, such as the connection between the business and the home, the large proportion of the family income obtained in kind from the farm, the general lack of adequate accounting, the lack of control over volume of production due to the weather and other uncontrollable influences, the inability to exert any purposeful control over prices or to employ concerted methods of restricting volume of production, the practice of selling "at the market" instead of producing in accordance with prearranged orders, etc.

In part, however, these elements of inelasticity were intensified by conditions of production in the tobacco colonies. In general, tobacco was produced by two quite different classes. One class consisted of pioneer or backwoods families operating largely by their own labor. In general, this class of farmers were largely self-sufficing, but produced a little tobacco as a means of satisfying by purchase a few simple wants that could not be provided for directly by their own labor. Prices influenced the behavior of these producers mainly through the direct balancing of the utility of things obtained against the disutility involved in producing the market crop, rather than indirectly through considerations of expenses, profits, and return on investment. Their reaction to price changes was likely to be very tardy.

The second class of producers consisted of established planters employing servant or slave labor, having debts and expenses to meet, and relying largely on production for sale to meet their obligations—in other words, a commercial and capitalistic system of farming. Having his fixed charges to meet, it was observed that for a considerable time after the beginning of a depression period the planter class actually increased the acreage planted, trying by the production of a larger quantity to make up for the smaller price. In time, however, loss of profits had its influence on the production policy of this class. While there was no other available staple to which they could turn, for in every one of these depression periods attempts to develop such staples as silk, wine, flax, hemp, and cotton proved futile, they could at least produce a larger part of their own supplies, particularly clothing, and when the depression lasted long enough there was a strong tendency toward greater self-sufficiency.

The maladjustment of production to price was promoted by the consignment system under which the planter was compelled to wait as much as two years before learning the results of the sale of a particular crop. It was further promoted by the general use of tobacco as a medium of exchange in the colonies and to some extent as a standard of value, and particularly by the legislative provisions for paying taxes, fees, quitrents, and other public charges at certain fixed rates.

Undoubtedly another factor which interfered seriously with the adjustment of supply and demand was the large proportion of the consumers' price which consisted of fixed charges for customs duties, cost of transport, and various market costs. In 1720 it was estimated that not counting customs duties a price of 4d. in Great Britain would yield but 1¾d. in Virginia. For Maryland tobacco a British price of 3d. would yield the planter only 1d. The addition of the duty, which at that time was 6⅓d., meant that for the Virginia planter to receive 1¾d. tobacco must sell in Great Britain at 10⅓d., and for the Maryland planter to receive 1d. his tobacco must sell at 9d. It is true most of the duty was recovered on re-exportation, but in continental markets other heavy charges were again imposed.

Attempted Solutions of the Problem

Many attempts were made to deal with the problem of marketing the tobacco surplus more effectively so as to bring greater advantages to the producer, including a vast amount of legislation, probably more than has ever been devoted to any other crop, with the possible exception of sugar.

ATTEMPTS AT MONOPOLY.—In an earlier part of this paper it was shown that the first decade of tobacco growing in the American colonies was on the basis of an abnormally high price level. It was an age of monopoly, and consequently the attempts to uphold this abnormally high level took the form of a series of monopolistic concessions calculated to maintain unity of control in merchandizing the product. There was also sufficient practical recognition of the laws of supply and demand to lead to provisions in the earlier proposals for restricting the quantity brought to market from the colonies and from Spain, and later to restrict the quantity grown in the colonies.

I shall not undertake to trace in this paper the various negotiations in connection with the proposed contract with Henry Somerscales in 1619; the contract with Sir Thomas Rowe and his associates in the following year, the Jacobs contract arranged in 1621–2; the long negotiations by the Virginia Company itself for an exclusive monopolistic privilege in marketing tobacco, which contract was finally nullified through the factional controversies in the Company itself; the Ditchfield contract of 1625, which failed because of the determined opposition of the Virginia planters; the Anis contract of 1627, which also met the strong opposition of the colonies; and finally the negotiations in 1638 for the Goring contract, in which the proponents attempted to popularize their proposal by suggesting the revival of the Virginia Company, a scheme which did not break down the determined resistance of the colonists.

While the colonists opposed these various attempts at monopolistic concessions, except that of the Virginia Company, which was a matter of controversy both in the Company itself and in the Colony, this opposition was due less to antagonism to the monopolistic solution than to the fact that the various proposals were made largely for the special benefit of the Crown and of a persistent group of courtiers who sought to fatten their purses at the expense of the planters.

Long after the idea of fiscal monopolies as a royal prerogative had been swept overboard by the civil wars and the accompanying changes in British constitutional principles, some interesting private attempts were made to employ monopoly in marketing as a means of coping with the problem of price depression.

In 1690 some adventurer who had traveled in Brazil and had learned the methods of curing tobacco in that country proposed the formation of a monopolistic company under royal charter for the production and marketing of "sweet-scented" tobacco cured by Brazilian methods. The scheme met with little encouragement by the Virginia authorities.

During the long depression which began in 1725 a notable attempt was made to bring about concerted action on the part of the London merchants in the handling of tobacco. The impulse for this attempt was largely the preponderant advantage enjoyed by the agent of the French fiscal monopoly of tobacco in purchasing annually fifteen thousand hogsheads of the dark variety of Oronoko tobacco.

The French, it was alleged, consistently took advantage of their position to play one merchant against another and thereby beat down the price. Not content with purchasing for their requirement in France, the shrewd French buyer bought whole shiploads, which he dumped on the Dutch market at less than cost in order to demoralize prices, and then on the basis of prices thus established he came into the London and output markets to purchase his annual supply. By these methods it was estimated that he deliberately incurred a loss of about £2,000 on tobacco shipped to the Dutch market, but saved about £50,000 on tobacco purchased for use in France. The evil was all the greater because the price determined for the French purchases tended to establish the market level for other classes of tobacco. Furthermore, the London merchants had been losing business to the outport merchants because their former clients, dissatisfied with the results of the consignment system, were turning to the method of selling in the colonies to the outport merchants.

A number of times previously the London merchants had organized for concerted action, and for some years had deducted three pence on each hogshead, which was supposed to be devoted to a common fund to pay the expenses of the tobacco lobby in Parliament and the other expenses of the merchants' organization. Apparently this charge had been made with the tacit consent of their colonial clients in the hope of substantial benefits, but the attempts of the merchants at concerted action in the market had always failed through inability to hold all the members in line. Yet the charge still continued and it was claimed that much of the proceeds had never reached the treasury of the organization.

The principal leaders in the movement for reorganization in 1727–9 were Henry Darnall, a Maryland merchant resident in London, and John Falconer, another London merchant. They developed a plan which involved provision for a salaried secretary, meetings by all the London merchants on the first Thursday of each month and by a board of twelve managers on the third Thursday of each month. Certain annual contributions were to be made by each merchant, from which he was allowed certain refunds for prompt attendance at meetings. Unused funds were to be employed to provide a dinner once or twice a year "to beget a good Friendship and Harmony among the Merchants; which Eating together, does more often produce among Mankind than bare Drinking."

It was proposed that careful statistics be collected of stocks on hand and shipments of tobacco to and from Great Britain. The merchants agreed to act in concert in dealing with the French, and in order to prevent them from turning to the outports for supplies, it was proposed to open correspondence with the outport merchants with a view to obtaining their support. In order to hold the London merchants in line the promoters expected to rely on the pressure of opinion among their clients in Maryland and Virginia. In order to solidify opinion in the colonies it was suggested that correspondence be opened with the various planters' clubs, of which, it was said, there was at least one in every county "for talking over affairs."

The organization was formed in April, 1728, according to these plans, and the agreement was signed by all the London tobacco merchants, twenty-nine firms in all. A minimum price for tobacco was agreed to. Very soon, however, some of the merchants were accused of dealing surreptitiously with the French. Then still others openly broke over on the ground of self-defence. Letters were written to the colonial planters, and for a time charges and counter-charges flew thick and fast.

Nearly a decade later, in 1737, another proposal was made, by a group of merchants (probably Scotch outport merchants) headed by Daniel McKircher, Esq., for a monopolistic selling agency to confront the buyers' monopoly enjoyed by the French tobacco concessionaires. Not only were British merchants at a great disadvantage in dealing as separate individuals with the French buyers, but the merchants themselves were put to unnecessary expense in that they were compelled to send their ships out to the colonies "by Way of Adventure, to procure their Lading," * * * involving expensive delays in the colony of five or six months and other great expenses in soliciting tobacco, the transportation at times of incomplete cargoes, storage in England until sale could be effected and various charges and losses involved in holding and merchandising the tobacco. The proponents estimated these unnecessary costs in England at £1-7s-11d. per hogshead of 732 pounds net weight.

It was proposed to have a single company which would arrange in advance for the required amount of tobacco and have it ready when the ships came out, thus effecting an economy in freight charges estimated at 25 per cent. The proponents of the plan had obtained the consent of the French buyers to purchase their usual quantity on the quay in London, paying 2d. sterling per pound cash. It was estimated that this was ¼d. less than the average price, but would involve economies in marketing and transport that would make the total net gain to the planter 13s.-8d. per hogshead.

The proposal met determined opposition in the colonies, probably largely on the part of the old-line British commission merchants, whose trade would have been largely displaced by the arrangement, and apparently the proposal was not put into effect.

LEGISLATIVE PRICE-FIXING.—In the early decades of the industry some attempts were made at crude legislative price-fixing. Two such acts were passed in 1632, two others in the following year, and other acts in 1639 and 1640. These were acts fixing the general price level for tobacco and prohibiting by penalties its exchange at a lower price. They are to be distinguished from the numerous rating acts, necessitated by the use of tobacco as currency, to determine the ratio of tobacco to sterling in payment of taxes, fees, quitrents, tavern rates, and ferry charges. In 1641 a royal ordinance inspired by the merchants put an end to these attempts at legislative price determination.

Our forefathers are not to be charged with complete ignorance of the laws of economics in the passage of these acts fixing the general price level of tobacco. In the first place, the several acts were associated with attempts at stinting or restricting the volume of production. In the second place, they were more or less justified by the uncertain conditions of marketing and the imperfection of marketing machinery. At a time when no general price level had as yet developed and when the individual planter was largely at the mercy of the merchant who chanced to call for his crop the legislative enactments served to define crudely the limits of bargaining and to supply a price criterion for the application of the laws against engrossing, forestalling and regrating.

RESTRICTION OF VOLUME OF PRODUCTION OR OF EXPORTS.—As suggested above, from an early period attempts were made to solve the surplus problem by stinting or restricting production, usually by allowing so many plants for each household, for each tithable or other unit of labor. Various arrangements for stinting were included in the later monopolistic contracts, as well as in connection with the price-fixing acts just described. In the legislation of 1639–40 designed to restrict production and fix prices, it became apparent that such legislation would be largely futile without an inter-colonial agreement with Maryland. This was the beginning of a succession of attempts to achieve such agreements.

There is evidence that Virginia legislation for stinting existed in the latter part of the seventeenth century and the early part of the eighteenth. The depression beginning in 1725 resulted in renewed attempts at control of volume of production. Virginia renewed an act in 1727, which had expired in 1725, for improving the staple of tobacco, probably involving destruction of inferior grades and stinting. A stinting act passed at the special session of the Maryland Assembly in 1726 encountered the opposition of the council because of the provision for scaling fees and debts by reason of the expected rise of prices. Another attempt in 1727 in which a compromise was effected on the scaling problem was vetoed by the proprietor. The continuing distress, which culminated in an outbreak of plant-cutting riots in Maryland, finally led to the successful passage of a stinting act in 1730, which, however, lapsed in 1732. The currency act of 1733 provided for the enforced destruction of 150 pounds per taxable during each of the two succeeding years. During this period also negotiations were carried on between Maryland and Virginia looking to mutual legislation for restricting the latest date of planting tobacco, in the interest of curtailing production.

The restriction of volume of production was also intrinsic in numerous acts passed from time to time in both colonies, partly for the purpose of improving quality, such as prohibitions against the packing of ground leaves and suckers, the tending and packing of second growth crops ("seconds"). In some of these acts it was provided that viewers should annually inspect the fields in their respective localities and insure the destruction of second growth tobacco. To some extent restriction of quantity was also achieved by the various acts against packing inferior tobacco and the destruction of such tobacco found in tobacco hogsheads. Restriction of quantity was also involved in the practice of stemming tobacco, which was strongly opposed by the British government because of resulting loss of revenues and prohibited in 1722 by act of Parliament. However, the act led to vigorous protest by the colonies, Virginia sending John Randolph to London especially to obtain repeal of the act, which he succeeded in achieving.

The aim of restricting the quantity of tobacco was also more or less present in the various acts in the early colonial period requiring the production of food crops (the two-acre acts), acts to exempt new settlers from taxation for a time on condition that they refrain from tobacco cultivation, and certain temporary legislation against the importation of slaves.

Attempts at Standardization and Improvement of Marketability

Probably more effective than the attempts at direct control of price and restriction of output were the efforts to improve the marketability of the product.

PROHIBITION OF SHIPMENTS IN BULK.—Among these measures we may include the long struggle to restrict the shipment of tobacco in bulk instead of in the hogshead. The former custom increased greatly in the latter part of the seventeenth century and early decades of the eighteenth by reason of the expansion of the industry into frontier regions where facilities for prizing in hogsheads were lacking, and by reason of the practice of pioneer farmers trading small miscellaneous lots of tobacco at neighborhood stores in exchange for goods brought by the outport ships.

The practice of shipping in bulk, which had increased rapidly with expansion of the industry into the back country, was strongly opposed by the administrative authorities, by the old-time commission merchants, and by the larger planters, because it was favorable to smuggling; because it was an obstacle to the standardization of quality; because a smaller number of ships for transportation were required, which did not appeal to the mercantilist ideals of the period; and because the earlier arrival of the bulk tobacco tended to disorganize the market, besides lending itself to cut-throat competition by small and irregular dealers. We may suspect that in part the opposition grew out of the general resistance of the old-line commercial agencies to the encroachments of the aggressive outport merchants, whose new and vigorous methods were tending to displace them in the trade.

The practice was defended on the ground of smaller cost of transport and because it was essential to the welfare of the poorer classes on the frontier and to the profits of the small outport merchants; and for many years this democratic resistance defeated attempts at prohibition in the colonies. The practice was prohibited by Parliament in 1698, but there was much evasion until the practice was prohibited by the inspection acts hereafter mentioned.

ATTEMPTS TO REGULATE SIZE AND SHAPE OF HOGSHEADS.—There was also a long struggle to regulate the size and shape of the hogshead and the time of shipment. Both of these points were of special concern to the merchants, for hogsheads of irregular shape and size were costly to transport because requiring an undue amount of cargo space. Carelessly made hogsheads came to pieces or warped apart in transit. Maryland long held out for a larger hogshead than was specified by Virginia laws on the ground that the character of Maryland tobacco did not admit of such close packing as in Virginia, while the Virginians attributed the difficulty to slovenly methods of packing in Maryland. Even an order by the Queen annulling the Maryland act and requiring that Maryland specifications be made identical with those of Virginia did not settle the problem.

ATTEMPTS TO REGULATE TIME OF COMPLETING HOGSHEADS.—The great and costly delays encountered by merchants in collecting tobacco in the colonies led to a great deal of legislation to require coopers to have hogsheads completed in sufficient time and other acts to confine shipment within certain specified periods. The practice of hurrying the completion of hogsheads by using unseasoned staves and heading necessitated also the passage of acts to compel the early cutting of timber for the purpose.

PROVISIONS FOR OFFICIAL INSPECTION BEFORE SHIPMENT.—It early became apparent that none of these measures for improvement of quality would be effective without a system of standardization by thorough inspection before shipment. As early as 1619 there was developed the practice of employing sworn viewers to inspect tobacco. From this time forward various temporary or partial measures for inspection were provided for, which cannot be traced in the present paper. No permanently effective system was achieved until the passage of the Virginia act of 1730, which marks an important milestone in the evolution of agricultural marketing machinery and practice.

The foundation for this important measure was laid by the warehouse act of 1712, which provided for the establishment of public warehouses at convenient points not more than one mile from navigable water. Though these warehouses might be privately owned, they were made public utilities. The rates and conditions of storage were fixed by law.

An inspection law was also passed in 1713 providing for licensed inspectors to enforce certain minimum standards, issuing warehouse receipts against tobacco. However, the measure excited tremendous opposition, including that of such important merchant planters as William Byrd (II), who reflected the attitude of the conservative consignment merchants, such as Micajah Perry, of London. These influences obtained in 1717 the royal veto of the measure.

Fortunately the warehouse act, slightly amended in 1720, still remained to serve as a nucleus, and the serious and protracted depression beginning in 1725 brought public sentiment to the support of the act of 1730. Variously amended from time to time, this act and the cognate warehouse act constituted the backbone of the colonial system of marketing until the Revolutionary War.

I cannot undertake here a detailed description of the system. Briefly, it involved several licensed and bonded inspectors stationed at public warehouses. They were authorized to open each hogshead; with the consent of the owner to sort out and destroy inferior tobacco, and lacking his consent to destroy the entire hogshead. The class and grade of the tobacco were then marked on the repacked hogshead. For the purpose of issuing warehouse receipts a distinction was made between "transfer" tobacco and "crop" tobacco. Against the former, general negotiable receipts were issued which did not entitle the owner to any particular hogshead, while the receipts for "crop" tobacco were specific in character, representing largely the consignment tobacco. When the receipts in course of circulation reached the hands of the exporter he could demand delivery and at that time require a second opening and inspection of the hogshead, and in case the tobacco was found below the standard, could enforce judgment against the inspector for compensation and costs. A scale of allowances for shrinkage was provided, and tobacco stored in public warehouses was publicly insured against loss by fire and other causes.

This was probably the most constructive type of marketing legislation passed in the colonial period, and its influence was profound. It contributed to improving the average quality of exports, standardized the commodity as a medium of exchange and of public payments and as a standard of deferred payments, and improved the system of customs administration. It gave Virginia growers and merchants a great advantage over those of Maryland. In 1743 Daniel Dulaney wrote that Maryland factors were moving to Virginia where they could buy better tobacco, though at a higher price. The French "regie" buyers also were turning more and more to Virginia to obtain their supply. The Council and Governor of Maryland informed the proprietor that unless Maryland took similar action the whole trade in tobacco would be lost to Virginia.

Maryland experimented for about a quarter of a century with a vacillating policy comprising acts against tending of seconds, suckers, and ground leaves, and acts imposing heavy penalties for false packing, enforced by the offer of rewards to informers. Finally, in 1747, the colony was forced to adopt the Virginia solution by the adoption of an inspection law closely modelled after that of the sister colony.

SUMMARY.—Through more than a century and a half great progress was made in the marketing of tobacco along the lines of more complete commercial organization and greater standardization. It is probable this progress accounts in part for the comparative freedom from protracted depression during the last three or four decades of the colonial period; but the market surplus problem, as we know it today, remained unsolved in spite of the numerous and varied efforts at solution which have been described. It continues as one of the outstanding economic problems of our own time.

17. CURRENCY FINANCE*

An Interpretation of
Colonial Monetary Practices

by E. James Ferguson

The production of agricultural surpluses for export stimulated the growth of urban centers, where merchants specialized
in the distribution of imports and exports. To facilitate trade
and finance growth, farmers and merchants needed currency
and credit. Though Britain expected to profit from trade with
America, it did not provide the colonies with an adequate money
supply. When the colonists resorted to local expedients, they
courted British disapproval and prohibition, but until the 1750's
they managed to evade English restraints through various
schemes. In the following essay, E. James Ferguson describes
how the Americans created a money supply, estimates how well
it worked, and rejects the view that paper money was necessarily cheap money or a means by which poor debtors at-

* *William and Mary Quarterly*, 3d series, vol. 10 (1953), 153–180. Footnotes
have been omitted except where they are necessary for an understanding of the text.

tempted to lighten their burdens by discharging obligations in inflated currency. How adequate were colonial monetary expedients for promoting economic growth? During and after the Revolution, Americans indulged in an orgy of currency creation and incorporated dozens of banks and insurance companies, which had not been possible earlier because of political restraints. This new financial system played an important role in stimulating economic development in the young republic.

For further reading: Curtis P. Nettels, *Money Supply of American Colonies before 1720* (1934); Richard A. Lester, "Currency Issues to Overcome Depressions," *Journal of Political Economy*, vol. 46 (1938), 324–375; B. Hammond, *Banks and Politics in America* (1957), chap. 1.

The accepted view of the financial and monetary history of the American colonies needs revision. It owes too much to the influence of nineteenth-century scholars who were themselves partisans in currency disputes. In their own day, William G. Sumner, Albert S. Bolles, Charles J. Bullock, and Andrew M. Davis stood for "sound money" against inflationist movements. One of their chief aims was to show the disastrous effects of wandering off the straight line of a sound-money policy. Hence, they studied those colonies whose money depreciated and relied on the opinions of such eighteenth-century controversialists as Dr. William Douglass, Thomas Hutchinson, and others in whose views they concurred. With the notable exception of Andrew M. Davis, who did a scholarly work on Massachusetts, they were interested in the colonies chiefly as background to the financial history of the Revolution. Their works in the latter field incorporated study in primary sources and were generally accepted as authoritative.

The pattern they stamped on historical interpretation still survives in its major outlines. Recent books sometimes modify their harsher judgments and bring in new material, but the interpretation rests largely on the story they told of paper money in Massachusetts, Rhode Island, and the Carolinas. These were the provinces where depreciation created a major problem. Neglect of other colonies whose experiments were more fortunate conveys the impression that paper money typically depreciated and was harmful to the community.

A correlated idea is that paper money was significant mainly as a ground of conflict between colonial debtors and creditors. No doubt this view is more readily accepted because it fits in with the Turner hypothesis. Here again, Massachusetts furnishes the prime example. The land bank controversy of 1740 is portrayed as a struggle of creditors against debtors, coastal merchants against back-country farmers. Other instances can be found in the early history of South Carolina.

While the debtor-creditor thesis has logical probability and a foundation in fact, it is nonetheless inadequate when viewed in a perspective embracing the whole development of the American colonies. Historians generally concede, for example, that in most provinces, a propertied aristocracy dominated the government. The debtor-creditor thesis, broadly considered, affords no sufficient explanation for the fact that in the half century before the Revolution, these aristocratic bodies regularly and persistently issued paper money. The thesis is also at odds with the fact that in the middle provinces, at least, mercantile groups strongly opposed the act of Parliament which prevented the colonies from making paper money a legal tender in private transactions. On the assumption that serious internal conflict existed between debtor and creditor, the stand taken by merchants would be inexplicable.

Several accounts of individual provinces appearing in the last few decades appraise the fiat money methods of the colonies in their setting. As the authors have stayed close to primary sources and have extended their range beyond New England, they depict a more successful use of paper money. The collective influence of these works has not been as great as one might suppose. Curtis P. Nettels has added a general study of monetary affairs; unfortunately, it covers only the period before 1720 when the colonies were just beginning to employ paper currency.

There are signs, however, that the dogmas which have prejudiced research are giving way. Fiat money is now the rule, and most economists have ceased to believe that currency must be convertible into gold or silver. Governments freely manipulate currency, as a means of economic control. In this frame of reference, the ways of the American colonies acquire new significance. An economist, Richard A. Lester, explores their use of paper money in the attempt to curb economic depression. He finds that their tactics were analogous to those of the New Deal and bore some ancestral relationship to present-day Keynesian doctrine. The most promising effort, however, is an unpublished doctoral dissertation by Leslie Van Horn Brock, which displays a grasp of colonial usages and attitudes seldom found in older studies. When such works as these attract more notice, other scholars may be persuaded to explore a field which is rich in implications for social and economic history.

Until more evidence is brought together, any general conclusions must be tentative. The formulations attempted in this paper are, therefore, exploratory and subject to correction. It seems possible, however, to qualify older interpretations and point out the tendency of future research. An effort will be made to show that in the middle colonies, from New York to Maryland, paper money was successful. Secondly, it will be argued that except in New England and the Carolinas, paper money did not engender any great conflict between broad classes of the population. Finally, the system of paper money will be described in general terms and an attempt made to define the essential features of "currency finance."

In judging the success of paper money, the first question is whether it depreciated. The answer cannot always be explicit. Different authors do not mean exactly the same thing by the word *depreciation*. Older historians were inclined to go by the rate of exchange. If currency passed below its legal rate in trade for hard money or in the purchase of bills of exchange, they considered that it had depreciated and inferred that too much had been issued or that people lacked confidence in fiat money. This was certainly true in colonies like Rhode Island, Massachusetts, and the Carolinas, where currency sank to low levels. In colonies where fluctuations in the value of money were only moderate, however, a discount on currency in exchange for specie or sterling bills did not necessarily imply that the currency was unsound. Historians of such provinces refer to paper money as stable, even though its value sometimes sank in relationship to specie.

It was normal to discount currency somewhat in exchange for hard money. First of all, the colonies sought to attract foreign coin by giving it a high legal value. They fixed such rates that hard money equivalent to £100 British sterling was legally worth from £133 to around £175 in the currency of different provinces. This was the legal rate. But hard money ordinarily commanded a premium beyond this, for it had more uses than paper. It was more negotiable in payments to foreigners and in inter-colonial transactions.

Besides a general preference for hard money, other factors sometimes worked to bring about a further discount on paper money. Detailed information on the processes of colonial trade is lacking, but it appears that most payments to Britain were made in bills of exchange, that is, drafts payable in Britain which the colonists procured largely by shipments of cargoes. The availability of sterling bills in America depended on the condition of trade. When British purchases fell off and the colonies shipped less than would pay for their imports, sterling bills became scarce and expensive, and people sought hard money to make payments abroad. Specie and bills of exchange rose in value relative to paper money. On the other hand, there were times during the French and Indian War when the colonies enormously increased the volume of their domestic currency, yet the exchange with specie remained constant or even improved because large British expenditures, decreased importations, and a greater supply of specie at hand reduced the need for hard money. Circumstances beyond the control of colonial governments affected the rate of exchange, regardless of how scrupulously the colonies managed their paper money or how good its credit was at home.

The most accurate test of the stability of paper money would be its value in exchange for commodities sold in colonial markets. An adequate price study exists for Pennsylvania, and there is some information for a few other colonies. Unfortunately, this kind of data is fragmentary, and historians usually have to depend on scattered figures and the casual remarks found in contemporary letters.

The weight of evidence suggests, however, that in the middle colonies fluctuations were not great enough to impair the credit or utility of paper money. Historians agree that Pennsylvania "maintained the system without fear of repudiation and to the manifest benefit of the province." It appears that for the half century before the Revolution, the domestic price level was more uniform than in any succeeding period of equal length. The emissions of New Jersey and Delaware are said to have been stable and to have passed usually at par with that of Pennsylvania. New York's currency was highly regarded, and the colony's ability to keep its bills at par was a "subject for special commendation."

Maryland's first emission of 1753 depreciated, even though well-secured, apparently because tobacco remained the primary medium of exchange. Later her bills rose in value and by 1764 were reported "locked up in the Chests of the Wealthy" for the sake of the interest falling due on them. Thereafter, in spite of heavy additions, the bills held their value. "As a colony," writes a modern scholar, "Maryland had solved the problem of a paper currency."

The provinces further south had trouble with their currency. Until 1755, Virginia supplemented the hard money in circulation with tobacco notes, which passed in local exchange and payment of taxes. But the coming of the French and Indian War forced the colony to emit paper money. The bills held their value until 1760, when a sharp break in tobacco prices marked the onset of a long and severe depression. For the next several years, planters could hardly sell their crops, and prices stayed very low. A shortage of the planter balances ordinarily arising from tobacco sales in Britain caused bills of exchange and specie to grow scarce, and their value rose in terms of the currency offered by planters obliged to make payments to British creditors. Virginia currency was discounted as much as 50 per cent to 60 per cent in purchase of bills of exchange. Although specie was extremely scarce, the colony did not put aside its plans to retire war-time paper emissions, and it probably contributed to the easement of conditions that the treasurer of the province, John Robinson, restored some £100,000 to circulation through secret loans to hard-pressed planters. Robinson's defalcations probably occurred in 1765 and 1766. It appears, however, that the decline in Virginia's currency in these and preceding years owed little to Robinson's private emissions, but was rather the result of trade depression. In the last years of the decade, the value rose, and by 1771 it was reported that the British merchants who had formerly complained of paper money were among its warmest advocates.

In the Carolinas, depreciation was severe, though it occurred for the most part early in the eighteenth century, when these colonies were thinly populated and undeveloped. Clearly, however, the legislature of North Carolina did little to sustain its first emissions, and the bills steadily depreciated. In 1748, they were called in to be exchanged for new bills at the rate of 7½ to 1. The new bills fluctuated thereafter around a point considerably below their nominal value, but were rising towards the end of the colonial period, when the British government kept the legislature under close rein.

A different situation prevailed in South Carolina, where all the depreciation occurred before 1731. The infant colony was then under heavy financial strain resulting from war. Debtor elements found the depreciation to their liking, however, and tried to maintain the downward trend. They were overcome after a bitter struggle. The currency was stabilized in 1731 at the rate of 7 to 1 of sterling, which remained unchanged until the Revolution. During its maturity, the province had a stable currency and a record of successful management.

Constancy of value was not, in many minds, the sole test of a currency. Another criterion is suggested by the remark of Thomas Pownall, that in spite of the depreciation in New England, "it was never yet objected that it injured them in trade." Thomas Hancock, one of the greatest merchants in America, seems at one time not to have been altogether convinced that paper money was an unmitigated evil, though he had dealt in a depreciated medium all his life. Of the legislation which placed Massachusetts on a sound money basis, he said: "This d——d Act has turn'd all Trade out of doors and it's Impossible to get debts in, either in Dollars or Province Bills." No study has been made of the economic effects of depreciation in the provinces where it occurred. It is possible that a steady and continuing inflation was not wholly injurious to an expanding country whose people seldom had fixed incomes or large stores of liquid capital.

Even if stability is taken as the sole rule in judging the success of colonial currency, the record is not entirely black. The depreciation in New England was mainly the fault of Rhode Island, whose emissions flooded the unitary economy of that area and undermined the currency of her neighbors. Elsewhere, North Carolina was the leading offender. The colonies, it must be said, did not have complete freedom to act. Each of them felt, in varying degree, the weight of British authority, which was always cast on the side of moderation in the use of currency. Nevertheless, the predominating fact was not the failure of paper money but its success and good credit—in the colonies from New York to Maryland, and in Virginia, as well as in South Carolina during its later development.

Serious conflicts between debtors and creditors did not arise when paper money stayed near par value. Ideally, perhaps, men of property would have preferred a circulation of coin or a currency backed by precious metals. Practically, however, most of them shared the popular belief that there was no alternative to the existing system. "Contrary to the traditions that historians have perpetuated," writes a modern student of economic thought, "a critical analysis of the contemporary literature indicates that the proponents as well as the critics were not poor debtors or agrarians, but for the most part officials, ministers, merchants, and men of substance and learning in general."

Pennsylvania's currency was esteemed by all classes and regarded as having contributed to the growth and prosperity of the colony. In his widely read work on colonial affairs, Thomas Pownall wrote that there "never was a wiser or a better measure, never one better calculated to serve the uses of an encreasing country . . . never a measure more steadily pursued, nor more faithfully executed for forty years together." Merchants and traders of Philadelphia formally opposed the restraining act of 1764 which prevented the colonies from making paper money legal tender. As colonial agent in England, Benjamin Franklin fought the enactment of the law and afterward wrote pamphlets urging its repeal. Franklin joined other colonial representatives and English merchants to argue the case for repeal before British ministers and members of Parliament. By 1767, the American agents planned to secure the introduction of a repealing act into Parliament. They gave up the idea only when it became known that Parliament would very likely insist that the price of such a concession must be the surrender by the colonies of permanent revenues to the crown.

Franklin told the House of Commons that restrictions on paper money were among the leading reasons why the American provinces had become alienated from the mother country. In 1774, the First Continental Congress cited the restraining act among the violations of colonial rights.

New York merchants also protested the restraining act. The assembly appointed a committee of New York county members, whose duties included corresponding with other provinces and the colonial agent with respect to the act. Governor Moore espoused the cause and repeatedly asked the Board of Trade to sanction an emission on the terms desired by the province. The assembly refused aid to British troops unless the crown approved a currency bill, and, according to Carl Becker, opposition to the Townshend Acts had one of its sources in this grievance. Popular unrest was stilled not only by the repeal of the duties, but also by a special act of Parliament which allowed the colony to issue paper money.

Public opinion in Maryland, according to historians of the province, was nearly unanimous in favor of paper money. Among the beneficiaries of the currency system were many of the most prominent men of the colony, who received loans from the government. The list included a "surprising number" of merchants. After Parliamentary restrictions were laid down in 1764, all classes concurred in the need for further emissions, and Maryland's agents in London tried to get the act repealed.

In spite of the notorious depreciation which afflicted North Carolina's emissions, paper money does not seem to have been a major factor in the sectional antagonisms of that colony. Both houses of a legislature presumably dominated by the "court house ring" petitioned the crown in 1768 to approve paper money legislation. At a time when the Regulator Movement in the backcountry had begun to split the colony into warring factions, Governor Tryon added his pleas to those of the legislature. His letters to the Board of Trade repeated familiar arguments, which, coming from less responsible sources, have often been dismissed as the pretence of debtors trying to evade their obligations. He said a larger circulating medium was necessary and that much distress arose from the lack of it.

In South Carolina, the early struggle between debtors and creditors was never quite forgotten, but in time the memory grew so dim that the contemporary historian, David Ramsay, could write: "From New-York to Georgia there had never been in matters relating to money, an instance of a breach of public faith." On the basis of his personal recollection, no doubt, he wrote that the use of paper money "had been similar from the first settlement of the colonies, and under proper restrictions had been found highly advantageous." Another historian of the province, Alexander Hewatt, an extreme foe of paper money at the time he wrote, acknowledged the benefit of currency emissions to a "growing colony" like South Carolina, provided they were kept within bounds.

Virginia's treasurer, Robert Carter Nicholas, expressed the view of a conservative planter. In a public defense of the government's conduct in emitting paper money, he declared that the outbreak of the French and Indian War had made it absolutely necessary. Sufficient funds could be obtained in no other way, and, though hesitant at first, the assembly found no other course open. Nicholas himself knew well the dangers of a paper medium and was conversant with the arguments against it, including the pamphlet of William Douglass, its ardent foe in New England. But Nicholas believed that the evils discovered in some places did not arise from paper money as such. "They have been chiefly, if not totally owing," he wrote, "either to these Bills of Credit not being established upon proper Funds, or to a Superabundance of them or to some Mismanagement." Granting a risk was involved, Nicholas believed that many countries had derived great benefit from paper money. He thought it had been helpful to Virginia.

Nicholas's opinion was much like that of a conservative New York merchant, John Watts, who was highly critical of the restraining act of 1764. Like many others, Watts thought the act would virtually put an end to paper money. "The use of paper money is abolished as an evil," he complained, "when, properly treated, it is the only medium we have left of commerce and the only expedient in an exigency. Every man of estate here abominates the abuse of paper money, because the consequences fall upon himself, but there is just the same difference in the use and abuse of it as there is in food itself . . ."

The writings of the post-Revolutionary era contain many allusions to the success of paper money in colonial times and the esteem in which it was then held. In 1786, a correspondent to a New York newspaper recalled how easily the provinces had maintained their paper money systems:

> Before the commencement of the late war, when public faith was still in possession of vestal chastity, divers of the states, then provinces, had large sums in circulation at full value, depending on funds calculated to redeem only five to ten per centum per annum of the amount issued; consequently it must be from ten to twenty years before the whole would be redeemed; and yet, tho' the money drew no interest . . . it circulated freely and at its full nominal value on a perfect equality with specie . . .

As this article appeared, the New York Chamber of Commerce made the same point in declaring its opposition to a paper money issue contemplated by the legislature. The Chamber of Commerce acknowledged that paper money had worked well in colonial times, but argued that this should not be taken as evidence that it would succeed under changed conditions.

An observation frequently made in these times was put down by David Ramsay in his *History of the American Revolution*. Noting that Continental currency held its value during the first year or two of the war, even though it had no security behind it, Ramsay explained: "This was in some degree owing to a previous confidence, which had been begotten by honesty and fidelity, in discharging the engagements of government." Alluding to the same fact, Financier Robert Morris observed: "There was a time when public confidence was higher in America than in any other country."

The inflation of the Revolution destroyed that confidence, at least among propertied men, for they believed that paper money could never be a reliable instrument in an era when the whims of the people dictated, as they said, the policy of the government. A great proportion of the people, however, never lost the old affection for paper money. "From the earliest settlement of America," declared a petition composed in 1785 for presentation to the Pennsylvania legislature, "most of our improvements have been aided by the medium of paper currency . . . and your petitioners are persuaded that . . . public faith might be restored, and the ancient system revived, to the great ease of the inhabitants and emolument of the community." Such an appeal invoked common knowledge.

It becomes clear that paper money occupied an important place in colonial affairs not because it embodied the aims of a particular class, but because it rendered important services to the community.

The circumstances which led to the adoption of paper money are well known. There was not enough hard money to provide a medium of trade for domestic transactions. Gold and silver coins flowed outward in purchase of British commodities and while in the colonies circulated mainly among merchants. Much business was done on the basis of book credits and debits, but specie was nearly always in short supply. Economic depression intensified the problem, for when cargoes did not raise enough to meet debts owed abroad, specie had to be shipped. Domestic trade became almost wholly barter. People who had specie could get an exorbitant premium, and those forced to make payments in hard money faced difficulty. Provincial governments could not collect taxes. The inhabitants felt the need of a medium of exchange which, unlike specie, would not "make unto itself wings and fly away."

The colonies, therefore, adopted paper money. It was issued by two different processes. The first method, in point of time, was the direct emission of fiat money by the government to pay expenses, particularly the costs of war. The other method, which we shall consider immediately, was the emission of money through a loan-office or "land bank."

The land bank was the primary social legislation of colonial America. It was a method of putting currency into circulation and at the same time affording loans to farmers which they could scarcely obtain from other sources. Provincial governments set up loan offices which advanced currency to farmers at low rates of interest, taking mortgages on real property as security. An individual could usually get only a limited sum. He repaid the loan in annual installments over a period of years. Frequently, though not always, the bills were legal tender in private transactions; in any case, they were almost always accepted in payments to the government for taxes, land, etc. As the annual installments due on the principal came back into the loan office, the bills were cancelled and retired, though they were often reissued, or successive banks established to keep up a continuous flow of loans. The colonies thus developed a medium of exchange out of "*solid* or *real* property . . . melted down and made to circulate in paper money or bills of credit."

The land banks of the middle colonies were, from all accounts, markedly successful. Pennsylvania managed one almost continuously after 1723 without mishap. For more than twenty-five years before the French and Indian War, the interest received by the government from money out on loan supported the costs of provincial administration, without the necessity of direct taxes. Relative freedom from taxation probably contributed to Pennsylvania's remarkable growth.

Other middle colonies also obtained good results. New Jersey enacted three separate loans up to 1735, and the interest enabled the government to exist without direct taxation for sixteen years before 1751. Delaware issued land bank notes from 1723 to 1746, with apparent benefit to the province. New York extended its land bank of 1737 until the last installment of the principal fell due in 1768, at which time all classes demanded its renewal. The bank was reinstituted in 1771 by virtue of the special act of Parliament, of which mention has already been made. Governor Tryon's report in 1774 showed that the interest from loans comprised about half the revenue of the province, an amount which nearly matched expenses in time of peace.

The notes which Maryland issued on loan in 1733 fell considerably below par, but later rose to nominal value. A modern historian writes:

> Considering the peculiar benefits to grain and tobacco culture, the conveniences offered to trade, the exceptionally high exchange that the bills maintained throughout most of their life, and the faithful redemption of every shilling at face value, it is hardly too much to say that this was the most successful paper money issued by any of the colonies.

A new bank was instituted in 1769, and the notes stayed at par until the Revolution.

Virginia never adopted a land bank. In North and South Carolina, land banks figured in the early depreciation of paper money, and it became the settled policy of the British government to disallow acts for their establishment. Similarly, as is well known, the land banks of the New England colonies, particularly those of Rhode Island, contributed to the decline of currency in that area and brought on the first statutory regulation of paper money by Parliament.

This system of agricultural credit so widely practiced in the colonies would seem to be a subject of considerable importance for social and economic history, yet it has not received the attention it deserves. The economist, Richard A. Lester, offers a general view of the use of land bank emissions to curb depressions, and it may be added that such a background of experience explains why even after the financial chaos of the Revolution, the common people still looked to paper money for relief from hard times. But the subject has further ramifications. Agriculture's need for credit facilities has been a constant factor in American history and a source of political unrest. Banks have served commerce and industry; until lately, agriculture remained at a disadvantage. It should be an interesting fact that colonial governments loaned money to farmers at low rates of interest. But no analysis has been made of the effects of land bank loans in the domestic economy, nor has anyone yet approached the general subject with sufficient breadth of view to place it in its relationship to the main currents of American development.

The revenue problems of colonial governments were lessened by land bank emissions; taxes were more easily collected when citizens had access to money. During the frequent wars of the eighteenth century, however, the provinces developed another use of paper money. They emitted it to pay governmental expenses. The procedure became a rationalized system of public finance.

Provincial revenues were normally small and inflexible. Officials drew fees rather than salaries, and the few public services were performed mainly by local government. Such provinces as Pennsylvania and New York spent no more than £5,000 a year apart from war expenses. Taxation was adjusted to limited needs. Imposts and excise taxes usually afforded a maintaining fund, while direct levies on polls and property raised what else was needed. None of these revenues could be freely expanded. Heavy duties on imports tended to drive off trade or cause

355

smuggling. Direct taxes were often hard to collect and slow coming in. Colonial governments found it difficult or impossible to borrow money from their own citizens. Private capital was tied up in lands or commodities. No banks or business corporations existed with liquid capital which could be enlisted in the public service. When a war or other emergency required large outlays, colonial governments knew no alternative but to issue paper money. Massachusetts hit upon this device in 1690, and eventually all the colonies took it up. "Currency finance" became the regular mode of financing government during war and often, as well, in time of peace.

Practice varied in details, but over the period in which the colonies experimented, they regularized their procedure in something like a system conducted on the basis of known principles. The one exception was Massachusetts, which went on a sound money basis in the 1750's. Elsewhere, methods fall into a pattern that can be described in general terms.

The essential feature of the system was that it avoided dealing in hard money. During a war, for instance, colonial legislatures printed, from time to time, the money needed to pay their expenses. Usually, the act which authorized the emission also appropriated sufficient taxes to withdraw the money from circulation. If expenses were large, the taxes for several years ahead might be pledged to the redemption of money issued during a single year.

The credit of the bills depended on several interrelated factors. Regardless of any promise on the face of the notes, the basic security was the fund assigned to withdraw the money. The holder had to be certain that all taxes and payments to the government taken together would be enough to create a general use for the bills and ensure a demand for them. He must rest easy in the knowledge that withdrawals would be continuous and that future governments would have the ability and the will to collect taxes. As this money was created and upheld by political acts, confidence in government was essential to its value.

Meanwhile, the value of the money was sustained by its current usages, as in paying fees, buying land from the province, or use in ordinary trade. So long as there was no great reason to question it, the people accepted currency in day-to-day transactions because it was the recognized medium of exchange. Colonial legislators, however, knew something about the quantity theory of money and understood that the amount must not exceed too far the requirements of trade at existing price levels, else depreciation would occur regardless of guarantees.

The system appears to have worked against the accumulation of public debt. The debt at any particular time consisted of bills of credit in circulation; to retire it, the government levied taxes payable in the certificates of indebtedness themselves. If the debt was large, paper money was apt to be correspondingly plentiful and widely distributed. The people were taxed in a medium readily accessible to them. As withdrawals reduced the supply of currency and it became concentrated into fewer hands, the debt was by that token rendered less onerous, until at some point the taxes imposed to cancel it could be discontinued and the remaining currency left in circulation. Under the benign operation of currency finance, the facility with which the public debt could be retired was in rough proportion to its size.

Other means than currency were used to anticipate future income. Colonial governments, and to a much greater extent the state governments of the Revolution, issued various kinds of warrants and certificates which, though often given an extensive circulation, did not serve as a medium of exchange to the same degree as paper money. With certain exceptions, however, these notes were issued and redeemed on the same terms as currency. In spite of variations, therefore, it is possible to trace a basic pattern in the financial methods employed by the colonies. They met expenses by issuing a paper medium, whether currency or certificates, directly to individuals in payment for goods and services. They redeemed this paper not by giving specie to those who held it, but by accepting it for taxes or other payments to the government. This was the system of currency finance.

It was not a system which would stand the strain of a prolonged and expensive war. Nonetheless, it sufficed for the wars in which the colonies engaged. During the French and Indian War, for example, New York emitted £535,000. Pennsylvania, whose currency normally stood at £80,000, issued £540,000. Virginia authorized £440,000. Other colonies made extraordinary contributions. The Board of Trade estimated that the North American provinces spent £2,500,000 sterling beyond their ordinary costs of government. About £800,000 of this represented expenditures of Massachusetts, the sound money colony. The remainder of £1,700,000 sterling consisted almost entirely of currency or certificates issued in the expectation that they would be retired only by acceptance for taxes and other payments to the government. In spite of the volume of this paper, little or no depreciation appears to have resulted in most provinces. The colonies benefited from expenditures of the home government, and from large British subsidies which put specie in their hands.

Debt retirement was rapid after the war. Virginia's currency was down to £206,000 by 1767, according to the treasurer's report, and though two small post-war emissions restored some money to circulation, only £54,391 was afloat in 1773. Pennsylvania, no longer tax free, made regular withdrawals until the Revolution. In New York, an acute shortage of currency existed by 1768. Elsewhere the provinces quickly freed themselves of their debts. A speaker in the House of Commons observed in 1766 that they had already retired £1,755,000, and that most of the remaining debt of £760,000 could be written off within two years.

How much this happy situation was due to British subsidies is hard to know. During the war, Parliament granted over £1,150,000 sterling for distribution among the American colonies, a sum which was nearly half of the £2,500,000 estimated as their war expenses. Even so, when one compares their real expenditures during the war with the sums involved in their ordinary fiscal operations, it appears that they made what was for them a most unusual effort, and the ease with which they retired their debts must in some measure be attributed to the peculiar facility offered by the methods of currency finance.

British policy on matters pertaining to colonial currency is a subject which has scarcely been touched. No doubt it was a factor of greater importance in imperial relations than is commonly understood. From the one considerable treatment available, it appears that most of the time the British government acknowledged the necessity of colonial emissions. Before 1740, the Board of Trade was "reluctantly sympathetic and essentially reasonable" in sanctioning both land bank loans and direct emissions. The Board, however, always opposed making currency a legal tender in private transactions, even though it approved laws for this purpose. Generally speaking, the Board tried to regulate colonial issues by ensuring that the amounts were reasonable, that funds for redemption were adequate, and that emissions were withdrawn within a limited period of time. Control was exerted largely through instructions to governors, who were ordered to refuse assent to laws which did not have a clause suspending their execution until approved by the crown.

Supervision was not effective and lapsed almost completely during frequent periods of war. As currency emissions were the only way the provinces could furnish aid, governors were permitted to approve acts without a suspending clause, provided the Board's other stipulations were satisfied. The colonies took advantage of their bargaining position, however, to procure the governors' assent to laws which did not comply with the Board's requirements. Neither governors nor the crown could afford to scrutinize too closely the modes by which assistance was rendered.

War still hindered the enforcement of policy, but British control tightened after 1740. Rhode Island's emissions were a flagrant abuse. The Board also appears to have been more susceptible to complaints of British merchants, some of whom claimed injury from legal tender laws. The same mercantile and creditor interests carried their appeals to Parliament, with the result that after 1750 the standing instructions of the Board of Trade were given statutory effect.

The act of 1751 applied only to New England. It did not abolish the paper money system even in that area, as is sometimes supposed, but merely established rules for carrying it on. Bills already in circulation were to be retired in strict accord with the terms of the issuing acts. When these were withdrawn, no paper money was to be legal tender. The provinces were allowed to emit bills from year to year to pay governmental expenses, provided they committed taxes sufficient to redeem them within two years. This clause was flexible enough to accommodate a moderate expansion of currency. In event of war or other emergency, all curbs were relaxed as to the amount which could be issued, provided enough taxes were appropriated to redeem the bills within five years. The act of 1751 left the colonies outside New England undisturbed. Within New England, its major effect was to prohibit legal tender laws and to rule out land banks.

The restraining act of 1764 came at the end of the French and Indian War, when the colonies had large sums outstanding. As first drafted, it would have placed all the provinces under the curbs imposed on New England. In its final form, it merely prohibited legal tender laws and required that existing legal tender currencies be sunk at their expiration dates. Many colonies protested, in the belief that the legal tender feature was an essential prop to their money. Experience was to show, however, that the restriction did not materially impair the workings of the currency system.

There is more than a hint that by this time Britain's policy as to paper money was subordinated to the larger purpose of securing a permanent civil list, and that attempts were being made to trade approval of colonial emissions for the grant of a fixed revenue to the crown. Even so, the colonies made headway against British restraints, though they could not again pass legal tender laws. New York was permitted to renew its land bank in 1771. After a long struggle, New Jersey exacted consent for the establishment of a land bank in 1774. Pennsylvania continued to emit currency and in 1773 renewed its land bank. Maryland issued £173,733 to pay war debts and over half a million dollars to finance improvements and to establish a land bank. Virginia's council annulled two land bank acts passed by the lower house, but the province emitted £40,000 for other purposes. North Carolina, closely confined by the British government, issued treasury notes and debenture bills, while South Carolina emitted "public orders" and "tax certificates," which were in effect a non-legal tender currency.

Parliament in 1773 legalized colonial monetary practices as carried on under the restrictive acts of 1751 and 1764. A question had arisen as to how far the prohibition of legal tender applied. To clarify the matter, Parliament passed an explanatory act which declared that the prohibition ruled out only those laws which made currency legal tender in private transactions. The colonies were allowed to make it legal tender in payments to the government. In stating the latitude permitted by existing law, Parliament defined the essential workings of the currency finance system. The act is worth quoting because it verifies the general survey given above:

Whereas the want of gold and silver currency in several of his Majesty's colonies and plantations in America may make it necessary, as well for the publick advantage as in justice to those persons who may have demands upon the publick treasuries in the said colonies for services performed, that such publick creditors should be secured in the payment of their just debts and demands, by certificates, notes, bills, or debentures, to be created and issued by the authority of the general assemblies . . . on the securities of any taxes or duties given and granted to his Majesty—for and towards defraying expences incurred for publick services; and that such certificates, notes, bills or debentures, should be made chargeable on the publick treasurers of the said colonies and received and taken by them as a legal tender in discharge of any such duties or taxes, or of any debts whatsoever, due to the publick treasuries . . . be it enacted . . . That . . . any

certificates, notes, bills or debentures which shall . . . be voluntarily
accepted by the creditors of the publick. . . may be made . . . to be a
legal tender for the publick treasurers . . . for the discharge of any
duties, taxes, or other debts whatsoever . . .

Had the Revolution not occurred, Britain might have reached a solution of colonial monetary problems. As early as 1754, Richard Jackson and Franklin exchanged plans to form one or more land banks based on capital loaned from the Bank of England or subscribed by private investors. It was expected that land bank notes would provide a circulating medium for the continent. Later, when the Stamp Act was under discussion, Franklin and Thomas Pownall broached a similar scheme, as an alternative way of gaining a revenue from the colonies. They envisaged a continental land bank with a branch office in each province, centrally managed in Britain. The bank was to issue legal tender notes on loan at 5 per cent interest, the principal to be repaid over a period of ten years. The notes would circulate as currency throughout the American colonies. Franklin and Pownall pressed this scheme for three or four years.

By 1767, it appears that the Secretary of Trade concurred in the idea that the restraining act of 1764 should be modified to permit the colonies to establish loan offices which would emit legal tender notes valid for all transactions except payment of sterling debts. A bill for this purpose was being prepared and the ground laid for its introduction into the House of Commons, when the colonial agents learned that the Commons would probably seize the opportunity to declare the income arising from the loan offices subject to the appropriation of the crown. As the colonial agents could not risk this outcome, they gave up the project. Saying he had hoped to make better use of his plan for a continental land bank, Pownall published the details of it in the 1768 edition of his *Administration of the Colonies*.

Any solution of the money problem under British auspices was forestalled by the Revolution. When it was too late, the British government instructed its peace commissioners of 1778 in a number of schemes which might have borne fruit if attempted earlier.

A view of the evidence suggests that generations of historical scholarship have fostered a mistaken impression of the monetary practices of the colonies. The efforts of the American provinces to create a medium of exchange, erect a system of agricultural credit, and equip their governments with the means of incurring and discharging responsibilities, hardly constitute a "dark and disgraceful" picture; nor, on the whole, is the record one of failure. Most of the colonies handled their currency with discretion and were successful in realizing the purposes associated with its use. Except for New England, where depreciation had given it a bad name, paper money was the "ancient system," which had long served well the needs of trade and the ordinary processes of government. Although mindful of its dangers, men of property accepted it as useful and necessary. In time of war, all the colonies but one were fully prepared to adopt the methods of currency finance as the only way of meeting an emergency. Emissions might then be over-large, as the Revolution was to prove, but the common need precluded any nice regard for the effect on contracts.

18. THE MOLASSES ACT AND THE MARKET
STRATEGY OF THE BRITISH
SUGAR PLANTERS*

by Richard Sheridan

British subjects, wherever they lived, were not free to do
business and pursue profit as they saw fit. An elaborate body of
law regulated the economic activity of the empire according to
the assumptions of mercantilism, which held that in the pursuit
of wealth England could intervene in the economic activity of
her colonies. While few questioned the validity of mercantilism
in the abstract, rival economic interests, in the mother country
and in the colonies, had their own notions of how the state
could best further the general welfare, usually by favoring one
group at the expense of a competitor. In the following essay,
Richard Sheridan explores the conflicts among those involved in
the production, distribution, and processing of sugar grown in
the British West Indies. He argues that mercantilism was not
simply a system by which a mother country exploited its colonies. In this case, two different groups of colonial interests

* *Journal of Economic History*, vol. 18 (1957), 62–83. Footnotes have been
omitted except where they are necessary for an understanding of the text.

clashed: North Americans who preferred to buy in the French sugar islands where the terms of trade were more favorable than in the British islands, and English sugar planters anxious to exclude the Americans from foreign sources. The sugar planters were equally determined to bolster the price of sugar in England by preventing British merchants from importing cheaper French sugar. Through political influence, they secured a protected market in Britain and Ireland and the passage of the Molasses Act (1733), which placed a prohibitive tax on French sugar imported into the American colonies. But the law was not enforced until the 1760's, probably because British merchants and politicians realized that as the Americans prospered in illicit trade, they gained additional means to pay for English imports. On balance, the mercantilist system may have benefited the Americans more than it burdened them, though the decisive determinants of the direction and rate of American economic development were the resource potentials in the colonies and the market opportunities abroad.

For further reading: Jacob Viner, "Power versus Plenty as Objectives of Foreign Policy in the Seventeenth and Eighteenth Centuries," *World Politics*, vol. 1 (Oct., 1948), 1–29; Oliver M. Dickerson, *Navigation Acts and the American Revolution* (1951); Lawrence A. Harper, *The English Navigation Laws* (1964); George L. Beer, *The Origins of the British Colonial System 1578–1660* (1908), *The Old Colonial System 1660–1688* (1912); Robert P. Thomas, "A Quantitative Approach to the Study of the Effects of British Imperial Policy upon Colonial Welfare," *Journal of Economic History*, vol. 25 (Dec. 1965), 615–638; Viola F. Barnes, *The Dominion of New England*; Richard Pares, *Yankees and Creoles: The Trade between North America and the West Indies before the American Revolution* (1956).

The Market Strategy of the British Sugar Planters

In the past few decades several approaches have been adopted with respect to the Molasses Act controversy of 1730–1733. It has been considered from the standpoint of Anglo-French commercial rivalry; as a conflict between two British colonial regions; as a measure designed to aid one group of British colonies at the expense of another; and as a source of precedents for parliamentary taxation of the colonies on the one hand and the colonists' refusal to comply with such taxation on the other. While the trade between North America and the French West Indies was the chief target of attack, it is not always realized that proponents of the Molasses Act had other objectives in mind. British sugar planters were not only at odds with North American merchants who traded with the foreign sugar islands, but also with Irish merchants who pursued a similar course of trade and with the buyers of sugar in England. Failure to achieve results by means of restrictive legislation in one area did not necessarily preclude success in others. The controversy needs to be understood in terms of the international sugar economy, the changing nature of the British market for sugar and rum, and the planters' attempt to adapt the Navigation Acts to these changes. From the planters' standpoint, the Molasses Act was only one of several measures that were needed to adapt the Navigation Acts to the realities of the market, so it may be unrealistic to consider any one act in isolation.

During the latter half of the seventeenth century the Navigation Acts were generally regarded with hostility by the sugar planters. This was a period of limited consumption in the home market, and as the acts of trade forced colonial sugar into England before it could be re-exported, the planters found it difficult to compete in foreign markets. Under these circumstances they evaded and violated the acts whenever possible. Foreign markets were larger than the home market, but in order to maximize profits British sugar had to by-pass the home market so as to save shipping costs and avoid payment of duties and handling charges. British sugar was therefore channeled to markets in continental Europe by way of North America, the Dutch and French West Indies, and to a lesser extent Ireland and Scotland. Although the English government passed laws to eliminate loopholes and tighten up enforcement of the Navigation Acts, considerable quantities of British sugar reached foreign markets without first being landed in England.

The early years of the eighteenth century witnessed a change in the nature of the markets for sugar that made it necessary for British planters to readjust their attitude toward the Navigation Acts. There was a long-run tendency for the English sugar demand to run ahead of the supply forthcoming from the colonies, and as foreign sugar was virtually kept out of England by prohibitive duties, English prices were generally higher than those on the Continent. After the Treaty of Utrecht in 1713, sugar production in the French colonies expanded much more rapidly than that of the British colonies. On the other hand, the per-capita consumption of sugar in England increased more rapidly than that of the Continent, owing to such factors as population growth, rising living standards, and the widespread consumption of tea, coffee, and punch. These forces were rather slow in taking effect, however, and for a time after Queen Anne's War English sugar prices experienced a temporary decline. Re-exports of British colonial sugar to foreign markets also fell off markedly, and the following table shows that they declined from nearly 40 per cent of total English sugar imports in 1698–1700 to less than 5 per cent in the period from 1733 to 1737.

English Sugar Imports, Re-exports, and British Empire Consumption
(Annual Averages for Selected Years)

YEARS	TOTAL IMPORTS (cwt.)	RE-EXPORTS TO FOREIGN COUNTRIES (cwt.)	RE-EXPORTS TO IRELAND AND BRITISH PLANTA-TIONS (cwt.)	TOTAL RE-EXPORTS (cwt.)	CON-SUMED IN BRITISH EMPIRE (cwt.)	PERCENTAGE IMPORTS RE-EXPORTED TO FOREIGN COUNTRIES
1698–1700	471,050	176,476	13,883	190,359	294,574	37.5
1716–1720	653,168	159,916	20,159	180,075	493,252	24.5
1728–1732	926,440	129,345	40,601	169,946	797,095	14.0
1733–1737	805,917	33,851	47,918	81,769	772,066	4.2
1748–1752	896,452	39,243	66,857	106,100	857,209	4.4
1753–1757	1,091,600	48,489	65,707	114,196	1,043,111	4.5

"This was due to French, Dutch, and Portuguese sugars being sold in Europe much cheaper than sugar from the English colonies," according to Frank Wesley Pitman. It is not surprising that these circumstances encouraged British planters to send the bulk of their sugar to the home market.

The above changes brought three major political issues to the forefront. The first arose over the attempts of English middlemen to introduce foreign sugar and rum into England by way of the British sugar colonies. By the early years of the eighteenth century English sugar prices were somewhat higher than those on the Continent of Europe, and this disparity was reflected in the price of sugar and its by-products, molasses and rum, in the sugar colonies of different European nations. The price of molasses and rum in the West Indies was also influenced by the fact that France prohibited the import of rum from her colonies so as to protect her brandy trade, while England was beginning to import substantial quantities of rum to satisfy the growing demand for that spirit. English middlemen took advantage of this situation and ordered their West India factors to exchange English manufactures and other plantation supplies for the cheaper foreign sugar products. The foreign commodities were then shipped to England or sold to North American traders disguised as commodities of British growth.

At the end of Queen Anne's War in 1713 large quantities of foreign sugar were reported to have been imported into England by way of the British sugar colonies. According to one account, which was written in 1732,

> Barbadoes used formerly to trade with the French and Dutch, and by taking off their sugars, prevented their seeking out for other Markets. They got by this means the Sugar Trade almost entirely into their own Hands, or at least had made themselves the common channel of that Trade.

The profitable interisland trade also attracted the merchants and factors of the Leeward Islands which were only a few miles distant from several foreign sugar islands. In April of 1722 the governor of St. Kitts described the nature of this trade as follows:

> There is a most pernicious and unlawful trade carried on between these Islands and the French Islands, which could not (otherwise) be supplied with provisions, materials for shipbuilding, horses and sugar works. . . . Our purchasing sugars from the French increases our duties, employs our ships, and has other advantages; but submits whether a present conveniency shall outweigh the strong probability of a future ruin.

The direction of interisland trade was thus reversed, and whereas foreign markets were formerly supplied with British sugar by way of the foreign sugar colonies, now foreign sugar entered England by way of the British sugar colonies. The effect of this trade was to raise the price of English manufactures and other plantation supplies to British planters, and to depress the price of sugar and other West India produce in island and home markets.

The second political issue arose over the North American and Irish trade with the foreign sugar colonies. Until the latter years of the seventeenth century it appears that North American and Irish merchants confined their Caribbean trade almost exclusively to the British sugar colonies. But early in the next century they began to trade with the foreign sugar colonies on an increasing scale. In addition to finding new markets for their plantation supplies, the Irish and North American traders were able to purchase the foreign sugar, rum, and molasses more cheaply. This trade assumed such large dimensions at the close of the war in 1713 that British planters complained that they were forced to pay abnormally high prices for lumber, horses, and provisions, and that they were deprived of the profitable North American and Irish markets for their sugar products.

The third political issue arose over the attempts of London sugar buyers, particularly the refiners and grocers, to form combinations for the purpose of depressing wholesale sugar prices in the metropolis. Although buying combinations were a persistent feature of the sugar trade, they became an object of planter hostility in the 1730's when shrinking export markets and expanded sugar production in the British colonies threatened to glut the home market. Undoubtedly these were the prime factors responsible for the temporary decline in the English price level, but there is so much evidence of sugar-buying combinations in the literature of the period that these organizations most probably aggravated the fundamental difficulty.

One planter wrote to the *Barbados Gazette* in 1735, complaining that

> Another great Misfortune (or rather a pernicious Evil) that Attends the Loss of our Exportation Trade, is that for Want of that Evacuation, our most general Market at Home has been overstocked with Sugars, which gives an Opportunity to the Buyers to enter into Combinations, to beat down the Price as low as they please. This practice is now grown too notorious to need Explanation, and is what every Shipper is fully apprized of, by his last Letters from London.

The Market Strategy of the British Sugar Planters

British planters thus had three main problems to solve: to keep foreign sugar from entering England by way of the British sugar colonies; to prohibit North American and Irish merchants from trading with the foreign sugar colonies; and to combat the English refiners and grocers who formed buying combinations to depress the price of sugar.

The planters first attacked the problem of introducing foreign sugar into England because it could be dealt with by political action in the sugar colonies. West India politics was mainly a struggle between merchants and planters, and the period from 1650 to 1750 witnessed a decided shift in power from the former to the latter. The change from an economy of small farmers to one of large sugar planters was accompanied by changes in marketing and finance. As more and more large planters took over the marketing of their produce through English commission agents, the number of local merchants and factors declined. The merchants appear to have been dominant in local politics during the transition to large-scale production of sugar, but their political influence declined along with their economic power. By the early years of the eighteenth century wealthy planters held a majority of seats in most of the island legislatures, and they used their influence to cut off a branch of trade that threatened to undermine their economic and political supremacy.

Barbadoes took the lead in attacking the interisland trade. In March of 1715 the legislature passed an act laying prohibitive duties on foreign sugar and other tropical commodities imported into that island. Antigua followed the lead of Barbados and passed a similar measure in November of 1715. This law was repealed when it failed to curb interisland trade, and in June of 1716 another act was passed which prohibited the importation of French and other foreign sugar, rum, molasses, and cotton. The Act of 1716 was disallowed by an Order in Council in May of 1719; and in 1721 Antigua passed another act laying prohibitive duties on the import of foreign sugar, molasses, rum, cotton, and ginger. In 1764 the Assembly of Antigua revived an earlier resolution and declared that every person engaged in such trade "is an Enemy to his Country and . . . is unworthy to be a Member of civil society."

In Jamaica the planters had difficulty in suppressing the interisland trade because it was supported by a powerful body of local merchants. In spite of strong opposition, however, the planters put through an act in 1715 to prevent fraudulent trade with St. Domingue. Another act was passed in 1726 which imposed heavy penalties for importing French sugar, indigo, and other tropical commodities and reshipping them to England. The planters found it difficult to enforce these acts, and in 1756 they passed an act which prohibited the import of foreign sugar, rum, and molasses. It provided that any violator "shall be deemed guilty of Felony and suffer Death as a Felon without benefit of Clergy." When the act was sent to England to be confirmed, the Privy Council was shocked by its harsh penalties and forthwith disallowed it.

It is difficult to say how effective these acts were in keeping foreign sugar out of English markets. While harsher penalties were a deterring influence, it is believed that the changing structure of the sugar trade was partly responsible for curtailing the trade. The growth of the commission system led to the decline of independent island merchants who were notorious for their participation in clandestine interisland trade. One of the consequences of these acts was to raise the price of sugar products in the British West Indies, and to force North American and Irish merchants to trade more extensively with the foreign sugar colonies.

Local political influence thus served the planters in their efforts to keep foreign sugar out of the home market. But political influence was needed in the English government if the planters were to combat the English buyers of sugar and prevent the North American and Irish merchants from trading with the foreign sugar colonies. Generally speaking, there were three classes of men who looked after the political interests of the planters in England—absentee planters, agents of the various colonial governments, and commission agents or merchants. During the seventeenth century these three groups were not very influential because few planters had as yet amassed enough wealth to become absentees, there were as yet only a few commission merchants, and the practice of appointing colonial agents was still in its infancy. Furthermore, the sugar colonies had few interests in common.

During the first half of the eighteenth century the West India interest gradually acquired more political influence in the home government. It became a general practice for colonial governments to appoint agents, many of whom were prominent planters, to look after their affairs in England. The agents were constantly soliciting the government in behalf of the planters, cultivating friendships with prominent politicians, submitting evidence to parliamentary committees and government officials, writing pamphlets, and welding together the West India interest so that its weight could be thrown on the side of the planters in any controversy affecting the sugar trade. Professor Penson records in this connection:

> At the time when the greatest successes were won for the West India interest, the agents were aided by the assistance of a powerful body of men, including Beckford, the intimate associate of the Elder Pitt, and a vast number of others whose wealth could command influence in British politics.

Commission merchants also increased in number and influence, and by the middle of the eighteenth century they were handling practically all of the sugar and other West India produce that was marketed in London. These merchants were generally recruited from prominent planter families, and many of them were diligent in pleading the case of the planters. Several wealthy commission merchants became prominent in the City of London and the House of Commons. William Beckford, Samuel Pennant, and Slingsby Bethell held the office of Lord Mayor of London; and there were a number of merchants like Beckford, Bethell, Henry Lascelles, Arnold Nesbitt, Richard Oliver, and Rose Fuller who were members of Parliament. The close community of interest among planters and commission merchants was borne out by a contemporary who wrote that English merchants who received consignments from the West Indies "commonly speak the language of those that employ them."

Absentee planters also played an active role in English politics during the eighteenth century. A West Indian estimated in 1732 that there were constantly one hundred gentlemen from Barbados in England. From the late 1730's to the mid-1760's a considerable number of planters from the Leeward Islands and Jamaica amassed sizable fortunes and retired to England. Not all of these absentees took an active part in English politics, but a substantial number became members of Parliament and worked actively to promote the sugar trade. The independent merchants and traders of London complained in 1754 that absentees were able

> to support contests in some of the richest and most populous cities in this Country. No less than three brothers from one of our Sugar-islands having offered themselves, one for London, one for Bristol, and one for Salisbury; and a fourth brother, according to what has

been published in the publick papers, intended for a Wiltshire Borough.

Contemporary and modern writers support the conclusion that the political influence of the West India interest was at its height from the early 1730's to the late 1760's. According to Professor Penson,

> It was not until the middle of the struggle of the years 1730–1733 over the illicit trade between the continental colonies and the French West Indies that the combination of strength that was so marked a feature of the middle of the latter part of the century came into evidence.

In February of 1744 it was noted in the *Parliamentary History* "how many were either by themselves or their friends, deeply concerned in one part or other of the sugar trade, and that the cause itself was always popular in the House of Commons."

The main problems that the planters hoped to solve by means of parliamentary legislation were said to be the North American and Irish trade with the foreign sugar colonies and the combination of London sugar refiners and grocers. These two problems need to be considered together because the planters understood that the solution of one would contribute to the solution of the other. In other words, if the planters had a forced market in Ireland and North America, they could channel part of their commodities to these markets and thus force English buyers to pay higher prices for the smaller proportion shipped to the home market. At the same time, the planters hoped to secure legislation that would confine the trade of North America and Ireland to the British sugar colonies so they would be able to purchase plantation supplies more cheaply. A pamphleteer for the Northern Colonies wrote in 1732 that the view of the sugar planters

> is to force the Northern Colonies into a Necessity of buying their Sugars, Rum and Molasses, of them at their own Rate, and in Consequence thereof, to confine the Northern Colonies would very greatly lessen the Quantity of Sugar usually sent to the Sugar Islands; and should the prohibition desired take place, the Sugar Planters might in great measure do the same to Great Britain itself in the Article of Sugar; for though that commodity is now near double the Price it was for many Years after the Sugar Islands were first settled, yet the entire Supply to the Northern Colonies would very greatly lessen the

Quantity of Sugar usually sent Home, and in all probability occasion a great Rise in its Price, and there would be but little, if any, for Re-exportation to other Markets, at least we could not then pretend to cope with those Kingdoms and States who have Sugar Colonies of their own.

The West India interest gained its first parliamentary victory in 1732 when an act was passed that granted liberty to export rum and other unenumerated commodities directly from the British sugar colonies to Ireland. A more important victory was gained the following year when the famous Molasses Act was passed in the face of strong opposition from the North American colonies. This act levied prohibitive duties on all foreign sugar, molasses, and rum imported into the American colonies. Moreover, it barred French sugar, molasses, and rum from Ireland; and other foreign and British sugar that was imported into Ireland had to be shipped from Great Britain in vessels that conformed to the Navigation Acts. The West India interest benefited from these and other restrictions upon the trade of Ireland.

Not content with a forced market for their commodities in Ireland and North America, the planters thought that an act granting liberty to ship plantation sugar directly to foreign markets would serve as an additional weapon against the English buyers of sugar. In 1735 a correspondent wrote to the *Barbados Gazette* the two things were needed if the planters were to secure relief from their misfortunes: "A more free and open Trade, with an easier Access to the Foreign Markets, [and] Some effectual method to prevent all unnatural combinations to depreciate the Commodity." He argued that the achievement of the first objective would in some measure contribute toward the second,

for whatever Sugars pass by the General Market, will keep that Market so much the thinner, and in some Degree help to break those evil Combinations. For the more the Commodity is dispersed, and the nearer it is laid to the Consumer, the better it will go off, since if the Market is not glutted in any one Place, the Price will be the better in all Places: But if too great a Quantity falls the Price at the most general Market, that will influence all the rest, and give Room for Combinations to beat it down still lower.

When a bill for a direct trade was introduced into Parliament in April of 1739, petitions against the bill were presented by the merchants of Bristol, Liverpool, London, Chester, Lancaster, and Whitehaven. The petitioners contended that such a trade would open the manufacturing countries of northern Europe to colonial shipping and curtail the sale of English manufactures in the colonies, and that it would hurt British navigation and the trade of English middlemen. The sugar refiners of London also presented a petition which complained that passage of the bill would raise the price of raw sugar in English markets and curtail the export of refined sugar. Pitman relates that the "planting interest denied that the passage of the bill would raise prices, and asserted that they could produce three times as much sugar as they did." After the contending interests were heard by the Lords and Commons, the bill was finally passed on June 12, 1739; and permission was granted to ship sugar directly from the plantations to any foreign port in Europe.

The question arises as to why the planters solicited Parliament for permission to export sugar directly to foreign markets when higher prices were realized from sales in the protected home market. Had the planters been organized into a cartel, they might have dumped sugar in foreign markets in order to keep up the price at home. There is no evidence, however, that such a cartel was formed; and individual planters were not willing to sell their sugar at lower prices in foreign markets merely to benefit other planters who patronized the home market. The evidence suggests that the motive of the planters was to force English refiners and grocers to pay higher prices by threatening to ship sugar to foreign markets. A Customs House document records that, between 1739 and 1753, only five ships carried a total of 777 hogsheads, 184 tierces, 253 casks, and 126 barrels of sugar to foreign markets south of Cape Finisterre; but that 48 licenses were granted to carry sugar to these markets. The reason for taking out so many unused licenses was explained in a letter from Rose Fuller in Jamaica to James Knight in London as follows:

> The great cause of it [the low price of sugar] is the combination of sugar bakers: they have it in their power to meet and agree what they shall give for our commodities, but all their combinations can never prevail if we can bring it about that sugars may not be quite so plenty in England as they have been of late years . . . we propose that every ship that comes from London to load here shall bring a license to carry sugars directly to foreign markets either to those to the southward or to the northward and as this license can be had for fifteen

shillings, if they make no use of it it will be but a small cost to the ship, and if it has no other effect it will at least alarm the bakers and keep them in a state of suspence what sugars will be sent to foreign markets.

If the Direct Export Act accomplished little more than to give the planters a weapon to harass the sugar buyers, the other measures were quite effective in expanding the protected market for West India commodities in the British Isles. This was especially the case with Ireland, where the planters were successful in diverting trade from the sugar colonies of France to those of Great Britain. Prior to 1732 Ireland carried on an extensive trade with France and the French sugar colonies. Large quantities of French spirits were imported into Ireland, and it appears that the English government imposed few if any restrictions upon this trade. Ireland was importing so much French wine and brandy in 1727 that the value of these imports exceeded the value of all Irish exports to France. French sugar planters benefited from the Irish trade, for Arthur Dobbs records that Ireland's exports to France during the year ending Lady Day, 1727 consisted of beef, butter, raw hides, and tallow to the value of £137,702, most of which products were then sent to the French West Indies to supply the needs of the planters. In return for these commodities, French wine, brandy, and sugar to the value of about £145,000 were imported into Ireland. After stating that France was more dependent upon Irish provisions for her sugar colonies than was Ireland dependent upon French wine and brandy, Dobbs proposed that

> if we had Rum and Sugars at the cheapest Hand from the [British] Plantations we should be encourag'd to distil Spirits from Sugar at Home, and to make Use of Rum instead of *French* Brandy. . . . This would increase our Demand for Sugars and Rum; and the Colonies would reap great part of the Benefit which France and the French Islands reap now by our Trade.

British sugar planters were also aware of the possibilities of the Irish market, and in the early 1730's they pushed through the above-mentioned acts of Parliament which restricted the foreign and colonial trade of Ireland and gave their commodities preferential treatment in that market. Apparently these measures were quite successful, for a contemporary wrote in 1745 that since the passage of the Act of 1732 "great

Quantities of British Rum have since been imported and consum'd there, instead of French Rum and French Brandy." Although substantial quantities of French rum were smuggled into Ireland after 1733, the legal imports, made up largely of British colonial rum, amounted to between one and two million gallons in the period from 1763 to 1772.

Ireland also became an important market for British plantation sugar after 1733. The sugar refiners and grocers of London alleged in their petition of 1754 that "the Home Consumption of Ireland is greatly increased of late years by the Increase of Refiners and Refining Houses." After 1733 Irish and North American vessels smuggled an undetermined quantity of French sugar into Ireland and some Portuguese sugar was entered legally, but it appears that Ireland was chiefly supplied with British plantation sugar that was re-exported from the mother country. In fact, the Irish market took off the greater part of England's sugar re-exports. If these re-exports are considered as part of the home consumption, between 95 and 97 per cent of the sugar imports of the British Isles were retained for home consumption in the period from 1733 to 1756.

In addition to Ireland, British planters had previously acquired a protected market for their commodities when the Art of Union brought Scotland within the scope of the Navigation Acts in 1707. Growing quantities of sugar and rum were channeled to that market. Glasgow became an important port for trade with the West Indies, and the sugar trade came to rank second in importance only to the prosperous tobacco trade of that port. The West India trade of Glasgow did not commence until about 1732, but by 1735 there were four ships from that port trading to Jamaica, one to Barbados, one to Antigua, and two to St. Kitts. During the greater part of the period from 1650 to 1750 it appears that Edinburgh, Leith, Dundee, and other east coast ports in Scotland were supplied with sugar by coastwise vessels from London. By the middle of the eighteenth century, however, the consumption of these port cities and the areas they supplied had increased to such an extent that direct trade was established with the British sugar colonies. Walter Tullideph, a sugar planter of Antigua, ordered his plantation attorneys to consign part of his sugar directly to merchants in Glasgow, Leith, and Dundee after he retired to Scotland in 1757. A sugar refinery was established at Edinburgh in 1751, and its articles of copartnership stated

The Market Strategy of the British Sugar Planters

That the Consumpt of SUGARS in the CITY of EDINBURGH, and the Neighbourhood thereof, is much increased; and that an Intercourse of Trade is now carried on between the Port of LEITH and the SUGAR-COLONIES in the BRITISH AMERICAN PLANTATIONS, whereby the Trade and MANUFACTURE of refining and baking SUGARS in EDINBURGH, or the Suburbs thereof, may be very beneficial.

The fourth forced market was the British North American colonies. Although the northern colonists were consuming larger quantities of sugar, the demand for British-grown sugar is often dismissed as insignificant in the period following enactment of the Molasses Act because it is assumed that clandestine traders adequately supplied these markets with sugar of French and Dutch growth. Contemporaries do report numerous violations of the Molasses Act, especially by merchants and traders from the New England and Middle Colonies, but at the same time the evidence suggests that the consumption of British Caribbean sugar in North America increased appreciably in the period before the American Revolution. Antigua, for example, was supplied with large quantities of provisions and lumber by North American traders during the years of peace from 1748 to 1756, and Tullideph wrote in April of 1751, "I never knew so much Sugar Ship't to North America, as hath been since I Arrived." Trade between North America and the British sugar colonies was interrupted during the Seven Years' War from 1756 to 1763; but in 1774 Edward Long, the historian of Jamaica, wrote, "it is well known that since the late war the consumption of it [sugar] in North America has been double what it used to be." Stricter enforcement of the Navigation Acts after the Seven Years' War and the Sugar Act of 1764 may have forced more sugar into North American markets.

Although foreign molasses practically displaced British molasses in North American markets, sizable quantities of British rum continued to be consumed in the northern colonies prior to the War of Independence. By far the greater part of the market was supplied with cheap rum which was distilled in the New England colonies from foreign molasses, but in all of the colonies there were some discriminating customers who insisted upon the quality rum that was imported from the British sugar colonies.

The evidence is too meager to warrant any conclusions concerning the North American market, but it is certain that British sugar planters gained an enlarged and protected home market that was far superior to the foreign market. They also gained room to maneuver against their enemies. It has been pointed out that planters repeatedly complained of the buying combinations of London sugar refiners and grocers, and that the Molasses Act and the Direct Export Act were intended, in part, at least, to break up these combinations.

To understand how planters exploited the opportunities afforded by these acts it is necessary to describe the changing nature of the sugar-marketing organization. Sugar was originally imported into London by merchants who traded on their own account with the West Indies. But as more and more planters marketed sugar through London commission agents, the independent merchants of that port declined in number until only a few remained by the middle of the eighteenth century. On the other hand, the transition to the agency system of marketing proceeded at a slower pace in the English outports and North America, and the sugar trade of these regions remained largely in the hands of independent merchants during the first half of the eighteenth century. The virtual elimination of independent London merchants meant that practically all of the sugar that was sold in the West Indies was purchased by the factors and supercargoes of outport and North American merchants. Under these circumstances large planters could either sell their sugar in the West Indies, in which event it by-passed the London market, or they could consign it to their London commission agents.

Although there was a long-run tendency for planters to market more sugar through commission agents, it appears that in some years the planters chose to sell the bulk of their sugar in the West Indies, and that to some extent their motive for doing so was to force up the price of that commodity in the London market. A writer on the trade of London and the outports alleged that many planters were selling sugar in the West Indies rather than consigning it to London agents. He recorded in 1749:

> The Trade carried on from the Out-Ports to America, tho' indeed more hazardous and less profitable, yet is less *precarious* than that carried on from London, as it does not depend so much upon the Humour of the Planters; who, if many of them now choose to sell their Commodities at a certain Price [in the West Indies] rather than to pay Freight, Insurance, Commission, and many other Charges, and afterwards run the risk of an uncertain Market, they doubtless have *their Reasons* for so *acting.*

The Market Strategy of the British Sugar Planters

Besides selling sugar in the West Indies, some of the larger planters by-passed the London market by consigning sugar and rum to commission agents in the English outports, Ireland, and Scotland. In the period from 1741 to 1767 Tullideph had agents at Bristol, Liverpool, Lancaster, Glasgow, Leith, Dundee, Cork, and Dublin to whom he consigned plantation produce. On several occasions he noted how the demand from these markets influenced the price of sugar in London. For example, he wrote from London in September of 1753 that "our Sugar Mercatt hath been a little brisker oweing to a demand from Leverpoole, Scotland, and Ireland."

Although London declined relatively to the outports as a sugar importer, she retained her supremacy as the great sugar market of Europe. It was here that buyers and sellers came into direct conflict with one another. Sugar refiners and grocers frequently entered into agreements to refrain from buying when prices were high, while planters retaliated by instructing their agents to hold sugar off the market when prices were low. "The bakers have stop't these 3 weeks past, which hath thrown a damp on the Sales, but they must soon come to mercatt again & then Sugars will be brisker," wrote Tullideph from London in July of 1754.

The planters were so successful in their attempts to raise the price of sugar that buyers were forced to seek parliamentary assistance. In March of 1753 the refiners, grocers, and other dealers in sugar of the cities of London and Westminster and the borough of Southwark presented a petition to the House of Commons detailing their grievances against the planters. A similar petition was presented by the grocers and refiners of Bristol, and a Committee of the Whole House was appointed to hear testimony. The following allegations were made by the London petitioners:

That the Price of *Muscovado* Sugar is become excessively high, owing to a deficient Importation from our Sugar Colonies in America. . . .

That ever since Lady-Day 1749, the Sugar Planters have received for their Sugars a much higher Price than what they did for many years before the Commencement of the late War. . . .

That the foreign Markets are supplied with Sugar from the *French* at less than half the Price it is here sold for, exclusive of all Duties paid here; and the Price of Sugars at the British Sugar

Colonies is more than double the Price of what it is at the *French* Sugar Colonies.

That the excessive Gain of the British Planters by a deficient Importation (all foreign Sugars being excluded by Duties which amount to a Prohibition) may be a Temptation to them to forbear breaking up more Land for Sugar Plantations, especially in the Island of Jamaica, where your Petitioners are informed large Tracts of Land fit for that Purpose do remain uncultivated.

Evidence was submitted to substantiate these allegations. For example, sugar at London was quoted at 44 shillings per hundredweight in 1753, as compared with an average of not more than 19 shillings "per C[wt]. English Weight and English Money" at Bordeaux, Rochelle, and Dunkirk.

After making these and other allegations the petitioners asked the House of Commons "to make it the Interest of the British Sugar Colonies to produce and send home a larger Quantity of Sugar to Great Britain . . . , or to grant any other Relief, as to their great Wisdom shall seem meet."

Although no remedial measures were taken by the British Government at this time, the well-substantiated charges of the London sugar buyers occasioned no little alarm among the planter interest. In April of 1754 Tullideph wrote of his fear that the supply of plantation sugar might not be adequate to satisfy the home consumption, "and if that ever happens to be our case, I fear our Enemies the Bakers & Grocers will make Application for leave to Import French Sugars." Four years later, in November of 1758, he wrote that "whenever any Commodity rises too high, various projects are formed to introduce it from other places & therefore whenever Sugars are from 45/ to 50/ [shillings per hundredweight] it is dangerous to expect more."

By this time the planters were afraid that their strategy had become too successful. They were confronted by a growing chorus of critics. Probably the leading critic was Joseph Massie, a voluminous writer of pamphlets on various economic questions of the day. In a pamphlet entitled *A State of the British Sugar-Colony Trade* of 1759, he enumerated the many favors that had been conferred upon the planters during the past thirty years. These included the liberty to import British colonial rum directly into Ireland; the prohibition of French sugar, rum, and molasses imports into Ireland; the high duties levied on all foreign sugars, rum, and molasses imported into the British North American colonies; the liberty to carry British sugar directly from the sugar colonies to any foreign port in Europe; the liberty of landing rum in Great Britain without "paying the Duty of Excise until such Rum be sold, or hath been landed Six Months"; and the prohibitory duties levied on all foreign sugars imported into Great Britain. After reciting these many benefits, Massie estimated that the "exorbitant Gain which the Sugar-Planters have made, over and above large Profits," amounted to £8,000,000 for the thirty-year period. Altogether, he estimated the "Loss that hath been brought upon the People of Great Britain, by the Misdoings of the British Sugar-Planters, within Thirty years past," to amount to £20,650,000.

Massie's pamphlet appeared at the zenith of the sugar planters' prosperity and political influence. After that time the West India interest slowly declined as a result of such factors as a marked expansion of sugar production in the British West Indies, the American War of Independence, the growing sentiment in favor of free trade, and the agitation to prohibit the British slave trade.

In conclusion, it appears that while the Molasses Act may be dismissed as a near failure in its application to the North American colonies, it cannot be so regarded with reference to the British Isles. Actually, it proved to be quite effective in expanding the protected home market to include Ireland. The success of the planter interest may be attributed to four main developments. First, the consumption of sugar and rum underwent considerable expansion in England as a consequence of population growth, rising living standards, and the widespread consumption of tea, coffee, and punch. Second, the supply of sugar forthcoming from the plantations tended to lag behind the demand. Third, changes in the Navigation Acts allowed sugar products to go to Ireland and Scotland; and fourth, comparatively little foreign sugar invaded the protected home market. These forces conspired to force British sugar prices well above the level prevailing upon the Continent of Europe, and the planter interest enjoyed a period of excessive profits which continued with little abatement from the late 1730's to the end of the Seven Years' War in 1763.

19. AMERICAN ECONOMIC GROWTH
BEFORE 1840*

An Exploratory Essay

by George R. Taylor

Once the American colonists won their independence, they enjoyed advantages which many of the new nations today lack. Well before the American Revolution the colonial economy, according to George R. Taylor's estimates, demonstrated a capacity for sustained growth so that when industrialization began in the nineteenth century, per capita income was well above that of most underdeveloped nations currently struggling to modernize traditional productive systems. The colonial achievement involved the development of an extensive, indigenous, and experienced merchant community and a vigorous urban sector, resources lacking in many of the new nations today. Another fruit of colonial economic growth was a high average standard of living, which impressed European visitors who remarked on

* *Journal of Economic History*, vol. 24 (1964), 427–444. Footnotes have been omitted except where they are necessary for an understanding of the text.

the healthiness, fecundity, and general prosperity of the Americans. As a result, when Americans struggled to create a stable political order in the decades after Independence, they enjoyed largely favorable economic conditions. The young republic did not have to worry about feeding its citizens or coping with impoverished elements threatening the social peace. The achievement of a relatively high standard of material comfort was thus a profoundly important legacy of the colonial period. Why was the American experience so different from that of other former European colonies?

In developing the subject of this paper, "American Economic Growth before 1840," I shall, relying for the most part on familiar materials, propose the hypothesis that economic growth per capita in the thirteen colonies of Britain in America advanced at a relatively rapid rate from about 1710 to 1775. I shall also suggest that the level of living remained relatively low in these colonies as late as about 1710 and that for the new nation output per capita over the years 1775 to 1840 improved slowly if at all.

Quantitative studies in economic history, particularly those having to do with growth over appreciable periods of time, necessarily involve, to an extent often forgotten or ignored, basic assumptions and value judgments. Even under the most favorable circumstances, data (never complete) have to be *manipulated* on the basis of *reasonable* assumptions. And price indices require *adjustment* because the importance of the items included changes over time. Moreover, rates of productivity or growth should, if one is to be precise, be designated as rates of *measured* growth, for much of the contribution made to better living standards, for example by improved technical knowledge and business organization, defies quantification. So, as students well know but sometimes forget, growth rates computed over appreciable time spans imply a spurious exactness.

Nevertheless, if the limitations are kept in mind, attempts to determine numerical rates of growth may prove interesting and useful even where considerable reliance must be placed on nonquantitative material. Despite faulty and imperfect information, students have combined careful analysis and bold assumptions to determine numerical values for the rate of economic growth in the United States since 1839. This accomplishment stimulates curiosity as to the rate of growth before that date, in a period when data were even less complete. Many detailed studies need to be made before important questions can be answered with assurance. This essay constitutes merely a probing of this area—an effort primarily directed to making a tentative estimate of the rate of per capita growth from about 1710 to 1775, using the quantitative and qualitative materials readily at hand. It is hoped that the speculative conclusions sketched will provoke further investigation.

Raymond W. Goldsmith, in his testimony in Washington before the Joint Economic Committee in 1959, focused his attention on the period 1839–1959. He concluded that the national product per head adjusted for price changes had averaged, in the one hundred twenty years since 1839, close to $1\frac{5}{8}$ per cent per year. Incidentally, he raised the question as to the rate of American economic growth before 1839 —a period for which quantitative data did not permit reliable measurement. He concluded, on the basis of two alternative lines of reasoning, that the long-run rate of $1\frac{5}{8}$ per cent could not be extended backward into the pre-1839 period. His two lines of reasoning are briefly summarized.

First, assuming that the average real income per person in 1760 could not have been less than half the level of 1860, it follows that the average rate of growth per person from 1760 to 1839 was only about six tenths of 1 per cent per annum. If this estimate approximates the true picture, it then follows that the trend line of growth from 1760 to 1839 was much flatter (rose less sharply) than it did thereafter. In fact, under this assumption it equaled only about one third the subsequent annual growth rate.

Following an alternative line of reasoning, Goldsmith concluded that a continuous rate of per capita growth as high as $1\frac{5}{8}$ per cent per year was inconceivable for the pre-1839 period. Assuming the post-1839 growth rate projected backward from that year implies cutting in half the per capita income every forty-three years. So, if the average income per person in 1839 was about $400, based on present prices (as he suggests), the income per capita would have been $145 in 1776, $80 in 1739, and $30 in 1676. Studies of American living levels indicate that these average incomes are absurdly small for the late colonial period and for seventeenth-century America as well.

On such reasoning Goldsmith concluded:

There seems little doubt, then, that the average rate of growth of real income per head was much lower than 1⅝ percent before 1839. If we consider periods of at least 50 years' length, it is questionable that we would find an average rate of growth as high as 1 percent in any one of them. There thus must have occurred a fairly sharp break in the trend of real national product per head some time before 1839. . . . I would hazard a guess . . . that the break occurred not very long before 1839 and that it reflects both the transition of the United States from a predominately agricultural to a more and more industrial country and the advent of the railroads.

Goldsmith's suggestions (he clearly regards them as no more than that) open up interesting lines of inquiry. Though his deductions as to pre-1839 growth are generally acceptable, I question his supposition that 1839 may have been preceded by an extended period of gradual growth at a rate of 0.6 per cent per year, as well as his conclusion that in no period of fifty years' duration before 1839 was the annual growth rate as high as 1 per cent. My own hypothesis is that until about 1710 growth was slow, irregular, and not properly measured in percentage terms; that from about 1710 to 1775 the average rate of growth was relatively rapid for a preindustrial economy (perhaps 1 per cent per capita or even a little higher); and that from 1775 until 1840, or possibly a decade earlier, *average* per capita production showed very little if any increase.

I

More than a century intervened between the first permanent settlement in Virginia in 1607 and the chartering of the Colony of Georgia in 1732. In any meaningful sense, economic growth in the British continental colonies must have been relatively slow and uneven during most of the seventeenth century. Not only did the machinery of government have to be established and gradually adapted to meet local conditions, but the early years were devoted to pushing back the Indians, learning to exploit immediate sources of income from fishing and trading in furs and deerskins, experimenting in raising agricultural crops, and the slow development of trade and communications both at home and with the rest of the Empire. By the Peace of Utrecht (1713) or a little later, the early costs of economic experiment had, in most colonies, become largely a matter of the past. The colonies stood at the beginning of an era of remarkable development. Growth before this time was, of course, important in laying the basis for future development, but it does not appear to have been generally very great in any absolute sense. Measurement in percentage growth rates for the seventeenth century is on the whole rather meaningless because increases must be computed from zero or at least from a very small base.

If productivity is measured by exports, the British West Indian possessions greatly surpassed the British North American colonies. But if size of population, the extent of settled territory, the number of independent farmers, and the development of an indigenous commerce and industry are compared, then, at least by the eighteenth century, a decided advantage lay with the mainland colonies of Great Britain. Perhaps the best overall evidence for the rapid increase in the gross product of the British North American colonies lies in the rapid population increase. It is estimated that the population in 1700 consisted of about 224,000 white persons and 28,000 negroes. By 1774, the whites numbered about 2,100,000 and the negroes 500,000. The large size of this white population of European origin on the eve of the Revolution deserves emphasis. It equaled more than one fourth that of the mother country and was perhaps sixty times that of the British Caribbean. In fact the white population of the thirteen colonies attained in the first three fourths of the eighteenth century a rapid and sustained growth unique in colonial history.

If one measures by gross product or by per capita productivity of the free population, a strong case can be made for the conclusion that rapid economic growth characterized the plantation areas of the southern colonies for the sixty years beginning about 1710 or a little later. If the slaves be included in the reckoning, the rate of per capita output would be reduced, for the number of slaves increased more rapidly than the whites during these decades.

Tobacco became the staple produce of tidewater Virginia and of Maryland soon after these colonies were founded early in the seventeenth century. Though the white population grew rapidly and a few great planters prospered, judging from contemporary reports, the average level of living for the white population improved slowly if at all until toward the end of the seventeenth century But the second and third quarters of the eighteenth century brought rapid growth and the great age of colonial tobacco culture. European markets for tobacco expanded greatly, and the increasing importation of African slaves after about 1680 apparently lowered the cost of tobacco production. By 1700, the slaves in Virginia totaled about 16,000. Their numbers had risen to 30,000 in 1730 (about 26 per cent of the total population); over 100,000 in 1750; and nearly 300,000 by 1790. The Maryland experience was similar. By 1770, the population of that colony reached 203,000, of which 64,000 were slaves.

This prosperous tobacco economy depended on slave labor. Most independent yeoman farmers either drifted out to the frontier or became the owners of at least a few slaves. The large plantations, some with hundreds of slaves, now increased in number and proved the most profitable producing units. Thomas J. Wertenbaker describes the situation as follows:

> . . . the Eighteenth century was the golden age of the Virginia slave holders. It was then that they built the handsome homes once so numerous in the older counties, many of which still remain as interesting monuments of former days; it was then that they surrounded themselves with graceful furniture and costly silverware, in large part imported from Great Britain; it was then that they collected paintings and filled their libraries with the works of standard writers; it was then that they purchased coaches and berlins; it was then that men and women alike wore rich and expensive clothing.

In the more southern plantation area, that centering in tidewater South Carolina, settlement came late in the seventeenth century and plantation rice culture expanded rapidly in the opening decades of the eighteenth century. To this plantation slave economy, indigo was added as a profitable crop in the late 1740's. The economic growth in this region after about 1715 appears to have been even more rapid than in the tobacco colonies. The average annual Carolina rice crop increased fourteen times from 1716–1720 to 1771–1775. Indigo production expanded tremendously after 1753. From 1747 to 1754, annual exports from Charleston averaged only about sixty-five thousand pounds, but by 1772–1775, the average had grown by more than twelve times. In commenting on the prosperity of this area just preceding the Revolution, Lewis C. Gray cites an estimate which places the return on rice production at nearly 30 per cent on the capital invested and even higher for indigo.

David Ramsay, a respected authority on South Carolina history, states that "few countries have at any time exhibited so striking an instance of public and private prosperity, as appeared in South-Carolina between the years 1725 and 1775." According to him, frugal and industrious planters doubled their capital every three or four years, "laborers on good lands cleared their first cost and charges in a few years," and immigrant settlers "commonly left their children in easy circumstances." These statements appear extreme and much further study is needed. But it seems probable that South Carolina during these years enjoyed a more rapid economic growth per capita than any other American colony—and perhaps than that of any other colony or county in the world. This statement seems justified if production growth is measured per white person. If all persons, both slave and free, are counted, it may still be true for the South Carolina plantation area and possibly for the whole southern plantation region.

II

The farming area of the thirteen colonies extended from the banks of the Kennebec River in southern Maine (then a part of Massachusetts) along the seacoast to Maryland in a strip of varying depth and then inland beyond the coastal plantations down the western piedmont and the mountain valleys to the Savannah River in Georgia. This vast region varied greatly as to time of settlement and development of population density. Individual ownership of small family-sized farms was the rule. And though many farms, especially those on the more remote frontier, were self-sufficient, this must not be overstressed. The colonial farmer, seldom far removed from water transportation, always sought to produce some marketable items. These he often supplemented by part-time activities such as hunting, trapping, and fishing; by exploiting the forests for masts, ashes, and naval stores; and in some of the northern colonies by digging iron from bogs and ponds.

Available clues point to rapid growth in this farming area following the initial difficulties of settlement and adjustment to new conditions. Population increased tremendously. Excluding persons living in the plantation region and in cities of 2,500 or more, the inhabitants of the colonial farming region numbered by 1775 approximately 1,700,000, making up about 80 per cent of the total white population of the thirteen colonies. Both immigration and rapid natural increase brought this white population (there were very few negroes) to a total actually greatly exceeding the number of settlers of European origin living in all other colonies at that time.

Along with this population expansion came a growing tide of products from land and sea. Although returns from hunting and trapping declined as the settled area spread, forest products increased greatly; and iron production, after growing slowly until about 1750, expanded so rapidly thereafter that, by 1775, one seventh of the world's annual iron production came from the American colonies. Except for such items as iron, forest products, and ships, Great Britain took very little of the surplus production of the middle and New England colonies. But other markets expanded during the eighteenth century—southern Europe, the West Indies, and the northern cities. Increasingly after about 1700, merchant traders operated a growing fleet of small trading vessels on the navigable rivers and on the bays and little harbors along the extended American coast, exchanging a variety of items from the outside world for local products.

Clearly the gross product of this farming region expanded greatly after the early decades of settlement. But determination of the per capita growth rate presents unusual difficulties. Perhaps two confident statements may be made. First, the farming population made up such a large proportion of the total that its per capita productivity assumes special importance. Second, the great extent of the farming area, the variety of products, and the differing conditions of production make estimates of productivity very difficult. A tremendous amount of study will be required before reliable conclusions can be drawn.

Some negative factors may be noted. Farming methods, whether cultivation of crops or the breeding of animals, improved very little during the colonial period and appear to have lagged behind those adopted in England during the eighteenth century. (On the other hand, colonial farm procedures often suited American conditions better than contemporary British critics realized.) Soil exhaustion became a problem, as the century advanced, in areas where good nearby lands could not be cleared. In eastern New England, where this situation early became most troublesome, wheat-growing soon gave way to corn or rye and to the raising of cattle and swine.

On the whole, I find the indications favorable to substantial economic per capita growth in the sixty years preceding the Revolution. The growth of population and the expansion of settlement point in this direction. The records left by contemporaries, though imperfect and at times contradictory, indicate an average level of living on farms in the thirteen colonies which was rising during the eighteenth century and probably was higher than in England in the decades preceding the Revolution. An indirect approach supports this conclusion. Richard B. Morris estimates that real wages of labor exceeded by 30 to 100 per cent the wages paid in England at the time. But urban workmen, even skilled craftsmen, were reportedly leaving the city to become farmers. Perhaps the freedom and independence of farm life helped to draw away these city workers, but they were also attracted by the high returns from farming.

It may also be argued that the people themselves, the farmers and their families, possessed characteristics favorable to economic growth The colonial farmers appear to have been relatively healthy and, at least in most of the New England and middle colonies, better educated than the general run of farm laborers in England. On small, individually owned farms, said Crèvecoeur, the owners developed a "restless energy" and a strong incentive to industry. Their vigor and achievement orientation undoubtedly contributed to their productivity. In a recent study, Theodore W. Schultz concludes that not land or the quantity of material capital but ". . . differences in the capabilities of the farm people are most important in explaining the differences in the amount and rate of increase of agricultural production."

Had the wealth and economic potential of the thirteen Atlantic colonies depended solely on farming, their growth history might have paralleled that of many another slowly developing agricultural settlement. However, along with increasing agricultural output and acting as an essential stimulant to it, urban centers arose in the New England and the middle colonies. Under the leadership of local merchants, an indigenous commercial economy developed, unique in colonial history and conducive to sustained growth.

The great commercial cities of western Europe played a major role in the colonial empires of the sixteenth and seventeenth centuries. But in none of the Continental European empires did colonial cities or the merchants living in them play a significant part in promoting and organizing colonial trade. This also held generally for the British colonies. Privileged English companies monopolized the trade to India and to Hudson Bay, and English and Scottish merchants held so firmly to the tobacco trade with Virginia and Maryland that colonials were largely excluded. Nor, despite the magnitude of the sugar trade, did independent centers of commercial activity spring up in the British West Indies. Bridgetown in Barbados, although the largest center of ocean trade in the British Caribbean, had only a few thousand inhabitants and its commerce was largely directed by merchants living in England or New England.

The single exception developed in New England and the middle colonies, where flourished not only major commercial cities like Boston, New York, and Philadelphia, but a host of smaller ones like Newport, Rhode Island; Albany; and Salem. By 1760, Boston—long the largest city in the thirteen colonies—had about 16,000 inhabitants; New York, 18,000; and Philadelphia, 24,000. By 1775, these three cities were major world-trading centers, and seventeen other American cities exceeded three thousand in population. These figures become most impressive when it is realized, as Carl Bridenbaugh points out, that Philadelphia in 1775, with 40,000 inhabitants, exceeded in size every English city save only London.

The rise of these commercial cities forms an important and complex story. Here it may merely be pointed out that the nature of the farming area made possible the rise of an indigenous colonial commerce, just as commerce simultaneously encouraged and forwarded the growth of the farming and extractive economy. The surplus products of the colonial farms did not consist of recognized staples with an assured English market but were diverse in their nature, collected over an extensive area, and shipped to many widely scattered home and foreign markets. Here was a commerce not well suited to monopolization, as was that from India or Hudson Bay, nor easily dominated by great British merchants, as was the direct trade from the tobacco and sugar colonies. The British merchants had little difficulty in retaining the lion's share of the commerce in enumerated commodities with the plantation areas. But in the export of various farm products and fish to southern Europe and the West Indies, in the growing intracolonial trade, and in the marketing of imported goods up and down the Atlantic coast, the Boston, New York, and Philadelphia merchants had the advantages of being on the spot and so able accurately to judge market needs and product quality, of dealing in small shipments and miscellaneous cargoes, and of relying less on factors, agents, and supercargoes than did the merchants of the mother country.

From their mentors, the British merchants, the American traders acquired a wealth of accumulated knowledge of management, of accounting, of communications, and of techniques essential to trading. The merchants of Boston, New York, Philadelphia, and other commercial centers provided leadership and promotion indispensable to the economy. Much more than wholesale dealers, exporters, importers, and shipowners, they performed most of the services which later became special branches of marketing, insurance, and finance. At almost every colonial seaport, but especially in New England, they promoted shipbuilding; and thanks in part to cheap and abundant raw materials, sailing vessels became a leading colonial export. Directly or indirectly, they promoted manufacturing activities supplementary to commerce and shipbuilding and employed many workmen in ropewalks, candlemaking and cooperage establishments, sail lofts, flour mills, bakeries, and distilleries. As long as the American merchants continued to enjoy wide trading privileges within the British Empire and the protection of the British navy, they prospered greatly, and American port cities increased in population and productivity. The available statistics on the commerce of the thirteen colonies, though incomplete and fragmentary, give many indications of relatively rapid growth after about 1710. No summary or sampling will be attempted here, though it may be pointed out that, as a market for British exports, the thirteen colonies surpassed the British West Indies for the first time in 1726–1730 and that their share of the total British exports rose from 4.4 per cent in 1701–1705 to 12.9 per cent in 1766–1770. And this came about at a time when British exports were expanding greatly.

So, what estimate can be made of the rate of per capita growth in the thirteen colonies as a whole? I hazard the opinion that the average level of living about doubled in the sixty-five years before the Revolution. This implies an average rate of increase of slightly more than 1 per cent per annum. This largely speculative conclusion finds some indirect support from the consideration of the post-Revolutionary years which now follows.

III

During the Revolutionary War, productivity fell off and remained relatively low during the Confederation period. Then it appears to have risen rapidly during the 1790's, so that by the first five or six years of the new century the average level of living was about where it had been in the early 1770's. Conditions continued good to 1807; but thereafter embargoes, non-intercourse acts, and the War of 1812 definitely depressed living standards. A brief expansion following 1814 ended with a sharp reaction in 1819–1820. A period of slow growth followed in the twenties, giving way to rapid improvement in the thirties. By 1836–1840, the level of living had, I believe, risen to (or somewhat above) the average reached in 1770–1774 and 1799–1804. Some of the chief developments from 1775 to 1839 supporting this conclusion may be briefly reviewed.

Little need to be said of the final twenty-five years of the eighteenth century. The American Revolution, like most wars, brought unexpected results. Caused in part at least by colonial resentment of British attempts to tax Americans and restrict their commerce, the struggle established independence (an object not generally sought when the war began) and resulted in considerable physical destruction, reduced foreign trade, and generally increased taxes. Freedom from foreign rule may be above price. But Americans, following 1783, discovered (as have many newly independent nations in more recent times) that political freedom, far from stimulating economic growth, may at least for a time actually retard it.

The gross product of the colonial economy apparently declined during the war years and made at best only a partial recovery by 1789. As population increased by about 40 per cent from 1775 to 1790, the average per capita income was doubtless lower in 1789 than it had been in 1774. In the decade before the break with England, the growing productivity of the rice and indigo plantations had continued without serious interruption. In the tobacco area, soil exhaustion and an increasing shortage of suitable new lands had begun to slow growth in the late colonial years. The Revolutionary War seriously hurt production in both plantation areas. The British armies in the South, following victories in 1779 and the capture of Charleston in February 1780, wrought widespread destruction from Georgia to the river valleys of eastern Virginia, and plantation production halted over wide areas when the British carried away 30,000 slaves from Virginia and nearly as many from South Carolina. During the period of the Confederation, plantation conditions improved slowly. Tobacco production in Virginia did not regain its prewar level until 1786. Wheat replaced tobacco as the chief product of eastern Virginia, as tobacco-growing spread into the far piedmont and the valley. Virginia tobacco exports in 1783–1790 averaged only slightly higher than in 1760–1775. Annual rice exports, 1783–1785, totaled less than half the average for 1770–1774, and indigo production fell off drastically with the withdrawal of the British bounty.

The war and its direct aftermath brought less positive damage in the middle and northern states. Some immediate benefits accrued. The French and British military forces provided an unusual market for the products of American farms. A new trade, formerly forbidden to Americans, developed with European Atlantic ports and with the non-British West Indian Islands. Wartime needs promoted the manufacturing of such products as iron, gunpowder, linens, cottons, and paper. And, at least for a time, New England ports and Philadelphia increased their commercial activity. Nevertheless, influences detrimental to productivity appear to have predominated. The aggregate population of the five leading commercial cities fell by more than 50 per cent during the first year of the conflict. The war disrupted coastwide trade, and foreign commerce became increasingly difficult as the British blockade of the coast became more effective.

With the return of peace in 1783, the newly independent country lost important colonial advantages. The British navy no longer protected American commerce, and Britain imposed trading restrictions including virtual exclusion from commerce with the British West Indies. Shipbuilding slumped as American-built ships were denied British registry, and whaling and fur trading declined also, in part due to British measures. Although Great Britain remained America's best customer, the market value of American goods imported by that country in 1784–1789 averaged less than for the years 1771–1775. Currency troubles, internal disorders including Shay's Rebellion, and interstate rivalries placed obstacles in the path of growth. A retardation of the rate of urban growth reflected the slowed economic development. From 1775 to 1790, the aggregate population of the three largest cities—Philadelphia, New York, and Boston—rose by less than 3 per cent, while the total population of the new nation increased by about 40 per cent. American cities of 5,000 or more population at the outbreak of the Revolution numbered twelve. No increase in this total had taken place by 1790.

For more than a decade, the Napoleonic Wars greatly stimulated the American economy. Rapidly rising prices and expanding trade characterized the early 1790's, and despite a brief setback in 1797–1798 conditions had improved so much by 1799–1800 that the general level of living probably approximated that of the early 1770's. For the years 1799–1839, data on which to base estimates of economic growth (while still fragmentary) became more abundant, and a number of attempts at measurement have been made. In 1939, Robert Martin published a statistical study purporting to show average per capita income to be less in 1839 than in 1799. An index of per capita income based on his calculations shows the following: 1799, 100; 1809, 96; 1819, 79; 1829, 77; and 1839, 92. Martin's results and his methods in securing them were reexamined in 1952 by Simon Kuznets, who concluded that, contrary to Martin, productivity per capita showed a rising trend over this period. Recently, more elaborate and detailed studies have been made of the statistical materials available for this period. Parker and Whartenby, on re-studying the whole problem, found the available statistics inadequate to support either Martin's or Kuznets' conclusions. Their calculations appear to throw real doubt on the assumption of a rising secular trend over this period, a conclusion challenged in a later study by Douglass C. North. My own estimate is that the average level of living in 1799–1806 was not again reached until the early 1830's at the earliest and, although some improvement came in that decade, the average for 1836–1840 was at best not much higher than that for the prosperous years around the beginning of the century. Only the chief considerations leading to this conclusion can be summarized here.

As late as 1840, about two thirds of the persons gainfully employed were in agricultural production. Therefore farm productivity trends take on special significance. An extensive statistical study made of this sector by Marvin W. Towne and Wayne D. Rasmussen found the average output per worker in agriculture very nearly the same in 1840 as in 1800. The authors make it clear that results for these years rest partly on the fragmentary statistical data available and very largely on assumptions regarded as reasonable. Their persuasive nonquantitative arguments in support of their conclusions are followed in part in the paragraphs which follow.

In Maryland and Virginia, the yield of tobacco and wheat fell off as the fertility of the soil became exhausted. Farther south, the invention of the cotton gin in 1793, the great European demand for raw cotton, and the suitability of considerable portions of the piedmont for cotton culture offset for a time the failure of other products, especially rice, to expand with population growth. But by the 1820's, and probably earlier, most cotton growing in the south Atlantic states yielded reduced per capita returns on increasingly impoverished soils. On the other hand, the migration of cotton growing to large plantations on the rich lands of the deep South brought an increased output per worker. At the same time throughout the South, small independent farmers and so-called poor whites increased in numbers and settled on marginal lands. Many, too poor to own slaves, engaged largely in subsistence farming, seldom producing more than enough to provide a meager living for their large families. I find little here to persuade me that average per capita productivity was rising in the southern states.

Nor does agricultural production in the North clearly demonstrate an upward trend per capita during this period. Most of the fertile river valleys leading down to the Atlantic had been cleared and cultivated even before the close of the colonial period. But population continued its rapid increase, and in the decades following the Revolution the areas with poorer soils in the middle Atlantic states and upland New England became dotted with farms. Not only were these lands often stony and difficult to clear, but their initial fertility soon disappeared, and transportation to market presented burdensome costs. By 1830, most of the upland areas of New England and of some of the middle Atlantic states had reached and passed their population peaks. The hard work of clearing the land, building roads and bridges, constructing houses and barns—all this had brought disappointing returns to the hopeful settlers. Individuals, families—and on occasion, whole settlements—now abandoned their homes in these areas and sought better lands in western New York and the Ohio River valley.

Three new developments in farming partially offset these unfavorable conditions. First, the growth of eastern cities brought some prosperity to nearby farmers by expanding the local market for perishable products. Second, at least after 1820, some increased yield may have resulted from the use of improved farm tools and machinery, especially the iron plow with interchangeable parts. But, although many improvements were being developed during this period, their use did not become sufficiently widespread appreciably to affect production until after 1840.

The growing migration westward to the rich soils and cheap lands of the Ohio Valley probably did little immediately to increase per capita productivity. The clearing of the land and the construction of dwellings, barns, roads, and bridges, was neither a quick nor an easy process, and the sparseness of settlement denied the advantages of specialization and the economies of scale. Moreover, the bulky farm products of the West had to be marketed a thousand miles or more down the river systems to New Orleans; and even though steamboats and canals reduced somewhat the transportation difficulties, effective relief did not come until after 1840, when the expanding demand of eastern cities and western Europe created the necessary market, and railroads began to contribute toward solving the transportation problem. All three of these mitigating factors developed too late appreciably to affect per capita farm production before 1840.

Probings in a number of other areas indicate that product increased less rapidly than population. This is evident, for example, in shipbuilding and the merchant marine engaged in foreign trade. Reexports from the United States reached their peak in the first decade of the nineteenth century and declined thereafter. And the average value of domestic exports from 1798–1802 to 1838–1842 failed to increase as rapidly as population.

On the other hand, it is obvious that in some sectors of the economy productivity expanded at a rapid rate between 1800 and 1840. Internal commerce experienced such an increase both coastwise and on the rivers, lakes, and canals. Turnpikes, canals, steamboats, and at least the beginnings of the railroads must have contributed toward increasing per capita output. Manufacturing also grew rapidly. Manufactures in homes under the putting-out system became extensive in New England and New York State during the first three or four decades of the nineteenth century and helped at least to some extent to offset declining agricultural productivity by providing part-time employment for women and children and winter employment for the men. But the chief productivity gains in manufacturing came from the introduction of improved machines and the factory system. Though important for the future, factory manufacturing constituted before 1840 a small fraction of total output. Also the rapid growth of cities, especially after 1820, contributed to the substantial enlargement of both regional and local markets, making possible economies of scale whose growing importance must not be overlooked even though they cannot be exactly measured.

As in colonial times and at least down to 1840, the great majority of Americans were farmers. The proportion of the gainfully employed in agriculture, after rising during the decade 1810–1820, appears to have declined thereafter. This shift of employment from agriculture to other sectors after 1820 contributed toward increased per capita productivity, as it has in more recent times. But the gains cannot be accurately measured and they came fairly gradually. They will surely be greatly exaggerated if attention is focused on the increased output of workers in textile factories. In absolute terms, the growth in factory employment was much less than in construction, in trade, and even in domestic service.

Sometime shortly before 1840 and probably during the decade of the thirties, the per capita productivity of the American economy began a strong upward trend. This improvement had by 1840 raised the average income to (or even moderately above) the level enjoyed in 1770–1774 and in the first years of the nineteenth century. This income level was a relatively high one. It was, by about 1840, clearly above that for France and not far below the English average. The estimate of $400 per capita (in dollars of current purchasing power) accepted by Goldsmith is actually well above the level now enjoyed in most Asian, African, and South American countries. As Gallman points out, "it is quite clear that the United States was not a poor country in 1839, even by modern standards."

Recognition of the high level of productivity attained by 1840 accords well with the hypothesis already developed that rapid economic growth took place in the period 1710–1775. Thus if per capita income was relatively low in 1710, as I believe plausible, and if per capita income in 1840 was about the same or at least not substantially higher than in the early 1770's, as was concluded above, then it follows that relatively rapid growth must have characterized the years from 1710 to 1775.

Like other attempts to estimate economic growth over long periods of time, the conclusions drawn in this paper depend partly on statistical measurement but largely on value judgments. They differ from calculations of growth rates for recent years chiefly in that they are more tentative and that they depend of necessity less on actual measurement and more upon qualitative judgment. The conclusions have been presented as plausible hypotheses. Their purpose is less to provide answers than to suggest tasks awaiting the best efforts of students—both those trained in statistical procedures and those more at home with an institutional approach.

Government and Politics

20. THE SHERIFF IN COLONIAL NORTH CAROLINA*

by Julian P. Boyd

Where was the locus of authority in the British empire?
Legally, supreme authority centered in the Crown and Parliament, which made and administered the laws that governed the
colonies. But from the beginning, power in America seemed to
drain away into local units of government: the towns, counties,
and provincial legislatures. In the following selection, Julian P.
Boyd analyzes the structure of politics in North Carolina. In
theory, power was supposed to rest in the hands of the Crown
and its officials, including the king's surrogate, the royal governor. In reality, colonists powerful in their localities imposed
their will on British officials. The sheriff was supposed to be the
king's agent, his appointee, but actually he became the instru-

* *North Carolina Historical Review*, vol. 5 (1928), 151–181. Footnotes have
been omitted except where they are necessary for an understanding of the text.

ment of local court house rings that dominated the counties. Through control over the tax system and elections, the sheriff enabled the local clique to which he belonged to dominate politics in its neighborhood, and together with similar groups elsewhere to challenge royal authority in the province. Though royal governors resisted these encroachments, which sapped their autonomy and authority, they repeatedly experienced frustration. In the end, the locus of authority was divided between America and England. Why did this occur?

For further reading: Charles S. Sydnor, *American Revolutionaries in the Making* (1965), also appearing under the title *Gentlemen Freeholders* (1952); Leonidas Dodson, *Alexander Spotswood, Governor of Colonial Virginia* (1932).

Of the several factors at work in colonial North Carolina in the process of fermentation which was to prepare the public mind for revolution, one of the most important was the effect on the government of the colony brought on by continual antagonism between the ruling class on the one hand and the officials of the crown on the other. This antagonism lasted throughout the period of royal control, and found constant expression in the frequent conflicts between the legislature and the royal governors over such economic and political questions as land, fees, money, and courts. One of the most dependable bulwarks on the side of the colonists in this struggle proved to be the county court of the justices of the peace, together with the small ring of officials attached to this court. For, as a general thing, the officials of the local governmental units belonged to the ruling class and exercised a controlling influence over the legislature. One of the most important of these local officials was the sheriff. The part he took in the political struggle going on in the colony was one of great importance. The influences which were at work through the sheriff, the politics of his office, his position in the colonial scheme of things, and his effect upon the royal government in North Carolina are some of the problems to be discussed in this paper.

There was probably no other officer in the colony, and certainly there was none under the jurisdiction of the county court, who exercised such plenary executive and administrative powers as the sheriff did. He was not only the executive officer of the county court, but, in theory at least, the representative of the crown in the county, just as the sheriff in England was. As a peace officer of the county, the full right of *posse comitatus* was vested in him. He also had important fiscal powers, being the collector of taxes for the colony, the county, and the parish. He was master of elections for members of the legislature and the local vestries, and throughout the colonial period exercised a growing influence over elections and over the legislature. He acted in most counties as vendue master, and possessed important powers in that office. Such offices made the sheriffalty a position of commanding importance in the county, and caused it to be the prized bit of patronage at the disposal of the county court.

It is also equally true that there was no other officer who made efficient royal government impossible quite so much as the sheriff did. Generally speaking, he impeded all effort at a sound fiscal policy. He frequently misappropriated and embezzled great quantities of the public money. He was a controlling factor in the elections, and at times returned the person of his own choice rather than that of the electorate. His influence was felt in nearly every phase of colonial life: it was even claimed that he retarded missionary endeavor by his lax and dilatory methods of handling the duties of his office.

The office of sheriff, however, was not a sinecure, even at best. Jails were very insecure in almost every county in the colony. The criminals were hardened and desperate, and at times openly flouted the law. Even when captured and placed in jail, they could not be kept there: escapes and jail deliveries were common. Riots and slave insurrections were frequently threatened. And what probably disturbed the sheriff more than unsettled conditions of law and order was the opposition which he met with in the collection of taxes, and the consequent reduction of commissions.

The Establishment of the Office of Sheriff

It was not until 1739 that the office of sheriff was created in the colony. Prior to that time, the duties which the sheriff exercised were vested in the provost marshal of the colony and his deputies, usually one in each county. The provost marshal of the colony was appointed by the king, was paid out of the public funds, and collected certain fees fixed by the legislature for himself and his deputies. The deputy marshals in the various counties were appointed by the provost marshal for the colony, usually with a certain sum being stipulated in the commission which the deputy was required to pay the provost marshal annually for the office. The deputy marshal was the executive officer of the court, and was obliged to execute all writs, warrants, executions, and orders of the court.

The important change in the office which took place in 1739 was not simply a change of name, but a change in the method of appointment. The old method whereby the office was farmed out through several steps, from governor to provost marshal to deputy marshal, and perhaps to several sub-deputy marshals, was abolished and the system was theoretically placed more under the control of the governor. The sheriff was nominally commissioned by the governor, but in actual practice the appointment was in the hands of the county court. Therein lay a very significant fact: the creation of the office of sheriff was evidence of the growing political power of the county court, and was the direct result of a popular demand for the establishment of the office.

The first notice of any agitation for the creation of the office of sheriff is found in a letter from Governor Johnston to the Board of Trade, in which he points out the impossibility of collecting the quit rents, if allowed to be paid in commodities, without establishing the office of sheriff. "There are," he wrote, "a thousand inconveniences in this wide extended country for want of sheriffs and the people are strangely bent on having them established by law." The popular demand prevailed, and in 1739 the General Assembly passed an act entitled "An Act for appointing Sheriffs in the Room of Marshals, of this Province, for prescribing the method of appointing them, and for limiting the time of their continuance in Office, and directing their Duty therein, and for Abolishing the Office of Provost Marshal of this Province." The preamble of the act showed it to be the result of a popular demand: "The Office of Provost Marshal hath been found to be very inconvenient in this extended Province, the Deputy Marshals not only neglecting, but frequently refusing, to do their duty . . . . which hath occasioned great Murmurs and Discontents among the Inhabitants of this Province."

The act gave the control of the appointment of sheriffs to the county courts by providing that in every precinct in the colony the court should recommend three persons "as they shall think most fit and able" to the governor, who was empowered to select one of the nominees to be sheriff for the next two years. A limitation was placed upon this nominating power which gives evidence of the control exercised by members of the county courts over the legislature; namely, the justices of the peace could not nominate a person to act as sheriff who was not a duly qualified member of their court. The sheriff, however, was not permitted to act as a justice or sit in the quarter sessions during his term of office. The act further provided that the sheriff should give bond to the king in the sum of at least five hundred pounds sterling, and that if any person nominated to the office refused to accept the appointment, he should thereby forfeit eight pounds proclamation money. If the county court refused to nominate three persons for the office, the governor was empowered to nominate any other justice, or anyone whom he might then appoint a justice, to fill the vacancy. The governor also had power to appoint in case of vacancy by death. This act would have abolished the office of provost marshal before sheriffs could have been appointed by the county courts, and to obviate this difficulty the legislature passed an amending act two days later providing that the governor with the consent of the council might appoint sheriffs for every county in the colony for the two succeeding years.

The first act, broadly defining the duties of the sheriff, provided that he should execute, by himself or through his deputy, all writs and precepts directed to him by the county court. The sheriff or his deputy was required to be in constant attendance at the court where his jurisdiction lay, otherwise to suffer amercement at the hands of the court. It was his duty to arrest any person for treason, felony, or any breach of the peace at any time, though he could not serve a writ on Sunday. The sheriffs of the various counties were obliged also to attend in turn the various meetings of the general court, according to rules established by that court, in order to serve writs and summon jurors to the court.

The act of 1739, providing for a specific term of years for the sheriff to hold office, was defective in that a sheriff would often go out of office before another could be appointed to succeed him. In order to remedy this an act was passed in 1745 which provided that the sheriffs should continue in office until their successors had been appointed and qualified. The most important provision of this act, however, was that amending the provision of the act of 1739 which confined the nominations for sheriff to the justices of the court. After 1745 the justices were empowered to recommend for sheriff any freeholder, excepting the members of the legislature and the members of the governor's council. The reason for this change, the law stated, was the difficulty of finding men to execute the office, since the persons nominated frequently chose to pay their fines rather than act in the office. This provision, however, did not prevent the courts from continuing to nominate justices of the peace for the office just as had been done under the act of 1739.

The acts of 1739 and 1745 only defined the duties of the sheriff as an officer of the court and prescribed the method of his appointment. There were many other acts passed subsequently which dealt with the office of sheriff directly or indirectly, and these had for the most part to do with his fiscal duties, such as collecting the taxes, settling with the treasurers and the county courts for the taxes collected, selling at public vendue the estates of deceased persons and property attached by him at the order of the court, attending to the prison and prisoners under his care, and other such duties. In addition to these powers conferred by statute, the sheriff enjoyed all other powers or duties conferred on him by the county court. He was sometimes ordered by the court to secure jailers, to repair the jail, the court house, or other public buildings, or to see that it was done, to let bids for the building of warehouses, ferries, jails, court houses, and other public buildings,—to do, in short, on the order of the court all those things necessary for the judicial and administrative government of the county.

The Appointment of the Sheriff

The importance of the sheriff in colonial government is nowhere shown so clearly as in the politics of appointment to the office. The governor nominally appointed the sheriff in the name of the king, but this control amounted to little in actual practice. The real appointive body was the county court.

The most striking indication of local control of the appointment to the office is shown in the fact that the justices of the court rarely nominated a person for sheriff who was not a justice of the peace. This practice, of course, was made mandatory by the law of 1739, but although that provision was repealed in 1745, the justices of the courts continued to nominate one another for the office down to the Revolution.

Another interesting fact is that the justices apparently had few scruples about voting for themselves in the nominations. At the nomination for sheriff in Pasquotank County in January, 1742, there were three persons present at the court, and the nomination which was returned to the governor contained only the names of these three men. There were numerous other instances of a like character. Toward the close of the royal period, however, there seems to have grown up in the county courts a prejudice against this practice of self-nomination. In response to such a nomination for sheriff in Tyrrell County in 1764, the court at a subsequent meeting passed the following order: "The Court being of opinion that as the former recommendation of Sheriff being entered by order of three members only & as one of them was recommended & at the first of the court, we recommend the following persons, Vizt: Wm. Carkeet, James Johnston, and Major John Hardison." This nomination prevailed, for James Johnston was made sheriff.

At any rate, it is certain that toward the close of the royal period the nomination of sheriff was no longer left to a small group within the court, but almost the entire court engaged in the nomination. Ordinarily at the quarter sessions of most of the counties there were about three to six justices on the bench, and rarely over eight, even in the most populous counties in the eastern section. But when the nomination of a sheriff was before the court, practically all of the justices in commission in the county were present. A good example is found in the Bute County quarter sessions in May, 1772. On Tuesday, May 12, there were only four justices present, including two of the three men later to be nominated. On May 13, the day of the nomination, there were twenty justices present, including all three of the nominees. On May 14, the justices had all returned to their plantations, for there was barely a quorum, three justices, left to attend to the ordinary administrative and judicial business of the court. In the same county in May, 1774, a similar situation occurred. At the opening of the court on the day of nomination, there were only three justices present. When the nominations were held, there were twenty-one justices present. A similar case occurred in Orange County in May, 1764.

With local politics thus entering into the nomination of the sheriff, the matter of appointment could hardly be said to have been under the direct control of any influence other than the county court. That nomination was considered as virtual election is shown not only by the above facts, but also by the fact that sometimes the courts returned only one nominee when the law required that three be returned. This local control is still further shown in the practice of nominating three men according to law, two of whom the justices knew would not accept the office if offered them. Then, too, there were personal and family politics working both upon the county court and the royal governors. An example of this is seen in the following letter from Robert Jones to Governor Dobbs: "I suppose you have not forgot the Sollicitation I formerly made in favor of my kinsman John Jones for the office of Sheriff of Northampton and Herewith you have a copy of the last Recommendations of persons fitly qualified to execute the said office in which you'll find him included. If you'll be so kind as to grant him a commission for that purpose, you'll do me an additional favor in sending it by the Bearer." Sometimes, too, the members of the legislature added their influence to the matter of getting sheriffs elected, especially when, due to lack of courts or other reasons, the justices failed to nominate.

The governor, however, did have a slight, though nominal control over the office. Every commission appointing a sheriff contained the specific phrase that such commission was issued during pleasure only, and could be revoked by the governor at any time. There were also various amendments to the laws as to the manner of appointing which gave a modicum of power to the governor. These acts, however, gave the governor power over appointments only in exceptional cases. In no sense did they give him any effective control over the manner of appointment, or give him the power of determining the matter of personnel.

The council, usually siding with the governor in upholding the prerogatives of the crown, was inclined to give him some power in the matter of appointing sheriffs. In 1774 it expressed the unanimous opinion that the governor had power to appoint sheriffs in case the law providing for their appointment had expired before the county courts could comply with such law. In 1749 the council made the unique order that "no future person keeping ordinary be recommended to the governor to be appointed Sheriff for any county within this Province." This order was sent to the various courts, but it is not at all certain that it was enforced. For even after a person was appointed sheriff by the governor, there was nothing to prevent the county court from granting him a license to keep an ordinary. This was frequently done.

As a matter of fact, the royal governors were not extremely anxious to assert their authority over the county courts or their officers too strongly, for by doing so, they would have aroused the hostility of the legislature, which was to a large extent made up of justices of the peace, sheriffs, clerks of court, and other members of the court ring.

Hence, rather than exercise the power of removal vested in them, the royal governors from time to time suggested that they should be given the right of appointment. The Board of Trade agreed with the governors in this, but nothing was done about it. The office was unequivocally in the hands of the local court party.

In general, the results of local control of the office of the sheriff, from the standpoint of the crown, tended toward a decentralized and weakened colonial government. These results might be briefly classified as follows: (1) a cumbersome, awkward, decentralized government resulting from an impairment of the governor's appointive power; (2) embezzlement and wastage of public funds by sheriffs; (3) lax and dilatory methods of administration of public, county, and parish taxes; (4) control of elections and influence over politics by the sheriffs; (5) the greater solidification of the county court ring; (6) various abuses in the administration of the office of sheriff, such as abuses of the fee system, the method of serving attachments, the jury system, and so on.

Impairment of the Appointive Power

The position of the Board of Trade in regard to the impairment of the appointive power of the governor is illustrated by a letter to Governor Tryon in 1770: "In regard to the Act for appointment of sheriffs, which we consider as part of the general system for the more effectual administration of Justice, as it does not leave a discretionary Power in the King's Governor of nominating a Sheriff in case he should think fit to reject those recommended by the Judges, it does improperly and as we conceive unnecessarily deviate from the rule & usage in the kingdom." The Board of Trade went on to threaten, after stating the obvious proposition that the chief representative of the crown in the county ought to be under the control of the crown, that unless the legislature remedied the objection, it would recommend the repeal of the act, "for no consideration of general Utility and convenience can justify an Acquiescence in a regulation that does not correspond with the Constitution of this Kingdom."

Replying to this letter, Governor Martin wrote:

. . . . The Sheriff's Office . . . . is held entirely by favour of the Magistrates as Members of the County Courts, they being impowered by a law passed in the year 1768 to nominate three persons, of whom the Governor is obliged to appoint one, under which regulation by their juggles and corruption the Governor is compelled to appoint the candidate they favour so that in fact the absolute nomination of the Sheriffs is in those little prostitute judicatures and the power of the King's Governor in the case is perfectly nugatory to remedy this defection in policy. The Lords of Trade by their letter to Governor Tryon of the 12th of December 1770 direct that it be recommended to the Assembly to amend that law by a provision vesting the appointment of the Sheriff in the Governor, and declaring that they should otherwise think it necessary to recommend it to His Majesty for his Royal disallowance. This Act, my lord, is so great a favorite with the Assembly, which is composed of justices of the peace, that there is no hope of its ever consenting to the proposed alteration, and embarrassed as the deliberations of that body have even been by faction since I came to this Country, I have had no opportunity to propose it.

On two other occasions Martin admitted the danger of this local control and his inability to cope with it in the legislature.

These letters of Martin show that the royal governors and the Board of Trade began to realize too late that a mistake had been made in 1739 when, in order to satisfy the demands of the court party, the office was placed under local control and kept there by subsequent acts. The price paid for this concession to popular demand in 1739 was a tendency toward decentralization of the administration from the standpoint of the crown and toward greater unity and greater solidification from the standpoint of the court party. The importance of the power controlling the appointment to this office, then, can hardly be overestimated. For, since the sheriff was the most important figure in the elections, the group controlling his office could obviously exert some influence over the legislature. This was exactly what happened, and throughout the royal period the justices of the peace held a place of dominance in the General Assembly. And, as Martin clearly saw, they were determined to submit to no law taking from them the power to appoint an officer who could maintain them in such an advantageous position.

The Sheriff and the Fiscal Administration

The sheriff was given authority to collect the parish, county, and colony taxes. Due to the decentralization of the fiscal administration and the local control of the office of sheriff, there was not even an efficient and systematic tax system for the colony, to say nothing of the individual counties, where local prejudices and politics ran riot. Toward the latter part of the royal period not only the governors, but even the legislature made attempts to remedy the evils in the system.

Most of the acts relating to the fiscal powers of the sheriff had to do specifically with the methods of accounting for the taxes collected. The first of these laws was passed in 1755. "There is at present," the preamble of the act stated, "no law whereby those who have been invested with the power of applying the Public Money, or the collectors of the same, can be compelled to a speedy execution of the said trusts, by Occasion whereof, the Public hath been greatly defrauded, & the faith thereof much depreciated." This act provided that in case the sheriff neglected or refused to account for taxes according to the various acts levying them, the superior court of the district might give judgment against the sheriff, on motion of the public treasurer of the district. The act also sought to correct certain abuses in the collection and accounting of the public taxes by the sheriffs. It was provided that since sheriffs had theretofore discovered taxables not in the lists given them by the county court clerks, and had kept such taxes for their own use, sheriffs so doing should account for the same on oath to the respective treasurers, county courts, and vestries. The act also gave the sheriffs full power in the collection of taxes. In cases where taxes were not paid when due according to law, the sheriff was permitted to distrain slaves, goods, and chattels. If the taxes were not paid within five days after such distress, the sheriff was empowered to sell the property after first giving notice of at least three days on the church door immediately after divine service. No "unreasonable distress," however, was to be made. No attachment of slaves was to issue unless there could not be found sufficient other property to settle the taxes due. To protect further the public money against improper uses the law raised the bond required of the sheriff from the one bond of £500 required by the law of 1739 to two bonds of £1000 each.

In 1759 another act was passed to correct the same evils. This act stated that "the continuing of sheriffs long in office, who do not regularly account for the Public Taxes they collect, is of great detriment to the Province." To remedy this evil it was provided that no county court should recommend to the governor any person who had served two years successively, unless he could produce a certificate from the treasurer of his district saying that he had fully accounted for and delivered all public taxes he had received as sheriff.

An act passed in 1760 sought to make more explicit the duty of sheriffs in settling their accounts. It provided that the sheriff in settling his accounts with the treasurer should deliver his account, signed and proved, of all the money he had received payable to the treasurer. This account the treasurer was required to produce in his settlement with the general assembly as a voucher for the money received by him. It was further provided that when the county court made allowance to the sheriff for such persons as had no visible estate, five justices of the peace should be present when the certificate of allowance was made.

In 1768 another effort was made to improve the cumbersome system. "Many of the Sheriffs of the Province," the act stated, "have heretofore applied to their own private uses, or otherwise embezzled, considerable sums of the Public Money, in the hopes of replacing the same when called for." To remedy this, it was provided that the sheriffs should deliver to the county court a regular account, signed by the treasurer of the district, ascertaining the amount of the public money received for the year preceding, together with an account of all disbursements, and that this account should be entered on the court minutes by the clerk. It was further provided that if the sheriff were removed from office for any reason excepting death, he should make an accounting with the treasurer immediately, otherwise he was to lose all commissions from the time of his last settlement. Another important provision of this act was that no person chosen as representative of his town or county should be recommended during his term of office for the office of sheriff by the county court. This provision obviously was aimed at the problem of reducing the growing influence of the sheriffs over the legislature.

In 1770 another act relating to the fiscal duties of the sheriffs was passed. The principal object of this act was to correct "the many hardships and inconveniences [which have] arisen from Sheriffs leaving the Province before they had accounted for Public, County, and Parish duties, whereby their securities have become lieable for same." The act simply provided that the persons who had signed the bonds of the absconding sheriff might collect all arrearages of taxes with practically the same powers of collection that the sheriff had. This act, of course, did not remedy the evil, but only provided for the relief of the persons signing the bonds of the sheriff.

In 1773 an act was passed for a still more rigid accounting for taxes collected by the sheriffs. This act provided that, when a sheriff failed to make payment of public monies due from him, the treasurer of·the district might then cause a writ of *scire facias* to issue against him, or, if he were deceased, against his executors or administrators. The act of 1755 had contained this same provision, but this act went further and required that in case the treasurer failed or neglected to bring suit against the sheriff for negligence in accounting, the treasurer himself was to stand liable for the arrearages of the sheriff. This last provision throws a flood of light on the political power of the sheriffs. For the treasurers depended largely for their re-election upon the sheriffs, and were therefore inclined to be rather lenient with them in accounting for the public taxes. Hence the only way to bring the treasurers to task was to hold them responsible for the overdue taxes if they permitted such to accrue.

In 1774 another act was passed to correct further abuses of the fiscal powers of the sheriffs. The practice of the county courts in allowing to the sheriffs a number of insolvents in the collection of their taxes led to the abuse of these taxes being collected and not reported. To correct this, the act provided that the sheriff should not be allowed more insolvents than were expressly sworn to in the list deposited with the clerk of court and kept for public inspection. If the sheriff returned any person as insolvent, and later proceeded to collect from such person any taxes for the year in which he was declared insolvent, he was to forfeit twenty pounds for every act of this kind.

All of these acts relating to the fiscal powers of the sheriff were passed as a result of the lack of an effective central control over the funds handled by the sheriff. The sheriffs' accounts were audited in a rather haphazard manner by neighbors and fellow justices of the peace and by treasurers dependent upon the sheriffs for re-election. In fact, so imperfect in operation was the system of supervision exercised over the sheriff in his fiscal capacity that it is a misnomer to speak of an auditing system, for no efficient or systematic method of checking up on the funds of the colony existed.

The whole process of assessing, or list-taking, collecting, and auditing the tax funds was in the hands of local officials. The county was divided into districts by the county court, and one justice, usually with one constable, was assigned to each district. The justice took a list of all the taxables in his district, or saw that the constable did it, and returned it to the county court. The court then took all the tax lists and turned them over to the sheriff, who was required to collect whatever taxes were levied by the colony, county, or parish. Frequently there were large numbers unlisted, due to increasing population and other causes. Unscrupulous sheriffs, no doubt, collected from such taxables at times and used the money for private purposes.

There were various methods whereby the courts settled for the taxes collected by the sheriffs. Sometimes the court itself received the account and passed upon it, often when there was hardly a quorum present, and at times when a former sheriff, sitting on the bench as a justice of the peace, would exhibit the account for taxes collected during his sheriffalty. Sometimes the court permitted the chairman of the court to settle with the sheriff. In some counties the clerk of court was given this authority. But the usual practice was for the court to appoint a committee of two, three, or four members to settle with the sheriff.

Examining the county court records, we find it a widespread condition that the sheriffs were delinquent in making their settlements, and at times were several years in arrears. A striking example of this is found in Carteret in 1747. At the July session of the court, the following entry was made in the court minutes: "At the request of Chas. Cogdell, Esq., Late Sheriff Desiring time to make up & pay to this Court the levys which he hath received, This Court hath ordered that the said Cogdell settle with Col Thos. Lovick and pay the sd Lovick such moneys due and that the sd Lovick pay the same unto such persons who hath a lawful claim." At the September term of court, Cogdell had not yet complied with this order of the court, and he was consequently ordered to appear before the next court. This order also was apparently disobeyed, for the December records show nothing of his appearance, and no further orders were issued. In the minutes for the March session, 1748, Cogdell was ordered to pay his arrearages within one month, or the clerk was authorized to issue process against him or his security. Apparently the delinquent Cogdell then settled his accounts after almost a year's active insistence on the part of the court that he make up the levies he had collected, for there are no further evidences in the records of his continued disobedience of the order. The Tyrrell court made a weak and ineffectual effort to call the sheriffs to account in December, 1766, by passing an order compelling the clerk of court to "prosecute the several sheriffs for the county tax who may be in arrear." There is nothing in the subsequent records to indicate that such prosecutions were made, or that settlements were made more punctually. An unusual admission of delinquency is found in the petition of Joseph Williams, sheriff of Duplin County for several years. In his petition to the legislature in 1761, he claimed that, as a result of his office, he "became debtor to the public in a large sum of money for the public taxes, but meeting with misfortunes," he was rendered unable to discharge the balance, which was about £230, without great detriment to himself and family. He claimed that he had already been obliged to dispose of several valuable slaves to reduce his indebtedness to the public, and since there was an execution in the hands of the sheriff against him, he prayed the assembly twelve months to pay the balance. Similar examples of delinquency were rather numerous.

The public, or colony, taxes were audited hardly more systematically than the county taxes. In general, the sheriffs settled with the public treasurers, and the treasurers in turn settled with the legislature. This led to several confusing practices, the chief of which was embezzlement. In a letter to the Earl of Shelbourne, Governor Tryon pointed out clearly the effect of the sheriffs on the fiscal system of the colony:

> The sheriffs have embezzled more than one-half of the public money ordered to be raised and collected by them (about £40,000) .... not £5,000 of which will possibly ever come into the Treasury, as in many instances the Sheriffs are either insolvent or retreated out of the Province. The Treasurer's lenity or rather remissness in the material part of their duty I construe to be founded on a principal of caution, for by not suing the sheriffs in arrears they obtain a considerable weight of interest among the connections of these delinquent sheriffs & which generally secures them a re-election in their office when expired.

Governor Tryon saw the weakness of the system of collecting the public taxes and the abuses to which it was liable. Consequently, he drew up a careful and systematic scheme for auditing the accounts of sheriffs and treasurers, modelled on the Virginia system. In presenting this plan to the Assembly in 1769, he said:

> The fact is too well-known to admit of denial considerable sums have been lost by negligence or insolvency of the sheriffs and other collectors with their sureties.

The plan was rejected by the Assembly. The cause was obvious to Tryon, and he courageously stated it in his final message to the assembly just before its adjournment:

> If ever carried, in any future session, into an Act of the legislature, it will be acknowledged the most beneficial session this Colony ever experienced, though it should be the only Act passed in that session. But this blessing is not to be obtained for the country while the Treasurers, late Sheriffs, and their sureties, can command a majority in the lower house.

Tryon used strong language before the assembly, but he did not overstate the facts. And there was one good result of his emphatic stand in 1769: the first complete and thorough-going investigation of the finances which the colony undertook. The assembly authorized John Burgwyn, clerk of the court of chancery and secretary to the council, to investigate the status of the fiscal system. The result was four reports. These reports revealed a startling condition of the finances of the colony, for most of which the sheriffs were directly responsible. The first report showing the delinquency of sheriffs indicated an outstanding indebtedness to the public on the part of these officials of £64,013 13s. 3d. This amount exceeded by over three thousand pounds the total amount of taxes collected in the colony from 1748 to 1770. The second report showing the amounts due from sheriffs was slightly improved, indicating a total arrearage for the colony of £52,455 1s. 7d. This widespread public defalcation was by no means confined to local officials in the counties in which the Regulators were active. In Currituck, for instance, an account had been standing since 1759 for £797 18s. 0d., against which judgment had issued, but Burgwyn reported the sheriff and his securities either dead or insolvent. Such notations occurred with deplorable frequency in Burgwyn's first report: "New Hanover, William Walker, Sheriff, 1759, £986 16s. 0d., Judgment, but no securities taken and nothing to be got . . . . Rowan, David Jones, Sheriff, 1757, £1205 8s. 0d., Judgment, both principal & securities bad . . . . Anson, Anthony Hutchins, Sheriff, 1763-1764, £472 4s. 8d., Neither principal nor securities worth a groat . . . . Cumberland, Isaiah Parvisol, Sheriff, 1763-1764, £652 12s. 1d., Principal died insolvent and securities not worth a groat." The majority of the old accounts shown in the first report had not been collected by the time of the second report, and in many instances had been increased.

These reports reveal the manner in which some of the officials whom the Regulators complained about protected each other. In 1759, Stephen Cade was sheriff of Dobbs County and incurred a debt due the public of £536 19s. 0d. A judgment was secured against this sum, but Burgwyn found that four of the sheriffs of Dobbs played into each others' hands, and that in levying the execution they always returned that there was nothing to be found. One of the securities of Cade assured Burgwyn that he had paid over two hundred and fifty pounds to one of these sheriffs, and that this amount had not been credited to the account. Cade was also sheriff of Johnston County in 1758, and left an arrearage of £970 6s. 1d., against which judgment had been secured with the same result as in Dobbs County. Neither of these accounts had been collected by the time of the second report.

This chaotic financial condition was not due in any sense to the fact that the sheriffs were "insolvent royal officials over whose appointment and in the approval of whose sureties the province had no voice whatever." It was precisely because of local control of the sheriff that such a state of affairs came about. For it was this local control and local politics that made impossible any systematic auditing of the sheriff's accounts, such as that which Tryon attempted to secure.

Aside from the effect of the fiscal and governmental system, this haphazard method of handling the funds had other results. In 1751, the treasurer of the northern district reported that work on the public buildings in New Bern had been suspended because the sheriffs had not paid in the money that they had collected. In 1763, James Reed, the Anglican minister, complained about not having had a stipend for nearly fourteen months, and said that:

> tho the sheriffs now have a whole years collection in their hands yet as there is no vestry to call them to account, they do not choose to part with the money on any terms or security whatsoever, the misfortune is they too often stand in need of it themselves. For the generality of the Sheriffs are very extravagant, to say no more, & very frequently spend the Public money not one in ten, I believe I might say in twenty, can ever make up their accounts, by which means the Clergy are frequently kept a long time out of their stipends.

Another North Carolinian wrote a friend in Pennsylvania in May, 1771, that:

there never was a people abused by authority more than this country has been . . . . the main substance . . . . was in the Sheriffs in most of the counties not having settled their accounts for eight or ten months past; so that by computation they were on the whole 80 or 100,000 pounds behind! The honest party in the administration appeared to the country too weak to bring these overgrown members to an account; therefore to strengthen their hands a great part of the country stopped payment of any taxes, but what were agreeable to law.

It is worth while to note that Tryon was liberal-minded enough to suggest that the pay of the sheriffs should be doubled in order to prevent embezzlement. In addressing the legislature in November, 1766, Tryon suggested that the emoluments of the public officers were too small and advocated that the commissions of the sheriffs especially be increased. "A Sheriff," he said, "as an Officer of the Revenue, and Being vested with many executive powers, holds an employment of great trust and importance; how far this trust has been executed with fidelity and punctuality in many counties, the Treasurers accounts will certify." He then recommended that the commissions be doubled on the collection of taxes "to prevent future neglect or embezzling," a fact which would be an inducement to "men of probity and responsibility to offer themselves as candidates for that active and important office." This was advice to which the ex-sheriffs and justices in the assembly could give ready attention. An act increasing the sheriffs' commissions was passed almost immediately.

As a matter of fact, the sheriff was one of the best paid officials in the colony, even when his office was conducted with strict honesty. His revenues came from several sources: (1) fees for the performance of orders of the court, such as making arrests, serving processes, executing attachments, and so on; (2) commissions for collecting the taxes; (3) a salary paid by the colony; (4) a salary paid by the county court for "extraordinary" services performed by the sheriff for which there were no fees allowed by act of the legislature; (5) commissions on the sales of estates for which he acted as vendue master; and (6) various other fees and commissions due to the linking up of the office with the county court ring, whereby the sheriff was given opportunity to administer estates of orphans, act as inspector for the county, hold militia offices, and so on.

By an act of 1740 the commissions of the sheriffs for taxes were placed at three per cent. Three years later this commission was raised to six per cent. It apparently remained at that rate until the increase made in 1766 to eight per cent. The salaries which the sheriffs received from the colony amounted to a stipend of from eight to ten pounds. The salary at first was eight pounds proclamation money but was later increased to ten pounds. The commissions allowed the sheriff as vendue master, according to Tryon, were not over "two per cent or 6d. in the pound. The courts, however, used a discretionary power in fixing the commissions of the sheriffs in this particular. Not the least of the sheriff's profits in office, however, came from his connections with the powerful court ring, for the sheriff frequently held several important positions. James Ellison, Sheriff of Beaufort, was also deputy surveyor for Granville, a justice of the peace, and inspector for the port of Bath. The sheriff was practically always a colonel in the militia. The sheriffs in the Granville district were for the most part not only deputy surveyors but also quit-rent collectors, for which office they received five per cent of all collections.

It is apparent, then, that the office of sheriff was very lucrative, due to the many fees, commissions, and other emoluments attached to it. What any one sheriff received in a year cannot, of course, be determined. But the liberality of the commissions and fees, to say nothing of the fraudulent abuses of these incomes, leads us to the conclusion that the office was very attractive financially.

The Sheriff's Control of Elections

One of the most important aspects of the sheriff's office was its influence over the politics of the colony. To understand this adequately it is necessary to inquire briefly into the suffrage laws of the colony.

By an act passed in 1715 the suffrage was made much more liberal than under later acts passed in the royal period. Persons twenty-one years of age, having resided in the precinct one year, and having paid the levies for the year preceding the election, could vote for burgesses. The voting was done by a method which lent itself admirably to political exploitation. The voter was given five votes; he wrote his choice of five names on a scroll of paper, or had it written for him, signed his name to the paper, and handed it to the deputy marshal taking the poll. In 1743, the manner of voting was somewhat altered. The use of a scroll was still retained, but the voter did not sign his name to it, although he did enroll his name in a book kept open by the sheriff at the same time that he voted. By this act, also, only freeholders were permitted to vote; the freehold necessary was fifty acres.

In 1760, the system was made even more advantageous for political influence by the sheriffs, for in that year the legislature passed an act requiring voting by the *viva voce* method. The candidates might, at any time after the election, look at the poll, and might require the sheriff to give them a copy of it. At about this time, the elections began to be held at the court house in each county; that is, directly under the eyes of the influential local court. Each writ of election issued to the sheriff contained directions that the election be held there.

It is natural to suppose that abuses would occur under such a system as this. The act of 1715 even anticipated this, and required that the marshals should attend the first three days of the legislature in order to explain disputed elections. It is significant to note, however, that there were less complaints of disputed elections during the proprietary period than during the royal period. Immediately after the establishment of the office of sheriff, the number of complaints of wrongly conducted elections increased so much that the legislature abandoned its original policy of hearing the petitions itself, and appointed a committee of privileges and elections, to which it referred all such matters. The findings of the committee in important cases were usually acted upon by the committee of the whole house.

Apparently the first complaints of mismanagement in elections came from the precincts of Currituck and Craven in 1731. In Craven, two justices of the peace were opposing each other: Joseph Hannis and Walter Lane. Lane was declared legally elected. In the Currituck election the house moved for a new writ of election to issue, and issued its warrant for Thomas Lowther, the marshal, on the ground that he had "misbehaved himself in the said election."

In 1735, Maurice Moore of New Hanover precinct petitioned the legislature that "he had the majority of Votes but the Marshal who took the Poll returned Mr. Job. How." The house considered the allegations of both sides, and resolved that Moore was legally elected by a majority of votes. Again, in 1739, the house acted contrary to the returns of an election officer. The committee of the whole house examined several witnesses and concluded that Robert Boyd, the returning officer for Bath, had conducted the election irregularly. The petitioner, Richard Rigby, was declared duly elected, and Boyd was summoned to the bar of the house to be "mildly reprimanded . . . . for obliterating the Poll for Bath Town & other misdemeanors in contempt of the Privileges of this House." At the same time Walter Lane of Craven County again protested his illegal defeat at the polls, and was declared legally elected. The same legislature summoned John Carter, a deputy marshal, "to attend upon a controverted election," and he replied by sending a "very abusive answer to this House."

Again in 1740 we find Walter Lane protesting an election in Craven on account of the fact that the sheriff voted in the election. The house admitted the sheriff's vote as proper, however, and the petition was rejected. At the same session a petition was presented by Griffith Jones, John White, and Robert Hamilton in behalf of themselves and the freeholders of Bladen County saying that Richard Everard was not qualified to be a member of the legislature, and gave as their specific charges that he "procured several unnaturalized Foreigners and others not qualified and they were polled by the Sheriff; and that the Sheriff was prevailed on to close the polls abruptly before several Freeholders had given their votes and who were at the polls for that purpose." The petition was put to a vote and rejected, apparently without debate.

A very significant protested election occurred in 1754 in Craven County. On December 16, of that year, four inhabitants of New Bern petitioned the legislature saying that they, among others, had voted for one Jeremiah Vail, but that James Davis, sheriff, had returned himself, "which we Apprehend is Quite Irregular and may be of Very bad President." The house declared Davis illegally elected. In the meantime the adherents of Davis had presented another petition to the assembly saying that they had voted for Davis while ignorant of the fact that his being sheriff would render him ineligible, and that, if he should be expelled, they desired a new writ of election to issue rather than to see Vail seated. This petition was signed by fourteen inhabitants. In the debate on the matter Samuel Swann objected to the motion for a new writ, and carried a motion to declare Vail seated.

Beginning in 1754 and lasting until 1773 there was an increasing number of disputed elections and charges of mismanagement on the part of sheriffs in the elections in the western counties, particularly in Anson and Granville. In December, 1754, William Hurst of Granville petitioned the legislature in a protest against the election of Robert Harris. In this petition Hurst declared that the sheriff had permitted many persons who were not freeholders to vote, thereby giving Harris a majority which he otherwise would not have had. Hurst further suggested that this was "greatly Subversive of the freedom of Elections, the Laws of this Province, the Rights and Liberties of the Subject." To this suggestion the legislature replied briefly that "The law does not allow of an Inquiry into the Facts contained in the sd Petition," and Harris was declared duly elected. Here, for the first time, the legislature made an unequivocal denial of its authority to go beyond the returns of an election officer, and thereby made tacit assertion of its connections with local politics.

In 1760, another contested election occurred in the same county. Several resolutions of the committee of privileges and elections in April of that year show that the sheriff of Granville had appointed Reuben Searcy as clerk in the election, and that Searcy had acted with great partiality "in a manner subversive of the rights and Freedom of Elections." The resolutions were adopted and a new writ issued. There was apparently no doubt as to the legality of inquiring into the returns of election officers; the language used by the committee, in fact, was almost identical with that used by Hurst in the contest just mentioned.

In the following years there were many elections in the conduct of which the sheriff was accused of partiality or mismanagement. In at least five of these cases the legislature appeared to find that the accusations were true, and either issued new writs or declared the petitioner legally elected. In four of the contested elections, however, the legislature declared that the petitions of protest could not be sustained. Three petitions apparently died in the committee. The causes of protest in all of the elections were practically the same. William Gray of Bertie, in 1760, said he was "duly Elected . . . . and that the Sheriff refused to return him." William Little of Anson protested that a "number of voices at the Election were refused or neglected to be received in favor of your Petitioner which would have given a Great Majority of Voices in his favor." Jacob Blount of Craven, in 1762, accused the sheriff of permitting several persons who were not freeholders to vote; and at least five persons admitted to the committee that they voted when they were not legally qualified to do so. In 1770, Thomas Respess of Beaufort accused the sheriff of illegally returning Wyriot Ormond when "he had a great majority of the votes of the freeholders of the town." In 1773, Thomas Stewart of Tyrrell said that the sheriff, "by suffering a number of persons to vote at the said election who were not possessed of a freehold in that county and several Freeholders to vote twice and by divers other illegal

and oppressive Acts . . . . procured a majority for one William Slade."
The petition of Peter Blinn, Gentleman, of Bath in 1766 claimed a
legal majority of the votes of the freeholders.

One of the most significant petitions coming to the assembly in protest of mismanaged elections by sheriffs was that of Thomas Wade of
Anson County in 1773. Because of the light which it throws on the
electoral procedure in colonial North Carolina, it is worth while to give
the matter detailed attention. Starting out with the broad allegation that
William Pickett, sheriff of Anson, did not conduct the election in a
proper and legal manner, Wade made several specific charges against
him: that he did not appoint inspectors of the election as required by
law to do; "that sundry evil-disposed persons were, with the connivance
of the sd Sheriff, placed in the passage to and from the Table where
the sd Poll was kept, who stopped and interrogated the freeholders in
their way to the Table . . . . who they intended to vote for; that if the
sd freeholders . . . . declared in Faviour of Mr. James Pickett, the brother
of him, and for Mr. Chas. Robinson, they were then assisted and helped
forward by those persons to give in their Votes;" if their vote was
unfavorable, they were "obstructed and hindered . . . . some of them
being violently pushed back, others of them pulled back by the hair of
their heads; and others so rudely and violently treated that great
numbers . . . . were detered from voting for the petitioner and many
of them from voting at all." Wade also charged that Pickett permitted
the clerk at the table where Wade's poll was kept "to be assaulted and
beaten in a very riotous manner as he sat at the table writing down the
names of the voters . . . and to be driven from the table and out of the
court house and detered from returning any more during the election,"
though not more than half of the freeholders had voted. He further
charged that a justice of the peace voluntarily required the sheriff to
take the leader who beat the clerk and put him in jail, and he refused
"to obey the command of the justice, or any ways to keep the peace, to
quell the sd riot, or conduct the sd Election with any order or de-
corum."

When the matter was discussed in the Committee in December,
1773, several depositions were heard. Only one of these affidavits declared that the election was just and impartial, and this was the statement of John Gwinn, the clerk who took the poll for Pickett's brother.
There were three others who testified that there had been fighting, and
that Thomas Wade, as a justice, had commanded the sheriff to take the

person who had started the riot. One of these, Robert Jarman, testified that he had voted for Wade, and as he did so, the sheriff whispered to him: "I see you vote against us, but pray don't make Interest against us." Jarman testified that he then went out and presently returned, when he saw one Sam Parsons standing by the clerk's table with a bottle in his hand, and as the people came in he whispered to them as if interrogating them, and that when Wade ordered him away he refused and seemed to be "in a passion." Going out and returning again, Jarman saw the two clerks, John Twitty and John Gwinn, standing at the table, one with a pistol in his hand and the other with a drawn sword, and said that he heard Wade "command the peace at sundry times," and command the sheriff to take the leader of the riot, and heard the sheriff's refusal. Wade then turned to the crowd to know if there was a deputy or a constable present. At that point Jarman again left the court house, "it appearing dangerous to stay in the house as it lookt as if murder would be done." Jarman asserted that many people had been unable to vote, as "they was not so fond of an Election as to fight for it." He believed Wade would have been elected if the election had been orderly.

When the committee in the assembly had heard these witnesses, they resolved that "the charges contained in the sd Memorial are not sufficiently supported by testimony so as to set aside the sd election." The house concurred in the resolution. In spite of this, one can scarcely doubt that the sheriff, being the brother of one of the candidates, did show some partiality in the election. The majority of the evidence submitted indicates that. At any rate, the incident serves to illustrate the powerful influence which sheriffs exercised over the elections.

As indicated by the Wade petition, the elections were probably very informal, one-sided affairs. Politics in its crudest sense no doubt found play in them. Since the elections were held at the court house, and under the immediate supervision of the influential court ring, and under the control of the most powerful officer in the ring, the poorer and more numerous class of freeholders probably would not dare to vote contrary to the wishes of the men who more or less determined their economic and social status. Another phase of the political exploitation of the elections no doubt took place in the ordinaries, or inns. Small, informal caucuses, where flip and punch flowed freely for those who promised to vote the right way, were probably held at these places, and elections were more or less determined before the drawing up of the electoral list.

Sheriffs were frequently the owners of ordinaries, and therefore in ready position to bring the aid of liquors to their elections.

The petition of Wade also indicates the importance of family politics. But there was still another political phase of the court ring which strengthened the power of the sheriffs; namely, the politics of the colonial militia. The county militia, like the county court, with which it was inseparably bound up, was virtually a close corporation. The officers were the justices of the peace, the clerks of court, and the sheriffs. They controlled the appointments to the militia so effectively that the governors were in the habit of sending blank commissions to the men already in command, and permitting these men to fill the commissions out for their subalterns and even for their successors. As a result, all of the offices drawing attractive fees were filled by local court officials. The sheriffs were prominent in the commissioned ranks of the militia. Alexander Mebane of Orange, Samuel Heighe of Pasquotank, Osborne Jeffries of Bute, John Gray of Orange, and many other sheriffs were commissioned officers in the militia. And the militia was often used to solidify the position of the court officials in the elections; one petitioner complains of the lax discipline of the militia, "which is wink'd at by the Officer's Commanding them, in order to Curry favour [to get their Votes at Elections] with the People . . . ."

Because of these facts, the court officials constituted the most unrepresentative form of local government which North Carolina has ever had. The suffrage was not only restricted legally, but in actual practice was so managed by the officials that nothing like free and representative suffrage existed. As a result even the legislature was of the same complexion as the local bodies, and could be said to be representative only in the sense that it was representative of the dominant class of local officials. The system of self-government which the colonists had thus developed through practice was one which could be easily exploited by the leaders. It is obvious that such an unrepresentative form of government, dominated by local leaders, could be brought to revolutionary pitch in short order if the officials desired it. This is precisely what happened in revolutionary North Carolina, and of the governing officials who were at the lead, the sheriffs were quite prominent.

21. THE ROLE OF THE LOWER HOUSES OF ASSEMBLY IN EIGHTEENTH-CENTURY POLITICS*

by Jack P. Greene

The most authoritative spokesmen for American interests were the lower houses of the colonial legislatures. Local cliques, such as those dominating the county courts, made sure they were well represented in Boston or Williamsburg by men who would advance and protect their interests. In the following essay, Jack P. Greene describes how these legislative bodies became powerful instruments of governance in America during the eighteenth century. Often they achieved power without conflicting with royal authority; sometimes a struggle with the governor became prolonged and bitter. Usually the legislature emerged triumphant, chipping away at another of the king's prerogatives. By the end of the colonial period, the American and British views of the imperial constitution had sharply diverged. Colonials insisted that their assemblies were lawmaking institutions inferior to none, not even Parliament, whereas the Eng-

* *Journal of Southern History*, vol. 27 (1961), 451–474. Copyright 1961 by the Southern Historical Association. Reprinted without footnotes by permission of the Managing Editor.

lish regarded them as subordinate bodies. These developments reflect the thrust of emerging colonial elites, who were constantly pressing for greater political authority, and the weakness of the royal government, which was ill equipped to exercise tight control over the colonists. The English were convinced that the best way to promote rapid development of the empire, whose wealth enriched England, was to pacify the Americans by granting them a measure of self-government. Few realized until too late where such a policy would lead.

For further reading: Jack P. Greene, *The Quest for Power: The Lower Houses of Assembly in the Southern Royal Colonies, 1689–1776* (1963); Leonard W. Labaree, *Royal Government in America* (1930).

The rise of the representative assemblies was perhaps the most significant political and constitutional development in the history of Britain's overseas empire before the American Revolution. Crown and proprietary authorities had obviously intended the governor to be the focal point of colonial government with the assemblies merely subordinate bodies called together when necessary to levy taxes and ratify local ordinances proposed by the executive. Consequently, except in the New England charter colonies, where the representative bodies early assumed a leading role, they were dominated by the governors and councils for most of the period down to 1689. But beginning with the Restoration and intensifying their efforts during the years following the Glorious Revolution, the lower houses engaged in a successful quest for power as they set about to restrict the authority of the executive, undermine the system of colonial administration laid down by imperial and proprietary authorities, and make themselves paramount in the affairs of their respective colonies.

Historians have been fascinated by this phenomenon. For nearly a century after 1776 they interpreted it as a prelude to the American Revolution. In the 1780's the pro-British historian George Chalmers saw it as the early manifestation of a latent desire for independence, an undutiful reaction to the mild policies of the Mother Country. In the middle of the nineteenth century the American nationalist George Bancroft, although more interested in other aspects of colonial history, looked upon it as the natural expression of American democratic principles, simply another chapter in the progress of mankind. The reaction to these sweeping interpretations set in during the last decades of the nineteenth century, when Charles M. Andrews, Edward Channing, Herbert L. Osgood, and others began to investigate in detail and to study in context developments from the Restoration to the end of the Seven Years' War. Osgood put a whole squadron of Columbia students to work examining colonial political institutions, and they produced a series of institutional studies in which the evolution of the lower houses was a central feature. These studies clarified the story of legislative development in each colony, but this necessarily piecemeal approach, as well as the excessive fragmentation that characterized the more general narratives of Osgood and Channing, tended to emphasize the differences rather than the similarities in the rise of the lower houses and failed to produce a general analysis of the common features of their quest for power. Among later scholars, Leonard W. Labaree in his excellent monograph *Royal Government in America* presented a comprehensive survey of the institutional development of the lower houses in the royal colonies and of the specific issues involved in their struggles with the royal governors, but he did not offer any systematic interpretation of the general process and pattern of legislative development. Charles Andrews promised to tackle this problem and provide a synthesis in the later volumes of his magnum opus, *The Colonial Period of American History,* but he died before completing that part of the project.

As a result, some fundamental questions have never been fully answered, and no one has produced a comprehensive synthesis. No one has satisfactorily worked out the basic pattern of the quest; analyzed the reasons for and the significance of its development; explored its underlying assumptions and theoretical foundations; or assessed the consequences of the success of the lower houses, particularly the relationship between their rise to power and the coming of the American Revolution. This essay is intended to suggest some tentative conclusions about these problems, not to present ultimate solutions. My basic research on the lower houses has been in the Southern royal colonies and in Nova Scotia. One of the present purposes is to test the generalizations I have arrived at about the Southern colonies by applying them to what scholars have learned of the legislatures in the other colonies.

This procedure has the advantage of providing perspective on the story of Southern developments. At the same time, it may serve as one guidepost for a general synthesis in the future.

Any student of the eighteenth-century political process will sooner or later be struck by the fact that, although each of the lower houses developed independently and differently, their stories were similar. The elimination of individual variants, which tend to cancel out each other, discloses certain basic regularities, a clearly discernible pattern— or what the late Sir Lewis Namier called a morphology—common to all of them. They all moved along like paths in their drives for increased authority, and, although their success on specific issues differed from colony to colony and the rate of their rise varied from time to time, they all ended up at approximately the same destination. They passed successively through certain vaguely defined phases of political development. Through most of the seventeenth century the lower houses were still in a position of subordination, slowly groping for the power to tax and the right to sit separately from the council and to initiate laws. Sometime during the early eighteenth century most of them advanced to a second stage at which they could battle on equal terms with the governors and councils and challenge even the powers in London if necessary. At that point the lower houses began their bid for political supremacy. The violent eruptions that followed usually ended in an accommodation with the governors and councils which paved the way for the ascendancy of the lower houses and saw the virtual eclipse of the colonial executive. By the end of the Seven Years' War, and in some instances considerably earlier, the lower houses had reached the third and final phase of political dominance and were in a position to speak for the colonies in the conflict with the imperial government which ensued after 1763.

By 1763, with the exception of the lower houses in the corporate colonies of Rhode Island and Connecticut, which had virtually complete authority, the Pennsylvania and Massachuestts houses of representatives were probably most powerful. Having succeeded in placing its election on a statutory basis and depriving the Council of direct legislative authority in the Charter of Privileges in 1701, the Pennsylvania House under the astute guidance of David Lloyd secured broad financial and appointive powers during the administrations of Daniel Gookin and Sir William Keith. Building on these foundations, it gained almost complete dominance in the 1730's and 1740's despite the opposition of the governors, whose power and prestige along with that of the Council declined rapidly. The Massachusetts House, having been accorded the unique privilege of sharing in the selection of the Council by the royal charter in 1691, already had a strong tradition of legislative supremacy inherited from a half century of corporate experience. During the first thirty years under the new charter first the benevolent policies of Sir William Phips and William Stoughton and then wartime conditions during the tenures of Joseph Dudley and Samuel Shute enabled the House, led by Elisha Cooke, Jr., to extend its authority greatly. It emerged from the conflicts over the salary question during the 1720's with firm control over finance, and the Crown's abandonment of its demand for a permanent revenue in the early 1730's paved the way for an accommodation with subsequent governors and the eventual dominance of the House under Governor William Shirley after 1740.

The South Carolina Commons and New York House of Assembly were only slightly less powerful. Beginning in the first decade of the eighteenth century, the South Carolina lower house gradually assumed an ironclad control over all aspects of South Carolina government, extending its supervision to the minutest details of local administration after 1730 as a succession of governors, including Francis Nicholson, Robert Johnson, Thomas Broughton, the elder William Bull, and James Glen offered little determined opposition. The Commons continued to grow in stature after 1750 while the Council's standing declined because of the Crown policy of filling it with placemen from England and the Common's successful attacks upon its authority. The New York House of Assembly began to demand greater authority in reaction to the mismanagement of Edward Hyde, Viscount Cornbury, during the first decade of the eighteenth century. Governor Robert Hunter met the challenge squarely during his ten-year administration beginning in 1710, but he and his successors could not check the rising power of the House. During the seven-year tenure of George Clarke beginning in 1736, the House advanced into the final stage of development. Following Clarke, George Clinton made a vigorous effort to reassert the authority of the executive, but neither he nor any of his successors was able to challenge the power of the House.

The lower houses of North Carolina, New Jersey, and Virginia developed more slowly. The North Carolina lower house was fully capable of protecting its powers and privileges and competing on equal terms with the executive during the last years of proprietary rule and under the early royal governors, George Burrington and Gabriel Johnston. But it was not until Arthur Dobbs' tenure in the 1750's and 1760's that, meeting more regularly, it assumed the upper hand in North Carolina politics under the astute guidance of Speaker Samuel Swann and Treasurers John Starkey and Thomas Barker. In New Jersey the lower house was partially thwarted in its spirited bid for power during the 1740's under the leadership of John Kinsey and Samuel Nevill by the determined opposition of Governor Lewis Morris, and it did not gain superiority until the administrations of Jonathan Belcher, Thomas Pownall, Francis Bernard, and Thomas Boone during the Seven Years' War. Similarly, the Virginia Burgesses vigorously sought to establish its control in the second decade of the century under Alexander Spotswood, but not until the administrations of Sir William Gooch and Robert Dinwiddie, when first the expansion of the colony and then the Seven Years' War required more regular sessions, did the Burgesses finally gain the upper hand under the effective leadership of Speaker John Robinson.

Among the lower houses in the older colonies, only the Maryland House of Delegates and the New Hampshire House of Assembly failed to reach the final level of development in the period before 1763. The Maryland body made important advances early in the eighteenth century while under the control of the Crown and aggressively sought to extend its authority in the 1720's under the leadership of the older Daniel Dulany and again in the late 1730's and early 1740's under Dr. Charles Carroll. But the proprietors were usually able to thwart these attempts, and the Delegates failed to pull ahead of the executive despite a concerted effort during the last intercolonial war under the administration of Horatio Sharpe. In New Hampshire, the House had exercised considerable power through the early decades of the eighteenth century, but Governor Benning Wentworth effectively challenged its authority after 1740 and prevented it from attaining the extensive power exercised by its counterparts in other colonies. It should be emphasized, however, that neither the Maryland nor the New Hampshire lower house was in any sense impotent and along with their more youthful equivalent in Georgia gained dominance during the decade of debate with Britain after 1763. Of the lower houses in the continental colonies with pre-1763 political experience, only the Nova Scotia Assembly had not reached the final phase of political dominance by 1776.

The similarities in the process and pattern of legislative development from colony to colony were not entirely accidental. The lower houses faced like problems and drew upon common traditions and imperial precedents for solutions. They all operated in the same broad imperial context and were affected by common historical forces. Moreover, family, cultural, and commercial ties often extended across colony lines, and newspapers and other printed materials, as well as individuals, often found their way from one colony to another. The result was at least a general awareness of issues and practices in neighboring colonies, and occasionally there was even a conscious borrowing of precedents and traditions. Younger bodies such as the Georgia Commons and Nova Scotia Assembly were particularly indebted to their more mature counterparts in South Carolina and Massachusetts Bay. On the executive side, the similarity in attitudes, assumptions, and policies among the governors can be traced in large measure to the fact that they were all subordinate to the same central authority in London, which pursued a common policy in all the colonies.

Before the Seven Years' War the quest was characterized by a considerable degree of spontaneity, by a lack of awareness that activities of the moment were part of any broad struggle for power. Rather than consciously working out the details of some master plan designed to bring them liberty or self-government, the lower houses moved along from issue to issue and from situation to situation, primarily concerning themselves with the problems at hand and displaying a remarkable capacity for spontaneous action, for seizing any and every opportunity to enlarge their own influence at the executive's expense and for holding tenaciously to powers they had already secured. Conscious of the issues involved in each specific conflict, they were for the most part unaware of and uninterested in the long-range implications of their actions. Virginia Governor Francis Fauquier correctly judged the matter in 1760. "Whoever charges them with acting upon a premeditated concerted plan, don't know them," he wrote of the Virginia burgesses, "for they mean honestly, but are Expedient Mongers in the highest Degree." Still, in retrospect it is obvious that throughout the eighteenth century the lower houses were engaged in a continuous movement to enlarge their sphere of influence. To ignore that continuity would be to miss the meaning of eighteenth-century colonial political development.

One is impressed with the rather prosaic manner in which the lower houses went about the task of extending their authority, with the infrequency of dramatic conflict. They gained much of their power in the course of routine business, quietly and simply extending and consolidating their authority by passing laws and establishing practices, the implications of which escaped both colonial executives and imperial authorities and were not always fully recognized even by the lower houses themselves. In this way they gradually extended their financial authority to include the powers to audit accounts of all public officers, to share in disbursing public funds, and eventually even to appoint officials concerned in collecting and handling local revenues. Precedents thus established soon hardened into fixed principles, "undoubted rights" or "inherent powers," changing the very fabric of their respective constitutions. The notable absence of conflict is perhaps best illustrated by the none too surprising fact that the lower houses made some of their greatest gains under those governors with whom they enjoyed the most harmony, in particular Keith in Pennsylvania, Shirley in Massachusetts, Hunter in New York, and the elder and younger Bull in South Carolina. In Virginia the House of Burgesses made rapid strides during the 1730's and 1740's under the benevolent government of Gooch, who discovered early in his administration that the secret of political success for a Virginia governor was to reach an accord with the plantation gentry.

One should not conclude that the colonies had no exciting legislative-executive conflicts, however. Attempts through the middle decades of the eighteenth century by Clinton to weaken the financial powers of the New York House, Massachusetts Governors Samuel Shute and William Burnet to gain a permanent civil list, Benning Wentworth to extend unilaterally the privilege of representation to new districts in New Hampshire, Johnston to break the extensive power of the Albemarle Counties in the North Carolina lower house, Dinwiddie to establish a fee for issuing land patents without the consent of the Virginia Burgesses, and Boone to reform South Carolina's election laws each provided a storm of controversy that brought local politics to a fever pitch. But such conflicts were the exception and usually arose not out of the lower houses' seeking more authority but from the executives' attempts to restrict powers already won. Impatient of restraint and jealous of their rights and privileges, the lower houses responded forcefully and sometimes violently when executive action threatened to deprive them of those rights. Only a few governors, men of the caliber of Henry Ellis in Georgia and to a lesser extent William Henry Lyttelton in South Carolina and Bernard in New Jersey, had the skill to challenge established rights successfully without raising the wrath of the lower houses. Clumsier tacticians—Pennsylvania's William Denny, New York's Clinton, Virginia's Dinwiddie, North Carolina's Dobbs, South Carolina's Boone, Georgia's John Reynolds—failed when pursuing similar goals.

Fundamentally, the quest for power in both the royal and the proprietary colonies was a struggle for political identity, the manifestation of the political ambitions of the leaders of emerging societies within each colony. There is a marked correlation between the appearance of economic and social elites produced by the growth in colonial wealth and population on the one hand and the lower houses' demand for increased authority, dignity, and prestige on the other. In the eighteenth century a group of planters, merchants, and professional men had attained or were rapidly acquiring within the colonies wealth and social position. The lower houses' aggressive drive for power reflects the determination of this new elite to attain through the representative assemblies political influence as well. In another but related sense, the lower houses' efforts represented a movement for autonomy in local affairs, although it is doubtful that many of the members recognized them as such. The lower houses wished to strengthen their authority within the colonies and to reduce to a minimum the amount of supervision, with the uncertainties it involved, that royal or proprietary authorities could exercise. Continuously nourished by the growing desire of American legislators to be masters of their own political fortunes and by the development of a vigorous tradition of legislative superiority in imitation of the imperial House of Commons, this basic principle of local control over local affairs in some cases got part of its impetus from an unsatisfactory experience early in the lower houses' development with a despotic, inefficient, or corrupt governor such as Thomas, Lord Culpeper, or Francis, Lord Howard of Effingham, in Virginia, Lionel Copley in Maryland, Sir Edmund Andros in Massachusetts, Seth Sothell in North Carolina, or the infamous Cornbury in New York and New Jersey. Clearly, the task of defending men's rights and property against the fraud and violence of tyrannical executives fell most appropriately to the representatives of those whose rights and property demanded protection.

But the quest for power involved more than the extension of the authority of the lower houses within the colonies at the expense of the colonial executives. After their initial stage of evolution, the lower houses learned that their real antagonists were not the governors but the proprietors or Crown officials in London. Few governors proved to be a match for the representatives. A governor was almost helpless to prevent a lower house from exercising powers secured under his predecessors, and even the most discerning governor could fall into the trap of assenting to an apparently innocent law that would later prove damaging to the royal or proprietary prerogative. Some governors, for the sake of preserving amicable relations with the representatives or because they thought certain legislation to be in the best interest of a colony, actually conspired with legislative leaders to present the actions of the lower houses in a favorable light in London. Thus, Jonathan Belcher worked with Massachusetts leaders to parry the Crown's demand for a permanent revenue in the 1730's, and Fauquier joined with Speaker John Robinson in Virginia to prevent the separation of the offices of speaker and treasurer during the closing years of the Seven Years' War.

Nor could imperial authorities depend upon the colonial councils to furnish an effective check upon the representatives' advancing influence. Most councilors were drawn from the rising social and economic elites in the colonies. The duality of their role is obvious. Bound by oath to uphold the interests of the Crown or the proprietors, they were also driven by ambition and a variety of local pressures to maintain the status and power of the councils as well as to protect and advance their own individual interests and those of their group within the colonies. These two objectives were not always in harmony, and the councils frequently sided with the lower houses rather than with the governors. With a weakened governor and an unreliable council, the task of restraining the representative assemblies ultimately devolved upon the home government. Probably as much of the struggle for power was played out in Whitehall as in Williamsburg, Charleston, New York, Boston, or Philadelphia.

Behind the struggle between colonial lower houses and the imperial authorities were two divergent, though on the colonial side not wholly articulated, concepts of the constitutions of the colonies and in particular of the status of the lower houses. To the very end of the colonial period, imperial authorities persisted in the views that colonial constitutions were static and that the lower houses were subordinate governmental agencies with only temporary and limited lawmaking powers—in the words of one imperial official, merely "so many Corporations at a distance, invested with an Ability to make Temporary By Laws for themselves, agreeable to their respective Situations and Climates." In working out a political system for the colonies in the later seventeenth century, imperial officials had institutionalized these views in the royal commissions and instructions. Despite the fact that the lower houses were yearly making important changes in their respective constitutions, the Crown never altered either the commissions or instructions to conform with the realities of the colonial political situation and continued to maintain throughout the eighteenth century that they were the most vital part of the constitutional structure of the royal colonies. The Pennsylvania and to a lesser extent the Maryland proprietors were less rigid, although they also insisted upon their theoretical constitutional and political supremacy over the lower houses.

Colonial lower houses had little respect for and even less patience with such a doctrinaire position, and whether or not royal and proprietary instructions were absolutely binding upon the colonies was the leading constitutional issue in the period before 1763. As the political instruments of what was probably the most pragmatic society in the eighteenth-century Western World, colonial legislators would not likely be restrained by dogma divorced from reality. They had no fear of innovations and welcomed the chance to experiment with new forms and ideas. All they asked was that a thing work. When the lower houses found that instructions from imperial authorities did not work in the best interests of the colonies, that they were, in fact, antithetic to the very measures they as legislatures were trying to effect, they openly refused to submit to them. Instructions, they argued, applied only to officials appointed by the Crown.

> Instructions from his majesty, to his governor, or the council, are binding to them, and esteemed as laws or rules; because, if either should disregard them, they might immediately be displaced,

declared a South Carolina writer in 1756 while denying the validity of an instruction that stipulated colonial councils should have equal rights with the lower houses in framing money bills. "But, if instructions should be laws and rules to the people of this province, then there would be no need of assemblies, and all our laws and taxes might be made and levied by an instruction." Clearly, then, instructions might bind governors, but never the elected branch of the legislature.

Even though the lower houses, filled with intensely practical politicians, were concerned largely with practical political considerations,

435

they found it necessary to develop a body of theory with which to oppose unpopular instructions from Britain and to support their claims to greater political power. In those few colonies that had charters, the lower houses relied upon the guarantees in them as their first line of defense, taking the position that the stipulations of the charters were inviolate, despite the fact that some had been invalidated by English courts, and could not be altered by executive order. A more basic premise which was equally applicable to all colonies was that the constituents of the lower houses, as inhabitants of British colonies, were entitled to all the traditional rights of Englishmen. On this foundation the colonial legislatures built their ideological structure. In the early charters the Crown had guaranteed the colonists "all privileges, franchises and liberties of this our kingdom of England . . . any Statute, act, ordinance, or provision to the contrary thereof, notwithstanding." Such guarantees, colonials assumed, merely constituted recognition that their privileges as Englishmen were inherent and unalterable and that it mattered not whether they stayed on the home islands or migrated to the colonies. "His Majesty's Subjects coming over to America," the South Carolina Commons argued in 1739 while asserting its exclusive right to formulate tax laws, "have no more forfeited this their most valuable Inheritance than they have withdrawn their Allegiance." No "Royal Order," the Commons declared, could "qualify or any wise alter a fundamental Right from the Shape in which it was handed down to us from our Ancestors."

One of the most important of these rights was the privilege of representation, on which, of course, depended the very existence of the lower houses. Imperial authorities always maintained that the lower houses existed only through the consent of the Crown, but the houses insisted that an elected assembly was a fundamental right of a colony arising out of an Englishman's privilege to be represented and that they did not owe their existence merely to the King's pleasure.

> Our representatives, agreeably to the general sense of their constituents, [wrote New York assemblyman William Smith in the 1750's] are tenacious in their opinion, that the inhabitants of this colony are entitled to all the privileges of Englishmen; that they have a right to participate in the legislative power, and that the session of assemblies here, is wisely substituted instead of a representation in parliament, which, all things considered, would, at this remote distance, be extremely inconvenient and dangerous.

436

The logical corollary to this argument was that the lower houses were equivalents of the House of Commons and must perforce in their limited spheres be entitled to all the privileges possessed by that body in Great Britain. Hence, in cases where an invocation of fundamental rights was not appropriate, the lower houses frequently defended their actions on the grounds that they were agreeable to the practice of the House of Commons. Thus in 1755 the North Carolina Lower House denied the right of the Council to amend tax bills on the grounds that it was "contrary to Custom and Usage of Parliament." Unintentionally, Crown officials encouraged the lower houses to make this analogy by forbidding them in the instructions to exercise "any power or privilege whatsoever which is not allowed by us to the House of Commons . . . in Great Britain."

Because neither fundamental rights nor imperial precedents could be used to defend practices that were contrary to customs of the mother country or to the British Constitution, the lower houses found it necessary to develop still another argument: that local precedents, habits, traditions, and statutes were important parts of their particular constitutions and could not be abridged by a royal or proprietary order. The assumptions were that the legislatures could alter colonial constitutions by their own actions without the active consent of imperial officials and that once the alterations were confirmed by usage they could not be countermanded by the British government. They did not deny the power of the governor to veto or of the Privy Council to disallow their laws but argued that imperial acquiescence over a long period of time was tantamount to consent and that precedents thus established could not be undone without their approval. The implication was that the American colonists saw their constitutions as living, growing, and constantly changing organisms, a theory which was directly opposite to the imperial view. To be sure, precedent had always been an important element in shaping the British constitution, but Crown officials were unwilling to concede that it was equally so in determining the fundamental law of the colonies. They willingly granted that colonial statutes, once formally approved by the Privy Council, automatically became part of the constitutions of the colonies, but they officially took the position that both royal instructions and commissions, as well as constitutional traditions of the mother country, took precedence over local practice or unconfirmed statutes. This conflict of views persisted throughout the period after 1689, becoming more and more of an issue in the decades immediately preceding the American Revolution.

If imperial authorities would not grant the validity of the theoretical arguments of the lower houses, neither after 1689 did they make any systematic or concerted effort to force a rigid compliance with official policies. Repressive measures, at least before 1763, rarely went beyond the occasional disallowance of an offending statute or the official reprimand of a rambunctious lower house. General lack of interest in the routine business of colonial affairs and failure to recognize the potential seriousness of the situation may in part account for this leniency, but it is also true that official policy under both Walpole and the Pelhams called for a light rein on the colonies on the assumption that contented colonies created fewer problems for the administration. "One would not Strain any point," Charles Delafaye, secretary to the lords justices, cautioned South Carolina's Governor Francis Nicholson in 1722, "where it can be of no Service to our King or Country." "In the Plantations," he added, "the Government should be as Easy and Mild as possible to invite people to Settle under it." Three times between 1734 and 1749 the ministry failed to give enthusiastic support to measures introduced into Parliament to insure the supremacy of instructions over colonial laws. Though the Calverts were somewhat more insistent upon preserving their proprietary prerogatives, in general the proprietors were equally lax as long as there was no encroachment upon their land rights or proprietary dues.

Imperial organs of administration were in fact inadequate to deal effectively with all the problems of the empire. Since no special governmental bodies were created in England to deal exclusively with colonial affairs, they were handled through the regular machinery of government —a maze of boards and officials whose main interests and responsibilities were not the supervision of overseas colonies. The only body sufficiently informed and interested to deal competently with colonial matters was the Board of Trade, and it had little authority, except for the brief period from 1748 to 1761 under the presidency of George Dunk, Earl of Halifax. The most useful device for restraining the lower houses was the Privy Council's right to review colonial laws, but even that was only partly effective, because the mass of colonial statutes annually coming before the Board of Trade made a thorough scrutiny impossible. Under such arrangements no vigorous colonial policy was likely. The combination of imperial lethargy and colonial aggression virtually guaranteed the success of the lower houses' quest for power. An indication of a growing awareness in imperial circles of the seriousness of the situation was Halifax's spirited, if piecemeal, effort to restrain the growth of the lower houses in the early 1750's. Symptomatic of these efforts was the attempt to make Georgia and Nova Scotia model royal colonies at the institution of royal government by writing into the instructions to their governors provisions designed to insure the continued supremacy of the executive and to prevent the lower houses from going the way of their counterparts in the older colonies. However, the outbreak of the Seven Years' War forced Halifax to suspend his activities and prevented any further reformation until the cessation of hostilities.

Indeed, the war saw a drastic acceleration in the lower houses' bid for authority, and its conclusion found them in possession of many of the powers held less than a century before by the executive. In the realm of finance they had imposed their authority over every phase of raising and distributing public revenue. They had acquired a large measure of independence by winning control over their compositions and proceedings and obtaining guarantees of basic English Parliamentary privileges. Finally, they had pushed their power even beyond that of the English House of Commons by gaining extensive authority in handling executive affairs, including the right to appoint executive officers and to share in formulating executive policy. These specific gains were symptoms of developments of much greater significance. To begin with, they were symbolic of a fundamental shift of the constitutional center of power in the colonies from the executive to the elected branch of the legislature. With the exception of the Georgia and Nova Scotia bodies, both of which had less than a decade of political experience behind them, the houses had by 1763 succeeded in attaining a new status, raising themselves from dependent lawmaking bodies to the center of political authority in their respective colonies.

But the lower houses had done more than simply acquire a new status in colonial politics. They had in a sense altered the structure of the constitution of the British Empire itself by asserting colonial authority and extending the constitutions of the colonies far beyond the limitations of the charters, instructions, or fixed notions of imperial authorities. The time was ripe for a re-examination and redefinition of the constitutional position of the lower houses. With the rapid economic and territorial expansion of the colonies in the years before

1763 had come a corresponding rise in the responsibilities and prestige of the lower houses and a growing awareness among colonial representatives of their own importance, which had served to strengthen their long-standing, if still imperfectly defined, impression that colonial lower houses were the American counterparts of the British House of Commons. Under the proper stimuli, they would carry this impression to its logical conclusion: that the lower houses enjoyed an equal status under the Crown with Parliament. Here, then, well beyond the embryonic stage, was the theory of colonial equality with the mother country, one of the basic constitutional principles of the American Revolution, waiting to be nourished by the series of crises that beset imperial-colonial relations between 1763 and 1776.

The psychological implications of this new political order were profound. By the 1750's the phenomenal success of the lower houses had generated a soaring self-confidence, a willingness to take on all comers. Called upon to operate on a larger stage during the Seven Years' War, they emerged from that conflict with an increased awareness of their own importance and a growing consciousness of the implications of their activities. Symptomatic of these developments was the spate of bitter controversies that characterized colonial politics during and immediately after the war. The Gadsden election controversy in South Carolina, the dispute over judicial tenure in New York, and the contests over the pistole fee and the two-penny act in Virginia gave abundant evidence of both the lower houses' stubborn determination to preserve their authority and the failure of Crown officials in London and the colonies to gauge accurately their temper or to accept the fact that they had made important changes in the constitutions of the colonies.

With the shift of power to the lower houses also came the development in each colony of an extraordinarily able group of politicians. The lower houses provided excellent training for the leaders of the rapidly maturing colonial societies, and the recurring controversies prepared them for the problems they would be called upon to meet in the dramatic conflicts after 1763. In the decades before Independence there appeared in the colonial statehouses John and Samuel Adams and James Otis in Massachusetts Bay; William Livingston in New York; Benjamin Franklin and John Dickinson in Pennsylvania; Daniel Dulany the younger in Maryland; Richard Bland, Richard Henry Lee, Thomas Jefferson, and Patrick Henry in Virginia; and Christopher Gadsden and John Rutledge in South Carolina. Along with dozens of others, these men were thoroughly schooled in the political arts and primed to meet any challenge to the power and prestige of the lower houses.

Britain's "new colonial policy" after 1763 provided just such a challenge. It precipitated a constitutional crisis in the empire, creating new tensions and setting in motion forces different from those that had shaped earlier developments. The new policy was based upon concepts both unfamiliar and unwelcome to the colonists such as centralization, uniformity, and orderly development. Yet it was, for the most part, an effort to realize old aspirations. From Edward Randolph in the last decades of the seventeenth century to the Earl of Halifax in the 1750's colonial officials had envisioned a highly centralized empire with a uniform political system in each of the colonies and with the imperial government closely supervising the subordinate governments. But, because they had never made any sustained or systematic attempt to achieve these goals, there had developed during the first half of the eighteenth century a working arrangement permitting the lower houses considerable latitude in shaping colonial constitutions without requiring crown and proprietary officials to give up any of their ideals. That there had been a growing divergence between imperial theory and colonial practice mattered little so long as each refrained from challenging the other. But the new policy threatened to upset this arrangement by implementing the old ideals long after the conditions that produced them had ceased to exist. Aimed at bringing the colonies more closely under imperial control, this policy inevitably sought to curtail the influence of the lower houses, directly challenging many of the powers they had acquired over the previous century. To protect gains they had already made and to make good their pretensions to greater political significance, the lower houses thereafter no longer had merely to deal with weak governors or casual imperial administrators; they now faced an aggressive group of officials bent upon using every means at their disposal, including the legislative authority of Parliament, to gain their ends.

Beginning in 1763 one imperial action after another seemed to threaten the position of the lower houses. Between 1764 and 1766 Parliament's attempt to tax the colonists for revenue directly challenged the colonial legislatures' exclusive power to tax, the cornerstone of their authority in America. A variety of other measures, some aimed at particular colonial legislatures and others at general legislative powers and practices, posed serious threats to powers that the lower houses had either long enjoyed or were trying to attain. To meet these challenges, the lower houses had to spell out the implications of the changes they had been making, consciously or not, in the structures of their respective governments. That is, for the first time they had to make clear in their own minds and then to verbalize what they conceived their respective constitutions in fact were or should be. In the process, the spokesmen of the lower houses laid bare the wide gulf between imperial theory and colonial practice. During the Stamp Act crisis in 1764–1766 the lower houses claimed the same authority over taxation in the colonies as Parliament had over that matter in England, and a few of them even asserted an equal right in matters of internal policy. Although justified by the realities of the colonial situation, such a definition of the lower houses' constitutional position within the empire was at marked variance with imperial ideals and only served to increase the determination of the home government to take a stricter tone. This determination was manifested after the repeal of the Stamp Act by Parliament's claim in the Declaratory Act of 1766 to "full power and authority" over the colonies "in all cases whatsoever."

The pattern over the next decade was on the part of the home government one of increasing resolution to take a firmer tone with the colonies and on the part of American lawmakers a heightened consciousness of the implications of the constitutional issue and a continuously rising level of expectation. In addition to their insistence upon the right of Parliament to raise revenue in the colonies, imperial officials also applied, in a way that was increasingly irksome to American legislators, traditional checks like restrictive instructions, legislative review, and the suspending clause requiring prior approval of the Crown before laws of an "extraordinary nature" could go into effect. Finally Parliament threatened the very existence of the lower houses by a measure suspending the New York Assembly for refusing to comply with the Quartering Act in 1767 and by another altering the substance of the Massachusetts constitution in the Massachusetts Government Act in 1774. In the process of articulating and defending their constitutional position, the lower houses developed aspirations much greater than any they had had in the years before 1763. American representatives became convinced in the decade after 1766 not only that they knew best what to do for their constituents and the colonies and that anything interfering with their freedom to adopt whatever course seemed necessary was an intolerable and unconstitutional restraint but also that the only security for their political fortunes was in the abandonment of their attempts to restrict and define Parliamentary authority in America and instead to deny Parliament's jurisdiction over them entirely by asserting their equality with Parliament under the Crown. Suggested by Richard Bland as early as 1766, such a position was openly advocated by James Wilson and Thomas Jefferson in 1774 and was officially adopted by the First Continental Congress when it claimed for Americans in its declarations and resolves "a free and exclusive power of legislation in their several provincial legislatures, where their right of representation can alone be preserved, in all cases of taxation and internal polity."

Parliament could not accept this claim without giving up the principles it had asserted in the Declaratory Act and, in effect, abandoning the traditional British theory of empire and accepting the colonial constitutional position instead. The First Continental Congress professed that a return to the *status quo* of 1763 would satisfy the colonies, but Parliament in 1774–1776 was unwilling even to go that far, much less to promise them exemption from Parliamentary taxation. Besides, American legislators now aspired to much more and would not have been content with a return to the old inarticulated and undefined pattern of accommodation between imperial theory and colonial practice that had existed through most of the period between 1689 and 1763. Rigid guarantees of colonial rights and precise definitions of the constitutional relationship between the Mother Country and the colonies and between Parliament and the lower houses on American terms, that is, imperial recognition of the autonomy of the lower houses in local affairs, would have been required to satisfy them.

Between 1689 and 1763 the lower houses' contests with royal governors and imperial officials had brought them political maturity, a considerable measure of control over local affairs, capable leaders, and a rationale to support their pretensions to political power within the colonies and in the Empire. The British challenge after 1763 threatened to render their accomplishments meaningless and drove them to demand equal rights with Parliament and autonomy in local affairs and eventually to declare their independence. At issue was the whole political structure forged by the lower houses over the previous century. In this context the American Revolution becomes in essence a war for political survival, a conflict involving not only individual rights as traditionally emphasized by historians of the event but assembly rights as well.

22. DEMOCRACY AND POLITICS
IN COLONIAL NEW YORK*

by Milton M. Klein

How democratic was colonial society? Historians sharply
disagree, as the following essay on New York politics indicates.
Was the right to vote restricted to a few by property and other
qualifications, or could a majority of the adult males satisfy
these tests? Yet even if a majority could vote, were they free
to cast their ballots as they desired, or were they influenced
by powerful neighbors on whom they depended? Even more
puzzling is the fact that many eligible voters rarely bothered
to exercise their rights. Finally, did those who voted have a
meaningful choice on election day between competing personalities who espoused alternative programs and policies for
managing public affairs? In the following essay Milton M. Klein
raises all these questions and illuminates the nature of political
rivalry in colonial New York. Though the author refers to competing groups as "parties," they are unlike modern political
parties and resemble much more closely what colonists called

* *New York History*, vol. 40 (1959), 221–246. Reprinted by permission of the
New York State Historical Association. Footnotes have been omitted except where
they are necessary for an understanding of the text.

"factions," small groups of individuals skilled at manipulation, who competed for short-term personal advantage without permanent organization, making and breaking alliances as expediency dictated. In contrast, political parties have permanent organization; they appeal for votes from economic, ethnic, religious, and other social groups, promising to use power to further the interests of their supporters.

For further reading: Robert E. Brown, "Democracy and Colonial Massachusetts," *New England Quarterly*, vol. 25 (1952), 291–313; John Cary, "Statistical Method and the Brown Thesis on Colonial Democracy," *William and Mary Quarterly*, 3d series, vol. 20 (1963), 251–276; Robert E. and B. Katherine Brown, *Virginia, 1705–1786: Democracy or Aristocracy?* (1964); Lawrence H. Leder, *Robert Livingston, 1654–1728, and the Politics of Colonial New York* (1961); Leonard W. Labaree, *Conservatism in Early American History* (1948).

The classic description of the political structure of colonial New York was provided by Carl Becker a half-century ago. In his doctoral dissertation and in two articles in the *American Historical Review*, Becker set forth the thesis that throughout most of the colonial period provincial politics were controlled by a few rich and powerful families whose wealth was based on land and commerce. This small coterie, linked among themselves by marriage, exercised a type of leadership that was "essentially medieval in nature—that is, informal and personal"; and political parties were consequently little more than "factions based on personal influence." Party allegiance was thus determined more by personal ties than by differences of political or economic principle, and "personal loyalty, rather than faith in a proposition was the key to political integrity."

Becker did single out one fundamental source of disagreement between political factions, the continuing dispute between governor and assembly, but he qualified this. While those supporting the executive at any particular moment might be designated the "court" or "British" party and those opposing him the "popular" or "anti-British" party, men moved into or out of the governor's "interest" not out of conviction or principle but rather as he was able to grant them special favors. When political leaders desired to enlarge their followings, Becker insisted, they did not appeal for popular support by party programs but rather engineered "prudential intermarriages" with other families of the aristocracy. The alliances thus created constituted the real sources of political strength.

The political stage could be monopolized by the aristocracy, according to Becker, because the bulk of the colony's population constituted a passive and inarticulate audience, or, at best, a well-trained and obedient claque. The suffrage was extremely limited, and the undemocratic landholding system of the colony placed most of the population in economic dependence upon a few great proprietors, who insured the political fidelity of their tenants by the coercive surveillance that open voting made possible. Nominations were managed by the aristocracy, tenants were herded to the polls to register their approval of hand-picked candidates, and if revolt should threaten, the leaders could meet it by deferring the election or holding it at odd times and inaccessible places.

The democratization of the political machinery, Becker maintained, took place in the last half of the eighteenth century, and particularly after 1765; and the evidences of the change were the rise of popular nominating devices like the mass meeting, the use of the press to rally popular support, and the disappearance of the "purely personal element" as the cement of political association. A newly articulate electorate took advantage of the democratized machinery to demand a larger share in the political process, and as the Revolution approached, the conflict between mother country and colony was fought alongside the local struggle between the old aristocracy and the new democracy.

Becker's analysis parallels that drawn for most of the other colonies, and his conclusion that the Revolution in New York had a dual character has been generalized into the oft-repeated and felicitous aphorism that the war was fought over the issue of "who should rule at home" as well as over the issue of "home rule."

Both the analysis and the conclusion are still attractive, but recent reappraisals of the political structure of colonial Massachusetts suggest the desirability of a fresh examination of the New York scene. No attempt can be made in a short paper to subject Becker's conclusions to exhaustive reexamination, but three questions arising from his analysis will be reconsidered here: (1) Were New York's political parties largely medieval-type personal factions? (2) Was the electoral machinery controlled by the aristocracy through the landlord-tenant relationship? and (3) Was the franchise severely restricted?

1

As Becker saw it, the political divisions of the first half of the eighteenth century were personal in character, and the so-called parties that developed during this period were no better than "factions based on personal influence." As evidence, Becker offered the well-known contest between the Livingston and De Lancey families, which appears to run like an unbroken thread through the colony's political history. Becker did not suggest the origin or the basis of the contest, but he saw these two families emerging, after fifty years of feuding among the various factions, as "the leaders in the struggle which was, though political in some degree, after all very largely personal in its nature . . . and that the struggle was personal rather than political is indicated by the fact that the parties were known by the names of their respective leaders."

The rivalry between the Livingstons and the De Lanceys was indeed long and bitter, but their disagreement was neither private nor personal in its origination, and the political parties that formed around them were rooted in substantial differences of a political and economic character. The contest began during the administration of Governor William Burnet (1720–1728), and it was inspired not by simple attachment or opposition to the governor's interest but rather by large differences between two rival economic groups over Indian policy and the fur trade.

Robert Livingston, the founder of that family's American fortunes and the first Lord of the Livingston Manor, was also the colony's Secretary for Indian Affairs. A fur trader in addition, he conceived an ambitious and far-sighted program of imperial-Indian relations designed to promote the interests of the Empire and of his own trade at the same time.

The heart of the Livingston program was a discontinuance of the traffic in furs that had developed between some traders in Albany and certain Montreal fur dealers. The latter got their skins from the Indians and from the French trappers (*coureurs de bois*) who lived among the western tribes. They then exchanged the pelts on a wholesale basis with the Albanians, who paid in English "stroud" and wares, which the natives preferred to the inferior French manufactures. In conducting this trade, both the Canadians and the Albanians ignored the interests of their home governments. French policy made the export of beaver from New France a legal monopoly and required all skins to be shipped to France; English policy demanded that the western Indians be diverted from their French allegiance, a policy that could hardly succeed as long as the natives depended upon Montreal for their supply of cloth, guns, and hardware.

Livingston was disturbed at the continuing business relationship between Albany and Montreal for economic as well as political reasons. As a "direct" or "retail" trader who sent his agents into the Indian country to secure skins directly from the native source, Livingston came into competition with those Albanians who conducted their trade "wholesale" through the Montreal merchants. He became convinced that unless the Indians could be induced to redirect the flow of furs to the English, France would ultimately dominate not only the fur trade but the Indians and the Continent as well. To prevent this, he suggested that a chain of fortified posts be built in the Indian country to impress the natives with British power and to serve as centers of the fur trade, that young New Yorkers be trained as scouts and "bushlopers" to compete with the *coureurs de bois,* and that Protestant missionaries be sent among the natives to counteract the work of the Jesuits. To make the program effective, a ban on trade between Albany and Montreal must be imposed.

Around Livingston rallied the other retail traders, the imperialists, and the land speculators with holdings in the Mohawk Valley. The success of the Livingston scheme would pacify the natives, encourage settlement in the back country, and boost land values. Men like Robert Livingston, Jr., Lewis Morris, and Cadwallader Colden joined to promote the new policy. They organized a "Livingston-Morris Party," secured the support of Governor Burnet, and launched the program with a law prohibiting trade with Canada and the establishment of a trading post and fort at Oswego, on Lake Ontario.

An opposition party was quickly organized by the wholesale traders and their allies, and its leadership was provided by Stephen De Lancey, Peter Schuyler, and Adolph Philipse. Schuyler was the spokesman of the Albanians who monopolized the traffic with Montreal; De Lancey and Philipse represented the New York merchants who supplied the traders with their English wares. The Livingston program threatened their interests in two ways. The prohibitory legislation would undermine the source of their prosperity, and the money for the new trading posts would be secured by fresh import levies that would fall most heavily on merchants like De Lancey who were so deeply involved in the Canada trade.

The immediate victory of the Livingstons was shortly nullified as the De Lanceys managed to win control of the assembly, to oust Livingston as speaker in favor of Adolph Philipse, and to secure a royal disallowance of the law barring trade with Canada; but the significance of the contest, in terms of the Becker thesis, is the politico-economic character of the party division and the superficial part that personal relationships played in the contest. Family ties, indeed, served less to clarify the lines of political divergence than to obscure them. Thus, Stephen De Lancey and Peter Schuyler, leaders of the anti-Livingston forces, were both related to Robert Livingston by marriage, the one as nephew, the other as brother-in-law; the De Lancey's son, Peter, married the daughter of Cadwallader Colden, a leader of the Livingston faction!

Kinship was equally inconspicuous in dictating the political loyalty of the second generation of the Livingston family. Philip Livingston inherited his father's wealth, but not his political principles. Himself a Canada trader, he was unenthusiastic about the Livingston-Burnet trade program. While he remained nominally allied with his father's former supporters, thus gaining a seat on the Governor's Council under Burnet, he also maintained good relations with the De Lanceys, not quite certain which of the Indian policies would become permanent. This happy faculty of keeping a discreet foot in both camps served Livingston especially well during the hectic days of the Zenger Trial. Personal relationship should have placed him in the camp of the Zengerite "popular" party, since its leaders were his father's old friends, Lewis Morris, James Alexander, Cadwallader Colden, and William Smith, Sr.; but as a member of the Executive Council, he found himself, perforce, one of the De Lancey "court" party. Publicly, Livingston professed his attachment to the De Lanceys, unwilling to jeopardize his place on the council; privately, he lent his aid to the Zengerites in their efforts to thwart Governor William Cosby. But Livingston's defection from the De Lanceys was not the result of his personal affection for or his family ties with the Alexander-Morris group. Cosby's high-handed tactics in challenging existing land titles simply threatened Livingston's own fortune.

Superficially, the dispute between Cosby and his critics revolved about the governor's attempt to collect the salary paid to Rip Van Dam, who had served as acting governor during the interval between Cosby's appointment and his arrival in New York. To collect, and to keep the case away from a jury, Cosby established a Court of Exchequer in which the proceedings could be conducted. Livingston, along with the Zengerite leaders, feared that the new juryless court might also be used to achieve Cosby's personal ambition to carve out a landed estate for himself. When Cosby began to resurrect old land titles and to demand quit rents long in arrears, Livingston took alarm. Some of his own land acquisitions from the Indians were so tainted that they could hardly stand the light of scrupulous examination. Land titles, he conceded, were "not drawn in right form" and "flaws may be found in Severall of them." To James Alexander, the mouthpiece of the Zengerites, he wrote that "If Mr. Van Dam had suffered himself to be devoured, certainly another Morcell would have followed, [and] no Person could have expected to escape." In extending his secret support to the Zenger leadership, Livingston confessed frankly that "we Change Sides as Serves our Interest best."

For the next two decades, the Livingstons pursued the same calculating political course, now allying with the De Lanceys, now opposing them, and at times preserving a cautious neutrality. When Governor George Clinton (1743–1753) turned upon Philip Livingston and attacked him for defrauding the Indians and trading with the enemy during King George's War, the family renewed their alliance with the De Lanceys. With the death of Philip Livingston, the second manor lord, in 1749, the personal ties between the Livingstons and the Alexander-Morris group became even stronger, but the family remained in the De Lancey fold while the old Zengerites moved into the circle of "the court." Not until 1754 did the descendants of Robert Livingston and his earliest political allies rejoin forces, and again it was "interest" not friendship that determined the Livingston choice. The De Lancey-controlled assembly refused to assist the family in its dispute with Massachusetts over the manor's boundary and was slow in soliciting Parliament to defer the new Iron Act long enough to allow the manor's iron works to be expanded. In deserting the De Lanceys once again, the Livingstons demonstrated how well they had learned the hard lesson that in politics there was "no such thing as friendship, abstracted from political Views."

In the light of the above evidence, it is difficult to accept Becker's assertion that "strictly speaking, . . . there were no political parties" but rather "two centers of influence," or that family connections provided the solid underpinnings of the colony's political structure. Contemporary observers were well aware of the tenuous character of family loyalty as the cohesive element in political organization. James Alexander himself confessed with a wisdom born out of long experience that "Interest often connects people who are entire strangers and sometimes separates those who have the strongest natural ties." William Smith, Jr., conceded that the Livingston party "did not always proceed from motives approved of by that family." And Cadwallader Colden, a veteran of New York's political battles, summed up his own extensive acquaintance with the colony's history in the observation that although parties "at different times have taken their denominations from some distinguished Person or Family who have appeared at their head," their roots lay in the "different political and religious Principles of the Inhabitants."

The Revolution may well have hastened the transformation of New York's political parties from "personal factions" to modern-type associations on "a basis of principle," as Becker suggested, but the process had been initiated early in the eighteenth century. The political rivalry between the Livingstons and the De Lanceys bears a closer resemblance to the later contests between Federalists and Democratic-Republicans than it does to the medieval feud between the Guelphs and the Ghibellines. And if Becker is right in insisting that the "essence of the aristocratic method" in politics is "that men are governed by personality rather than by principle," then colonial New York's early political parties were less aristocratic than democratic.

2

Next to the marriage relationship, the principal instrument of aristocratic political control, according to Becker, was "the economic relation of tenant to proprietor." New York's undemocratic system of landholding, perhaps the most undemocratic of all the colonies, appears at first glance to substantiate Becker's thesis. A few individuals engrossed vast estates, manorial and non-manorial; most small farmers held their lands as tenants rather than as owners; and the terms of many leases were irritating and onerous, involving personal services of a medieval nature and restrictions on the sale and use of the property. From these conditions, Becker drew the inference that tenant voters were politically dependent upon the will of their economic overlords. The inference was never specifically documented, Becker being content with the statement: "That tenant voters would be largely influenced by lords of manors is perhaps sufficiently obvious."

Economic power certainly endowed the great proprietors with a large share of political influence, but landlord control was neither automatic nor absolute, nor were lessees universally at the mercy of the owners because of stringent conditions of tenure. The leases on the Livingston Manor were generally considered among the most burdensome, but even here some tenants held their lands on generous terms. In 1737, for example, Philip Livingston granted land to some German families rent-free for the first nine years and supplied each of them with three horses, two cows, and provisions for a year besides. Three years later he offered leases "gratis" and others rent-free for the first ten years in order to attract "good people." On the James Duane estate, such liberal terms were not unusual.

Tenants on all the estates were usually permitted to begin farming without any down payment, rents were often nominal, and non-payment was not always followed by eviction. In 1757, William Smith, Jr., reported that on the Van Rensselaer and Livingston Manors, rents had "as yet been neither exacted nor paid" even though they amounted to only a tenth of the produce of the leaseholds. The total rent on a 160 acre farm was seldom more than twenty-five dollars, and some lands rented for as little as two or four pounds per 100 acre.

Tenant status did not render the small farmers politically impotent, nor did it preclude their political independence. On the Westchester County manors there was a considerable amount of self-government, the "inhabitants" of Philipsburgh, for example, meeting regularly to "mak[e] town laws" and to choose constables, collectors, assessors, poundmasters, clerks, and highway overseers. Even where political "bossism" prevailed, it was not impossible for the small farmers to revolt against the "organization" nominee and threaten to set up a candidate of their own. In 1748 such an incipient revolt occurred among the farmers of Canajoharie against the Albany County machine, and two years later a similar protest movement originated among the tenants of Henry Beekman, Jr., in Ulster and Dutchess Counties. Beekman's machine was a well-disciplined one, but not even his political control was foolproof. In 1751 he expressed fears that unless his friends united around his nominee for the assembly seat, the place would go to "one w[hi]ch we will Like worse."

According to Becker, once the political "bosses" of the counties selected the candidates for provincial office, the tenant voters followed "their lead as a matter of course." But if the landlords were so sure of the votes of their tenantry, one wonders why they went to such considerable extents to buy votes. Not even the most powerful of the political machines or the greatest proprietor could guarantee success in an election campaign without a large war chest. By 1753, the business of "election jobbing" and political bribery was so widespread that it became the subject of public protest from one anguished citizen who was outraged that so many voters should be willing to barter away their prized and traditional franchise for no more than "Beer and Brandy," "a Pound of Beef," or "a Treat" and "a Frolick."

The practice was common in Beekman territory, Henry Beekman regularly providing his tenants with free beef, bacon, cider, and rum a day or two before the polls opened. In Albany, votes were bought at prices that ranged from a mere bottle of wine to as much as forty pounds! Perhaps the most revealing evidence to dispute Becker's contention that tenants merely registered the wishes of the great proprietors is the experience of Robert Livingston in 1761. Despite his economic power as lord of the manor, Livingston could not guarantee the political adherence of his tenants unless they were paid for their votes. "The Camps will not move to an Election without being payed for their time," he advised his friend, Abraham Yates, Jr., who was running for the assembly seat in Albany County. At forty shillings a man, however, Livingston had no doubts that "they may be had." He warned Yates quite plainly that unless sufficient funds could be raised, the election would be lost, "for money are the Senues of War, in this as well as in other affairs."

Just as Becker appears to have overestimated the extent of political control that stemmed from proprietorship, so did he exaggerate the role that open voting played in insuring landlord control. Becker's statement that "Every voter was watched, we may be sure, and his record was known," is another of those irritating generalizations based largely on assumption rather than proof. As a matter of fact, there is little evidence to suggest that tenants considered *viva voce* voting either oppressive or undemocratic, or that the great proprietors regarded it as essential to their political control.

There were many small farmer uprisings in the eighteenth century, culminating in the "Great Rebellion of 1766," but the complaints of the tenantry always centered around land titles, rents, security of tenure, and their personal obligations to the manor lords. The secret ballot was never one of the demands of the dissidents. How lightly the aristocracy considered the practice as an instrument of political control is revealed by the attempt, in 1769, to pass a secret ballot bill in the assembly. The bill was given its strongest endorsement in the house by the Livingston party, the traditional spokesmen of the landed interest, and was attacked by the De Lanceys on the grounds that it would enable "crafty and subtle" lawyers to *influence* the voters! The question was argued most heatedly in New York City where landlord control was not a significant issue; and among the most ardent supporters of the measure, in addition to the Livingstons, were the Sons of Liberty, a group that was entirely out of sympathy with the tenants during their "rebellion" a few years earlier.

When the written ballot was ultimately incorporated into the New York State Constitution of 1777, it was done at the suggestion not of a representative of the tenantry but of John Jay, whose conservatism is epitomized in his comment that "those who own the country ought to govern it." The innovation did not work any great change in tenant voting habits or in landlord control. Van Rensselaer tenants continued to elect the patroon or a member of his family to the state legislature, and for twenty-one years they chose a Van Rensselaer to represent them in Congress.

If *viva voce* voting was an essential ingredient of the undemocratic political structure of New York, then there is patent incongruity in the failure of both the aristocracy and tenantry to recognize it as such. Undoubtedly the landed aristocrats exercised great influence in the colony's politics, but their influence is better ascribed to voter illiteracy and indifference than to open balloting or the landlord-tenant relationship. It is not without significance that when in 1788 a tenant in Albany County recalled publicly that he had often in the past given his "assent" to the will of his landlord "in supporting his political importance," he added: "I was ignorant of my own rights."

3

Becker's contention that suffrage restrictions left over half the adult white male population without any political privileges is difficult to corroborate because of the few census returns and the even fewer election statistics available for the colonial period. The figure is open to considerable question, however, based upon Becker's own reckoning. The unfranchised, he claimed, included the smaller freeholders, the leasehold tenants, and the "mechanics," and this resulted in an electorate so narrow that in 1790 it comprised only twelve per cent of the total population. The latter figure is, in the first place, deceptive, since the "total" population included women, children, and Negroes. A recent calculation of the electorate in New York City in 1790 discloses that virtually 100 per cent of the *adult white males* qualified under the suffrage requirement of the state constitution of 1777. Moreover, Becker was absolutely wrong in excluding the mechanics of New York City and Albany on the ground that they were neither freeholders nor freemen, and in casually dismissing the number of freemen in these cities as "insignificant."

The freemen of Albany and New York City were those merchants and handicraftsmen who had been admitted to the freedom of the town by the municipal corporation. The practice was a European one, intended originally to reserve the benefits of town industry to its inhabitants, but in New York freemanship quickly lost its original character. Wholesale traders were early exempt from its limitations, the city never enforced the monopoly, and by the eighteenth century an increasing number of tradespeople were carrying on business in open violation of the law. New Yorkers continued to seek the privilege, however, for the political rather than the economic benefits it bestowed: freemen along with freeholders could vote in municipal and provincial elections and hold municipal office.

In New York City, freemanship was conferred liberally, and the number of freemen who participated in the city's elections was scarcely "insignificant." Indeed, freemen played a decisive role at the polls. The privilege was not restricted to skilled laborers, the term "handicraftsman" being interpreted so loosely that among those admitted under this category were carmen, porters, painters, fishermen, boatmen, gardeners, yeomen, and mariners, along with others classified simply as "laborers." The cost of purchasing the freedom of the town might well have served to bar mass admissions. In Albany it ranged from thirty-six shillings to three pounds twelve shillings for merchants, and from eighteen to thirty-six shillings for handicraftsmen. In New York City, rates fluctuated similarly, merchants paying from twenty shillings to five pounds and handicraftsmen from six shillings to one pound four shillings, with three pounds and twenty shillings being the respective averages. However, skilled laborers did not find the sum excessive during a period when they earned an average of more than seven shillings a day, and natives of the city and those completing an apprenticeship in the city were even less concerned with the cost, since they could secure their freedom by simply paying the clerical fee of about two shillings. Finally, in New York City, those citizens "that are poor and not able to purchase their Freedoms" were admitted "gratis," by a decree of the Common Council in 1703.

These liberal regulations permitted an increasing number of mechanics and laborers to secure the freedom of the city. By the middle of the eighteenth century, they comprised two-thirds of all the admissions; in 1765, they made up almost half the new freemen. Still another index of the increasing accessibility of freemanship is the rising number of persons admitted as "Registrants" rather than "Purchasers," the former being those who because of their birth or apprenticeship in New York merely had to have their names recorded on the rolls and pay the nominal clerical fees. From 1735 to 1740, three times as many new freemen were registered as purchased their freedom, and in 1765 twice as many were admitted by registration as by purchase.

Albany's regulations paralleled those of New York City, freemanship here too proving more important as a political than as an economic institution. The town fathers were less interested in barring non-freemen from the economic life of the city than in encouraging them to purchase their freedom. Here also the privilege was extended liberally, natives of the city paying only a few shillings to be registered and others being admitted free. In 1702, for example, the right was conferred by action of the Common Council on the entire military company stationed at the fort! About the only persons disfranchised in Albany as a result were bound servants and foreigners not naturalized.

Freemanship played a vital role in the political life of the two largest cities of the colony of New York. In New York City itself, admissions to freemanship serve as a kind of barometer of political activity, rising in periods of political excitement and falling during the calms between political storms. Freemen were not "an insignificant portion of the electorate," as Becker believed, nor was the institution of freemanship a handmaiden of the aristocracy's system of political control. In the elections of 1768 and 1769 in New York City, no less than two-thirds of the voting electorate were freemen. Freemanship was not an obstacle to popular participation in politics but rather a democratic device which opened the polls to all classes of citizens and gave virtually all the adult white males the opportunity of exercising the franchise.

Outside of Albany and New York City, the franchise was probably more restricted, but perhaps not nearly as much as Becker indicated. The large number of tenant farmers who made up the bulk of the rural population were not necessarily barred from voting by the colony's suffrage restrictions. In 1699 the legislature limited the right to vote in provincial elections (apart from the freemen of New York City and Albany) to freeholders over twenty-one years of age who possessed lands or tenements to the value of forty pounds, free of all encumbrances; but two years later it defined as "freeholder" any person who held land for his own life or that of his wife's, mortgages notwithstanding. The modification amounted to a liberalization since it qualified all those tenants whose leases ran for a term of lives or for at least twenty-one years.

The number of persons thus enfranchised is difficult to determine in the absence of sufficient tax rolls. However, all the tenants on the Livingston and Van Rensselaer Manors undoubtedly qualified as freeholders, leases on the former being for at least one life and those on the latter being freehold estates. The status of the tenants on the Van Cortlandt and Philipse Manors is less clear, but whatever the terms of their leases, the tenants of the Westchester County manors were regarded as politically powerful. In any case contemporaries were unable to draw clear distinctions in tenant status, Lieutenant Governor Cadwallader Colden reporting to the Board of Trade in 1765 that all the farmers in the province were regarded as holding their lands in "fee simple." This would presumably have made all of them eligible to vote providing their lands were of sufficient value.

Just how many estates were valued at forty pounds or more is not known, but contemporaries like the historian, William Smith, Jr., complained that the great proprietors had a tendency to rate their lands "exorbitantly high." On the manors, where the assessors were selected locally, it would not be difficult for the manor lords to secure courtesy valuations of forty pounds for as many of their leaseholds as they desired. Certainly tenants played an important and at times a decisive role in elections in Albany, Westchester, and Dutchess Counties, but in the absence of fuller statistical data, their precise numerical significance is unknown. A few figures are available, but they are disappointingly inconclusive. In Westchester County in 1763, for example, less than 25 per cent of the adult white male population was able to meet the *sixty-pound* freehold qualification for service on juries. In Albany County in 1720, however, about 44 per cent of the adult white males were listed as freeholders in a census of that year, and in New York City at least 48 per cent were freeholders in 1768.

If disfranchisement under the existing suffrage requirements was a source of tenant discontent, it was singularly missing, along with *viva voce* voting, among the grievances loudly voiced by rural leaseholders during the agrarian disturbances of the 1750's and 1760's.

One other basis of disfranchisement is worth noting. Catholics and Jews were both barred from the polls by actions of the assembly in 1701 and 1737, respectively, but the effect of these restrictions was minimal. The number of Catholics in the colony was insignificant, and the law seems not to have been applied to Jews with any regularity. In the city of New York, where virtually all of the Jews of the province resided, the poll lists of 1761, 1768, and 1769 carry such Jewish names as Moses Benjamin Franks, Baruch Hays, Judah Hays, Solomon Hays, Benjamin Laziere, Hayman Levy, Isaac Moses, Aaron Myer, and Isaac Myer.

Somewhat more information exists for those who *did* vote than for those who *could* vote. In New York City, voting returns for four years disclose the following degrees of participation:

	ADULT WHITE MALES	NUMBER OF VOTES	PER CENT OF ADULT WHITE MALES
1735	1465	812	55.4
1761	2581	1447	56.1
1768	3589	1924	53.6
1769	3733	1515	40.6

In Westchester County, figures are available for the famous poll of 1733 on the green of St. Paul's Church, Eastchester, in which Lewis Morris, recently deposed from the chief justiceship by Governor Cosby because of his role in the Van Dam affair, ran for the assembly seat. In that election, which became a *cause célèbre* in the Zenger Trial, participation was smaller than in the New York City polls already noted:

ADULT WHITE MALES	NUMBER OF VOTES	PER CENT OF ADULT WHITE MALES
1276	420	32.9

If participation in elections during the colonial period was only as extensive as it was in 1788, when about half of those eligible in New York City voted, then the electorate of the colony was still an extremely broadly based one, amounting to virtually all the adult white males in New York City (and probably in Albany), and to about 65 per cent in the rural counties. The latter figure, moreover, may well be an underestimate in view of the fact that transportation difficulties, political indifference, and illiteracy kept rural participation in elections below the level of New York City's. The *qualified* electorate in the rural areas may quite possibly, then, have been as large as that of New York City and Albany.

4

While there is no intention of suggesting that the reappraisal offered in this paper is conclusive, there appears to be enough evidence to warrant redrawing the conventional picture of colonial New York's politics. Surely Becker's relegation of early political parties to quasi-feudal factions of a personal nature requires reconsideration in view of the continuing economic self-interest, rather than the ties of blood and marriage, which explains the political tergiversations of great families like the Livingstons and De Lanceys. Their political somersaults placed them alternately within or outside the circle of "the court," but this was purely incidental. The De Lanceys could shift from the gubernatorial to the popular side without disturbing the essential bases of their party organization, and the Livingstons could similarly pose as champions of prerogative or flaming representatives of the people depending upon their own political or economic principles. That such political gyrations disturbed family ties or personal relationships was also quite incidental. Coldens married De Lanceys and Livingstons married Alexanders without reconciling existing political enmities between the respective families.

One of the Livingstons diagnosed the fundamental bases of the colony's political alignments with acute perception when he noted of the Morrises that they "set their witts to work to gain a party" only when their personal interests were "touched." Kinship took but second place to "interest."

There appears considerable exaggeration, too, in Becker's impression of early parties as highly informal in character and undisciplined in organization. Party machinery seems to have been well developed long before 1765, with party "bosses," campaign chests, vote-getting devices, and patronage rewards all in existence. Appeals for popular support on the grounds of "principle" and through the medium of the press were common in the late 1740's and early 1750's. "Paper war" accompanied almost every election. That of 1750 in Westchester County produced a particularly heavy barrage of pamphlets and broadsides. Two years later, the election campaign in New York City was so violent that the printer of one of the local newspapers, the *Gazette*, made public apology for the many vituperative essays that appeared in its columns. During 1754–1755, the controversy over the founding of King's College generated so much literary heat in the *New York Mercury* that its printer was frequently compelled to publish supplements to carry the non-controversial news and regular advertisements.

The frequency with which political leaders resorted to the press and the regularity with which they lured voters to the polls with financial blandishments suggest a far greater degree of political independence among the small farmer electorate than Becker assumed. The economic bond between landlord and tenant was never so strong that shrewd party leaders could afford to take the latter's allegiance for granted. Even so firmly entrenched a political leader as Henry Beekman was careful to solicit the wishes of his constituents and to introduce legislation in the assembly that would prove "Beneficiall for the county." Other party leaders were equally aware of the strength of the independent voter. When the triumvirate of young lawyers, William Livingston, William Smith, Jr., and John Morin Scott, undertook to thwart the Anglican scheme to establish King's College on terms favorable to the Church of England, their political strategy was to arouse the country voters to deluge the assembly with petitions against the plan and thus to maintain such "an unremitting pressure from their constituents" as to keep "irresolute" assemblymen "warm in their attachment to the anti-Episcopal cause." And while they sought support from the wealthy landlords who controlled political machines in the rural counties, their major appeal was addressed to the small farmers themselves, with local lawyers, public officials, and Presbyterian clergymen acting as their agents and campaign managers.

The electorate was not only more articulate and more active than Becker believed, but it was also more extensive. Even the incomplete figures offered in this paper indicate a franchise that was surprisingly broadly based, particularly in New York City and Albany where about one-third of the adult white male population of the colony resided, and an electorate that took advantage of its suffrage in at least as great a measure as did the qualified voters under the new state constitution after the Revolution.

The Revolution in New York was not "the open door through which the common freeholder and the unfranchised mechanic and artisan pushed their way into the political arena," to use Becker's language, simply because the door had never really been closed throughout most of the colonial period. The local aristocracy did occupy a commanding position in the colony's politics, and they continued to do so after independence; but the explanation for their political leadership must be sought in factors other than the strength of family ties, their economic power as landlords, or an excessively restricted franchise.

23. HISTORIANS AND THE PROBLEM OF EARLY AMERICAN DEMOCRACY*

by J. R. Pole

In the following essay, J. R. Pole argues that it is historically incorrect to think that the colonies were democratic just
because a large proportion of the adult males could vote.
Though government was not insensitive to public sentiment
and the exercise of political power was not restricted to a
hereditary aristocracy, most Americans deferred to the wisdom
and authority of their betters, those whose wealth, training,
family connections, talents, and position entitled them to lead.
Deference, not democracy, was the basis of colonial government.
Subordination of inferiors to superiors was weakened by the
absence of a hereditary aristocracy and consequent confusion
concerning who was entitled to respect. The upper strata of
colonial society were recruited from self-made men and their
heirs. But those who achieved position could not be certain to
retain it or pass it on to the next generation, since family fortunes in America fluctuated, lacking the institutional supports
that buttressed hereditary ruling groups in Europe. This insta-

* *American Historical Review*, vol. 67 (1962), 626–646.

bility in the upper strata, as old families declined and new ones ascended, weakened their ability to command deference, especially since prominent colonials often competed with one another for a favored position.

The earliest national period of United States history combines two themes. It is a period of revolution and also of constitution making. Charter governments, whether royal or proprietary, give way to new governments which claim to derive the whole of their authority from the American electorate. The Americans, though working from experience, build for the future. This fact is of cardinal importance for any attempt to understand their work or the state of mind in which it was undertaken.

The claim of the new government raises a problem that was not solved by the mere exercise of effective, but revolutionary powers. Was their authority strictly compatible with the doctrine that governments derive their just powers from the consent of the governed? What was meant by "consent"? How was such consent obtained or certified?

The attempt to answer these questions leads the historian into a reconstruction of the character of these early institutions and an inquiry into the ideas by which they were governed. In the light of subsequent American development, it has led historians to address themselves to the problem of deciding whether or not these institutions were democratic. Whether or not we choose to adopt this particular definition, whether or not we regard it as a useful tool of analysis, the underlying problem is one that the historian cannot easily avoid. No history of the American Revolution and of constitution making could be written without discussion of the doctrines on which the Americans based their resistance, the question of what meaning these doctrines bore for the different American participants, and of the degree of participation, the attitude and purposes of different elements in American society.

There is a problem of the relationship of ideas to institutions; there is a previous problem of the ideas themselves. I do not think that the broad and undifferentiated use of the term "democracy" helps either to describe the institutions or to explain the ideas. I do not even think that our analysis of these matters will be much affected by the use of this concept. But the thesis has been advanced[1] that the American colonies were already full-fledged democracies before the American Revolution began, from which it follows that the cardinal principle of the Revolution was a defense of democratic institutions against royal or parliamentary tyranny. It is a thesis that has the advantage of an attractive simplicity, and it is one that can be supported by a good deal of evidence, especially if that evidence is read without much relation to the context of eighteenth-century political ideas. It also has the merit of providing the occasion, and in order that the argument should not go by default, the necessity of a more searching inquiry into the realities.

To use the word "democracy" is to raise, but not I think to solve, a problem of definition. And it is not an easy one. There is so little agreement about what is meant by "democracy," and the discussion has such a strong tendency to slide noiselessly from what we *do* mean to what we *ought* to mean, that for purposes of definition it seems to be applicable only in the broadest sense. And this sense has the effect of limiting, rather than of advancing, our understanding of the past.

But I must certainly admit that if I did think the word "democracy" in fact did justice to the problem, then I would have to accept it despite the risks involved. More than this: we ought to have some agreement as to what meaning it can be made to bear. It makes good sense in a purely comparative view to call the American colonies and early states democratic when contrasting them with the Prussia of Frederick II or the Habsburg Empire; they were in the same sense democratic compared with France or with England, with which they had so much in common. There might be less unintended irony in calling them part of the "free world" than in doing the same today with Spain, Formosa, or the Union of South Africa. In the broad strokes we use to differentiate between tyrannies and free states the term will serve as a starting point, but not as a conclusion. It is interesting, when one begins to look more closely at the structure of the complex societies of the eighteenth century, how rapidly these broad distinctions lose their value and cease to serve any analytical purpose. As R. R. Palmer has recently remarked, surveying the Western world before the French Revolution, "No one except a

---

[1] Robert E. Brown, *Middle-Class Democracy and the Revolution in Massachusetts, 1691-1780* (Ithaca, N. Y., 1955), esp. 401–408.

few disgruntled literary men supposed that he lived under a despotism."[2]
When one considers how complex the machinery of administration, of
justice, for the redress of grievances and, if any, of political representation must become in any ancient and intricately diversified society, it
is easy to feel that the more democratic virtues of the American societies
were related, more than anything else, to their relative simplicity and
lack of economic and functional diversity. But a closer inspection, not
only of the structure, but of the development, of colonial institutions
reveals a tendency that puts the matter in another light; for these institutions were unmistakably molded in the shape of English institutions
and were conforming themselves, both socially and politically, to the
conventions of the period.

The alternative view, which I want to suggest, does not confine
itself merely to rejecting the "democratic" interpretation by putting in
its place a flat, antidemocratic account of the same set of institutions.
What it does, I think, is to see the democratic elements in their proper
perspective by adding a further dimension without which the rest is
flat, incomplete, and, for all its turbulence, essentially lifeless. This is
the dimension of what Cecelia Kenyon has called "institutional
thought."[3]

To take this view, one has to free oneself from a tendency that has
become very difficult to resist. I mean the strong, though wholly anachronistic tendency to suppose that when people who were accustomed
to ways and ideas which have largely disappeared into the past felt
grievances against their government, they must necessarily have wanted
to express their dissatisfaction by applying the remedies of modern
democracy; and, again, that when their demands were satisfied, the
aspirations thus fulfilled must have been modern, democratic aspirations.

The idea that the great mass of the common people might actually
have given their consent to concepts of government that limited their
own participation in ways completely at variance with the principles of
modern democracy is one that lies completely outside the compass or
comprehension of the "democratic" interpretation. That interpretation

---

[2] R. R. Palmer, *The Age of the Democratic Revolution* (Princeton, N. J., 1959),
51.

[3] Cecelia M. Kenyon, "Men of Little Faith: The Anti-Federalists on the
Nature of Representative Government," *William and Mary Quarterly*, XII (Jan.
1955), 4.

insists on the all-importance of certain democratic features of political life, backed by certain egalitarian features of social life having a strong influence on political institutions. What it misses is that these features belonged within a framework which—to polarize the issue at the risk of using another broad term—was known to the world as Whiggism. The institutions of representative government derived from the time when the Whig concept of representative government was being worked out in England and, both by extension and by original experience, in the American colonies (and when the foundations were laid for the Whig interpretation of history). Even where democratic elements were strong and dominant, the animating ideas belonged to a whole Whig world of both politics and society. More than this, the colonial and early national period in which they played so important a part was pervaded by a belief in and a sense of the propriety of social order guided and strengthened by principles of dignity on the one hand and deference on the other. It was, to use the term coined by Walter Bagehot in his account of Victorian England, a deferential society.[4]

There is, of course, nothing very new about the theory that early American society was relatively egalitarian and that this situation was reflected in political institutions and conduct. It was a view that became fashionable in the days of George Bancroft. But it has been reformulated, with formidable documentation, in Robert E. Brown's work on Massachusetts and in his attack on Charles Beard.[5] To regain our perspective it seems necessary for a moment to go back to Beard.

Beard, as we know, distinguished in his study of the Constitution between two leading types of propertied interest, basically those of land and commerce. Commercial property was supposed to have been strongly represented in the Constitutional Convention, landed property outside. The opposition in some of the state ratifying conventions was supposed to have arisen from the outraged interests of the landed classes.

Despite intense opposition in certain states, the Constitution was eventually ratified. But here Beard went further. He asserted that ratification was not a true expression of the will of the people. He based this argument on the prevalence of property qualifications for the suffrage,

---

[4] See also E. S. Griffith, *History of American City Government: Colonial Period* (New York, 1938), 191; Clifford K. Shipton, review of Brown, *Middle-Class Democracy, Political Science Quarterly*, LXXI (No. 2, 1956), 306–308.

[5] Robert E. Brown, *Charles Beard and the Constitution: A Critical Analysis of "An Economic Interpretation of the Constitution"* (Princeton, N. J., 1956).

which meant that only a minority of freeholders and other owners of property could participate in the elections to the ratifying conventions, which in consequence were not truly representative. There are two elements in Beard's hypothesis, as Brown has pointd out.[6] On the one hand, Beard advances the alleged clash between the mercantile and landed interests, with the mercantile coming out on top because of the power conferred by its economic advantages; on the other, he implies the existence of a connection between the landed opposition to ratification and the supposedly disfranchised masses, whose silence so damagingly detracts from the authority of the Constitution. It is not my purpose to discuss the question as to whether Beard's argument has stood the test of recent scrutiny. Another aspect, which may be called that of the moral consequences of Beard's work, deserves more consideration than it has received.

The Philadelphia Convention was described by Thomas Jefferson as "an assembly of demi-gods," a judgment to which posterity murmured "Amen." There are, however, marked disadvantages about being descended from demi-gods; they not only lack a sense of humor, but they set an appallingly high standard. What a relief it must have been, after the first shock of Beard's iconoclasm had died down, to find that they were only human after all! Beard had questioned the Constitution at two points. In the first place, by implying that it was the work of men motivated by private economic interests he made it possible to reconsider its wisdom and justice; but in the second place, when he denied that it had received the sanction of a genuine popular ratification he made it possible—perhaps obligatory—to question the authority of the Constitution precisely because it did not owe its origin to the only recognized source of such authority in the whole science of government as understood in America: the consent of the governed.

To this problem, Brown's critique of Beard is directly relevant. He not only pursues Beard with a determination that recalls John Horace Round's pursuit of Edward Freeman, but in his work on Massachusetts, he makes a thorough and painstaking investigation of the institutions of that province, in which he reaches the conclusion that colonial Massachusetts was already so fully democratic that no case can be made for an interpretation of the American Revolution there in terms of an internal "class war." It is in this connection that Brown broadens his

---

[6] *Ibid.*, 50–51, 53–55, 180–181, 194.

front to develop an attack on Carl Becker.[7] The Revolution was a war of secession, fought for the preservation of American democracy against the antidemocratic policy of the crown. Nothing more, and nothing less. The joint foundations of all this are the wide extent of the suffrage franchise and the wide distribution of middling quantities of property.

The consequences are obvious. If the states, and not only the states but the colonies, were ruled by the consent of the governed, then Beard's unenfranchised masses disappear, and the Constitution is restored to its high place not only in the affection of the American people, but in their scale of approbation.

American history has been written not merely as the story of the people who went to, and lived in, America. It has been developed as the history of liberty. Innumerable books carry in their titles the message that colonial development was a progress toward liberty; since the Revolution, it has sometimes been possible to discern in accounts of American history a certain messianic quality, which some have felt to have been reflected periodically in American diplomacy. History written in this way frequently finds itself obliged to ask how a man, or a movement, stands in relation to the particular values for which American history is responsible. A recent study of Alexander Hamilton's place in the origins of political parties, for example, speaks of the need to determine Hamilton's "rightful place in our history."[8] It becomes important, not just to write a man's biography or to assess his contribution, but to place him correctly on the eternal curve upon which American political performances seem to be graded.

The writing of history thus becomes a matter, not only of finding out what actually happened, but of judging the past. It is a process that cuts both ways. For earlier generations of Americans were keenly—almost disconcertingly—aware of the example they were setting for their descendants. (There is a town meeting entry in Massachusetts, in 1766, which calls the attention of future generations to the sacrifices the townsmen were making for their liberties.[9]) They knew that they would

---

[7] Brown, *Middle-Class Democracy*, Chap. iv.

[8] Joseph E. Charles, "Hamilton and Washington," *William and Mary Quarterly*, XII (Apr. 1955), 226. A further example in connection with Hamilton, whose career provokes this kind of judgment, is found in the title of Louis M. Hacker's *Alexander Hamilton in the American Tradition* (New York, 1957).

[9] Lucius R. Paige, *A History of Cambridge, Massachusetts, 1630–1877* (New York, 1883), 137.

be judged. They were not only building institutions, they were setting standards, for the future. This can become a nerve-racking business. As has been remarked in a different connection (by a writer in the *Times Literary Supplement*) the past and the present seem to watch each other warily as from opposite boxes at the opera, each suspecting the other of being about to commit a *faux pas*.[10]

The two great instruments of American nationhood were the Revolution, with its banner, the Declaration of Independence, and the Constitution. Baptism and confirmation. It would be hard to imagine a more important commitment, not only for the interpretation of the American experience, but one might almost say for the emotional stability of the interpreter, than to place his own values in their proper relation to these events, or if that cannot be done, then to place these events in their proper relation to his values.

Accordingly, historians have brought the problem of values firmly into their assessment of history. They ask, "How democratic was early American society?" And they do not hesitate to reply, if their findings tell them so, that it was not democratic enough. Or, which is still more confusing, that it was struggling forward toward a fuller ideal of democracy. Accounts of this period repeatedly explain that such features of government as property qualifications for the suffrage and political office were still regarded as necessary at that time. "Still." These people had the right instincts; they were coming on nicely; but, unlike ourselves, they had not yet arrived.

There thus develops a tendency to adopt a completely anachronistic note of apology for the insufficiency of democratic principles in early American institutions.[11]

I would like here to anticipate the objection that I am advocating that moral judgments should be taken out of historical writing. Neither do I deny that major developments can and ought to be traced to their minor origins. Moral judgments about the past are not necessarily anachronistic. It is not, I think, unhistorical to believe that some of the acts of treachery and cruelty or of violent aggression which comprise so

---

[10] "Imaginative Historians: Telling the News about the Past," *Times Literary Supplement, Special Supplement on The American Imagination*, Nov. 6, 1959.

[11] Even Brown does so. In pointing out how few men were disfranchised in Massachusetts he significantly remarks, "We cannot condone the practice of excluding those few," though he rightly adds that it makes a tremendous difference whether they were 95 per cent or 5 per cent. Brown, *Middle-Class Democracy*, 402.

great a proportion of recorded human activity were morally wrong, or even to maintain that they influenced the course of events for the worse. But when judgments of moral value are applied to complex social systems, they expose the judge to a peculiar danger of self-deception, perhaps even of self-incrimination. The historian must not only be careful, he must also be highly self-critical, when he embarks on assessments of the moral shortcomings of the past.

The reading of values into historical analysis is particularly liable to deception when the values of the present are themselves made the basis for the selection of materials, which are then judged in the light of the values in question. This may happen when the importance of different institutions or opinions is estimated on the basis of our own opinion of the role they ought to have played in their own time.

Without doubt there is a place for such judgments. There is a place for criticism of the Hanoverian House of Commons—rather a large place. But when we discuss that body our task is not that of apologizing for the fact that the bright light of nineteenth-century democracy had not yet broken on such persons as Pitt or Burke or Shelburne or Fox. Our problem, as I understand it, is that of reconstructing the inner nature of political society in their age and of asking how far Parliament answered the needs of that society, and how far it did not. And that is a matter of what history was actually about, not what it ought to have been about. The historian has a responsibility to the past, but it is not that of deciding within what limits he can recommend it to the approbation of his readers.

The American Revolution was certainly a war for self-determination. But self-determination and democracy are not interchangeable terms, though they can be confused with a facility that has not been without its significance in American diplomacy. A society need not be democratic in order to achieve a high degree of internal unity when fighting for self-determination. Again, a measure of democracy, or a wider diffusion of political power, may well be brought about as an outcome of such a struggle. Such a development was in fact one of the most important consequences of the American Revolution.

It must be acknowledged that the sources of colonial history supply an impressive quantity of material that can be marshaled against my own views of this subject, though not enough as yet to weaken my conviction of the validity of historical evidence.

Much evidence of this sort comes from New England, and Massachusetts is rich in examples. In 1768 General Thomas Gage wrote to Viscount Hillsborough, "from what has been said, your lordship will conclude, that there is no government in Boston, there is in truth, very little at present, and the constitution of the province leans so much to democracy, that the governor has not the power to remedy the disorders which happen in it."[12] The next year Sir Francis Bernard wrote to Viscount Barrington,

> . . . for these 4 years past so uniform a system for bringing all power into the hands of the people has been prosecuted without interruption and with such success that all fear, reverence, respect and awe which before formed a tolerable balance against the power of the people, are annihilated, and the artificial weights being removed, the royal scale mounts up and kicks the beam. . . . It would be better that Mass. Bay should be a complete republic like Connecticut than to remain with so few ingredients of royalty as shall be insufficient to maintain the real royal character.[13]

In 1766 Thomas Hutchinson reported: "In the town of Boston a plebeian party always has and I fear always will command and for some months past they have governed the province."[14] Describing elections in 1772, Hutchinson told Hillsborough, "By the constitution forty pounds sterl. —which they say may be in clothes household furniture or any sort of property is a qualification and even into that there is scarce ever any inquiry and anything with the appearance of a man is admitted without scrutiny."[15]

The franchise was certainly broad. Brown has shown that in many towns as many as 80 per cent of the adult male population, in some more than 90 per cent, were qualified by their property to vote in provincial elections.[16] Three towns appear in the nineties, three in the fifties, the rest in between. These findings tend to confirm and strengthen the impression that prevailed among contemporaries, that Massachusetts was a hotbed of "democratical" or "levelling" principles: the more so after the Boston junta got control of the General Court.

---

[12] *Correspondence of General Thomas Gage . . .*, ed. Clarence E. Carter (2 vols., New Haven, Conn., 1931, 1933), I, 205.

[13] Quoted by R. V. Harlow, *History of Legislative Methods before 1825* (New Haven, Conn., 1917), 39–40.

[14] Brown, *Middle-Class Democracy*, 57.

[15] *Ibid.*, 291.

[16] *Ibid.*, 50.

These expressions raise two issues, one of definition, the other of interpretation.

The point of definition first: when the indignant officers of government described these provinces as "democratical," they were of course not talking about representative government with universal suffrage. They shared not only with their correspondents, but in the last analysis even with their political opponents, the assumption that the constitutions of the colonies, like that of Britain, were made up of mixed elements; they were mixed constitutions, in which the commons were represented in the assembly or commons house. In each constitution there were different orders, and the justification, the *raison d'être*, of such a constitution was that it gave security to each. When they said that the government was becoming "too democratical" or "leaned towards democracy" they meant that the popular element was too weighty for the proper balance of a mixed constitution. They used these expressions as terms of abuse. Not that that matters: we may be impressed by their indignation, but we are not obliged to share it. What is more important to the historian is that the leaders of these movements which took control of the assemblies were in general prepared to accept the same set of definitions.

This they demonstrated when they came to establish new constitutions. The theory of mixed government was maintained with as little adulteration as possible. The difference they had to face was that all the "orders" now drew their position in the government from some form of popular representation. Most of the new constitutions represented the adaptation of institutions which undeniably received their authority from the people, an authority conceived, if not in liberty, then certainly in a revolutionary situation, to the traditional and equally important theory of balanced government.

This does not dispose of the second point, that of interpretation. Suppose that, in this form of mixed government, the "democratical" arm actually gathers up a preponderance of political power. This, after all, was what happened in the Revolution and had been happening long before. Does this give us a democracy? It is a question of crucial importance and one to which one school of thought returns an uncritically affirmative answer. Much of the power and internal influence within each colony was indeed concentrated in its assembly. This concentration reflected, or rather represented, the distribution of power and influence in the colony in general. If the domestic distribution of power tends toward oligarchy rather than democracy—to use the language of the time—then the power of that oligarchy will be exercised in, and through, the assembly itself: just as in the House of Commons. A difference of degree, not of kind. And in fact this most significant aspect of the domestic situation in the colonies applied with hardly less force in leveling Boston than in high-toned Virginia.

In Virginia one feels that an immigrant from England would at once have been at home.[17] There were many instances of hotly contested elections, of treating and corruption, of sharp practice by sheriffs. It would not be difficult, however, to adduce evidence of democratic tendencies in Virginia elections. Especially in the spring elections of 1776 there were many signs that the freeholders were taking their choice seriously, and several distinguished gentlemen were either turned out of their seats or given a nasty fright. But it is an unmistakable feature of Virginia elections that although the freeholders participated often quite fully, the contests were almost invariably between members of the gentry. To seek election to the House of Burgesses was to stake a distinct claim to social rank. Virginia elections were of course conducted viva voce under the friendly supervision of the local magnates. The comparatively broad base of politics in Virginia makes it all the more instructive to look into the real concentration of political power. There were two main areas: the House of Burgesses and the county courts (not taking account of the council and governor).

Effective power in the House of Burgesses was concentrated in a few hands. The house began to use the committee system in the late seventeenth century and had brought it to a high efficiency well before the middle of the eighteenth.[18] The famous Virginia ruling families of this era always occupied a large share of the key positions, enough to ensure their own domination. Before the Revolution, of some hundred members who regularly attended the house, only about twenty took an active part in proceedings. Three families, the Robinsons, the Randolphs, and the Lees, provided most of the leaders. A very recent study shows that of 630 members between 1720 and 1776, only 110 belonged throughout

---

[17] Charles S. Sydnor, *Gentlemen Freeholders* (Chapel Hill, N. C., 1952); David J. Mays, *Edmund Pendleton 1721–1803* (2 vols., Cambridge, Mass., 1952); J. R. Pole, "Representation and Authority in Virginia from the Revolution to Reform," *Journal of Southern History*, XXIV (Feb. 1958), 16–50.

[18] Harlow, *Legislative Methods*, 10–11.

the period to the "select few who dominated the proceedings of the house."[19]

These men, many of whom were linked by ties of family, had the characteristics of a strong social and political elite. They were large landowners and generally were substantial slaveowners. Some were merchants. A few, such as Edmund Pendleton, had arrived by intellectual ability and hard work combined with legal training. But Pendleton had the patronage of a great family. All those with ambition were land speculators. This gave them an interest in western development, an interest which no doubt extended to the policy of making western areas attractive to the prospective settler. Probably for this reason they wanted to extend the suffrage, which they twice tried to do in the 1760's by reducing the amount of uncleared land required as a qualification. The crown disallowed these acts, though on other grounds. This reform was completed in the first election law after the Revolution. Despite the famous reforms pressed through by Jefferson, no concessions were made on matters of fundamental importance. It is a striking tribute to the tremendous security of their hold on the country that in the new state constitution there was no provision for special qualifications for membership in the legislature. The qualifications of voters and of representatives for the time being remained as before. It is a silent piece of evidence, possibly, but one that speaks loudly of their eminent self-confidence.

Life in the counties was dominated by the county courts, which touched the interests of the common people far more closely than did the remote and occasional meetings of the legislature. The courts, which knew little of any doctrine of separation of powers, exercised all the main functions of both legislative and judicial administration. These included tax assessment, granting licenses, supervising highways, and authorizing constructions. They had nothing elective in their nature. Membership was by co-option. The courts made the important county nominations for confirmation by the governor. And the county courts were made up of the leading men of the county, representing at the local level the material of which the House of Burgesses was composed at the central. They seem on the whole to have worked well enough. And

---

[19] Jack P. Greene, "Foundations of Political Power in the Virginia House of Burgesses, 1720–1766," *William and Mary Quarterly*, XVI (Oct. 1959), 485–506; quotation from p. 485.

it is likely that if they had in fact been elected by the freeholders, their membership would have been about the same. Assuredly they were not tyrannical; equally certainly they were not democratic. They were a good example of what is usually meant by oligarchy.

What happened in the American Revolution in Virginia was that the policies of the British government clashed with the interests of this ambitious, proud, self-assured, and highly competent provincial government. In arguing its case, both to the British authorities and to its own people, this government appealed to the principles on which it claimed to be founded, which were philosophically the same and historically comparable to those of Parliament itself. For historical reasons, the Virginia Whigs were somewhat closer to the radical, or popular side, of the Whig spectrum. But in Virginia as in other provinces, it was the principles generally understood as Whig principles that were at stake, and it was these principles which were affirmed and re-established in the new set of domestic state constitutions.

From time to time, as the war went on, the upper classes felt tremors of alarm in which they revealed something of their relationship to the common people.

Thus John Augustine Washington, writing to Richard Henry Lee of the difficulties of getting the militia to obey a marching order, and the secret proceedings by which they bound themselves to stand by each other in refusing to leave the state, remarked: "I fear we have among us some designing dangerous characters who misrepresent to ignorant, uninformed people, the situation of our affairs and the nature of the contest, making them believe it is a war produced by the wantonness of the gentlemen, and that the poor are very little, if any interested."[20] Another of Lee's correspondents, on the need to arouse popular support, wrote: "The spark of liberty is not yet extinct among our people, and if properly fanned by the Gentlemen of Influence will, I make no doubt, burst out again into a flame."[21]

These hints, these references which illuminate the assumptions of political life, often reveal more than formal expositions of doctrine, or even the official records.

These "Gentlemen of Influence," the ruling class, were prepared to extend the suffrage when it suited their interest to do so in the 1760's,

---

[20] Quoted in Pole, "Representation and Authority in Virginia," 28.
[21] *Ibid.*, 28–29.

but refused to take the same step when it would have opened the question of political power, a generation later. The first demands for reform, in both suffrage and distribution of representation, began to appear about the turn of the century. And these demands were met with a prolonged and bitter resistance, leading only to reluctant and unsatisfactory concessions even in the famous constitutional convention of 1829–1830. The struggle was carried on until a more substantial extension of political rights was at last achieved in 1850. The forces that Virginia's political leadership so long and so determinedly held at bay can, I think, without exaggeration, be called the forces of democracy.

It is a very familiar fact about the early state constitutions that they were generally conservative in character, in that they retained much of the principles and structure of the governments of the colonies. The colonies were already self-governing in the main, and this self-government was administered by representative institutions. When one's attention is confined to these institutions, it can soon become rather difficult to see in what respect they were not, in a common-sense use of the word, democratic. After all, they were accessible to the people, they received petitions and redressed grievances, they possessed the inestimable right of free speech, and in the battles they fought, they were often engaged, in the interest of the colonies, against royal governors.

All these features were not merely consistent with, they were the formative elements of, the great Whig tradition of Parliament since the Glorious Revolution and before. They were, like so many other things, derivable from Locke. With certain exceptions, such as the difficulty of the Regulator rising in North Carolina, it would be true that colonial assemblies lay closer to the people than did the British House of Commons. For one thing, there were far more representatives per head of population in the colonies than in Britain. Parliament had 1 member to every 14,300 persons, the colonies approximately 1 to every 1,200.[22] And this meant that legislative methods and principles were more likely to be familiar to the ordinary colonist. To put it in contemporary terms, the colonies, on the whole, had a great many more constituencies like Middlesex or Westminster, except that they were mostly country and not town constituencies. It might be very close to the mark to press the analogy further and say that they had a great many constituencies that

---

[22] Mary P. Clarke, *Parliamentary Privilege in the American Colonies* (New Haven, Conn., 1943), 268.

very much resembled Yorkshire—the Yorkshire of Sir George Savile, the Yorkshire of Christopher Wyvill.

What does seem striking about these in many ways highly representative colonial assemblies is, as I suggested earlier, the determination and sureness of touch with which they assumed the characteristics of Parliament. These were characteristics originally designed to secure the liberty of the people's representatives: free speech in debate, freedom of members from arrest or molestation, and freedom of the assembly from abuse by breach of privilege. But there were all too many occasions on which it must have seemed that these safeguards were designed to secure the assemblies against abuse, in the form of free speech and fair comment, by their own constituents.[23]

The colonial assemblies became extraordinarily sensitive to the question of privilege. Strictly from an institutional viewpoint, they were deliberately building on the tradition of Parliament. But institutional studies always seem to tempt the historian to arrive at his answer the short way, by examining structure, without asking questions about development.

Much research has recently been done on what Palmer calls the "constituted bodies"[24] which held a strong and growing position in the Western world in the eighteenth century. They were numerous and differed greatly, one from another, and from one century to another— first of all the variety of political or judicial bodies: diets, estates, assemblies, parlements; then the professional associations or guilds; as well as religious orders, and those of the nobilities of Europe.

There seems strong reason for holding that the colonial assemblies were behaving in close conformity with the other bodies of this general type. At their best they were closer to local interests, but no less characteristically, they displayed a remarkable diligence in the adoption of parliamentary abuses. They would send their messengers far into the outlying country to bring to the bar of the house some individual who was to be humbled for having committed a breach of privilege, which very often meant some private action affecting the dignity or even the property of the sitting member. Criticism of the assemblies, either verbal or written, was a risky business. The freedom of the colonial press was very largely at the mercy of the assembly's sense of its own dignity,

---

[23] *Ibid.*, 127.
[24] Palmer, *Democratic Revolution*, 27–44.

so much so that a recent investigator doubts whether the famous Zenger case,[25] which is supposed to have done so much toward the establishment of freedom of the press in the colonies, really had any general significance or immediate consequences. The fact is that restrictions on free press comment on assembly actions were not the policy of the crown but the policy of the assemblies.

Expulsions from colonial assemblies were frequent. And in case a parallel with the action of the Commons in the Wilkes case were needed to round off the picture, we may remark that colonial assemblies repeatedly excluded members who had been lawfully elected by their constituents.[26]

There was another feature in which these assemblies showed their affinity with the outlook of their times. In spite of the amount of choice open to the electors, there was a growing tendency for public office, both the elective and the appointive kinds, to become hereditary. It was of course very pronounced in Europe; it is surely no less significant when we see it at work in America. The same family names occur, from generation to generation, in similar positions. And this was no less true in New England than in Virginia or South Carolina or Maryland.

If this was democracy, it was a democracy that wore its cockade firmly pinned into its periwig.

One of the most interesting consequences of the revolutionary situation was that it demanded of political leaders a declaration of their principles. Thus we get the famous Virginia Bill of Rights, the work of George Mason; the Declaration of Rights attached to the 1780 constitution of Massachusetts; and the constitutions themselves, with all that they reveal or imply of political ideas; and in the case of Massachusetts we can go even further, for there survive also, in the archives of that state in Boston, the returns of the town meetings which debated that constitution and in many cases recorded their vote, clause by clause.

This constitution, in fact, was submitted to the ratification of what counted then as the whole people—all the adult males in the state. The constitutional convention had been elected on the same basis. The constitution which was framed on this impressive foundation of popular sovereignty was certainly not a democratic instrument. It was an articu-

---

[25] Leonard W. Levy, "Did the Zenger Case Really Matter? Freedom of the Press in Colonial New York," *William and Mary Quarterly*, XVII (Jan. 1960), 35–50.

[26] Clarke, *Parliamentary Privilege*, 194–96.

late, indeed a refined expression, of the Whig view of government—of government-in-society—as applied to the existing conditions in Massachusetts, and as interpreted by John Adams.

The property qualifications for the suffrage were, in round figures, about what they had been under the charter. In practice they proved to have very little effect by way of restricting participation in elections. The introduction of decidedly steeper qualifications for membership in the assembly meant that that body would be composed of the owners of the common, upward of one-hundred-acre family farm, and their mercantile equivalent. The pyramid narrowed again to the senate, and came to a point in the position of governor. These restrictions were new, but gave little offense to the general sense of political propriety; the suffrage qualifications were objected to in about one-fifth of the recorded town meeting debates.[27]

The house and senate represented different types of constituency, and the difference is one of the clues to institutional thought. The house represented the persons of the electorate living in corporate towns, which were entitled to representation according to a numerical scale of population; very small communities were excluded. The town remained the basic unit of representation. The senate, on the other hand, represented the property of the state arranged in districts corresponding to the counties; the number of members to which each county was entitled depended, not on population, but on the taxes it had paid into the state treasury. The result in distribution of representatives in the senate was not actually much different from the apportionment that would have been obtained by population,[28] but the intention was there, and the plan conformed to the principles of political order by which the delegates were guided.[29]

---

[27] The constitution of 1780 is discussed in: S. E. Morison, "The Struggle over the Adoption of the Constitution of Massachusetts, 1780," Massachusetts Historical Society *Proceedings*, L. (Boston, 1916–17), 353–412; Robert J. Taylor, *Western Massachusetts in the Revolution* (Providence, R. I., 1954); J. R. Pole, "Suffrage and Representation in Massachusetts: A Statistical Note," *William and Mary Quarterly*, XIV (Oct. 1957), 560–92. The town meeting records are in Volumes CCLXXVI and CCLXXVII in the Massachusetts Department of Archives, the State House, Boston.

[28] As noted by Palmer, *Democratic Revolution*, 226.

[29] It may be permissible to mention that Brown, in his study of this constitution, omits to note this provision for tax payment as the basis of county representation. In itself, this may seem a small clue, but the thread leads into another world of political ideas than that of modern democracy. Brown, *Middle-Class Democracy*, 393.

New York, which established popular election of its governor, and North Carolina took the matter further by differentiating between the qualifications of voters for the senate and the house of representatives.

How then are we to explain the paradox of popular consent to a scheme of government which systematically excluded the common people from the more responsible positions of political power? The historian who wishes to adopt the word "democracy" as a definition must first satisfy himself that it can be applied to a carefully ordered hierarchy, under the aegis of which power and authority are related to a conscientiously designed scale of social and economic rank, both actual and prospective; if this test fails him, then he must ask himself whether he can call the system a democracy, on the ground that it was a form of government established with the consent of the governed. Those who wish to argue this line have the advantage of finding much serviceable material that can be adopted without the rigors, or the risks, of a historically-minded analysis. It is possible to concentrate all attention on those aspects of the system which we would now call democratic, to assert that these elements exerted a controlling influence and that all the rest was a sort of obsolescent window dressing. Such a view may not be particularly subtle, but on the other hand it is not absolute nonsense. It is, perhaps, the easiest view to arrive at through an extensive reading of local economic records in the light of a clear, but vastly simplified interpretation of the political process; but it leaves unfulfilled the rather more complex task of perceiving the democratic elements in their proper place within a system conceived in another age, under a different inspiration.

In the Whig philosophy of government the basic principle, preceding representative institutions, is the compact. The people already owned their property by natural right, and they are supposed to have come into the compact quite voluntarily to secure protection both to their property and to their persons. For these purposes government was formed. What was done in Massachusetts seems to have been a solemn attempt to re-enact the original compact in the new making of the state. It was even possible to deploy the theory of compact as an excuse for seizing other people's property: in 1782 the legislature of Virginia resolved that the estates of British subjects might be confiscated because they had not been parties to the original contract of the people of that state.[30] And

---

[30] Edmund Randolph to James Madison, Richmond, Dec. 27, 1782, Madison Papers, Manuscript Division, Library of Congress.

the Virginia constitution had not even been submitted for popular ratification!

Massachusetts and New Hampshire, in fact, were the only states in which popular ratification was sought for the revolutionary constitution. In a society whose moral cohesion was supplied by the sense of deference and dignity, it was possible for the broad mass of the people to consent to a scheme of government in which their own share would be limited. Some of them of course expected to graduate to the higher levels; government was not controlled by inherited rank.

This factor—the expectation of advancement—is an important feature of the American experience; it is one which is often used to excuse the injustice of exclusion from government by economic status. The *Address* that the Massachusetts convention delegates drew up in 1780 to expound the principles on which they had acted makes the point that most of those excluded by the suffrage qualification could expect to rise sufficiently in their own property to reach the level of voters. The exclusion of the artisan and laborer from the assembly was, however, more likely to prove permanent.

It would be a mistake to suppose that the body of citizens included in the electoral system at one level or another, or expecting to gain their inclusion, was really the whole body. There are always farm laborers, journeymen, migrant workers, and one may suspect that the numbers excluded by law were larger than the terms of the *Address* suggest. But even if we are disposed to accept the high level of popular participation in elections as being weighty enough to determine our definitions, it is surely wise to pause even over the legal disfranchisement of one man in every four or five, and in some towns one man in three.

This constitutional scheme was derived from a mixture of experience, theory, and intention. It is the intention for the future which seems to call for scrutiny when we attempt a satisfactory definition of these institutions.

In the first place there is the deliberate disfranchisement of the small, perhaps the unfortunate, minority; the fact that the number is small is not more significant than that the exclusion is deliberate. In the second place, there is the installation of orders of government corresponding to orders of society; the fact that the lines are imprecise and that the results are uncertain is again not more significant than that the scale is deliberate.

It was a rule of Whig ideology that participation in matters of government was the legitimate concern only of those who possessed what was commonly called "a stake in society." In concrete terms this stake in society was one's property, for the protection of which government had been originally formed. As a means to that protection, he was entitled, under a government so formed, to a voice: to some form of representation.

But there is a further problem. To put it briefly, what is to happen if the expected general economic advancement does not take place? Accumulations of wealth were far from being unknown; what if the further accumulation of wealth and the advance of the economy were to leave an ever-increasing residue of the population outside the political limits set by these constitutions? It is unlikely that their framers were ignorant of such possibilities. The growth of Sheffield, Manchester, and Leeds was not unknown; London was not easy to overlook; the Americans had close ties with Liverpool and Bristol. The fact is that a future town proletariat would be specifically excluded by the arrangements that were being made.

The historian who insists that this system was a model of democracy may find that the advance of the economy, a tendency already affecting America in many ways, leaves him holding a very undemocratic-looking baby. In the Philadelphia Convention, James Madison bluntly predicted that in future times "the great majority" would be "not only without landed, but any other sort of, property"—a state in which they would either combine, to the peril of property and liberty, or become the tools of opulence and ambition, leading to "equal danger on the other side."[31] The objection became common when state constitutions were under reform. Opponents of suffrage extension in the constitutions of the 1820's, who included many of the recognized leaders of political life, had a better right than their opponents to claim to be the legitimate heirs of the Whig constitution makers of the revolutionary era.

The constitution of the two legislative houses was based on the view that society was formed for the protection of persons and their property and that these two elements required separate protection and separate representation. This was one of the leading political commonplaces of the day. It is implied by Montesquieu; Jefferson accepts it in his *Notes on Virginia*; Madison held the view throughout his career; Hamilton

---

[31] *Records of the Federal Convention*, ed. Max Farrand (4 vols., New Haven, Conn., 1927), II, 203–204.

treated it as a point of common agreement.[32] It is worth adding that it lay behind the original conception of the United States Senate in the form envisaged by the Virginia plan, a form which was subverted when the Senate became the representative chamber of the states. The whole subject was, of course, familiar to John Adams, who went on thinking about it long after he had drawn up a draft for the constitution of his state in 1780.

John Adams, as he himself anticipated, has been a much-misunderstood man. But it is important that we should get him right. No American was more loyal to Whig principles, and none was more deeply read in political ideas.

Adams is often said to have been an admirer of aristocracy and of monarchy. His admiration for the British constitution was easy to treat as an admission of unrepublican principles. But he really believed in the British constitution as it ought to have been, and he prudently averted his gaze from what it was in his own day. If Adams had lived in England in the 1780's, he would have been an associator in Wyvill's parliamentary reform movement, rather than a Foxite Whig.

Adams was profoundly impressed with the advantages enjoyed by birth, wealth, superior education, and natural merit, and the tendency for these advantages to become an inherited perquisite of the families that enjoyed them. He was equally clear about the corrupting influence of this sort of power. For this reason he wanted to segregate the aristocracy in an upper chamber, a process which he called "a kind of ostracism." The strong executive in which he believed was intended as a check not on the commons so much as on the aristocracy.

He developed this view of the function of the upper chamber in his *Defence of the Constitutions of the United States* (1786–1787). It is not wholly consistent with the view given in the *Address*[33] attached to the draft Massachusetts constitution of 1780, in which the line taken was that persons and property require separate protection in different houses. This view is itself a reflection of more than one tradition. It reflects the traditional structure of the legislature—council and as-

---

[32] Charles de Secondat, Baron de Montesquieu, *Oeuvres complètes* (Paris, 1838), *De l'esprit des lois*, 267; James Madison, *Writings*, ed. Gaillard Hunt (9 vols., New York, 1910), V, 287; Hamilton's speech in *Debates and Proceedings of Convention of New York, at Poughkeepsie 1788* (Poughkeepsie, N. Y., 1905), 26.

[33] This, however, was the work of Samuel Adams. (William V. Wells, *The Life and Public Services of Samuel Adams* [3 vols., Boston, 1865], III, 89–97.)

sembly, lords and commons; it reflects also the idea that the state is actually composed of different orders (a word of which John Adams was fond) and that these orders have in their own right specific interests which are entitled to specific recognition. They are entitled to it because it is the purpose of the state to secure and protect them: that in fact was why the state was supposed to have come into existence.

Adams once, in later years, wrote to Jefferson: "Your *aristoi* are the most difficult animals to manage in the whole theory and practice of government. They will not suffer themselves to be governed."[34] Yet in spite of his intense distrust of them, I think his attitude was two sided. I find it difficult to read his account of the role played in society by the aristocracy without feeling that there was to him, as there is to many others, something peculiarly distinguished and attractive about these higher circles, elevated by nature and sustained by society above the ordinary run of men. And had he not, after all, sons for whom he had some hopes? Some hopes, perhaps, for the family of Adams?

Governor Bernard had lamented the disappearance from prerevolutionary Massachusetts of those balancing factors, "Fear, reverence, respect and awe." Disappearance at least toward the royal authority. They did not disappear so easily from domestic life. There is nothing which reveals these deferential attitudes more fully than in respect to birth and family, given on trust. Adams therefore tells us much, not only of himself but of his times, when he draws attention to inequality of birth:

> Let no man be surprised that this species of inequality is introduced here. Let the page in history be quoted, where any nation, ancient or modern, civilized or savage, is mentioned, among whom no difference was made, between the citizens, on account of their extraction. The truth is, that more influence is allowed to this advantage in free republics than in despotic governments, or would be allowed to it in simple monarchies, if severe laws had not been made from age to age to secure it. The children of illustrious families have generally greater advantages of education, and earlier opportunities to be acquainted with public characters, and informed of public affairs, than those of meaner ones, or even than those in middle life; and what is more than all, a habitual national veneration for their names, and the characters of their ancestors, described in history, or coming down

---

[34] Quoted in Palmer, *Democratic Revolution*, 273, n. 52.

by tradition, removes them farther from vulgar jealousy and popular envy, and secures them in some degree the favour, the affection, the respect of the public. Will any man pretend that the name of Andros, and that of Winthrop, are heard with the same sensations in any village of New England? Is not gratitude the sentiment that attends the latter? And disgust the feeling excited by the former? In the Massachusetts, then, there are persons descended from some of their ancient governors, counsellors, judges, whose fathers, grandfathers, and great-grandfathers, are mentioned in history with applause as benefactors to the country, while there are others who have no such advantage. May we go a step further,—Know thyself, is as useful a precept to nations as to men. Go into every village in New England, and you will find that the office of justice of the peace, and even the place of representative, which has ever depended only on the freest election of the people, have generally descended from generation to generation, in three or four families at most.[35]

Deference: it does not seem, in retrospect, a very secure cement to the union of social orders. Yet to those who live under its sway it can be almost irresistible.

It was beginning to weaken, no doubt, in Adams' own political lifetime. "The distinction of classes," Washington said to Brissot de Warville in 1788, "begins to disappear." But not easily, not all at once, not without a struggle.

It was this which collapsed in ruins in the upheaval of Jacksonian democracy. And that, perhaps, is why the election of so ambiguous a leader was accompanied by such an amazing uproar.

---

[35] John Adams, *Defence of the Constitutions of the United States* . . . (3 vols., Philadelphia, 1797), I, 110–11.

24. THE WARD-HOPKINS CONTROVERSY AND THE AMERICAN REVOLUTION IN RHODE ISLAND*

An Interpretation

by Mack E. Thompson

Was class conflict the dynamic force behind political rivalries in colonial America? In the following essay, Mack E. Thompson finds that such a hypothesis cannot explain events in pre-Revolutionary Rhode Island. Though historians and students commonly use the concept of class, does that term have any clear and consistent usage? What is a class? Do occupational groups form classes and are they homogeneous? Or are the economic interests of merchants and farmers too heterogeneous and internally divided for them to form coherent, unified political and economic groups? Men whose economic interests appear to be similar often disagree over the best ways of furthering them. Moreover, people are members not only of occupa-

* *William and Mary Quarterly*, 3d series, vol. 16 (1959), 363–375. Footnotes have been omitted except where they are necessary for an understanding of the text.

tional groups but also of ethnic, religious, and geographic groups that subject them to pressures which may reinforce or counterbalance one another. In Rhode Island there was political rivalry between two similar coalitions of heterogeneous elements, one centered in Providence, the other in Newport, the colony's leading commercial centers. This rivalry emerged as the colony's primarily agricultural economy became more complex and developed a commercial sector. Economic development promoted differentiation in the colony's social structure, stimulating new centers of influence where enterprising newcomers entered politics to advance their interests. In other colonies, demographic changes brought the influx of new elements in the population, the emergence of self-conscious ethnic and religious elements, and the growth of newly settled regions anxious to share power with the older areas. These and other sources of social differentiation generated political rivalry.

For further reading: David S. Lovejoy, *Rhode Island Politics and the American Revolution 1760–1776* (1958); Theodore Thayer, *Pennsylvania Politics and the Growth of Democracy, 1740–1776* (1952); William S. Hanna, *Benjamin Franklin and Pennsylvania Politics* (1964).

From 1755 to 1770 the colony of Rhode Island was torn by an internal political struggle that historians usually refer to as the Ward-Hopkins controversy, since the two factions contending for political supremacy were led by Samuel Ward from Westerly and Newport and Stephen Hopkins from Providence. Those who consider the American Revolution as an internal social and political conflict as well as a revolt from political obedience to England seem to see their thesis substantiated by the Ward-Hopkins controversy. Their assumption is that in pre-Revolutionary Rhode Island the people were sharply divided politically along economic class lines. One author states that Rhode Island was "a battleground for conservative merchants and radical farmers," and that "radicalism won victories earlier than in the other colonies." "When the break with England came," this author concludes, "Newport and the Narragansett country remained loyal, whereas the agrarian north, which was in control of the government, declared Rhode Island's independence of Britain two months before the radical party was able to achieve that end in the Continental Congress. Throughout the revolutionary period the Rhode Islanders were staunch defenders of democracy and state sovereignty." In other words, the colony was taken into the Revolution by northern agrarian radicals who had earlier won a victory for democratic rights against southern conservative merchants. The purpose of this paper is to offer an alternative interpretation of the Ward-Hopkins controversy and the Revolution in Rhode Island.

It is true that Rhode Island was split politically along geographic lines. Hopkins's supporters were located in the northern towns and Ward's in the southern. But to view the north's rise to political power as a victory for agrarian radicalism is to miss entirely the significance of Stephen Hopkins's political success. Fundamental to an understanding of domestic politics in Rhode Island is a clear picture of the colony's economic growth during the middle half of the eighteenth century.

To speak of the north as "agrarian" and the south as "mercantile" is a fairly accurate description of Rhode Island in 1720, if we mean that commercial activity was confined largely to Newport and the Narragansett country in the south. Before that date, and for some years after, only in Newport, on Aquidneck Island in Narragansett Bay, did there exist in Rhode Island an urban community with a fairly sizable population employed in commerce and manufacturing. And only in the southern part of the colony, in the Narragansett country, were there substantial numbers of capitalistic farmers. In the rest of the colony an overwhelming majority of the people were engaged in subsistence agriculture, and commercial activity was relatively unimportant.

Until the 1750's the agrarian interests managed to have a decisive voice in the formation of public policy because the architects of the colony's government in the seventeenth century had fashioned a system to serve the needs of an agricultural population, and their charter had placed control of the central government in the hands of men residing in small farming communities. As long as Rhode Island's economic base remained predominantly that of subsistence agriculture the most important unit of government was town, not colony, government. With few exceptions the problems of these people could be solved by the town council. For decades the powers of the General Assembly were neither numerous nor vigorously exercised except in the area of monetary policy. From 1710 to 1751 Rhode Island farmers passed nine paper money bills or "banks" in an attempt to solve their monetary problems. They were forcefully but unsuccessfully opposed by the commercial interests in Newport.

But the Rhode Island economy was not static. During the half century preceding the Revolution, external as well as internal events caused a remarkable economic growth that profoundly altered long existing political conditions. Newport, already one of the five leading ports in America by 1720, continued to grow. As the West India market expanded and the number of trading ships to Newport increased, Narragansett planters geared their production to meet the demands of agricultural exporters. Increasingly these planters turned from subsistence to capitalistic farming, sending their surpluses to Newport for distribution. Opportunities in manufacturing, particularly distilling, shipbuilding, and ropemaking, caused many farmers to diversify their activities and in some cases to leave the land altogether. Long existing cultural, religious, and family affinities between the Newport and Narragansett residents were strengthened by intimate economic association, and the planters of Narragansett drifted slowly into political alliance with merchant, mechanic, and professional classes of Newport. Newporters or men closely identified with the interests of that town began to monopolize the governorship and other important offices in the colonial government. They also tried to run the General Assembly in their own interests but were never quite able to wrest control from the grip of the small farmers.

While Newport was expanding its commercial activities and extending its economic and political influence into the southern agricultural communities, in the north, on the banks of the Seekonk and Providence Rivers, another commercial center was rising. For almost a century Providence, the oldest town in the colony, had remained an agricultural community, but in the second quarter of the eighteenth century it responded to the same influences that were making Newport one of the leading ports in British North America. By the mid 1750's Providence was a thriving port with a young and enterprising group of merchants.

Providence's economic growth is not surprising. In some respects that city was more advantageously located than Newport. Providence not only had a protected outlet to the sea, but her merchants could draw on a larger hinterland for their cargoes than could Newport's. In response to increased demand for exports, several Providence merchants began to manufacture candles, chocolate, barrel hoops, rum, and rope and to serve as middlemen, supplying Newport merchants with cargo they could not find on the island or in the Narragansett country across the bay. By the early 1750's Providence was prepared to challenge Newport for economic leadership of the colony.

It is against this background of economic change that Rhode Island politics must be projected. Newport's continued expansion and Providence's rise as an important commercial center were both cause and effect of the violent political controversy that erupted in 1755 and continued for over a decade. In that year the freeman elected Stephen Hopkins, one of Providence's leading merchants, to the governorship, an office he held for nine of the next thirteen years. His election shows that a realignment of political forces had taken place—the hitherto fairly unified agrarian interest had disintegrated, and two composite factions, one in the north and another in the south, had appeared. The new factions were made up of cross sections of society—large and small farmers, merchants and tradesmen, professional men and other freemen. The previous division of political forces along agrarian-commercial lines was no more. Hopkins's election also shows that political leadership had finally passed from the agrarian-small town interests to commercial and manufacturing groups and that the chief instrument for the promotion of economic growth was likely to be the General Assembly rather than the town council. Although rural towns continued to exert considerable influence in the political life of the colony, thirty years passed before they again consolidated to seize control of the government.

With the disintegration of agrarian solidarity and the growth of two factions composed of men from both the urban and rural areas, political success went to the man who could reconcile conflicting interests within his own section and attract a majority of the few uncommitted freemen. As the contest between the north and south developed, leaders of both sides realized that the voters holding the balance of power were concentrated most heavily in the farming communities in the central part of the colony, equidistant from the two commercial centers of Newport and Providence. Stephen Hopkins, one of the most accomplished politicians in colonial America, was more successful in appealing to these freemen and better able to prevent any serious defections in his party than was his opponent, Samuel Ward.

The climax to the prolonged struggle came in the election of 1767, when Hopkins decisively defeated Ward for the governorship and dealt the southern party a shattering blow from which it never recovered.

Hopkins's success was the result of a combination of factors. By 1767, after controlling the government for two consecutive years, Ward and his followers in Newport had alienated the Narragansett planters and farmers by refusing to support a measure to regulate interest rates, and some of the latter began to look elsewhere for political leadership. Ward's party was further discredited by the gerrymandering activities of Elisha Brown, the deputy governor.

Hopkins helped his cause by collecting a large election fund and conducting an energetic campaign. Personal influence, money, and liberal amounts of rum were brought to bear, and where possible, the old, the sick, and the infirm were carried to the polls to cast their ballots for Hopkins-party men. Freemen were not only paid to vote for Hopkins and his supporters but "many persons that is stranious for Mr. Ward who may be agreed with for a Small Sum to Lay Still," were also approached. One Hopkins-party campaign worker, "Clostly Engaged in the Grand Cause" in Cumberland, reported that he would "be short with Regard to the Necessary argument (haveing Last Evening fell into Company with Two men who was against us Last year, who was hard to Convince of their Error, but I over come them) shall want five Dollars more which I must have; for I must meat the above two men To morrow morning almost up to Woonsoketfalls where I expect to Settle Some things very favourable To the Campaign . . . ." He ended his urgent letter with the candid remark: "am Engaged Clostly in makeing freemen and hope I shall merrit the Beaver Hat."

Hopkins's success in 1767 was materially aided by the growing identification of outlying towns with Providence as a result of the economic opportunities that flourishing port offered. Providence's economic growth may be compared to an expanding whirlpool; when it began slowly to spin in the second quarter of the century, it drew nearby agricultural communities into its vortex. In the next decades, as its force increased, it slowly but inexorably sucked more distant towns into its center. Political sympathies apparently were swept along with economic interests, for these towns eventually supported Stephen Hopkins and the northern party. Southern response to this economic and political alignment was what triggered the Ward-Hopkins controversy and kept it alive for over a decade.

Stephen Hopkins's elections to the governorship in 1755 and in subsequent years was not a victory for social and political radicalism. On issues commonly associated with radicalism there was little discussion and almost no discussion at all directly relating to internal political controversies. During Hopkins's numerous administrations no new laws were passed or even introduced in the General Assembly abolishing or lowering the property qualifications for the vote. The people were apparently not concerned with such issues. And ironically, on the most important problem of the period, currency, the men who assumed the leadership in solving it were not the southern "conservative merchants" but the northern "radical farmers." Stephen Hopkins, one of Providence's leading merchants, and the Browns of Providence, Obadiah and his four nephews, Nicholas, Joseph, John, and Moses, who operated one of the largest shipping firms in the colony, led the fight for currency reform. By the early 1760's Stephen Hopkins's northern followers were committed to a program of sound money and in 1763 they were able to push through the assembly the first bill to regulate currency in the history of the colony. While some southerners supported currency reform, the Browns would never have been able to pass the bill without the support of representatives from the nearby agricultural towns, a fact which points up the composite nature of the northern faction. Subsequent legislation provided Rhode Island with a stable currency until the Revolution.

To see in Rhode Island political controversy a class struggle—agrarian radicals fighting conservative merchants—is to see something that did not exist. That came only in the post-Revolutionary years and had its roots in the changes brought about by the war and the success of the Revolution. This is not to say that before 1776 there were no class distinctions or that members of the lower classes did not resent advantages enjoyed by the upper classes; but there is little evidence that such distinctions or sentiments resulted in social tensions serious enough to label revolutionary.

Briefly stated, then, the chief cause for the intense political struggle in Rhode Island before the Revolution was the desire of men in the north and the south to gain control of the government to promote private and public interests. When the southern and northern economies expanded, and merchants, tradesmen, and capitalistic farmers emerged whose needs could no longer be satisfied by the town meeting, they began to compete with one another for control of the colonial government. The General Assembly could bestow many profitable favors on deserving citizens; it could issue flags of truce to merchants authorizing them to exchange French prisoners and provisions in the West Indies;

it could determine which merchants could outfit privateers; it could grant monopolies to enterprising businessmen; it could vote funds to build or repair lighthouses, bridges, schools, and to make other local public improvements; it could alter the apportionment of taxes to the benefit of towns in particular sections. These and other powers only the General Assembly had. The section that controlled the government could use the assembly as an instrument to promote its economic and cultural growth.

A good illustration of this interpretation of domestic politics in Rhode Island occurs in the struggle that took place in 1769 and 1770 over the permanent location of the College of Rhode Island. After considerable discussion, the choice of sites for the college narrowed to Providence and Newport. The contestants considered the controversy one more episode, and perhaps the last, in the long drawn-out competition for economic and political leadership between the north and the south. In a letter to the town councils of Scituate and Glocester, Stephen Hopkins and Moses Brown of Providence wrote:

When we consider that the building the College here will be a means of bringing great quantities of money into the place, and thereby of greatly increasing the markets for all kinds of the countries produce; and, consequently, of increasing the value of all estates to which this town is a market; and also that it will much promote the weight and influence of this northern part of the Colony in the scale of government in all times to come, we think every man that hath an estate in this County who duly weighs these advantages, with many others that will naturally occur to his mind, must, for the bettering of his own private interest, as well as for the public good, become a contributor to the College here, rather than it should be removed from hence. . . .

We are more zealous in this matter as we have certain intelligence that the people in Newport, who are become sinsible of the importance of this matter, are very deligently using every method in their power to carry the prize from us, and as the few remaining days of this month is the whole time in which we can work to any purpose, we hope none will slumber or sleep. We think ourselves in this matter wholly engaged for the public good; and therefore hope to be borne with when we beg of you and all our neighbors, to seriously consult their own interest and pursue it with unremitted zeal.

The governing body of the College of Rhode Island eventually voted to make Providence the permanent home of the institution. In the 1770 election, Samuel Ward, his brother Henry, who was the colony secretary, and a few other southern politicians made a determined effort to capture control of the government in order to get a charter for a college in Newport. They failed and their bill to charter a second college was defeated by deputies committed to northern leadership.

To say that the central theme of the Ward-Hopkins controversy was the political struggle between similar interests in two different sections does not necessarily assume a uniformity of motives on the part of the participants. Undoubtedly some men on both sides were propelled above all else by the financial rewards public office afforded, by personal animosities, and by desire for social prestige, while others devoted their time and money to politics because of a sense of public responsibility or simply because they enjoyed the game of politics. But what bound the men of each party together was their recognition that the promotion of their own section, and thus their own interests, could best be done through control of the government. Social and economic classes could co-operate for this purpose in the two sections. In fact, co-operation, not dissension, between classes is the distinctive characteristic of pre-Revolutionary political life in Rhode Island.

If we turn now to consider the claim that Rhode Island split into radical and conservative camps over British attempts to extend Parliamentary authority to America, we find that the facts do not bear out this claim. Rhode Island was one of the first colonies to react to the Sugar Act of 1764 and to the Stamp Act of the following year. In the General Assembly, members of the two factions united to petition the Lords Commissioners for Trade and Plantations for their repeal. This early response set the tone for resistance to subsequent Parliamentary legislation and ministerial attempts to enforce customs regulations.

The political leaders of both factions opposed British policy with equal vigor. Stephen Hopkins made a strong defense of American rights in *The Rights of the Colonies Examined,* and the General Assembly sent this pamphlet to the colony's agent in England for use in the move for repeal of the Stamp Act. Hopkins's subsequent service for the cause of American independence is too well known to necessitate further comment. His political opponent, Samuel Ward, was no less a patriot. In fact, Ward held the governorship during the Stamp Act crisis when the colony successfully prevented the use of stamps. He made every effort to frustrate attempts of the king's officers to enforce the Acts of Trade and was an outspoken critic of British trade regulations. When the First Continental Congress met in Philadelphia in September 1774, Ward and Hopkins attended as delegates from Rhode Island.

Stout resistance by these key figures to Parliament's attempts to extend its authority to the American colonies was emulated by the second rank of leaders of both factions and strongly supported by the freemen. The only person of importance in the north who attempted to abide by the Stamp Act was John Foster, a justice of the peace and clerk of the Inferior Court of Common Pleas for Providence County, who refused to open his court and transact business without stamps. A crowd of angry people gathered before his house and threatened to ride him out of town on a rail unless he changed his mind. This was enough to convince Foster of his error. In 1769 after the Townshend Acts were passed and again in 1772, royal officials trying to perform their duties were roughly treated by the northerners; and in 1773, when British naval vessels were patrolling Narragansett Bay in an effort to stop contraband trade, John Brown, the leading merchant in Providence, and a number of citizens, burned the revenue vessel, the *Gaspee,* to the water's edge. Royal investigators could get no assistance from Rhode Islanders in their search for the culprits. In the south, in Newport, throughout the period 1765–75, the people frequently demonstrated their hostile attitude toward British policy and supporters of the Crown.

One of the striking things about anti-British leadership in Rhode Island is its continuity. The same people who successfully organized the opposition to the Stamp Act and the Townshend Acts led the resistance to the Tea Act and the Intolerable Acts and declared Rhode Island's independence. For the most part these leaders were not radical agrarians but members of the commercial and professional classes of both Providence and Newport. This does not mean that the farmers were pro-British. There was stronger loyalist sentiment among the merchants in Newport than among the farmers in the agricultural communities. What it does mean is that the farmers were content to follow the lead of men like Hopkins and Ward. The merchants, shipowners, and lawyers who were the leaders in domestic politics were also the leaders in the Revolutionary movement.

Articulate supporters of Parliament supremacy in Rhode Island during the 1760's were almost without exception royal government employees. They constituted an infinitesimal percentage of the population and exerted no influence within the colonial government and very little outside it. And when they did speak out, they made every effort to hide their identity and to cloak their real intentions. If discovered, they were either forced into silence or hounded out of the colony. During the five years before the outbreak of violence, supporters of British policy were even less noticeable than during the earlier period. Even Joseph Wanton, Rhode Island's Episcopalian governor who eventually went over to the British, was a strong defender of American liberties throughout these years. When Rhode Island declared its independence, the few citizens who could not accept the decision either withdrew from active participation in public affairs or left the colony.

The colony's vigorous, continuous opposition to British policy proves that Rhode Islanders were trying to preserve a system with which they were well satisfied, rather than to change it. The struggle for home rule in Rhode Island was not paralleled by any fight between agrarian and commercial classes to determine who should rule at home. The transition from colony to commonwealth was made with practically no changes in the existing institutions, leadership, or social structure. And there were few demands for any changes. The struggle for democratic rights came in the postwar decade and its origins must be sought in the changes produced by the war and independence and not in the Ward-Hopkins controversy.

25. SUCCESSION POLITICS IN MASSACHUSETTS, 1730–1741*

by John A. Schutz

One index of the turbulence and instability of colonial politics is the experience of the royal governor, whose tenure in
office was insecure because he was constantly threatened by
forces in America and England that sapped his authority and
threatened his continued rule. In the following essay, John A.
Schutz analyzes how royal governors were made and unmade.
The governor's task was to uphold the royal prerogative, advance British interests, faithfully execute the laws and instructions formulated in London, keep the Americans content and
productive, and remain in office long enough to enjoy its financial rewards and perquisites. Governor Jonathan Belcher of
Massachusetts found it impossible to discharge all these responsibilities at the same time. A patronage appointee, the governor
was enmeshed in the complexities and uncertainties of factional
politics in England and America. To get into office, one had to
have connections among English politicians who dispensed

* *William and Mary Quarterly*, 3d series, vol. 15 (1958), 508–520. Footnotes
have been omitted except where they are necessary for an understanding of the text.

lucrative positions in the colonies as well as support from Americans whose influence in London could aid one's claim. Yet once in office, the governor lacked sufficient patronage to buy off all the potentially dangerous opposition in America and to protect himself from others eager to replace him. In England, hungry office seekers joined a governor's provincial enemies and exploited the shifts within English politics that altered the control of patronage. Royal officials owed their jobs to patrons in England, and when these lost influence they could no longer protect the men they had once helped. Threatened at home, the governor was also undermined in the colony he ostensibly ruled. Because so much patronage was controlled in England, he lacked sufficient jobs to offer the ambitious and troublesome elements in America. He tried to build a corps of faithful supporters by dispensing what favors were available, but these were rarely enough. Moreover, he found it expedient to sacrifice British interests to gain local popularity, as Governor Belcher did by catering to religious prejudices and colluding with merchant allies to steal the King's timber. Yet when Belcher faithfully attempted to follow his instructions and to prevent colonists from expanding the money supply, he sealed his doom by making many new enemies and strengthening the hands of his old foes, who finally secured his removal. In the end, Belcher had failed to uphold the laws, guard the prerogative, keep his subjects obedient and content, or retain his job. His experience was not unique; it was shared by other Crown officials throughout the colonies who profoundly weakened royal authority in America.

For further reading: John A. Schutz, *William Shirley, King's Governor of Massachusetts* (1961). Compare with Jere R. Daniell, "Politics in New Hampshire under Governor Benning Wentworth, 1741–1767," *William and Mary Quarterly*, 3d series, vol. 23 (1966), 76–105; J. R. Pole, *Political Representation in England and the Origins of the American Revolution* (1966); M. Eugene Sirmans, *Colonial South Carolina, A Political History, 1663–1763* (1966).

Succession Politics in Massachusetts, 1730-1741

When Jonathan Belcher was recalled from the governorships of Massachusetts and New Hampshire in 1741, the provinces were nearly in revolution. So bitter and desperate had politics become in that year that they obscured the hard-bitten battles of the ten previous years. The turbulence of politics during the 1730's was partly caused by Belcher's personality and partly by the instability of his rule. His uncanny knack for acquiring enemies bred more than the usual discontent—a circumstance dramatized by his habit of magnifying incidents so that even small matters took on the character of celestial struggles. Though his tactics in annoying the opposition were somewhat less than celestial in character, so too were those of his enemies, who used forged documents, slander, and half truths as they tried to remove him from his offices.

There was reason, if not justification, for their unscrupulous methods. As rival groups seeking control of the governorships, they wanted a share of the spoils: contracts, offices, favorable legislation, and official support of their wishes in communications with the British government. To win these rich prizes, they found it essential to have the power of the governor on their side. They calculated carefully their relative influence with Jonathan Belcher, the incumbent, and with a half-dozen contenders for the office, including William Shirley, and they estimated the weight these men might have with the legislature, the people, and the British authorities in obtaining their desires.

But the governorships, whether they were in the hands of Belcher or others, were filled by the leading politicians of England, who made appointments to office and determined tenure according to their desires and fancies. While these facts concerning appointments were well known to Americans, they hoped nonetheless to circumvent the system. They wanted a sympathetic governor, with connections in Boston and London, who could satisfy the aspirations of the controlling groups of both communities.

Some of these groups, in 1730, liked Belcher very much, not only because he was already governor but because he had alliances with members of the Walpole administration. His friendship with Samuel Shute, a former governor of Massachusetts; with Lord Townshend, brother-in-law of the prime minister; and with many New Englanders made him a most valuable person to know. They welcomed his views on hard money, his willingness to back favorable legislation for the Quakers, his loyalty to the British government. They prized, too, his social position as a leader of New England merchants, his educational attainments as a Harvard graduate, and his family connections with many influential politicians.

Other groups, opposing the governor, were at first without a substitute for Belcher, but were later attracted to William Shirley, who had come to Boston in 1731 and was an officeholder there. They liked his ties with the Duke of Newcastle, a rising and ambitious English politician who was then allowing nothing to stand in the way of his attaining the prime ministership. They admired Shirley's energy, his legal ability, and his audacity. His position as advocate general of the Vice-Admiralty Court, admittedly, was a humble one, yet it indicated to those who knew patronage politics that he could expect better preferment in the future. In short, he was a man worth watching; he was a possible successor to Belcher if and when the British government wanted to make a change of governors.

Belcher, however, was apparently well entrenched in his position and showed a miraculous capacity to endure the politics of office. His success was due undoubtedly to a ruthless use of patronage. Lifelong friendships were sometimes abandoned—at the risk of creating fierce hatreds —but he was willing to take the risk and formed a solid bloc of supporters. He built a party that included such eminent families as the Wendells, Partridges, Edward Hutchinsons, Stoddards, and Pepperrells. He even laid plans for the future by appointing the sons of these men to minor offices and by sending his younger son, Jonathan, to London where the lad was to study law and prepare to be an English politician. By 1733, Belcher was boasting openly: "I have no compliments to make to my enemies, who if they want any favour from the Governor must stroke down their stomachs and ask for themselves."

Not everything, however, went according to plan. Shortly after his appointment to the governorships, his major patron, Lord Townshend, was driven from the Walpole administration and, even worse, his good friend, Samuel Shute, died. Belcher was unsettled by these events because he was uncertain who would protect his interests in London should there be trouble in Massachusetts or New Hampshire. No New England governor, he well knew, could afford to be long without a protector when political enemies regularly took their grievances home. For the time being, he would count upon Walpole's good nature and King George II's reputed policy of never allowing a competent official to be removed without a hearing. But he took steps immediately to employ an agent in London to look after his welfare. He also asked his son to solicit help from prospective patrons like the Duke of Newcastle and Lord Wilmington.

These actions revealed rather than relieved his feelings of insecurity, for he was reminded frequently that he was not master of patronage in his own colonies. In a most personal way this was brought home to him in 1733 when his son, Andrew, was removed as naval officer of Boston harbor, an office often given to relatives of the incumbent governor. An ordinary spoilsman from England pushed the younger Belcher out of the post. In addition, Belcher's lieutenant governors received their positions in spite of his known opposition. In fact, the New Hampshire appointee, David Dunbar, was a bitter enemy—"a lump of malice and perfidy," complained Belcher, "and every thing else that's vile. . . ."

With so much valuable patronage passing out of his hands—sometimes into those of his enemies—Belcher was most perplexed about what to do for his friends. In bewilderment, he asked the Board of Trade to consider his predicament. "How is it possible . . . ," he wrote in May 1733, "to support the King's power and authority if such insults upon it must be indured, and how can the hands of the King's Governor be strengthened if men so diametrically opposite to him must be let into the government to clog every thing he proposes for the King's service and for the good of his subjects?"

Furthermore, the governor found himself in the uncomfortable position of being forced to give away good patronage to strangers in order to win their friendship. Anthony Reynolds, the young and adventurous son of the Bishop of Lincoln, was appointed collector of customs in New Hampshire in the hope that the Bishop would use influence with the ministry. William Shirley, the protégé of the Duke of Newcastle, had received his first office at Boston in 1731, because Belcher needed the Duke's assistance and wished as well to make use of Shirley's excellent law acquaintances to introduce his son to the London bar. By 1733 Belcher was unhappily recommending Shirley as advocate general of the Vice-Admiralty Court, a strategic position in the regulation of commerce that should have gone to a close friend.

While Belcher had every reason to be worried about his London support, he kept repeating to himself what he had heard King William III was accustomed to say in the thick of politics: "Steady, steady, and all will be well." With such thoughts, he consoled himself that his English political alliances would take care of themselves if he could master local politics. But here again he was perplexed to find a carry-over into colonial affairs of his weak position in England. He was not fully in control of local politics because many key men in the administration were not personally loyal to him and because his uncertain standing at home was well known in Boston. In addition, he had not enough offices to distribute, not enough power to settle problems of finances and administration, and not enough control over the legislature to guide its policies.

In spite of these handicaps Belcher sought local political alliances. He pledged himself to a sound money program, which pleased his merchant associates and found favor among his London supporters. But it could not be established without much spade work in the Massachusetts legislature. The colony was then facing some very serious credit problems because of its unfavorable balance of trade. There was no adequate supply of hard currency for domestic needs, since most of it was drained off to make up the annual trade deficit with European creditors. To provide a circulating medium, therefore, the colony had emitted bills of credit for governmental and business purposes. Under proper supervision, these bills were a satisfactory substitute, but the problem of stabilizing their value was not easily solved. Ordinarily, yearly taxes were pledged as security and the collection of taxes provided a method for redeeming them. Unfortunately, the legislature was often tempted by political considerations to issue bills of credit in lieu of taxes, without taking the necessary precautions to insure their value. When this occurred, devaluation was certain to take place, with devastating effects upon the price and credit structure and with harmful repercussions on the whole money market. Creditors were often ruined by the cheap money—to the delight of many debtors—and salaried officials were severely embarrassed.

To ameliorate these conditions took superhuman effort and considerable time, and Belcher had also to be careful not to take sides, but to insist that sound money would bring benefits to everyone. Over the years he had consistently protested against this inflationary policy and had urgently pleaded for controls, with only partial success. In 1737, however, he secured what he believed to be a great victory when the legislature approved a budget with stricter safeguards for the issuance of paper money. In jubilation he wrote: "I say, it is the best Supply Bill [that] has been made for more than 30 years past, and did the whole Province know the happiness it leads to, and had it in their own power to do, they would knight the Governor for this good Deed. Old Toper, and his Clan, curse and gnash their Teeth at it."

Belcher was just as ready to win some friends among those landowners of Maine and New Hampshire who were disputing the claim of the British navy to cut white pines on their lands. These pines, standing mostly on private lands, became the property of the Crown on reaching a certain size. Since it was not clear which trees were to be reserved, all sorts of legal difficulties arose between the landowners and the king's surveyors. Some of Belcher's relatives and friends had large interests in the disputed areas. Appointing sympathetic justices of the peace, he allowed them to make off with much valuable timber. In effect, he was siding with timber smugglers against British laws and British officials— a most peculiar position for a British governor.

In religious affairs Belcher had quickly secured relief for his Quaker associates—some of whom were related to him through marriage—and firmly assured his Congregational supporters that he would not favor the Anglican Church. In fact, he forced his daughter's husband to renounce the Church and become a Congregationalist as a condition for his approval of the marriage. Still, in spite of his hostility toward the English Church, he was far too astute to break openly with the religious arm of the British government—or to carry his quarrels with Roger Price, its leading minister in Boston, into official channels. While no one could easily ignore Price, who had few equals as an antagonist, Belcher was determined to do as little as possible to help the Church, and as for Price, "he is such a trifling, insignificant spark that I don't intend to give myself any further trouble about him."

Though himself not very hostile to individuals because of their faith, Belcher drove men like William Shirley, Charles Apthorp, Robert Auchmuty, and other influential Bostonians into the courts where they sought relief for the Anglican Church. Some of these people, with excellent connections in London, were so disturbed by the discriminatory laws that they filed protests with the home authorities. Belcher's policy separated him as well from the British officeholders, most of whom were Anglicans.

These men of the Anglican Church seemed far from Belcher's major concerns as governor until he was confronted with a series of riots in the forest country of New Hampshire in 1734. To his embarrassment, an investigation conducted by Shirley in his capacity as advocate general soon revealed that Belcher's friends and relatives—such eminent people as the Frosts of Maine—were the smugglers. Though the law was vague and the Frosts were taking advantage of this fact, Belcher counted upon the advocate's friendship and understanding of local politics to soften the report to the British authorities. But Shirley probed deeper and, worse still, prepared cases against the Frosts with the aid of two fierce enemies of the administration, Samuel Waldo and David Dunbar.

One might have expected Waldo, an enormously wealthy New England landowner, to be a member of Belcher's party, but he was the agent of an English firm, Joseph Gulston's, supplying masts to the royal navy. In order to cut the pines, Waldo took his crew upon private lands. Their entry was often violently resisted, and Waldo was forced to battle the landowners in the courts, where he spared neither himself nor his vast wealth in support of the Admiralty's case against them.

Dunbar, the surveyor general of the king's woods, was directly responsible to the king for the protection of the royal forests. An impulsive man whose impossibly bad temper had been cultivated during years of service in the British army, he was well connected in London, with a powerful and loyal friend on the Board of Trade. Besides his duties in guarding the forests, he was lieutenant governor of New Hampshire under Belcher. From the first, his relations with the governor were made uncomfortable by many issues, including a recognition of his claim to be acting governor during Belcher's long absences in Massachusetts. With that authority Dunbar would have been able to enforce more successfully the forest laws by means of his own appointees as justices of the peace. It would, of course, have embarrassed Belcher even more in his desire to protect his friends in the timber-smuggling business. As it was, Dunbar became a leader, if not the leader, of a New Hampshire opposition to Belcher's administration.

With angry men such as these working against him, Belcher resorted to time-hardened tactics of delay. By influencing the judges and controlling the council in every way he could, he increased the red tape, but he was unable to prevent appeals to the Privy Council in England. Still, the costs of English litigation were prohibitive, and his enemies were straining their resources in shouldering such a burden. Somehow they made their appeals—perhaps with the aid of Shirley's London friends—and obtained remarkably rapid hearings, winning favorable decisions by 1736. Nonetheless, Belcher was positive that he could handle the local situation by using other methods of delay to keep Waldo and Dunbar embroiled in the courts for years to come. That strategy, instead, forced his enemies to seek further assistance at home by personal appeals to the ministers, thus transferring their battleground to London.

With these disputants and their friends Belcher was involved in another issue. It concerned the undefined Massachusetts–New Hampshire boundary, which ran through an area rich in timber and farm land. Speculators in both colonies, perturbed about the disposition of the region, had sought Belcher's help. With the usual desire to please everyone, he pleased no one, and least of all the New Hampshire legislature, which promptly engaged John Thomlinson to lobby for them in London.

Thomlinson's instructions bore the mark of Wentworth family influence. The Wentworths were Belcher's bitter rivals, men of wealth and commerce, high in the officialdom of the colony. Deprived of office by the governor, they sided with dissident elements whenever there was a promise of embarrassing him. Common cause was made with Dunbar and Waldo, with the royal timber cutters and the local landowners, and with an assortment of disaffected groups. The Wentworths were Thomlinson's friends and business associates, ready always to supply him with information hostile to the Belcher administration. Even without the benefit of their help, Thomlinson was an extraordinarily good selection. Not only was he on excellent terms with the merchants trading with New England, but he understood the intricacies of British politics and possessed much skill in applying public pressure. His friendship with the Wentworths tied the boundary issue to their family aspirations, and the Wentworths began dreaming of recapturing their former offices.

As Waldo, Dunbar, and Thomlinson went about their separate tasks, details of their actions were reported to Belcher by his London agents. They discovered early that it was not only the men they needed to guard against but also William Shirley's wife, who went to London in 1736 to petition for more patronage for her husband and family. "Mrs. Gypsy," as Belcher called her, was the daughter of a London merchant and had the aggressiveness of a tradesman, a talent she employed to bring Belcher's antagonists together as her husband's friends. Using her acquaintance with the Duke of Newcastle, she passed their protests against Belcher to the Duke, and she provided them with strategic introductions. But more important to her husband's future, she played the role of peacemaker for these men, whose interests often clashed, directing their bitterness away from each other and toward Belcher. By 1738 she had persuaded them that the one way to win their fight was to support her husband as Belcher's successor in Massachusetts.

Having reached their decision, they set out to cause Belcher as much trouble as possible. Threats and disclosures were released from time to time, usually planned to keep Massachusetts and New Hampshire constantly unsettled. Forged letters slandering his administration were circulated privately; numerous legal documents were presented in court to expose his smuggler friends and to magnify the rivalry between the two colonies. These tactics, though often anticipated by Belcher, were not easily met. "Every now and then," he wrote, "they spring a new mine, and if you knew as much of the trouble and plague and charge as I do, you'd pity the Governour. . . . A separate government is now openly and violently pushed for, and Benning [Wentworth] to be your man, and the present face of affairs meditate a greater probability of it than any thing heretofore . . . there's nothing the rascals won't attempt to accomplish their malice."

While Belcher was keenly aware of the low character of the opposition's tactics, he probably did not realize the extent to which preparations were being made to unseat him from his governorships. Negotiations were being carried on by Waldo, Shirley, Thomlinson, Wentworth, and many others, with decisions concluded on patronage in Massachusetts and New Hampshire and agreements reached with the royal contractors in London respecting the forest laws. The interests of these men were soon made known to the Admiralty in a memorial critical of Belcher's enforcement of the forest laws. Charles Apthorp, Robert Auchmuty, and other friends of Shirley's met officials of the Anglican Chuch in both London and Boston, emphasizing to them his record of devoted service to the Church and soliciting their support. About the same time, they took steps to strengthen Shirley's position with an appointment as warden of King's Chapel.

As Belcher followed the mounting opposition in London, he tried to direct his counterattack through friends there. He circularized the major ministries with an account of Dunbar's activities in New England, elaborating the many instances in which the surveyor had embittered local politics for selfish gain. "I can't see," he complained to Lord Wilmington, "what advantage it can be to His Majesty's service, or to the ease of his Ministers, to have persons put into post[s] in one and the same Government, who will be continually thwarting and opposing one another."

It was difficult to describe his own feelings toward Dunbar and to arouse the proper anxiety in his friends. To his own son, Jonathan, who was receiving regular letters, he felt impelled to cut Dunbar's figure with these words: "Dunbar . . . is certainly the most malicious, perfidious creature, that wears human Shape." But Belcher knew that it was not enough to expose and vilify Dunbar: he had to be certain of the favorable opinion of the ministers. Dunbar had "to be taken care of," to be sure, but Robert Walpole and the Duke of Newcastle must be kept steady, Lord Wilmington encouraged to continue "his goodness," and the Board of Trade "baffled" in every possible way. Dunbar's patron, Martin Bladen, was particularly strong in the Board of Trade, but Bladen's master was Walpole, and if Walpole remained friendly, let "the Apes, Loons, and little creatures" rant.

Friends were mobilized, petitions presented, and ministers warned. The Quaker merchants, through the good offices of Belcher's Quaker brother-in-law, were asked to lend their assistance, and this they gladly did. Letters to Sir Charles Wager of the Admiralty (and pickles for his wife) had good effect and gifts of fish, wine, plants, and seeds, as well as personal calls by son Jonathan, kept Belcher's name favorably before those who could help him.

While Belcher seemed to be holding his own in England, difficulties increased in Massachusetts. The smuggled merchandise of his merchant friends was seized and condemned in action after action before the Vice-Admiralty Court. Sugar, molasses, cloths, and cheeses, among other items, were sold at public auction as their owners looked on helplessly. Losses were cruelly large, sometimes representing the savings of a lifetime.

As the crisis heightened, Belcher was repeatedly threatened by friend and foe alike, each wanting him to do something drastic. Ultimately, he was forced to confer with Shirley, whose staff was undertaking the prosecutions. On begging Shirley to abandon the campaign against the smugglers, he was not only rebuffed but lectured on the duties of a royal governor in combating the illicit trade. Desperate and angry, he lashed out at Shirley, but there was little else he could do except attack members of the Vice-Admiralty Court in an attempt to secure their removal. This he began with a lengthy and bitter denunciation of the judge, Robert Auchmuty.

The weakness of Belcher's position gave rise to other disputes. Those enemies who formerly had held their grudges in private were now less

afraid to make them public. In the legislature a group of his enemies refused to adjust his salary rate to allow for the growing inflation; another
group criticized his handling of the boundary difficulties with New
Hampshire; and, worst of all, the two houses became embroiled in a
controversy over his recommendations in the annual budget, neglecting
in the meantime to pay the necessary salaries and other costs of government.

In complete defiance of the governor's known policy, two associations
of merchants took credit matters into their own hands. They formed in
1740 two private banks which issued paper money that would apparently
meet the urgent need for credit and a fluid currency. The first bank, the
Land Bank and Manufactury Scheme, was founded by nearly four hundred important men, including John Colman, John Choate, Robert Hale,
and Robert Auchmuty. They planned an emission of £150,000 in bills of
credit to be secured by the good faith and property of the subscribers. In
their haste to get the bank established, they paid little attention to such
essentials as the circulation of the bills, reserves for their retirement, and
the administration of the company.

The very crudeness of this plan aroused the Boston merchants, who
assailed it with all the oratory at their command and then offered a plan
of their own, the Silver Scheme. Under the leadership of Edward Hutchinson, James Bowdoin, and Edmund Quincy, some one hundred persons
formed a company which proposed to issue £120,000 in silver notes that
would be acceptable by them for merchandise and business transactions
—a much more conservative and workable plan than that of the other
inflationists.

While Belcher feared the reaction of the British government to both
schemes, he considered the Land Bank the more inflationary and the
more dangerous of the two. After a futile threatening of its shareholders
with all sorts of penalties, he was forced to remove them not only from
appointive offices but from the elective offices of the Massachusetts
House of Representatives as well. No greater purge had ever been undertaken in the colony's history, and it cut deep into the community's political life. The bitterness of the Land Bank's supporters knew no bounds
when they heard that Belcher had encouraged the intervention of Parliament in his attempt to suppress the banks.

These hard-fisted measures all but destroyed Belcher's usefulness in
Massachusetts. His enemies relentlessly pursued him, exposing his past
errors of judgment and openly predicting his removal. In desperation,

Belcher turned to his patrons for help, but he found neither the sympathy nor the support he needed. "It is strange," he observed in his bitterness, that "the ministry will be so teased and plagued with every ill-natured fellow that conceives a prejudice at a Governour. Why won't they see through their spight and malice, and bid them be quiet?"

By this time, however, Belcher's friends in government were unable to help him or, perhaps, unwilling to sacrifice their good relations with Newcastle. The Duke, as the leader of a war party, was rapidly winning popular favor throughout Great Britain. This was Newcastle's first great bid for power, and he was making the most of his opportunity. With his rise to prominence, he was in a position to reward his followers, among them Shirley, whom he turned to for assistance in New England in connection with the War of Jenkins' Ear.

Such favoritism shown to Shirley was but another setback for Belcher. It further weakened his control of local patronage and multiplied again his differences with the legislatures. It also served to notify merchants looking for rich contracts, recruiting fees, military commissions, and offices of state that Shirley was the new power in Massachusetts. Still, Belcher was of stout heart when he calculated his position in the spring of 1741: "I find great things have been done this winter, and that Sir R[obert] is staunch, and Lord President [Wilmington] made soft and easy. I hope my enemies will become tired, gnash their teeth, and melt away."

Before the foregoing words had reached his agents in London, Belcher had been recalled. Abandoned by his friends, he lost both governorships; Shirley succeeded him in Massachusetts, while Benning Wentworth became the governor of the separate colony of New Hampshire. There was no sympathy for Belcher in the New England trading community, which immediately celebrated the change of governors with tavern parties in London and in Boston. Attending one London party were such men as Waldo, Thomlinson, and Apthorp, who stayed in England long enough to arrange other alliances in Shirley's behalf. And Mrs. Shirley completed Belcher's political demise by securing Lord Wilmington's patronage and the removal of certain Belcher appointees at Boston.

Without friends and full of bitterness, Belcher admitted that his removal was a "terrible shock." He blamed his loss of office upon the falsehood, hypocrisy, and treachery" of the politicians and merchants who had not stood by him in times of crisis. His support of hard money, he felt, had been the test of his loyalty to the Crown, but he had been sacrificed because of his subsequent unpopularity. "I am now close at the heels of sixty and much inclined to retirement and solitude, yet I have hints . . . that give distant hopes of the ministry's making some provision for me, but if they should not, perhaps by a trip to Great Britain I might in one shape or other do something for myself." Six years later, with the help of another patron, he became governor of New Jersey.

26. THE BRITISH GOVERNMENT
AND COLONIAL UNION, 1754*

by Alison Gilbert Olson

The growth of a far-flung empire that stretched from London
to Philadelphia to Calcutta had not been planned. Nor did the
British develop an efficient, centralized bureaucracy to administer their possessions. Most of the American colonies had been
settled by private rather than public enterprise and, though
some became royal colonies with a Crown-appointed governor,
others remained corporate colonies that elected their governors,
or proprietary colonies whose governors were selected by a
proprietor such as the Penn family. Not until the end of the
seventeenth century did the British establish a permanent
administrative body to oversee colonial affairs. The Board of
Trade (1696) was an advisory organ; it usually suffered from
weak leadership, and had to compete with other agencies such
as the Treasury and Admiralty, which also had jurisdiction in
colonial affairs. The greatest obstacle to the centralization of
colonial administration was indifference as well as fear of pro-

---

* *William and Mary Quarterly*, 3d series, vol. 17 (1960), 22–34. Footnotes have
been omitted except where they are necessary for an understanding of the text.

voking controversy in Parliament and the colonies. The last effort
to reorganize colonial affairs before the 1760's was the Albany
Plan of Union (1754), whose genesis and fate are analyzed in
the following essay. In peacetime, each colony assumed responsibility for defending its frontiers and dealing with the Indians,
but by the middle of the eighteenth century, as England and
France moved toward the decisive struggle for control of North
America, increased commitment and coordination of resources
devoted to the contest became necessary. An intercolonial congress was one means of pooling, enlarging, and integrating colonial financial and defense efforts. The initiative came not from
England but from colonial officials and statesmen, but the circumstances of English domestic politics doomed the proposal.
Ignorance of American affairs and political rivalry between the
President of the Board of Trade and the head of the ministry
had earlier frustrated efforts to tighten control over the colonies,
and when the approach of war increased the pressure for imperial reorganization, fears that such a proposal would alienate
the Americans and arouse a storm of opposition in Parliament
led a prudent ministry to do nothing. England thus entered the
Great War for Empire (1754–1763) without modernizing the
structure of imperial administration, a task delayed until after
the French were beaten.

For further reading: Oliver M. Dickerson, *American Colonial Government, 1696–1765* (1912); Stanley M. Pargellis,
Lord Loudoun in North America (1933); Lawrence H. Gipson,
British Empire before the American Revolution, vol. 5 (1942),
chaps. 4, 5; Robert C. Newbold, *The Albany Congress and Plan
of Union of 1754* (1955); John Shy, *Toward Lexington* (1966),
chap. 1.

The Albany Congress of 1754 drew up a plan to unite the American
colonies under a federal government. This plan was a link between the
Confederacy of New England and the Articles of Confederation; it
was also the last major plan for federal union prepared by the colonists
themselves before 1763, when the overhaul of the British imperial
system made federation under British hegemony unattractive to them.

Furthermore, since many features of the plan of union were embryonic in the "Short Hints" Benjamin Franklin drew up for the Congress, the Albany Plan provided Franklin's admirers with a superfluous demonstration of the great man's versatility. For these reasons historians have studied extensively the conception and preparation of the plan, while they have overlooked the reasons for its rejection.

The Albany Commissioners approved the plan "pretty unanimously," yet not a single colonial assembly voted in its favor. Particularism and fear for charter rights alone can scarcely explain this discrepancy. The Commissioners began the plan by requesting an act of Parliament along the lines prepared. Ever since Charles I had established the Committee of Foreign Plantations, British governments had been concerned to develop a plan of union acceptable to the American colonists. Here, presumably, was one, already approved by representatives of ten of the colonies, yet the cabinet never even presented the Albany Plan to Parliament. Was the plan too democratic for the ministers, as Benjamin Franklin claimed? Or did the ministers themselves approve the plan and abandon it only after the colonial legislatures had failed to vote their endorsement, as Robert Newbold has recently surmised?

Both assumptions are open to question. Newbold did not have access to British sources, and Franklin's London informants were either ignorant or uncommunicative about the fate of the Albany Plan. Had either Franklin or Newbold examined the cabinet correspondence for the summer and autumn of 1754, he would have realized that the principle of effecting intercolonial union through an act of Parliament had been fully discussed and rejected by the British government only a month before copies of the Albany Plan arrived in London.

From the middle of August 1754 until nearly the end of September, the leading minister and his advisers had discussed a plan of union drawn up jointly by the cabinet and the Board of Trade. They approved the principle of intercolonial co-operation, but they dared not risk the government's majority in the House of Commons by presenting it as legislation. The debate would uncover latent fears of colonial independence. While a strong government could weather the vote, the ministry in power was weak: it faced a newly elected Parliament with strong speakers in opposition, it had no effective manager on the ministry's side, and it could count on only uncertain support from the King.

Initially the Albany Congress was ordered by the Board of Trade and the Secretary of State in two directives sent out in the summer of

1753. On August 12, 1753, Lord Halifax, president of the Board of Trade, received word from the Governor of Virginia that the French were building fortresses on the Ohio to connect their lines of defense along the Mississippi and the St. Lawrence. Two weeks later Halifax apparently conferred with the three ministers most concerned with colonial affairs—the Duke of Newcastle, First Lord of the Treasury, and the Earl of Holdernesse and Sir Thomas Robinson, both Secretaries of State. As a result of this conference Holdernesse prepared a circular letter to colonial governors instructing them to correspond with each other on matters of defense and to warn their legislatures of the urgent need for mutual military assistance. In September Halifax called together the Board of Trade to discuss reports of an unsatisfactory conference between Governor George Clinton of New York and the neighboring Indian chiefs. The Board then sent out its own circular letter on September 18 advising the other colonies to unite with the Governor of New York in promoting a joint Indian congress.

Neither the Board of Trade nor the cabinet imagined that the colonists would take advantage of an Indian congress to prepare a plan for permanent political union. When Governor William Shirley of Massachusetts sent copies of a speech he had delivered in April 1754 urging the Massachusetts assembly to consider the Albany Congress as just such an opportunity, the cabinet did not know what to make of it.

Shirley had told the assembly that "Such an union of councils besides the happy effect it will probably have upon the Indians of the Six Nations, may lay a foundation for a general one among all His Majesty's Colonies for the mutual support and defense against the present dangerous enterprizes of the French on every side of them." Did Shirley intend the Albany Congress to provide a model for future congresses? Or did he mean that the commissioners should petition the British government to determine quotas of troops provided by each colony in case of a French attack? The cabinet was not sure. And so, in a meeting held on June 13 to consider Shirley's speech, the cabinet decided to expand upon his idea and to commission the Board of Trade to prepare a plan of colonial union.

For several years the Board had been awaiting such an invitation. A union of mainland colonies under one executive would facilitate administration from England; if that executive were responsible to the Board of Trade alone, the Board would unquestionably increase its prestige and power relative to the Treasury and the Admiralty.

But the Board could not take the initiative in drawing up such a plan with any promise of a favorable reception by the ministry. The Board's powers were purely advisory. The acceptance of their advice depended primarily on the personal relations of its president with the First Lord of the Treasury, and at best Halifax's relations with the Duke of Newcastle were distant. An ambitious administrator in an ineffective administration, a rather poorly connected critic of government by connection, Halifax had found his potentially broad-visioned colonial policy consistently obstructed by procedural difficulties. In his five years at the Board frustration had turned to irascibility. Newcastle avoided his company; Newcastle's closest adviser, the Earl of Hardwicke, regarded his political abilities with contempt.

Repeatedly Halifax's requests for a regular seat in the cabinet had been turned down; repeatedly he had solicited a vacant Garter, only to be put off and eventually recommended as one of seven nominees for three vacancies. Early in September 1754 he invited Newcastle to visit his country home at Horton and Newcastle did not reply. When he read that month of Colonel George Washington's defeat on the Ohio he expected the Privy Council to meet; yet Newcastle sent him no announcement of plans. Consequently, the Board of Trade had very little hope of seeing any of its recommendations for colonial union adopted by the cabinet.

Halifax seems to have hoped that preparing a plan of union might increase his chances of obtaining a cabinet position. In the summer of 1753 he had drawn up a plan ("The Proceedings of the French in America have been of two heads . . ."), which provided for the sending of a commander in chief to the colonies and for Parliamentary legislation uniting in one fund all revenues collected in the colonies. Having discreetly circulated copies of his plan to several ministers in April 1754, Halifax came to the meeting on June 13, hoping his plan would be the basis for cabinet instructions to the Board. Instead, he was humiliated. The cabinet accepted only his suggestion of sending a commander in chief, the least original part of Halifax's plan and, in any event, the one feature of any plan of union on which the government had the least flexibility. Some chief executive must represent the British government, and he must necessarily be a military officer. To appoint a civil governor over a proprietary or corporate colony would be a violation of charter rights, and vacating charters by act of Parliament had been tried with total lack of success in 1701, 1702, 1706, and 1715.

The King, who could at any time assume the functions of commander in chief himself, had the right to appoint such an officer over any part of his dominions. For the rest of Halifax's plan the cabinet substituted its own equally vague provisions giving to a colonial congress (rather than to Parliament) the allocation of financial quotas.

On June 22, Horatio Walpole, Auditor-General of the Plantations, wrote Newcastle:

Now I am upon this subject, I beg leave to add, that as our possessions on the continent in America are one continued chain of Colinys, and altho under different governments, of different kinds, belong to the Crown of Gr. Britain, and altho jealous of one another as all neighbors generally are in their private concerns, have one and the same interest with respect to those provinces in America who are possessed by foreign powers, especially the French that are so strong and border upon them; I am persuaded that such a plan of union might be formed between the Royale, Proprietary and Charter Governments, under the protection and with approbation of the Crown of Gr. Britain, for their mutual security and Defense, against the encroachment of their foreign neighbours by a convention, for settling the respective proportions of assistance to be furnishe[d] by them all in defense of any one of them, that shall be attacked or threatered to be attacked as might be a standing security in all dangerous emergencys.

[Three days later, he wrote further.] In the meantime the governors in the several colonys upon the whole continent should be instructed and desired to send the best accounts they can of whatever may be thought useful towards framing a plan of such an union, or confederacy, the heads of the principal articles should be concerted and drawn here by the Board of Trade and the execution of it for obtaining the direction and management of some able person of Quality [illegible] to be sent from hence with a commission from his Majesty to negotiate this allegiance with the several governments and under proper instructions endeavour to induce them all to concur in it.

Newcastle assured him:

I am very glad to be able to tell you that the principles upon which we have proceeded, and the Resolutions which we have taken are entirely agreeable to your letter. The first point we have laid down is that the colonies must not be abandon'd.

516

We have also given orders some time ago to the Board of Trade to prepare a scheme for a general concert amongst the Northern Colonies, and for settling the proportions, which each Province should contribute, for their constant defence, and in case of any emergency or attack . . . and it is intended to send a proper person of weight to be Governor of New York; who may, as you propose, have the conduct of this scheme for a general concert; and be, as it were, a sort of general or commander-in-chief of the whole. Ld. Willoughby was some time ago thought of, but he absolutely refused it, I find the person most approved of is Col. Cornwallis, if he would undertake it.

The Board filled in details on the cabinet's plan in July, and on August 15 Halifax sent the finished draft to Newcastle. The plan proposed that the governors of all North American colonies be instructed to propose to their provincial legislatures that commissioners be elected to meet and discuss the critical need for intercolonial defense. The commissioners would consider particularly the building and manning of western forts; they would prepare an estimate of the cost, and on the basis of trade, population, wealth, and revenue, they would determine the quota of each colony. A commander in chief (also acting as commissioner for Indian affairs) would supervise the construction of the forts; for this purpose he could draw directly upon the provincial treasurers for the amount of the quotas. If any colony were suddenly attacked, it was to draw up an estimate of extraordinary expenses. The commissioners would convene, study, and possibly revise the estimate, and divide the anticipated expenses among all the colonies in proportion to the percentage represented by their original quotas.

When the commissioners had agreed upon the plan for fortifications, the quotas, and the procedure for handling emergencies, they were to forward copies of the agreement to the governors and the colonial legislatures. They, in turn, would consider the plans, suggest possible alterations, and return the report to the commissioners within two months. After revision the final copy of the agreement was to be sent to London for the King's approval.

For six weeks after receiving his copy of the plan Newcastle rushed from one adviser to another soliciting opinions on it. He was too ignorant of colonial affairs to analyze the merits of the plan himself and too lacking in self-confidence to trust his own judgment anyway. He needed constant reassurance of his favor with strategic friends, and seeking advice was one of his more subtle and subconscious methods of courting flattery. In desperate fear of offending anyone important, the timid minister would thank each adviser effusively, avow wholehearted concurrence with his comments, and pass on his suggestions unmodified to the next adviser. From conference to conference his reactions to the bill were altered; from day to day his morale rose or fell with the warmth of response from his confidants.

His advisers represented three groups—the cabinet, noncabinet politicians, and the royal family. Only two advisers were from the cabinet, first, because Newcastle deliberately kept a weak cabinet and second, because the stipulations most important to the cabinet had already been made in June. Like most eighteenth-century prime ministers the Duke wanted a mediocre cabinet with strong advisers outside it. His fellow ministers were not only men of uninspired talent, they were also peers with little feeling for the temper of the Commons—a feeling indispensable to eighteenth-century political leadership. So jealous was Newcastle of cabinet competitors that he was even relying on the pathetically unimaginative Sir Thomas Robinson, Secretary of State, to be his manager in the next House of Commons, ignoring the vastly superior claims of William Pitt and Henry Fox to cabinet positions.

As a result, there were only two cabinet members worth consulting on colonial affairs—the Earls of Hardwicke and Granville. Hardwicke was a lawyer who scarcely knew where the colonies were, but he was willing to risk an opinion, however narrow, on any question where he considered his assistance indispensable to Newcastle. Granville, on the other hand, had a fine mind and a ruined reputation—the ideal combination for Newcastle's cabinet. As Baron Carteret, audacity, brilliance, charm, and royal favor had made him leading minister for a tantalizing year in 1742; but disillusionment, premature old age, alcohol, and a new peerage had gradually reduced him to the position of political spectator.

Granville and Hardwicke were the first advisers to whom Newcastle showed the finished plan. As might have been expected, they heartily supported it. Granville apparently favored it without alteration; Hardwicke suggested only minor changes for simplification. He thought that determining a quorum for the meetings of commissioners was premature and unnecessary, and that summoning all the commissioners to approve supplies before an invaded colony could begin its defense was ridiculously cumbersome. Instead he suggested that an invaded colony be able to bill its confederates after the emergency had been met. These changes were minor; Hardwicke even thought Halifax could incorporate them without returning to the Board.

Sometime after Granville and Hardwicke had approved the basic plan, Newcastle consulted his political friends outside the cabinet— William Murray, Alderman William Baker of London, Charles Townshend, and George Onslow. Townshend and Baker were presumably asked because of their knowledge of colonial affairs, since Townshend had been a member of the Board of Trade and Baker was a North American merchant. Townshend was already the more notorious; Baker was certainly the more reliable. Contemptuous of deliberation, Townshend's impatient mind glanced over subjects with terrifying superficiality. He understood neither the colonists' resentment of external regulation nor Parliament's fear of colonial independence.

Onslow and Murray, on the other hand, were consulted for their understanding of the House of Commons. As speaker of the House, Onslow knew its temper as no one else did. As the government's manager there, Murray, an ambitious lawyer better known for his later career as Lord Chief Justice Mansfield, was the only ministerial speaker capable of holding his own in debate with Pitt and Fox.

All four men were particularly concerned with enhancing the power of Parliament vis-a-vis the Empire and the King. While Hardwicke and Granville were sympathetic to the colonists' desires for considerable self-government, Murray and Townshend were later associated with the most extreme assertion of Parliamentary supremacy over the colonies, and even Baker later supported the Declaratory Act in 1766.

Townshend, Murray, and Baker, therefore, agreed with the cabinet that the North American colonies must be united, but they favored initiating the plan in Parliament. The cabinet had intended to send it to the colonial legislatures for their voluntary implementation. To Townshend, Murray, and even Baker, this was folly. No colony would make financial sacrifices demanded by commissioners of other colonies. At best the colonial assemblies might water down their quotas beyond all utility; at worst they might even refuse to nominate their own commissioners. If their quotas were inadequate George II might blame the cabinet for putting him in the awkward position of having to veto the whole plan; if the colonists entirely refused to co-operate Parliament would have to legislate in opposition to their expressed wishes. Parliament, therefore, should initiate the plan.

This argument was strengthened by the news of Washington's defeat on the Ohio after a month's siege when every other colony had refused to send aid to his Virginia militia. The news reached London on September 8, 1754; a week later Charles Townshend wrote Newcastle that "I am sure I can convince your Grace from past experience in like cases that the Provinces are more likely to accept such a candid and just plan sent from hence in an act of Parliament than to form one in any meeting by their deputies or in their assemblies." When Newcastle talked with Murray and Baker later in the month he found them both heartily agreeing with Townshend.

An act of Parliament was not what the cabinet or the Board of Trade had originally intended, but even the Board had admitted that if the plan were rejected by the colonies, "We see no other method that can be taken but that of an application for an interposition of the authority of Parliament."

At first sight, presenting the plan directly to Parliament appeared entirely feasible. On closer consideration, however, three difficulties were manifest. The bill would be controversial, the ministry had such weak leaders in the Commons that it could scarcely risk controversy, and, moreover, the ministry could not wait until Parliament opened in November before making arrangements to recruit colonial militia.

On September 9 (immediately after he received the news of Washington's surrender) Newcastle called on his friend the Speaker of the House to find out just how controversial a bill for intercolonial union would be. The Speaker thought any such bill would provoke considerable debate on the "ill consequence to be apprehended from uniting too closely the northern colonies with each other, an Independency upon this country to be feared from such an union." Apparently 1754 was a year in which English fear of an American revolt was enjoying one of its periodic revivals. Horace Walpole, for example, was criticizing New York as a "free, rich, British Settlement and in such opulence and such haughtiness that suspicions had long been conceived of their meditating to throw off their dependence on their mother country." From the American merchants, or from country gentlemen who feared an increase in their land taxes if the colonial uprising had to be subdued by force, the government might expect serious opposition to the bill.

Equally important, that opposition would almost certainly be managed jointly by the two greatest orators in the House of Commons—Pitt and Fox. Nominally both men held ministerial appointments, Pitt as Paymaster of the Forces and Fox as Secretary at War. Neither position, however, carried with it an obligation to support the government's legis-lation in Parliament, and neither man was in a mood to defend it volun-tarily. In the spring Newcastle's ever-present jealousy of cabinet rivals had led him to frustrate the ambitions of Pitt and Fox by filling two cabinet-level vacancies—the Secretaryship of State and the Chancellor-ship of the Exchequer—with political nonentities. To win Fox over, Newcastle had offered him the lead in the House of Commons, but as the offer did not include access to Secret Service money, Fox declined it. Hence at the very time when Newcastle was considering whether to prepare Parliamentary legislation for uniting the colonies he was also frantically excited about the ministry's weakness in the newly elected House of Commons where Pitt and Fox were lying in wait for the cabinet's inarticulate newcomers.

Moreover, Newcastle knew that he could not possibly arrange for the opening of Parliament before November, and the news of Washington's surrender made it imperative that reinforcements be sent to the American frontier before then. Even if the bill could be passed early in November, it would still be difficult to transmit a copy of the plan to the colonies, assign each colony's quota of troops, and train the new recruits in time for a spring campaign. Hardwicke and Granville thought this was feasi-ble; the Duke of Cumberland thought the colonists incapable of training an army over the winter and favored sending two regiments of Irish troops instead. Newcastle was as usual undecided. Finally, at a meeting with Hardwicke, Cumberland, and Robinson on September 26, he yielded to Cumberland and ordered the Irish regiments sent to North America.

This order was the death warrant for the Board of Trade's plan to unite the colonies. As long as North America was in a state of emer-gency, rationalized the irresolute minister, why not avoid the contro-versy which a bill for intercolonial union would excite? On September 28 he wrote Murray, "You will have heard all that is passed, about the General Concert for establishing some provision for the joint defense of our Northern Colonies, but as no scheme of that kind can be of service in the present exigency, that may be a matter of future consider-ation." Robinson's circular letter to the governors of North America a month later explained only that regiments were being sent "until such time as a Plan of General Union of H. M.'s Northern colonies for their common defense can be perfected."

Ten days after Newcastle had abandoned the plan in the cabinet con-ference with Cumberland, copies of the Albany Plan arrived in London.

The first person to receive a copy was Charles Townshend, to whom it had apparently been sent by a friend in New York. Robinson received a copy several days later, and Newcastle, on October 12. For at least three weeks Newcastle was too busy to look at the plan. He was occupied fully with the budget, the address from the throne, and the negotiations for a government spokesman in the Commons. Somewhat uncertainly he wrote to Townshend on November 2, "There is a representation from the Commissioners who met at Albany which may forword our work of engaging the colonels [*sic*] to take some care of themselves. I have not had time to examine it, but if I am not mistaken it is so far conformable to your own idea that they themselves propose that what they would have done should be by an act of Parliament here."

Meanwhile, the Board of Trade had considered the minutes of the Albany Congress and sent their comments on to the cabinet. While they wrote at length about the immediate need for appointing Indian commissioners, they forwarded without comment the plan "Which, as far as their sense and opinion of it goes, is complete within itself . . . we shall not presume to make any observations on it." In fact, there was no need to register formal approval. The Board's recommendation of intercolonial military union the summer before was on record, and any formal statement on the Albany Plan would be without further effect. Halifax knew that Newcastle had seen the plan. Moreover, it was futile to hope that Newcastle would support it.

The Albany Plan incorporated many features of the government's proposal—a chief military executive and a commissioner for Indian affairs, both to be paid by the crown, provisions for arranging Indian treaties binding on all the colonies and for the building of western forts with funds voted by an intercolonial assembly and collected by the treasury officials of each separate colony. More important, it disposed of some of the difficulties involved in putting the government's plan into effect—it had already been accepted by intercolonial commissioners, and it requested an act of Parliament.

On the other hand, the governmental union projected by the Albany Plan went far beyond anything the English government would dare present to Parliament. It provided for a Grand Council of delegates from the mainland colonies. The number of delegates from each colony was to be proportional to the colony's share of taxes. Delegates were to be elected by the colonial assemblies every three years; the Council would meet annually to discuss Indian affairs, provide for building forts and patroling the seacoast, and levy indirect taxes binding directly the inhabitants of every colony in the union. The President-General could veto its acts, but he could not prorogue it or select its speaker. The plan thus projected a union in which the legislative assembly would have more power than the separate colonial assemblies had in relation to their governors but less power than Parliament enjoyed vis-a-vis George II. The danger of the government proposed, therefore, was not in its democracy but in the anticipated permanence of its institutions, the regularity of its intercolonial meetings, and the federal nature of its authority.

The Board of Trade's plan had provided the minimum possible administrative union capable of obtaining the colonists' voluntary consent to taxation for their own defense and capable of obtaining some intercolonial co-operation against emergency attacks. The Albany Plan provided an extensive legislative union. Members of Parliament who already feared American independence would have even less interest in the Albany Plan than in the one prepared by the Board of Trade.

Equally important, the old problems connected with the passing of the Board of Trade's plan remained—a new House of Commons in which it would be impossible to pass a controversial bill without an experienced manager, the outbreak of hostilities in America, and the alleged impossibility of recruiting colonial militia in time for a spring campaign.

Correspondence concerning the bill is lacking because Newcastle and his advisers were all in town during November. It seems clear, however, that while Newcastle was still considering the scheme (in a conference with the King) as late as December 6, he had not really been inclined to any plan of union since the meeting with Cumberland on September 26 and possibly since his meeting with the Speaker of the House of Commons on September 9.

It is misleading, then, to consider the Albany Plan out of the context of the Board of Trade's plan which was discussed before it. To do so is to give the ministry and the Board far less credit for interest in colonial union than they deserve. The Albany Plan was evidently little discussed by the cabinet; the reason for this is not that the plan itself was too democratic or that the cabinet was awaiting the approval of colonial legislatures, but that the feasibility of uniting the colonies had been thoroughly considered before copies of the plan ever arrived in England.

Patterns of Provincial Society

27. THE ARISTOCRACY IN COLONIAL AMERICA*

by Arthur M. Schlesinger

Even though in the American colonies, as in Europe, the
social order was hierarchically arranged, the American social
structure was not a replica of the British. In the following essay,
Arthur M. Schlesinger examines the nature of the top strata, the
colonial elites, and suggests similarities and differences between
American and English aristocracies. The American upper crust
was a sudden creation; European aristocracies had deeper historical roots. Membership in the American upper strata was
usually the result of achievement rather than inheritance, and
the opportunities for gaining the keys to the club were considerable. Newcomers were constantly pushing their way into the
leading circles, and the younger sons of established families

* *Proceedings of the Massachusetts Historical Society*, vol. 74 (1962), 3–21.
Footnotes have been omitted except where they are necessary for an understanding
of the text.

could not expect to perpetuate the family's place unless they worked hard to preserve the material foundations of its position. Neither leisured *rentiers* nor coupon clippers, the leading colonials were active estate managers and enterprising businessmen. These circumstances made the upper groups unstable as new families ascended and older ones declined. This impermanence and insecurity generated anxieties and tensions whose dimensions and consequences historians have yet to explore.

For further reading: Carl Bridenbaugh, *Myths and Realities, Societies of the Colonial South* (1963); J. Henretta, "Economic Development and Social Structure in Colonial Boston," *William and Mary Quarterly,* 3d series, vol. 22 (1965), 75–92; E. Evans, "The Rise and Decline of the Virginia Aristocracy in the Eighteenth Century: The Nelsons," Darrett B. Rutman, ed., *The Old Dominion* (1965), 62–78; Jackson T. Main, *Social Structure of Revolutionary America* (1965); N. Dawes, "Titles as Symbols of Prestige in Seventeenth Century New England," *William and Mary Quarterly,* 3d series, vol. 6 (1949), 69–83.

For many years historical students have been so interested in discovering evidences of democracy in the colonial period that they have tended to distort the actual situation. This paper is an attempt to correct the balance.

The colonists unhesitatingly took for granted the concept of a graded society. It was the only kind they had known in Europe, and they had no thought of forgoing it in their new home. Indeed, they possessed a self-interested reason for retaining it. In this outpost of civilization it was man alone, not his ancestors, who counted. Even the humblest folk could hope to better their condition, for the equality of opportunity which they now had attained meant, as well, the opportunity to be unequal. The indentured servant, the apprentice, the common laborer, everyone in fact but the Negro bondsman, could expect to stand on his own feet and get on and up in the world.

Other factors, however, precluded a faithful duplicating of Europe's stratified order. As David Ramsay pointed out in his *History of the American Revolution* (1789), no remnants of the feudal age existed to thwart or hinder men's advancement. The occasional nobleman who went to America deserted his accustomed "splendor and amusements" only for temporary exile, usually to cash in on a colonial proprietary-ship or a royal governorship. Thomas Fairfax, settling in Virginia from England in 1747 at the age of fifty-four, was unique among the permanent comers in bearing so high a rank as baron, but he lived out the remaining thirty-four years of his life for the most part unobtrusively on his distant Shenandoah Valley estate.

Some settlers, however, notably in Virginia, were the untitled younger sons or kinsmen of peers, while to the northward many belonged to the English landed or mercantile gentry. By Old World standards, though, they were members of the upper middle class and at best could provide but the entering wedge for an aristocracy. They not only lacked noble rank but suffered from want of a royal court to act as a stimulus and model. Nor could they rest their social edifice, as did the privileged caste at home, on a hereditary class of landless peasants and destitute workingmen. The enslaved blacks alone served the purpose, but they were to be found mainly in the South, where indeed the patrician order achieved its fullest development.

In the case of a few of the early colonies the English government sought by fiat to establish artificial class distinctions, but these efforts, occurring in the middle third of the seventeenth century, all came to grief. The London authorities, accustomed to titles of nobility at home, were blind to the very different conditions existing in the overseas wilderness. The people were sparse, strong-willed, and still scrambling for a living; the thought of a social strait jacket imposed from above outraged their mettlesome self-respect and, by the same sign, operated to deter prospective settlers.

One attempt was John Locke's blueprint of a quasi-feudal order in the Carolinas. Another took the form of the power granted Lord Baltimore as proprietor of Maryland to confer "whatever titles" he pleased. In the first instance the purpose was avowedly to "avoid erecting a numerous democracy"; the Maryland charter, on the other hand, put the case positively, asserting that short of such a provision "every access to honors and dignities may seem to be precluded, and utterly barred, to men well born." Baltimore, however, for reasons unknown, never exercised the prerogative. Consequently, the plan of an American-based peerage, which collapsed after a brief trial in the Carolinas, did not even make a beginning in Maryland.

For the settlers to build a structured society on their own initiative and in their own interest was, however, quite another matter. This they proceeded to do in colony after colony as rapidly as time and circumstances permitted. In the case of Massachusetts, though, they did not have to wait. Not only did the founders themselves belong to Britain's rural and urban gentry but, as good Puritans, they considered their superior station divinely ordained. In the words of their first governor, John Winthrop, "God Almightie in his most holy and wise providence hath soe disposed of the Condicion of mankinde, as in all times some must be rich some poore, some highe and emminent in power and dignitie; others mean and in subieceion." Accordingly, the men so favored immediately assumed the key positions in government and society, sharing the honors with the foremost clergymen.

They overreached themselves, however, when they sought to legalize class differences in dress. Despite the heavy penalties for disobedience, ordinary people in this new land did not understand that they were to be permanently ordinary. To no avail did the legislature in 1651 express "utter detestation" that men "of meane condition, education and callings should take uppon them the garbe of gentlemen by the wearinge of gold or silver lace" and the like, and that "women of the same rank" should "wear silke or tiffany hoodes or scarfes." Both there and in Connecticut, which had somewhat similar regulations, the resistance to them was so stubborn that they were presently allowed to fall into disuse.

In all other respects, however, the aristocracy retained its primacy, and as the years went on, families with fortunes newly made on land or sea won admittance to the circle. The traveler Joseph Bennett wrote in 1740 of Boston, "both the ladies and gentlemen dress and appear as gay, in common, as courtiers in England on a coronation or birthday." And the author of *American Husbandry,* surveying the entire New England scene in 1775, reported that, though social demarcations were less conspicuous than abroad, "gentlemen's houses appear everywhere" and on the "many considerable land estates . . . the owners live much in the style of country gentlemen in England."

In New York, while the colony was still New Netherland, the Dutch West India Company had introduced a system of patroonships—immense tracts along the Hudson which the possessors were to cultivate with tenants bound to them by a semifeudal relationship. But only a few of the grants were actually made before the British took over in 1664, and of these Rensselaerswyck, in what is now Albany County, was the only one to work out well. The English governors in their turn followed the Dutch example to the extent of awarding enormous estates to favored individuals; and on this basis a privileged class evolved which divided political and social pre-eminence in the province with the leading merchants and lawyers of New York City.

Although the historical background in Pennsylvania was different, the outcome there, too, was the same. Despite the lowly antecedents of most of the Quaker settlers and their devotion to "plain living," an aristocracy of great landholders and merchant princes likewise arose. John Smith, an old-time Friend looking back from the year 1764, sadly depicted the change as it had come over Philadelphia. During the first twenty years, he said, as the members began to accumulate means, they commenced "in some degree conforming to the fashions of the World," and after another score of years, when "many of the Society were grown rich," vanities like "fine costly Garments" and "fashionable furniture" became usual. Indeed, the foremost families, not content with handsome urban residences, maintained in addition country estates as retreats from the intense heat of the Philadelphia summers.

But the Southern aristocracy attained the closest resemblance to the English landed gentry. There, in a predominantly rural economy, men on the make enjoyed the decisive advantage of an extensive servile class as well as of broad acres. There, also, to a degree unknown in the North, the Virginia patrician William Fitzhugh spoke for his class in avowing that his children had "better be never born than ill-bred." Josiah Quincy, Jr., visiting South Carolina in 1773, wrote that "The inhabitants may well be divided into opulent and lordly planters, poor and spiritless peasants and vile slaves." The Bostonian, however, overlooked the fact that, different from the other Southern provinces, the select circle in this particular one also included successful merchants, thanks to Charleston, the only important seaport south of Philadelphia.

Thomas Jefferson, analyzing from a more intimate knowledge the free population of Virginia, listed at the top "the great landholders"; next, "the descendants of the younger sons and daughters of the aristocrats, who inherited the pride of their ancestors, without their wealth"; thirdly, "the pretenders, men, who, from vanity or the impulse of growing wealth, or from that enterprise which is natural to talents, sought to detach themselves from the plebeian ranks"; next, "a solid and independent yeomanry, looking askance at those above, yet not venturing to jostle them"; and, finally, the "degraded" and "unprincipled" overseers, the smallest group. The description would have pertained equally well to Maryland.

The Southern gentry, however, possessed an energy and resourcefulness uncharacteristic of its Old World prototype. To maintain its position the members had to be men of affairs—tireless and responsible directors of a system of agricultural labor alien to the homeland, which, moreover, was used for the raising of staple crops uncultivated there and grown on great and often scattered plantations. They could not, however much they wished, constitute in the same sense a leisure class.

Two concepts of land inheritance derived from English law furnished potential support for an aristocratic order. The principle of primogeniture ensured that the total family realty would descend automatically to the eldest son in default of a will. This arrangement prevailed not only throughout the South but also in New York and Rhode Island, and, in the modified form of a double share for the oldest boy, existed in all the remaining colonies but New Jersey. Entail, the other aspect of the system, enabled an owner to leave his estate intact to a specified heir or line of heirs. This practice had legal sanction everywhere. As a matter of fact, however, neither method was much used, for where land was so plentiful there did not exist the same need as in the mother country to guard against dissipating a patrimony. Moreover, these devices, even when employed, did not work the same hardship on the disinherited, who usually by their own means could acquire independent holdings and thereby actually enlarge the economic base of the upper class.

The English-appointed governor and his entourage in the provincial capital formed the apex of the social pyramid. These personages and their womenfolk emulated the pomp and circumstance of the royal court at home and furnished a pattern for the great landholders, mercantile princes, and the like who composed the native aristocracy. A beadroll of such families in the eighteenth century would include among others the Wentworths of New Hampshire, the Bowdoins, Quincys, Hutchinsons, Olivers, Faneuils, and Hancocks of Massachusetts, the Redwoods, Browns, and Wantons of Rhode Island, the Trumbulls and Ingersolls of Connecticut, the De Lanceys, Schuylers, Van Rensselaers, Livingstons, and Coldens of New York, the Logans, Allens, Morrises, Willings, Pembertons, and Shippens of Pennsylvania and, in the plantation colonies, the Dulanys and Carrolls of Maryland, the Byrds, Randolphs, Carters, Masons, Pages, Fitzhughs, Harrisons, and

Lees of Virginia, and the Rutledges, Pinckneys, Draytons, Laurenses, and Izards of South Carolina.

Families like these buttressed their position by matrimonial alliances both within and across provincial boundaries. To cite a few cases, the New Yorker John Franklin married Deborah Morris of Philadelphia, and her fellow townsman William Shippen wedded Alice Lee of the Old Dominion. The Allens of Philadelphia, the Redwoods of Newport, the New York De Lanceys, the Ervings of Boston, and the Izards of Charleston took mates in three or more colonies. The rare instances of gentle-folk marrying beneath their station scandalized their friends and kinsmen. To William Byrd II, for example, it was nothing short of a "tragical Story" when a wellborn Virginia girl in 1732 played "so senceless a Prank" as to marry her uncle's overseer, "a dirty Plebian."

By custom and official usage members of the gentry enjoyed the privilege of attaching certain honorific tags to their names. As in England, they alone could qualify as "Gentlemen," and they only had the right to the designations "Esquire" and "Master," although the latter term tended in ordinary speech to be pronounced "Mister." The common man, for his part, contentedly answered to "Goodman"—his day of being called "Mister" was yet to come. Equal consideration for class distinctions governed the allotment of pews in Congregational churches, where persons resisting their assignments were sometimes haled into court. And at Yale until 1767 and Harvard until 1772 even the order of reciting in class and the place of students in academic processions bore a relation to the social standing of their parents.

Not being to the manner born, most people aspiring to gentility had to learn from scratch how to act like their betters. Luckily manuals for the purpose lay at hand. The great majority were English importations, but to meet the rising demand colonial printers, as the years went by, put out their own editions. These treatises followed originals appearing in France and Italy, where since the age of chivalry the standards of approved behavior had been set for the whole of Europe. Among the writings most often listed in American booksellers' announcements and the inventories of private libraries were Henry Peacham's *The Compleat Gentleman* (1622), Richard Brathwaite's *The English Gentleman* (1630), Richard Allestree's *The Whole Duty of Man* (1660), and, for feminine guidance, Lord Halifax's *The Lady's New Year's Gift: or, Advice to a Daughter* (1688), the anonymous *Ladies Library* (1714), the *Friendly*

Instructor (1745) by an unknown, and William Kenrick's *The Whole Duty of Woman; or, a Guide to the Female Sex from the Age of Sixteen to Sixty* (1761). Even the commonsensical Benjamin Franklin wrote his wife from London in 1758 that he wanted their daughter Sally to "read over and over again the *Whole Duty of Man,* and the *Lady's Library,*" and we know that George Washington as late as 1764 purchased an American reprint of the *Whole Duty of Man.*

These handbooks held up integrity, courage, justice, courtesy, and piety as the hallmarks of the gentleman, with modesty, chastity, tenderness, godliness, and the duty of submission to one's husband as the essentials of a gentlewoman. Wifely docility not only befitted the innate inferiority of the sex but attested lasting penance for the first woman's disobedience. If her yokefellow proved unfaithful, wrote Lord Halifax, she should "affect ignorance" of it; if he were a sot, she should rejoice that the fault offset her own many frailities; if he were "Cholerick and Ill-humour'd," she should avoid any "unwary Word" and soothe him with smiles and flattery; if he lacked intelligence, she should take comfort in the thought that "a wife often made a better Figure, for her Husband's making no great one." The writers, when treating behavior in company, instructed the ladies what to wear, how to arrange a dinner, what diversions were proper, and how to converse (with the admonition: "Women seldom have Materials to furnish a long Discourse. . . .").

Having discovered how to conduct themselves, the gentry further evidenced their status by the elegance of their attire. The pains they took to ape the latest court styles appear in their elaborate orders to English tailors and the loud complaints over the pattern or fit or color of the garments commissioned. George Washington, for one, cautioned his London agent, "Whatever goods you may send me, let them be fashionable, neat and good of their several kinds." According to the Englishman Daniel Neal in 1747, "there is no Fashion in London but in three or four Months is to be seen at Boston," and William Eddis after a few years in Annapolis wrote similarly in 1771 that he was "almost inclined to believe" that a new mode spread more rapidly among "polished and affluent" Americans than among "many opulent" Londoners.

Subject to the season's vagaries in matters of detail, gentlemen wore cocked hats, white ruffled silk shirts, and embroidered broadcloth frock coats, with knee breeches of fine texture and gorgeous hues, silk hose fastened with ornamental garters, and pumps displaying gold or silver buckles. Powdered wigs, an added adornment, began to lose favor about 1754, when George II discarded his, to be followed by the vogue of letting one's natural hair grow long and powdering it and queuing it behind or tying the tail in a small silk bag.

Gentlewomen on festive occasions tripped about on dainty high-heeled slippers in rustling ·gowns of imported brocade, bombazine, sarsenet, shalloon, damask, velvet, taffeta, and other expensive fabrics. They stiffened their bodices with whalebone stays and stretched their skirts over great hoops of the same material. They kept abreast of the latest English dress designs by means of clothed dolls sent over from London, and shortly before the Revolution they had the additional help of engraved pictures. Indicative of the irresistible sweep of style, the Yearly Meeting of Friends in 1726 at Philadelphia futilely decried the "immodest fashion of hooped petticoats" and such improprieties as "bare necks" and "shoes trimmed with gaudy colors."

An object of special pride was milady's coiffure, a structure pains-takingly erected on a concealed crepe roller or cushion. In preparation for a ball or party she would have her hair dressed the day before and perhaps sleep in a chair that night to keep it in condition. For going about outdoors the first families maintained their own equipages, stylish vehicles variously called chaises, calashes, chairs, and landaus, or, still more grandly, they traveled in coaches-and-four and berlins attended with liveried drivers and footmen.

The apparel of the simple folk similarly evinced their status. The men, their hair short-cropped, typically wore caps, coarse linen shirts, leather coats and aprons, homespun stockings, and cowhide shoes with either long or short buckskin breeches, while the women's garments were of equal cheapness and durability. The French Revolution in its impact on America was in the years ahead to go far toward removing class differences in male attire, but portents of what awaited revealed themselves in unexpected ways in the events leading up to the rupture with Britain. Thus, to conceal their participation in the Stamp Act vio-lence at Boston in August, 1765, "there were fifty gentlemen actors in this scene," wrote Governor Francis Bernard, "disguised with trousers and jackets on." Their motive was doubtless to escape the possible legal consequences of their connivance, but it was probably just a desire for sheer creature comfort which caused the South Caro-lina Assembly in 1769 to permit the members to forgo wigs and knee breeches in order to transact committee business in caps and trousers—

like "so many unhappy persons ready for execution," objected a newspaper commentator.

For those on top of the heap the Anglican Church held a compelling attraction. Just as it was the allegiance of the upper class at home, so it was that of the Crown officials sent to America. The dignified ritualism of the Book of Common Prayer, with its setting of fine music, exerted an undoubted appeal, but the social prestige of membership probably formed the greater magnet. At any rate hundreds of Congregationalists, Presbyterians, Quakers, Lutherans, and others, as they moved upward in the world, forsook the faith of their fathers for the more stylish communion.

Other evidences of snobbishness were even clearer. An English nobleman passing through the colonies never failed to stir the social waters. Thus Lord Adam Gordon, one of the few members of Parliament ever to visit America, conquered all before him as he journeyed from Charleston to Boston in 1765; and Lord Charles Hope on a similar excursion in 1766 met with a like reception. Four years later Sir William Draper crowned his New York stay by wedding Susannah De Lancey.

Two crucial moments in life—marriage and death—afforded special opportunities for ostentation. Weddings were celebrated with banqueting, innumerable toasts, and like festivities sometimes extending over several days. A funeral obliged the bereaved family to provide the assemblage with such souvenirs of the occasion as mourning gloves, scarves, and gold rings as well as quantities of food and drink. At the burial of John Grove of Surrey County, Virginia, in 1673 the liquor consumed equaled the cost of a thousand pounds of tobacco. Governor Jonathan Belcher of Massachusetts in 1736 distributed more than a thousand pairs of gloves in honor of his wife, but Peter Faneuil overtopped him two years later with three thousand at the services for his uncle Andrew. In addition, the grief-stricken friends would don appropriate attire for a further period at their own expense.

As this costly fashion seeped downward in society, it placed an excessive burden on families who, desiring to pay as great respect to their departed, could ill afford the outlay. To ease their plight the Yearly Meeting of Friends at Philadelphia in 1729 recommended to their co-religionists that "wine or other strong liquors" be furnished "but once." The Massachusetts legislature went so far in a series of statutes between 1721 and 1741 as to prohibit under heavy fine the "very extravagant" expense of gloves, scarves, rings, rum, or wine.

But custom proved too stubborn; and no real change came about until the colonists, provoked by the Sugar Act of 1764 and its successors, saw a chance to strike back at Britain by disusing (among other things) the mourning materials they had hitherto imported.

Now public meetings from New Hampshire to Georgia urged "the new mode" on all who loved their country. The *Boston News-Letter*, March 9, 1769, observed with special gratification that the rich Charlestonian Christopher Gadsden had worn simple homespun at his wife's obsequies and that "The whole expence of her funeral, of the manufacture of England, did not amount to more than 3l. 10s our currency." At another South Carolina funeral the people in attendance spiritedly declined to accept the gifts which the family had provided. The First Continental Congress in 1774 climaxed these efforts by subjecting to boycott all persons who distributed scarves or went "into any further mourning-dress, than a black crape or ribbon on the arm or hat, for gentlemen, and a black ribbon and necklace for ladies." From this blow the practice never recovered.

One aspect of Old World patrician life, the *code duello*, the Americans did not achieve or even want to achieve. Perhaps because of their generally more humane disposition they instinctively recoiled from the settlement of disputes by personal combat. Though occasional duels took place during the century and a half, these typically involved royal officers on overseas assignment or recent comers not yet fully Americanized, unless perchance they partook of the shabby character of the encounter between the Charleston youth and a sea captain over what the *South-Carolina Gazette*, September 6, 1735, termed their "pretensions to the Favours of a certain sable Beauty."

The few affrays involving colonial aristocrats deeply shocked public sentiment and, if death resulted, provoked criminal prosecutions. What was apparently the earliest such affair cost the life of Dr. John Livingston of New York in 1715 at the hands of Governor Dongan's nephew Thomas, whom the court two days afterward found guilty of manslaughter. In 1728 occurred a sword fight between two Boston young men in which Henry Phillips killed Benjamin Woodbridge over differences not then or since revealed. Before the grand jury could bring in an indictment for murder (which it did a month later), the victor fled to France with the help of Peter Faneuil, a kinsman by marriage. Some years following, in 1770, Dr. John Haly of Charleston fatally shot Peter De Lancey, the deputy postmaster, in a duel in the candlelit parlor of a tavern. Though he, too, like Dongan, was convicted of manslaughter, he avoided the consequences through the pardon of the governor. In 1775 came the last instance, also between two South Carolinians, but this one differed markedly from the earlier clashes in that Henry Laurens, while willing to accept the challenge of John Grimké, declined as a matter of principle to fire on him. Happily he escaped unscathed. No one could have foreseen as the colonial period ended that the discredited practice would under altered circumstances find wide favor in the next generation.

The continuous recruitment of the top stratum of the community from beneath reveals sharply the basic aspect of colonial society: its fluidity, the incessant movement of people upward. The American aristocracy, however undemocratic when once it took form, was undeniably democratic in the method of its forming. The only class struggle in that far day was the struggle to climb out of a lower class into a higher one, for, as Nathaniel Ames put it in one of his almanacs,

> All Men are by Nature equal,
> But differ greatly in the sequel.

The self-made man thus began his career in America, to become in time a national folk hero. In the absence of England's officially prescribed ranks it was, above all, the acquisition of wealth which elevated a family to the social heights. Extensive land grants and other perquisites from the government, obtained perhaps through favoritism or fraud, might expedite the process. Further help could, and often did come, from lucrative marriages. Newspapers, with no thought of impropriety, would describe a bride as "a most amiable young Lady with a handsome Fortune," sometimes stating the amount, though, of course, the unions not infrequently joined couples already well-to-do. But, for the most part, it was industry and ability applied imaginatively to beckoning opportunities that ensured the outcome.

As early as 1656 John Hammond, a Briton who had spent many years among the Virginia and Maryland settlers, wrote that "some from being wool-hoppers and of as mean and meaner imployment in England have there grown great merchants, and attained to the most eminent advancements the Country afforded." And a century later, in 1765, the scholarly officeholder Cadwallader Colden similarly said of New York that "the most opulent families, in our own memory, have arisen from the lowest rank of the people." If a writer in the *Pennsylvania Evening-Post*, March 14, 1776, is to be credited, half the property in the city of Philadelphia belonged to "men whose fathers or grandfathers wore LEATHER APRONS." Indeed, Colden believed that "The only principle of Life propagated among the young People is to get Money, and Men are only esteemed according to . . . the Money they are possessed of." And even the pious *New-England Primer* taught:

> He that ne'er learns his A, B, C,
> For ever will a Blockhead be;
> But he that learns these Letters fair
> Shall have a Coach to take the Air.

Some examples of nobodies becoming somebodies will make the matter more concrete. Thus Henry Shrimpton, a London brazier, so expanded his interests and activities after settling in Boston in 1639 that when dying twenty-seven years later he left an estate of nearly £12,000, and with this nest egg his son Samuel (who in filial gratitude displayed a brass kettle on his "very stately house") succeeded before his death in 1698 in making himself the town's richest citizen. The Belcher family of Massachusetts progressed in three generations from the vocation of innkeeping at Cambridge to mercantile greatness in Boston and then to the officeholding eminence of grandson Jonathan, who served as royal governor of Massachusetts and New Hampshire from 1730 to 1741 and of New Jersey from 1747 to 1757.

In a like number of generations the Reverend John Hancock, an impecunious Lexington minister, apprenticed his son Thomas to a Boston bookseller; and Thomas, opening his own establishment in 1723 and later branching out into more profitable lines, amassed a fortune of £100,000 sterling, which at his demise in 1764 he willed to his nephew John, making him the Croesus of the patriot movement in Massachusetts. By the same token, Connecticut's Roger Sherman, another signer of the Declaration of Independence, started out as a shoemaker's apprentice and, after following the trade on his own for some years, turned to surveying, the law, and other fields which won him independent means.

In the Middle colonies Robert Livingston, son of a poor parson in Scotland and founder of the renowned New York clan, began his American career in 1673 at the age of twenty-one as town clerk in the frontier village of Albany and within another twenty-one years owned a princely domain of 160,000 acres. The great Manhattan merchant John Lamb, an associate of Livingston's descendants in Revolutionary days and general in the Continental army, was the American-born child of a Londoner who in 1724 had escaped hanging for burglary through commutation of his sentence to indentured service overseas.

Isaac Norris, the progenitor of the notable Pennsylvania family, arrived in Philadelphia from England in 1691 with a little more than £100 and in less than a quarter-century became the colony's principal landholder. George Taylor, coming as an indentured servant from Ireland in 1736, first worked at an iron furnace in Chester County, then, setting up in the trade with a partner, accumulated his ample means. He was another man of humble pedigree to sign the Declaration of Independence. The meteoric rise of Benjamin Franklin, the runaway apprentice from Boston, has become a legendary American success story.

Though the economic life of the Southern colonies differed markedly from that of the North, the outcome there too was the same. Thus the Irish-born Daniel Dulany, talented lawyer and political leader in early eighteenth-century Maryland, commenced his American years in 1703 as a penniless eighteen-year-old lad under indenture. In neighboring Virginia, John Carter, an English newcomer in 1649 of obscure antecedents, laid the material basis of one of that province's first families; his son Robert of Nomini Hall, known to his contemporaries as "King" Carter, owned some 300,000 acres, 700 slaves and over 2,000 horses and other livestock at the time of his decease in 1732. William Byrd, the forerunner of another Virginia dynasty, came from England in 1671 at the age of nineteen with the bequest of some land from an uncle, which he made the springboard for a great fortune in tobacco culture and trading before his death in 1704.

In South Carolina the Manigaults, Allstons, and Laurenses, among others, conformed to the familiar pattern. The first American Manigault, a French Huguenot emigré from London in 1695, originally tried farming, then made good at victualing and more remunerative ventures, and in 1729 he bequeathed an estate which his son Gabriel by the mid-eighteenth century built into the largest fortune in the province. By contrast, Jonathan Allston was "a gentleman of immense income, all of his own acquisition," according to Josiah Quincy, Jr., who visited his plantation in 1773. Henry Laurens, like the younger

Manigault, owed the silver spoon in his mouth at birth to his father, in this case a Charleston saddler who had amassed riches in that and other undertakings.

But only a few Americans ever achieved the accolade of English noble rank, and this came about under circumstances so fortuitous as to make it the despair of other colonists. William Phips, who had risen from shepherd boy and shipwright's apprentice on the Maine frontier to prosper as a shipbuilder in Boston, was knighted in 1687 for raising in Haitian waters a Spanish galleon laden with £300,000 of treasure, of which the Crown awarded him £16,000 as well as his title. John Randolph, a distinguished Virginia lawyer and planter, obtained his knighthood in 1732 for his statesmanlike skill in negotiating certain differences between the London government and his colony. William Pepperrell, a business leader and landholder in Massachusetts and Maine, won the status of baronet in 1746 in return for commanding the victorious American forces against the French fortress of Louisbourg. A more dubious case was that of the well-to-do New Jersey officeholder William Alexander, who on the basis of tenuous evidence laid claim to being the sixth Earl of Stirling. Ignoring the rejection of his contention by a House of Lords committee in 1762, he continued to profess the title, and it was as Lord Stirling that he rendered valuable service to the American cause as a general in the War for Independence.

In a special category was the Cinderella-like story of Agnes Surriage. This comely, sixteen-year-old maiden, a barefoot servant in a Marblehead tavern in 1742, so captivated Charles Henry Frankland at first sight that the English-born revenue officer in Boston sent her to school at his own expense. Then he lived with her as his mistress in an elegant mansion he had built for her in Hopkinton. Even his inheritance of a baronetcy in no wise altered the relationship, but something that occurred while the couple were abroad in 1755 wrought the miracle, causing Sir Henry at long last to make Agnes his wife. According to tradition it was her daring rescue of him during the Lisbon earthquake. Boston society, hitherto scandalized, now forgot her past and as Lady Frankland received her with open arms. Warm-hearted by nature, she had by all accounts become through the years a person of cultivation and charm. Her unusual tale has fascinated numerous chroniclers, including Oliver Wendell Holmes, who recounted it in ballad form in *Songs in Many Keys* (1865).

The Aristocracy in Colonial America

Governor Francis Bernard of Massachusetts, seeing in the creation of an American peerage an opportunity to "give strength and stability" to supporters of Britain, urged the proposal on the Ministry in 1764 soon after the difficulties with the colonists arose. "Although *America*," he conceded, "is not now (and probably will not be for many years to come) ripe enough for an hereditary *Nobility*; yet it is now capable of a *Nobility* for life." Indeed, in men like Thomas Hutchinson, Philip Livingston, Franklin, and Henry Laurens (to name no others) the colonies possessed personages who by Old World standards could qualify for even heritable rank. But whatever fate might have befallen the scheme if it had been put forward and adopted earlier, it could hardly have succeeded at so late a juncture. With the colonists already fearful of British designs on other counts, anybody who accepted an honorific dignity at this stage would have forfeited all public esteem. He would have marked himself indelibly as one who had sold out to the government. But the matter never came to a test, for the Ministry quietly shelved the suggestion.

By 1776 the colonial aristocracy had endured for more than a century and a half in the oldest regions, for over a century in others, and had sunk deep roots elsewhere. With the passage of time it had consolidated its position and constantly replenished its vitality with transfusions of new blood. Its members had not, moreover, used their station exclusively for self-aggrandizement and outward show but, as a class, had considered themselves trustees for the common good, identifying their welfare with that of the community at large. In the case of the Southern gentry the need to superintend the lives of hosts of slaves served to heighten this sense of stewardship, making them feel as fit to rule as were the guardians to whom Plato had entrusted his republic.

In all the colonies men of quality occupied responsible posts in every sphere of official activity: the executive department, the provincial and local lawmaking branches, the armed forces, the judiciary. True, the alternative would have been to allow ill-prepared and possibly rash underlings to seize the reins, but the deeper reason lay in the conviction that only the rich and wellborn possessed the required wisdom and capacity. In no less degree they provided the cultural leadership. They not only exemplified for all to see the refinements of living, but they set standards of tasteful architecture and well-kept grounds and through their patronage enabled portrait painters to pursue their calling. In like fashion they assembled the best private libraries and afforded their sons superior intellectual advantages. And from their largess came the principal benefactions to religion and education, to charity and projects of community improvement.

Nor did their role in any of these respects excite resentment among the mass of the population. Men in every walk of life not only accepted the concept of a layered society, but believed in its rightness. The clergy preached it; all classes practiced it. Whatever might be the shortcomings of the English aristocracy—and colonial editors repeated from the London press lurid accounts of its immoralities and profligacy—the American variety was no privileged group living off the unearned increment of ancestral reputations. They, by and large, had mounted the heights through shrewdness and ability and had stayed there by the continued exercise of those faculties. The ordinary citizen deemed it only proper to accord them deference. Very rarely did their real or alleged abuses of authority provoke popular opposition, and such occasions seldom lasted long.

The quarrel with the mother country had nothing to do with the stratified character of British society, only with the objectionable policies of certain individuals in positions of power. Not even the fiery Tom Paine condemned it in his tract *Common Sense* when blasting the titular head of the system as "the royal brute." Nor did the framers of the Declaration of Independence do so later that year. Though they proclaimed that all men are created equal, they merely rebuked their brethren at home for suffering George to act a "tyrant" toward his American subjects.

To be sure, in the events foreshadowing this final crisis the colonial gentry betrayed divided sympathies, notably in New York and Pennsylvania, some siding ardently with Britain or at least seeking to prevent an irreparable break. But the well-informed Thomas McKean, himself a Signer, stated in retrospect that almost two-thirds of the country's "influential characters"—that is, the overwhelming majority— had favored the American cause.

The heritage of a common history and culture bound the upper-class patriots to the homeland no less than it did the loyalist minority; but, unlike the latter, they had developed a passionate attachment to colonial self-government, a fierce jealousy of any encroachments on the authority which they had so long and capably wielded. Besides, the new taxation and trade legislation, falling heaviest on the well-to-do, supplied a clear economic motive which was intensified by the conviction that, if the present enactments went unchallenged, worse ones would follow. The phenomenal progress of the colonies during the many years that London had permitted them virtual autonomy thoroughly justified in their minds implacable resistance to the ministerial innovations.

To counteract the measures, however, they required the support of the humbler elements; but this they were accustomed to enjoy. Sometimes to their alarm these allies threatened the orderly course of opposition by gratuitously resorting to riot and violence, but the men of quality were invariably able to regain control. In recognition of their role the Continental Congress, when the war broke out, unanimously chose a Virginia aristocrat as commander in chief of the armed forces, and in due course a grateful Republic named him its first President. The revolt against upper-class dominance was to come in later times.

28. THE CONTRIBUTION OF THE PROTESTANT CHURCHES TO RELIGIOUS LIBERTY IN COLONIAL AMERICA*

by Perry Miller

By the end of the colonial period, tolerance of religious diversity had become the rule in America even in communities where an established church enjoyed a privileged position and state support. The first generation of Englishmen who settled in Virginia and Massachusetts brought with them little respect for the consciences of dissenters. Everywhere colonists, imitating Old World practice, established a church which embodied the one true faith, as they understood it: Anglicanism in Virginia, Congregationalism in Massachusetts. Those who came among them and did not submit to the reigning faith did so at their peril, for heresy was no more permitted in the New World than in the Old. In the following essay, Perry Miller explains how and why religious bigotry gave way to tolerance. Though a few favored tolerance because they believed it was a good thing, most abandoned efforts to maintain religious unity because it

* *Church History*, vol. 4 (1935), 57–66. Footnotes have been omitted except where they are necessary for an understanding of the text.

was impractical and difficult if not impossible to achieve without sacrificing other more compelling goals.

For further reading: Evarts B. Greene, *Religion and the State* (1959).

While endeavouring to formulate these remarks I have come to sus-
pect that there may possibly lurk in the title of my paper a misleading implication. The word "contribution" would seem to connote on the part of the Protestant churches a deliberate and concerted effort toward the triumph of religious liberty. Those of us who prize ecclesiastical freedom would like to feel that our colonial ancestors of their own free will and choice undertook the march to liberty. Liberal-minded historians in particular are prone to sing the praises of this individual or that church for furthering this advance; they are inclined to gloss over or to apologize for the men and the institutions that hindered it.

Such an attitude, though inspired by the most admirable of motives, has been, I am convinced, an encumbrance to the student of history. There is no way to deny—and as far as I can see, no use in denying—
that Protestants coming to this country in the seventeenth century were almost unanimous in their conviction that toleration was a dangerous and heathen notion. They came fresh from Europe of the Reformation, where experience had demonstrated that if two divergent churches were permitted to exist within striking distance of each other, it would only be a question of time before throats were cut. And Protestants were far from deploring this belligerency. If you believe, as men believed in that era, that you are altogether on the Lord's side, and that your enemies are and must be entirely on the devil's, you can see no virtue in the idea of tolerating them. Statesmen knew that a policy of toleration would not work; theologians were grimly determined that it never should work. As the Reverend Nathaniel Ward of Ipswich in Massachusetts Bay emphatically declared:

> He that is willing to tolerate any Religion, or descrepant way of
> Religion besides his own, unless it be in matters merely indifferent,
> either doubts of his own, or is not sincere in it. He that is willing to

tolerate any unsound Opinion, that his own may also be tolerated, though never so sound, will for a need hang God's Bible at the Devil's girdle.

When a Protestant church came into a colony at the beginning of settlement, with no other churches on the ground, with a clear field before it, that church deliberately set up an exclusive régime, it conscientiously strove to establish one official church in absolute uniformity, it frankly employed the civil power to compel all inhabitants to conform and contribute. Both Virginia and Massachusetts furnish examples of this disposition. The Anglicans in the one colony and the Puritans in the other, entertaining utterly different conceptions of polity and theology, were at one in their philosophy of uniformity. Among the early enactments of the House of Burgesses was a statute demanding that there "be a uniformity in our Church as near as may be to the Cannons in England, both in substance and in circumstance, and that all persons yield obedience under pain of censure." Puritan ministers and the Puritan settlement at Nansemond were driven out, and in 1671 that picturesque and outspoken governor, Sir William Berkeley, reported with glowing pride that no free schools disgraced the landscape in Virginia: "I hope we shall not have [them] these hundred years: for learning has brought disobedience and heresy and sects into the world." This, quite clearly, is nipping religious liberty in the bud.

The Puritans were equally clear and decisive. Many writers have already called attention to the fact that though the Puritans came to New England to escape persecution, they did not come to bestow upon those who disagreed with them any such immunity within the confines of their colonies. John Cotton patiently explained their position to Roger Williams thus: anybody in possession of his senses must recognize what is true and what is false when a learned Congregational minister demonstrates truth and falsehood to him. If a man, after such instruction, then maintains certain errors, he deserves punishment, not for being in error, but for persisting in it. In his heart of hearts, his own better judgment must acknowledge as much, even if he won't admit it. Accordingly, the laws of Massachusetts and the explicit pronouncements of her apologists pile up incontrovertible evidence that the leaders of the Bay Colony were intentionally and consistently intolerant; the banishment of Williams and Anne Hutchinson, the fining of Dr. Child, the whipping of Obadiah Holmes, and the dangling bodies of four

Quakers hanged on Boston Common attest the fidelity with which the Puritans scouted the idea of toleration.

Speaking still as a historian, I must confess my gratitude to such men as Berkeley and Cotton. We know, at any rate, where we stand with them. With many figures of this stripe for our authorities, we can confidently assert that the Protestant *intention* in America was not towards religious toleration, let alone liberty. Yet it is also true that the colonies of Virginia and Massachusetts were the exceptions; they were the only colonies in which a program of intolerance had any real success, the only colonies in which a religious uniformity was achieved, and even in them for a relatively short time. The colonial period witnessed a fairly steady growth of practical religious freedom. From time to time some men in one or another of the churches might foresee the end and even approve. But by and large, I can find very little evidence that the Protestant churches ever really entertained the conception of complete liberty as their ultimate goal, or that they often moved in that direction unless forced to do so by the pressure of events or by the necessities of the social environment. As I say, there are exceptions, notably of course Williams and Penn, but the contribution of the majority of the Protestant churches must in the final analysis be described as inadvertent.

My time is limited, and it would manifestly be impossible to relate the whole narrative here. I wish therefore only to indicate, however briefly, what seems to my mind to be three important factors determining the development of religious liberty in America. To enumerate them roundly, they seem to me to have been, first the practical situation of the sects in the colonies, second the influence and interference of England, and third the shift in issues and concerns produced by the introduction or development of both the rationalistic and evangelical temper in the eighteenth century.

Most of the colonies were not as fortunate as Virginia or Massachusetts; they did not begin with unsettled expanses, or they could not people them with men of only one persuasion. The proprietors of the Carolinas, for instance, intended some day to establish the Church of England in their domains, but from the beginning had to reckon with a hopeless variety of creeds, Puritans from England and from New England, Huguenots, Dutch Calvinists, Scotch Calvinists, Quakers and several sorts of Baptists. The uniformity for which the noble proprietors hoped was impossible, unless they were prepared to expel nine-tenths of their settlers. So religious principle gave way to economic interest; practical toleration became the rule. The official clique still contemplated a full establishment of the Anglican church and in 1704 felt themselves strong enough in South Carolina to enact legislation excluding dissenters from the assembly and establishing an ecclesiastical court. A revolution was averted only when these acts were annulled by Parliament and toleration was restored.

The story in New York is much the same. The Dutch had been fairly tolerant and hospitable, following the national policy at home. When the English took over the colony, the number of sects already flourishing precluded any effective establishment. As Governor Dongan complained in 1687:

> Here bee not many of the Church of England; few Roman Catholics; abundance of Quaker preachers, men and women especially; Singing Quakers; Ranting Quakers; Sabbatarians; Anti-Sabbatarians; some Anabaptists; some Independents; some Jews; in short, of all sorts of opinions there are some, and the most part of none at all. The most prevailing opinion is that of the Dutch Calvinists. . . . As for the King's natural born subjects that live on Long Island, and other parts of the Government, I find it a hard task to make them pay their Ministers.

The governors did what they could, but the best they could wring from a predominantly Dutch Calvinistic assembly was the peculiar Ministry Act of 1693, which established in four counties six Protestant churches, not necessarily Anglican. Very few denominations were clearly advocating religious liberty on principle in New York; they were all opposing an established church, and the result was that religious liberty in large measure they all had. Circumstances placed insuperable obstacles in the way of intolerance. Where a multiplicity of creeds checkmate each other, they find themselves to their surprise maintaining religious liberty.

Indeed, the reasons that made uniformity difficult or ineffective in the Carolinas or in New York ultimately made it impossible in Virginia and Massachusetts. The established order in Virginia was never a very efficient organization; as early as 1629 the Burgesses were endeavouring to stop the clergy from "drinking or ryott" or "playing at dice." Meantime the dissenters began trickling in, Quakers and Baptists, and then the Scotch-Irish with their militant Presbyterianism streamed down the

Shenandoah. Many of these were valuable settlers, particularly on the frontier, and the government had to give them allowance, either by express enactment or by tacit agreement. In Massachusetts also Quakers and Baptists forced an opening, and Anglicans came to stay in the train of the royal governors. By the 1730's the province had to allow some dissenters from the established Congregational order to pay their rates to churches of their own persuasion.

Thus in the colonies a generous amount of liberty or at least of toleration had come to prevail by the time of the Revolution. But this situation was hardly the result of conscious and deliberate theory; it was the result of circumstances. Diversity of belief compelled it. Rhode Island is, of course, an exception to this statement, thanks to the teachings of Roger Williams. Inspiring a figure as Williams may be, he nevertheless devised theories that were not palatable to the majority of Protestant churches in his day. Williams may speak for the essentially individualistic tendency inherent in all Protestantism; in the perspective of time we may see that his was the only solution for the ecclesiastical problem in a Protestant world, but Protestants in the colonies did not want to think so. If we desire to state accurately the "contribution" of the Protestant churches in all colonies beside Rhode Island and Pennsylvania to the development of religious liberty, we are forced to say that they made it inevitable by their dogged persistence in maintaining their own beliefs and practices. They persisted so resolutely that the governments had either to exterminate them or to tolerate them. In this connection it is worth noting that once a sect was tolerated it was generally ready to thrust itself into intolerance if it could get the upper hand. The Anglicans in Maryland, for example, given toleration by the Catholic proprietor in 1649, spent every effort to secure a Protestant establishment and the disfranchisement of their benefactors. Once the Church of England was established in Maryland, we have the old story again; the dissenting sects that had opposed the proprietor's church at once banded together, with the Catholics this time, to antagonize the royal governor's. By 1776 the established church in Maryland had become a shadow. The New Side Presbyterians and the Baptists in eighteenth century Virginia brought down upon their own heads the official persecution to which they were subjected by their own scurrility in assaulting the deplorable established church. "They treat all other modes of worship with the utmost scorn and contempt," complained the broad-minded Governor Gooch in 1745. The Protestant churches in

America finally accepted the idea of religious liberty because they had become habituated to it. Most of them had not moved toward it with intelligent foresight; they had been forced to accustom themselves to it, because experience demonstrated the futility of exclusive domination by any one church, because settlers were too valuable to be antagonized over-much by acts of conformity, and because there were simply so many Protestant organizations that no power on earth could whip them into a system of uniformity.

A second source of liberal developments in colonial America is to be found in the example of English opinion and English law. The many sects that sprang up like mushrooms in the frenzied years of the Civil Wars had banded together with the English Independents against the Presbyterians to demand toleration. The dissenters were finally given toleration by the Parliament and the Established Church in the act of 1689. Though this act by no means created religious liberty, it marked the demise in England of that philosophy of absolute uniformity and enforced conformity which had characterized all Protestant churches during the Reformation.

It is with this development of opinion in England that we are to connect the experiment of William Penn. The Quakers were one of the enthusiastic groups that came into being during the wars. They began their existence when the idea of toleration had already been embraced by the Independents. Although in the first flush of their zeal the Quakers had flung themselves against all other churches in a spirit that betrayed little comprehension of toleration, they soon aligned themselves with the Independents. Their peculiar theology made it possible for them to admit, much more easily than other creeds could do, that men might be holy and good even if they belonged to other organizations. In that spirit Penn founded his colony, on an explicit theory of liberty for all churches, though his conceptions were still not as broad as those of Williams and he would not enfranchise Jews or give harbor to atheists. His plan was a little too broad for the home government, so that in 1705 the colony yielded to compulsion from Queen Anne and required the test-oath to be taken by office-holders, thus excluding Catholics from official positions.

Yet if the English government was instrumental in curtailing religious liberty in Pennsylvania, the act of 1689 fashioned a weapon by which minority groups in other colonies could pry loose the laws of conformity. The dissenters of South Carolina successfully appealed to the Whigs in Parliament to block the exorbitant acts of 1704. Francis Makemie, by demanding a license to preach in Virginia under the terms of the act of 1699, compelled the Burgesses to incorporate them into Virginia law. Samuel Davies appealed to the act again in 1753 to procure liberty for itinerant ministers. The Royal charter of Massachusetts, drawn up in 1691, guaranteed that "there shall be liberty of conscience allowed, in the worship of God, to all Christians (except Papists)." When Connecticut in 1708 grudgingly gave toleration to dissenters from the Congregational system, it specifically cited "the act of William and Mary." Thus once more, liberty was forced upon the colonies from without. The Quakers were intentionally libertarian; the other churches used English principles and laws for self-protection. In the end they furthered the growth of religious liberty, but not with malice aforethought; they achieved that end in the course of securing relief and opportunities for themselves.

The eighteenth century saw a steady extension of toleration in the colonies until with the Revolution established churches collapsed, in Massachusetts and Connecticut somewhat belatedly. But again an examination of the activity and statements of the churches before the Revolution does not offer much evidence that they took the lead. In the shift of the general intellectual climate, and the pressure of one or two political factors, religious liberty came to seem attractive. A complete account of this transformation would entail a chapter in intellectual history that has yet to be written; lacking that chapter we can here only enumerate a few of the factors. Before the Revolution the dissenting churches were thrown into co-operation and alliance against the threat of an Anglican bishop; this served to lessen the hostility of one toward another. Furthermore, in this century the question of church-polity ceased to be a serious issue; the young Jonathan Edwards would as soon serve in a Presbyterian as in a Congregational parish. Probably the most irritating of controversies was thus minimized. Then also, the differences between the sects began to seem of minor significance in the face of the towering danger of scientific rationalism and deism, which threatened all traditional creeds alike. Against the spread of "infidelity" all the churches drew closer together. Finally the movement for religious liberty was carried to a speedy triumph in the Revolutionary decades because the leadership was taken by a rational aristocracy, shot through with deistical beliefs, willing to see any number of religions have their freedom because they believed in none of them. As Nathaniel

Ward had said, nothing is easier than to tolerate when you do not seriously believe that differences matter. So the Adamses, Masons, Franklins, and Jeffersons could advocate dis-establishment and religious liberty in a spirit which is, from an orthodox Christian point of view, simply cynical. As James Madison cheerfully put it: "In a free government, the security for civil rights must be the same as that for religious rights; it consists in the one case in a multiplicity of interests and in the other in the multiplicity of sects." At the same time the transformation of religious issues wrought by the Great Awakening and the introduction of revivalistic evangelicalism had created a situation in which the new Protestant groups were able to see clearly that a policy of religious liberty offered them definite advantages. Evangelical Baptists and New Side Presbyterians, and eventually the Methodists, came to perceive that they were opposing conceptions of institutionalized civic religion inherited from the previous century; they had to demolish established churches along with intricate theological structures in order to have the track cleared for their own program of spiritual regeneration and impassioned zeal. I do not think it has ever been sufficiently emphasized, or that it can be too much stressed, that there is a subtle and close connection between the shift of vital religious interest from elaborate intellectual systems of theology to the simplified emotional fervor of the new revivalism and the turning of Protestant Americans from a concern with ecclesiastical exclusiveness to the demand for liberty to all churches. It is not only that two or three more militant minorities now existed to contend for privileges against vested institutions, but that the whole bent and temper of this evangelicalism required that organization, external regulation and formal discipline become subordinated to the reawakening of the spirit and the revivifying of morality. It is in Massachusetts where the ruling classes most stoutly resisted what they considered the crude mysticism of the camp meetings that the retention of an established church was the most protracted. Such apparent champions of religious liberty as the Baptists Backus and Manning, or the Presbyterian Davies, have about them an apparent liberalism which is inspiring to behold, which yet can easily be made too much of. The truth of the matter was that they understood the situation, they realized that old institutions had to be replaced by less systematized forms if the sort of religious incitement they prized was to have full opportunity. James Manning—symbolizing the vast difference of evangelical Protestantism in the eighteenth century from Puritanism of the seventeenth, as we have seen that Puritanism incarnated in Nathaniel Ward—said to the Massachusetts delegates to the Continental Congress in October, 1774, "Establishments may be enabled to confer worldly distinctions and secular importance. They may make hypocrites, but cannot create Christians." So for the time being such leaders often made common cause with the rational aristocracy to attack established order and medieval theology. Yet all the time they were perfectly aware that their cause would not be lost, but in reality furthered, if various denominations were allowed to practise it in various ways. In terms of an ideal of ethics rather than of evangelical emotion, the same ultimately became true of the Unitarians. As Professor Hall has remarked, "It was easier for Harvard College to take up Unitarianism than it would have been to introduce at that date sports on Sunday."

It therefore seems to me that it is possible to speak too glibly of the "contributions" of Protestant groups to religious liberty; we can be easily betrayed by our own approbation for the idea into prizing and unduly exalting such instances of advance as we can find in our forebears. It has often seemed to me that the worshippers of Roger Williams have done more harm than good not only to the Puritans of the Bay but to their hero himself by their extravagant laudation of his ideas without at the same time maintaining sufficient historical perspective upon the general intellectual background from which he so dramatically emerged. Exceptionally liberal men in Protestant ranks undoubtedly exist, and they deserve all honor and veneration; but by and large Protestants did not contribute to religious liberty, they stumbled into it, they were compelled into it, they accepted it at last because they had to, or because they saw its strategic value. In their original intention, Protestants were intolerant; because of the sheer impossibility of unifying colonies made up of a hodge-podge diversity, because of the example of toleration set and enforced by England, and because of a complete shift in the intellectual situation in the eighteenth century, whereby religious liberty became a perfect solution for new issues—for these reasons, the Protestant churches did not so much achieve religious liberty as have liberty thrust upon them.

29. DENOMINATIONALISM*

The Shape of Protestantism in America

by Sidney E. Mead

Religious tolerance encouraged diversity, attracted dissenters to American shores, and made it increasingly difficult for state churches to maintain their privileged place. In some provinces, such as Pennsylvania, church and state were separated from the beginning. But elsewhere the European tradition of a state church prevailed, and people were taxed to maintain the dominant faith. By the end of the colonial period, however, few of the established churches could resist the forces pressing for separation of church and state, a principle embodied in the new state and federal constitutions of the revolutionary era. If a church was no longer supported by the state, how was it to survive, be financed, and recruit members? In the following essay, Sidney E. Mead argues that denominationalism became the institutional form through which American Christianity

* *The Lively Experiment* by Sidney E. Mead. Copyright © 1963 by Sidney E. Mead. Reprinted by permission of Harper & Row. Footnotes have been omitted except where they are necessary for an understanding of the text.

organized its resources and activities once the ties between church and state were severed. Denominations were voluntary associations of like-minded individuals seeking to further a common goal. Voluntarism became a characteristically American method by which private associations conducted affairs that in Europe were functions of government. This pattern of organization had profound effects on the life of churches in America.

For further reading: Sidney E. Mead, *The Lively Experiment* (1963) ; William W. Sweet, *Religion in Colonial America* (1942) ; H. Richard Niebuhr, *The Kingdom of God in America* (1959) ; *Religion in American Life*, J. W. Smith and A. L. Jamison (eds.) (1961), vol. 1.

The Christianity which developed in the United States [after 1800] was unique. It displayed features which marked it as distinct from previous Christianity in any other land. In the nineteenth and twentieth centuries the Christianity of Canada most nearly resembled it, but even that was not precisely like it.

Professor Latourette's generalization applies primarily to the institutional forms rather than to the theology of Christianity in the United States, which latter has been surprisingly derivative—lacking in originality, uniqueness, and distinctiveness.

The basis of this institutional uniqueness has been the "free church" idea. The phrase "free churches" is used in various and confusing ways—sometimes to designate those churches of congregational polity, sometimes those peculiarly distinguished by their "liberal" views. But most properly the phrase designates those churches under the system of separation of Church and State. Here the qualifying word "free" is used in the basic sense of independent and autonomous, and in the context of long tradition thus designates those churches that are independent of the State and autonomous in relation to it.

The denomination is the organizational form which the "free churches" have accepted and assumed. It was evolved in the United States under the complex and peculiar situation that there existed between the Revolution and the Civil War.

The denomination, unlike the traditional forms of the Church, is not primarily confessional, and it is certainly not territorial. Rather it is purposive. And unlike any previous "church" in Christendom, it has no official connection with a civil power whatsoever. A "church" as "church" has no legal existence in the United States, but is represented legally by a civil corporation in whose name the property is held and the necessary business transacted. Neither is the denomination a "sect" in any traditional sense, and certainly not in the most common sense of a dissenting body in relationship to an Established Church. It is, rather, a voluntary association of like-hearted and like-minded individuals, who are united on the basis of common beliefs for the purpose of accomplishing tangible and defined objectives. One of the primary objectives is the propagation of its point of view, which it in some sense holds to be "true." Hence to try to divide the many religious bodies in the United States under the categories of "church" and "sect" is usually more confusing than helpful, especially since by long custom "church" is commonly used in a way that implies approbation, and "sect" in a way that implies derogation.

Keeping these considerations in mind, however, I have for the sake of variety followed the practice common in America when discussing the Protestant bodies, of using the words "church," "sect," and "denomination" as synonymous.

It is the purpose of this paper to delineate some elements that were woven into the denominational structure during the formative years, and to suggest how these elements have conditioned the thought, life, and work of American Protestantism down to the present.

I

In Christendom from the fourth century to the end of the eighteenth Christianity was organized in an Established Church or Churches. The one Church reached its peak in expression and power during the twelfth and thirteenth centuries. At that time it actually possessed and wielded tremendous tangible, overt power in the affairs of men, and more subtly tremendous and formative cultural power in the souls of men. The heart of this Church was creedal or confessional belief in supernatural power mediated to men through the sacraments. It claimed inclusiveness and universality as the one true Church of Christ on earth, but by the same token it was necessarily exclusive. Outside the Church and its sacraments there was no salvation, although this had to be asserted with humility because ultimately only God knew his own with certainty.

The Reformation broke up this tangible unity of the one Church in Christendom. On the one hand its claim to be, not a revolt *from* the Church but merely an attempt to reform the church within and on the true principles of the Church itself, was inherently valid. But on the other hand the true principles of the Church had become so inextricably mingled with the organizational forms and practices that honest re-formation meant revolt from the existing institution. This movement coincided with the emergence into self-consciousness of the modern nations, back of which were the complex economic, social, and political movements that ushered in and have shaped modern western civilization.

Inevitably the spiritual reformation and consequent institutional fragmentation of the Church developed affinities with the rising national consciousnesses—and found physical protective power in the new states to oppose the physical power controlled by Rome. Thus the one re-formation of the Church found diverse expressions in the nations—Lutheranism within the realms of the German princes and the Scandinavian countries, Anglicanism in England, Reformed in Geneva and Scotland, and so on.

The conflict culminated in the Thirty Years War that devastated Europe. The Westphalian settlements of 1648 marked a grudging recognition of the necessity to live-and-let-live within the several territorial areas. The basis for the churches that thus emerged was both confessional and territorial. And each of these churches in its own territory and in its own way continued to make the claims traditionally made by the one true Church. Each as a Church assumed the traditional responsibilities, and each clung to the long established principle of religious uniformity enforced by the civil power within a commonwealth. These were the churches of the "right-wing."

Meanwhile in the turmoil of re-formation had emerged certain "heretical" individuals and movements that, appealing to the commonly accepted authority of Scripture, began to claim freedom of religious belief and expression as a right. These were the "sects" of the "left-wing." They were voluntary groups without status or social responsibility and power. From the viewpoint of the official churches they were schismatic as well as heretical, and hence thought to be subversive of all order and government whether civil or ecclesiastical. And so almost universally strenuous repressive measures were invoked against them.

II

Representatives of practically all the religious groups of Europe, both "right" and "left" wing, were transplanted to that part of America that was to become the United States. There they learned in a relatively short time to live together in peace under the genial aegis of the Dutch and English combination of patriotic-religious fervor, toleration, cynicism, simple desire for profits, efficacious muddling through, and "salutary neglect" that made up the colonial policy of these nations. The eventual result was that by 1787, after independence was won, it was recognized that if there was to be a *United* States of America, then religious freedom had to be written into the new national constitution.

It was of course recognized that this was a departure from the prevailing tradition of almost fourteen hundred years standing in Christendom. But by this time many both within and without the religious groups were in a mood to agree with Thomas Jefferson:

As to tradition, if we are Protestants we reject all tradition, and rely on the scripture alone, for that is the essence and common principle of all the protestant churches.

Even so, the transplanted offshoots of Europe's State Churches —the "right-wing" groups—retained their position of prestige and dominance in the new land throughout the colonial period. At the close of the Revolution the four largest and most powerful religious groups were the Congregationalists, the Anglicans, the Baptists, and the Presbyterians. Of these four, the Baptist "sect" held nowhere near the position of power and respect accorded the other three. Fifth in size were the Lutherans, sixth the German Reformed, and seventh the Dutch Reformed. Meanwhile the Methodist body, still in swaddling clothes in the Anglican manger, was twelfth in size.

To be sure the dominant, powerful and respected "right-wing" churches had experienced considerable internal change during the vicissitudes of the colonial period, and especially during the upheavals growing out of the great revivals. But there was as yet little indication and less awareness that the church patterns of America would be markedly different from those of Europe. Hence Ezra Stiles' prediction in 1783 that no doubt the future of Christianity in America would lie about equally with Congregationalists, Presbyterians, and Episcopalians, seemed eminently plausible.

The radical change in the relative size of the religious bodies in America took place during the brief period between roughly 1787 and 1850. By the latter date the Roman Catholic church, which at the close of the Revolution was tenth in point of size and everywhere except in Pennsylvania laboring under some civil restrictions, was the largest. Second in size were the Methodists, followed by the Baptists, Presbyterians, Congregationalists, and Lutherans. Seventh in size were the Disciples—an upstart group less than twenty years old. The Protestant Episcopal church had fallen to eighth place, while perhaps most amazing of all, Joseph Smith's Mormons were ninth.

Since this configuration of relative size has persisted in the United States for about a century—with a few notable exceptions such as the Congregationalists' drop from fifth to ninth place—we may speak of this period as the "formative" years for the American denominations. The story of the numerical growth and geographical expansion of the several ecclesiastical institutions, while by no means complete in every detail is sufficiently well established for the immediate purposes of this paper.

III

Our concern is with the mind and spirit of these "free" churches —their genius which was woven from many diverse strands during this formative period and has continued largely to define their direction, life, and work down to the present.

Religious freedom and the "frontier" provided the broad ideological and geographical setting in which these developments took place. The first meant the removal of traditional civil and ecclesiastical restrictions on vocal and organizational expressions of the religious convictions and even the whimsies of all men. The "frontier" provided the necessary space and opportunities in which such expressions could thrive. It was this combination of freedom and opportunity in all areas that made this period what Whitehead called it, the "Epic Epoch of American life"—the period of "Freedom's Ferment" as Alice Felt Tyler most aptly dubbed it.

My general interpretation is based upon the view that what individuals and groups do when given freedom depends upon what they are (their character) when such freedom is offered. Hence an understanding of the development of what we note as characteristic traits of the denominations that took place during the formative period, hinges in large part upon a delineation of characteristic attitudes and practices that came to be accepted during the colonial period. In keeping with this suggestion I shall now take up in somewhat schematic fashion several important elements, ideas or practices, that went into the making of the denominations, and which together gave and still gives them their distinctive character.

A

The first to be noted is the "sectarian" tendency of each American denomination to seek to justify its peculiar interpretations and practices as more closely conforming to those of the early Church as pictured in the New Testament than the views and policies of its rivals. This tendency is closely related to a kind of historylessness exhibited, as Professor Latourette has pointed out, in the "marked tendency" of American Protestantism during the nineteenth century "to ignore the developments which had taken place in Christianity in the Old World after the first century."

This anti-historical bias itself has long historical roots. Roman Catholicism developed the idea of the Bible as the Word of God within the context of the Church which through apostolic succession from Peter was the bearer of the tradition. The purity and authority of the Church in speaking out of the tradition, was in turn guarded by the sacraments of baptism and ordination. Thus the Church, as the continuing, tangible historical reality, always stood as interpreter of the Word to the individual, and in this sense spoke out of the tradition with authority equal to that of the Bible.

The Reformers, in revolt against the Church as it then existed, appealed over the practices of the Church to the Word as found in the Bible. But the Reformation which took shape in the "right-wing" Lutheran, Anglican, and Reformed versions, held the doctrine of the Word together with doctrines of the Church and Ministry in such fashion as to guard against individual "enthusiasm" and to preserve the sense of the unbroken historical continuity of Christianity.

The "left-wing" sects, in their fight for existence against almost universal opposition, sought a source of unquestioned authority that would undercut all the tradition-based claims of both Roman Catholics and "right-wing" Protestants over them. They found it in the Bible, which as the commonly recognized Word of God, they proposed to place directly in the hands of the Spirit-guided individual Christian as his only necessary guide to faith and practice. The common thrust of these groups was toward *"no creed but the Bible"* and the right of "private judgment," under grace, in its interpretation. In practice this meant appeal over the authority of all churches and historical traditions subsequently developed to the authority of the beliefs and practices of primitive Christianity as pictured in the New Testament.

In America, although the churches of the "right-wing" were everywhere dominant during the colonial period, the situation in the long run played into the hands of the "left-wing" view. For there, under the necessity to live side by side with those from other lands and different backgrounds, the angularities of the transplanted national and religious traditions tended to cancel each other out. Crevecoeur clearly delineated this tendency, and attributed it to the fact that

> zeal in Europe is confined; here it evaporates in the great distance it has to travel; there it is a grain of power inclosed, here it burns in the open air, and consumes without effect.

Nevertheless as Christians, whether Lutheran, Anglican, Congregational, Presbyterian, Baptist, Quaker, or what not, all shared the Bible—the center and symbol of a common Christian beginning and heritage, and for all the highest authority. Hence each in defense of its peculiar way against the others, was increasingly pressed to fall back on this one commonly recognized authority and to argue that its denominational teaching and way most closely conformed to the Biblical patterns. Thus in America where, unlike their European parents, the transplanted "right-wing" churches never possessed or were soon shorn of effective coercive power to suppress dissent and enforce uniformity, their leaders were almost forced to enter the argument if at all pretty much on the terms originally set by the "left-wing" groups.

Meanwhile the common sense of opportunity to begin all over again in the new land, which was so characteristic a feature of the mind of the early planters, also worked to erase the sense of continuity with the historic Church and to accentuate appeal to the teachings of Jesus and the practices of primitive Christianity. For even to nominal or cultural Christians of the 17th century, this opportunity was bound to be interpreted as an occasion ordained by God to begin again at the point where mankind had first gone astray—at Eden, the paradise of man before the fall. Here is deeply rooted the commonly observed and usually irritating assumption of innocence on the part of many Americans.

But to ardent churchmen and Biblicists the opportunity was bound to be seen as a providential chance to begin over again at a selected point in history where it was thought the Christian Church had gone astray. John Cotton was not unusual in speaking of the churches formed by the Puritans in New England as exceptionally close to what would be set up "if the Lord Jesus were here himself in person."

Both the Pietistic and Rationalistic movements of the eighteenth century, each in its own way, worked to the same general end. The personal religious experience emphasized by the Pietists was assumed to be a duplication of the experience of New Testament Christians. And rationalistic social and political leaders and reformers, in their battle against existing ecclesiastical institutions, soon learned to appeal to the pure moral teachings of Jesus (whom they saw as the first great Deist) as the norm by which these could be judged and found wanton. In essence the views of Pietists and Rationalists were so close together that both could agree with the Unitarian Joseph Priestley that the story of the Christian Church was largely a sordid history of the "corruptions" of pure Christianity through the inventions and contrivances of clever men. Thus both reached the same conclusion, namely that the forms, practices and traditions of the historic church were neither binding nor of particular interest to the present.

Hence, in summary, in the constellation of ideas prevailing during the Revolutionary epoch in which the denominations began to take shape were: the idea of pure and hence normative beginnings to which return was possible; the idea that the intervening history was largely that of aberrations and corruptions which was better ignored; and the idea of the opportunity to begin building anew in the new land on the true and ancient foundations. It is notable that the most successful of the definitely Christian indigenous denominations in America, the Disciples of Christ, grew out of the idea of a "new reformation" to be based, not on new insights, but on a "restoration" of the practices of the New Testament church—on which platform, it was thought, all the diverse groups of modern Christendom could unite insofar as they could shed the accumulated corruptions of the Church through the centuries. Typically American, this beginning over again was not conceived as a new beginning, but as a picking up of the lost threads of primitive Christianity.

But the common view of the normative nature of the pure moral teachings of Jesus or New Testament religious experience and organizational forms, which undercut appeal to all intervening traditions, actually provided few restrictions on the ardent men and women who were busily engaged in building new churches in the new land.

For the actual content of the Rationalists' pure religion and morals of Jesus, although Jefferson happily thought it was "as easily distinguished" from other matters in the Gospels "as diamonds in a dunghill," turned out to be surprisingly like current Deistic Views. The Pietist as easily found his kind of emphasis on religious experience indigenous in the New Testament. And both found their version of "the church" to be identical with the Church of the Bible. Hence those in both camps were free to move with the tides of history, pragmatically, experimentally—incorporating as much of the traditional and the new in their structures as to each seemed valid and desirable. Here is part of the explanation of the often puzzling combination of Biblical authoritarianism with experimental and pragmatic activism in American religious life.

Men of some historical learning and consciousness, like the doughty John W. Nevin of the German Reformed Church's Mercersburg Seminary, protested that the "sectarian" appeal to

> private judgment and the Bible involves of necessity, a protest against the authority of all previous history, except so far as it may seem to agree with what is thus found to be true; in which case, of course, the only real measure of truth is taken to be, not this authority of history at all, but the mind, simply, of the particular

sect itself. . . . A genuine sect will not suffer itself to be embarrassed for a moment, either at its start or afterwards, by the consideration that it has no proper root in past history. Its ambition is rather to appear in this respect autochthonic, aboriginal, self sprung from the Bible, or through the Bible from the skies.

But by 1849 when this was published, such were passing voices crying in the lush wilderness of the American free church, sectarian system that had no mind to be bound by the past, and little thought that wisdom might be found even by American churchmen between the first and the nineteenth centuries.

Thus in spite of almost universal appeal to the authority of the Bible, and a tendency to literalistic interpretation of it, the architects of the American denominations appear to have been surprisingly unbound by the past, by tradition. But it must be added that their freedom in this respect was largely the appearance or feeling of freedom possible only to those ignorant of their rich history. Hence in a sense the very freedom which they felt and acted upon, a freedom without historical perspective, served many times to bind them to the tendencies of the moment that appeared to be obvious. Hence in all innocence they built into the life of the denominations what time and tide happened to bring to their shores. And each tended to sanctify indiscriminately all the various elements of doctrine and practice that it for whatever reason adopted, under the supposition that it but followed a blueprint revealed in the Word of God.

B

The second element to be noted is the voluntary principle. Voluntaryism is the necessary corollary of religious freedom which, resting on the principle of free, uncoerced consent made the several religious groups voluntary associations, equal before but independent of the civil power and of each other. What the churches actually gave up with religious freedom was coercive power—the revolution in Christian thinking which they accepted was dependence upon persuasion alone.

The religious groups were somewhat prepared to accept such dependence by their experiences during the great colonial revivals that swept the country from the 1720's to the Revolution. The revivals in

every area led to a head-on clash between the defenders of the forms
and practices of "right-wing" Protestantism and the revivalists, and
in every case the revivalists triumphed, insofar as the acceptance of
revivalism, however reluctantly, was concerned. Meanwhile the revivals
had demonstrated the possibilities of and had taught confidence in
dependence upon persuasion alone. Once this battle was won in the
churches, the principle of voluntaryism became a leaven in the mind
and practices of the religious groups, conditioning their development.

Conceiving the church as a voluntary association tends to push
tangible, practical considerations to the fore, by placing primary
emphasis on the free uncoerced consent of the individual. Thus a recent
history of Congregationalism published by that denomination's press,
declares that

> a Congregational church is a group of Christians associated together
> for a definite purpose, not because of peculiarities of belief

and the members of local churches

> are not asked to renounce their previous denominational teachings but
> are asked to join in a simple covenant pledging cooperation and
> fellowship.

Hence the center of a denomination, as of any other voluntary association, is a tangible, defined objective to which consent can be given.
During the actual struggles for religious freedom, the common objective was recognition of the right to worship God in public as each
saw fit and without civil restraints or disabilities. Once this was
achieved, each group was free to define its own peculiar objectives.

In relation to the voluntary principle Christianity itself tends to
be conceived primarily as an activity, a movement, which the group is
engaged in promoting. If the group *has* a confessional basis, its attitude
toward it is likely to become promotional and propagandistic, as for
example, witness Missouri Synod Lutheranism. Anything that seems
to stand in the way of or to hinder the effectiveness of such promotion
is likely to be considered divisive and a threat to the internal unity and
general effectiveness of the group. For example, insofar as theology is
an attempt to define and clarify intellectual positions it is apt to lead
to discussion, differences of opinion, even to controversy, and hence

to be divisive. And this has had a strong tendency to dampen serious discussion of theological issues in most groups, and hence to strengthen the general anti-intellectual bias inherent in much of revivalistic Pietism. This in turn helps to account for the surprising lack of inter-denominational theological discussion, or even consciousness of theological distinctiveness among the many groups. "Fundamentalism" in America, among other things, was a movement that tried to recall these denominations to theological and confessional self-consciousness. But it was defeated in every major denomination, not so much by theological discussion and debate as by effective political manipulations directed by denominational leaders to the sterilizing of this "divisive" element.

Voluntaryism further means that a powerful selective factor is at work in the choice of denominational leaders, since such leaders finally gain and hold support and power in the group through persuasion and popular appeal to the constituency. This means that whatever else top denominational leaders *may be,* they *must be* denominational politicians. Tocqueville was surprised to find that everywhere in America "you meet with a politician where you expected to find a priest." Similar factors are of course at work in the American Republic at large and all the factors that Lord Bryce pointed out as militating against the great man's chances of becoming President of the United States operate in the same fashion in the selection of a President of the American Baptist Convention.

Voluntaryism also means that each group has a kind of massive and stubborn stability, inertia, and momentum of its own, deeply rooted in and broadly based on the voluntary consent and commitment of the individuals composing it. Here is the real basis for the tremendous vitality of these denominations. This is likely to become evident in periods of internal stress or of threat to the existence of the group from the outside—as some proponents of mergers have learned to their consternation.

The acceptance of religious freedom by the churches had one important implication that has seldom been noticed. Written into the fundamental laws of the land at a time when rationalism permeated the intellectual world, it embodied the typically rationalist view that only what all the religious "sects" held and taught in common (the "essentials of every religion") was really relevant for the well being of the society and the state. Obversely this meant that the churches implicitly accepted the view that whatever any religious group held *peculiarly* as a tenet of its faith, must be irrelevant for the public welfare. Thus in effect the churches accepted the responsibility to teach that the peculiar views or tenets or doctrines that divided them one from another and gave each its only reason for separate and independent existence, were either irrelevant for the general welfare or at most possessed only a kind of instrumental value for it. It is little wonder that a sense of irrelevance has haunted many religious leaders in America ever since.

C

The third element to be noted is the place of the mission enterprise in the life of the denominations.

Since the free churches of America are voluntaryistic and purposive the defined objectives of a group are peculiarly definitive and formative.

It is a commonplace that Pietism became dominant in the American churches at the beginning of the nineteenth century. Pietism as a movement in the churches stressed personal religious experience and commitment, expressed in Christian works of evangelization and charity. Hence a concomitant of Pietism wherever it appeared—in German Lutheranism, in English Methodism, in American colonial revivals—was always a renewed interest in missions. Thus the tendency of Pietism as of voluntaryism, is to place the central emphasis on the objectives of the group, which is to make the missionary program of a denomination, both home and foreign, definitive for it.

Missions of course, are an aspect of the broad work of evangelization —the winning of converts through persuasion leading to conversion. But since conversion always takes place in the context of a group, it necessarily has two aspects, the conversion of the individual to God, and the individual's commitment to what the particular group is doing, which defines for him the nature of the Christian life in practice. The two aspects are separable, and the second may come to outweigh the first, placing the denomination under pressures to accept as members all who will cooperate in furthering the work of the local church or denomination—as witness the above quoted Congregationalists' conception of their church. For this reason the originally very exclusive sectarian denominations in America have tended always to move in the direction of loosely inclusive membership.

Further, the fact that the denomination is a voluntary association, has an effect upon the conduct of the over-all evangelistic or mission program it envisages. Since all depends upon persuasion, various aspects of the program, for example, home and foreign missions, necessarily compete for attention and funds within the denomination. Similarly, the several areas of the foreign field compete, with the result noted by H. W. Schneider, that

> in the twentieth century, as well as in the nineteenth, the most popular missionfields were still those areas in which "heathenism" was most spectacular—India, China, and "darkest Africa."

Just as voluntaryism and sense of mission forms the center of a denomination's self-conscious life, so they provide the basis for the interdenominational or superdenominational consciousness and cooperation which has been such an outstanding aspect of the American religious life. This is seen in the host of inter- or super-denominational societies—the American Board of Commissioners for Foreign Missions, The American Home Mission Society, the Bible Society, the Tract Society, the American Sunday School Union, the Temperance Society, the Colonization and Anti-Slavery Societies, the Y.M.C.A., and the Federal and National Councils. Very typical is the statement of the Interchurch World Movement launched in 1919 as a

> cooperative effort of the missionary, educational, and other benevolent agencies of the evangelical churches of the United States and of Canada to survey unitedly their present common tasks and simultaneously and together to secure the necessary resources of men and money and power required for these tasks.

The genius of these movements is the same as that of the individual denominations, namely, to instrument certain defined objectives, in this case of such nature and extent as to enlist the support of individuals in many different denominations. It should be noted that most of these societies were not formed by the cooperative activity of denominations as such, but rather as voluntary associations of individuals from various denominations. In this sense they have been superdenominations, many times in recognized competition with the denominations, as witness for example the Old School Presbyterian attitude toward the

A.H.M.S. and the Baptist attitude toward some of the work of the Bible Society.

There have been of course, outstanding examples of genuine co-operation of denominations as such, as for example the Congregational-Presbyterian Plan of Union of 1801 and the later Accommodation Plan, and more recently the Federal and National Councils. But the basic genius is the same, in this case cooperative work for the accomplishment of tasks too large for one group to do alone.

Here is the basis for the persistent American view that an ecumenical movement must begin with working together rather than with agreement on fundamental theological propositions; on "life and work" rather than "faith and order." This is the way to which American churchmen tend to be committed because of the nature of their long and successful experience in interdenominational cooperation.

Since the missionary enterprise plays such a central and definitive role in an American denomination's self-conscious conception of itself, even slight changes in the basic conception of it, works subtle changes in the character of the denomination itself. Hence an understanding of the changing motifs of missions in America contributes greatly to an understanding of many denominational developments and reactions thereto.

During the formative period of 1783 to 1850, the most prevalent conception of the missionary enterprise in all the evangelical denominations was that of individualistic winning of converts one by one to the cause of Christ. To be sure it was assumed by most that, as Rufus Anderson, Secretary of the A.B.C.F.M. put it in 1845

> that point being gained, and the principle of obedience implanted, and a highly spiritual religion introduced, social renovation will be sure to follow.

And he went on specifically to reject as a direct objective of missions the "reorganizing, by various direct means, of the structure of that social system of which the converts form a part."

Similarly, as Wade C. Barclay's second volume of his *History of Methodist Missions* makes clear, the Methodists commonly accepted Wesley's injunction to his preachers which was written into the first discipline—"You have nothing to do but save Souls." And Bishop McKendree in 1816 had anticipated Rufus Anderson's general position in his answer to the question "What may we reasonably believe to be God's design in raising up the Preachers called Methodists?," which was, "to reform the continent by spreading scriptural holiness over these lands." One cannot say, therefore, that these leaders gave no thought to "social renovation"—but believing as they did that it was not of the essence of the work of the free churches but would automatically follow upon the dissemination of "scriptural holiness," one can say that they took a great deal for granted that time did not bear out.

This general conception of the mission enterprise largely defined the objectives of all the evangelical denominations during the first three quarters of the nineteenth century. In a real sense each became a great missionary organization devoted to pressing the claims of the Gospel as it saw them wherever and however opportunity offered. By the same token, every member was a missionary, either actively and directly as a consecrated worker in the field, or through his enlistment in and support of the common enterprise. Thus the General Assembly declared in 1847, that

> The Presbyterian Church [U.S.A.] is a missionary society, the object of which is to aid in the conversion of the world, and every member of this church is a member of the said society and bound to do all in his power for the accomplishment of this object.

It was this that shaped and gave direction to each budding denomination.

But during the last quarter of the nineteenth century and the opening years of the twentieth, real belief in the all-sufficiency of this kind of missions declined, at least among those of the top leadership in most of the large denominations. During this period enlightened theological Professors hand in hand with "Princes of the Pulpit" responding to the impact of scientific thinking in the garb of evolution and to the deplorable economic and social conditions in the burgeoning industrial society shaped the "new theology" and the "social gospel." Inevitably as their views came to prevail the conception of the work of the Church underwent changes, and missions were metamorphosed from the simple task of winning converts to which, it was assumed, all else would be added, to the complex task of participating actively in social betterment and reconstruction. Foreign missions, from being simple outposts of Christian evangelization, became outposts of the latest technological, medical, agricultural and educational knowledge and practice being developed in the United States. This view of missions received most frank expressions in the "layman's inquiry" published in 1932 as *Re-Thinking Missions.* "We believe," the inquiry states,

> that the time has come to set the educational and other philanthropic aspects of mission work free from organized responsibility to the work of conscious and direct evangelism. We must . . . be willing to give largely without preaching, to cooperate whole-heartedly with non-Christian agencies for social improvement.. . . .

This of course was conceived as "Christian" work—but by what standards? Why should the devoted young medical missionary in Japan, China, or India be closely examined regarding his views of the Trinity or the Virgin Birth, or on any other "merely" theological views for that matter? Meanwhile as Professor Winthrop Hudson has made clear, in the United States itself Christianity was so amalgamated and identified with the American way of life that it was difficult for denominational leaders to distinguish what was peculiarly "Christian" in the work from the general culture. In this situation Christian missions were easily metamorphosed into attempts at intercultural penetration. "The Christian" said the laymen's inquiry

> will therefore regard himself as a co-worker with the forces within each such religious system which are working for rightousness.

In the long run the results were somewhat embarrassing since while the younger churches throve in every mission land, yet in general it was easy for the East, for example, to accept the technology while in reaction rejecting the Christianity which had been assumed to be inseparable from it. In brief, the revolt of the "colonial" missionary countries of the East, armed with the latest "Christian" know-how of the West, somewhat undercut belief in this kind of missions, which meant the undercutting of the denominations' conception of their life and work at home.

Here is one root of much of the present confusion and distress in the American denominations. No longer really believing either in the sole efficacy of a simple Christian evangelization, or in the salutary effects of cultural interpenetration under Christian auspices, their purposive core and sense of direction is destroyed and they are set adrift. The one hopeful element in the picture is that this, among other things, is pressing even American churchmen to re-examine the meaning of the Church not only as "life and works" but also as "faith and order."

The same principle applies to such outstanding interdenominational movements within the country as the Y.M.C.A. and the Federal Council. The "Y," a product of the revivalism of the second quarter of the nineteenth century, had as its original objective the evangelization of uprooted men in the traditional fashion. Beginning with this primary purpose it added libraries, reading rooms, inexpensive hotels, and recreational and other facilities as a means thereto. But as belief in simple evangelization declined the facilities themselves tended to take the leading role in the program, until today the primary appeal of the "Y" is likely to be as a community welfare organization which is somewhat embarrassed by its earlier evangelistic emphasis.

The Federal Council originating in 1908, was described by one of its historians as, in effect a marriage of American church unity or cooperative movements with the concern for social service. Thus it reflects the changed conception of the primary work of the Church at the time of its origin as Walter Rauschenbusch clearly stated. It was conceived by such leaders as Graham Taylor as a cooperative movement among the churches in the interests of social justice, and C. Howard Hopkins referred to it as "the climax of official recognition of social Christianity. . . ." Its first outstanding pronouncement was its "Social Creed of the Churches" adopted in the meeting in Chicago in 1912.

On the one hand then, the Council can be seen as an expression of the basic genius of the American religious organizations—cooperation in the interests of effective evangelization. But on the other hand it reflects the changed conception of "evangelization" from the traditional winning of individual souls to Christ coupled with charitable amelioration of distress to the winning of people to concern for social justice based if necessary upon radical social reconstruction. Inherent in the change was the tendency to substitute social-action for the Christian Gospel of redemption which Visser't Hooft pointed out in his study of *The Background of the Social Gospel in America* in 1928.

This tendency was vigorously combatted in the denominations by the Fundamentalist movement which insofar was right in conception, but which protested on the basis of a theological position generally so archaic and bankrupt that it had no prospect of widespread appeal to intelligent people. It succeeded merely in helping to identify Christianity with stubborn, recalcitrant reactionism in wide areas of America, and in making "Bible belt" a phrase for ultrasophisticated Menckenites to conjure with.

More recently a much more profound and truly sophisticated theological movement, commonly associated with the names of Reinhold Niebuhr and Henry Nelson Wieman has risen in the denominations, which bids fair to do justice both to the Christian tradition and the American activistic genius.

But meanwhile, under the stress of continuing social and political crisis, a genuinely reactionary movement has arisen both inside and from without the denominations which would limit the churches' work to the earlier conception of individualistic soul-winning. This explains the causes and nature of recent attacks on the denominations and the Council as exemplified in John T. Flynn's *The Road Ahead*, which accuses the churches of furthering "creeping socialism" instead of confining themselves to saving souls.

D

The fourth element to be noted is revivalism.

In the English colonies as uniformity enforced by the civil power broke down (e.g., in New England and Virginia) or where it was not, or not for long, attempted (e.g., in Rhode Island, New Amsterdam-New York, and Pennsylvania), and hence where the religious groups were, or were increasingly dependent upon persuasion and popular appeal for recruitment and support, revivalism soon emerged as the accepted technique of the voluntary churches. Not without protest of course, as witness the long and bitter opposition in all the old line churches, but notably in Congregationalism, Presbyterianism and Anglicanism, where doughty Protestant traditionalists correctly sensed that the revivalists "stressed evangelism more than creed," and attempted like King Canute and about as effectively to exercise a measure of control over the incoming tides.

Early revival leaders in the colonies like the Tennents among the Presbyterians and Jonathan Edwards of the Congregationalists, who were long accustomed to sober but effective periods of spiritual refreshing in their parishes, apparently stumbled upon the practice, as witness, for example, Edwards' narrative of "surprising" conversions. But they and especially their followers of lesser stature and more tenuous traditional roots, became apt and even enthusiastic pupils and imitators of the glamorous free-wheeling Anglican revivalist, George Whitefield, whose career, like the Sorcerer's great broom in the hands of a less skillful manipulator, was multiplied in innumerable splinters.

But if the situation in the colonies tended to work for the acceptance of revivalism in all the churches, the situation under religious freedom in the new nation tended to make it imperative. As Professor Garrison has succinctly put it,

> With 90 per cent of the population outside the churches, the task of organized religion could not be limited to encouraging "Christian nurture" . . . in Christian families, or to ministering to old members as they moved to new places farther west. It had to be directed toward that 90 per cent. What they needed first was not nurture or edification, but radical conversion, . . . [and since they followed] no chiefs, . . . they had to be brought in one by one.

"It is small wonder," he correctly continues, "that the revivalists put on all the heat they could and with some notable exceptions, appealed to the emotions more than to the intelligence." There is the heart of the matter. Revivalism in one form or another became the accepted technique of practically all the voluntary churches, the instrument for accomplishing the denominations' objective of evangelism and missions.

Now a commonly accepted practice, whatever the reasons originally given for it, eventually reveals implications of a systematic nature— and revivalism tended strongly to influence the patterns of thought and organization of the groups affected. The "revival system" came to be much more than just a recruiting technique. Some colonial churchmen correctly sensed this, and many of their predictions regarding the effects of revivalism on the churches were fulfilled in the years following independence. What they saw was that revivalism tends to undercut and to wash out all the traditional churchly standards of doctrine and practice.

There are several reasons why this is so. First, revivalism tends to produce an oversimplification of all theological problems, both because the effective revivalist must appeal to the common people in terms they can understand, and because he must reduce all the complex of issues to a simple choice between two clear and contrasting alternatives. Said one convert of "Priest [John] Ingersoll," as the father of the famous agnostic was called, "He made salvation seem so plain, so easy, I wanted to take it to my heart without delay." How simple it could be made is indicated by "Billy" Sunday's proclamation:

> You are going to live forever in heaven, or you are going to live forever in hell. There's no other place—just the two. It is for you to decide. It's up to you, and you must decide now.

Second, the revivalist gravitates almost inevitably toward the idea that "whosoever will may come," and this tendency coupled with the necessarily concomitant stress on personal religious experience in "conversion," tends to make man's initiative primary. Revivalism thus tends to lean theologically in an Arminian or even Pelagian direction with the implicit suggestion that man saves himself through choice. As John W. Nevin complained in *The Anxious Bench*, published in 1843, under revivalism it is the sinner who "gets religion," not religion that gets the sinner.

Thus in the hands of New England revivalists in the line of Timothy Dwight, Lyman Beecher and Nathaniel W. Taylor, Calvinism was "modified" almost beyond recognition by the emphasis placed on their interpretation of "free-will." The foundation of their theological system, said Beecher, was that even God exerts only persuasive power over men. This general emphasis in turn bolsters the voluntaryistic notion that converted men by choice create the church—an idea paralleled in the political realm by the notion that the people create the government. And finally an extremely ardent revivalist may take as condescending an attitude toward God as he takes toward the President of the Republic, as when Charles G. Finney declared that "the devil has no right to rule this world" and the people ought "to give themselves to God, and vote in the Lord Jesus Christ, as governor of the Universe."

Third, revivalists are strongly tempted (and have commonly yielded) to stress results and to justify whatever means will produce them. Even Edwards defended the preaching of terrifying "hell-fire" sermons with the comment that he thought it not amiss to try to frighten men out of hell. And Finney and his friends justified their "new measures" largely on the ground that they got results, namely conversions. Lyman Beecher and his alter-ego, Nathaniel W. Taylor, almost made "preachableness" in revivals normative for doctrines, and D. D. Williams has pointed out that for some of their revivalistic heirs in New England

> the ultimate standard for judging every doctrine and every practice of Christianity was thus first, Will it help or hinder the salvation of men?

This pragmatic emphasis on results reached a peak in the eminently persuasive albeit muddled thinking (when judged by any rigorous standards) of Dwight L. Moody who reputedly said he was an Arminian up to the cross but Calvinist beyond—and who declared forthrightly that "It makes no difference how you get a man to God, provided you get him there." This emphasis culminated in the spectacular career of "Billy" Sunday and his professional imitators with their elaborate techniques for assessing *their* contribution to the Kingdom of Heaven and the Church of Christ on earth by counting the number of *their* converts. It is probably small wonder that the outstanding historian of Christianity in America, a Methodist, rather easily equated the numerical size of the several denominations with their significance and influence in the American culture.

Fourth, revivalism as voluntaryism, tended to bring a particular type of leader to the fore—men close to the people who could speak their language and rouse their emotions. During this formative period it is notable that educated, cultured, dignified religious leaders and ecclesiastical statesmen, men like Timothy Dwight, John Witherspoon, William White—tend to be replaced in the denominations by demagogic preachers and revivalists—men like Peter Cartwright, C. G. Finney, Henry Ward Beecher, Joseph Smith.

This tendency should be seen in the context of the general leveling or equalitarian trend of the times. The parallel development in the political sphere is striking. With the passing of the older revolutionary leaders, the removal of restrictions on popular suffrage, the removal of the barriers between the people and the government, the shift from Federalism and Jeffersonianism to Jacksonian democracy, the "orator" able to appeal in Congress to his peers declined in importance and the popular leaders of the masses increased in influence. Lord Bryce in commenting on the Presidency contrasts the "intellectual pigmies" who followed Jackson with the men of education, administrative experience, largeness of view, and dignity of character who had preceded.

Finally, as revivalism came to pervade the denominations with its implication that the Christian life was a struggle across dull plateaus between peaks of spiritual refreshing, not only was "Christian nurture" in the churches slighted, it was given a reverse twist. Bushnell pointed this out in his complaint that far from encouraging the child to grow up in the Church as a Christian, never knowing himself to be otherwise, the revival system encouraged him to grow up in flagrant sin in order that by contrast he would better know himself as a Christian through the crisis experience of conversion. Thus the revivalists' emphasis that Christ came to save sinners, had the effect of encouraging the Church to nurture flagrant sinners in its bosom in order that they might be "gloriously saved."

Not only did revivalism thus tend to a neglect of the Christian nurture of children in the Church, it tended also to have an adverse effect on the minister as a shepherd of his flock. For inevitably the sober local pastor tended increasingly to be judged by his ability to create the proper build-up and setting for the periodic revival campaigns in his church. And naturally ardent members of the congregation were quick to compare him unfavorably with the more colorful, albeit less responsible, roving evangelists. Many a church prayed the prayer, "Lord, send us a man like Finney!" And the stock answer to decline and apathy in a local church was to import a forceful revivalist to "revive us again!" just as the stock answer to troubles in the country was the importation of a morally impeccable plumed knight in shining armor to lead a great crusade for spiritual renovation and to throw the rascals out.

Fifth, it is perhaps somewhat anti-climactical to suggest here that revivalism tended to foster an anti-intellectual bias in American Protestantism. The over-simplification of issues, plus the primary emphasis on a personal religious experience, and on tangible numerical results, left little room or encouragement for the traditional role of the Church and its ministers in intellectual leadership.

Revivalism with these tendencies was a central element in the structure of the Protestantism that gained religious freedom and was an important factor in shaping the exercise of that freedom in subsequent years and in forming the denominations. There were those in the formative years who, from the viewpoint of "classical" Protestantism, regarded the sweep of the "revival system" with alarm and voiced a strong and cogent protest. Most notable perhaps was John W. Nevin of the Mercersburg Seminary who in 1843 published his *The Anxious Bench* as an attack on the whole "new measure" revival system which he contrasted with the "system of the Catechism." Similarly Horace Bushnell, a Connecticut Congregationalist, voiced a milder protest in his work on *Christian Nurture* published in 1847. But by and large revivalism made a clean sweep in practically all the denominations. Lyman Beecher noted with some amazement that even Emerson's "corpse cold" Unitarians in Boston attempted to hold revivals, but was inclined to agree with Theodore Parker that they lacked the essential piety and warmth for the work and hence succeeded only in making themselves a bit ridiculous. Among the denominations the Presbyterians probably made the most consistent and determined stand against the more radical effects of the system, and suffered fragmentation, ridicule, and abuse for their defense of traditional standards of doctrine and polity. Even Lutheranism, its confessionalism undercut by rationalism and pietism, was swept by revivalism, as the replies to Nevin's work indicate and despite the efforts of confessionally minded men from within was probably saved from becoming just another typical American denomination by the great influx of new Lutheran immigrants.

Surveying the scene as a whole, the historian of Presbyterianism in America was not far wrong when he said that "The Great Awakening . . . terminated the Puritan and inaugurated the Pietist or Methodist age of American Church History."

E

The fifth element to be noted is the churches' general flight from "Reason" in reaction against the Enlightenment during the Revolutionary Epoch, and the concomitant triumph of Pietism in most of them.

The two live movements affecting Christianity during the eighteenth century were Rationalism (Deism in religion) and Pietism. During that century the foremost politico-ecclesiastical issue in America was religious freedom. Confronting this practical issue, Rationalists and Pietists could combine forces against the defenders of the right wing or traditional position of Establishment, in spite of basic theological differences. This they did, bringing the issue to successful culmination in the provisions for religious freedom written into the new constitutions of the States and the Federal Government. In brief, it is not too far wrong to say that rationalists conceived and shaped the form of the new government, while pietistic sentiments were riding to dominance in the churches.

But once religious freedom was accomplished and a popular interpretation of the French Revolution in America brought the theological issue of "Reason" *versus* Revelation to the fore, pietism rapidly realigned itself with classical, right-wing, scholastic orthodoxy in opposition to rationalists and all their works—now included under the blanket term "infidelity." By and large, except perhaps for Unitarianism, the bulk of American Protestantism turned against the ethos of the Enlightenment, and thereafter found itself either indifferent to or in active opposition to the general spirit and intellectual currents of modern western civilization. Thereafter the bulk of American Protestantism was moulded primarily by pietistic revivalism and scholastic orthodoxy. The former made personal subjective religious experience basic, while scholastic orthodoxy defined the professed interest and content of theology. This provides a fair definition of evangelical Protestantism in America.

This triumph of pietistic revivalism in the American denominations, associated as it was with the strong reaction against the ideas and spirit of the Enlightenment which were to inform modern civilization, has had far reaching effects on their thought and life. Pietism as a movement has been peculiarly amorphous in character and intellectually naive. The early leaders, intent on cultivating individual Christian piety in the churches—whether Spener and Francke in German Lutheranism, or the Wesleys in English Anglicanism—never conceived their work except as a movement within the saving forms of a church in the interest of revitalizing its Christian life. Only so does Wesley's use of the text, "Is Thine heart . . . as my heart? . . . If it be, give me thine hand" makes sense. And if the context of a church is absent this can and has led to strange bedfellows for Christians. For Pietism, cut off from the forms of a traditional church and itself the guiding genius of a denomination, has successively loaned itself to whatever live movement seemed to give structure to current problems and their solutions.

Thus, as suggested, it loaned itself to the battle for religious freedom as structured by the Rationalists in the eighteenth century. During the Revolutionary Epoch when the issue seemed to be "reason" *versus* revelation, it as easily loaned its warm heart to hard headed reactionary scholastic orthodoxy and its structuring of that issue. However this alignment was largely on the theological question, and at the same time on the side of "moral and social ideals and attitudes" the emerging modern age was accepted. Here is the real basis for that strangely divided or schizophrenic character of American Protestantism that has baffled so many historians and observers. The two Randalls, John Herman Senior and Junior, stated the situation clearly in their *Religion and the Modern World* of 1929:

> Western society confronted the disruptive forces of science and the machine age with a religious life strangely divided. On the side of moral and social ideals and attitudes, of the whole way of living which it approved and consecrated, Christianity had already come to terms with the forces of the modern age. . . .
>
> On the side of beliefs, however, Christianity in the early 19th century had not come to terms with the intellectual currents of Western society. It found itself, in fact, involved in a profound intellectual reaction against just such an attempt at modernism. . . .
>
> Thus it was that Christianity entered the 19th century with its values belonging to the early modern period, to the age of commerce and individualism, and its beliefs thoroughly medieval and pre-scientific.

This schizophrenia has affected every area of the American denominational life and work. It helps to explain why during the course of the nineteenth century the denominations so easily came to sanctify the ideals and spirit of the rising industrial, acquisitive, bourgeoise society until by the end of the century there was almost complete identification of Christianity with "the American way of life" until, as Henry May put it, "In 1876 Protestantism presented a massive, almost unbroken front in its defense of the social status quo."

It also helps to explain why Protestants could accept the "democratic way" with passionate fervor in practice, but fail to develop a critical Protestant theory of the Christian individual as a ruler. Yet in the democracy every man as a citizen, even though a Christian, is by definition a responsible ruler and cannot be set over against the magistrate and the State as under some other forms. The extent of this failure on the part of American Protestantism is indicated by the fact that when, following the Civil War, some churchmen, motivated at least by humanitarian concerns addressed themselves to pressing social problems they soon found as did Walter Rauschenbusch for example, that if they were to embark upon "Christianizing the Social Order" they had to find or create "A Theology For the Social Gospel." And if they be criticized, as they often are, for being more creative than Christian in this respect, it should also be remembered that there was little in the then current theology of the pietistic orthodoxy of the denominations upon which to build such a theology.

But again, when it was widely accepted that, as Francis Greenwood Peabody put it in 1900,

> the social question of the present age is not a question of mitigating the evils of the existing order, but a question whether the existing order itself shall last. It is not so much a problem of social ameliora- tion which occupies the modern mind, as a problem of social trans- formation and reconstruction

then wide areas of the predominantly pietistic churches easily loaned themselves to identification of the Christian Gospel with this endeavor. Men like George D. Herron, and even Walter Rauschenbusch, came close to blurring the line between Christianity and Socialism, as their heirs sometimes tended to equate it with "New Deals," with "Fair Deals," and "Crusades."

More recently we have seen a clash between the earlier evangelical pietistic view that separation of Church and State means that the churches shall confine themselves to "saving souls" and say nothing about social, economic, and political problems, and the later identifi- cation of the Christian message with concern for social betterment and reconstruction. Thus Stanley High professed to speak for those who were shocked by what took place at Amsterdam—

> But the most disturbing fact in this listing of alleged capitalist evils [by the Amsterdam Conference] is the revelation of how far the church—at least in the persons of its ecclesiastical leadership at Amsterdam—has transferred its concern from the spiritual business of converting man to the secular business of converting man's insti- tutions.

The nature of the reaction against the eighteenth century during the Revolutionary Epoch, also meant that the "free churches" accepted religious freedom in practice but rejected the rationalists' rationale for it. And finding within the right-wing scholastic orthodox tradition that they fell back upon little theological basis for the practice, the denominations have never really worked out a Protestant theological orientation for it. Here is the basis for a widespread psychosomatic indigestion in American Protestantism, since it can neither digest the Enlightenments' theory nor regurgitate its practice.

A. N. Whitehead noted that "the great Methodist movement"—roughly equivalent to my "pietistic-revivalism"—marks the point at which "the clergy of the western races began to waver in their appeal to constructive reason." In comments above on voluntaryism and revivalism it was suggested how and why these tended to foster a general anti-intellectualism in the denominations. The present comments on the reaction against the eighteenth century suggest how and why such anti-intellectualism was made official. In brief, at this point evangelical Protestantism, as defined above, parted company with the intellectual currents of the modern world. Thereafter the former defined "religion," while the latter defined "intelligence." Hence since around 1800 Americans have in effect been given the hard choice between being intelligent according to the standards prevailing in their intellectual centers, and being religious according to the standards prevailing in their denominations.

This is really no secret. In fact, one of the most commonly accepted generalizations is that the churches during the nineteenth century largely lost the intellectuals. In America as early as 1836, Orestes A. Brownson noted, that

> Everybody knows, that our religion and our philosophy are at war. We are religious only at the expense of our logic [or knowledge].

At about the same time, a more orthodox brother expressed approximately the same sentiment in more euphemistic fashion. "There is," he said

> an impression somewhat general—that a vigorous and highly cultivated intellect is not consistent with distinguished holiness: and that those who would live in the cleanest sunshine of communion with God must withdraw from the bleak atmosphere of human science.

Or, as he finally put it more bluntly toward the end of the same article, "It is an impression, somewhat general, that an intellectual clergyman is deficient in piety, and that an eminently pious minister is deficient in intellect." His article, contrary to his purpose, leaves one with the feeling that the impression was not unfounded.

And only yesterday Hugh Hartshorne upon his retirement after many years spent as a Professor of Psychology of Religion in the Yale Divinity School, stated as his mature conclusion that what is called "theological education" in America "is neither theological [according to theological standards] nor education [according to accepted educational standards]." Not unnaturally many, unable to achieve such clarity or accept the situation with such candor, became schizophrenic trying to be intelligent in the schools and religious in the churches. They could be whole in neither. A student entering our theological schools recently, said to me, "In college all my basic interests were religious, but I couldn't seem to find a place to express them in any denomination." Exactly so.

This situation helps to explain why educational leaders in our great Universities, the centers of our burgeoning intellectual life, have never quite known what to do with theological schools in their midst which pretended to train ministers for local parishes. Meanwhile, "practical" churchmen in the United States have by and large been suspicious of nothing more than University education for ministers, unless at every point it could be made obviously applicable to the immediate practical concerns of the churches.

Hence it might be said that the real patron of administrators in University related Seminaries is Janus—who aside from his exceptional physical and mental equipment which enabled him always to face in two directions at once and to speak from either of two mouths, is described as the "guardian of portals and patron of beginnings and endings." Indeed, such Seminaries have been possible largely because men so gifted have been willing to engage in a kind of consecrated duplicity which has permitted the long-range intellectual task of theological reconstruction required by the Universities to be carried on under the guise of ministering directly to the practical needs of local parishes. Whether or not the work of these men abstractly considered is "good" or "evil" is a question purely "academic." It is a necessary work, and I am willing to leave the question of their ultimate salvation with the pronouncement of highest authority that "with God all things are possible." But we ought to be aware that the very success of their necessary work is apt to lure some into the supposition that a kind of subterfuge is of the essence of the religious life in the modern world. Here is the knotty problem that our tradition poses for us.

F

The sixth and final formative element to be noted is the situation of competition between the denominations. In good rationalistic theory, which was basic, competition among the several religious sects, each contending for the truth as it saw it, was of the essence of the free-church idea under the system of separation of Church and State—and was, indeed, the true guarantee of the preservation of "religious rights," as James Madison suggested in the 51st Federalist Paper.

The free-churches were not reluctant to accept this view, and situation, since "in the existence of any Christian sect" the

> presumption is of course implied, if not asserted . . . that it is holding the absolute right and truth, or at least more nearly that than other sects; and the inference, to a religious mind, is that right and truth must, in the long run, prevail.

If theoretical considerations made competition between the religious sects acceptable, the practical situation made it inevitable and intensified it. At the time the declarations for religious freedom were written into the fundamental laws of the land there was a large number of religious bodies, each absolutistic in its own eyes. To them such freedom meant the removal of traditional civil and ecclesiastical restraints on free expression and propaganda. These free-churches were confronted with a rapidly growing and westward moving population, around 90 per cent of which was unchurched. This offered virgin territory for evangelization. The accepted technique was revivalism, a way of reaching and appealing to individuals gathered in groups for their individual decision and consent.

These factors combined, worked to intensify the sense of competition between the free, absolutistic groups in the vast free market of souls—a competition that helped to generate the tremendous energies, heroic sacrifices, great devotion to the cause, and a kind of stubborn, plodding work under great handicaps that transformed the religious complexion of the nation. But it cannot be denied that, as L. W. Bacon said of a specific situation during the colonial period that many times the fear that the work of the gospel might not be done seemed a less effective incitement to activity than the fear that it might be done by others.

This of course was competition between Christian groups sharing a common Christian tradition and heritage, and indeed, really in agreement upon much more than they disagreed on. It was not competition between those of rival faiths, but competition between those holding divergent forms of the same faith—and probably not the less bitter for being thus a family quarrel. This fact meant that ever changing patterns of antagonism and competition were developed, and, by the same token, ever changing patterns of alignments and cooperation.

Robert Baird in his *Religion in America,* first published in America in 1844 at the time when the competition was most keen, divided all the denominations into the "Evangelical" and the "Unevangelical." The former

when viewed in relation to the great doctrines which are universally conceded by Protestants to be fundamental and necessary to salvation . . . all form but one body, recognizing Christ as their common head.

The latter "either renounce, or fail faithfully to exhibit the fundamental and saving truths of the Gospel."

Roman Catholics belong to the latter classification for although "as a Church [they] hold those doctrines on which true believers in all ages have placed their hopes for eternal life" yet they "have been so buried amid the rubbish of multiplied human traditions and inventions, as to remain hid from the great mass of the people. According to Baird, then, Roman Catholics stood in a special category. The great unbridgeable division was between those who "recognize Christ as their head" and those who did not. Notable among the latter were Unitarians, but Universalists, Swedenborgians, Jews, Deists, Atheists, and Socialists were also included. This commonly accepted schematic categorization set the patterns of competition and cooperation among and between the groups.

A Roman Catholic threat could unite all the other groups—even the Evangelical and Unevangelical—in a common front of opposition, especially when as in the west attention was directed to the supposed social and political threat of the Catholic Church to "free institutions." On the other hand, evangelicals might upon occasion borrow a weapon

or accept aid and comfort from Roman Catholics in opposition to Un-
evangelicals. Evangelicals would of course unite against Unitarians and
Universalists. Conservative Unitarians might in the stress of conflict with
"the latest form of infidelity," seek substantial aid from the staunchest
of the orthodox, as when Andrews Norton of Harvard had the Princeton
Presbyterian attacks on Transcendentalism reprinted in Boston. Baptists
and Methodists, although the outstanding. antagonists on the frontier,
might easily combine against Presbyterians and Episcopalians. But
finally each sect stood by itself against all others, a law unto itself in
defense of its peculiar tenets which it inherently held as absolute.

The general effect of such competition was an accentuation of minor
as well as substantial differences—the subjects of baptism and its proper
mode, ecclesiastical polity, the way of conducting missionary work,
pre and post millennialism, "Vater unser" versus "Unser Vater" in the
Lord's prayer—and a submergence of the consciousness of a common
Christian tradition. Further, such competition helped sometimes to make
sheer stubborn perpetuation of peculiarities a chief objective of a group
long after real understanding of and hence belief in them had faded into
limbo. And lastly, it many times produced a somewhat less than charitable attitude toward other Christian groups, and even the kind of
sardonic jealousy reflected in the reputed remark of the Baptist revivalist who in commenting on his meetings said, "We won only two last
night, but thank God the Methodists across the street did not win any!"
In the long run these more questionable results of the competition have
been most obvious and most generally lamented.

Nevertheless, it must be recognized that such competition and conflict is inherent in the system of free churches, and as Talcott Parsons
had observed, it would exist "even if there were no prejudice at all. . . .
a fact of which some religious liberals do not seem to be adequately
aware." In contemporary terms, this is "a struggle for power among
[the] religious denominations," as each tries to extend itself. So long
as the total membership of the denominations was but a fraction of the
total population, this aspect of the competition was largely obscured.
But as the percentage of total church membership rises higher and
higher, it becomes increasingly clear that each may be seeking to extend
itself at the expense of others, as for example, when Southern Baptists
"invade" Northern (now American) Baptist territory, and Roman Catholics "invade" traditionally Protestant rural areas.

Meanwhile, however, other factors noted in this paper have tended to a general erosion of interest in the distinct and definable theological differences between the religious sects that historically divided them, until increasingly the competition between them seems to be related to such non-theological concerns as nationality or racial background, social status, and convenient accessibility of a local church. Finally what appears to be emerging as of primary distinctive importance in the pluralistic culture is the general traditional ethos of the large families, Protestant, Roman Catholic, and Jewish. Thus so far as Protestants are concerned, in the long run the competition between groups inherent in the system of separation of church and state, which served to divide them, may work to their greater unity.

30. COLLEGE FOUNDING IN THE AMERICAN COLONIES, 1745–1775*

by Beverly McAnear

College founding in America began with Harvard in 1636; by the end of the colonial period ten institutions of higher learning had been established, compared with only two in England. The proliferation of colleges in America reflected provincialism and denominational diversity; groups in various colonies created local institutions to advance the interests of a particular religious sect, competitively coexisting with others in the community. Potential leaders of society were educated within an institution where faculty, curriculum, and tone reflected the preferences of a particular faith. Except for the instruction of clergymen, colonial colleges were generally not professional schools, for neither law nor medicine required formal education at that time. The older colleges, Harvard, William and Mary, and Yale were chartered by colonies which had a state church, so these institutions had close ties with the established faith. The later colleges, founded in settlements where no one group

---

* *Mississippi Valley Historical Review*, vol. 42 (1955), 24–44. Footnotes have been omitted except where they are necessary for an understanding of the text.

was dominant or enjoyed state support, were forced to seek more diverse sources of backing and open their doors to men of different denominations, because excluded groups were politically powerful enough to block or jeopardize the granting of a charter by the legislature.

For further reading: Bernard Bailyn, *Education in the Forming of American Society* (1960); R. Hofstadter, *Academic Freedom in the Age of the College* (1955); Samuel Eliot Morison, *Three Centuries of Harvard* (1936); Louis L. Tucker, *Puritan Protagonist: President Thomas Clap of Yale College* (1962); Richard M. Gummere, *The American Colonial Mind and the Classical Tradition* (1963).

In the year 1745 there were but three colleges in all of British North America. Yet by the beginning of the Revolution the virus that Ezra Stiles labeled "College Enthusiasm" had so widely infected the American colonists that seven new colleges had been firmly established; plans had been laid for three more which were to open during the Revolution; and at least six abortive projects had been undertaken by responsible people. Thus by 1776 every province and nearly every popular religious sect was planning and had arranged for financial backing for a school of its own. In addition to the older three—Harvard, Yale, and William and Mary—those actually giving instruction were: Dartmouth College in New Hampshire; the College of Rhode Island, now Brown University; King's College, from which Columbia University has descended; Queen's College, soon to bear the name of Rutgers; the College of New Jersey, destined to become Princeton University; the Academy and College of Philadelphia, still living as the University of Pennsylvania; and Newark Academy, ultimately to reappear as the University of Delaware.

This interest in the founding of colleges coincided with a growth of the spirit of rationalism that sought intellectual stimulation in sources other than theological—a spirit eagerly capitalized on by college promoters who urged the establishment of non-sectarian institutions. Sectarian discussion, such as the Old Light–New Light controversy, further spurred on the founding of colleges consecrated to the religious approach of the partisans. Finally, college founding was helped along by the years of prosperity after 1748, which made fund raising easier, and by the growth of civic and humanitarian spirit, which provided the stimulus. Between 1745 and 1765 most of the campaigns were organized by Yale graduates; after 1765 College of New Jersey men began to take the lead. Men educated in Great Britain and some who were not college men were also among the founders of the new colleges. Except for the role of Harvard graduates in the founding of Dartmouth and the part played by the College of Philadelphia in the establishment of Newark Academy, the graduates of the other American colleges did not figure prominently in the movement.

Regardless of their educational background, college promoters became interested in advancing higher education through affiliation either with a library company or with a church. Most organizers—and they were the most successful—were ministers interested in the advancement of their own sect. Clerical leaders campaigned for Dartmouth, Queen's, New Jersey, Newark, and, in their final stages of organization, for Rhode Island and King's. The reasons emphasized by clerics for establishing colleges were to educate ministers, to raise the level of general culture and morals through the influence of the clerical alumni, and to convert the Indians. They maintained that a college was a religious society whose basic and chief duty was to train its students to be religious and moral men. The study of nature was to be subservient to the inculcation of religion; the one was only a threshold to the other, and religious instruction therefore was to be emphasized. They freely promised toleration to all Protestant Trinitarian sects, but they demanded clerical administration and the dominance of one sect.

Those promoters identified with one of the library companies were usually laymen, often without much formal education. Colleges and libraries were at that time a natural conjunction of interests, for some of the library companies were originally designed as organizations which would not only circulate books but which would also provide popular lecture courses, particularly on scientific subjects. Men affiliated with libraries were concerned with the foundation of Rhode Island, King's, and Philadelphia, and with abortive proposals for colleges at Newport and Charleston. They argued that a college should properly be considered a civil society committed to the duty of training youths for service to the commonwealth, and the value of any type of training was to be measured according to its ultimate usefulness to the graduates in civil life. The best attribute of an educated man was an independent mind; free inquiry was therefore to be encouraged and religious instruction prohibited. To assure freedom, religious toleration and nonsectarianism were to be maintained, and even direct state control was proposed.

To their basic appeal for support each group of promoters added virtually the same arguments. College alumni would provide superior public servants and the very presence of the college and its faculty would raise the cultural level of the province. The students' love of their native province would be protected against the alienation that might result from new attachments formed during their school years in distant parts, and thus the best minds of the colony would be saved for the service of their birthplace. Money would not flow out of the province to enrich the residents of college towns in other provinces. And, finally, a local school would provide a less expensive education for ambitious sons of residents.

Almost inevitably a movement to launch a college aroused religious and political rivalries. Many of the quarrels concerned the sectarian affiliation of the proposed college; and in these contests the Anglicans and Presbyterians were the most combative. In addition to their involvement in the Old Light-New Light controversy raging in the Calvinistic churches, some of the schools became involved in provincial or imperial political questions which had nothing to do with higher education, and some college promoters were confronted with the monopolistic claims of institutions already established. Once aroused by these contentions, factions which had been aligned in the opening days of a college lived on to blight its growth. These feuds account in great measure for the failure of all the newer colleges to gain annual provincial appropriations, and they caused the failure of many of the proposals for new colleges even though neither money nor public interest was lacking.

Factional division usually began with a dispute over the terms of a charter of incorporation and the nomination of the first trustees. Incorporation was necessary to protect the institution's property and to permit the granting of degrees; and the religious loyalties of the trustees usually determined the ecclesiastical affiliation of the college. The founders of New Jersey and Dartmouth objected so stubbornly to the inclusion of royal officers of Anglican faith among the trustees that they were almost denied their charters. A furious battle over the method of organization of the college cost King's thousands of pounds of endowment and all hope of future provincial support.

In drafting their charters, King's, Dartmouth, and Queen's used the College of New Jersey charter of 1748 as a model; Rhode Island drew upon the Harvard and Yale charters, in addition to New Jersey's; and Newark turned to the charter of Pennsylvania. Ironically, no one seems to have known at the time whether the colonial governors had the power to grant charters of incorporation and therefore whether the college charters were valid.

The building lot for the college was invariably provided by a public or semi-public organization in order to attract the college to its town. The difficulties that New Jersey College experienced in its attempts to secure a sizable sum in four different New Jersey villages indicate that the custom was not well established in the 1740's. But it caught on quickly, and Queen's was embarrassed by bids from New Brunswick, Tappan, and Hackensack, while Rhode Island felt obliged to hold an auction to terminate five months of competitive controversy.

As soon as money was available, a college hall, containing classrooms and a dormitory, was erected. To supervise construction, some colleges relied on artisans or amateur architects, but Rhode Island, New Jersey, and Philadelphia retained the services of the Philadelphia architect and builder, Robert Smith. The plans drawn by Smith and William Shippen, a physician and amateur architect of Philadelphia, were repeated elsewhere and virtually created in America the collegiate Georgian style. Essentially their design was an adaptation of that for King's College, Cambridge University. During the twenty-five years before the Revolution, five of these schools spent approximately £15,000 sterling for the erection or remodeling of buildings. "This they chose to do," President John Witherspoon of the College of New Jersey wrote, "though it wasted their Capital, as their great Intention was to make effectual Provision, not only for the careful Instruction, but for the regular Government of the Youth." A pretentious building was also desirable because it afforded publicity, and its inclusion of dormitory space and commons reduced student expenses.

The cost of the original hall invariably reduced the college to a state of near insolvency. Indeed, Philadelphia and Rhode Island invested in their buildings literally the last penny in the till. As a result, trustees tended to limit the materials for classroom demonstrations in physics, surveying, and astronomy. Thanks to the persistence of their presidents, however, by 1775 the scientific instruments of King's, New Jersey, and Philadelphia were equal to or better than those possessed by Harvard, Yale, and William and Mary. The other new colleges owned little or no scientific apparatus.

A greater handicap was the inadequacy of libraries. By the time of the Revolution, the Harvard library, with more than 4,000 volumes, was probably the largest college library in the colonies. Yale was not far behind, but William and Mary must have had less than 3,000. While Philadelphia, King's, and New Jersey, with perhaps 2,000 books each, made at least a respectable showing, library facilities at the other newly established institutions were either virtually or completely non-existent.

Nearly all the books in the libraries of the newer colleges had been presented: none customarily bought more than occasional titles. The only important purchases were three consignments for New Jersey, one of which was so costly that the trustees deemed it an extravagance and charged the bill to the president. To make matters more difficult, these libraries were largely the gifts of benevolent clergymen, and the weight of theology hung heavy upon them. "But few modern Authors, who have unquestionably some Advantages above the immortal ancient, adorn the Shelves," wrote a college official in 1760. "This Defect is most sensibly felt in the Study of Mathematics, and the Newtonian Philosophy." Philadelphia and New Jersey sought to remedy matters by assessing the students a library fee, but the income must have been small.

By the time the trustees of a college had built the hall and provided furniture, scientific equipment, and a library, they had invested approximately £5,000—perhaps the equivalent of $350,000 today. By 1776 the physical properties of all the infant colleges probably represented the expenditure of something approaching £25,000—an investment which produced virtually no income, since student rents could hardly have paid for maintenance.

In assembling a faculty, the trustees were apt to seek a president who had been trained in a British university, but since the necessary income was often lacking they were forced to be content with the product of an American college. The president bore the heaviest share of the burden of the school. He did a good part of the teaching and conducted the college's religious exercises. He was also the chief and sometimes the only administrative officer, and he was obliged to gather money and recruit students. To supplement his income, he often served as the pastor of a neighboring church. Such arrangements were discouraged by the trustees, however, and as the college grew more prosperous, pressure was placed on the president to confine himself to college affairs.

The other members of the faculty (seldom more than three) were usually younger men destined within a few years to be clergymen. Most were American trained, though Anglican schools secured some British-educated tutors. Lack of money prevented the hiring of a more stable, better trained faculty, since almost any profession promised greater returns and better social status. The hardest position to fill was that of the science instructor. Few men with the necessary training were to be found in the colonies, and hence the post was often vacant. Each instructor normally was assigned a given class of students to whom he imparted knowledge on all subjects except the natural sciences. This arrangement demanded, however, that a faculty member undertake a considerable degree of specialization of subject matter, because the curricula emphasized given branches of learning in different years.

One of the president's most perplexing tasks was the enrollment of students. To an even greater extent than the present-day college, colonial institutions relied upon income from tuition to provide vitally needed revenue. But to recruit students, it was necessary to popularize the value of higher education. Prior to 1745 not many parents in the British North American colonies sent their sons to college. This was especially true for the Middle Colonies. To attract public attention, some use was made of printed publicity. Ministers were pressed to act as recruiting agents for the college identified with their sect. Alumni, especially where they were schoolmasters or pastors, were able to help the recruiting for New Jersey, but most of the other colleges were too young to have many graduates.

The overwhelming majority of entrants were attracted by the college nearest their homes. The difficulty and expense of travel, the emotional complications inherent in distant separation from home, and local pride perhaps influenced students and furnished talking points for recruiting agents. But provincialism could be defeated if a distant college offered a cheaper education. Those colleges which grew most rapidly and attracted most students from other provinces were those which charged least. New Jersey and Rhode Island had the lowest charges, and Eleazer Wheelock permitted some Dartmouth students to work for their expenses. Hence these three colleges showed the most rapid increase in enrollment. Apparently New Jersey was also aided by its custom of admitting applicants as juniors, thus waiving costly residence at college for the first two or three years of a boy's work. Philadelphia and King's were the most expensive and therefore always had small student bodies, largely drawn from their immediate vicinity.

Despite ardent campaigning, the enrollment in all these infant colleges was small. The opening class in any of them could hardly have been more than five to eight boys. Succeeding classes naturally increased enrollment, and the prosperous years of the early 1770's greatly aided recruitment. Even so, most of the newer schools prior to the Revolution had at best an attendance of only forty or fifty students. By all odds, the most successful was New Jersey, which grew to an enrollment of about one hundred. Yet, despite this rapid growth, New Jersey was still smaller than her older rivals, for after 1755 the student bodies of Harvard and Yale had often exceeded one hundred and fifty. Approximately four sevenths of all college students of 1775 were enrolled in the three oldest institutions.

Upon appearance at college, the prospective student was required to pass an entrance examination, usually administered by the president. The requirements of the new colleges seem to have been copied from those of Yale; for Rhode Island, King's, and New Jersey the requirements were almost identical. Essentially, the test demanded ability to translate elementary Latin and Greek and a knowledge of arithmetic— this last being a contemporary innovation. It is doubtful that an applicant was ever sent home, though sometimes extra work was prescribed.

Many of the students admitted were mere boys. From 1750 to 1775 the median age of the entrants at Yale was only sixteen or seventeen; at Philadelphia it was sixteen; and at King's only fifteen. Eleven- and twelve-year-old freshmen were not unknown, and John Trumbull satisfied the Yale entrance examination at the age of seven years and five months. Because of the competition for students the colleges were in danger of becoming grammar schools. As a step toward remedying this difficulty, the governors of King's in 1774 ruled that after the admission of the class of 1778 entrance would be refused any applicant younger than fourteen "except upon account of extraordinary qualifications."

As a general rule, only freshmen were admitted. Though there were exceptions in every college, only Dartmouth, New Jersey, and possibly Philadelphia made a practice of admitting students to advanced standing. These boys had usually studied with a minister because such a training was less expensive than college residence. For admission to advanced standing, the college required payment of fees for the earlier years and passage of an entrance examination. The examination seems to have been largely a formality. Writing to a friend, one such candidate at New Jersey reported: "After examinations on the usual *authors*, when I and they, who were examined with me, received admission into the junior-class, we were told, that we should have been examined on the *Roman antiquities*, if it had not been forgotten." Witherspoon disliked the system and unsuccessfully sought to abolish it.

Rhode Island, King's, and New Jersey also patterned their curricula after the Yale model, a program that reflected the course of study developed in the English dissenting academies. Actually colleges, these institutions had broken away from complete concentration upon the classics and Aristotelianism and had instituted Newtonianism, social sciences, and modern languages. All four colleges required the same course of studies in the first two years: principally Latin, Greek, and Hebrew. That they assigned much more time to these subjects than did the English academies indicates an effort to repair the deficiencies of their matriculants who, compared to their English counterparts, were retarded about a year and a half. In the final two years, the American colleges emphasized natural sciences, mathematics, and metaphysics. President Samuel Johnson at King's apportioned three fourths of the time of juniors and seniors to mathematics and the natural sciences, while Yale provided but one year, and Rhode Island and New Jersey considerably less than a year. To complete the studies for the senior year, Yale provided metaphysics and divinity, and New Jersey and Rhode Island oratory, composition, and almost certainly divinity. This difference in emphasis is partly explained by the desire of the dissenting colleges to train preachers and in part by the lack of scientific equipment and instructors. All devoted some time to logic, ethics, geography, and public speaking.

At Philadelphia a more independent approach to the curriculum was undertaken by President William Smith, who was influenced by Dr. Samuel Johnson, the great English writer, and by Robert Dodsley's *Preceptor*. Nonetheless, the subjects prescribed by Smith were much the same as those offered elsewhere, except that he placed much greater stress upon oratory and the social sciences and did not regularly offer courses on religion.

Between 1765 and 1775 the American institutions showed great capacity to adapt their curricula to trends appearing in the English academies. Stress was placed on English grammar and composition by requiring polished written translations and original products of the students' pens, and greater weight was placed on oratory. English literature, however, was never taught formally. Some schools began to offer modern foreign languages as electives, and with their growing popularity classes in Hebrew were deserted. Greater attention was also paid to history by Witherspoon at New Jersey and by President James Manning at Rhode Island, though, as was the case in England, apparently only ancient history was taught. In brief, during these thirty years the college moved to some degree from ancient to modern languages, from divinity to the social sciences, and from metaphysics to natural sciences. Only Dartmouth and King's seemed to find the older ideas the better.

Most colleges organized their courses into a four-year curriculum. Smith, however, instituted at Philadelphia the then current English innovation of a three-year college. In actual fact, Philadelphia's program of study was abbreviated by pushing back into the academy some of the courses taught elsewhere to college freshmen. Newark also seems to have required only three years' residence, but similar experiments in truncation by Witherspoon at New Jersey and Manning at Rhode Island were soon abandoned.

Classes began early and lasted through the day, punctuated by morning and evening prayers. Instruction was based upon recitations from and elaborations of textbooks, though the lecture method was used by some presidents in teaching the seniors. The college library was rarely used by undergraduates, and New Jersey claimed distinction for its policy of encouraging seniors to browse in the library. To stimulate scholarship, King's, New Jersey, and Philadelphia set up prizes to be awarded for excellence in specified subjects, and Manning wanted to adopt the plan at Rhode Island. But the system proved ineffective, and it was allowed to die.

Regular attendance, payment of fees, and proper deportment—or due regret for improper deportment—seemed almost invariably to yield a diploma on the scheduled day. "To the frequent scandal, as well of religion, as learning," wrote a contemporary critic, "a fellow may pass with credit through life, receive the honors of a liberal education, and be admitted to the right hand of fellowship among the ministers of the gospel. . . . Except in one neighbouring province, ignorance wanders unmolested at our colleges, examinations are dwindled to mere form and ceremony, and after four years dozing there, no one is ever refused the honors of a degree, on account of dulness and insufficiency." In 1756 there were 172 students enrolled at Yale, and all but seven eventually received degrees. Elsewhere, virtually automatic progress by the student likewise seems to have been the rule; only at King's and Philadelphia was the mortality rate high.

All the younger colleges claimed to be non-sectarian and insisted that full religious toleration was granted to all Protestants. Therefore all were advertised as "free and Catholic" or as "Catholic, Comprehensive, and liberal." Nevertheless, all students were required to take courses in divinity or the Bible, and all attended college prayers twice a day. College laws also required attendance at church on Sunday. Tolerance demanded that the student be permitted to attend the church of his own choice, though in some instances there was only one church in town. Thus while sectarians could and did freely accuse each other of proselytizing, none could charge these college administrators of ignoring the injunction laid down by one of their trustees that *"Liberty be not made a Cloak of Licentiousness."*

Most students lived in the college hall, two or three to a room or suite of rooms. Meals were served in the college refectory, usually situated in the basement of the college hall. The only important meal came at mid-day; it consisted essentially of meat and potatoes. The evening meal was based upon left-overs from noon, and breakfast brought only bread and butter. While this community life was recommended by the college authorities, many students preferred the more expensive but freer method of boarding out in adjacent homes. Such freedom, however, sometimes created special problems of discipline.

Relations between the faculty and the students seem to have been reasonably good, although there were, of course, exceptions. Provost William Smith, of Philadelphia, gained a reputation for harshness; Eleazer Wheelock, of Dartmouth, ruled with the care but without the indulgence of a father; and Robert Harpur, the science instructor at King's, was hated and tormented on general principles. But the newer colleges were free of the student riots which occurred at Harvard and Yale.

The students found their college days profitable and enjoyable, and letters written after graduation to former schoolmates bore the impress of nostalgia. Extra-curricular activities revolved around clubs devoted to literary and bibulous exercises. Oratory was perhaps the most popular interest, and students sharpened their oratorical prowess in nightly practice for the seniors' grand performance on commencement day. Singing and the writing of verse were also fashionable; and the score for the New Jersey commencement of 1762 is one of the earliest examples of college music now extant. In their songs and some of their poetry the students frequently gave expression to sentiments which suggest that college pride had already been born.

However valuable students found college life to be, their fathers regarded the expense of maintenance with no little concern. During the years between 1746 and 1772 the charges of the College of New Jersey for room, board, and tuition—£9 per year—were the lowest of any college. But college fees gradually increased, and after 1772 an economical parent found that the lowest bill, £12, was presented by the College of Rhode Island. The highest annual charges made by any of the newer colleges were those of King's—£18. And room, board, and tuition, of course, represented only a fraction of a student's total expenses. Firewood, candles, and washing cost £3 more; books and stationery, clothing and travel, and pocket money, too, increased the cost. Thus in 1775 the lowest cost of educating a boy ranged from £25 to £35 a year; it might easily amount to £55 or even more for spend-thrifts. But the highest expense in America was mild compared to charges in England, where advanced education cost over £100 annually.

For colonial days these were large sums in terms of personal cash income. An able carpenter with good employment earned about £50 a year; a captain in the royal army, £136; a college instructor, £100; and a good lawyer, £500. Some relief was afforded by the extension of credit, and only too often greater relief was gained by parents who defaulted payment of the indebtedness. A little money for needy students was raised through church collections and subscriptions by the Baptists at Rhode Island and the Presbyterians at New Jersey. But none of the infant colleges had annually appointed scholars, and it appears that only at Dartmouth did any number of students work to pay their expenses. Therefore, sooner or later, the father had to pay, and clearly only the well-to-do could easily afford to do so. Indeed, some contemporary commentators believed that only the sons of the wealthy should go to college.

The greatest problem faced by the college administrators was that of getting the money necessary to keep the college open, for students' fees paid only a small part of the cost of a boy's education. In their search for the requisite funds, promoters of the new colleges found that tapping the provincial treasury yielded only a trickle of cash. Harvard, Yale, and William and Mary all had been given both grants and annual subventions by their respective provincial governments or by the King. Among the newer colleges, only Dartmouth, King's, and Philadelphia were voted money from public treasuries, and King's alone was treated generously. None ever received an annual public subsidy, despite repeated applications.

Appeals to the general public by means of subscription lists and lotteries brought some funds, and occasional bequests added more; but the receipts from these sources were usually needed to meet recurring deficits. To gain capital for investment, efforts were made to raise funds in Europe and the West Indies. Between 1745 and 1775 the seven new colleges received well over £72,000 in gifts from thousands of people solicited by hundreds of well-wishers. Over the same period approximately two sevenths of these funds were invested in income-producing endowment; about three sevenths were used in meeting current operating expenses; and the remaining two sevenths were absorbed in the erection of buildings. With the exception of King's, which was able to meet its running expenses with the income from its investments, all were operating on deficit budgets after 1770; and at the same time the raising of funds for colleges became increasingly difficult.

The most obvious effect of the work of the pioneer educators who were responsible for the establishment and operation of these newer colleges was the great increase in the number of college-trained men in the colonies. From 1715 through 1745 the three older colleges graduated about fourteen hundred men, but in the following thirty-one years over thirty-one hundred gained bachelors' degrees in British North America. Almost nine hundred of these degrees (28 per cent of the total number) were granted by the seven new colleges. These schools therefore were responsible for about half the increase of college-trained men during these decades.

Behind the growing interest in college attendance was increasing economic prosperity. Each advance in college enrollment followed by three or four years the initial point on a rise of the index of commodity prices. Mounting colonial wealth aided the establishment of colleges in provinces from which the older colleges had drawn few students. Probably over 90 per cent of the graduates of Harvard, Yale, and William and Mary came from eastern New Hampshire, Massachusetts, Connecticut, and Virginia. Rhode Island and the middle provinces were relatively fallow fields, and to the boys in those areas the younger colleges represented opportunity. Therefore, the advance in enrollment beginning in 1769 redounded to the advantage of the newer rather than the older colleges, and from 1769 through 1776 they graduated approximately 40 per cent of the bachelors of arts.

This sudden popular interest in a college degree brought repeated demands that college bills should not be so high as to exclude the sons of the less well-to-do. This insistence sprang in part from a belief that the duty of the college was to open the gates of opportunity to youths of merit regardless of their fathers' social and economic position. One of the college propagandists argued: "The great Inducement to Study and Application . . . is the Hope of a Reward adequate to the Expence, Labour and Pains, taken. In Countries where Liberty prevails, and where the Road is left open for the Son of the meanest Plebeian, to arrive at the highest Pitch of Honours and Preferments, there never will be wanting such Emulation, and of Course great Men. . . . Such at this Day, is Great Britain." Some extended the argument, maintaining that all classes of society needed some type of education beyond that of the common school.

These democratic concepts of education were being applied at the time to a class society which it was assumed educated men would buttress. Such efforts as were made to reduce the barrier of high cost came from the dissenting colleges. Groups of dissenters in England had long aided poor students financially, and the Baptists and Presbyterians in America followed the custom. Furthermore, ministers were badly needed in the colonies and usually they could be recruited only among the sons of farmers. A costly education, therefore, would handicap the Presbyterian and Baptist churches. Inevitably the administrators of dissenting colleges were forced to yield to pressure to keep their fees down, and hence their graduates included a goodly number of sons of artisans and farmers of modest means. Thus the requirements of religious sects gave effect to the demand for democratization of higher education.

One concern of this increased interest in higher education was the improvement of professional training. New Jersey was the first of the younger colleges to build a curriculum designed to train preachers, and it is not surprising, therefore, that about half of the pre-Revolutionary graduates of New Jersey entered the ministry. Rhode Island and Newark followed New Jersey's precedent, and President Smith at Philadelphia read lectures in divinity as a special course for candidates for the ministry. Through the influence of President Witherspoon, New Jersey was also the first of the new colleges to introduce formal graduate training in divinity, a program already long established at William and Mary.

Philadelphia in 1765 and King's in 1767 undertook to supply professional training in medicine, though on an undergraduate level. But physicians had a poor economic and social status, and so the medical schools were never overflowing with students. By 1776, Philadelphia had graduated but ten students and King's twelve. Perhaps it was as well, for one of the abler graduates of King's recommended in his thesis the prescription of a specific he had not the courage to administer.

This advance in educational standards also influenced the legal profession, and in 1756 the New York bar began to demand college work as a requisite for admission. By 1776 one third of those entitled to plead before the provincial courts held the degree of bachelor of arts. Formal training in civil law, the common law, or municipal law was never undertaken in any colonial college, although King's, Philadelphia, and the advocates of the proposed college at Charleston all dreamed and planned for the establishment of such courses.

The colleges likewise raised the standards of secondary education. Throughout the period, criticism of the preparation of college matriculants was constant, and, in an effort to gain more satisfactory material, all the new colleges maintained their own grammar schools. These secondary schools were also essential to the colleges as "feeders" of matriculants. As the years passed, the number of independent grammar schools in the middle and southern provinces increased sharply, and the graduates of the newer colleges, particularly New Jersey, were in great demand as masters.

These college founders also made significant contributions to colonial interdependence. Hundreds of students crossed provincial boundaries to enroll in their alma maters. Half of Newark's enrollment came from provinces other than Delaware; 40 per cent of Philadelphia's from homes outside of Pennsylvania. New Jersey attracted men from North Carolina and Massachusetts. So heavy a migration was a significant change, for the three older colleges had drawn nearly all their students from relatively restricted areas. In the years immediately preceding the Revolution, students migrating northward were passed by northern-born graduates, particularly of Yale and New Jersey, moving to southern provinces. In Virginia and North Carolina, New Jersey men began a new cycle of college founding. Thus the younger colleges stimulated interprovincial migration of able men, trained in much the same intellectual pattern.

The history of higher education during these three decades, then, is dominated by the establishment of successful colleges and the development of promotional techniques. Each successive college was founded more easily and with better planning than its predecessors; problems were foreseen and precedents were available and accepted. Once opened, they carried on until subjected to military interference during the Revolution. These colleges significantly increased the cultural level of the population and raised the educational standards of the professions. The founders advanced the practice and idea of democratic higher education. They transplanted the essentials of the educational system of the English dissenting academies and saw the system take root; and virtually the entire task had been the accomplishment of men born and bred in America. They believed that they were strengthening the bonds of an empire in which America should be subsidiary, not subordinate to England. From the beginning many had hoped the colleges would further the creation of cultural autonomy in America. In 1770, for example, Ezra Stiles tabulated the various degrees granted by the several American colleges and concluded: "Thus all the learned degrees are now conferred in the American Colleges as amply as in the European Colleges." As the colonial epoch closed, many Americans proudly felt that they had achieved educational self-reliance.

31. THE CULTURE OF EARLY PENNSYLVANIA*

by Frederick B. Tolles

Did the American colonists produce a distinctive and vital culture, or was cultural achievement a task left to later, more comfortable generations? According to Frederick B. Tolles, a unique cultural life took shape in early Pennsylvania from interaction of the diverse religious and ethnic groups which populated William Penn's "Holy Experiment." Religious freedom and economic opportunity attracted to Pennsylvania waves of English, Welsh, Germans, and Scotch-Irish who brought with them traditions of worship and modes of living. Migrating in groups, they did not disperse throughout the colony but concentrated in areas where they were a self-conscious and often dominant element. This pattern of settlement made it easier to perpetuate their distinctive cultures, which differentiated them sharply from other groups. In an open society where no group was permanently entrenched in positions of privilege, these elements mingled and often competed. Thus Philadelphia became not only a leading commercial center, one of the largest cities

* *Pennsylvania Magazine of History and Biography*, vol. 81 (1957), 119–137. Footnotes have been omitted except where they are necessary for an understanding of the text.

in the British Empire, but also a city where cultural pluralism flourished. According to one European visitor, such cultural and ethnic intermingling was one of the sources of the "new race of men" appearing in America.

For further reading: Max Savelle, *Seeds of Liberty* (1965); Daniel J. Boorstin, *The Americans: The Colonial Experience* (1958); Louis B. Wright, *The Cultural Life of the American Colonies, 1607–1763* (1957); Oliver W. Larkin, *Art and Life in America* (1949); Brooke Hindle, *The Pursuit of Science in Revolutionary America, 1755–1799* (1956).

Benjamin West has a lot to answer for. Everyone knows his painting of William Penn's treaty with the Indians; it is one of our national icons, "as indelibly impressed on the American mind," it has been said, "as . . . Washington's crossing of the Delaware." The lush greens of its foliage, the tawny flesh tones of its noble savages, the sober drab of its Quaker plain dress have fixed forever in our consciousness a stereotype of early Pennsylvania. There he stands under the great elm at Shackamaxon, portly and benignant, the Founder of the Quaker commonwealth, eternally dispensing peace and yard goods to the Indians. If it is mostly legend—for there is no documentary record of a treaty at Shackamaxon—it is at least an inspiring one, quite as much so as that of Pocahontas laying her lovely head on Captain John Smith's breast or Squanto instructing the Pilgrim Fathers in the mysteries of maize culture. And whatever its faults as a document or as a painting, it has the merit of a certain truth to history, for, unlike the founders of Jamestown and Plymouth, the Quaker founders of Pennsylvania did contrive by fair dealing and generosity to stay at peace with the local Indians for three quarters of a century. As a matter of fact, it is worth pausing a moment to note that the autumn of 1956 marked the two-hundredth anniversary of the ending of that remarkable experiment in peaceful race relations.

What is wrong, then, with West's vast, idyllic canvas as a symbol of early Pennsylvania? It is not the anachronisms that bother me. True, the architectural background is composed of brick buildings

603

that could not have been standing in 1682; true, West portrays Penn as stout and middle-aged when in fact he was still young and athletic, and dressed him in the Quaker Oats costume of shadbelly coat and cocked hat that Friends did not wear for half a century to come. No, the mischief lies in the aura, the atmosphere, of the painting—the air of smug and stupid piety combined with the stolid respectability of the successful bourgeois. No one will deny that the early Quakers were a "God-fearing, money-making people"—least of all I, who have written a book on the proposition that they had one foot in the meetinghouse and the other in the countinghouse. It is probably unfair to demand of a painter that he project the life of the mind on his canvas; perhaps it takes a modern abstractionist to portray a pure idea. Yet I cannot help regretting that the most widely current stereotype of early Pennsylvania should suggest a cultural and intellectual desert.

Besides, early Pennsylvania was not, of course, just Quaker. Everyone who has seen *Plain and Fancy* knows about the Amish, who have been here for a long time, and everyone who has a taste for the quaint and the indigestible knows about "hex signs" on barns (which have nothing to do, of course, with witches) and shoofly pie. If we don't know about the Scotch-Irish, it is not for want of zeal on the part of their descendants, who would have us believe that they fought the Indians and won the American Revolution all by themselves. And if we happen to be Bryn Mawr graduates we are vaguely conscious that the college campus and its surroundings were once peopled by Welshmen, who left the landscape strewn with odd-sounding place names like Llanerch, Bala-Cynwyd, and Tredyffrin (many of which, incidentally, were chosen from a gazetteer by a nineteenth-century president of the Pennsylvania Railroad looking for distinctive names for his suburban stations).

What I want to suggest is that early Pennsylvania had a genuine and important culture or complex of cultures, that there was something more to it than simple Quaker piety and commercialism on the one hand and ethnic quaintness on the other. I am going to side-step one basic problem by refusing to define exactly what I mean by "culture." The anthropologically minded will be annoyed by my irresponsible tendency to use the term now as Ruth Benedict would use it and again perhaps as Matthew Arnold would use it. In justification of this slipshod procedure I can only plead that I am merely an unscientific historian, not a "social scientist."

The Culture of Early Pennsylvania

"Early Pennsylvania" I will define more strictly. By this term I shall mean Pennsylvania east of the Susquehanna and south of the Blue Mountains in the period down to about 1740. But I must immediately point out that this area was never a self-contained or self-conscious regional unit. It was part of a larger geographical whole. The men in the gray flannel suits have been trying hard in recent years to impress upon us the concept "Delaware Valley, U.S.A." The colonial Pennsylvanian knew without being told that he lived in the valley of the Delaware. He first saw his new home from the deck of a ship sailing up the great river. His prosperity and his comfort depended in large measure on the commerce that carried his farm products down the river to the West Indies and southern Europe, that brought back up the river the textiles and hardware he needed and could not manufacture for himself. The Delaware united West Jersey, Pennsylvania, and the Lower Counties (which eventually became the state of Delaware) into a single economic province, and linked it with the rest of the Atlantic community. It also unified the valley into a single "culture area." The Quakers' Yearly Meeting embraced Friends on both sides of the river, and met alternately at Philadelphia on the west bank and Burlington on the east. The Anglicans also thought of the valley as a unit, a single missionary field to be saved from "Quakerism or heathenism." I shall restrict myself, however, to that portion of it which originally formed the province of Pennsylvania proper—the counties of Bucks, Philadelphia, and Chester.

The Founder of Pennsylvania, we must be clear, was neither a narrow-minded religious zealot on the one hand nor a mean-spirited Philistine on the other. William Penn was a man of broad intellectual culture in Matthew Arnold's sense, educated at Oxford, on the Continent, and at Lincoln's Inn; he was a Fellow of the Royal Society and the associate not only of kings and courtiers, but of the reigning intellectuals of the day—men like Samuel Pepys, the diarist, John Locke, the philosopher, Sir William Petty, the political economist. He was a man of wide reading. The list of books he bought to bring to America on his second visit suggests his range; it included the poems of Milton, a copy of *Don Quixote*, the works of John Locke, the latest travel books by William Dampier and Father Hennepin, the Roman histories of Livy and Suetonius. Penn was a good Quaker and a shrewd real-estate promoter, but he was also—though one would scarcely guess it from Benjamin West's canvas—a Restoration egghead, as much at home with the philosophers of the Royal Society as with the Indians of the Pennsylvania forest. The example of such a man was enough to insure that Pennsylvania would not be a cultural desert. And Penn's commitment to a sophisticated ideal of religious freedom meant that the intellectual life of his colony would never stagnate for want of controversy and the creative clash of opinions.

It is true that, by and large, the English Quakers who sailed with Penn on the *Welcome* or followed him on other ships did not come, as he did, from the leisure class. Quakerism in the seventeenth century took root in the lower orders of society, among the yeoman farmers, husbandmen, artisans, shopkeepers, hired servants, men and women who worked with their hands. The farmers among them, poverty-stricken dalesmen from the moors of northern England, headed straight for the rich uplands of Bucks and Chester counties. (As late as the middle of the eighteenth century, the people of Chester still spoke in a broad Yorkshire dialect.) Within a few years they were producing flour and meat for export. With the proceeds they built those neat stone farmhouses with their projecting pent roofs and door hoods that are so charming when one comes upon them in the midst of the split-levels and ranch houses of Philadelphia's exurbia.

They had little beyond the rudiments of reading and writing, these rural Friends, and few books beyond the Bible and Barclay's *Apology*. They had little time for reading, and besides, their Quakerism enjoined upon them a sober, plain way of life. But if their lives seem drab, remember the clean lines, the satisfying proportions, the functional perfection of the stone meetinghouse where they gathered on First Day to worship God in the living silence. In that simple structure form followed function with a faithfulness that Frank Lloyd Wright might envy, and every superfluity was stripped away to leave its purpose revealed in utter purity. The Pennsylvania Friends even anticipated a favorite device of the modern architect: they installed sliding panels with which they could break up the "flow of space" and convert their oblong meetinghouses into two rooms for the men's and women's meetings for business.

Howard Brinton calls the period from 1700 to 1740 the Golden Age of Quakerism in America. He is thinking primarily of the rural Quakers of Bucks and Chester counties when he describes, with a touch of nostalgia, the "unique Quaker culture" of the period.

The Culture of Early Pennsylvania

In the Quaker communities the meeting was the center, spiritually, intellectually and economically. It included a library and a school. Disputes of whatever nature were settled in the business sessions of the meeting. The poor were looked after, moral delinquents dealt with, marriages approved and performed. . . . Each group, centered in the meeting, was a well-ordered, highly integrated community of interdependent members. . . . This flowering of Quakerism was not characterized by any outburst of literary or artistic production. Its whole emphasis was on life itself in home, meeting and community. This life was an artistic creation as beautiful in its simplicity and proportion as was the architecture of its meeting houses. The "Flowering of New England" has been described in terms of its literature, but the flowering of Quakerism in the middle colonies can be described only in terms of life itself.

Quaker life in Philadelphia soon fell into a different pattern. Eventually the cleavage between rural and urban Quaker culture would split the Society of Friends into two factions, Hicksite and Orthodox (and one might even suggest that the recent healing of the schism was made easier by the blurring of that sharp line of cleavage in our twentieth-century suburban culture). The material basis for the rise of urban Quaker culture was Philadelphia's amazing growth and prosperity. Last of the major colonial cities to be founded, William Penn's "green country town" quickly outstripped New York, Newport, and Charleston, and by 1740 was pressing the much older town of Boston hard for primacy in wealth and population.

By 1740 the Quakers were already a minority group in the Quaker City, but they had been the prime movers in the town's economic expansion and they still controlled a large share of its trade and its visible assets. Most of the early immigrants had been craftsmen and shopkeepers. They practiced the economic ethic of Poor Richard long before Benjamin Franklin, that Johnny-come-lately, arrived in Philadelphia. Working diligently in their callings, they quickly transformed a primitive frontier village into a complex provincial market town and business center. The tons of wheat and flour, the barrels of beef and pork, the lumber, the bales of furs that poured into Philadelphia from the farms in the hinterland provided, of course, the substance of Philadelphia's flourishing export trade. But it was the diligence and business acumen of the Quaker merchants that translated those raw goods into prosperity for the whole region.

But prosperity, it must be admitted, had its effects on Philadelphia Quakerism. As wealth increased, plainness—what Friends called "the simplicity of Truth"—declined. As early as 1695 Philadelphia Yearly Meeting was warning its male members against wearing "long lapp'd Sleeves or Coates gathered at the Sides, or Superfluous Buttons, or Broad Ribbons about their Hatts, or long curled Perriwiggs," and cautioning women Friends against "Dressing their Heads Immodestly, or Wearing their Garments undecently . . . or Wearing . . . Striped or Flower'd Stuffs, or other useless and Superfluous Things." Obviously, the Yearly Meeting wouldn't have bothered to discourage its members from wearing these abominations unless some Friends were actually doing so. But the clever Quaker could find ways to outwit the meeting, could practice conspicuous consumption without violating the letter of the discipline. In 1724 Christopher Saur, the German printer, noted that "plainness is vanishing pretty much" among the Philadelphia Friends. It was still noticeable in their clothes, "except," he added, "that the material is very costly, or is even velvet." In other words, the Philadelphia Friends were becoming worldly, and there were Jeremiahs—especially among the country Friends—who insisted that vital Quakerism varied inversely with the prosperity of its adherents.

I am not concerned at the moment with moral judgments. I am concerned with "culture," loosely defined, and I must therefore point out that the Quaker aristocrats of Philadelphia were receptive not only to the fashions of the "world's people," but to their architecture, their books, their ideas as well, though there was always something sober and substantial about Quaker houses, libraries, and intellectual pursuits, as there was about Quaker clothes. If rural Pennsylvania Quakerism flowered in ordered and beautiful lives, the Quakerism of Philadelphia flowered in many realms of the mind and spirit, particularly in the fields of organized humanitarianism, science, and medicine. Since they had no use for a learned clergy, the Quakers were slow to establish colleges: Haverford, which began as a secondary school in 1833, did not become a college until 1856; Swarthmore was not founded till 1864, and Bryn Mawr came still later, in 1885. But the humane and learned institutions which gave Philadelphia its cultural pre-eminence in the pre-Revolutionary years—the American Philosophical Society, the Library Company, the Pennsylvania Hospital, even the College of Philadelphia, which became the University of Pennsylvania—all owed more than a little to the solid and generous culture of the Quaker merchants.

If I limit myself to mentioning the cultural interests and achievements of just one Philadelphia Quaker—James Logan—it is because he is the one I know best. I will not contend that Logan was either a typical Philadelphian or a representative Friend. The breadth and reach of his mind would have made him an exceptional man in any time or place; and as for his Quakerism, he sat so loose to it that Philadelphia Monthly Meeting had to deal with him repeatedly for breaches of the discipline. But a résumé of James Logan's contributions in the realm of "high culture" should lay to rest any lingering suspicions that early Philadelphia was a Sahara of the intellect.

Logan came to Philadelphia in 1699 as William Penn's secretary. At one time or another over the next half century, he occupied nearly every responsible public office in the province, including those of chief justice and acting governor. He was Pennsylvania's leading fur merchant, her ablest and most respected Indian diplomat. He was the builder of Philadelphia's most distinguished early Georgian mansion—the house called Stenton, which still stands in its elegant Quaker simplicity amid the ugliness of industrial North Philadelphia. He assembled a library of three thousand volumes which I do not hesitate to call the best-chosen collection of books in all colonial America. Unlike most other colonial libraries, it is still intact at the Library Company of Philadelphia. And unlike many other colonial libraries, it was a scholar's working library. Logan's marginal annotations make it clear how closely he studied his learned books in many tongues. He carried on a correspondence in Latin—the universal language of scholarship—with Dr. Johann Albertus Fabricius of Hamburg, the most erudite classicist of his age, and his commentaries on Euclid and Ptolemy were published in Hamburg and Amsterdam. He made a translation of Cicero's essay on old age which Benjamin Franklin, its publisher, hailed as "a happy omen that Philadelphia shall become the seat of the American Muses." He designed and carried out some experiments on the generation of Indian corn that botanists all over Europe cited for a century or more as proof that sex reared its head in the plant kingdom. He was certainly one of the first Americans to understand and use Sir Isaac Newton's method of fluxions, or calculus. He made contributions to the science of optics, which were published in Holland, and several of his scientific papers were read before the

Royal Society of London and printed in its *Philosophical Transactions*. He crowned his intellectual life by writing a treatise on moral philosophy which, unfortunately, was never finished and never published. That treatise, which exists only in fragments, may have been suggested by an offhand remark of the great John Locke that it should be possible to construct a rational science of morals: Logan called it in typical eighteenth-century fashion, "The Duties of Man Deduced from Nature."

James Logan, I repeat, was not a typical Philadelphia Quaker, but the example of such a man—and remember he was the leading public figure of his day—could not fail to stimulate others to the intellectual life. Indeed, the three men who are usually called Philadelphia's first scientists—Benjamin Franklin, John Bartram, the botanist, and Thomas Godfrey, the inventor of the mariner's quadrant—all owed a great deal to Logan's encouragement and patronage.

Here then, were two conflicting, or at least divergent, Quaker cultures in early Pennsylvania. A third—perhaps we should call it a subculture—flourished transiently in the frontier region, west of the Schuylkill, known as the "Welsh Tract." It is difficult to form an accurate picture of the early Welsh community. There are massive works on the subject, but they are all heavily genealogical in emphasis, and read more like stud books than works of history. They seem more concerned with providing a suitable ancestry for later generations of Philadelphians than with disclosing the actual outlines of life in the Welsh Tract.

Were the settlers of Merion, Haverford, and Radnor rich or poor? We get no clear answer because the truth is obscured by a conflict of myths. On the one hand, to fit the legend of America as a land of opportunity, a haven for the oppressed, they must be poor men, fleeing from persecution. On the other hand, to satisfy our itch for highborn ancestors, they must be aristocrats, country squires, gentlemen to the manner born. The size of some of the early landholdings and the inventories of some personal estates suggest that a few wealthy Welshmen did take up their residence on the Main Line in the 1680's and 1690's. But alongside the purchasers of two and three thousand acres who signed themselves "gentleman" were scores of yeomen, grocers, tailors, and the like, who settled on one hundred or one hundred fifty acres. The bulk of the Welsh immigrants were probably of "the middling sort" of people who gave the North American colonies and eventually the United States their overwhelmingly middle-class character.

Neither poverty nor persecution really explains that emigration from Wales which started as soon as William Penn opened the doors of Pennsylvania and lasted till some Quaker communities in Wales were all but depopulated. Professor A. H. Dodd, a learned student of Welsh history, has pointed out that if poverty had been at the root of this folk movement, it would have stemmed from the economically backward regions of Anglesey and Caernarvon rather than from fertile and prosperous Merionethshire, Radnorshire, and Montgomeryshire. And had persecution been the main impetus, the stream of emigration would have slacked off with the coming of toleration in 1689, instead of continuing as it did into the next century.

If we would identify the fundamental "cause" of the Welsh migration, we must recognize that it was not the "pushing" factors of poverty or persecution at home, but the strong "pulling" force of a dream— the powerful but delusive dream of a new Wales in the western wilderness, in which, as the Welsh immigrants put it themselves, "we might live together as a civil society to endeavor to decide all controversies and debates amongst ourselves in a Gospel order, and not to entangle ourselves with laws in an unknown tongue." So the first Welsh settlers extracted from William Penn a verbal promise that they should have a 40,000-acre enclave west of the Schuylkill where they could speak their own language, practice their own customs, and hold their own courts in splendid isolation.

Their attempt to transplant their ancient culture and preserve it intact did not prosper. Within a few decades they had lost their identity and merged with the fast-growing American society around them. They blamed William Penn for the failure of their dream. It was true that his governor, confronted with a solid Welsh voting bloc, followed the time-honored principle of divide and rule: he split the Welsh Tract in two by running a county line through the middle of it, throwing Haverford and Radnor into Chester County, leaving only Merion in Philadelphia County. But the experiment, one suspects, was doomed from the start. The Welsh, after all, were a bilingual people, as fluent in English as in their own tongue; they kept their records in English, and there is little evidence that distinctive Welsh laws or customs were observed in the Tract. It was not long before David ap Rees became David Price, Ellis ap Hugh became Ellis Pugh, and Edward ap John became plain Edward Jones.

It is not clear how long even such national traits as the love of music persisted. Thomas Allen Glenn found it pleasant "to think that often through the wild woodland of Colonial Merion there has echoed the burthen of some ancient British war song, chanted ages ago in battle against the legions of Imperial Rome." But Charles H. Browning, who compiled the fullest account of Welsh life in Pennsylvania, could not find "even a tradition that the Welsh Friends over the Schuylkill were inclined to music, singing and dancing." There is a revealing story about Edward Foulke, one of the pioneer settlers of Gwynedd. While he was still in Wales and not yet joined with the Quakers, people used to collect on Sundays at his house at Coed-y-foel in Merionethshire to join him in song, for Edward was a fine singer. But he and his wife presently became uneasy in their minds about this idle way of spending the Lord's Day. Thereafter, when his musical friends gathered and he was tempted to "undue levity," he would get out the Bible and read it aloud. It was surprising, says an old account, how quickly "the light and unprofitable portion of his visitors" melted away. When Edward Foulke came to the Quaker settlement of Gwynedd in 1698, it is safe to assume that he left his harp behind. The war songs of the ancient Britons may have rung out in the Merion woods, but the echo that Thomas Allen Glenn thought he caught over the centuries was more likely the sound of the psalms of David sung in the Baptist chapels of the Welsh Tract. In any case there is little reason to think that the Welsh Friends after a few decades in America differed much from their English coreligionists.

The original settlers of Germantown seem to have suffered a like fate. The late Professor William I. Hull was convinced that they were predominantly Dutch, not German, in culture, and Quaker, not Mennonite, in religion. But whatever their origins, they quickly became Philadelphia Friends, like the Welsh. Their very names they Anglicized from Luykens to Lukens, from Kunders to Conard, from Schumacher to Shoemaker. Those Dutchmen who were not assimilated to Anglo-Saxon Quakerism were presently swallowed up by the great tide of Swiss and Germans who came to Pennsylvania after 1709—the people who, to add to the general confusion, are known as the "Pennsylvania Dutch."

I cannot here attempt a definition or characterization of Pennsylvania Dutch culture. All I can do is make a few observations about it and suggest two excellent books on the subject—Fredric Klees's *The Pennsylvania Dutch* and the symposium called *The Pennsylvania*

Germans, edited by Ralph Wood. In the first place, Pennsylvania Dutch culture was never a single entity, a uniform way of life. Though we tend to think of it as a unity, it was and is a congeries of cultures with roots in many different geographical areas and religious traditions. Among the immigrants from continental Europe who came to Pennsylvania in a trickle during the first twenty-five years and in a flood thereafter were Alsatians and Württembergers and Swiss, a scattering of French Huguenots who had lived temporarily in the Rhine Valley, and, ultimately, some Bohemians, Silesians, and Moravians, who came to America by way of Saxony. In religious terms they fell into three broad categories: the sects or plain people, the church people, and the Moravians. All of them were pushed out of central Europe by religious persecution and economic hardship; all were pulled toward Penn's colony by the promise of religious freedom and economic opportunity. It is the sects—the Mennonites, the Amish, the Dunkers, the Schwenkfelders, the Protestant monks and nuns of Ephrata, the mystical Society of the Woman in the Wilderness—who have attracted most attention because of their peculiarities. But it was the church people—the Lutherans and the Reformed—who predominated, and it was they who established the characteristic Pennsylvania Dutch way of life. When Count Zinzendorf, the leader of the Moravians, came to Pennsylvania with a noble ecumenical dream of uniting all the German religious groups, he soon discovered how stubborn these theological and cultural differences were.

What these people had in common was chiefly that they spoke a different, a "foreign," tongue. They were, said a supercilious Philadelphian, "so profoundly ignorant as to be unable to speak the English language." Hence arose the familiar stereotype, the notion that they were boors, stupid, stolid clods—in a word, "the dumb Dutch." Yet they were beyond all comparison the best farmers in colonial America. From the beginning their great barns, their neat farmyards, their care in fencing their livestock, their systematic rotation of crops, their infallible instinct for fertile limestone soil, their industry and good management drew favorable comment in a land notorious for wasteful and slovenly farming. "It is pretty to behold our back settlements," wrote Lewis Evans in 1753, "where the barns are large as palaces, while the owners live in log huts; a sign, though, of thriving farmers." Evans' reference to the log cabin is a reminder that we owe that symbol of the American frontier to the Germans and to the Swedes, who had settled earlier along the Delaware River. It was no invention of the American pioneer, but a cultural importation from the forest lands of central and northern Europe. As a matter of fact, we are indebted to the Pennsylvania Dutch for the two other major symbols of the frontier—the Conestoga wagon, and the so-called Kentucky rifle. And consider their rich and various folk art. Beside the gay and colorful designs of tulips and hearts, distelfinks and peacocks with which they covered their dower chests and pottery and baptismal certificates, most of what passes for early American folk art seems pale and anemic. Finally, be it remembered that the plain people of the Pennsylvania Dutch country have maintained a vital and satisfying religious life longer than almost any other group in America. Even today the simple piety of a Mennonite farmer is a real and impressive thing in the midst of much false and superficial religiosity.

Theirs was a peasant culture, and it has kept its peasant character for two centuries in a country where peasantry has always been alien. Professor Robert Redfield's generic description of peasant values describes their outlook pretty accurately: "an intense attachment to native soil; a reverent disposition toward habitat and ancestral ways; a restraint on individual self-seeking in favor of family and community; a certain suspiciousness, mixed with appreciation, of town life; a sober and earthy ethic." Unquestionably, early Pennsylvania Dutch life was limited, lacking in intellectual quality, wanting in many of the higher values of civilized life. And yet, having said that, one immediately asks: where in early America except in the Moravian towns of Bethlehem and Nazareth and Lititz could one hear Bach and Handel, Haydn and Mozart, performed by full orchestra and chorus?

The tide of German immigration set toward the full around 1710 and reached the flood at mid-century. Hardly had the old settlers begun to adjust to these newcomers with their strange tongue and stranger ways before they became aware of a new inundation of land-hungry immigrants—the people who have always been known in America as the Scotch-Irish—Scottish and Presbyterian in culture, Irish only in that they had been living for a longer or shorter period in Ulster. They came in waves, the first after 1717, the second about ten years later, the third around the year 1740. Their coming in such crowds and their free-and-easy attitude toward details like land titles took even James Logan aback, although he was a Scotch-Irishman himself. They simply squatted, he complained, wherever they found "a spot of vacant ground." When challenged to show title, he added, a little sadly, their standard response was that it was "against the laws of God and nature that so much land should lie idle while so many Christians wanted it to labor on and raise their bread."

It was actually James Logan who assigned them their historic role in America. It happened that the Indians across the Susquehanna were growing restive just as the first wave of Scotch-Irish settlers was reaching Philadelphia. Though Logan was a Quaker, he did not share William Penn's faith in pacifism. Recalling from his own childhood how gallantly the Protestants of Ulster had defended Londonderry and Inniskillen against the Roman Catholic forces of James II, he "thought it might be prudent" to plant a settlement of these tough, bellicose Ulstermen on the Susquehanna "as a *frontier* in case of any disturbance." Logan used the term "frontier" with a specific, limited meaning; he meant a border garrison, a strong point on the edge of hostile territory. But the word was destined to vibrate with special overtones for Americans as the outer edge of settlement crept across the continent. And on nearly every American frontier, the Scotch-Irish —those doughty, Bible-quoting, whisky-drinking, gun-toting, Indian-fighting Presbyterians whom James Logan planted in his garrison town of Donegal on the Susquehanna—would be the defenders of the marches, the tamers of the wilderness, the advance agents of the white man's civilization.

They were not crude, uncultivated roughnecks, these Scotch-Irish frontiersmen. They were pious Presbyterians, and they insisted on a learned ministry and a literate congregation. "The schoolhouse and the kirk went together," says Carl Wittke, "wherever the Scotch-Irish frontier moved." "These fortresses against ignorance and the devil," adds Louis B. Wright, "paralleled a chain of blockhouses and forts against the French and Indian. The Scots were as eager to fight one as the other." New Englanders have a habit of attributing the spread of popular education over the country to the heirs of the Yankee Puritan. But some of the credit rightfully belongs to the Scotch-Irish Presbyterian, who kept the lamp of learning lighted on many an American frontier. As early as 1726 the Reverend William Tennent established a "Log College" on Neshaminy Creek in Bucks County, and the "Log College" was the seed out of which Princeton University grew.

A cultural map of the settled portion of Pennsylvania in 1740 would show a band of Quaker country roughly parallel with the Delaware River and extending back twenty-five or thirty miles, its western outposts near Coatesville, Pottstown, and Quakertown. Behind it would be a broad belt of Pennsylvania Dutch country, anchored at Bethlehem to the northeast and at Lancaster to the southwest. Still farther west in the Susquehanna Valley would be a sparse strip of Scotch-Irish settlement, overlapping on its eastern side with the Pennsylvania Dutch country and swinging eastward in upper Bucks County, near where Neshaminy Creek joins the Delaware. There were a hundred thousand people in all, perhaps more. Scattered over these broad ·culture areas would be small pockets of people with different backgrounds—English and Welsh Baptists in the Quaker country, a handful of Roman Catholic and Jewish families in Philadelphia, four or five thousand Negroes, slaves and freedmen, and, here and there, some remnants of the ancient inhabitants of Pennsylvania—the Lenni Lenape or Delaware Indians.

Two of these "pocket groups" demand special mention. Along the Delaware south of Philadelphia lived several hundred descendants of the "old colonists"—the Swedes, Finns, and Dutch who had brought the white man's culture to the Delaware Valley long before William Penn. By the end of a century, however, they had lost most of their distinguishing characteristics and had merged with the English culture around them. In Philadelphia there was a strong and growing Anglican community, which worshiped in style in the Palladian elegance of Christ Church. Already some of the leading Quaker families had moved so far from their plainer country brethren that they began to drift over to the more fashionable Church of England. The cultural traditions of early Pennsylvania, it is clear, were in constant flux, forever forming new combinations, new patterns, in the prevailing atmosphere of social freedom and economic plenty. The variety and interrelations of these traditions give early Pennsylvania culture its peculiar significance in the development of American life.

It was this region primarily that Hector St. John de Crèvecoeur had in mind when he asked his famous question, "What then is the American, this new man?" and sketched out the answer which has done duty for most of us ever since. The American, said Crèvecoeur, is the product of a "promiscuous breed" of "English, Scotch, Irish, French, Dutch, Germans, and Swedes." Settling in the New World, he leaves behind him "all his ancient prejudices and manners [and] receives new ones from the new mode of life he has embraced, the new government he obeys, and the new rank he holds." Here, says Crèvecoeur, "individuals of all nations are melted into a new race of men, whose labors and posterity will one day cause great changes in the world." The prophecy in Crèvecoeur's last words has unquestionably come true, but his account of the process by which his American, "this new man," was created is too simple.

The familiar image of the melting pot seems to imply "a giant caldron in which foreigners are boiled down into a colorless mass—as insipid as any stew." Clearly that is not an accurate image of early Pennsylvania. To be sure, some groups melted. The Welsh apparently did. So did the Dutch in Germantown and the Swedes along the Delaware. But the Germans, by and large, did not. Indeed they seem to have become self-consciously German for the first time in Pennsylvania: "the impact of American life," says Caroline Ware, "tends to accentuate rather than to obliterate group consciousness" among immigrants. Some Philadelphia Quakers became Episcopalians, but the great majority did not; and there was never any *rapprochement* between the Quakers of the east and the Scotch-Irish Presbyterians of the west. Indeed, the political history of colonial Pennsylvania is a story of continuous struggle, not primarily between social classes or economic groups, but among cultural and religious blocs. Not assimilation but what might be called "selective interaction" was the rule. It seems likely, for example, that the plain dress and the plain architecture of the Amish— or at least some elements thereof—were not brought to America by the immigrants, but were borrowed, once they had arrived, from the broadbrim hat, the plain bonnet, and plain meetinghouse of the Quakers. By way of return, the Pennsylvania Dutchman put scrapple and sticky cinnamon buns on Quaker City breakfast tables. It has even been suggested that we owe apple pie to the Pennsylvania Dutch, though as a New Englander, I shall require further evidence before I can accept *that* revolutionary thesis. In any case, this process of selective borrowing seems to be how American civilization was created, and there is no better laboratory in which to observe it at work than early Pennsylvania.

My final observation takes me from the popular culture of bonnets and scrapple back to the level of "high culture." It is fairly well known that from about 1740 to the end of the eighteenth century Philadelphia was the intellectual and cultural capital of North America. In science, in medicine, in humanitarianism, in music and the drama and *belles lettres* its pre-eminence was unquestioned. How shall we explain this remarkable quick maturing in the youngest of the colonial towns? Not simply, I submit, on the ground that it was the largest and most prosperous city in the American colonies. I for one have never been convinced that high culture is a function of a high rate of income. Nor can we attribute it *all* to that displaced Bostonian, Benjamin Franklin. No, I think we shall find the source of colonial Philadelphia's flowering in the richness, the variety, and above all, in the creative interaction of the elements in its cultural hinterland.

There is nothing in Benjamin West's idyllic painting of Penn and the Indians that foreshadows the Philadelphia of Franklin and Rittenhouse, of Benjamin Rush and Charles Brockden Brown, of the American Philosophical Society and the Pennsylvania Hospital and the College of Philadelphia. But William Penn, it should be clear by now, was more than a benign dispenser of peace and yard goods to the Indians. By opening the doors of Pennsylvania to people of every nation and every religion, he established a situation of cultural pluralism and thereby created the conditions for cultural growth. And the atmosphere was freedom.

32. ENGLAND'S CULTURAL PROVINCES*

Scotland and America

by John Clive and Bernard Bailyn

Though Scotland and America were far from the centers of intellectual and cultural life in Europe, both participated in the eighteenth-century Enlightenment, producing some of its major and minor luminaries. To account for this phenomenon, John Clive and Bernard Bailyn made a comparative analysis of Scottish and American cultural development, arguing that common experiences in both societies nourished cultural vitality. Despite many important differences, both these societies relied on the leadership of men who had pushed their way forward to positions of eminence which in England were usually the privilege of the well-born. The opportunities for the ambitious unleashed resources of human genius and imagination that under other conditions might not have borne fruit. And because such individuals were not intimately part of conventional culture, they often let their minds wander along original

* *William and Mary Quarterly*, 3d series, vol. 14 (1957), 200–213. Footnotes have been omitted except where they are necessary for an understanding of the text.

paths which established elites avoided. Just as important as the social origin of the Scottish and American Enlightenment were the cultural provincialism and isolation of these societies which men worked hard to overcome. Independence from Britain only intensified the American dilemma after the Revolution, but it was already apparent in the colonial period: how could a people with a growing sense that they were "a new race of men," liberated from tyranny that oppressed people elsewhere, create an indigenous culture worthy of those who Hector St. John de Crèvecoeur claimed were "the western pilgrims . . . carrying along with them that great mass of arts, sciences, vigour, and industry which began long since in the east; they will finish the great circle."

The question of the origin of the "Scottish Renaissance"—that remarkable efflorescence of the mid-eighteenth century, with its roll call of great names: Hume, Smith, Robertson, Kames, and Ferguson— is one of those historical problems which have hitherto stubbornly resisted a definite solution. This may be due to its very nature; for, as the greatest of recent historians of Scotland has remarked, "We recognize as inadequate all attempts to explain the appearance of galaxies of genius at particular epochs in different countries." This is not to imply that attempted explanations have failed to be forthcoming. On the contrary, ever since a learned Italian named Carlo Deanina applied himself to the problem in *An Essay on the Progress of Learning among the Scots* (1763), historians have suggested different reasons for that striking and apparently sudden outburst of creative energy. Macaulay saw the principal cause for what he considered "this wonderful change" from the barren wastes of seventeenth-century theology in the act passed by the Estates of Scotland in 1696, setting up a school in every parish. Buckle, sounding a suitably Darwinian note, observed the energies displayed in the Scottish political and religious struggles of the seventeenth century surviving those struggles and finding another field in which they could exert themselves.

There is something to be said for both these points of view. The national system of education, though in practice never quite as ideal as in conception, enabled many a poor farmer's boy to go on to one of the universities as well prepared as his socially superior classmates. Nor can it be denied that in spite of the Fifteen and the Forty-five the general atmosphere of eighteenth-century Scotland was more conducive to peaceful pursuits than that of the strife-torn decades of the seventeenth century. But it requires no more than a little reflection on cultural history to perceive that neither peace nor public education, nor their conjunction, guarantees the intellectual achievements suggested by the word "renaissance."

Similar objections may be advanced concerning some of the other so-called "causes" of Scotland's golden age. Thus it is certainly true that the eighteenth century, in contrast to the seventeenth, was for Scotland a period of increasing economic prosperity. However, the disastrous Darien scheme of the 1690's ate up that capital fuel without which even the most rigorous Protestant ethic could not become economically efficacious. The immediate effect of the Union of 1707 was not the expected sudden prosperity, but increased taxation and loss of French trade. Nor, until much later, was there a compensating expansion of commerce with England and the colonies. Real economic advancement did not come until the latter half of the century, too late to serve as a satisfactory reason for the first stages of Scotland's great creative period. As for the influence of "New Light" Hutcheson, his Glasgow lectures—effusions on the marvelous powers of the "moral sense" by an enthusiastic disciple of Shaftesbury—no doubt "contributed very powerfully to diffuse, in Scotland, that taste for analytical discussion, and that spirit of liberal inquiry, to which the world is indebted for some of the most valuable productions of the eighteenth century." But holding them solely responsible for the Scottish enlightenment is surely expecting a little too much even from the most lucid philosopher. Furthermore, it is worth noting that, after Hutcheson's first year at Glasgow, at least one contemporary observer singled him out for praise because he was maintaining the cause of orthodox Christianity in a university shot through with free thought. The fact is that, by the time Hutcheson began his lectures, considerable breaches had been made in the dam of orthodox austerity so laboriously constructed during the embattled decades of the previous century.

Adequate explanation of the origins of the Scottish renaissance, therefore, must take account not only of a variety of social factors at the moment of fullest flowering, but also of the conditions of growth in the preceding period. Thus broadened, the problem seems to involve the entire history of Scotland for the better part of a century. The numerous elements that entered into the renaissance must be brought together. But the interpretation of broad historical movements of this kind is not simply a matter of listing factors. A knowledge of their configuration is equally important. Comprehension of Scotland's renaissance must rest on an appreciation of the essential spirit of the time and place, as well as on the accumulation of cultural data.

The underlying unity of this renaissance, the profound impulses that elevated the life of a nation, require deeper study and thought than they have yet received. We do not propose to solve such problems in these few pages. We seek, merely, possible perspectives in which to perceive them, and we find an approach suggested by the subject of the present symposium. For the American colonies, too, enjoyed a flowering in the eighteenth century—not a renaissance, but yet a blossoming worthy of the designation "golden age." British North America produced no Hume or Adam Smith, but in Edwards and Franklin, Jefferson, Madison, and Adams, Rittenhouse, Rush, Copley, West, Wythe, and Hutchinson it boasted men of impressive accomplishment. Its finest fruit, the literature of the American Revolution, has justly been called "the most magnificent irruption of the American genius into print."

The society in which the achievements of these men were rooted, though obviously different from that of Scotland in many ways, was yet significantly related to it. Elements of this relationship struck contemporaries much as they have later scholars. "Boston," writes one critic, "has often been called the most English of American cities, but in the eighteenth and early nineteenth centuries it was a good deal more like Edinburgh than like London. . . . The people, like those of Edinburgh, were independent, not easily controlled, assertive of their rights. . . ." In Boston, New York, and Philadelphia, as in Edinburgh and Glasgow, private clubs, where pompous, often ridiculously elaborate ritual threw into bold relief the fervor of cultural uplift, were vital social institutions. Similar to the quality of social mobility that led Dr. Alexander Hamilton to berate New York's "aggrandized upstarts" for lacking "the capacity to observe the different ranks of men in polite nations or to know what it is that really constitutes that difference of degrees" was the spirit of "shocking familiarity" in Scotland of which Boswell, on his continental tour, took care to warn Rousseau.

Such remarks tell much and suggest more. They lead one to pursue the question of the social similarities bearing on intellectual life into richer, if more remote regions. They suggest the value of a comparison of the cultural developments in Scotland and America from the standpoint of the English observer in London. Certain common social characteristics of these flowerings, thus isolated, might throw new light on the basic impulses of the Scottish renaissance and prove of interest to historians of both regions.

We find, first, a striking similarity in the social location of the groups that led the cultural developments in the two areas.

Whatever else may remain obscure about the social history of colonial America, it cannot be doubted that advance in letters and in the arts was involved with social ascent by groups whose status in Europe would unquestionably have been considered inferior or middling. Despite the familial piety that has so often claimed nobility for *arrivé* forbears, and with it a leisured, graceful intimacy with the muses, there were few cultivated aristocrats in the colonies to lead intellectual and artistic advances. Throughout the North, the middle-class origins of the literati were unmistakable.

Who led the cultural advance in the northern towns? Ministers, of course, like William Smith, Provost of the College of Philadelphia, who carried with him from Aberdeen not only a headful of learning but frustrated ambitions that developed into a common type of cultural snobbery; like Samuel Johnson, President of King's College, who grew up in Connecticut where, he wrote in his poignant *Autobiography*, "the condition of learning (as well as everything else) was very low," and whose "thirst after knowledge and truth" alone saved him from a hopeless provincialism; or like the supercilious Mather Byles, scion of a local intellectual dynasty, who snapped the whip of sarcasm over a mulish populace while proudly displaying a note from Alexander Pope elicited by fawning letters and gifts of hackneyed verse.

Equally important were lawyers like John Adams, William Livingston, and James DeLancey, whose cultural even more than political ascendancy was assured "in a Country," Cadwallader Colden wrote in 1765, "where few men except in the profession of the Law, have any kind of literature, where the most opulent families in our own memory, have arisen from the lowest rank of people. . . ." Along with these two professional groups, there were a few of the leading merchants, or, more frequently, their more leisured heirs, like the versifer Peter Oliver or his politician-historian cousin, Thomas Hutchinson. These men, potentates on the local scene, were no more than colonial businessmen in the wider world of British society. Even the brilliant classicist and scientist, James Logan of Philadelphia—"aristocrat" by common historical designation—would have been but a cultivated Quaker burgher to the patrons of arts and letters in London.

If such were the leaders in the northern port towns, who followed? The numerous cultural associations, the clubs, were recruited from the professional middle and tradesman lower-middle classes. Franklin's famous Junto was a self-improvement society of autodidacts. Its original membership included a glazier, a surveyor, a shoemaker, a joiner, a merchant, three printers, and a clerk. And though Philadelphia's merchants derided the Junto as the "Leather Apron Club," they themselves, in their own societies, like their fellows in Annapolis's Tuesday Club, or Newport's Literary and Philosophical Society, could not help finding relaxation in most un-aristocratic self-improvement.

But it is, of course, in the South where the brightest image of the aristocrat, the landed gentleman as the man of letters, has appeared. Wealth in land and slaves, we have been told again and again, combined to create a class of leisured aristocrats—the Byrds, the Carters, the Lees—whose lives glowed with vitality in letters as in politics. But careful study has shown this to be a myth. "The most significant feature of the Chesapeake aristocracy," writes Carl Bridenbaugh,

> was its middle-class origin. . . . Leisure was a myth; endless work was a reality quite as much for successful planter-gentlemen as for their lesser confreres—and the same held for their womenfolk as well. . . . Those who have appointed themselves custodians of the historical reputation of this fascinating region have generally insisted that it produced that which, by its very nature, it could not produce—a developed intellectual and artistic culture rivaling that of any other part of the colonies. . . . They led a gracious but not a cultured life. . . . The Chesapeake society produced a unique bouorgeois aristocracy with more than its share of great and noble men; they were, however, men of intellect, not intellectuals.

What of the deeper South—the society of colonial Carolina? "Families of actual gentle birth were even fewer [here] than in the Chesapeake country; the bourgeois grown rich and seeking gentility set the style. . . . The striking aspects of colonial Charles Town were the absence of cultural discipline and the passiveness of the city's intellectual and artistic life." If Carolina's rising merchant-planter families produced "the only leisure-class Society of colonial America" where alone "enjoyment, charm, refinement—became the *summum bonum*," they yet failed to furnish even a few recruits to the arts and sciences.

How sharp is the contrast to Scotland, with its ancient landed families and tighter social organization?

It would be wrong to ignore the share of the aristocracy in the cultural life of eighteenth-century Edinburgh; but, due to special circumstances, its role remained contributory rather than decisive. The Scottish nobility and gentry had largely remained Jacobite and Episcopalian, even after the re-establishment of the Church of Scotland. This meant that they were unencumbered by those ascetic proclivities against which even moderate Presbyterians still had to struggle. Too poor to travel abroad, they spent their winters in what was no longer the political but still the legal and ecclesiastical capital, where they wrote and sang ballads, sponsored assemblies and diverse entertainments— fostered, in short, an atmosphere of ease and social grace. But if they were masters of the revels, they were masters of little else. While Jacobitism kept conscientious younger sons out of professions requiring an oath to the House of Hanover, poverty forced many of them to earn their living as tradesmen. "Silversmiths, clothiers, woollen drapers were frequently men of high birth and social position." Economic necessity of this sort helped to create in the Old Town of Edinburgh a society in which social demarcations were far from sharply drawn, in which status was as much a function of professional achievement as of birth. Thus Peter Williamson's first *Edinburgh Directory* (1773–1774), listing citizens in order of rank, was headed by the Lords of Session, Advocates, Writers to the Signet, and Lords' and Advocates' Clerks. The category of "noblemen and gentlemen" followed after.

This order of precedence was symptomatic of the fact that in the course of the century, social and cultural leadership had fallen to the professional classes, and especially to the legal profession. A good example of the close connection between Law and Letters is provided by an analysis of the membership of the Select Society, founded in 1754 for the dual purpose of philosophical inquiry and improvement in public speaking. By 1759, this society (then numbering 133 members) had come to include all the Edinburgh literati; and out of 119 who can be readily identified by profession, at least forty-eight were associated with the law in one way or the other. Along with university professors and members of the Moderate party among the clergy, it was the lawyers who played the principal role both in the mid-eighteenth and early nineteenth-century stages of the Scottish enlightenment; one need only mention the names of Kames, Mackenzie, Monboddo, Scott, Jeffrey, and Brougham. That Scotland retained its own legal system after the Union, that the law thus became the main ladder for public advancement, and that there prevailed a great interest in legal studies had other less direct though no less important consequences. The traditionally close involvement of Scottish and Roman law, as well as the liberal influences brought home from Holland by generations of Scottish law students at Utrecht and Leyden, proved to be forces conducive to fresh currents of philosophical and historical thought. In his Glasgow lectures on moral philosophy, Francis Hutcheson presented "the most complete view of legal philosophy of the time." And those early public lectures Adam Smith delivered in Edinburgh after his return from Oxford (1748–1751) in which he first enunciated the principle of the division of labor had as their actual subject matter "jurisprudence," or the philosophy of law. To these lectures, the first part of Robertson's *History of Charles V* owed a great deal. A considerable part of the intellectual history of Scotland in the eighteenth century might be written in terms of direct and indirect legal influences. There was no doubt about the fact that, as one traveler commented late in the century, it was the lawyers who "indeed, in some measure give the tone to the manners of the Scotch Metropolis," that they, "in short, are the principal people in that city."

The similarity in social origins between the Scottish and American literati became evident at a time when another more complicated relationship between the two societies was being formed. Trade, migration, and cultural exchanges mark one phase of this relationship. But these direct transfers of goods, persons, books, and ideas reflect the profound fact that Scotland and America were provinces, cultural as well as political and economic, of the English-speaking world whose center was London. From this common orientation flowed essential elements of cultural growth.

English sovereignty over the American colonies meant not only regulations and fees, but also the presence of a particular group of men who dominated the stage of colonial affairs. They had first appeared in large numbers in the seventies of the previous century, when, after the settlement of the Restoration government, England had attempted to lace together the scattered segments of its Atlantic empire. To accomplish this, she had dispatched to the centers of settlement royal officials —governors, admirals, customs officials, inspectors of forests, collectors general and particular, minor functionaries of all sorts—empowered to assert the prerogatives of sovereignty. In the course of a half-century, the more highly placed of these men, together representing officialdom, became focuses of society in the port towns. Their influence was immense. Not only did they represent political power and economic advantage, but, in most urban centers, they were models of fashion. More than links between governments, they brought England with them into the heart of colonial America. As the brightest social luminaries in the provincial capitals, they both repelled and attracted. Social groups as well as political factions formed around them.

Officialdom, usually considered a political influence, was in fact a most important shaping force on the formation of colonial society. These agents of imperialism could not help but influence the growth of the arts in the colonies. Arbiters of taste, they attracted, patronized, helped to justify those who devoted themselves to letters, arts, and the graces of life.

In Scotland, too, the political connection with England led public men to become cultural go-betweens. Here, though, it was not an enforced officialdom that mattered; only the hated excisemen correspond in position, and Boswell was unusual in wanting more official Englishmen in Scotland to make the Union more complete. The situation, in fact, was reversed; but the effects were similar. The sixteen peers and forty-five members of Parliament who represented Scotland at Westminster (and who had such a hard time making ends meet in London) brought back English books and English fashions. They were catalysts in the process that gave Edinburgh its own *Tatler*, as well as its coffeehouses and wits, and, later in the century, its gambling clubs and masquerades.

Officialdom in the colonies, Scottish Members of Parliament, the Union of 1707—political relationships between England and her dependencies thus brought about cultural links as well. The existence of imperial agents and local representatives to the cosmopolitan center served also to emphasize the provincial character of life in both regions. Scotsmen and Americans alike were constantly aware that they lived on the periphery of a greater world. The image they held of this world and of their place in it was perhaps the most important, though the subtlest, element common to the cultural growth of America and Scotland in the eighteenth century.

Life in both regions was similarly affected by the mere fact of physical removal from the cosmopolitan center. For, though the Scottish border lay less than three hundred miles from London, as late as 1763 only one regular stagecoach traveled between Edinburgh and the British capital. The trip took about two weeks, or fully half the traveling time of the express packet from New York to Falmouth, and those few who could afford to make it considered it so serious an expedition that they frequently made their wills before setting out. As far as the English were concerned, Smollett's Mrs. Tabitha, who thought one could get to Scotland only by sea, represented no great advance over those of her countrymen earlier in the century to whom "many parts of Africa and the Indies . . . are better known than a Region which is contiguous to our own, and which we have always had so great a concern for." Even toward the middle of the century, there were occasions when the London mailbag for Edinburgh was found to contain only a single letter.

But isolation, as Perry Miller has pointed out, "is not a matter of distance or the slowness of communication: it is a question of what a dispatch from distant quarters means to the recipient." News, literature, and personal messages from London did not merely convey information; they carried with them standards by which men and events were judged. In them, as in the personal envoys from the greater European world, was involved a definition of sophistication. *Tatlers* and *Spectators* were eagerly devoured in Edinburgh as in Philadelphia. Scottish ladies, like their American counterparts, ordered all sorts of finery, from dresses to wallpaper, from England. There were Americans who echoed the Scottish minister's complaint that "all the villainous, profane, and obscene books and plays, as printed in London, are got down by Allan Ramsay, and lent out, for an easy price, to young boys, servant weemen of the better sort, and gentlemen." Franklin's excitement at first reading the *Spectator* and his grim determination to fashion his own literary style on it is only the most famous example of the passion with which Americans strove to imitate English ways. "I am almost inclined to believe," wrote William Eddis, "that a new fashion is adopted earlier by the polished and affluent Americans, than by many opulent persons in the great metropolis. . . ."

Communications from England exerted such authority because they fell upon minds conscious of limited awareness. A sense of inferiority pervaded the culture of the two regions, affecting the great no less than the common. It lay behind David Hume's lament (in 1756) that "we people in the country (for such you Londoners esteem our city) are apt to be troublesome to you people in town; we are vastly glad to receive letters which convey intelligence to us of things we should otherwise have been ignorant of, and can pay them back with nothing but provincial stories which are in no way interesting." And it led Adam Smith to admit that "this country is so barren of all sorts of transactions that can interest anybody that lives at a distance from it that little intertainment is to be expected from any correspondent on this side of the Tweed." It rankled deeply in those like the seventeenth-century cosmopolite John Winthrop, Junior, who longingly recalled in "such a wilde place" as Hartford, Connecticut, the excitement of life in the European centers. The young Copley felt it profoundly when he wrote from Boston to Benjamin West in London, "I think myself peculiarly unlucky in Liveing in a place into which there has not been one portrait brought that is worthy to be call'd a Picture within my memory, which leaves me at a great loss to gess the stil that You, Mr. Renolds, and the other Artists pracktice." The young Scot returning to Edinburgh after a journey to the continent and London felt he had to "labour to tone myself down like an overstrained instrument to the low pitch of the rest about me."

The manners and idioms that labeled the provincial in England were stigmas that Scotsmen and Americans tried to avoid when they could not turn them, like Franklin in Paris, into the accents of nature's own philospher. There was no subject about which Scotsmen were more sensitive than their speech. Lieutenant Lismahago may have proved to his own satisfaction that "what we generally called the Scottish dialect was, in fact, true, genuine old English," but Dr. Johnson laughed at Hamilton of Bangour's rhyming "wishes" and "bushes," and when, in 1761, Thomas Sheridan, the playwright's father, lectured in Edinburgh (and in Irish brogue) on the art of rhetoric, he had an attentive audience of three hundred nobles, judges, divines, advocates, and men of fashion. Hume kept constantly by his side a list of Scots idioms to be avoided, and was said by Monboddo to have confessed on his deathbed not his sins but his Scotticisms.

By 1754, the emergence of American English, adversely commented on as early as 1735, was so far advanced that the suggestion was made, facetiously, that a glossary of American terms be compiled. The scorn shown by Englishmen for Scots dialect was not heaped upon American speech until after the Revolution. But well before Lexington, Scottish and American peculiarities in language were grouped together as provincial in the English mind, a fact understood by John Witherspoon when he wrote in 1781, "The word Americanism, which I have coined . . . is exactly similar in its formation and signification to the word Scotticism." The same equation of verbal provincialisms underlay Boswell's recounting of an anecdote told him "with great good humour" by the Scottish Earl of Marchmont:

> . . . the master of a shop in London, where he was not known, said to him, "I suppose, Sir, you are an American." "Why so, Sir?" (said his Lordship.) "Because, Sir (replied the shopkeeper,) you speak neither English nor Scotch, but something different from both, which I conclude is the language of America."

The sense of inferiority that expressed itself in imitation of English ways, and a sense of guilt regarding local mannerisms was, however, only one aspect of the complex meaning of provincialism. Many Scotsmen and Americans followed the Reverend John Oxenbridge in castigating those who sought to "fashion your selves to the flaunting mode of *England* in worship or walking." In the manner of Ramsay of Ochtertyre's strictures on eighteenth-century Scottish authors, they inveighed against the slavish imitation of English models, such "a confession of inferiority as one would hardly have expected from a proud manly people, long famous for common-sense and veneration for the ancient classics." Awareness of regional limitations frequently led to a compensatory local pride, evolving into a patriotism which was politically effective in the one area, and, after the Forty-five, mainly sentimental in the other, due to the diametrically opposed political history of the two —America moving from subordination to independence, Scotland from independence to subordination. It was the conviction that life in the provinces was not merely worthy of toleration by cosmopolites but unique in natural blessings that led Jefferson, in his *Notes on Virginia*, to read the Count de Buffon a lesson in natural history. It was a kindred conviction that, in spite of its "familiarity," life in Edinburgh had a congeniality and vigor all its own, that made Robertson refuse all invitations to settle in London. Hume, too, in the midst of his Parisian triumphs, longed for the "plain roughness" of the Poker Club and the sharpness of Dr. Jardine to correct and qualify the "lusciousness" of French society. Hume's complex attitude toward his homeland is significant; it is typical of a psychology which rarely failed to combat prejudice with pride.

For Scotsmen, this pride was reinforced by the treatment they received in England, where their very considerable successes remained in inverse proportion to their popularity. One day, Ossian, Burns, and Highland tours might help to wipe out even memories of Bute. Meanwhile, in spite of their own "Breetish" Coffee House, life in London was not always easy for visitors from north of the Tweed. "Get home to your crowdie, and be d—d to you! Ha'ye got your parritch yet? When will you get a sheepshead or a haggis, you ill-far'd lown? Did you ever see meat in Scotland, saving oatmeal hasty pudding? Keep out of his way, Thomas, or you'll get the itch!" The young Scotsman thus recounting his London reception added that there was little real malice behind such common jibes. But Boswell's blood boiled with indignation when he heard shouts of "No Scots, No Scots! Out with them!" at Covent Garden. Yet only a few months later, he may be found addressing a memorandum to himself to "be *retenu* to avoid Scotch sarcasting jocularity," and describing a fellow countryman as "a hearty, honest fellow, knowing and active, but Scotch to the very backbone."

The deepest result of this complicated involvement in British society was that the provincial's view of the world was discontinuous. Two forces, two magnets, affected his efforts to find adequate standards and styles: the values associated with the simplicity and purity (real or imagined) of nativism, and those to be found in cosmopolitan sophistication. Those who could take entire satisfaction in either could maintain a consistent position. But for provincials, exposed to both, an exclusive, singular conception of either kind was too narrow. It meant a rootlessness, an alienation either from the higher sources of culture or from the familiar local environment that had formed the personality. Few whose perceptions surpassed local boundaries rested content with a simple, consistent image of themselves or of the world. Provincial culture, in eighteenth-century Scotland as in colonial America, was formed in the mingling of these visions.

The effect of this situation on cultural growth in the two regions cannot, of course, be measured. Undoubtedly, provincialism sometimes served to inhibit creative effort. But we suggest that there existed important factors which more than balanced the deleterious effects. The complexity of the provincial's image of the world and of himself made demands upon him unlike those felt by the equivalent Englishman. It tended to shake the mind from the roots of habit and tradition. It led men to the interstices of common thought where were found new views and new approaches to the old. It cannot account for the existence of men of genius, but to take it into consideration may help us understand the conditions which fostered in such men the originality and creative imagination that we associate with the highest achievements of the enlightenment in Scotland and America.